Literature and Psychoanalysis

This is what analytical discourse is all about: what can be read. What can be read beyond what the subject has been incited to say. (. . .) In analytical discourse, the signifying utterance is given another reading than what it means.
Jacques Lacan

Reading is dramatized not as an emotive reaction to what language does, but as an emotive reaction to the impossibility of knowing what it might be up to.
Paul de Man

LITERATURE AND PSYCHOANALYSIS

The Question of Reading: Otherwise

Edited by Shoshana Felman

The Johns Hopkins University Press
Baltimore and London

Johns Hopkins edition published 1982 in hardcover
and paperback
Second printing, paperback, 1985
Third printing, paperback, 1989

The Johns Hopkins University Press
701 West 40th Street
Baltimore, Maryland 21211
The Johns Hopkins Press Ltd., London

Library of Congress Cataloging in Publication Data
Main entry under title:

Literature and psychoanalysis.

    "Originally appeared as a double issue, nos. 55/56 of
Yale French studies"—T.p. verso.
    1. Psychoanalysis and literature. I. Felman, Shoshana.
PN56.P92L5   1982   801′.92   81-48196
ISBN 0-8018-2753-1
ISBN 0-8018-2754-X (pbk.)

Contents

When this volume first appeared as a special issue of *Yale French Studies*, nos. 55/56 (1977), the awakening American interest in the new interpretive possibilities put forward by the French psycho-analytic context was far less evident than it is today. Now that the theoretical renewal opened up by contemporary French thought is attracting ever-growing intellectual attention in this country, now that the work of Jacques Lacan is becoming better known, the timeliness of a volume that concretely illustrates and pragmatically tests these new methods of interpretation and that collectively appraises the Lacanian contribution not just as a source of informa-tion, but, mainly, as a source of inspiration—as an unprecedented lesson in reading—is all the more apparent.

Literature and Psychoanalysis: The Question of Reading—Other-wise. Why *Otherwise?* Because the very thrust of this volume is to propose, on the one hand, a truly different, *other* approach to read-ing (reading otherwise), and on the other hand, a truly different, *other* approach to the question of the relation between psychoanalysis and literature (raising the question otherwise; relating otherwise the two disciplines; inferring in a different manner the methodological and theoretical implications of the relation).

The question hitherto neglected is, indeed, how to relate psycho-analysis and literature otherwise than at the (all-too-frequent) cost of banalizing both; how to put in contact the very genius of psycho-analysis and the (very different) genius of the thing called literature —of that which makes texts literary—without reducing their basic otherness, without compromising the differences between them which make, precisely, for the specificity of their genius.

Otherwise suggests, then, that what is at stake in the different manner of this volume is the very question of the relation between otherness and wisdom. Psychoanalysis and literature, in attempting to derive each other's wisdom without compromising the other's otherness, here renew the question not just of their respective meaning(s), but of their respective meaningfulness.

In testifying time and again—in innumerable letters—to their "exhilaration" and "excitement" over the fact that the collection opened up new avenues for their own research, readers of these essays have revealed that the volume answers a profound intellectual need in this country: a need both to uncramp the orthodoxy of psychoanalytic models and to revitalize the theory and practice of literary criticism. "The volume has made an enormous difference in my sense of the vitality of psychoanalytic interpretation," writes one reader. "The field has been given renewed potential."

It is my hope that the present republication, in its rethinking of the dialogue between psychoanalysis and literature, will continue to contribute to a furthering of our understanding both of the vitality of texts and of the textuality of life.

S.F., *October 1981*

This volume has a triple purpose:

1) To familiarize the American public with the new theoretical orientation of modern French psychoanalysis (inspired in particular by Jacques Lacan's innovative reinterpretation of Freud);

2) To initiate a dialogue, an exchange and an interaction between French and American thought, through the contact established here between French and American contributions;

3) By means of this interaction, to de-center and to displace *both* the French and the American contexts and their ways of treating the topic (literature/psychoanalysis), so as to *put the topic in motion,* and thereby to open it up to new theoretical possibilities.

To bring into communication the American and the French *styles of thought* is doubtless a complex operation, a difficult, risky, perhaps a dramatic, *enterprise of translation.* Translation, however, is what psychoanalysis is all about; the unconscious itself, in Freud's writings, is often compared to a foreign language, and Freud has literally defined the basic fact of repression as a constitutive "lack of translation." The barrier between languages foreign to each other is therefore the locus (and sometimes the means, or the alibi), of repression.

Thus, let the reader be patient (i.e., refrain from repressing too soon); let him suspend, for a moment, his natural disbelief in the face of a foreign (cultural and theoretical) *style.*

In a belated manner, and through its own deferred action, through its own unpredictable outcome, this issue will thus also have been a sort of dramatization, a theoretical *acting out,* of the very conditions of possibility, and of impossibility, of translation.

S.F., *March 1977*

"Love," says Rimbaud, "has to be reinvented." It is in much the same spirit that we would like here to reinvent the seemingly self-evident question of the mutual relationship between literature and psychoanalysis. We mean indeed to suggest that not only the approach to the question, but also, the very relationship between literature and psychoanalysis — the way in which they inform each other — has in itself to be reinvented.

Let us outline this suggestion in a series of programmatic remarks, the purpose of which would be to analyze and to put in question the apparently neutral connective word, the misleadingly innocent, colorless, meaningless copulative conjunction: *and,* in the title: "Literature and Psychoanalysis." What does the *and* really mean? What is its conventional sense, its traditional function, in the usual approach to the subject? In what way would we like to *displace* this function (to reinvent the "and"), — what would we like it to mean, how would we like it to *work,* in this issue?

Although "and" is grammatically defined as a "coordinate conjunction," in the context of the relationship between "literature and psychoanalysis" it is usually interpreted, paradoxically enough, as implying not so much a relation of coordination as one of *subordination,* a relation in which literature is submitted to the authority, to the prestige of psychoanalysis. While literature is considered as a body of *language* — to *be interpreted* — psychoanalysis is considered as a body of *knowledge,* whose competence is called upon *to interpret.* Psychoanalysis, in other words, occupies the place of a *subject,* literature that of an *object;* the relation of interpretation is structured as a relation of master to slave, according to the Hegelian definition: the dynamic encounter between the two areas is in effect, in Hegel's terms, a "fight for recognition," whose outcome is the sole recognition of the master — of (the truth of) psychoanalytical theory; literature's function, like that of the slave, is to *serve* precisely the *desire* of psychoanalytical theory — its desire for recognition; exercising its authority and *power* over the literary field, holding a discourse of masterly competence, psychoanalysis, in literature, thus seems to seek above all its own *satisfaction.*

Although such a relationship may indeed be satisfying to psychoanalytical theory, it often leaves dissatisfied the literary critic, the reader of a text, who feels that, in this frame of relationship, literature is in effect *not recognized* as such by psychoanalysis; that the psychoanalytical reading of literary texts precisely *misrecognizes* (overlooks, leaves out) their literary specificity; that literature could perhaps even be defined as that which remains in a text precisely *unaccounted for* by the traditional psychoanalytical approach to literature. In the literary critic's perspective, literature is a subject, not an object; it is therefore not simply a body of language to interpret, nor is psychoanalysis simply a body of knowledge with which to interpret, since psychoanalysis itself is equally a body of language, and literature also a body of knowledge, even though the mode of that knowledge may be different from that of psychoanalysis. What the literary critic might thus wish, is to initiate a real exchange, to engage in a real *dialogue* between literature and psychoanalysis, as between two different bodies of language and between two different modes of knowledge. Such a dialogue has to take place outside of the master-slave pattern, which does not allow for true dialogue, being, under the banner of competence, a unilateral monologue of psychoanalysis *about* literature.

In an attempt to disrupt this monologic, master-slave structure, we would like to reverse the usual perspective, and to consider the relationship between psychoanalysis and literature *from the literary point of view*. We would not presuppose, as is often done, that the business of defining, of distinguishing and of relating literature and psychoanalysis belongs, as such, to psychoanalysis. We would like to suggest — and the following articles will try to demonstrate this proposition each in its specific manner — that in much the same way as literature falls within the realm of psychoanalysis (within its competence and its knowledge), psychoanalysis itself falls within the realm of literature, and its specific logic and rhetoric. It is usually felt that psychoanalysis has much or all to teach us about literature, whereas literature has little or nothing to teach us about psychoanalysis. If only as a working hypothesis, we will discard this presupposition. Instead of literature being, as is usually the case, submitted to the authority and to the knowledge of psychoanalysis, psychoanalysis itself would then here be submitted to the literary perspective. This reversal of the perspective, however, does not intend to simply reverse the positions of master and slave in such a way that literature now would *take over* the place of the master, but rather its intention is to disrupt altogether the position of mastery as such, to try to avoid *both* terms of the alternative, to deconstruct the very structure of the *opposition,* mastery/slavery.

The odd status of what is called a "literary critic" indeed suffices to mix and shuffle the terms of the alternative. It could be argued that people who choose to analyze literature as a profession do so because they are unwilling or unable to choose between the role of the psychoanalyst (he or she who analyzes) and the role of the patient (that which is being analyzed). Literature enables them not to choose because of the following paradox: 1) the work of literary analysis resembles the work of the psychoanalyst; 2) the status of what is analyzed — the text — is, however, not that of a patient, but rather that of a master: we say of the author that he is a master; the text has for us authority — the very type of authority by which Jacques Lacan indeed defines the role of the psychoanalyst in the structure of transference. Like the psychoanalyst viewed by the patient, the text is viewed by us as "a subject presumed to know" — as the very place where meaning, and *knowledge* of meaning, reside. With respect to the text, the literary critic occupies thus at once the place of the psychoanalyst (in the relation of interpretation) *and* the place of the patient (in the relation of transference). Therefore, submitting psychoanalysis to the *literary* perspective would necessarily have a subversive effect on the clear-cut polarity through which psychoanalysis handles literature as its other, as the mere object of interpretation.

There is another point on which literature can inform psychoanalytical discourse in such a way as to deconstruct the temptation of the master's position and the master-slave pattern. There is one crucial feature which is constitutive of literature but is essentially lacking in psychoanalytical theory, and indeed in theory as such: irony. Since irony precisely consists in dragging authority as such into a scene which it cannot master, of which it is *not aware* and which, for that very reason, is the scene of its own self-destruction, literature, by virtue of its ironic force, fundamentally deconstructs the fantasy of authority in the same way, and for the same reasons, that psychoanalysis deconstructs the authority of the fantasy — its claim to belief and to power as the sole window through which we behold and perceive reality, as the sole window through which reality can indeed reach our grasp, enter into our consciousness. Psychoanalysis tells us that the fantasy is a fiction, and that consciousness is itself, in a sense, a fantasy-effect. In the same way, literature tells us that authority is a *language effect,* the product or the creation of its own *rhetorical* power: that authority is the *power of fiction;* that authority, therefore, is likewise a fiction.

The primacy granted here to the literary point of view would therefore not simply mean that literature, in its turn, would claim — as has been done — priority and authority over psychoanalysis as its influential *historical source,* as its ancestor or its predecessor in the discovery of the unconscious; but rather, the reversal of the usual perspective is here intended to displace the whole pattern of the relationship between literature and psychoanalysis from a structure of rival claims to authority and to priority to the scene of this structure's deconstruction.

In view of this shift of emphasis, the traditional method of *application* of psychoanalysis to literature would here be in principle ruled out. The notion of *application* would be replaced by the radically different notion of *implication:* bringing analytical questions to bear upon literary questions, *involving* psychoanalysis in the scene of literary analysis, the interpreter's role would here be, not to *apply* to the text an acquired science, a preconceived knowledge, but to act as a go-between, to *generate implications* between literature and psychoanalysis — to explore, bring to light and articulate the various (indirect) ways in which the two domains do indeed *implicate each other,* each one finding itself enlightened, informed, but also affected, displaced, by the other.

In its etymological sense, "implication" means "being folded within" (Latin: im-plicare = in + fold): it indicates, between two terms, a spatial relation of *interiority.* Application, on the other hand, is based on the presumption of a relation of exteriority; a presumption that, in the case of literature and psychoanalysis, can be shown to be a deceptive one. From the very beginning, indeed, literature has been for psychoanalysis not only a contiguous field of external verification in which to test its hypotheses and to confirm its findings, but also the constitutive texture of its *conceptual* framework, of its theoretical body. The key concepts of psychoanalysis are references to literature, using literary *"proper"* names — names of fictional characters (Oedipus complex, Narcissism) or of historical authors (masochism, sadism). Literature, in other words, is the language which psychoanalysis uses in order to *speak of itself,* in order to *name itself.* Literature is therefore not simply *outside* psychoanalysis, since it motivates and *inhabits* the very names of its concepts, since it is the *inherent reference* by which psychoanalysis names its findings.

However, the relation of *interiority* conveyed by the interimplication of literature and psychoanalysis is by no means a simple one. Since literature and psychoanalysis are *different* from each other, but, at the same time, they are also "enfolded within" each other, since they are, as it were, at the same time outside and inside each other, we might say that they compromise, each in its turn, the interiority of the other. The cultural division, in other words, of scholarly "disciplines" of research is by no means a natural geography: there are no *natural* boundaries between literature and psychoanalysis, which clearly define and distinguish them; the border between them is undecidable since they are really *traversed* by each other.

Each is thus a potential threat to the interiority of the other, since each is contained in the other as its *otherness-to-itself*, its *unconscious*. As the unconscious traverses consciousness, a theoretical body of thought always is traversed by its own unconscious, its own "unthought," of which it is not aware, but which it contains in itself as the very conditions of its disruption, as the possibility of its own self-subversion. We would like to suggest that, in the same way that psychoanalysis points to the unconscious of literature, *literature, in its turn, is the unconscious of psychoanalysis;* that the unthought-out shadow in psychoanalytical *theory* is precisely its own involvement with literature; that literature *in* psychoanalysis functions precisely as its *"unthought"*: as the condition of possibility *and* the self-subversive blind spot of psychoanalytical *thought*.

The articles that follow are heterogeneous, varied in their interests and in their insights. What they have in common is that none of them simply takes for granted the relationship between literature and psychoanalysis: they all reflect upon the textual and theoretical encounter between literature and psychoanalysis not as an answer, but as a question, questioning at once its possibilities and its limits. They thus suggest, each in its specific, different manner, how the question of the relationship between literature and psychoanalysis might begin to be articulated — *otherwise:* how psychoanalysis and literature might indeed begin to be rethought, both in their otherness and in their common wisdom.

SHOSHANA FELMAN

Jacques Lacan

Desire and the Interpretation of Desire in *Hamlet*

The Object Ophelia

As a sort of come-on, I announced that I would speak today about that piece of bait named Ophelia, and I'll be as good as my word.

Our purpose, as you remember, is to show the tragedy of desire as it appears in *Hamlet,* human desire, that is, such as we are concerned with in psychoanalysis.

We distort this desire and confuse it with other terms if we fail to locate it in reference to a set of co-ordinates that, as Freud showed, establish the subject in a certain position of dependence upon the signifier. The signifier is not a reflection, a product pure and simple of what are called interhuman relationships — all psychoanalytic experience indicates the contrary. To account for the presuppositions of this experience, we must refer to a topological system without which all the phenomena produced in our domain would be indistinguishable and meaningless. The illustration shows the essential co-ordinates of this topology.

The story of *Hamlet* (and this is why I chose it) reveals a most vivid dramatic sense of this topology, and this is the source of its exceptional power of captivation. Shakespeare's poetic skill doubtless guided him along the way, step by step, but we can also assume that he introduced into the play some observations from his own experience, however indirectly.

Shakespeare's play contains one shift in the plot that distinguishes it from previous treatments of the story, including both the narratives of Saxo Grammaticus and Belleforest and the other plays of which we possess fragments. This shift involves the character Ophelia.

Ophelia is present, to be sure, from the beginning of the legend on. She appears in the early versions, as I've said, as the bait in the trap that Hamlet doesn't fall into, first because he's warned in advance, and then because Ophelia herself refuses to have any part of it, having long been in love with the prince, according to Belleforest's version. Perhaps Shakespeare merely extended her function in the plot, which is to capture Hamlet's secret by surprise. But she thus becomes one of the innermost elements in Hamlet's drama, the drama of Hamlet as the man who has lost the way of his desire. She provides an essential pivot in the hero's progress toward his mortal rendezvous with his act — an act that he carries out, in some sense, in spite of himself. There is a level in the subject on which it can be said that his fate is expressed in terms of a pure signifier, a level at which he is merely the reverse-side of a message that is not even his own. Well, Hamlet is the very image of this level of subjectivity, as we shall see even more clearly in what follows.

1

Our first step in this direction was to express the extent to which the play is dominated by the Mother as Other [*Autre*], i.e., the primordial subject of the demand [*la demande*]. The omnipotence of which we are always speaking in psychoanalysis is first of all the omnipotence of the subject as subject of the first demand, and this omnipotence must be related back to the Mother.

The principal subject of the play is beyond all doubt Prince Hamlet. The play is the drama of an individual subjectivity, and the hero is always present on stage, more than in any other play. How is the desire of the Other manifested in the very perspective of this subject, Prince Hamlet? This desire, of the mother, is essentially manifested in the fact that, confronted on one hand with an eminent, idealized, exalted object — his father — and on the other with the degraded, despicable object Claudius, the criminal and adulterous brother, Hamlet does not choose.

His mother does not choose because of something present inside her, like an instinctive voracity. The sacrosanct genital object that we recently added to our technical vocabulary appears to her as

Jacques Lacan

an object to be enjoyed [*objet d'une jouissance*] in what is truly the direct satisfaction of a need, and nothing else. This is the aspect that makes Hamlet waver in his abjuration of his mother. Even when he transmits to her — in the crudest, cruellest terms — the essential message with which the ghost, his father, has entrusted him, he still first appeals to her to abstain. Then, a moment later, his appeal fails, and he sends her to Claudius' bed, into the arms of the man who once again will not fail to make her yield.

This fall, this abandon, gives us a model that enables us to conceive how it is that Hamlet's desire — his zeal with respect to an act that he so longs to carry out that the whole world becomes for him a living reproach for his perpetual inadequacy to his own will — how this zeal always flags. The dependence of his desire on the Other subject forms the permanent dimension of Hamlet's drama.

To get a better grip on the problem we must go into a psychological detail that would remain utterly enigmatic if it were not placed in the total orientation that determines the direction and meaning of the tragedy: how this permanent dimension touches the very nerve and sinew of Hamlet's will — which would appear in my diagram as the hook, the question mark, of the *Che vuoi?* of subjectivity constituted and articulated in the Other. [1]

---

[1] Lacan refers repeatedly in these sessions of his seminar to a series of diagrams with which his audience is already familiar from the previous year. Three of the diagrams are reproduced here as they appear in the text "Subversion du sujet et dialectique du désir dans l'inconscient freudien" (1960; in Jacques Lacan, *Écrits* [Paris: Seuil, 1966], pp. 793-827; graphs, pp. 805, 808 [not reproduced here], 815, 817). The reader is referred both to the theoretical development provided by the essay and to the remarks on these graphs in the "Table commentée des représentations graphiques" prepared by Jacques-Alain Miller for inclusion in the second and succeeding editions of the *Écrits* ("Les graphes du désir," pp. 907-908). Cf. also the English edition, *Ecrits: A Selection* (Norton, 1977) pp. 334-335.—Tr.

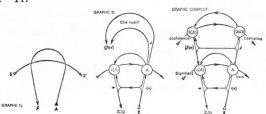

13

The end-term that buttresses this model of the subject and his question, is symbolized on our graph by the barred subject ($) in the presence of the object a — in the economic system of the psyche we call this the fantasy. Desire, which can be situated on the line A [$◇D] at a variable indeterminate point, finds in the fantasy its reference, its substratum, its precise tuning in the imaginary register.

There is something mysterious about the fantasy; indeed, it's ambiguous and paradoxical. It is on one hand the end-term of desire, and on the other hand, if we approach it from one of its aspects, it's actually located in the conscious: ambiguous indeed. Insofar as the fantasy marks every human passion with those traits which we call perverse, it appears in a sufficiently paradoxical form to have long ago motivated the rejection of the phantasmatic dimension as being on the order of the absurd. In this respect an essential step was taken in the present age when psychoanalysis undertook the interpretation of the fantasy in its very perversity. This interpretation was made possible only by placing the fantasy in an economy of the unconscious — this is what you see in the graph.

On this graph the fantasy is hooked up on the circuit of the unconscious, a very different one from the circuit commanded by the subject, which I call the level of the demand [*demande*]. In the normal state of affairs, nothing from the unconscious circuit is carried over to the level of the message, of the signified of the Other, which is the sum and module of the significations acquired by the subject in human discourse. The fantasy is not communicated to the message level: it remains separate and unconscious. When, on the other hand, it does cross over to the level of the message, we find ourselves in an atypical situation. The phases in which the fantasy makes this crossover are of a more or less pathological order. We shall give a name to these moments of crossover, of communication, which, as the diagram indicates, can take place only in one direction. I underscore this essential statement, because our purpose here is to refine our understanding and application of this apparatus.

For now, let us consider only how the moment in which Hamlet's desire becomes distracted and deflected functions in Shakespeare's tragedy, insofar as this moment must be related back to the precise adjustments of his imaginary register. Ophelia's place in this constellation is on the level of the letter *a* as it appears in our representation of the fantasy. [....]

With respect to the object *a*, at once image and pathos, the subject feels himself to be in an imaginary situation of otherness. This object satisfies no need and is itself already relative, i.e., placed in relation to the subject. It is obvious from simple phenomenology (and this is something to which I shall return in a few moments) that the subject is present in the fantasy. And the object is the object of desire only by virtue of being the end-term of the fantasy. The object takes the place, I would say, of what the subject is — symbolically — deprived of.

This may seem a bit abstract to those who have not accompanied us along the road that has led up to this point. What is it that the subject is deprived of? The phallus; and it is from the phallus that the object gets its function in the fantasy, and from the phallus that desire is constituted with the fantasy as its reference.

The object of the fantasy, image and pathos, is that other element that takes the place of what the subject is symbolically deprived of. Thus the imaginary object is in a position to condense in itself the virtues or the dimension of being and to become that veritable delusion of being [*leurre de l'être*] that Simone Weil treats when she focuses on the very densest and most opaque relationship of a man to the object of his desire: the relationship of Molière's Miser to his strongbox. This is the culmination of the fetish character of the object of human desire. Indeed all objects of the human world have this character, from one angle at least. [....]

The opaque character of the object *a* in the imaginary fantasy determines it in its most pronounced forms as the pole of perverse desire. It is the structural element of perversions, insofar as perversion is characterized by the complete emphasis in the fantasy on the strictly imaginary term, *a*. In parentheses with it we also encounter *a* plus *b* plus *c* and so forth: the most elaborate combinations of sequelae, of lingering traces combined by chance, by means of which a fantasy has crystallized and functions in a perverse desire. But however bizarre the fantasy of perverse desire may appear to you, never forget that the subject is always in some way present and involved in that fantasy. In the fantasy the subject always stands in some relationship to the pathos of existence — to the suffering of existing itself or that of existing as a term in a sexual configuration. For a sadistic fantasy to endure, the subject's interest in the person who suffers humiliation must obviously be due to the possibility of the subject's being submitted to the same humiliation himself. This is the phenomenological point to which I was alluding a few moments ago. It's a wonder indeed that people could ever think of avoiding this dimension and could treat the sadistic tendency as an instance of primal aggression pure and simple.

2

The time has come to articulate the true opposition between perversion and neurosis.

Perversion is indeed something articulate, interpretable, analyzable, and on precisely the same level as neurosis. In the fantasy, as I have said, an essential relationship of the subject to his being is localized and fixed. Well, whereas in the perversion, the accent is on the object *a,* the neurosis can be situated as having its accent on the other term of the fantasy, the $.

The fantasy is located at the extreme tip, the end-point of the subject's question, as if it were its buttress [*butée:* lit., abutment], just as the subject tries to get control of himself in the fantasy, in the space beyond the demand. This is because he must find again in the very discourse of the Other what was lost for him, the subject, the moment he entered into this discourse. What ultimately matters is not the truth but the hour [*l'heure*] of truth.

This is what permits us to specify the factor that most profoundly distinguishes the fantasy of neurosis from the fantasy of perversion.

The fantasy of perversion is namable. It is in space. It suspends an essential relationship. It is not atemporal but rather outside of time. In neurosis, on the contrary, the very basis of the relationships of subject to object on the fantasy level, is the relationship of the subject to time. The object is charged with the significance sought in what I call the hour of truth, in which the object is always at another hour, fast or slow, early or late.

I have said before that hysteria is characterized by the function of an unsatisfied desire and obsession by the function of an impossible desire. But beyond these two terms the two cases are distinguished by inverse relationships with time: the obsessive neurotic always repeats the initial germ of his trauma, i.e., a certain precipitancy, a fundamental lack of maturation.

This is at the base of neurotic behavior, in its most general form: the subject tries to find his sense of time [*lire son heure*] in his object, and it is even in the object that he will learn to tell time [*lire l'heure*]. This is where we get back to our friend Hamlet, to whom everyone can attribute at will all the forms of neurotic behavior, as far as you want to go, i.e., up to character neurosis. The first factor that I indicated to you in Hamlet's structure was his situation of dependence with respect to the desire of the Other, the desire of his mother. Here now is the second factor that I ask you to recognize: Hamlet is constantly suspended in the time of the Other, throughout the entire story until the very end.

Do you remember one of the first turning-points we focussed on when we were beginning to decipher the text of *Hamlet*? During the play scene the king becomes unsettled and visibly reveals his own guilt, incapable of viewing the dramatization of his own crime. Hamlet relishes his triumph and mocks the king. But on the way to the meeting he has already arranged with his mother, he comes upon his stepfather in prayer: Claudius is shaken to the depths of his being by the scene that has just shown him the very countenance and program of his deed. Hamlet stands before this Claudius, who by every indication is not only in no state to defend himself but also does not even see the threat that hangs over his head. And Hamlet stops, because it's not time. It's not the hour of the Other: not time for the Other to render his "audit" to heaven. That would be too kind, from one point of view, or too cruel, from another. That might not avenge his father properly, because prayer, being a gesture of repentance, might open up the way to salvation for Claudius. In any case, one thing is sure: Hamlet, who has just managed to "catch the conscience of the king" as planned—stops. Not for a moment does he think that his time has come. Whatever may happen later, this is not the hour of the Other, and he suspends his action. Whatever Hamlet may do, he will do it only at the hour of the Other.

Hamlet accepts everything. Let's not forget that at the beginning, in the state of disgust he was already in (even before his meeting with the ghost) because of his mother's remarriage, he thought only of leaving for Wittenberg. A recent commentary on a certain practicality that is becoming more and more typical of present-day life, used this as an illustration, noting that Hamlet was the best example of the fact that many dramatic crises can be avoided by the prompt issuance of passports. If Hamlet had been given his papers to travel to Wittenberg, there would have been no drama.

When he stays on, it is the hour of his parents. When he suspends his crime, it is the hour of the others. When he leaves for England, it is the hour of his stepfather. It's the hour of Rosencrantz and Guildenstern when he sends them on ahead to death—with a casualness that amazed Freud—by means of a bit of hocus-pocus that he brings off not half badly. And it is the hour of Ophelia, the hour of her suicide, when the tragedy will run its course, in a moment when Hamlet has just realized that it's not hard to kill a man, the time to say "one" ... he won't know what hit him.

He receives word of an event that in no way seems to promise an opportunity to kill Claudius: a tournament, the rules of which have been worked out to the last detail. They tempt him with the stakes—all precious objects, swords, fittings, and other things that have value only as luxuries; this should be followed in the text, for these are the nuances of the world of the collector. Hamlet's sense of rivalry and honor is aroused by the assumption that Laertes is the more skillful swordsman and by the handicap thus granted to Hamlet in the terms of the wager. This complicated ceremony is a trap for him to fall into, laid by his stepfather and his friend Laertes: we know this, but Hamlet does not. For him, going along with the wager will be a lark, like playing hookey. Still, he feels a slight warning signal in the region of his heart: something troubles him. For a moment here the dialectic of foreboding brings its special accent to the play. But, all in all, it is still at the hour of the Other, and what's more, for the sake of the Other's wager (for it is Claudius, not Hamlet, whose possessions are at stake), wearing the king's colors, for his stepfather's sake, that Hamlet enters into this supposedly friendly combat with a man considered to be a better swordsman than he. Thus Claudius and Laertes have aroused his sense of rivalry and honor, as part of a trap that is calculated to be foolproof.

Thus he rushes into the trap laid by the Other. All that's changed is the energy and fire with which he rushes into it. Until the last term, until the final hour, Hamlet's hour, in which he is mortally wounded before he wounds his enemy, the tragedy follows its course and attains completion at the hour of Other: this is the absolutely essential framework for our conception of what is involved here.

This is the sense in which Hamlet's drama has the precise metaphysical resonance of the question of the modern hero. Indeed, something has changed since classical antiquity in the relationship of the hero to his fate.

As I have said, the thing that distinguishes Hamlet from Oedipus is that Hamlet *knows*. This characteristic explains, for example, Hamlet's madness. In the tragedies of antiquity, there are mad heroes, but, to the best of my knowledge, there are no heroes—in tragedy, I say, not in legends—no heroes who feign madness. Hamlet, however, does.

I am not saying that everything in his madness comes down to feigning, but I do underscore the fact that the essential characteristic in the original legend, i.e., in the versions of Saxo Grammaticus and Belleforest, is that the hero feigns madness because he knows that he is in a position of weakness. And from that moment on, everything hinges on the question of what's going on in his mind.

However superficial this characteristic may seem to you, it's still the thing that Shakespeare seized on for his *Hamlet*. He chose the story of a hero who is forced to feign madness in order to follow the winding paths that lead him to the completion of his act. The person who knows is indeed in such a perilous position, marked for failure and sacrifice, that he is led to feign madness, and even, as Pascal says, to be mad along with everyone else. Feigning madness is thus one of the dimensions of what we might call the strategy of the modern hero.

Thus we arrive at the point at which Ophelia must fulfill her role. If the structure of the play is really as complex as I have just portrayed it as being, you may be wondering, what is the point of the character Ophelia? Ophelia is obviously essential. She is linked forever, for centuries, to the figure of Hamlet.

Some people have reproached me for the timidity with which they feel I've been proceeding. I don't think that's the case. I wouldn't want to encourage you to produce the sort of hogwash that psychoanalytic texts are full of. I'm just surprised that nobody's pointed out that Ophelia is *O phallos*, because you find other things equally gross, flagrant, extravagant, if you just open the *Papers on Hamlet,* which Ella Sharp unfortunately left unfinished and which it was perhaps a mistake to publish after her death.

Since it's getting late, I just want to stress what happens to Ophelia in the course of the play.

We first hear Ophelia spoken of as the cause of Hamlet's sad state. This is Polonius' psychoanalytic wisdom: Hamlet is sad, and that's because he's not happy, and if he's not happy, it's because of my daughter. You don't know her—she's the very finest there is—and I, of course, as a father, could never permit her to....

We first encounter Ophelia—and this makes her quite a remarkable figure already—in the context of a clinical observation. She indeed has the good fortune to be the first person Hamlet runs into after his unsettling encounter with the ghost, and she reports his behavior in terms that are worth noting.

> My lord, as I was sewing in my closet,
> Lord Hamlet, with his doublet all unbraced,
> No hat upon his head, his stockings fouled,
> Ungartered, and down-gyvèd to his ankle,
> Pale as his shirt, his knees knocking each other,
> And with a look so piteous in purport
> As if he had been loosèd out of hell
> To speak of horrors — he comes before me.
> ... ...
> He took me by the wrist and held me hard.
> Then goes he to the length of all his arm,
> And with his other hand thus o'er his brow
> He falls to such perusal of my face
> As 'a would draw it. Long stayed he so.
> At last, a little shaking of mine arm
> And thrice his head thus waving up and down,
> He raised a sigh so piteous and profound
> As it did seem to shatter all his bulk
> And end his being. That done, he lets me go,
> And with his head over his shoulder turned
> He seemed to find his way without his eyes,
> For out o' doors he went without their helps
> And to the last bended their light on me.

(Act II, Sc. I)

And Polonius cries out: This is love!

This distance from the object that Hamlet takes in order to move on to whatever new and henceforth difficult identification, his vacillation in the presence of what has been until now the object of supreme exaltation, gives us the first stage, which is, to use the English word, one of "estrangement."

That's all we can say. Nevertheless, I don't believe that it's excessive to designate this moment as pathological, related to those periods of irruption, of subjective disorganization which occur when something in the fantasy wavers and makes the components of the fantasy appear. This experience, called depersonalization, in the course of which the imaginary limits between subject and object change, leads us to what is called in the strict sense the fantastic dimension [*le fantastique*].

This dimension arises when something from the imaginary structure of the fantasy is placed in communication with something that normally reaches the level of the message, i.e., the image of the other subject, in the case in which that image is my own ego. Moreover, some authors like Federn note with great precision the necessary correlation between the feeling of the subject's own body and the strangeness of that which arises in a certain crisis, a certain rupture, when the object as such is attained.

I may have forced things here a bit for the purpose of interesting you by showing you how this episode is related to certain types of clinical experience. But I assure you that without reference to this pathological schema it is impossible to locate what Freud was the first to elevate to the level of analysis under the name of *das Unheimliche,* the uncanny, which is linked not, as some believed, to all sorts of irruptions from the unconscious, but rather to an imbalance that arises in the fantasy when it decomposes, crossing the limits originally assigned to it, and rejoins the image of the other subject.

In the case of Hamlet, Ophelia is after this episode completely null and dissolved as a love object. "I did love you once," Hamlet says. Henceforth his relations with Ophelia will be carried on in that sarcastic style of cruel aggression which makes these scenes —and particularly the scene that occupies the middle of the play— the strangest in all of classical literature.

In this attitude we find a trace of what I mentioned a moment ago, the perverse imbalance of the fantasmatic relationship, when the fantasy is tipped toward the object. Hamlet no longer treats Ophelia like a woman at all. She becomes in his eyes the childbearer to every sin, a future "breeder of sinners," destined to succumb to every calumny. She is no longer the reference-point for a life that Hamlet condemns in its essence. In short, what is taking place here is the destruction and loss of the object. For the subject the object appears, if I may put it this way, on the outside. The subject is no longer the object: he rejects it with all the force of his being and will not find it again until he sacrifices himself. It is in this sense that the object is here the equivalent of, assumes the place of, indeed is—the phallus.

This is the second stage in the relationship of the subject to the object. Ophelia is at this point the phallus, exteriorized and rejected by the subject as a symbol signifying life.

What is the indication of this? There's no need to resort to the etymology of "Ophelia." Hamlet speaks constantly of one thing: child-bearing. "Conception is a blessing," he tells Polonius, but keep an eye on your daughter. And all of his dialogue with Ophelia is directed at woman conceived as the bearer of that vital swelling that he curses and wishes dried up forever. The use of the word "nunnery" in Shakespeare's time indicates that it can also refer to a brothel. And isn't the relationship of the phallus and the object of desire also indicated in Hamlet's attitude during the play scene? In Ophelia's presence he says of her to his mother, "Here's metal more attractive," and wants to place his head between the girl's legs: "Lady, shall I lie in your lap?"

Considering the great interest of iconographers in the subject, I don't think it excessive to note that the list of flowers in the midst of which Ophelia drowns herself, explicitly includes "dead men's fingers." The plant in question is the *Orchis mascula,* which is related to the mandrake and hence to the phallic element. You'll find "dead men's fingers" in the *Oxford English Dictionary,* both under "finger" and in an entry of its own under "D," where Shakespeare's allusion is duly cited.

The third stage, to which I have already directed your attention several times, is the graveyard scene, in the course of which Hamlet is finally presented with the possibility of winding things up, of rushing to his fate. The whole scene is directed toward that furious battle at the bottom of the tomb, which I have stressed repeatedly, and which is entirely of Shakespeare's own invention. Here we see something like a reintegration of the object *a*, won back here at the price of mourning and death.

I should be able to finish up next time.

(15 April 1959)

Desire and Mourning

Thus, for Hamlet, the appointment is always too early, and he postpones it. Procrastination is thus one of the essential dimensions of the tragedy.

When, on the contrary, he does act, it is always too soon. When does he act? When all of a sudden something in the realm of events, beyond him and his deciding, calls out to him and seems to offer him some sort of ambiguous opening, which has, in specific psychoanalytical terms, introduced the perspective we call flight [*fuite*] into the dimension of accomplishment.

Nothing could be clearer on this score than the moment in which Hamlet rushes at whatever it is moving behind the arras and kills Polonius. Or think of him awakening in the dead of night on the storm-tossed ship, going about almost in a daze, breaking the seals of the message borne by Rosencrantz and Guildenstern, substituting almost automatically one message for another, and duplicating the royal seal with his father's ring. He then has the amazing good luck to be carried off by pirates, which enables him to ditch his guards, who will go off unwittingly to their own execution.

We recognize here a phenomenology that is familiar to us from our experience and our conceptions: the phenomenology of the neurotic and his relation to his life. But I have sought to lead you beyond these characteristics, however striking they may be.

24

1

I wanted to open your eyes to one structural trait that is present throughout the play: Hamlet is always at the hour of the Other.

That, of course, is just a mirage, because, as I've said, there's no such thing as an Other of the Other [*il n'y a pas d'Autre de l'Autre*]. [2] In the signifier there is nothing that guarantees the dimension of truth founded by the signifier. For Hamlet there is no hour but his own. Moreover, there is only one hour, the hour of his destruction. The entire tragedy of *Hamlet* is constituted in the way it shows us the unrelenting movement of the subject toward that hour.

Yet the subject's appointment with the hour of his destruction is the common lot of everyone, meaningful in the destiny of every individual. Without some distinguishing sign, Hamlet's fate would not be of such great importance to us. That's the next question: what is the specificity of Hamlet's fate? What makes it so extraordinarily problematic?

What does Hamlet lack? Can we, on the basis of the plan of the tragedy, as composed by Shakespeare, pin down and spell out this lack in a way that goes beyond all the approximations that we have a way of permitting ourselves and that produce the general fuzziness not only of our terminology but also of how we act with our patients and of the suggestions we make to them?

Nevertheless, let's start with an approximation. You can say in simple, everyday terms what Hamlet lacks: he's never set a goal

[2] This often repeated Lacanian formula helps to distinguish the Other (capitalized) from the other (lower case) in Lacan's own discourse and from earlier uses of the terms by other authors. The Lacanian Other is in no way the complement or the negation of the subject, nor itself essentially a subject. Although the subject may take actual persons, beginning with the father, as incarnations of the Other, the Other functions only in the symbolic register, only in the context of language, authority, law, transgression, and sanction. All this makes it impossible for the Other to have an Other of its own. — Tr.

for himself, an object—a choice that always has something "arbitrary" about it.

To put it in commonsensical terms, Hamlet just doesn't know what he wants. This aspect is brought out in the speech that Shakespeare has him pronounce at one of the turning-points in the drama, the moment when he drops out of sight, the brief interval when he goes away on this nautical excursion from which he will return most rapidly. He has no sooner left for England, still obediant, in compliance with the king's orders, than he encounters the troops of Fortinbras, who has been present from the beginning in the background of the tragedy and who at the end will come to gather the dead, to tidy up, to restore order. In this scene our friend Hamlet is struck by the sight of these courageous troops going off to conquer a few acres of Polish soil for the sake of some more or less pointless military pretext. This gives Hamlet pause to consider his own behavior.

> How all occasions do inform against me
> And spur my dull revenge! What is a man,
> If his chief good and market of his time
> Be but to sleep and feed? A beast, no more.
> Sure he that made us with such large discourse,

—the expression that is glossed "reason" is "large discourse," fundamental discourse, what I have referred to in other seminars as "concrete discourse"—

> ... such large discourse,
> Looking before and after ...

—now here's where the word "reason" comes in—

> ... gave us not
> That capability and godlike reason
> To fust in us unused. Now, whether it be
> Bestial oblivion ...

—"bestial oblivion," one of the key-words by which to measure Hamlet's existence in the tragedy—

26

> ... or some craven scruple
> Of thinking too precisely on th' event—
> A thought which, quartered, hath but one part wisdom
> And ever three parts coward — I do not know
> Why yet I live to say, "This thing's to do,"
> Sith I have cause, and will, and strength, and means
> To do't. Examples gross as earth exhort me.
> Witness this army of such mass and charge,
> Led by a delicate and tender prince,
> Whose spirit, with divine ambition puffed,
> Makes mouths at the invisible event,
> Exposing what is mortal and unsure
> To all that fortune, death, and danger dare,
> Even for an eggshell. Rightly to be great
> Is not to stir without great argument,
> But greatly to find quarrel in a straw
> When honor's at the stake. How stand I then,
> That have a father killed, a mother stained,
> Excitements of my reason and my blood,
> And let all sleep, while to my shame I see
> The imminent death of twenty thousand men
> That for a fantasy and trick of fame
> Go to their graves like beds, fight for a plot
> Whereon the numbers cannot try the cause,
> Which is not tomb enough and continent
> To hide the slain? O, from this time forth,
> My thoughts be bloody, or be nothing worth!

(Act IV, Sc. IV)

Such is Hamlet's meditation on the object of human action. This object leaves the door wide open to us for all of what I shall call the particularizations that we shall consider. That is true dedication—shedding one's blood for a noble cause, for honor. Honor, too, is portrayed correctly: being totally committed by one's word. As for the gift, we as analysts cannot overlook this concrete determination, cannot help being struck by its weight, be it in flesh or in commitment.

What I'm trying to show you here is not merely the common form of all this, the least common denominator: it's not a question of formalism. When I write the formula $\$ \Diamond a$ at the end of the question that the subject, in search of his last word, asks in the Other, this is not something that is actually open to investigation, except in that special experience. which we call psychoanalytic experience and which makes possible the exploration of the unconscious circuit running along the upper track of the graph.

What we're concerned with is the short circuit in the imaginary register between desire and that which is across from it, i.e., the fantasy. I express the general structure of the fantasy by $\math$\mathcal{S} \Diamond a$, where $\mathcal{S}$ is a certain relationship of the subject to the signifier—it is the subject as irreducibly affected by the signifier—and where $\Diamond$ indicates the subject's relationship to an essentially imaginary juncture [*conjoncture*], designated by a, not the object of desire but the object *in* desire.

Let's try to get some notion of this function of the object in desire. The drama of Hamlet makes it possible for us to arrive at an exemplary articulation of this function, and this is why we have such a persistent interest in the structure of Shakespeare's play.

This is our starting point: through his relationship to the signifier, the subject is deprived of something of himself, of his very life, which has assumed the value of that which binds him to the signifier. The phallus is our term for the signifier of his alienation in signification. When the subject is deprived of this signifier, a particular object becomes for him an object of desire. This is the meaning of $\mathcal{S} \Diamond a$.

The object of desire is essentially different from the object of any need [*besoin*]. Something becomes an object in desire when it takes the place of what by its very nature remains concealed from the subject: that self-sacrifice, that pound of flesh which is mortgaged [*engagé*] in his relationship to the signifier.

This is profoundly enigmatic, for it is ultimately a relationship to something secret and hidden. If you'll permit me to use one of those formulas which come to me as I write my notes, human life could be defined as a calculus in which zero was irrational. This formula is just an image, a mathematical metaphor. When I say "irrational," I'm referring not to some unfathomable emotional state but precisely to what is called an imaginary number. The square root of minus one doesn't correspond to anything that is subject to our intuition, anything real—in the mathematical sense of the term—and yet, it must be conserved, along with its full function. It's the same ˙ with that hidden element of living reference, the subject, insofar as, taking on the function of signifier, he cannot be subjectified as such.

The notation $\$$ expresses the necessity that S be eclipsed at the precise point where the object a attains its greatest value. This is precisely why we can grasp the true function of the object only by surveying its various possible relationships to this element. It would be excessive, perhaps, if I were to say that the tragedy of Hamlet took us over the entire range of those functions of the object. But it definitely does enable us to go much further than anyone has ever gone by any route.

2

Let's start with the ending, the meeting place, the hour of the appointment.

The final act, in which Hamlet finally puts the full weight of his life on the line, as the price for being able to accomplish his action—this act that he activates and undergoes, has something in it of the moment at the end of the hunt when everyone moves in for the kill. At the moment when his act reaches completion, he is also the deer brought to bay by Diana. A plot has been hatched out between Claudius and Laertes with incredible audacity and malice, whatever the reasons of each, and with the assistance of that loathsome insect, the ridiculous toady who comes to Hamlet to propose the tournament, that plot now closes around him.

This is the structure—extraordinarily simple. The tournament puts Hamlet in the position of being the one who, in the wager, takes up the side of Claudius, his uncle and stepfather. He thus wears another man's colors.

The tournament involves, rightly, certain stakes. In the dialogue between Hamlet and the man who comes to tell him of the conditions of the contest, nothing is spared to dazzle you with the quality, number, and array of the objects wagered. Hamlet bets Laertes six Barbary horses, against which Laertes stakes "six French rapiers and poniards," a complete outfitting for duelists, along with "hangers"—the scabbards, I suppose. Three have what the text calls "most delicate carriages," an especially elegant expression to refer to the loops from which the sword hangs. It's the sort of word a collector would use, and the same as the word for the support of a cannon.

These precious objects, gathered together in all their splendor, are staked against death. This is what gives their presentation the character of what is called a *vanitas* in the religious tradition. This is how all objects are presented, all the stakes in the world of human desire — the objects *a*.

I have indicated the paradoxical and even absurd nature of the tournament that is proposed to Hamlet. Yet he seems just to lie down and roll over, one more time, as if there were nothing in him to stand in the way of his being constantly and fundamentally at somebody else's beck and call: "Sir, I will walk here in the hall. If it please his majesty, it is the breathing time of day with me. Let the foils be brought, the gentleman willing, and the king hold his purpose, I will win for him an I can; if not, I will gain nothing but my shame and the odd hits" (Act V, Sc. II).

This is something that shows us the very nature of the fantasy. At the moment in which Hamlet is on the point of resolution —finally, as ever, on the verge of resolution—there he is, hiring himself out to someone else, and, what's more, getting nothing in return, doing it all for free, even though the other person is precisely his enemy, the man that he must defeat. He stakes his resolution against the things that interest him least in the world, and he does this in order to win for someone else.

The others think they can charm Hamlet with these objects, these collector's items, and they are doubtless wrong. Still, they are making an effective appeal to what does interest him. He is interested for the sake of honor—what Hegel calls the fight for pure prestige [3]—interested for the sake of honor in a contest that pits him against a rival whom he moreover admires. We cannot help pausing for a moment to consider the soundness of the connection advanced by Shakespeare, in which you will recognize the dialectic of what is already a long-familiar moment in our dialogue, the mirror stage.

What is expressly articulated in the text—indirectly, it is true, i.e., within a parody—is that at this point Laertes is for Hamlet his double [*semblable*]. When Osric, the tedious courtier who brings the proposal of the duel, speaks to Hamlet of his adversary, depicting the eminence of the man to whom he will have to show his mettle, Hamlet cuts him off: "Sir, his definement suffers no perdition in you, though, I know, to divide him inventorially would dozy th' arithmetic of memory, and yet but yaw neither in respect of his quick sail" (Act V, Sc. II). He delivers an extremely precious, flowery speech, parodying the style of the man he's addressing. He concludes: "I take him to be a soul of great article, and his infusion of such dearth and rareness as, to make true diction of him, his semblable is his mirror, and who else would trace him, his umbrage, nothing more."

The image of the other, as you see, is presented here as completely absorbing the beholder. The particular value of this passage, inflated with its Gongoristic conceits, is that this is Hamlet's attitude towards Laertes before the duel. The playwright situates the basis of aggressivity in this paroxysm of absorption in the imaginary register, formally expressed as a mirror relationship, a mirrored reaction. The one you fight is the one you admire the most. The ego ideal is also, according to Hegel's formula which says that coexistence is impossible, the one you have to kill.

---

[3] "*Lutte de pur prestige.*" See the presentation of section B, IV, A of Hegel's *Phenomenology of Mind* in Alexandre Kojève, *Introduction à la lecture de Hegel*, ed. Queneau (Paris: Gallimard, 1947), pp. 11-34, esp. 18, 22, 24. — Tr.

Hamlet responds to this necessity only on a disinterested level, that of the tournament. He commits himself in what we might call a formal, or even a fictive way. He is, in truth, entering the most serious of games, without knowing it. In that game he will lose his life—in spite of himself. He is going out—again, without knowing it—to meet his act and his death, which, but for an interval of a few moments, will coincide.

Everything that he saw in the aggressive relationship was only sham, a mirage. What does that mean? It means that he has entered into the game without, shall we say, his phallus. This is one way of expressing the particularity of Hamlet as subject in the play.

He does enter into the game, nevertheless. The foils are blunted only in his deluded vision. In reality there is at least one that isn't, that has been marked to be given to Laertes when the weapons are handed out: it has a real point and, what's more, is poisoned.

The off-handedness of a screenwriter is here coupled with what we might call the formidable intuition of the playwright. Shakespeare doesn't actually bother to explain how the poisoned weapon gets from the hand of one of the duelists into that of the other—this must be one of the difficulties in playing the scene. In their scuffle after Laertes scores the hit from which Hamlet will die, the point changes hands. No one bothers to explain such an amazing incident, and no one needs to. Because the important thing is to show that Hamlet can receive the instrument of death only from the other, and that it is located outside the realm of what can actually be represented on the stage. The drama of the fulfillment of Hamlet's desire is played out beyond the pomp of the tournament, beyond his rivalry with that more handsome double, the version of himself that he can love. In that realm beyond, there is the phallus. Ultimately the encounter with the other serves only to enable Hamlet to identify himself with the fatal signifier.

The funny thing is, it's there in the text. There's talk of foils as they are being handed out: "Give them the foils, young Osric. Cousin Hamlet,/ You know the wager?" Earlier Hamlet himself says, "Give us the foils." Between these two moments, Hamlet

makes a play on words: "I'll be your foil, Laertes. In mine igno-
rance/ Your skill shall, like a star i' th' darkest night,/ Stick fiery
off indeed" (Act V, Sc. II). The French translator does what he
can: "*Laerte, mon fleuret* [fencing foil] *ne sera que fleurette* [little
flower] *auprès du vôtre.*" But the word "foil" here clearly does not
mean a fencing foil; the word has a meaning—indeed, a fairly
common one—that we can trace back to its specific occurrences in
Shakespeare's day: "foil" is the same word as the Old French
feuille, used preciously to designate a container for something
precious, i.e., a jewel case. Thus the passage means: I shall be
there solely to set off your stellar brilliance against the blackness
of the sky. These are the very conditions of the duel: the odds are
set at 12 to 9, i.e., Hamlet is given a handicap. But why the pun
on "foil"? It's no accident that it's there in the text.

One of Hamlet's functions is to engage in constant punning, word
play, double-entendre—to play on ambiguity. Note that Shakespeare
gives an essential role in his plays to those characters that are called
fools, court jesters whose position allows them to uncover the most
hidden motives, the character traits that cannot be discussed frankly
without violating the norms of proper conduct. It's not a matter
of mere impudence and insults. What they say proceeds basically
by way of ambiguity, of metaphor, puns, conceits, mannered speech
—those substitutions of signifiers whose essential function I have
been stressing. Those substitutions lend Shakespeare's theater a
style, a color, that is the basis of its psychological dimension. Well,
Hamlet, in a certain sense, must be considered one of these clowns.
The fact that he is a particularly disturbing character should not
keep us from realizing that his is the tragedy that brings about this
fool's, this punster's annihilation. Without this dimension, as
someone has pointed out, more than eighty per cent of the play
would disappear.

This constant ambiguity is one of the dimensions in which
Hamlet's tension is achieved, a tension that is concealed by the
masquerade-like side of things. For Claudius, the usurper, the essential thing is to unmask Hamlet's intentions, to find out why

he is feigning madness. Still, we must not neglect the *way* in which Hamlet feigns madness, his way of plucking ideas out of the air, opportunities for punning equivocation, to dazzle his enemies with the brilliance of an inspired moment—all of which give his speech an almost maniacal quality.

The others then start to build on this themselves, even to tell tales. What strikes them in what Hamlet says is not its discordance but on the contrary its special pertinence. It is in this playfulness, which is not merely a play of disguises but the play of signifiers in the dimension of meaning, that the very spirit of the play resides.

Everything that Hamlet says, and at the same time the reactions of those around him, constitute as many problems in which the audience is constantly losing its bearings. This is the source of the scope and import of the play.

I remind you of all this to convince you that there is nothing arbitrary or excessive about allowing this last little pun on the word "foil" all its force. Hamlet's pun touches the immediate question [*Hamlet fait jeu de mots avec ce qui est alors en jeu*]: the distribution of the weapons. He says to Laertes, "I'll be your foil." And, sure enough, what will appear a moment later but the very foil that wounds him mortally and that also will permit him to complete his circuit and to kill both his opponent and the king, the final object of his mission. In this pun there lies ultimately an identification with the mortal phallus.

Here then is the constellation in which the final act is situated. The duel between Hamlet and his more handsome double is on the lower level of our graph, *i(a)—m.* Here the man for whom every man or woman is merely a wavering, reeking ghost of a living being, finds a rival his own size. The presence of this customized double will permit him, at least for a moment, to hold up his end of the human wager: in that moment, he, too, will be a man. But this customizing job is only a result, not the beginning: it is the consequence of the immanent presence of the phallus, which will be·able to appear only with the disappearance of the subject himself. The subject will succumb even before he takes it in hand to become himself a murderer.

One question arises: what enables him to have access to this signifier in this way? To reply, we shall return once more to our crossroads, this most unusual crossroads, which I have mentioned before, i.e., to what takes place in the graveyard. [. . . .]

3

Let me ask you to return to the graveyard scene, to which I have already referred you three times. There you will see something utterly characteristic: Hamlet cannot bear Laertes' display of sorrow at his sister's burial. It is the ostentatiousness of Laertes' mourning that makes Hamlet lose control, that staggers him, that shakes him so profoundly that he cannot put up with it any longer.

This is the first rivalry and the most authentic by far. Whereas Hamlet approaches the duel with the whole apparatus of chivalry and a blunted foil, at the graveyard he goes for Laertes' throat, leaping into the hole into which Ophelia's body has just been lowered.

> Show me what thou't do.
> Woo't weep? woo't fight? woo't fast? . . . .
> I'll do't. Dost thou come here to whine?
> To outface me with leaping in her grave?
> Be buried quick with her, and so will I.
> And if thou prate of mountains, let them throw
> Millions of acres on us, till our ground,
> Singeing his pate against the burning zone,
> Make Ossa like a wart! Nay, an thou'lt mouth,
> I'll rant as well as thou.

Thereupon everyone is scandalized and rushes to separate the warring brothers. And Hamlet continues:

> Hear you, sir.
> What is the reason that you use me thus?
> I loved you ever. But it is no matter.
> Let Hercules himself do what he may,
> The cat will mew, and dog will have his day.

> (Act V, Sc. I)

There's a proverbial element here which I think derives all its force from analogies that some of you are capable of drawing—I cannot go into them here.

Later, speaking with Horatio, Hamlet will explain that he couldn't stand to watch Laertes make such a spectacle of his mourning. This brings us to the heart of something that will open up an entire problematic.

What is the connection between mourning and the constitution of the object in desire? Let's go at the question by way of what is most obvious to us, which will perhaps seem the most remote from the center of what we're seeking here.

Hamlet has acted scornfully and cruelly toward Ophelia, and then some. I have already stressed the demeaning aggression and the humiliation that he constantly imposes on her, once she has become for him the very symbol of the rejection of his desire. Then, suddenly, the object regains its immediacy and its worth for him:

> I loved Ophelia. Forty thousand brothers
> Could not with all their quantity of love
> Make up my sum. What wilt thou do for her?

> (Act V, Sc. I)

These are the terms in which he begins his challenge to Laertes. Here, too, is a characteristic that presents Hamlet's structure in a different form and completes it: only insofar as the object of Hamlet's desire has become an impossible object can it become once more the object of his desire.

In the desires of obsessional neurotics we have already encountered the impossible as object of desire. But let's not be too easily satisfied with these overly obvious appearances. The very structure at the basis of desire always lends a note of impossibility to the object of human desire. What characterizes the obsessional neurotic in particular is that he emphasizes the confrontation with this impossibility. In other words, he sets everything up so that the object of his desire becomes the signifier of this impossibility.

But something even deeper demands our attention.

Jacques Lacan

Freudian formulations have already taught us to formulate mourning in terms of an object-relationship. Indeed, is it not striking that it was Freud who first stressed the object of mourning, after all those years in which psychologists had lived and thought?

The object of mourning derives its importance for us from a certain identification relationship that Freud attempted to define most precisely with the term "incorporation." Let's see if we can rearticulate the identification that takes place in mourning, in the vocabulary that we've learned to use in our work so far.

If we pursue this route, armed with our symbolical apparatus, we will gain perspectives on the function of mourning that I believe to be new and eminently suggestive, perspectives to which you would otherwise have no access. The question of what identification is must be elucidated by those categories which I have set forth in these seminars over the years, i.e., the symbolic, the imaginary, and the real.

What is the incorporation of the lost object? What does the work of mourning consist in? We're left up in the air, which explains the surcease of all speculation along the path that Freud nevertheless opened up in "Mourning and Melancholia." The question hasn't been posed properly.

Let's stay with the most obvious aspects of the experience of mourning. The subject who descends into the maelstrom of sorrow finds himself in a certain relationship to the object which is illustrated most clearly in the graveyard scene: Laertes leaps into the grave and embraces the object whose loss is the cause of his desire, an object that has attained an existence that is all the more absolute because it no longer corresponds to anything in reality. The one unbearable dimension of possible human experience is not the experience of one's own death, which no one has, but the experience of the death of another.

Where is the gap, the hole that results from this loss and that calls forth mourning on the part of the subject? It is a hole in the real, by means of which the subject enters into a relationship that is the inverse of what I have set forth in earlier seminars under the name of *Verwerfung* [repudiation, foreclosure].

Just as what is rejected from the symbolic register reappears in the real, in the same way the hole in the real that results from loss, sets the signifier in motion. This hole provides the place for the projection of the missing signifier, which is essential to the structure of the Other. This is the signifier whose absence leaves the Other incapable of responding to your question, the signifier that can be purchased only with your own flesh and your own blood, the signifier that is essentially the veiled phallus.

It is there that this signifier finds its place. Yet at the same time it cannot find it, for it can be articulated only at the level of the Other. It is at this point that, as in psychosis—this is where mourning and psychosis are related—that swarms of images, from which the phenomena of mourning arise, assume the place of the phallus: not only the phenomena in which each individual instance of madness manifests itself, but also those which attest to one or another of the most remarkable collective madnesses of the community of men, one example of which is brought to the fore in *Hamlet,* i.e., the ghost, that image which can catch the soul of one and all unawares when someone's departure from this life has not been accompanied by the rites that it calls for.

What are these rites, really, by which we fulfill our obligation to what is called the memory of the dead—if not the total mass intervention, from the heights of heaven to the depths of hell, of the entire play of the symbolic register. [. . . .]

Indeed, there is nothing of significance that can fill that hole in the real, except the totality of the signifier. The work of mourning is accomplished at the level of the *logos:* I say *logos* rather than group or community, although group and community, being organized culturally, are its mainstays. The work of mourning is first of all performed to satisfy the disorder that is produced by the inadequacy of signifying elements to cope with the hole that has been created in existence, for it is the system of signifiers in their totality which is impeached by the least instance of mourning.

Jacques Lacan

This explains the belief we find in folklore in the very close association of the lack, skipping, or refusal of something in the satisfaction of the dead, with the appearance of ghosts and specters in the gap left by the omission of the significant rite.

Here we see a new dimension in the tragedy of *Hamlet:* it is a tragedy of the underworld. The ghost arises from an inexpiable offense. From this perspective, Ophelia appears as a victim offered in expiation of that primordial offense. The same holds for the murder of Polonius and the ridiculous dragging around of his body by the feet.

Hamlet then suddenly cuts loose and mocks everyone, proposing a series of riddles in particularly bad taste which culminates in the expression "Hide fox, and all after," a reference to a sort of game of hide-and-seek. Hamlet's hiding of this body in defiance of the concerned feelings of everyone around him, is here just another mockery of that which is of central importance: insufficient mourning.

Next time we shall have to spell out the connection between the fantasy and something that seems paradoxically distant from it, i.e., the object-relationship, at least insofar as mourning permits us to shed some light on this connection. The ins and outs of the play *Hamlet* will enable us to get a better grasp of the economy —very closely connected here—of the real, the imaginary, and the symbolic. [. . . .]

(22 April 1959)

Phallophany

The tragedy *Hamlet* is the tragedy of desire. But as we come to the end of our trajectory it is time to notice what one always takes note of last, i.e., what is most obvious. I know of no commentator who has ever taken the trouble to make this remark, however hard it is to overlook once it has been formulated: from one end of *Hamlet* to the other, all anyone talks about is mourning.

Mourning is what makes the marriage of Hamlet's mother so scandalous. In her eagerness to know the cause of her beloved son's "distemper," she herself says: "I doubt it is no other but the main,/ His father's death and our o'erhasty marriage." And there's no need to remind you of what Hamlet says about the leftovers from "the funeral baked meats" turning up on "the marriage tables": "Thrift, thrift, Horatio."

This term is a fitting reminder that in the accommodations worked out by modern society between use values and exchange values there is perhaps something that has been overlooked in the Marxian analysis of economy, the dominant one for the thought of our time—something whose force and extent we feel at every moment: ritual values. Even though we note them constantly in our experience, it may be useful to give them special consideration here as essential factors in human economy.

I have already alluded to the function of ritual in mourning. Ritual introduces some mediation of the gap [*béance*] opened up by mourning. More precisely, ritual operates in such a way as to make this gap coincide with that greater *béance,* the point *x,* the symbolic lack. The navel of the dream, to which Freud refers at one point, is perhaps nothing but the psychological counterpart of this lack.

Nor can we fail to be struck by the fact that in all the instances of mourning in *Hamlet,* one element is always present: the rites have been cut short and performed in secret.

For political reasons, Polonius is buried secretly, without ceremony, posthaste. And you remember the whole business of Ophelia's burial. There is the discussion of how it is that Ophelia, having most probably committed suicide—this is at least the common belief—still is buried on Christian ground. The gravediggers have no doubt that if she had not been of such high social standing she would have been treated differently. Nor is the priest in favor of giving her Christian burial ("She should in ground unsanctified have lodged/Till the last trumpet. For charitable prayers,/ Shards, flints, and pebbles should be thrown on her" [Act V, Sc. I]), and the rites to which he has consented are themselves abbreviated. We cannot fail to take all these things into account, and there are many others as well.

The ghost of Hamlet's father has an inexpiable grievance. He was, he says, eternally wronged, having been taken unawares—and this is not one of the lesser mysteries as to the meaning of this tragedy—"in the blossoms of [his] sin." He had no time before his death to summon up the composure or whatever that would have prepared him to go before the throne of judgment.

Here we have a number of "clues," as they say in English, which converge in a most significant way—and where do they point? To the relationship of the drama of desire to mourning and its demands.

This is the point that I would like to focus on today, in an attempt to delve into the question of the object such as we encounter it in psychoanalysis—the object of desire.

1

There is first of all a simple relationship that the subject has to the object of desire, a relationship that I have expressed in terms of an appointment. But you will not have failed to notice that we are approaching the question of the object from quite a different angle when we speak of the object such as the subject identifies himself with it in mourning—the subject, it is said, can reintegrate the object into his ego. What does that mean? Aren't we dealing here with two phases which are not reconciled in psychoanalytic theory? Doesn't this call for an attempt to get deeper into the problem?

What I have just said about mourning in *Hamlet* must not obscure the fact that at the bottom of this mourning, in *Hamlet* as in *Oedipus,* there is a crime. Up to a certain point, the whole rapid succession, one instance of mourning after another, can be seen as consequences of the initial crime. It is in this sense that *Hamlet* is an Oedipal drama, one that we can read as a second

Oedipus Rex and locate at the same functional level in the genealogy of tragedy. This is also what put Freud, and his disciples after him, onto the importance of *Hamlet*.

Indeed, the psychoanalytic tradition sees in Oedipus' crime the quintessential charting of the relationship of the subject to what we call here the Other, i.e., to the locus of the inscription of the law. This same tradition places Hamlet at the center of its consideration of the problem of origins. This is a good point at which to recall certain essential details of how the relationship of the subject to the original crime has been articulated for us up till now.

Instead of taking the usual course of leaving things in a state of fuzzy confusion, which doesn't make theoretical speculation any easier, we must make distinctions. There are two stages.

The first is that of the crime, perfectly illustrated by *Totem and Taboo,* which deserves to be called the Freudian myth. We can even say that Freud's construction may well be the sole example of a full-fledged myth to have emerged in our historical age. This myth shows us an essential connection: the order of the law can be conceived only on the basis of something more primordial, a crime. This is also the meaning for Freud of the Oedipal myth.

For Freud, the primal murder of the father forms the ultimate horizon of the problem of origins. Note, too, that he finds it relevant for every psychoanalytic issue, and he never considers a discussion closed until it is brought in. This primal patricide, which he places at the origin of the horde and at the origin of the Judaic tradition, clearly has a mythic character.

The connection between the law and the crime is one thing. Another is what develops from this connection when the tragic hero—both Oedipus and each one of us potentially at some point of our being, when we repeat the Oedipal drama—renews the law on the level of tragedy, and, in a sort of baptism, guarantees its rebirth. This is the second stage.

The tragedy of Oedipus satisfies perfectly the definition I have just given of myth as ritual reproduction. Oedipus, who is actually completely innocent, unconscious and unaware, manages without realizing it—in a sort of dream that is his life (life is a dream)—to renew the channels of access from crime to the restoration of order. He takes on the punishment himself and at the end seems to us to be castrated.

This is the element that remains hidden if we restrict ourselves to the first stage, that of the primal murder. Indeed, the most important thing is punishment, sanction, castration—the hidden key to the humanization of sexuality, the key with which we are accustomed by our experience to make the accidents of the evolution of desire fall into place.

It is not without interest to take note of the dissymmetries between the tragedy of Oedipus and the tragedy of Hamlet. It would be too elaborate an exercise to list them in detail, but I shall nevertheless give you a few indications.

In *Oedipus,* the crime takes place at the level of the hero's own generation; in *Hamlet,* it has already taken place at the level of the preceding generation. In *Oedipus,* the hero, not knowing what he's doing, is in some way guided by fate; in *Hamlet,* the crime is carried out deliberately.

The crime in *Hamlet* is the result of betrayal. Hamlet's father is taken by surprise in his sleep, in a way that is utterly foreign to the current of his waking thoughts. "I was cut off," he says, "even in the blossoms of my sin." He is struck by a blow from a sector from which he does not expect it, a true intrusion of the real, a break in the thread of destiny. He dies, as Shakespeare's text tells us, on a bed of flowers, which the play-scene will go so far as to reproduce in the opening pantomime.

The sudden intrusion of the crime is somehow, paradoxically, compensated for by the fact that in this case the subject *knows.* This is not one of the less puzzling aspects of the play. The drama of Hamlet, unlike that of Oedipus, does not start off with the question "What's going on?," "Where is the crime?," "Where is the criminal?" It begins with the denunciation of the crime, with the crime as it is brought to light in the ear of the subject. We can express the ambiguity of this revelation in the form used in our algebra for the message of the unconscious, i.e., the signifier of barred A [S($\cancel{A}$)].

In the normal form, if we can put it that way, of the Oedipal situation, the S($\cancel{A}$) is embodied by the Father, since he is the expected source of the sanction from the locus of the Other, the truth about truth. The Father must be the author of the law, yet he cannot vouch for it any more than anyone else can, because he, too, must submit to the bar, which makes him, insofar as he is the real father, a castrated father.

The situation at the beginning of *Hamlet* is completely different, even though it can be represented by the same notation. The Other reveals himself from the beginning as the barred Other. He is barred not only from the world of the living but also from his just retribution. He has entered the kingdom of hell with this crime, this debt that he has not been able to pay, an inexpiable debt, he says. And indeed, this is for his son the most frightening implication of his revelation.

Oedipus paid. He represents the man whose heroic lot is to carry the burden of requited debt. On the contrary, Hamlet's father must complain for all eternity that he was interrupted, taken by surprise, cut off in midstream—that to him the possibility of response, of retribution, is forever sealed off.

You see that our investigation, as it moves along, leads us to ask questions about retribution and punishment, i.e., about what is involved in the signifier phallus in castration.

Freud himself indicated, perhaps in a somewhat *fin de siècle* way, that for some reason when we lived out the Oedipal drama, it was destined to be in a warped form, and there's surely an echo of that in *Hamlet*.

Consider one of Hamlet's first exclamations at the end of the first act: "The time is out of joint. O cursèd spite/ That ever I was born to set it right!" "O cursèd . . ."—the word "spite," which appears throughout Shakespeare's sonnets, can only be translated "*dépit*," grudge, vexation—"he did it out of pure spite." But let's be careful here. To understand the Elizabethans one must first turn

Jacques Lacan

certain words around on their hinges so as to give them a meaning somewhere between the subjective one and the objective one. Today the word "spite"—as in "he did it out of pure spite"— has a subjective meaning, whereas in "O cursèd spite" it's somewhere in between, between the experience of the subject and the injustice in the world. We seem to have lost the sense of this reference to the world order. "O cursèd spite" is what Hamlet feels spiteful toward and also the way that the time is injust to him. Perhaps you recognize here in passing, transcended by Shakespeare's vocabulary, the delusion of the *schöne Seele,*[4] from which we have not escaped, far from it, all our efforts notwithstanding. When I referred to the sonnets just now, it was not purely gratuitous. So—I translate: *"O malédiction, que je ne sois né jamais pour le remettre droit."*

This justifies and deepens our understanding of *Hamlet* as possibly illustrating a decadent form of the Oedipal situation, its decline. This is the same word that we find in Freud's expression, *der Untergang des Ödipus-Komplexes,* the decline or dissolution of the Oedipus complex—in the life of each individual, he means. This is the title he gives to one of his texts, not a long one, which I'd like to bring to your attention now. You'll find it in Volume XII of the *Gesammelte Werke* [*Standard Edition*, XIX, 173-79].

2

Thus in 1924 Freud himself calls attention to what is ultimately the puzzle of the Oedipus complex. It's not simply that the subject wanted, desired to kill his father and to violate his mother, but that that is in the unconscious.

[4] Allusion to Hegel's dialectic of the withdrawn, contemplative "beautiful soul" (*Phenomenology of Mind,* tr. Baillie [New York: Harper & Row, 1967], pp. 663-67, 675-76, 795), generally considered itself an allusion in turn to a variety of eighteenth- and early nineteenth-century writers, primarily in Germany. In several other contexts, Lacan links this dialectic to others in the *Phenomenology* ("master-slave," "law of the heart") and stresses that the beautiful soul denounces the perceived disorder of the world around him without recognizing that this disorder is a reflection of his own inner state. See *Écrits,* pp. 171-73, 281, 292, 415.—Tr.

How does that come to be in the unconscious? How does it come to reside there so that the subject, during an important period of his life, the latency period, which is the source of the construction of his entire world, is no longer concerned by the Oedipal situation at all—to such an extent that Freud could admit, at least at the beginning of his treatment of the issue, that in an ideal case this lack of concern is a happy, definitive resolution of the whole business?

Let's begin with what Freud tells us; then we'll see whether it's grist for our mill.

When does the Oedipus complex, according to Freud, go into its *Untergang*, that decisive event for all of the subject's subsequent development? When the subject feels the threat of castration, and feels it from both directions implied by the Oedipal triangle. If he wants to take his mother's place, the same thing will happen —remember that he is aware of the fact that woman is castrated, this perception marking the completion and maturity of the Oedipus complex. Thus, with regard to the phallus, the subject is caught in an impossible dilemma with no avenue of escape.

Thus the phallus is this thing that is presented by Freud as the key to the *Untergang* of the Oedipus complex. I say "thing" and not "object," because it is a real thing, one that has not yet been made a symbol, but that has the potential of becoming one.

Freud's presentation of the problem puts the female child in a situation that is not at all dissymmetrical with that of the male. With respect to this thing, the subject enters into a relationship that we may call one of lassitude—the word is in Freud's text— where gratification is concerned. As for the boy, he decides he's just not up to it. And as for the girl, she gives up any expectation of gratification in this way—the renunciation is expressed even more clearly in her case than in his. All we can say is expressed in a formulation that doesn't come out in Freud's text but whose pertinence is everywhere indicated: the Oedipus complex goes into its decline insofar as the subject must mourn the phallus.

This serves to illuminate the later function of this moment of desire. The scraps and fragments of the Oedipus complex, more or less incompletely repressed, emerge in puberty in the form of neurotic symptoms. But that's not all. It is the common experience of analysts that the genital normalization of the subject, [5] not only in the economy of his unconscious but also in the economy of his imaginary register, depends on the decline of the Oedipus complex. If the process of genital maturation is to turn out well, the Oedipus complex must be terminated as completely as possible, for the consequence of this complex in both man and woman is the scar, the emotional stigma, of the castration complex. We may be able to shed some light on the decline of the Oedipus complex as mourning for the phallus if we refer to what Freud's writings tell us about the mechanism of mourning. There's a synthesis to be made here.

What defines the limits of the objects for which we may have to mourn? This, too, has not been worked out yet. We can certainly imagine that the phallus is not just one more object to be mourned like all the others. Here, as everywhere else, it has a place of its own, a place apart. This place is what we want to determine, to determine against a background. Then the place of the background itself will become apparent as a result.

Here we're on completely new ground, where we encounter what I call the question of the place of the object in desire. This is the question that I have been exploring [*que je laboure*] with you by means of a series of concentric strokes; I put various stresses on it to give it various resonances, and our analysis of *Hamlet* should help us to pursue it further.

What gives the phallus its particular value? Freud replies, as always, without the slightest precaution—he bowls us over, and thank God he did it till the day he died, for otherwise he never could have finished what he still had to lay out [*tracer*] in his field

<hr/>

[5] See the article "Stade (ou Organisation) génital(e)" in Jean Laplanche and J.-B. Pontalis, *Vocabulaire de la psychanalyse* (Paris: Presses Universitaires de France, 1967). — Tr.

of work—Freud replies that it's a narcissistic demand [*exigence*] made by the subject.

At the moment of the final outcome of his Oedipal demands, the subject, seeing himself castrated in any case, deprived of the thing, prefers, as it were, to abandon a part of himself, which will henceforth be forever forbidden to him, forming the punctuated chain of signifiers that forms the top of our diagram. If the love relationship that is caught up in the parental dialectic recedes, if the subject permits the Oedipal relationship to founder, it is because—says Freud—of the phallus, of that phallus that is introduced so enigmatically from the beginning of the narcissistic stage on.

What does that mean to us, in terms of our vocabulary?

There's no point in referring back to all of this unless it permits us to shed some light on what Freud must leave out. He leaves it out because he needs to get to the heart of the matter and doesn't have time to dwell on his assumptions. This is moreover the way that all action, generally speaking, is founded, especially all true action, which the action that concerns us here should be.

Well, in terms of our discourse, "narcissistic" has something to do with the imaginary register. Let's start by saying that the subject must explore [*faire le tour de*] his relationship to the field of the Other, i.e., the field organized in the symbolic register, in which his demand for love has begun to express itself. It is when he emerges from this exploration, having carried it to the end, that the loss of the phallus occurs for him and is felt as such, a radical loss. How does he respond then to the necessity [*exigence*] of this mourning? Precisely with the composition of his imaginary register and with nothing else—a phenomenon whose similarity to a psychotic mechanism I have already indicated. [. . . .]

The position of the phallus is always veiled. It appears only in sudden manifestations [*dans des phanies*], in a flash, by means of its reflection on the level of the object. For the subject, of course, it's a question of to have it or not to have it. But the radical position of the subject at the level of privation, of the subject as subject of desire, is not to be it. The subject is himself, so to speak, a negative object.

We can say that the forms in which the subject appears at the levels of castration, of frustration, and of privation, are forms of alienation, but we must provide for each of the three a characterization that distinguishes it perceptibly from the others. At the level of castration, the subject appears in a blackout [*syncope*] of the signifier. It's something else when he appears at the level of the Other, in a state of submission to the law of one and all. It's something else again when he himself must situate himself in desire. The form of his disappearance has in this case a singular originality, well suited to prompt us to formulate it further on.

This is indeed the direction in which the course of the tragedy *Hamlet* is taking us.

3

Indeed, the "something rotten" with which poor Hamlet is confronted is most closely connected with the position of the subject with regard to the phallus. And the phallus is everywhere present in the disorder in which we find Hamlet each time he approaches one of the crucial moments of his action.

There's something very strange in the way Hamlet speaks about his dead father, an exaltation and idealization of his dead father which comes down to something like this: Hamlet has no voice with which to say whatever he may have to say about him. He actually chokes up and finally concludes by saying—in a particular form of the signifier that is called "pregnant" in English, referring to something that has a meaning beyond its meaning—that he can find nothing to say about his father except that he was like anyone else. What he means is very obviously the opposite. This is the first indication, the first trace, of what I want to talk about here.

Another trace is that the rejection, deprecation, contempt that he casts on Claudius has every appearance of *dénégation*. [6] The torrent of insults that he unleashes on Claudius—in the presence of his mother, namely—culminates in the phrase "a king of shreds and patches." We surely cannot fail to relate this to the fact that, in the tragedy of Hamlet, unlike that of Oedipus, after the murder of the father, the phallus is still there. It's there indeed, and it is precisely Claudius who is called upon to embody it.

Claudius' real phallus is always somewhere in the picture. What does Hamlet have to reproach his mother for, after all, if not for having filled herself with it? And with dejected arm and speech he sends her back to that fatal, fateful object, here real indeed, around which the play revolves.

For this woman—who doesn't seem to us so very different from other women, and who shows considerable human feelings—there must be something very strong that attaches her to her partner. And doesn't it seem that that is the point around which Hamlet's action turns and lingers? His astounded spirit, so to speak, trembles before something that is utterly unexpected: the phallus is located here in a position that is entirely out of place in terms of its position in the Oedipus complex. Here, the phallus to be struck at is real indeed. And Hamlet always stops. The very source of what makes Hamlet's arm waver at every moment, is the narcissistic connection that Freud tells us about in his text on the decline of the Oedipus complex: one cannot strike the phallus, because the phallus, even the real phallus, is a *ghost*.

We were troubled at the time by the question of why, after all, no one assassinated Hitler—Hitler, who is very much this object that is not like the others, this object *x* whose function in the homogenization of the crowd by means of identification is de-

[6] Lacan's translation of Freud's term *Verneinung*, usually translated in English as "negation." Its use here suggests that Hamlet's hostile references to Claudius can be interpreted as indications of repressed admiration. See Freud's 1925 essay, "Negation" (*Standard Edition*, XIX, 235-39), and the corresponding article in Laplanche and Pontalis.—Tr.

monstrated by Freud. Doesn't this lead back to what we're discussing here?

The question at hand is the enigmatic manifestation of the signifier of power, of potency: the Oedipal situation, when it appears in the particularly striking form in the real that we have in *Hamlet,* with the criminal, the usurper, in place and functioning *as* usurper. What stays Hamlet's arm? It's not fear—he has nothing but contempt for the guy—it's because he knows that he must strike something other than what's there. Indeed, two minutes later, when he arrives at his mother's chamber and is beginning to give her all holy hell, he hears a noise behind the curtain, and he lunges out without looking first.

I don't recall now what astute commentator pointed out that Hamlet cannot possibly believe that it's Claudius, because he's just left him in the next room. Nevertheless, when he has disemboweled poor Polonius, he remarks: "Thou wretched, rash, intruding fool..../ I took thee for thy better." Everyone thinks that he meant to kill the king, but in the presence of Claudius, the real king and the usurper as well, he did after all hold back: he wanted something or someone better, wanted to cut him off, too, in the blossoms of his sin. Claudius, as he knelt there before him, wasn't quite what Hamlet was after—he wasn't the right one.

It's a question of the phallus, and that's why he will never be able to strike it, until the moment when he has made the complete sacrifice—without wanting to, moreover—of all narcissistic attachments, i.e., when he is mortally wounded and knows it. The thing is strange and obvious, recorded in all sorts of little riddles in Hamlet's style.

Polonius for him is merely a "calf," one that he has in some sense sacrificed to the spirit of his father. When he's stashed him under the stairs and everyone asks him what's going on, he goes into a few of his jokes, which are always so disconcerting for his adversaries. Everyone wonders whether what he says is really what he means, because what says gets them all where they're the touchiest. But for him to say it, he must know so much that they can't believe it, and so on and so forth.

This is a position that must be quite familiar to us from the phenomenon of the avowal made by the subject. He speaks these words which up till now have remained as good as sealed to the commentators: "The body is with the king"—he doesn't use the word "corpse," please notice—"but the king is not with the body." Replace the word "king" with the word "phallus," and you'll see that that's exactly the point—the body is bound up [*engagé*] in this matter of the phallus—and how—but the phallus, on the contrary, is bound to nothing: it always slips through your fingers. [....]

> Hamlet: The king is a thing —
> Guildenstern: A thing, my lord?
> Hamlet: Of nothing.

(29 April 1959)

French text edited by Jacques-Alain Miller, from transcripts of Lacan's Seminar. Translated by James Hulbert.

Daniel Sibony

Hamlet: A Writing-Effect

To be or to produce a writing-effect: that was the question. But what is a writing-effect?

Indeed it is always possible to say that when the signifier starts to play for itself and its precipitations become dense enough to carry the continuity of their game and its discontinuities, then spoken language is caught by or caught up in writing-effects that slice through it and jam its works, no matter what. And after all, isn't the smallest writing-effect the joke, the play on words that trips up the One, the straw that broke the camel's back: a frozen mass of expectation both diverts it and makes it yield up a smidgen of the *real* .... Still, this says nothing about what is at stake in an instance of writing (it does, though: the pleasure of the joke, or *jouissance* [enjoyment/use/bliss/orgasm] — but just exactly which *jouissance*?) or the mechanism of a piece of writing, what makes it stand up as such — the solid, rigid forms that it produces to support the presence of the words that cling to it.

So let's start off with an archaic form, associated with the representation [*mise en scène*] of the repudiated sacrifice, which suggests a stain as well, a bond, and the thing that most frustrates the topologist—a *knot:* [1] in a word, writing. It's worth noting that it sounds like the word of negation, both in English and in French *(knot/not; nœud/ne):* this *not* proves to be at the center of every writing-effect, doubtless because of its reversals, which reintroduce the limits of the body and that final incompletion which marks desire: *je crains qu'il* ne *se défasse,* or *qu'il* ne *revienne* [2]—who,

---

[1] In France, the question of knots and their relevance for psychoanalytic theory dates from Lacan's introduction of the problem in recent years of his seminar. See his *Encore* (Paris: Seuil, 1975), pp. 107-123.—Tr.

the ghost with the lifted visor? But who is he, and is writing inseparable from this ghost story in which the son's downfall is in his failure to translate-betray [*traduire-trahir*] his name (in which Hamlet subverts the traditional identifications associated with the phallus, the identification of having it with being it, and that of not having it with the dead being [*l'être morte*], [3] the unfathomable mother . . .)?

So why is it—since there are objects that lead directly to what writing questions, the knot, a soft empty spool of unrecognized threads, an erectile ball—why is it so strangely difficult, as Lacan says, to manipulate it? This is a particularly difficult question, not easy to define, especially since it is taken up at the point at which it serves notice on space, the space of drives, the body: follow a knot with your eye, tie your gaze in a knot, and it's your gaze that comes untied. At any rate, this bit of deception that makes you mistake one knot for another when they are *perhaps* different, or that keeps you from associating one with the other when they are the same—this bit of deception is very close to another, more intrinsic sort of deception: that in general there is no algorithm that makes it possible to go from one to the other, an algorithm and thus a way of writing that would bridge the gap between the two forms and would annul in one whatever could not be reduced to the other, or would provide a measurement of this difference. Curiously, it is this lack of a writing-bridge which helps to establish the knot as a form of writing. We should remember this hollow space from which any writing is set in motion, from which it spreads or is expected, despite the possibility that the program that it brings about may involve metaphor and fill up the hollow-(ing) of writing [*ce qui de l'écriture évide*]. This writing already

---

[2] In French, certain expressions of fearing are frequently followed by an extra *ne* in the noun clause that follows. English translations of the examples in the text show that the *ne* is not logically necessary: "I am afraid that it will come untied" or "that he will return." Cf. the Latin *nē* and the English *lest,* as well as Lacan, *Écrits* (Paris: Seuil, 1966), pp. 663-64, 800. — Tr.

[3] Play on *"lettre morte"*: dead letter; something invalid, not understood, or treated as being of no consequence. — Tr.

Daniel Sibony

seems to be one boundary of its own rewriting, as well as a support for its own possible translatabilities.

This paradox is only an apparent one, one that we also see elsewhere—everyone knows the connection between the proper name and the writing-effect, and that this connection is not unrelated to the fact that the proper name is unchanged from language to language, even if it doesn't happen to be *written* in the same way. Now, it's obvious that between two languages, two living languages equipped with speaking bodies of determined sex, the bridges are burnt—fortunately; otherwise God would be an inmate crying out in this madhouse, would no longer be at a distance ... or else there would be one fundamental language and that would be slaughter —but not *because of* paranoia (for if there were a fundamental language, then indeed there would be no paranoia). So the bridges are burnt, and all the more so when languages seem relatively close: you know this little speech in which Kafka, when presenting a Yiddish poetry reading to a German-speaking Jewish audience who *of course* did not understand Yiddish, says to them: "I can see the fear in your eyes." I have said elsewhere [4] that that fired them up for the Gehenna of desire, the embarrassment [*géhenne/gêne; gêne éthique/génétique*], ethical or not, of their desire [or "of their delusion": *du leur/du leurre*]. It's not so far from writing—to think that with one strange language one can stage or represent others— in this case one other, German—by *disrupting* the limits of its auto-erotic music, of its self-comprehension (the air with which it understands itself), by using skillful clamor to fondle its terrible "innocence"; to think that with an explosion it confers upon its shaken sons (shaken by having seen the realization of their fantasies of maternal prostitution) the mission of reintegrating it into its *natural* enclosures by breaking into the real with total, cannibal comprehension. . . .

---

[4] "Remarques sur l'affect 'ratial'" in *Éléments pour une analyse du fascisme,* comp. Macciocchi (Paris: Union Générale d'Éditions, 1976), II, 159. — Tr.

And now, what if these foreign languages that worry about their doubling [*doublure*], were estranged fragmentations *within* one and the same language? They are like blocks cut up in pieces, adrift, because different writings separate them; and indeed, the thing a language can stand the least is to be inhabited by fragmentation. Their collisions, overloadings, and proximities give the measure of the internal destructibility of the language, the histories that it can have, the cracks in its climax [*jouissance*]—in short, the increasing levels of writing that it sustains and that the writer as artist has the perversion of tracking down. Find the rebellious, inadmissable foreign languages that run through the language, free the animals that give it life [*les animaux qui l'animent*], and you will have its cutting lines [*lignes de coupure*] and thus the movement of its internal translations, the style of its various kinds of writing, the a-symmetries that throw it out of equilibrium and go beyond it; that the unconscious does *not* know contradiction [*que l'inconscient ne connaît pas la contradiction*] proves that it is a carving up of language, a cut-and-paste job performed on languages foreign to one another. One would think that these cracks in language are a matter of sex, but it's not that simple: if it's true that all writing depends for its effect on referring to the sexual hole [*le trou sexuel*], and hence to perversion, it cannot be ruled out that writing might survive only by betraying that perversion which it entails. But it is certain that something is being engendered; this is even represented in a somewhat droll event in the holy scriptures, in which, in fact, it is very rare that we do not find any given literary writing-effect represented or personified, which moreover makes the thing unreadable. In the Bible, though, there is this woman who feels too much movement in her belly and simply goes off to ask God about it, who functions as the levy station [*lieu de prélèvement*] for utterances [*énonciations*] (and even annunciations) that are untenable in language, to be told that precisely that will produce two foreign languages, which starts up the murder of the brother all over again.

This is to say that the presence of these two mutually foreign blocks conditions every writing-function, not only because these blocks are signifiers—which they are of necessity—but because they support different levels of utterance and produce holes in the signifier, where bodies come to swarm. Is it possible then to say that a piece of writing takes effect only from another, by the third form by means of which it calls forth or revives [*suscite ou resuscite*] the other writing? This would be all the more prevalent the greater the distance between this writing and its reading of itself. Consider simply the embarrassment that you feel when you perceive the distance between speaking and writing, between the density of your voice as it reads your text, and your speech [*parole*], which is its double. Is it merely the presence of this double which makes your voice strange, foreign? Or are you not rather thrust into a ghostly representation *conceived* by the other [*l'autre*], a representation whose identification consumes you? Consider also the theatrical or ritual representation occasioned by the reading of a text when the reading is (of necessity) foreign to the text. For it is obvious that *writing* is different from *reading,* and the two coincide only when it is necessary to protect a piece of writing from the tenacious danger of its translatabilities. Doubtless, there is no "real" writing—i.e., none that is sufficiently involved with the "real" of sexual identity [*sexuation*]—which does not perform a vivisection in the gap between reading and writing and which, as a new way of writing, does not live exclusively from its fundamental lack of self-identity, self-possession, self-adequacy.

We are familiar with the fantasy in which a subject, apparently male, imagines his sexual organ thrust from within into the organ of another man, so that he hopes to have an erection himself from the other man's erection: quite a provocative little vision, one that covers not merely submission to the enjoyment [*jouissance*] of another person, nor merely the representation of a phallic transmission—a very special sort of interlocking or gestation, it is a kind of success of the erotic relationship in its parasitic aspect. And if the comparison made by our psychoanalytic forebears which likened writing to the manipulation of the penis were still valid, this fantasy would be a caricature model of writing in writing, one that would tend rather to signify its hopelessness.

Is there any writing that bridges the gap between two signifiers? There is of course the bar,[5] but it is there only as an abstract presence in place of what might be written there. We know that some people have even taken this as a process of fabrication to construct bridges between words that are *almost* the same [*semblables*], to produce sentences that retain this fatal "almost" of the double and to narrate or reveal the pure manifestation of this coupling. This is brought off best by showing that there are no bridges, and moreover that a bridge that must pass from a simple being to his double, must cross the fatal surface from here to the beyond. Thus these bridges are always in a state of ruin, impossible bridges, including the bridge that it is *literally* madness to cross and from which one of Kafka's first heroes plunges to death by drowning as Kafka himself thus enters the stream of writing. Ultimately these bridges may function well only in mathematics, for the simple reason that they lead nowhere and that the only ones who use them are the engineers who build them, and that in mathematics the task is all the easier and the pleasure all the greater because the mathematician moves from one block to another that is *supposed* to be different and because he declares at the beginning (a = a) that he will ignore the strangeness of the thing to itself.

Thus the question involves what happens between two different pieces of writing in the sudden manifestation of their proximity, their doubling, the trampling or the forced fertilization of one by the other, or the derivation of one from the other; this event

[5] Line separating the numerator and the denominator in a fraction or used in similar notation. See for example Lacan, "L'instance de la lettre dans l'inconscient ou la raison depuis Freud" in *Écrits*, esp. pp. 499, 501, 515. In other contexts the same word refers to the slash that cancels a number or a letter, implying its impairment, "fading," or unconsciousness. — Tr.

Daniel Sibony

is the cutting that each one brings about and the abyss whose hollowness is shown by the doubled being of their presence.

Now, in the effect of the written poetic object, everything is in ruins; things are stopped up, and the real impasse (that of the sexual relationship)[6] is present; but between the simplest level of forced fertilization and the explosions of writing that escape writing, there are possibilities. Think of Joyce and Kafka: obviously neither of them believed in the sexual relationship, without which a certain kind of writing cannot be produced; but in the case of one, woman remained the rock, the granite boundary that runs along the path to the good place along which man loses his way, whereas Joyce smashes through all these boundaries and leads us to the bed where Molly, the woman, weaves her monologue. And it is no accident that this sent him, the man who wrote it, into *Finnegans Wake,* because ultimately the stubborn question that keeps returning, like the real, is indeed the way that he is hooked to language, the possibility of creating new inner limits that stun it: writing that stuns language. Hamlet proclaims it in his own vocal range, in his own fashion: "O wonderful son, that can so stonish a mother!" But even Hamlet does not believe in this state of wonder, for he adds: "But is there no sequel at the heels of this mother's admiration?"

I shall speak of *Hamlet* as a model that follows and provides differentiated veins through the bedrock of writing, veins whose movement can be related to the materiality of the piece of writing that is represented [*l'écrit mis en scène*]. (It is moreover rare for great writing not to erode the literal pathways that run through it and not thus to change the backdrop of its expression.) Thus there is a representation of the function of writing as such, organized around its own generation in written form, self-productive of the flashes and discontinuities that give it life by means of their repeti-

---

[6] "Sexual relationship" is one translation of *"rapport sexuel,"* the plural of which might be translated "sexual relations," as in "to have sexual relations with someone." (*Rapport* can also mean "bond," "ratio," "report," "profit.") (Cf. Lacan, *Encore,* p. 57 et passim, and his "...ou pire" in *Scilicet* 5 (1975), p. 7. For Lacan, there is no *"rapport sexuel,"* i.e., sexual relations do not relate the sexes.)—Tr.

tion: it is self-generating, autogenous, autoerogenous, and at the same time it spreads its interpretation in written objects, mazes strung throughout history, picking up more or less consistent forms of writing to offer its threads [*fils*] and its derivations [*filiations*] to be picked up by other writing. This interaction of the riggings of writing leads to essential discontinuities: what *matters* in the written work of art, as in every radical writing-effect, are the discontinuities that it reveals, that it turns up in language, the possible outcomes from which new reckonings and new numbers are possible. From this discovery, the subject tries to produce something that will enable him to account for himself, something that will imply and provide a reference-point for [*qui suppose et supporte*] effects of sublimation which cannot readily be confused with the lukewarm evaporation of drives or with repression pure and simple. These cutting lines open up unexpected levels of expression and make them function, in whatever material form the levels of expression embody the cutting lines. This implies that such kinds of writing are not to be interpreted, because they come into being by "overcoming" interpretation and cutting across it. One's only option is to follow up on it with another piece of writing, so as to capture in this new representation the movement by means of which the various followups produce the interpretation of the spoken Name [7] that they do not pronounce. This is of enormous interest to the analyst, who sometimes deludes himself [8] that he is there to read and decipher texts: it is indeed a question of the fury [9] of the text, the aberrant or raging writing of the symptom, ill from its own necessity; and the analyst can sustain this lie only by drifting, unawares, towards the place where a divine stylet writes and crosses out magic mental blocks: [10] nothing less than the phallus in person. We know this

---

[7] Untranslatable play on words: "*du Nom-dit qu'elles ne disent pas.*" The coined expression "*Nom-dit*" is pronounced the same as "*non-dit*," unuttered. — Tr.

[8] "*Se donne le doux leurre*": "*le doux leurre*," the sweet delusion, suggests "*douleur*," pain, sorrow, trouble. — Tr.

[9] "*L'ire*" (fury, wrath) is a pun on "*lire*," to read. — Tr.

[10] "*Blocages magiques*" suggests "*bloc magique*," Freud's *Wunderblock*, or mystic writing-pad. See his essay "A Note upon the 'Mystic Writing Pad' " (publ. 1925) in the *Standard Edition*, XIX, 227-232. — Tr.

Daniel Sibony

comic—and not joking [*d'esprit*]—effect which attaches to an interpretation when the fact of giving the interpretation suggests that one holds the ember with which it was written—in which case a minimum of modesty, if not of prudence, leads one to postpone it. We shall return elsewhere to the import of this fantasy, which precisely fails to recognize the function of writing as an object sliced out of language, the effect of a decomposition of desire and the cause of a different desire.

As if by chance, every time that anyone has said anything psychoanalytically or poetically consistent about *Hamlet,* it has been by relating it to the nodalities of a different piece or body of writing: Freud, Joyce, Lacan. Freud, in a learned footnote in his *Interpretation of Dreams,* walks right into the middle of this plot, this fratricide, as if the murder of Gonzago, which took place in Vienna (and the text of which is after all the nucleus of the play), this writing within writing, this theater of the theater, whose motive and trap the maddened writing of (young) Hamlet sought in the past—as if the murder of Gonzago were plunged into the future and there received its echo, emanating from another dead father, Freud's father Jakob, whose death made his son's writing take the detour of dreams and the interpretation of desire— writing that forces him to move the infernal regions [11] but nevertheless to go out of Egypt into the desert of Moses. [12] Or Lacan: who has continued this writing in the graphs of its desire [13] and could equally well attempt to chain up the beast again with his knots. In each case, Hamlet's neurosis is isolated, the basic inhibition that

[11] Reference to Freud's use of the *Aeneid,* VII, 312 ("If I cannot bend the Higher Powers, I will move the Infernal Regions") as the epigraph to *The Interpretation of Dreams.* — Tr.

[12] It is in this statement that Freud echoes literary writing, and not, as it is commonly believed, in the exquisite pleasure of finding his little Oedipuses in literature. Moreover, Freud demonstrates, in and by his own language, that a decisive writing-step [*pas-d'écriture*] regarding another piece of writing, whether that other writing has the texture of a symptom or the symptom of a text, that such a step is brought about only by cutting across, by renaming, differently, the no to which it clings, along with its lies.

[13] See the illustrations reproduced in the first note to the Lacan text in this issue, p. 13. — Tr.

keeps him from acting, from knowing what he wants, caught up in desire for his mother, etc., etc.; his neurosis is illuminated either directly by the Oedipal complex or in the distress of the subject in the face of the desire of the [Lacanian] Other, forced to choose between being the phallus and being no one. Joyce, then, swept up this writing in the waves of his own, in the wake of *Ulysses,* and strangely enough not only does this not make him elude the clinical aspect of this text all that much—but when he says "Khaki Hamlets don't hesitate to shoot," what is he doing if not reaching, by means of whatever commands Hamlet, that which, in this structure, actually constitutes religion, i.e., in the Christian way, whose soldiers dream of getting off the shot that will fill their mother with an ultimate orgasm [*jouissance*]? Religion and war here celebrate the mother's complaint, or her fiction, for which filial devotion is not enough. Thus Joyce transmits more than merely his own cry— "Mother, let me live"—and this is what distinguishes his writing from chaotic incantation: in that separation which puts him in the loci from which writing originates or is generated, he tries to *get* both the exile and its law. He goes beyond the vicinity of two exiles, Hebrew and Irish: he returns, exposes, and flushes out these foreign wordbeasts [*animots*] that had burrowed into language and thus challenges the Allmother to recognize them as her offspring.

If we were willing, only for a moment, to accept that all writing refers back to an implicit "program," we would distinguish at least three such programs. In a minimal program, the pure object would retain "all" the negations [*dénégations*] that would rewrite it in meaning or interpretation—with the delusion [14] (and why not) of being the object and even the cause of desire: a sort of ready-made writing. At the opposite pole would be an extreme, maximal program, *à la* Joyce: attaining the innumerability of the proper name in a destroyed language, and rushing to his death, he rests his last

[14] Written *"avec le leur"* (rather than *"leurre"*), "along with their own." — Tr.
[15] First word of *Genesis,* in Hebrew: "In the beginning. . . ." — Tr.

Daniel Sibony

word on the first riverrum past and the bar where Eve and Adam get drunk on *berechit* [15] and he thinks he can say to someone else "Carry on for me"; for here this writing connects up with another or pursues indeterminacy, alongside Moses or in his wake. The first sort of writing has no program but itself, defying meaning and enjoyment [*jouissance*]. (Even mathematics, while continuing to build its bridges and its chasms, continues to border on the indeterminacy of paternity. [16]) The knot that Lacan manipulates, the Borromean knot, [17] is one figure of this indeterminacy, and if he pronounces it to sound like Nebo, why not? Nebo refers to the second (or the $n + 1$) murder of Moses, because Mount Nebo is the site of Moses' death, or rather his *point of view* for seeing the promised land, and to the fact that he didn't give a damn [*il s'en foutait*] about what Joyce was to call this "sunken cunt of the world," this area around the Dead Sea, [18] and that for him this remnant of the promise was only an object fallen from the law, destined to locate its mad idealizations and its offal. Between the extremes of these two programs, which touch in absolute indeterminacy, there are programs of compromise, and particularly that of writing which does not pass periodically through indeterminacy nor through its own blind spot, and which is sealed by the voice of meaning, repressed or not. Consider the Japanese writer Mishima, who finally drew the ink for his murderous stylet from his own body.

There's something like this in *Hamlet:* it is the representation of a desperate attempt to write which propels the play and writes it in a scattered array of scenes, of mirrored stories, of texts quoted, acted out, written, thwarted, etc.... From this point of view, the pattern of the characters and the forces that hold them in place and move them around (the study of which provides relatively easy satisfaction for anyone who pursues it)—all these lines are merely strands of writing woven together, used to recall, rename, overstate, and re-count the characters, until their final destruction. Thus the

[16] Cf. Daniel Sibony, *Le nom et le corps* (Paris: Seuil, 1974).
[17] See again Lacan, *Encore*, pp. 107-123; illustration of the Borromean knot, p. 112. — Tr.
[18] "*La mer morte*"; cf. "*la mère morte*," the dead mother — Tr.

different forms of madness that run through the play (and among which feigned madness is not the least severe) are like static incarnations of the general madness that jams the works of the play, the madness of writing. One of the qualities of artistic writing that is conscious of its enigma, is that it draws every interpretative reading towards that revived enigma, as if into a trap, and that the writing infects the interpretation with the writing-effect from which it emanates: its madness. Now, Shakespeare begins his play with these endless rewritings and renamings. [19] Thus it is important to understand *Hamlet* as a writing-maze in which the main question is what makes it tick—what is the mainspring of this flurry of writing? If, moreover, we relocate the center of this writing-maze at the core of the play that it detonates, it can be said that the amazing block [*blocage*] in which Hamlet finds himself and which goes far beyond his famous inhibition—for, after all, he doesn't spend all his time failing to avenge his father: he pokes into his mother with all the vigor of his tongue ("thou dar'st *wag* thy tongue against me," she says, "wag" being the word for moving or brandishing the tail), [20] he kills someone, he drives someone else mad, he feigns or thinks he feigns madness, and brings on the final bloodbath—but the important thing is that we can see Hamlet's block fall into place like a pure and simple writing device [*dispositif*] for Shakespeare to write across the surface of, for him to hook up with other devices and to cut across with analogies that are more and more "potent" to the point of silence, and to turn this too-perfect writing pad [*bloc d'écriture*] into a tool for breaking down and ravaging space. This device belongs to a kind of unconscious that is purely writing-oriented and that makes spoken language come out in a form in which writing and reading are one and such that the command that is slipped into it, to which the subject is anchored, no matter what its content is—or rather it can undergo every sort of transformation—the important thing is that the com-

---

[19] *Renommées.* The usual meaning of *renommée* is fame, renown; Sibony plays with this ambiguity repeatedly in the rest of this text. — Tr.
[20] "*Queue,*" which also means "prick." — Tr.

Daniel Sibony

mand must involve the subject in the unsignifying [*asignifiant*]
filling-up of what surpasses the Other or is missing in his knowledge
about his orgasm [*jouissance*]; this is the only recourse against the
monstrous desire of this woman who is almost fifty when the play
begins. Thus the question is not to decide whether Hamlet *is* more
hysterical or obsessed and why he is inhibited, and so on and so
forth, but rather to measure the double import of the event that
accompanies the ghost, both for the subject who endures it and
for the writing that generates it and that it generates.

Hamlet is the game of the wandering inkblot in which dodge and
seeming *drown* in implied, generic suicide, the inkblot that Shakespeare pursues in order to divert it, to shunt it off its track, using
a language that is foreign to itself. He circles around a hole—the
hell in which the father never stops *burning,* the hole from which
the raging mother [21] has spat up the ghost who knows too much into
the base fetor and the orgy-sounds—circles around it with a sting-
ing, darting kind of writing, a burning that transports them all onto
the stage that is dazzled by the necessity of dying, into the dizziness
of broken mirrors, until the final bloodbath.

The knowledge that all the "supposing" is about [22] is the exploded excess of the Other's knowledge about his death, which
subjugates the son to the point of nothingness, and transforms the
inkblot of the commandment into a dazzling leftover scrap of
the writing that deals with the unbearable aspect of what the Other
knows about the possibilities of that being written down.

Here writing deconstructs the bar of the signifier and is the
dramatization of its cutting edge.

In *Hamlet,* Shakespeare's achievement is producing senseless
bridges, i.e., impassable ones, built from what poetic writing is made
for inventing—this slicing out from language, the object of which
remains invisible. These are senseless bridges between two systems

---

[21] *La mère démontée* — "the dismounted [and hence randy] mother"
— is a pun on the commonplace "*la mer démontée,*" the raging sea. — Tr.

[22] "*Le savoir dont il serait supposé,*" i.e., the critical fund of knowledge
supposedly had by the mythical authority in the Lacanian expression "*le
sujet supposé savoir.*" See Lacan, "La méprise du sujet supposé savoir" in
Scilicet, No. 1 (1968), pp. 31-41. — Tr.

[*dispositifs*]: one the system of young Hamlet's capture in and through writing, and the other the system of the One wave of writing that continues forever. The bridges link up one piece of writing which is the defeat of the signifier and another which produces multiple representations and cuts off the signifiers at the very level of writing itself; every successful writing-machine is utterly deadly because it reminds us in the future of the death that will come about in the past. One could say that Shakespeare, with his multiple game [*jeu*] of writing, intercedes (but with whom?—that's the question) to make his man go backwards until a certain knowledge of his already-consummated death-to-desire becomes distantly legible. The machine that is commanded here functions successfully, unless the commander begins to desire, in which case it becomes the materialization of the impasse of his desire.

What is usually considered a summons to take revenge, and what we usually fool ourselves into thinking is without any direct effect, is in reality merely a particular instance of what emerges here as a form of instant writing: the consummation of a death-to-desire in the writing of a mortal epiphany. What is dizzying about the play is that Shakespeare invents a character who is merely a presence in the essential emptiness of madness, and creates him this way so that he can traverse the emptiness and the madness that is essential to writing. And his madness is his mad attempt to name that being without a name; thus his madness hovers constantly on the edge of language as constituted by that which is written. On that edge of language, Hamlet's doublings mark out the great scene of history, from Eden to the wars of modern times, paradise, garden, tree of death and drowning, serpent, where Adam, the shrewish ghost, the name of the father who was poisoned, and even Eve, the life-giving mother of all life, has her double in Ophelia, so that beyond all incest all men might be completely enclosed between these two poles of *The* woman. [23]

[23] The expression "*La* femme" designates, in modern French psychoanalytic theory, an impossible unity and completeness; woman (without capital) is distinguished from man in part precisely by the nature of this impossibility. See for example, Lacan, *Encore*, p. 68 et passim, and Lacan, *Télévision* (Paris: Seuil, 1974), pp. 60ff. — Tr.

Daniel Sibony

Let us therefore not interpret: let us see the lines of interpretation in the hollow spaces of writing.

Memory-writing: at the very beginning the King-Cain starts up the machine for returning the repressed, and his political discourse is accompanied by [*se double de*] sex and incest; it seems that if only political discourse is directed to its true addressee, it will admit to its hermaphroditic function. The King speaks of the "green memory" of the death of his dear brother Hamlet, of lost territories, of young Prince Fortinbras who is restlessly eager to regain them, and of "our most valiant brother," who came by them legitimately. This little evocation of childhood years is for Hamlet's benefit, and its content is insane from the beginning: Claudius had every right to possess Hamlet's mother, who is none other than his sister, sister-in-law, or, moreover, his wife, present here, and this Hamlet-Fortinbras with his "weak supposal of our worth" who wants to recover what was legally taken from his father! (He has just spoken of having taken the Queen to wife.) He then *writes* to Fortinbras' uncle in order to have him restrain his nephew [24]—he *writes to himself* and gives his plan: I'm keeping my eye on you—I know that it was murder, but everyone knows that! Know then that I have marked you down. Fortinbras thinks that the death of our dear brother left us helpless. (You little piece of scum, you think that I feel guilty, well I am guilty, but as long as I can take advantage of it [*en jouir*]. . . .) This is a first draft: *we are in the midst of writing, with all the sketch-marks visible.* He sends two messages, and later two messengers, to explore what he knows. [25] Ant it is not Hamlet but Laertes who responds: "Dread lord," you frighten me, I flee. And Hamlet responds—but to his mother, not to the King—"I know not 'seems.'" I wear an "*inky* cloak": I am submerged in writing and in me that goes beyond seeming. The machination comes to life, and the King turns the argument around:

---

[24] Here are lines of letters that run throughout the text, but in this case it is writing that is made to function in that which is written, the ghost, the letter of the father.

[25] All of this can be done on the stage as a series of slips, "goofs," substitutions.

fathers have a way of dying, the "common theme," "Your father lost a father,/ That father lost, lost *his*"—lost his *what?* The point is that the late king did not satisfy The woman.... This is the tradition of the "death of fathers," going back to "the first corse": fathers get killed; and this is spoken with the irritation and impatience that one has for a double (Your grief is a ploy), a double presented as a successor. Thus Claudius speaks to Hamlet from the depth of his own death: "think of us as of a father" and "let the world take *note!*" Hamlet is taken literally in the doubling of this discourse, in which he is told to "Be as ourself," and his first thought, when he is alone, is of suicide: because a written law forbids suicide, he will make suicide into writing, with the unfathomable desire of his mother as his first theme—paradise lost, "an unweeded garden," her always hot for it, his father more a tender sort, jealous of the very wind lest it hurt her face, and she had to take this Greek god, this Hercules, and here I am, no Hercules at all. What matters here is not so much Hamlet's conversion into a phallus, his desperate plunge into his mother's hole, but rather the *start of a memory,* the memory of this total forcing ("Must I remember?"), the beginning of the astounding return of the repressed: let's move right to this *mortal epiphany which will petrify Hamlet in his writing.* On one side is the orgy, the satyr-Hercules in the process of ramming it into his mother, and on the other is Hamlet, holding forth fastidiously on excesses of temperament and slight flaws in character, and speaking strangely about birth—you can't do anything about it, it's not your fault, you don't choose your origin—and there's the ghost. His friends warn him that if he follows it he risks falling right into the sea, and that the place where they are standing by the sea is enough to "put toys of desperation into every brain," and they repeat: You know that people go mad just looking down at the sea with its tossing and roaring. And the orgy sounds keep coming from the next room, where holiness and harlotry link hands.

The first words of the ghost are "Mark me"—write me—(glossed "listen to me," which is fine, as long as we see the paradox of listening to writing that is about to be produced), and his last words are "Remember me." We all know the conventional idea that we write things down to retain them, to remember them; here, Hamlet writes to forget, or lest *he* return, [26] mistakable, unrecognized— which drives him to write, *to retain:* the desire to forget, to make sure of the repressed, at the risk of being overwhelmed by its return, and even if the event disturbs this pleasure of retention with a tiresome reading. Standing before the ghost, who comes to revive that excess of knowledge that the Other has, Hamlet takes out his tablets, the tables of his memory, to rid it of every other trace, so that this trace can reside there alone as a pure injunction, expressible only in the infinite series of its own negations [*dénégations*]. It is thus a lethal trace, but one whose death must be made eternal. In fact, he doesn't take dictation, like the prophets in their paranoid constructions [*montages*]; on the contrary, he destroys the gap of the utterance in the trace and all his playfulness will never be enough to exhume this gap. From the start (as soon as its signifier appears) vengeance is put under the sign of compulsion (and of the pseudo-hallucinatory effects that compulsion induces: consider the Ratman, who in the middle of the night calls up the figure of his father—living in the other world—to show him his half-erection in the mirror; but the analogy should not be carried too far, even though Hamlet cries "A rat!" when he thrusts his sword into the double father-puppet, under the sign of an erotic thrust at his mother, who cries out for help as if he were about to mount her; a rat?).

Thus the question of revenge and its attainment is settled in advance as soon as it appears, by infinite negation [*négation*]. Its attainment is not even inhibited, but deferred, and it is in this form that it must serve as a reference-point, a support, in signification for the subject, as the cross for his ascension; and if he gets his revenge, he uses up this signifying wisp and goes utterly unsupported. Thus if he avenged his father, he would go mad, and to

[26] *"De crainte qu'il ne revienne":* cf. note 2 above. Note once more the resemblance between *ne* and *noeud.* — Tr.

defer this madness is to simulate it. He learns what he must do—he comes to know the hollow of his desire, in the form of the empty commandment that turns him into a stain, a blot, a pure mark, not translatable, a mark that merely repeats an initial impasse of translation. But learning in this form what must be done literally implies that he can no longer know what he wants, or that what he wants is unknowable to him, or that he can do nothing more with this knowledge (which Shakespeare indicates with the air of ill-guarded secrecy that pervades the play); when we say to someone, "You don't know what you want," this means that for him the Other knows too much: this is what produces fundamental *malleability,* the depressive state of "absentmindedness" and an indifference to any possible knowledge. Another example of this submission to an empty commandment (Mark me; remember me) is seen in the way he dies: he takes what might seem to be a whim on the part of Claudius, who is hostile to him, namely the tournament in which Claudius has bet on him—he takes this as a "must"; he replies with an elegant pun: "I'll be your foil" (i.e., the setting to your jewel, and your weapon). But the ghost does not only say that he knows the story of the murder: he ties it implicitly to the woman who is the mother of all life, the Eve who brings forth the first murderer as her uncastratable son; and from *this immortal mother —no transmission here: it's always the same one*—arises the insatiable version whom Hamlet worships. This carryover to the murder of the father, lurking in the unconscious and controlling the opening of the text toward its indefinite inscription, is so obvious, that Hamlet's impatience is from the very beginning the sign that there is no question of avenging the murder: "Haste me to know 't, that I, with wings as swift/ As meditation or the thoughts of love,/ May sweep to my revenge"; if he means a meditation on the afterlife, that's a lengthy process, and if it's his father's love he means, then he has a long wait in store: he's talking about eternity. And as to the story going around about his father's death, it's the most desperate ode to the phallus, which will be accompanied [*doublé*] by another bit of writing, the holy scriptures [27] (disavowing them and thus retranslating them): the fall from paradise, sleeping *A-dame* in his garden—that's how the story goes—busying himself, sheltered from desire, when a serpent stung him, introduced by a woman's hand—some apple—the violent intrusion of desire in the woman whom he and his innocent life in paradise could not satisfy. Everybody believed the story, and "the whole ear of Denmark is rankly abused," and he took it in the ear, too, screwed by his brother (ear/anus); the phallus is transmitted into an impasse—this is indeed what makes Hamlet's cryptograph suicidal—and to "abuse" an innocent ear, like a young virgin—what a divine idea! Indeed this is the crime of which Ophelia's father and brother accuse Hamlet in the previous scene when they warn Ophelia (the Other-woman, the pure one): with beauteous words doth he abuse your ears; thus Hamlet suddenly seems to be in league with the serpent —one knot more. The radical effect of this writing is that it summons us, it invites reading and then suddenly capsizes that reading, breaking it with an unexpected fracture, while writing continues on its own course on a different level; as certain objects—a knot, say—break up and elude the gaze of the beholder, this writing finally breaks up (with) reading and thus jams up the spoken word. It is a limit-case of writing, so far from meaning that it does not even feel obligated to exclude meaning. Let's say that like another great body of writing (the Bible), Shakespeare's writing does not fear meaning because it has every means to put an end to meaning, should it be necessary, and is thus a text *mad with meaning.* This writing is made to intercede with the real, to be impossible castration in linguistic form, and the play of signifiers spins on madly until every word spoken is revealed to be caught up and compromised in it. Words are jarred loose from their fixed usage [*jouissance à demeure*], taken up in the threads of divergent, foreign chains of signifiers. Still, Shakespeare starts from that extreme fact of writing (the commandment, the ghost) in which his man finds himself caught up in a severe crush where all the signifiers are equiv-

[27] *Écriture:* writing; *l'Écriture sainte:* the Holy Scriptures. — Tr.

alent, and this block is processed, cut up in the theatrical rearranging that multiplies utterances and blows up the bridges that we imagine between them.

And Shakespeare plays at smashing together all the available chains of signifiers and various mutually exclusive writings, e.g., Hebrew scripture and Greek mythology, in order to draw new traces from them; the result is the immaculate conception, penetration by the divine phallus, the sole phallus worthy of Her. Niobe, to whom Hamlet's mother is also compared, is the first mortal woman, the mother of all living men, the Greek Eve, but she, Niobe, couples with Zeus right off, combining the roles of Eve and the Virgin Mary (and multiplying the stakes of the "crime"). The ghost, whose sole revelation is the statement: Know that I know who killed me, that I have not died from this knowledge which from now on will obsess you—this ghost provides an odd disclaimer to the rumor going around about the death of Hamlet's father: although people say that he was bitten by a serpent, it is true, and the rumors give an interpretation of what happened, for the phallic beast was indeed present like a serpent with all his seductiveness at the origin of the crime, with all the diabolical power of his wit [esprit], of the joke [mot d'esprit], i.e., of pure sexuality. The murderer proceeds with the overwhelming power of a phallus ("O wicked wit and gifts, that have the power/ So to seduce!") against which there is no recourse. Hamlet has one of those fantasies, one of those sweet, sad, stubborn delusions [doux leurres] told to him: his father wasn't able to stand up to that; in the face of that maternal power, he was worthless. And the rumors about his death are marked by a deception that is the deception of desire itself. Moreover, what he asks is impossible: don't let her screw (she's over forty-five but it's a question of the desire of the whole species), don't let it happen, and be especially careful about this: Taint not thy soul—What? Kill the image of the father without thinking of possessing the mother? It's absurd. "Leave her to heaven, and let her play with her crown of thorns," the impotent man moans. This ghost is amazing—I mean, coming with his story of Berechit and the first so-called sin, the impossible genesis of desire, the beginning of fratricides, floods, acts of incest, and the law—"What a falling-off!" And now when the ghost fades away with the reminder that Hamlet's father is in debt up to his neck, that he has made no reckoning but that the deficit is *real*—to all this, Hamlet responds with an entire topos of writing; a few sentences contain it all—write, erase, record, memory, forgetting, tablet, all pressures past, book, copy, and on top of all that "thy commandment alone shall live," and on his tablets he writes the empty law that one may smile and smile and be a villain. He wants so much to remember, that in this simulated act he makes a clean slate of his memory and becomes himself the walking symbol of the impossible repression of the murder. He puts right down on his notebook the mark *that is not to be translated* (translated, transported from one language to another, from one prison to another), not to be communicated (like a secret). It is thus the mark that never ceases to be rewritten as is. It's not so much that Hamlet's inhibited as that this mark isn't, that it cannot be inhibited, that it cannot stand to be seconded by any other mark. That's what seeing the ghost is all about: a cryptogram of Hamlet's neurosis, comparable to Joyce's "Write it all down." In the case of *Hamlet*, the commandment will burn and consume them all as a mark of the lack in the memory of the Other. The mortal hole at the hollow center of the mother of all life becomes the inkblot with which the poet records his journey across a certain knowledge about death. The ghost is precisely the suddenly overabundant hole of this knowledge. And the other poet, Mallarmé, who loses his son, "the son who died without knowing"—but what is this knowledge whose excess remains, unbearable, for those who live on? He then recalls ancient Egypt, where, beyond embalming, it's an art in itself to thwart death by writing. What of this Egyptian write-it-all-down? Did they want to gain, with death, the beauty of speed? Here writing absorbs its own failure and seeks to saturate it.

"What do you seek, sweet beloved vision—coming often to me, bending—as if to listen to the secret of my tears—the knowledge that you are dead—which you do not know? No, I shall not tell you—for then you would vanish—and I would remain to cry alone, the two of us in one, you, the child, crying for yourself in me, the future man that you will not be, who remains without life or joy." "I who know bear a terrible secret in his stead!" [28]

It's foolish to believe that writing is thwarting childbirth or playing at childbirth across the abyss of paternity. Of course writing cuts across and supports the flaky layers [*feuilletages*] of narcissism, even in their encounter with the knowledge thought to be held by the Other (in transference). Mourning is the unfolding of the narcissistic body; Hamlet is the writing of that impossible entity which is mourning, taken just at its beginning, in absolute form, and thus *normal*. And in mourning for the father there is the flickering of the loss of name: a representation of the subject as a nameless thing, the degradation of the unnamable. The paradox is that mourning seeks its own completion, and yet from the very beginning it is directed toward eternity, narcissistic timelessness. The ghost is the emptiness of a command that is uttered: mark me, write me, write your name—which Shakespeare resolves with fame, reputation [*la renommée, le renom*].

There are a thousand ways of opposing death with writing. The Egyptian way is said to be the one that *embodies* death, gives it the corporeal form of life itself; this is the attempt to be the life of death. *Hamlet* subtly combines the continually problematic existence of the dead father with the devastating presence of the living mother, this mortally living body. Writing leaps back and forth across this impossible interval, doubling, multiplying, with no escape save annihilation.

The play is swarming with murders and corpses, and long before the last act: the cemetery, the tour of the skeletons, Ophelia's burial, the "brothers'" fistfight in an empty grave—to say nothing

[28] Stéphane Mallarmé, *Pour un tombeau d'Anatole* (Paris: Seuil, 1961), pp. 247-48, 264 [= ms. pp. 149, 150, 166] — Tr.

of the final slaughter—there's a stench of corpses in Hamlet's father's kingdom ("there's some*thing* rotten..."), and the very Heavens poke their nose in to inhale these smells (of sacrifice?) from Cain's crime, which is "rank" (reeking and luxuriant): "it smells to heaven." Writing oscillates between a name that cannot be inscribed and the dead body, a corpse-effect whose intrusion into the real is the sign and signature of this impasse. There are many scenes of the dance of death—where is the body? The body, the dead body, find the body, bring the body.... The ghostly epiphany is also an epitaph: Hamlet falls [*tombe*] by way of writing, and the tomb is the point at which name and body are wed in their common impasse. An army will die "to gain a little patch of ground/ That hath in it no profit but the name"; a tomb, the very space of the war, a piece of the mother's body on which the brothers fight, and all these soldiers will kill one another for an "eggshell" (sic) and "go to their graves like *beds.*" In this writing clinic, what matters is to wrest a name from this cut-up body, and die doing it. And all this is spewed forth by the apparition that is the question of what the dead father knows, the father who has come to say "You know that I am burning..."; desire emerges only in its consummation. Even Hamlet's scene with his mother—a quintessential acme of all literature—takes place before the body of a false father and culminates with the ghostly body of the real father... which his mother (hardier than all those soldiers) neither sees nor hears.

All the supposed symmetries of the play are false: hence their cutting edge [*d'où leur tranchant*], the delusion [*leurre*] of false mirrors. For example:

MOTHER: Hamlet, thou hast thy father much offended.
HAMLET: Mother, you have my father much offended.

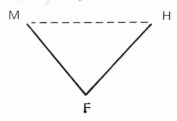

There are already four of them, and Hamlet's desire for his mother is as plain as black and white, transparent—no need to "interpret" it: "And (would it were not so) you are my mother." But then the space of this false symmetry is split up, and the mother-father-Hamlet trio no sooner appears than it is dislocated, stretched out of shape by the fratricide that takes place between the two fathers. Expelled from the fictitious triangular space, mother and son are in two mutually foreign planes that touch dispairingly, separated by the mirror of a murder that renames the splitting of their space,

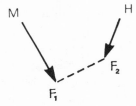

and this dissymmetrical split continues: a third incestuous father is there, waiting impatiently.

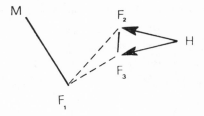

The line between Hamlet and his father is not drawn as being translatable; this, indeed, is why it imposes itself as this havoc of writing in the ghost scene, ordering not direct revenge but revenge of a craftier sort, in which he must *be the written reference-point* [*support scripturé*] *of the name* and thus avenge his father in his very being. The ghost *is* the command that thus functions as an expression of writing, and this line, which is at times the symbol of an equivalency between father and son in their common failure in the face of The woman—this line blows up here into a mere fragment doubled by mirrors; this beginning of writing preserves it in the fiction of its origin, and Hamlet, dislodged from all reference in signification, must pay with his consummation for the supposed existence of such a reference-point. He cannot decide to act because it is a pure decision, consummate and carried out in advance, a precipitate burning of the murder, so much a part of every act, so complete and definite in vengeance, that if he carried it out he would be giving himself up. He depends on that act the way a suckling depends on his mother, or the way a speaking being [29] depends on language; and he is already consummating the simulation of that madness which keeps him from becoming involved in action. (The simulation of madness is indeed an ingenious way of defining a man who seeks to go beyond all seeming.)

A typical scene of that dissembling madness: Hamlet, on the way to his mother's chamber, sees the King in prayer. He could kill him, but he postpones the murder, for to kill him would be to send him straight to paradise (again!), whereas his father was killed in the blossoms of his sins and his "audit" is surely a heavy one.... Of course, it is possible to say that he doesn't know what he wants, and after all wanting to kill someone and take over his position is wanting to wound oneself through him; and can he moreover know what he wants when he has this dead father who knows so much for him? But let's look at things literally, letter by letter, where their madness bursts forth: the text is mad not with this incredible ratiocination but from the fact that it writes about a subject that is out of place at the same time that it expels him, and even as he is saying "I": "and am I then revenged?" Here madness, as poetic language puts it into play, is not the loss of meaning but that movement by which each statement, weighed down by writing, uproots and transports its utterance with itself,

---

[29] "*L'être parlant*": expression preferred in French psychoanalysis to *être pensant* or *être humain*, because of the role of language in the constitution of the human being. — Tr.

cornering the subject in the extreme position in which he changes places every time he changes statements. Caught up in this fragile adherence to language, the subject is merely the sad scene of what is said for him in his spoken word; sense cannot save him, and nonsense (feigned madness) does not protect him. It widens the gaping void each time: to kill the paternal rival, the jealous son demands that he be in the blossoms of his sin, i.e., in bed with the insatiable mother: they must be screwing. It's fairly routine for a man to throw his rival onto the woman he loves; but in this case it's not a matter of a character trait but rather like the wake of mobility in language of a life-and-death question. And what is this "ideal" vengeance from which the victim is to reap neither residue nor profit? Once more we have the fiction of a dead man's knowledge about his death, murder enriched by its traces in a knowledge that writes it down. A new fiction sprouts, the fiction of a chain supposedly cut off, a reckoning that would be just: the harried fiction of killing someone *rightly,* i.e., without coming away with the slightest guilt—all the guilt remaining with the victim who has not yet repented, who has not mourned for [*fait le deuil de,* i.e. relinquished] the pleasure [*jouissance*] that produces the guilt.... Here writing, retained by knowledge in the drifting away of its positions and suppositions, surrounds the whole problematic of war, religion, sacrifice, prayer. In any case it is this evasion of the madness of murder that is madness itself: brushing aside all disturbing clutter, finding regions where knowledge is sure (so it's no surprise that everything ends up in heaven with everyone gone to the great beyond). It is the ignorance of his father's account ("And how his *audit* stands, who knows save heaven?") that gives immobile breath to this speech of Hamlet's: to kill the other by *giving* him death like a dead end, the impossibility of traversal— but it almost amounts to giving him life, if indeed life is propelled by lethal dead ends that force us to make our way around them.... To kill without residue is to kill the residue: this prefigures the dead end of writing or the drowning of its absolute success. (Here is the measure of Freud's stroke of genius in linking the preservation of the remains, from the murder, with the function of guilt as purveyor of bliss [*jouissance*].)

The ghost is the death of the father as suspended by a knowledge that goes beyond it—from which a remmant of knowledge emanates to haunt the space of madness: the play of the game [*le jeu du jeu*], insofar as it is by definition the activity that defers death at the same time that it summons it as a figure of the real to be responsible for this game.

Hamlet is the play that cannot be staged [*la pièce injouable*], not so much because of its real and unprecedented richness (every staging of the play can only be a section of the staging that the play itself is—arbitrary choices must be made) but in a more precise sense: if indeed the game [*jeu*] seeks to thwart [*déjouer*] death, Shakespeare in *Hamlet* thwarts the game itself. This has nothing to do with thwarting death by writing.

Two procedures animate the play: that of writing and that of the game.

The game: what is called the play within the play is only a culmination of the scissure whereby, in several scenes, *one group* of characters sets itself apart [*s'écarte*] or hides, in order to see or, especially, to hear the other. There is always an extra ear, the organ into which the subversive poison is, in the epiphany, regurgitated from an immemorial inkblot, the memory of the dead, the nocturnal pit [*trou*] that says listen, listen, listen, and the other who takes notes and understands nothing of this ghost escaped from the repression of murder. So these different ways of listening mean that nothing of course is communicated to the character who sets himself apart, but they increase the levels of utterance. And the character of Hamlet is in itself a play within a play. He spends his time setting himself apart from what he presents to the view and hearing of others, and hence to himself: he is, like everyone else, duped by that distance. And is the spectator himself so sure of his place, since the play thrusts him on stage from time to time? Thus there is *game,* shown, played as such, played to the death (even the final massacre begins with the playing of a bet, and even the murder of Polonius is presented as a game: "a rat? Dead for a ducat, dead!") and, at the same time, *writing,* put into play as an object. (There are countless texts, letters, and tablets, including the letter that is supposed to kill its bearer, for which Hamlet substitutes another letter which he signs with the paternal seal, not without recalling that the art of writing, so despised, has something to its credit.) The writing-effect is, at the extreme, the ghost, and the ultimate effect of the game is the play within the play and the constant procession behind the curtains; but the essential thing is that the game (within the game) maintains the fiction of readability, and that death alone links the two functions of writing and game. This is fictive readability, pointless at best: when Polonius hides to listen in on Hamlet's meeting with his mother, he does not know to what an extent he's already read everything and understood nothing. His last line to Hamlet's mother is "Tell him ... that your grace hath screened and stood between/ Much heat and him," and he puts himself precisely in between the son and the mother in heat (but isn't the special appeal of the game the deafness of the players to the signifier that holds them?), the mother who once again will cause the old man to be killed, and as innocently as could be, by crying murder when Hamlet has only evoked the *mirror* he is about to set before her. Surely a mirror isn't death, is it? But indeed it is, if the one who beholds it is life itself, with nowhere to run, and if mirrors in no way impair the vise of her orgasm [*jouissance*]. It's no use her saying, in the very midst of the ghostly visitation, "O Hamlet, thou hast cleft my heart in twain": she doesn't believe a word of it; one must imagine her on the ground, cleft, open, irresistible for this little preacher whose sermon is caught up short. It is an irreparable naïveté on the son's part to appeal to religion against the true mother-sources of religion. What's more, a visitation to stir things up is not out of order here: the son has shaken the mother, for lack of a decisive word to speak; he is no more than the appendage of their joint masturbation. The ghost appears in the place of the thing that doesn't come. She of course has no trouble plunging it into herself with a "What shall I do?" when he's just told her, only he didn't know that he was *asking* [*demandait*] something of her.

Hamlet cannot read the book of himself, because he writes it with his own suicide. It is the boundary of the game which the poet doubles to get his writing to pass through the perversion in which he risks being swallowed up like someone playing with his mother, or rather with that question asked of death, the risk of which he provokes. Hamlet is that block of extreme playfulness which Shakespeare disperses and wears down with maximal differentiations. The player's dread of an answer or of a cessation of questions is, in Hamlet's case, the dread of *acquitting* himself of the debt (as if he could), or else the dead father will die; yet he knew himself that he was dead.

The player (as the lower limit of the writer-poet) plays with his mother's phallus in the sense that he remains an adherent to her masturbation, to the masturbation of language. With this frozen, and even sterile, phallus, he wants to fertilize the great indifference of numbers, whereas the writer will attempt to fertilize a dead language with the senseless recurrences of sense. But the stakes run together in the struggle with death for the knowledge it has of itself. If winning, for the player, is resurrection, one sees in *Hamlet* the first glimmer of something that must have delighted someone like Joyce in that fundamental betrayal by the writer-poet of the perverse contract: it is not a question of rousing the dumbness of numbers or of masturbating language, but of making language crack beneath the names of the father [*les noms du père*] that he forces it to produce. This permanent forcing aspires to go beyond the perverse position by turning it around: for writing as denial of the name of the father, Joyce substitutes the dismentalment (so demented) [*démentellement (tellement dément)*] of language by the names of the father.

If Hamlet, the character, is a squandering of the signifier in the mark, the inked block [*bloc encré*] which submerges it, one may further illustrate the relationship of the signifying cut and the return of the trace as the encounter with a double, by the little topological fiction of a man who goes off at sunrise towards the mountain and arrives at the top at sunset; he stays there a certain length of time (to do what? Perhaps to meditate on the desolation of writing), but one morning he goes back down at sunrise and takes the same path back to his point of departure in the course of the day. Whatever, then, the irregularities of his course, in one direction or the other, whatever his stops and backtrackings, there is a place in this path that he passes twice at the same hour of the day, once going, once returning. (Imagine that he projects for himself, on the way back, the film of his journey out; there is a moment when the image he observes on his animated memory is that of the real place where he finds himself at that moment.) Or, there is a place where he meets his memory at the very hour of its "first" marking—and an hour when he coincides with his image at the same place. If now another man comes down instead, the son of the first, or the substance of his shadow, there is a place that he passes at the hour of his father; one can foresee what havoc there would be if things happened this way (according to the principle that the continuous image of a connected space cannot be split up). This catastrophe, in which the imaginary would assume an inscriptive value and inscription would sink to the level of the imaginary, is avoided by the fact that that space which is the image of time (of that fictive day), is discontinuous. That space is none other than that of language since, when it comes to mountains, our heroes know how to scale only statements (more rarely, utterances); the most simple discontinuous space is (0,1) or *fort-da,* where the anguish of the child playing with the absence of the mother produces this symbolic germ. Thus one effective signifier (and, after all, there's a whole chain of them) is sufficient for this meeting with the double, on the return path, to lose its real consistency. One level of utterance is sufficient—lacking which, the being who is subjected to this encounter, sees the event towards

which he is rushing in the future, surge into the present as already
completed, and he is unaware that he has neither inscribed it nor
even thought it except by virtue of that "rush" which "completes"
the thing written, and the fiction that in order to be it is enough
that the thing be "thought." Here the being, in his entirety, *acts
as* signifier and is reabsorbed into the mark. He speaks as if he
were reading writing that was inscribed only by virtue of his speaking it. Every trace glimpsed ("thought") is anticipated as double,
and the unconscious trace is maintained only by being redoubled
indefinitely, and speech, by reading [*de lire*] in advance, marks the
lack that was still not written. "Hamlet reading the book of himself"—that's where it's enclosed, and in the *book*-scene, in which
the retroactive dizziness of writing is heightened: Shakespeare
writes the thing, literally, with the object, writing, and with the
unsuccessful writing of the object. What Hamlet reads are "words,
words, words" (remember the English word "sword"), and what
a *shame* it is to write that—what? The incest by which we are
doomed from childhood, in which the comic father of course doesn't
recognize his labored flattery of Ophelia, his daughter to whom he
will give a book for her to pretend to be reading, a little hand-
prop for her "devilish" innocence, or the air which they sing to each
other? ("Will you walk out of the air, my lord?" "Into my grave?"
returns Hamlet—and indeed what can save us from this "air"? But
for the other it's not in the score [*musique*]: "that's out of the air"
—what Hamlet is telling him [*ce que Hamlet lui chante*] is that in
reascending the course of time he comes upon his own tracks.) And
to complete the resonances he puts into position, since one writing
is read only by means of another, Shakespeare refers to yet another
book, the Scriptures, not to the text but to the crudest of its sexual
interpretations. "Old Jephthah," he calls him, but the old man
doesn't know anything of that *other* text: Jephthah is the whoreson
who has won a war against the tribe descended from the screwing
between the drunken Noah and his daughter; well, that Jephthah,
having only one daughter and guessing that she will be the one
to come and greet him on his return, vows to God to sacrifice the

first person who greets him, and he does it—that rather than let her screw elsewhere.

This technique of making one writing resonate upon another in order to produce the hollow sound of their mutual indebtedness is one of the ways to undo the crushing of the name or rather that crushing signifier, the ghostly equating of the written and the spoken: that ghost, that excess of paternity in language. The result is a delirious labor of doubling [*doublure*], in reality a feigned madness of dubbing [*doublage*]: not a single complete "family," but all the possible segments are there, all the relations, thanks to the resulting multiplicity of positions. (Not even the role of director is missing, nor that of the actor, in the most violent sense of the word, the one who plays "with" his essential images which reveal him and thrust him forward, and the player [*joueur*] who is consumed in the question that he puts to destiny, and the writer who plays at attempting the mortal encounter and dies by succeeding; and the role of spectator and observed spectator and the living role of the dead father and of the son living his death....) So many transferences are at work, never the mother-father-son trio as such but the doubles and trios neither fit nor stick together but are always jammed up, crystals crushed into new mirrors, flat fictive mirages and false symmetries (so much is symmetry indeed the gearwork of writing, functioning as the denial of sexual a-symmetry: consider Arabic calligraphy and the pleasures of symmetry with which it eroticizes language.)

Another effect of the paternal excess is life in the deluded symmetry of the beyond. The famous dialogue is "insignificant," hence absolute, "undramatic" in that it offers or repeats the formula of the drama. It is the absurd assertion of death as a last-minute denial [*dénégation*] of suicide; for, after all, we "ordinarily" shrink back from death because it divests us of our sufferings and the gain we anticipate from their suppression; that is, at least, if one doesn't follow in the footsteps of the great Egyptian high priest with his arsenal of aromatics and writings inside coffins. What then causes this sweet prince to shrink back from death (which no one

Daniel Sibony

is urging him to bring upon himself)? The dreams and nightmares
that the dead perhaps have, if indeed they sleep, nightmares from
which they cannot awake, thus in which they cannot die. The act
of death being annulled (it is only an entrance into sleep), the
waking hours of life become identified with a pure defense against
nightmares, that is to say, against the irrepressible intrusion of
desire; death comes only at the risk of impairing those defenses
against desire, and his horror of death derives from the fact that
death might let desire exist while removing the possibility of suppressing it. It is thus the simple horror of desire, insofar as desire
is engendered by a law. To die, to sleep—to sleep, to dream—to
expose oneself to the disturbance produced by desire, with no recourse but flight... into death? In short, the most certain death
is still life, for there at least one is sure of being vigilant against
desire and hence of being dead. One mustn't take lightly this little
inquiry into death, for not only have entire civilizations (at the
origin, they say) enjoyed [*joui*] and hence thought of nothing but
these sepulchral (and, specifically, written) longings, but the beyond
imposes itself here as the effect of the impossibility of the Other's
being dead to knowledge about his orgasm [*jouissance*], and in that
very impossibility the question haunts the shadow borne by his
son and is the single reference-point of his sexual enjoyment [*jouissance*], for he speaks to us of slaves who don't revolt, and why?
Because what they want is to want to revolt, and not to revolt,
and if they saw it through to the end they would therefore no
longer be able to revolt. It's not so crazy (consider politics) but
the difficulty is getting it to take hold. Then again, if to live is
to be vigilant (since life equals debt) the idea that after death one
would still owe [*doive*]—what?—implies that life is immortal and
what makes it that way is the injunction with which it circumvents
writing and the injunction of the play which causes the mad desire
for the mother to culminate in suicide: the son completes the cycle,
poisoned by the father, both Hyperion and satyr, pierced through
like the comic father by a blow dealt by one of his doubles. He
accomplishes the act when, with his mother dead, the stake has

disappeared, at the very moment when, like the father, he will be dead and know it, when the object of mourning, whose half-erection he has sustained up till that point, wavers. Note the contiguity of the writing-device with death, precisely because the two are no longer confused; even though it starts here, openly, with a murder —a successful one, that everyone goes along with, a murder pardoned, redeemed, trinitied, but no, there is one upon whom it falls: "Why me?" says Hamlet, in that Biblical and no doubt amused accent of Shakespeare's, whose wave of writings seems too aware of its impasses to be suicidal, even if it begins for him with the death of his son. (Let's not be too hasty to see in it the narcissistic murder of the child: read the sonnets, the necessity of a son, without which writing is at some point threatened, without that other one than you, vibrating with a strange warmth which is yours, extinguished for you, lost.) No, here poetic writing is completely involved in a calculation, across the precipitated play of the signifier, in the production of other scenes where the suicidal function of writing operates as such, other spaces, constricted knots of the orgasm [*jouissance*] of the Other, knots occupied by his unfathomable body or plural corpse, knots signed with a single stretch of writing in which every act is outside time. One must agree that the underlying "mystery" is indeed dizzying (though entirely chartable) if its mysticism is the temptation of the short-cut, the straight trail, and if, at the other pole, the mathematician Cantor, whose writing attests violently to that presence of the One in writing, when he too had cracked up at the death of his son and was up against undecidable questions in writing about set theory, oddly went and shut himself up in a psychiatric clinic in order to elucidate at leisure the question haunting him: was Shakespeare the true father of his works, or, in other words, is Shakespeare the true name, the *proper* name of their author? That he should debate this problem, all the while playing, in the midst of his depressive attack, with his excrement, and that he should leave the clinic with the germ of a theory of proper infinities and of "successive

Daniel Sibony

powers," is what makes the (written) thing moving without mere pathos [donne ... son pathétique sans pathos].

Let's take a brief look at Joyce's revival of *Hamlet*, the fabric that is woven by his mixture of writing and the story that it reveals. If a piece of writing does not tell stories [*histoires*], does not recount them, how could it literally punctuate time, to the point of taking on the density of history [*l'histoire*]? There is in Joyce a step toward the extreme of writing without history, which resonates with the unbearable blanks and dead spots of history.

Hamlet as a text is sparked by repetition and doubles, not so much to rile interpreters but so that across these doubles the inexpressible, which need not be spoken, might be inscribed as an intaglio [*en creux*] in language, and so that that which is fundamentally indeterminable in the function of the father might be retained in the inextricable knottiness of texts. What's more, every poet reties this knot without knowing that he is producing the tether that already binds him. This hollow [*ce creux*] is the very space hollowed out by his writing. Why was the figure of the ghost with the lifted visor so important for Joyce that he, too, produces this Hamlet, but differently, and becomes enthusiastic about the fact that Moses wrote his tables of the law in "the language of the outlaws"? What if that figure were Shakespeare, with his language, in which he, better than anyone, sustained the wager of writing? This language which Joyce was going to force to yield to the pressure of writings—is this the destroyed language that made him, the father of an Ophelia, lose an Ophelia? Was it necessary for the madness of his language to have already been uttered and attested to by the mad Lucia? Insane, she lies [*démente-ellement*] in language: did he ever believe in the madness of his daughter? In any case, in this tragic game that language plays with writing beyond the murder of the father or his images, there is in language, when it has relinquished its maternal envelope, that multiple proliferation of the name which makes writing operate at the very limit of doubles and feigning, in a movement toward that limit.

And it is far more complex than narcissistic calculations in which the writer as poet would sacrifice his real progeny in order to preserve it in writing, whereas this blemish [*cette tare*], this art [*cet art*], the flesh and blood of a living woman would spare him. We must hear Joyce's voice vibrate with enthusiasm when he reads his text in which Moses is drawn from the great Egyptian mother, if we are to imagine what is at stake.

And when in the question of *who* Hamlet is (a question reduced to the level of "clergymen's discussions of the historicity of Jesus"), Hiesos Kristos is evoked, that "magician of the beautiful" who claims that "this verily is that," who wants *re-noun* [*la renommée*]: well, well, he too wants to remake the names of things, make language yield to that which is inaudible in a proper name, the Christian re-elaboration of the function of the father: "I am the fire upon the altar. I am the sacrificial butter." (This comes just after we have been told that Aristotle, "one should hope," not only "was once Plato's schoolboy" but also "has remained so" [*mais le "reste" aussi*].) Thus we have on the horizon "the Christ with the bridesister, moisture of light, born of an ensouled virgin."

Hamlet is the art of transforming the death of the father (or his murder) into suicide, the result of which is massacre and even the concentration camp. It is no madder to transform murder into suicide than to prove suicide inherent in every death. Indeed, that's enough to drive you mad: in one family they traditionally cut open the veins of the dead to assure themselves (!) that the dead are indeed dead. At least in the Other, it will not be said that they didn't die on purpose. (One humorist said that his mother had given birth to him on purpose.) In any case, Joyce did have a feeling for this element of religious massacre, situating the points of murderous certainty, the son's envelope in his devotion to his mother, and "nine lives are taken for his father's one, Our Father who art in purgatory." "The bloodboltered shambles in act five is a forecast of the concentration camp sung by Mr Swinburne" ("swine" plus "burn"). Is this a successful repetition of the golden calf or the sacrificial lamb? ("I am the fire . . . .") Or is it a dress-

Daniel Sibony

rehearsal [*répétition générale*] on the stage [*scène*] of the unconscious, of the monstrous orgasm [*jouissance*] of which the
Christian, Western world was "purged" in the *anus mundi*? This
indeed is what makes it a monstrous meeting-place in writing, writing that arouses the compulsions of preceding "texts," launches
ghost stories and oscillating systems, and lends itself to their
resonances, rediscovering unconscious availabilities [*disponibilités*]
and pseudo-periodical functions of the letter. From this point of
view, *Hamlet* is a success: it must simply be followed up. Shakespeare himself, by exploding sacred writing with the fire of multi-
valent utterances, had ravaged theatrical space, the stage of the
Globe, and had smashed the place of shelter against that of exposure, depopulated holy places, and demolished the altar of the
body. Joyce provides himself with a keyboard of almost infinite
range, and of all that horde, drunken with memory and writing,
that awakens with the twentieth century, he combines the maximum
of fair play [*non-duperie*] with patient submission to the names
of the father [*noms du père*] that are retained in language—which
leads to new statements, as the result of forcing language to yield.

Is a writing-effect the *knothing* that arises between irreducible
utterances, [30] when knot and thing meet in nothingness, the thing
exploded in language and the knot separated from its pure phallic
dimension?

In any event, *Ulysses* begins with a vague air of Elsinore, and
for Dedalus his mother's "deathbed," which comes up in the middle
of the discussion about Shakespeare, whose wife buried him, we
know, with two coins on his eyes. Only he, Dedalus, does not
acquiesce: there's no worshipping his mother or saving his father

---

[30] As when Hamlet places his head between Ophelia's legs, after hinting
that he could put his prick there:
Hamlet: Do you think I meant country matters?
Ophelia: I think nothing, my lord.
Hamlet: That's a fair thought to lie between maids' legs.
Ophelia: What is, my lord?
Hamlet: Nothing.
And later (the next time he makes an off-color joke): "You are naught,
you are naught."

from his loss and repeating, with him or his like, erotic outpourings at his mother's deathbed. On her deathbed, which comes back to him, along with the sheeted mirror, she had asked him to pray. No. And now she returns to him in a dream, her face tortured, a cantankerous *mater* before an empty cross? He turns her implied accusations against her. "Ghoul! Chewer of corpses! No, mother. Let me be and let me live." The whole book ends with the marriage, in no way mystical, of Bloom and Molly: "and yes I said yes I will Yes."

But to endure the existence of the Other (the labor of the son) or of his desire (Eve) is not without paradox, for this existence is also the subject's and thus presents the danger for him that it may cost him that existence. Here is the dawning of the double suicide in which the maintenance of a double name (Hamlet) is affirmed and at the same time, in this suicide, the search for a narcissistic reference-point is linked with the artist's weaving of his own image, while the mother is restored to her place in the biological realm: *"As we, or mother Dana"* (he refers to the mother, the woman, or the totality of women, as a whole—let's see what he does with them) *"weave and unweave our bodies* [. . .] from day to day, their molecules shuttled to and fro, so does the artist weave and unweave his image. And as the mole on my right breast is where it was when I was born, though all my body has been woven of new stuff time after time"—the mole, the *mark* is thus constant throughout tyings and untyings [*nouements et dénouements*]—*"so through the ghost of the unquiet father the image of the unliving son looks forth."* The axis of death is cut by three layers of drives [*feuillets pulsionnels*]: death as a drive [*pulsion*] which moves the healthy shuttle of the cells, as a drive which produces the encounter of the artist with his written image which he ties and unties, and finally as a drive which introduces the transparent and reflecting glass in which the subject sees himself from the ghostly image that inhabits him, the image of the unquiet father. The death of the father looks at him but revives narcissistic identification and at the same time a delusion of mastery over this death, by means of knowledge.

Daniel Sibony

This is where the transformation of death into suicide reveals what is at stake: those who are killed, insofar as *suicide appears to be the highest point of knowledge about one's own death,* or who simply have died in their sleep, *"cannot know the manner of their quell unless their Creator"—in this case the son who has turned prophet for the occasion* ("O my prophetic soul!")—*"endow their souls with that knowledge,"* and in that respect Hamlet tends to go to extremes: he's never done being consubstantial with this father. The limit-point of this indefinite suspension is Christ: "He Who Himself begot, middler the Holy Ghost, and Himself sent himself, Agenbuyer, between Himself and others, Who, put upon by His fiends, stripped and whipped, was nailed like bat to barn-door, starved on crosstree"—see Eve's desire to eat of this forbidden fruit: every descent from the cross attests to it—"Who let Him bury, stood up, harrowed hell, fared into heaven and there these nineteen hundred years sitteth on the right hand of His Own Self but yet shall come in the latter day to doom the quick and dead when all the quick shall be dead already." Here we have the horizon, the absolute boundary of Hamlet, and, always in the background, his suicidal devotion to his mother: the father is radically "out," "acted out."

There is a reciprocal effacing of the son in the father: "through the ghost of the unquiet father the image of the unliving son looks forth." Now, it is precisely in connection with this capturing of the son's image in the hallucinated presence of the dead father that the *instant of creation* is evoked, in which paternity of (and in) writing is at stake. That instant from which the artist must emerge (the "coal," a burning bush, is "fading") imposes itself in a rejection (or renunciation) of time: "in the future, the *brother* of the past, I may see myself as I sit here now but by reflection from that which then I shall be." The father's murderer is his brother, his double, his other half, and in the play he invokes the first murder and the curse on Cain, and thus implicitly his devotion to the maternal orgasm [*jouissance*] of the woman he covets, a common theme of "nature" and "reason," "whose common theme/ Is death of fathers, and who still hath cried,/ From the first corse till he that died to-day,/ 'This must be so' ": *in short, a father means fatality, fate, and Hamlet will undertake the staging of that fatality.* But strangely enough, Joyce asks the question "Was he mad?" not about Shakespeare as writer but about Hamlet: "Fatherhood, in the sense of conscious begetting, is unknown to man. It is [...] an apostolic succession, from only begetter to only begotten. On that mystery and not on the madonna which the cunning Italian intellect flung to the mob of Europe the church is founded and founded irremovably because founded, like the world, macro- and microcosm, upon the void. Upon incertitude, upon unlikelihood." And even upon indeterminacy. *"What's in a name?"* says Buck Mulligan, and Stephen resumes: "That is what we ask ourselves in childhood when we write the name that [...] is ours."

It is by letting his double, Dedalus, speak to other men about another writer and his double (Hamlet) that Joyce indulges in that madness of writing which consists in drawing from his own tracks a reference-point, a means of access to the chain of living beings. The relationship to what is written is transformed into a relationship to the double when there is no remnant, nothing left over; the artistic effect seeks to make this remnant emerge, to invent this remnant in its repetition.

If Hamlet, by redistributing the pieces in the maddest, most fluid substitutions, replays the levels of utterance that are *mater*ialized in the drama of desire, by breaking his frozen writings against one another, Joyce rewrites and retranslates these foreign traces, exploding at those points where they don't fit. As an indication of this, consider this dream of his wife, Nora: "At a performance in the theatre/ A newly discovered play by Shakespeare/ Shakespeare is present/ There are two ghosts in the play./ Fear that Lucia may be frightened"—and the curious "interpretation" that he gives of it: "The [presence] of Shakespeare [...] is a suggestion of fame" [*renommée*], "his certainly (it is the tercentenary of his death) mine not so certainly [sic]. The fear for Lucia (herself in little) is fear that either subsequent honours" [*renommée*] "or the future development of my mind or *art* or its extravagant excursions into forbidden territory may bring unrest into her life." It is a woman who is afraid lest her daughter should become unsettled [*que sa fille ne se trouble*]. Lucia was to reach the bottom, the bottomless hole in language that is driven mad by her father. They each reach the bottom, but one by diving, the other by drowning herself.

Translated by James Hulbert
with the assistance of Joshua Wilner.

Shoshana Felman

Turning the Screw of Interpretation

What does the act of turning a screw have to do with literature? What does the act of turning a screw have to do with psychoanalysis? Are these two questions related? If so, might their relationship help to define the status of literature? It is these rather odd questions that the present study intends to articulate, so as to give them a further turn, to investigate and interrogate them on the basis of Henry James's famous short novel, *The Turn of the Screw.*

I. An Uncanny Reading Effect

> I didn't describe to you the purpose of it
> (...) at all, I described to you (...) the *effect*
> of it — which is a very different thing.
>
> (H. James, *The Sacred Fount*)

> The mental features discoursed of as the
> analytical are, in themselves, but little suscep-
> tible of analysis: we appreciate them only
> in their effects.
>
> (E. A. Poe, *The Murders in the Rue Morgue*)

The plot of *The Turn of the Screw* is well known: a young woman answering a want ad in a newspaper goes to meet a "perfect gentleman," a "bachelor in the prime of life," who hires her to take charge of his niece Flora and his nephew Miles, two little orphans who live in a secluded country house belonging to him. The young woman is to become the children's governess, but under the strict condition set down by her employer—"the Master"—that she assume "supreme authority" for her two charges, that is, that she solve singlehandedly any problems concerning them, without at any time turning to him for help or even contacting him for any reason. This condition is no sooner accepted than it begins to weigh heavily upon the governess (who is also the narrator)—especially when a letter arrives informing her, without giving the reason, that little Miles has been expelled from school: this unexplained punishment makes the child's apparent innocence seem somehow mysterious, suspect, ambiguous. In addition, the governess discovers that the house is haunted: several times she finds herself confronted by strange apparitions, whom, with the help of information about the house's past history gleaned from the housekeeper, Mrs. Grose, she finally identifies as the ghosts of two servants, Peter Quint and Miss Jessel, now dead, but formerly employed by the Master in this very house, and whose shady intimacy had, it seems, "corrupted" the children. The governess becomes steadily more convinced that the ghosts have come back to pursue their nefarious intercourse with the children, to take possession of their souls and to corrupt them radically. Her task is thus to *save* the children from the ghosts, to engage in a ferocious moral struggle against "evil," a struggle whose strategy consists of an attempt to catch the children in the very act of communing with the spirits, and thereby to force them to admit that communion, to confess their knowledge of the ghosts and their infernal complicity with them. Total avowal, the governess believes, would exorcise the children. The results of this heroic metaphysical struggle are, however, ill-fated: Flora, the little girl, caught by the governess in presence of the phantom of Miss Jessel, denies seeing the vision and falls seriously ill following the vehement accusations directed at her by the governess, whom she thenceforth holds in abhorrence; Miles, the little boy, on the other hand, having seemingly "surrendered" by pronouncing—under the governess's pressure—the *name* of Peter Quint face to face with his ghost, at that very moment dies in the arms of the governess as she clasps him to her breast in moral triumph. It is with this pathetically ironical embrace of a corpse that the story ends.

If the strength of literature could be defined by the intensity of its impact on the reader, by the vital energy and power of its *effect, The Turn of the Screw* would doubtless qualify as one of the strongest—i.e., most *effective*—texts of all time, judging by the quantity and intensity of the echoes it has produced, of the critical literature to which it has given rise. Henry James was himself astounded by the extent of the effect produced on his readers by his text, the generative potency of which he could measure only *a posteriori*. Ten years after the first appearance of *The Turn of the Screw,* in his New York Preface (1908), he writes:

Indeed if the artistic value of such an experiment be measured by the intellectual echoes it may again, long after, set in motion, the case would make in favour of this little firm fantasy — which I seem to see draw behind it today a train of associations. I ought doubtless to blush for thus confessing them so numerous that I can but pick among them for reference. [1]

Few literary texts indeed have provoked and "drawn behind them" so many "associations," so many interpretations, so many exegetic passions and energetic controversies. The violence to which the text has given rise can be measured, for example, by the vehement, aggressive tone of the first reactions to the novel, published in the journals of the period: "The story itself is distinctly repulsive," affirms *The Outlook* (LX, October 29, 1898, p. 537; *Norton,* p. 172). And *The Independent* goes still further:

The Turn of the Screw is the most hopelessly evil story that we have ever read in any literature, ancient or modern. How Mr. James could, or how

---

[1] Unless otherwise specified, all quotes from The New York Preface and from *The Turn of the Screw* are taken from the Norton Critical Edition of *The Turn of the Screw* (ed. Robert Kimbrough), New York: Norton, 1966; hereafter abbreviated "*Norton.*" As a rule, all italics within the quoted texts throughout this paper are mine; original italics alone will be indicated.

any man or woman could, choose to make such a study of infernal human debauchery, for it is nothing else, is unaccountable ... The study, while it exhibits Mr. James's genius in a powerful light, affects the reader with a disgust that is not to be expressed. The feeling after perusal of the horrible story is that one has been assisting in an outrage upon the holiest and sweetest fountain of human innocence, and helping to debauch — at least by helplessly standing by — the pure and trusting nature of children. Human imagination can go no further into infamy, literary art could not be used with more refined subtlety of spiritual defilement. (*The Independent*, LI, January 5, 1899, p. 73; *Norton*, p. 175)

The publication of *The Turn of the Screw* thus meets with a scandalized hue and cry from its first readers. But, interestingly enough, as the passage just quoted clearly indicates, what is perceived as the most scandalous thing about this scandalous story is that *we are forced to participate in the scandal*, that the reader's innocence cannot remain intact: there is no such thing as an innocent reader of this text. In other words, the scandal is not simply *in* the text, it resides in *our relation to the text*, in the text's *effect on us*, its readers: what is outrageous in the text is not simply that *of which* the text is speaking, but that which makes it speak *to us*.

The outraged agitation does not, however, end with the reactions of James's contemporaries. Thirty years later, another storm of protest very similar to the first will arise over a second scandal: the publication of a so-called "Freudian reading" of *The Turn of the Screw*. In 1934, Edmund Wilson for the first time suggests explicitly that *The Turn of the Screw* is not, in fact, a ghost story but a madness story, a study of a case of neurosis: the ghosts, accordingly, do not really exist; they are but figments of the governess's sick imagination, mere hallucinations and projections symptomatic of the frustration of her repressed sexual desires. This psychoanalytical interpretation will hit the critical scene like a bomb. Making its author into an overnight celebrity by arousing as much interest as James's text itself, Wilson's article will provoke a veritable barrage of indignant refutations, all closely argued and based on "irrefutable" textual evidence. It is this psychoanalytical reading and the polemical framework it has engendered that will henceforth focalize and concretely organize all subsequent critical discussion, all passions and all arguments related to *The Turn of the Screw*. For or against Wilson, affirming or denying the "objectivity" or the reality of the ghosts, the critical interpretations have fallen into two camps: the "psychoanalytical" camp, which sees the governess as a clinical neurotic deceived by her own fantasies and destructive of her charges; and the "metaphysical," religious, or moral camp, which sees the governess as a sane, noble saviour engaged in a heroic moral struggle for the salvation of a world threatened by supernatural Evil. Thus, as John Silver astutely puts it, "If the ghosts of 'The Turn of the Screw' are not real, certainly the controversy over them is." [2]

Would it be possible to say, indeed, that the *reality of the debate* is in fact more significant for the impact of the text than the reality of the ghosts? Could the critical debate itself be considered a *ghost effect*? Even more than the debate's content, it is its *style* which seems to me instructive: when the pronouncements of the various sides of the controversy are examined closely, they are found to repeat unwittingly—with a spectacular regularity—all the main lexical motifs of the text. Witness the following random examples, taken from a series of polemical essays:

—The motif of a danger which must be averted:

> The *danger* in the psychoanalytic method of criticism lies in its apparent plausibility.
>
> (Nathan Bryllion Fagin) [3]

—The motif of a violent aggression inflicted upon an object by an injurious, alien force:

> The Freudian reading of Henry James' 'The Turn of the Screw' (...) *does violence* not only to the story but also to the Preface.
>
> (Robert Heilman) [4]

---

[2] "A Note on the Freudian Reading of *The Turn of the Screw*, in: *A Casebook on Henry James's "The Turn of the Screw,"* ed. Gerald Willen, New York: Thomas Y. Crowell Company, 1969, 2nd edition; p. 239. This collection of critical essays will hereafter be abbreviated *"Casebook."*

[3] "Another Reading of *The Turn of the Screw*," in *Casebook*, p. 154.

[4] "The Freudian Reading of *The Turn of the Screw*," in *Modern Lan-*

Shoshana Felman

—The motif of attack and defense, of confrontation and struggle: in a rebuttal to the Freudian reading, Oliver Evans proposes that Wilson's theory be

> *attacked* point by point.
>
> (Oliver Evans) [5]

—The motif of final victory, of the enemy's defeat:

> Here is one place where I find Freud completely *defeated*.
>
> (Katherine Anne Porter) [6]

It could perhaps be objected that a vocabulary of aggression, conflict, and maybe even danger, is natural in a conflictive critical debate, and that it is just a coincidence that this vocabulary seems to echo and repeat the combative spirit which animates the text. Such an objection could not, however, account for some other, more specific, more peculiar stylistic echoes of the text which reemerge in the very language of the critics, in the very style of the polemic: the motif, for instance, of neurosis and of madness, of hysterical delusion. Robert Heilman thus accuses Wilson of alleged "hysterical blindness" (FR, MLN, p. 434), which alone would be able to account for the latter's errors in interpretation. Wilson, argues Heilman, is misreading James's use, in his New York Preface, of the word "authority." In Heilman's view, James's statement that he has given the governess "authority," is referring but to her *narrative* authority, to the *formal* fact that the story is being told *from her point of view,* and not, as Wilson would have it, to "the relentless English 'authority' which enables her to put over on inferiors even purposes which are totally deluded." How is this misreading possible? "Once again," explains Heilman, "the word *authority* has brought about, in an unwary liberal, an emotional spasm which has resulted in a

guage Notes, LXII, 7, Nov. 1947, p. 433. This essay will hereafter be referred to as: *"Heilman,* FR, MLN."

[5] "James's Air of Evil: *The Turn of the Screw,"* in *Casebook,* p. 202.

[6] "James: *The Turn of the Screw.* A Radio Symposium," in *Casebook,* p. 167.

kind of hysterical blindness" (FR, MLN, p. 434). Wilson's reading is thus polemicized into a *hysterical* reading, itself viewed as a neurotic symptom. What is interesting—and seems to me instructive—about this, is that it is the very critic who *excludes* the hypothesis of neurosis from the *story,* who is rediscovering neurosis in Wilson's critical *interpretation* of the story, an interpretation which he rejects precisely on the grounds that *pathology as such cannot explain the text:*

> It is probably safe to say that the Freudian interpretation of the story, of which the best known exponent is Edmund Wilson, no longer enjoys wide critical acceptance. (...) We cannot account for the evil by treating the governess as pathological... [7]

But the hypothesis of madness, or "pathology," which is indeed brought up by the governess herself, is not nearly so easy to eliminate as one might think, since, expelled from the text, it seems to fall back on the text's interpreter, and thus ironically becomes, through the very critical attempt at its elimination, ineradicable from the critical vocabulary, be it that of the "Freudians" or that of the "metaphysicians."

Another textual motif which crops up unexpectedly in the very language of the critical controversy is that of *salvation.* While insisting on the fact that *The Turn of the Screw* is in truth a drama of salvation, that is, a rescue operation to save the children from the evil ghosts, Robert Heilman writes:

> *The Turn of the Screw* may seem a somewhat slight work to call forth all the debate. But there is something to be said for the debate. For one thing, it may point out the danger of a facile, doctrinaire application of formulae where they have no business and hence compel either an ignoring of, or a gross distortion of, the materials. But more immediately: *The Turn of the Screw* is *worth saving.* (FR, MLN, p. 443).

The rescue operation, the drama of salvation described by the text thus *repeats itself* in the critical arena. But *from what* must the text

[7] Robert Heilman, "*The Turn of the Screw* as Poem," in *Casebook,* p. 175.

be saved? From being reduced, explains Heilman, to "a common-place clinical record." But again, let us notice the terms of the objection, which associates the psychoanalytical reading's abuses with the more general abuses of science as such:

We run again into the familiar clash between scientific and imaginative truth. This is not to say that scientific truth may not collaborate with, subserve, and even throw light upon imaginative truth; but it is to say that the scientific prepossession may seriously impede the imaginative insight. (FR, MLN, p. 444).

Another critic, repeating and emphasizing the term "prepossession," agrees: "We must agree, I think, that Freudian critics of the tale are *strongly prepossessed*." [8] But what precisely is a "prepossessed" critic if not one whose mind is in advance in the *possession* of some demon, one who, like James's children, is himself *possessed*? Possessed—should we say—by the ghost of Freud? It is clear, in any case, that the urgency of rescuing, of *saving the text,* in a critical account like Heilman's, strongly resembles the exorcistic operations of the governess *vis-à-vis* her "possessed" charges, and that the critical confrontation appears itself as a kind of struggle against some ghost-effect that has somehow been awakened by psychoanalysis. The scene of the critical debate is thus a *repetition* of the scene dramatized in the text. The critical interpretation, in other words, not only elucidates the text but also reproduces it dramatically, unwittingly *participates in it*. Through its very reading, the text, so to speak, acts itself out. As a reading effect, this inadvertent "acting out" is indeed uncanny: whichever way the reader turns, he can but be turned by the text, he can but *perform* it by *repeating* it. Perhaps this is the famous trap James speaks of in his New York Preface:

It is an excursion into chaos while remaining, like Blue-Beard and Cinderella, but an anecdote—though an anecdote amplified and highly emphasized and returning upon itself; as, for that matter, Cinderella and Blue-Beard return. I need scarcely add after this that it is a piece of ingenuity pure and

[8] Mark Spilka, "Turning the Freudian Screw: How Not to Do It," in *Norton,* pp. 249-250.

simple, of cold artistic calculation, an *amusette* to catch those not easily caught (the "fun" of the capture of the merely witless being ever but small), the jaded, the disillusioned, the fastidious. (*Norton*, p. 120).

We will return later on to this ingenious prefatory note so as to try to understand the distinction James is making between naive and sophisticated readers, and to analyze the way in which the text's return upon itself is capable of trapping *both*. Up to this point, my intention has been merely to suggest—to make explicit—this uncanny trapping power of Henry James's text as an inescapable *reading-effect*.

Taking such reading-effects into consideration, we shall here undertake a reading of the text which will at the same time be articulated with a reading of its readings. This two-level reading—which also must return upon itself—will be concerned with the following questions: What is the nature of a reading-effect as such? and by extension: what is a reading? What does the text have to say about its own reading? What is a "Freudian reading" (and what is it *not*)? What in a text *invites*—and what in a text *resists*—a psychoanalytical interpretation? In what way does literature *authorize* psychoanalysis to elaborate a discourse about literature, and in what way, having granted its authorization, does literature *disqualify* that discourse? A combined reading of *The Turn of the Screw* and of its psychoanalytical interpretation will here concentrate, in other words, not only on what psychoanalytical theory has to say about the literary text, but also on what literature has to say about psychoanalysis. In the course of this double reading, we will see how both the possibilities and the limits of an encounter between literature and psychoanalytical discourse might begin to be articulated, how the conditions of their meeting, and the modalities of their not meeting, might begin to be thought out.

II. What is a Freudian Reading?

> The Freudians err in the right direction.
>
> (Mark Spilka)

Shoshana Felman

I would like, as a starting point, to begin by subscribing to the following remarks by Mark Spilka:

> My concern (...) is with the imaginative poverty of much Freudian criticism, its crudeness and rigidity in applying valid psychological insights, its narrow conception of its own best possibilities (...) Over the past four decades Freudian critics have made James's tale a *cause célèbre*. The tale sustains the *"cause"* through erotic ambiguities. Since it also arouses childhood terrors, and perhaps arises from them, we may say that the Freudian approach works here or nowhere. Yet opponents charge that Freudian critics have reduced the tale to a "commonplace clinical record." Though they are perfectly correct, my own charge seems more pertinent: these Freudian critics have not been sufficiently Freudian. (*Norton*, p. 245).

These subtle, challenging remarks err only in the sense that they consider as resolved, non-problematic, the very question that they open up: how Freudian is a Freudian reading? Up to what point can one be Freudian? At what point does a reading start to be "Freudian enough"? *What* is Freudian in a Freudian reading, and in what way can it be defined and measured?

The one characteristic by which a "Freudian reading" is generally recognized is its insistence on sexuality, on its crucial place and role in the text. The focal theoretical problem raised by a psycho-analytical reading would thus appear to be the definition of the very status of sexuality as such *in a text*. Wilson's reading of *The Turn of the Screw* indeed follows this interpretative pattern of accounting for the whole story in terms of the governess's sexual frustration: she is in love—says Wilson—with the Master, but is unable to admit it to herself, and thus obsessively, hysterically projects her own desires upon the outside world, perceives them as exterior to herself in the hallucinated form of fantasmatic ghosts.

The theory is, then, that the governess who is made to tell the story is a neurotic case of sex repression, and that the ghosts are not real ghosts but hallucinations of the governess. [9]

---

[9] Edmund Wilson, "The Ambiguity of Henry James," in *The Triple Thinkers*, Penguin, 1962, p. 102. This essay will hereafter be referred to as *Wilson*.

In order to reinforce this theory, Wilson underlines the implicitly erotic nature of the metaphors and points out the numerous phallic symbols:

Observe, also, from the Freudian point of view, the significance of the governess's interest in the little girl's pieces of wood and of the fact that the male apparition first takes shape on a tower and the female apparition on a lake. (*Wilson*, p. 104).

What, however, was it in James's text that originally called out for a "Freudian" reading? It was, as the very title of Wilson's article suggests, not so much the sexuality as "The *ambiguity* of Henry James." The text, says Wilson, is ambiguous. It is ambiguous, that it, its meaning, far from being clear, is itself a *question*. It is this question which, in Wilson's view, calls forth an analytical response. The text is perceived as questioning in three different ways:

1) *Through its rhetoric*: through the proliferation of erotic metaphors and symbols *without* the direct, "proper" naming of their sexual nature. [10]

2) *Through its thematic content* — its *abnormal* happenings and its fantastic, strange manifestations. [11]

3) *Through its narrative structure* which resembles that of an enigma in remaining, by definition, elliptically incomplete. [12]

Solicited by these three modes of textual questioning — narrative, thematic, and rhetorical — the "Freudian" critic, in Wilson's view, is called upon to *answer*. In the case of the narrative question

[10] Cf., for example, *Wilson*, p. 126: "Sex *does* appear in his work — even becoming a kind of obsession," but we are always separated from it by "thick screens."

[11] Cf. *ibid.*, p. 126: "The people who surround this observer tend to take on the diabolic values of *The Turn of the Screw*, and these diabolic values are almost invariably connected with sexual relations that are always concealed and at which we are compelled to guess."

[12] Cf. *ibid.*, p. 108: "When one has once got hold of the clue to this meaning of *The Turn of the Screw*, one wonders how one could ever have missed it. There is a very good reason, however, in the fact that nowhere does James unequivocally give the thing away: almost everything from beginning to end can be read equally in either of two senses."

of the elliptical, incomplete structure of the enigma, he answers with the riddle's missing word, with the mystery's solution: the governess's sexual desire for the Master. In the case of the thematic question of uncanny strangeness, of fantastic happenings, he answers with a *diagnosis*: the ghosts are merely the symptoms of pathological, abnormal sexual frustration and repression. In the case of the rhetorical question of symbolic ambiguity, he answers with the "proper name," with the *literal* meaning of the phallic metaphors.

Considered from the "Freudian point of view," sexuality, valorized as both the foundation and the guidepost of the critical interpretation, thus takes on the status of an *answer* to the *question* of the text. Logically and ontologically, the answer (of sexuality) in fact pre-exists the question (of textuality). The question comes to be articulated (rhetorically, thematically, and narratively) only by virtue of the fact that the answer is as such *concealed*. Indeed the question is itself but an answer in disguise: the question is the answer's hiding place. The Freudian critic's job, in this perspective, is but to pull the answer out of its hiding place — not so much to give an answer *to* the text as to answer *for* the text: to be *answerable for* it, to answer *in its place,* to replace the question with an answer. It would not be inaccurate, indeed, to say that the traditional analytical response to literature is to provide the literary question with something like a reliably professional "answering service."

Such an operation, however, invites two fundamental questions: Does "James" (or James's text) authorize this way of answering *for* him? Does "Freud" (or Freud's text) authorize this way of answering *through* him?

The question of the possibility of answering for the text, as well as that of the status of such an answer, is in fact raised by James's text itself in its very opening, when Douglas, having promised to tell his dreadful story, intimates that it is a *love story,* which was confided to him by the heroine (the governess):

Mrs. Griffin, however, expressed the need for a little more light. "Who was it she was in love with?"

"The story will tell," I took upon myself to reply. (. . .).

"The story *won't* tell," said Douglas; "not in any literal, vulgar way." (Prologue, *Norton*, p. 3; James's italics).

In taking upon himself "to reply," to make *explicit* who it was the governess was in love with, in locating the riddle's answer in the governess's repressed desire for the Master, what then is Edmund Wilson doing? What is the "Freudian" reading doing here if not what the text itself, at its very outset, is precisely indicating as that which it *won't* do: "The story *won't* tell; not in any literal, vulgar way." These textual lines could be read as an ironic note through which James's text seems itself to be commenting upon Wilson's reading. And this Jamesian commentary seems to be suggesting that such a reading might indeed be inaccurate not so much because it is incorrect or false, but because it is, in James's terms, *vulgar.*

If so, what would that "vulgarity" consist of? And how should we go about defining not only an interpretation's accuracy, but what can be called its *tact*? Is a "Freudian reading" — by definition — tainted with vulgarity? *Can* a Freudian reading, as such, avoid that taint? What, exactly, makes for the "vulgarity" in Wilson's reading? Toward whom, or toward what, could it be said that this analysis lacks tact?

"The difficulty itself is the refuge from the vulgarity," writes James to H. G. Wells (*Norton*, p. 111). And in the New York Preface to *The Turn of the Screw,* he elaborates further the nature of that difficulty, of that tension which underlies his writing as a question:

Portentous evil — how was I to *save that,* as an intention on the part of my demon spirits, from the drop, the *comparative vulgarity,* inevitably attending, throughout the whole range of possible brief illustration, the offered example, the imparted vice, the cited act, the limited deplorable presentable instance? (*Norton*, p. 122).

Shoshana Felman

What is vulgar, then, is the *"imputed* vice," the "offered example," that is, the explicit, the specific, the unequivocal and immediately referential "illustration." *The vulgar is the literal,* insofar as it is unambiguous: "the story won't tell; not in any *literal, vulgar* way." The literal is "vulgar" because it *stops* the *movement* constitutive of meaning, because it blocks and interrupts the endless process of metaphorical substitution. The vulgar, therefore, is anything which misses, or falls short of, the dimension of the symbolic, anything which rules out, or excludes, meaning as a loss and as a flight, — anything which strives, in other words, to eliminate from language its inherent silence, anything which misses the specific way in which a text *actively* "won't tell." The vulgarity that James then seeks above all to avoid is that of a language whose discourse is outspoken and forthright and whose reserves of silence have been cut, that of a text inherently *incapable* of silence, inherently unable to hold its tongue.

If vulgarity thereby consists of the *reduction of rhetoric* as such, of the elimination of the indecision which inhabits meaning and of the *ambiguity* of the text, isn't that precisely Wilson's goal? Isn't Wilson's critical and analytical procedure that, precisely, of a *literalization* (i.e., in James's terms, of a "vulgarization") of sexuality in the text? Wilson, in fact, is quite aware of the text's rhetorical, undecidable question:

The fundamental question presents itself and never seems to get properly answered: What is the reader to think of the protagonist? (*Wilson,* p. 112).

But he only points out that question in order to *reduce* it, *overcome* the difficulty of the ambiguity, *eliminate* the text's rhetorical indecision by supplying a prompt *answer* whose categorical *literality* cannot avoid indeed seeming rudimentary, reductive, "vulgar." What are we to think of the protagonist?

We find that it is a variation on one of his [James's] familiar themes: the thwarted Anglo-Saxon spinster; and we remember unmistakable cases of women in James's fiction who deceive themselves and others about the origins of their aims and their emotions. (...)

107

James's world is full of these women. They are not always emotionally perverted. Sometimes they are apathetic. (. . .)

Or they are longing, these women, for affection but too inhibited or passive to obtain it for themselves. (*Wilson,* pp. 110-111).

Is this type of literalization of textual sexuality what a "Freudian point of view" is really all about? Invalidated and disqualified by James, would this "vulgarizing" literalization in truth be validated, authorized, by Freud? If for James the *literal* is *vulgar,* can it be said that from a Freudian point of view the *sexual* as such is *literal?* In order to investigate this question, I would like to quote, at some length, Freud himself, in a little-known text which appeared in 1910 under the title " 'Wild' Psychoanalysis":

A few days ago a middle-aged lady (. . .) called upon me for a consultation, complaining of anxiety-states. (. . .) The precipitating cause of the outbreak of her anxiety-states had been a divorce from her last husband; but the anxiety had become considerably intensified, according to her account, since she had consulted a young physician in the suburb she lived in, for he had informed her that the *cause* of her anxiety was her *lack of sexual satisfaction.* He said that she could not tolerate the loss of intercourse with her husband, and so there were only three ways by which she could recover her health—she must either return to her husband, or take a lover, or obtain satisfaction from herself. Since then she had been convinced that she was incurable (. . .)

She had come to me, however, because the doctor had said that *this was a new discovery for which I was responsible,* and that she had only to come and ask me to confirm what he said, and *I should tell her that this and nothing else was the truth* (. . .). I will not dwell on the *awkward predicament* in which I was placed by this visit, but instead will consider the conduct of the practitioner who sent the lady to me (. . .) connecting my remarks about "wild" psycho-analysis with this incident. [13]

It is tempting to point out the analogy between the rather comical situation Freud describes and the so-called "Freudian" treatment of the governess by Wilson. In both cases, the reference to Freud's theory is as brutally and as crudely literal, reducing the psychoanalytical explanation to the simple "lack of sexual satisfaction."

---

[13] " 'Wild' Psycho-Analysis," in *The Standard Edition of the Complete Psychological Works of Sigmund Freud,* Vol. XI (1910), pp. 221-222. This edition will hereafter be abbreviated *Standard.*

Shoshana Felman

Here therefore is Freud's own commentary on such procedures. Curiously enough, Freud, like James, begins with a reminder that the validity of an interpretation is a function not only of its truth, but also of its *tact:*

Everyone will at once bring up the criticism that if a physician thinks it necessary to discuss the question of sexuality (...) he must do so with tact. (*Standard*, p. 222).

But tact is not just a practical, pragmatic question of "couch-side manner"; it also has a theoretical importance: the reserve within the interpretative discourse has to allow for and to indicate a possibility of error, a position of uncertainty with respect to truth.

Besides all this, one may sometimes make a wrong surmise, and *one is never in a position to discover the whole truth.* Psycho-analysis provides these definite technical rules to replace the indefinable "medical tact" which is looked upon as a special gift. (*Standard*, p. 226).

The "wild psychoanalyst" 's analysis thus lacks the necessary tact, but that is not all.

Moreover, the physician in question was ignorant of a number of *scientific theories* [Freud's italics] of psycho-analysis or had misapprehended them, and thus showed how little he had penetrated into an understanding of its nature and purposes.
    (...) The doctor's advice to the lady shows clearly in what sense he understands *the expression "sexual life" — in the popular sense,* namely, in which by sexual needs nothing is meant but the need for coitus (...) *In psychoanalysis the concept of what is sexual comprises far more; it goes lower and also higher than its popular sense.*
    (...) Mental absence of satisfaction with all its consequences can exist where there is no lack of normal sexual intercourse (...)
    (...) By emphasizing exclusively the somatic factor in sensuality he undoubtedly simplifies the problem greatly. (*Standard*, pp. 222-223).

Sexuality, says Freud, is not to be taken in its literal, popular sense: in its analytical *extension,* it goes "lower and also higher" than its literal meaning, it extends both beyond and below. The relation between the analytical notion of sexuality and the sexual act is thus not a relation of simple, literal adequation, but rather a relation, so to speak, of *inadequation:* the psychoanalytical notion of sexuality, says Freud, comprises both *more* and *less* than the literal sexual act. But how are we to understand an *extension* of meaning which inclûdes not only *more,* but also *less* than the literal meaning? This apparent paradox, indeed, points to the specific complication which, in Freud's view, is inherent in human sexuality as such. The question here is less that of the meaning *of* sexuality than that of a complex *relationship between sexuality and meaning;* a relationship which is not a simple *deviation* from literal meaning, but rather, a *problematization of literality as such.*

The oversimplifying literalization professed by the "wild psychoanalyst" thus essentially misconstrues and misses the complexity of the relationship between sex and sense. It entails, however, another fundamental error, which Freud goes on to criticize:

A second and equally *gross misunderstanding* is discernable behind the physician's advice.

It is true that psycho-analysis puts forward *absence of sexual satisfaction* as the cause of nervous disorders. *But does it not say more than this?* Is its teaching to be ignored as too complicated when it declares that *nervous symptoms arise from a conflict between two forces* — on the one hand, the libido (which has as a rule become excessive), and on the other, a rejection of sexuality, or a repression (which is over-severe)? No one who remembers this *second* factor, which is *by no means secondary in importance,* can ever believe that sexual satisfaction in itself constitutes a remedy of general reliability for the sufferings of neurotics. *A good number of these people are, indeed, (. . .) in general incapable of satisfaction (Standard,* p. 223).

Nervous symptoms, Freud insists, spring not simply from a "lack of sexual satisfaction" but from a *conflict between two forces.* Repression is constitutive of sexuality: the *second* factor is by no means *secondary* in importance. But the second factor as such is precisely the *contradiction* of the first. Which means not only that the literal meaning—the first factor—is not simply first and foremost, but also, that its *priority,* the very *primacy* in which its literality is founded, its very *essence of literality,* is itself *subverted* and *negated* by the second, but not secondary, meaning. Indeed, sexuality being constituted by these *two* factors, *its meaning is its*

Shoshana Felman

own contradiction: the *meaning* of the sexual as such is *its own obstruction,* its own deletion.

The "lack of satisfaction," in other words, is not simply an *accident* in sexual life, it is essentially inherent in it: "All human structures," says Lacan, after Freud, "have as their essence, not as an accident, the restraint of pleasure—of fulfillment." [14]

Here, then, is another crucial point which Wilson misses, *opposing* as he does sexuality to the "lack of satisfaction," considering the frustration of the governess (defined as the "thwarted Anglo-Saxon spinster") as an abnormal *accident* to be treated as pathogenic. What would "the abnormal" be, however, in Wilson's view, if not precisely that which is *not literal,* that which *deviates* from the *literal*? Literal (normal) sex being viewed as a simple, positive *act* or *fact,* it is simply inconceivable that it would constitutively miss its own aims, include its own negation as its own inherent property. For Wilson, sex is "simple," i.e., adequate to itself. [15] Wilson can thus write of *The Sacred Fount,* another enigmatic Jamesian story—"What if the hidden theme of *The Sacred Fount* is *simply sex* again?" (*Wilson,* p. 115). But for Freud, as we have seen, not only is the status of sexuality not *simple:* composed as it is by two dynamically contradictory factors, sexuality is precisely *what rules out simplicity as such.*

It is indeed because sexuality is essentially the violence of its own non-simplicity, of its own inherent "conflict between two forces," the violence of its own division and self-contradiction, that it is experienced as anxiety and lived as terror. The terrifying aspect of *The Turn of the Screw* is in fact linked by the text itself, subtly

[14] Jacques Lacan, "Discours de clôture des journées sur les psychoses chez l'enfant," in *Recherches,* special issue on "Enfance aliénée," 11 décembre 1968, pp. 145-146; translation mine. Unless otherwise indicated, all quotations from Lacan's works in this paper are in my translation.

[15] And if that adequation does not appear in James's work, it is, in Wilson's view, because James, too, like the governess, missed out on the simplicity of the normal status of normal sex and knew only the lack of satisfaction involved in its pathological manifestations: cf. *Wilson,* p. 125: "*Problems of sexual passion* (...) were beginning to be subjects of burning interest. But it is probable that James had by this time (...) come to recognize *his unfittedness for dealing with them* and was far too honest to fake."

but suggestively, precisely to its *non-simplicity*. After having promised to tell his story, Douglas adds:

"It's quite too horrible." (...) "It's beyond everything. Nothing at all that I know touches it."
"For sheer terror? I remember asking. He seemed to say *it was not so simple as that;* to be really at a loss how to qualify it (Prologue, p. 1).

If, far from implying the simplicity of a self-present literal meaning, sexuality points rather to a multiplicity of conflicting forces, to the complexity of its own divisiveness and contradiction, its meaning can by no means be univocal or unified, but must necessarily be *ambiguous*. It is thus not rhetoric which disguises and hides sex; sexuality *is* rhetoric, since it essentially consists of ambiguity: it is the coexistence of dynamically antagonistic meanings. Sexuality is the *division and divisiveness of meaning;* it is meaning *as* division, meaning *as* conflict.

And, indeed, what is the *subject* of *The Turn of the Screw* if not this very conflict which inhabits meaning, the inherent conflict which structures the relationship between *sex* and *sense*? "The governess," John Lydenberg pertinently writes, "may indistinctly consider the ghosts as the essence of evil, and, as Heilman points out, she certainly chooses words which identify them with Satan and herself with the Saviour. But our vantage point is different from the governess's: we see her as one of the combatants, and as the story progresses we become even more uncertain who is fighting whom." [16]

In thus dramatizing, through a clash of meanings, the very functioning of meaning as division and as conflict, sexuality is not, however, the "text's meaning": it is rather that through which meaning in the text *does not come off,* that which in the text, and through which the text, *fails to mean,* that which can engender but a *conflict of interpretations,* a critical debate and discord precisely like the polemic which surrounds *The Turn of the Screw* and with which we are concerned here. "If analytical discourse," writes

[16] J. Lydenberg, "The Governess Turns the Screws," in *Casebook*, p. 289.

Lacan, "indicates that meaning is as such sexual, this can only be a manner of accounting for its *limits*. Nowhere is there a last word. (...) Meaning indicates only the direction, point only at the sense toward which if fails." [17]

III. The Conflict of Interpretations: the Turns of the Debate

> Et ma tête surgie
> Solitaire vigie
> Dans les vols triomphaux
> De cette faux
>
> Comme rupture franche
> Plutôt refoule ou tranche
> Les anciens désaccords
> Avec le corps
>
> (Mallarmé, *Cantique de St-Jean*)

In repeating as they do the primal scene of the text's meaning as division, the critics can by no means master or exhaust the very meaning of that division, but only act the division out, perform it, be part of it.

To participate in a division is, however, at the same time, to fight *against* division: it is indeed to commit oneself to the elimination of the opponent, and through him, to the elimination of the heterogeneity of meaning, the very scandal of contradiction and ambiguity. One after another, the critics thus *contest* Wilson's reading by negating or denying his assumption that the very *meaning* of *The Turn of the Screw* can at all be *divided* or equivocal:

"Almost everything from beginning to end," [Wilson] declares, "can be read equally in either of two senses." "Almost everything": *But what if there is one thing, one little thing, that cannot be read in either of two senses, that can be read only in one sense?* What then? How strange that Mr. Wilson does not see that any such fact (...) could be the sharp little rock on which *his theory must split* (A. J. A. Waldock). [18]

---

[17] J. Lacan, *Le Séminaire — Livre XX: Encore* (1972-73), Paris: Seuil, 1975, p. 66. This work will henceforth be referred to as *Encore*.
[18] "Mr. Edmund Wilson and *The Turn of the Screw*," in *Casebook*, p. 172.

The Freudians misread the internal evidence almost as valiantly as they do the external. In the story, of course, there are passages that it is possible to read ambivalently; but *the determining unambiguous passages* from which the critic might work are so plentiful that *it seems hardly good critical strategy to use the ambiguous ones as points of departure* (Robert, Heilman, FR, MLN, p. 436).
Granted that the text has various levels of meaning, it would appear on the whole unwise to have them mutually contradictory (Alexander Jones). [19]

The attempt, however, to eliminate contradiction itself partakes of the contradiction: the affirmation of meaning as *undivided* is simultaneously one that *excludes* the position of the opponent; the homogeneity of meaning can be asserted but through the expulsion of its heterogeneity. In precisely trying to *unify* the meaning of the text and to proclaim it as unambiguous, the critics only mark more forcefully its constitutive *division* and duplicity. Contradiction reappears with ironical tenacity in the very words used to banish it:

[My] interpretation (. . .) has the virtue of *extreme inclusiveness,* though I fear *there is no room in it* for (. . .) Mr. Wilson (Oliver Evans, *Casebook,* p. 211).

But here again, to affirm contradiction in the very act of denying it, as does the *critics' story,* their story of the "true" interpretation of the story, is precisely to bear witness to the *double bind* which is constitutive of the very framework of the *governess's narrative,* to be caught in the dynamically conflictive impasse which confronts the governess herself *as narrator.* To affirm contradiction in the very act of denying its existence in the text is therefore to repeat, oneself, the *textual act,* to perform the very act of textuality triggered by the ambiguity of sexuality. It becomes thus clear that the critical debate, in its intentions and contentions, itself partakes of the textual *action.* "The Turn of the Screw," writes James, "was an action, desperately, or it was nothing" (New York Preface, *Norton,* p. 121). The *actors,* or the agents of this textual action, are indeed the readers and the critics no less than the characters. Criticism, to use Austin's terminology, here consists not of a state-

[19] "Point of View in *The Turn of the Screw,*" in *Casebook,* p. 301.

ment, but of a performance of the story of the text; its function is not *constative,* but *performative.* Reading here becomes not the cognitive observation of the text's pluralistic meaning, but its "acting out." Indeed it is not so much the critic who comprehends the text, as the text which comprehends the critic. Comprehending its own criticism, the text, through its reading, orchestrates the critical disagreement as the performance and the "speech *act*" of its own disharmony. "Irony," as Roland Barthes, in a different context, puts it, "irony is what is immediately given to the critic: not to see the truth, but, in Kafka's terms, to be it." [20]

In thus dramatizing, through their contradictory versions of the text's truth, the truth of the text as its own contradiction, James's critics, curiously enough, all hold *Freud* responsible for their disagreement: "Freud" is indeed believed to be the cause and is referred to as the demarcation line of their polemical divergence. The studies of *The Turn of the Screw,* according to their own self-presentation, divide themselves into so-called "Freudian" and so-called "anti-Freudian" readings. Thus it is that while Ezra Pound calls James's story "a Freudian affair," [21] while Wilson—as we have seen—invites us to "observe the Freudian point of view," and while Oscar Cargill celebrates "Henry James as a Freudian Pioneer" in the very title of the first version of his study of *The Turn of the Screw,* Katherine Anne Porter, on the other hand, singles out *The Turn of the Screw* as an illustration of Freud's "defeat": "Here is one place," she argues, "where I find Freud completely defeated" (*Casebook,* p. 167). So does Robert Heilman strike at Freud himself through Wilson, in entitling his polemical essay against the latter, "The Freudian reading of *The Turn of the Screw,*" an essay whose opening line marks well the generalization of the methodological reproach at stake: "The Freudian reading of Henry James's *The Turn of the Screw* (...) does violence not only to the story but also to the Preface" (FR, MLN, p. 433). In a counter-attack on

[20] *Critique et Vértié,* Paris: Seuil, 1966, p. 75.
[21] Quoted by Harold C. Goddard in "A Pre-Freudian Reading of *The Turn of the Screw,*" in *Norton,* p. 182.

Heilman and other "anti-Freudian essays" listed in a footnote under this terminological heading, John Silver proposes "to lend support to Mr. Wilson's interpretation" in an essay which he entitles: "A Note on the Freudian Reading of *The Turn of the Screw*" (*Casebook,* p. 239). Between "Freudians" and "anti-Freudians," in the critical debate around *The Turn of the Screw,* Freud's ghost significantly and ironically thus seems to have become the very mark and sign of divisiveness and of division. It is as though "Freud" himself, in this strange polemic, had become the very *name* of the critical disagreement, the uncanny *proper name of discord.*

This symmetrical polar opposition between "Freudians" and "anti-Freudians" itself rests, however, on an implied presupposition, which is, in truth, as problematic, and as paradoxical, as the debate itself. The paradox can be summed up as follows: Whereas the two opposing critical sides believe themselves to be in spectacular *disagreement* over *James's* "true meaning," they demonstrate in fact a spectacular *agreement* over *Freud's* "true meaning," which, unlike that of James, is considered by both sides to be transparent, unequivocal, incontrovertible. But in reality the "true Freud" is no more immediately accessible to us than the "true James." For "Freud" is equally a text, known only through the difficulties and uncertainties of the act of reading and of interpretation. What, indeed, if it were not enough to call oneself a "Freudian" in order to *be* one? And what if it were not enough to call oneself an "anti-Freudian," either, in order to, in truth, become one? In this sense, Freud's name can hardly be considered a *proper* name, but becomes in effect nothing other than a *ghost,* as ambiguous as James's ghosts, to the extent that it conveys not an established truth or a referential *knowledge,* but an *invitation to interpretation.* A "Freudian reading" is thus not a reading guaranteed by, grounded in, Freud's knowledge, but first and foremost a *reading of Freud's "knowledge,"* which as such can never *a priori* be assured of knowing anything, but must take its chances *as* a reading, necessarily and constitutively threatened by error.

Shoshana Felman

In thus examining the paradigm of the so-called "Freudian reading of *The Turn of the Screw*" and its distortion of Freud's theory as we could here but begin to *read* it in Freud's *text,* our intention has been to displace and dislocate the much-repeated, central question of the polemic: "is the Freudian reading true or false?" by suggesting that *we do not yet even know what a Freudian reading really is.*

The question, therefore, can no longer be simply to decide whether in effect the "Freudian" reading is true or false, correct or incorrect. It can be both at the same time. It is no doubt correct, but it misses nonetheless the most important thing: it is blind to the very textuality of the text. The question of a reading's "truth" must be at least complicated and re-thought through another question, which Freud, indeed, has raised, and taught us to articulate: what does such "truth" (or any "truth") leave out? What is it *made to miss*? What does it have as its function to overlook? What, precisely, is its residue, the *remainder* it does not account for? Since, as we have seen, the critical scene of the polemic is both repetitive and performative of the textual scene, it can in fact be said that it is the very "falseness" of the readings which constitutes their "truth." The Freudian reading is no doubt "true," but no truer than the opposed positions which contradict it. And it is "false," indeed, to the extent that it *excludes* them. These opposed positions which assert the text's contradiction in the very act of denying it, are thus "true" to the extent that they are "false." And a new, far more troubling question can no longer be avoided, with respect to James as well as with respect to Freud, and indeed *because of* both: is a reading of *ambiguity* as such really *possible*? Is it at all possible to read and to interpret ambiguity *without reducing it* in the very process of interpretation? Are reading and ambiguity in any way *compatible*?

It should be noted that the expression "Freudian reading" is *itself* an ambiguous expression which can refer either to Freudian *statements* or to Freudian *utterance:* a reading can be called "Freudian" with respect to *what it reads* (the *meaning* or thematic *content* it derives from a text) or with respect to *how it reads* (its interpretative *procedures,* the techniques or *methods* of analysis it uses). While it is almost exclusively in the first of these two senses that the concept "Freudian reading" is understood and used in the American cultural context, in France, it is on the contrary rather in the second sense that a new reading of Freud has been elaborated by Jacques Lacan. For Lacan, indeed, the unconscious is not only *that which must be read,* but also, and primarily, *that which reads.* Freud's discovery of the unconscious is the outcome of his *reading* of the hysterical discourse of his patients, i.e., of his being capable of reading in this hysterical discourse *his own unconscious.* The discovery of the unconscious is therefore Freud's discovery, within the discourse of the other, of what was actively reading within himself: his discovery, in other words, or his reading, of what was reading—in what was being read. The gist of Freud's discovery, for Lacan, thus consists not simply of the revelation of a new *meaning*—the unconscious—but of the *discovery of a new way of reading:*

[Freud's] first interest was in hysteria. (. . .) He spent a lot of time listening, and, while he was listening, there resulted something paradoxical, (. . .), that is, a *reading*. It was while listening to hysterics that he *read* that there was an unconscious. That is, something he could only construct, and in which he himself was implicated; he was implicated in it in the sense that, to his great astonishment, he noticed that he could not avoid participating in what the hysteric was telling him, and that he felt affected by it. Naturally, everything in the resulting rules through which he established the practice of psychoanalysis is designed to counteract this consequence, to conduct things in such a way as to avoid being affected. [22]

In the light of this Lacanian insight, I would like to propose a re-reading of *The Turn of the Screw* which would try to replace the conventional idea of a "Freudian reading" with a different type of reading, one whose necessity and possibilities have been precisely opened up by Lacan's re-reading of Freud's discovery of reading.

---

[22] Transcribed from a recording of J. Lacan's talk at the "Kanzer Seminar" (Yale University, Nov. 24, 1975), which has been translated into English by Barbara Johnson.

Shoshana Felman

Throughout this paper, Lacan's works will be periodically referred to, not so much as an authoritative body of theoretical knowledge, but as a remarkably rich and complex analytical *text,* whose value lies for us less in any reified form of its pronouncements than in the suggestiveness of its rhetoric, less in what it states than in what it *understates,* leaves *open,*—in its linguistic silences and their possible interaction with James's text.

Our reading of *The Turn of the Screw* would thus attempt not so much to *capture* the mystery's solution, but to follow, rather, the significant path of its flight; not so much to solve or *answer* the enigmatic question of the text, but to investigate its structure; not so much to name and make *explicit* the ambiguity of the text, but to understand the necessity and the rhetorical functioning of the textual ambiguity. The question underlying such a reading is thus not *"what* does the story mean?" but rather *"how* does the story mean?" How does the meaning of the story, whatever it may be, rhetorically take place through permanent displacement, textually take shape and take effect: *take flight.*

IV. The Turns of the Story's Frame: a Theory of Narrative

> It appeared that the narrative he had prom-
> ised to read us really required for a proper
> intelligence a few words of prologue.
>
> *(The Turn of the Screw)*

> Literature is language (...); but it is language
> around which we have drawn a frame, a
> frame that indicates a decision to regard with
> a particular self-consciousness the resources
> language had always possessed.
>
> (Stanley E. Fish)

The actual story of *The Turn of the Screw* (that of the governess and the ghosts) is preceded by a prologue which is both posterior and exterior to it, and which places it *as* a story, as a speech event, in the context of the "reality" in which the story comes to be told.

With respect to the story's *content,* then, the prologue constitutes a sort of *frame,* whose function is to situate the *story's origin.*

The narrated story is thus presented as the *center* of the *frame* —the focal point of a narrative space which designates and circumscribes it from the outside as *its inside.* Placed *around* the story which becomes its center, the narrative frame, however, frames *another* center within its *literal* space:

> The story had held us, *round the fire,* sufficiently breathless (. . .) He began to read to our hushed *little circle,* (. . .) kept it, *round the hearth,* subject to a common thrill (pp. 1 and 4).

Since the narrative space of the prologue organizes both a *frame around the story* and a *circle around the fire,* since the fire and the story are both placed at the very *center* of the *narration,* the question could arise as to whether they could be, in any way, considered *metaphors of each other* in the rhetorical constellation of the text. This hypothesis in turn opens up another question: if the content of the story and the fire in the hearth *are* metaphors of each other, how does this metaphorical relation affect the centrality of the two terms?

Before pursuing these questions further, let us take another look at the prologue's status as the story's "frame." The prologue, in fact, frames the story not only spatially but also temporally: while it takes place long *after* the governess's story, it also tells of events which had occurred *before* it: the meeting between the governess and the Master which sets up the determining conditions of the subsequent events. The frame picks up the story, then, both *after its end* and *before its opening.* If the function of the frame is to determine the story's *origin,* then that origin must somehow be both anterior and posterior to the story.

Anterior to the story but recounted and accounted for *a posteriori,* the story's origin seems to depend on the authority of the story teller, i.e., of the narrator, who is usually supposed to be both the story's literal source and the depositary of the knowledge out of which the story springs and which the telling must reveal.

But while the prologue's function would thus seem to be to *relate* the story to its narrator, the prologue of *The Turn of the Screw* rather *disconnects* the story from the narrator since it introduces not *one* narrator, but *three:* 1) the person who says "I," the first person "general narrator" who transmits to *us* the story with which he himself had no direct connection, and which he heard from Douglas; 2) Douglas, who reads the story to the circle around the fire, but who did not participate in it himself. Douglas had known the governess, the story's heroine, as his sister's governess long after the story had taken place, and had been secretly in love with her although she was ten years his senior. It was, however, only later, on her deathbed, that the governess confided to him a written account of her story. 3) The third teller of the story is thus the governess herself, who is the first-person narrator of her own written narrative.

Having received and read the manuscript, Douglas had in turn kept the governess's story secret for forty years, until that night around the fire when at last, to his privileged circle of friends and most especially to the general narrator, he decided to reveal it. And finally, long after his own telling of the story around the fire, Douglas, on his own deathbed, confided the treasured manuscript to his friend the narrator, who tells us in the prologue that the story he is transmitting to us is his own transcription, made still later, of that manuscript, which he had heard Douglas read before the fire.

The existence of the story is thus assured only through the constitution of a *narrative chain,* in which the narrators relay the story from one to the other. The story's origin is therefore not assigned to any one voice which would assume responsibility for the tale, but to the deferred action of a sort of *echoing effect,* produced—"after the fact"—by voices which themselves re-produce previous voices. It is as though the frame itself could only multiply *itself,* repeat itself: as though, in its infinite reproduction of the very act of narration, the frame could only be its own self-repetition, its own self-framing. If the tale is thus introduced through its own reproduction, if the story is preceded and anticipated by a repetition of the story, then the frame, far from situating, as it first appeared, the story's *origin,* actually situates its *loss,* constitutes its infinite deferral. The story's origin is therefore situated, it would seem, in a *forgetting* of its origin: to tell the story's origin is to tell the story of that origin's obliteration. But isn't this forgetting of the story's origin and beginning, and the very story of this forgetting, constitutive, precisely, of the very story of psychoanalysis and of *analysis as a story*? *The Turn of the Screw* would seem to be very like a psychoanalytical tale. Through the spiral threads of its prologue, the story indeed originates in a frame through which it frames itself into losing its own origin: as is the case with the psychoanalytical story of the unconscious, it is here the very loss of the story's origin which *constitutes* the origin of the story. The New York Preface, in its turn, both underlines and illustrates this point: added *a posteriori* as a second preface to the beginning of the story, it is like a prologue to the prologue, an introduction to the introduction, as if to make up for the missing origin or beginning, but succeeding only in repeating, in beginning once again the tale of the constitutive loss of the tale's beginning.

The starting point itself — the sense (...) of the circle, one winter afternoon, round the hall-fire of a grave old country house where (...) the talk turned, *on I forget what homely pretext,* to apparitions and night-fears, to the marked and sad drop in the general supply (...). The good (...) ghost stories appeared all to have been told (...) Thus it was, I remember, that amid our lament for a beautiful *lost form,* our distinguished host expressed the wish *that he might but have recovered for us* one of the scantiest of *fragments* of this form at its best. He had never forgotten the impression made on him as a young man by the withheld glimpse, at it were, of a dreadful matter that had been reported years before, and with as few particulars, to a lady with whom he had youthfully talked. The story would have been thrilling *could she but find herself in better possession of it,* dealing as it did with a couple of small children in an out-of-the-way place, to whom the spirits of certain "bad" servants, dead in the employ of the house, were believed to have appeared with the design of "getting hold" of them. This was all, but *there had been more,* which my friend's old converser *had lost the thread of* (...). He himself could give us but *this shadow of a shadow* — my own appreciation of which, I need scarcely say, was exactly *wrapped up in that thinness* (*Norton,* pp. 117-118).

A narrative frame which thus incarnates the very principle of repetition of the story it contains, and, through that repetition, situates both the loss of the story's origin and the story's origin *as* its own loss, is clearly not a simple backdrop, staging, from the circumstancial *outside,* the *inside* of the story's content, but constitutes rather a complication, a problematization of the relationship itself between the inside and the outside of the textual space. On the one hand, as Alexander Jones points out, the "outside" frame expands the "inside" of the story, bringing into it both the storyteller and the reader:

By placing himself within the confines of the story as "I," the narrator, James makes himself one of the characters rather than an omniscient author. *No one is left on the "outside" of the story,* and *the reader is made to feel that he and James are members of the circle around the fire (Casebook,* p. 299).

In including not only the content of the story but also the figure of the reader within the fireside circle, the frame indeed leaves no one *out:* it pulls the outside of the story into its inside by enclosing in it what is usually outside it: its own readers. But the frame at the same time does the very opposite, pulling the inside outside: for in passing through the echoing chain of the multiple, repetitive narrative voices, it is the very *content,* the *interior* of the story which becomes somehow *exterior to itself,* reported as it is by a voice inherently alien to it and which can render of it but "the shadow of a shadow," a voice whose intrusion compromises the tale's secret intimacy and whose otherness violates the story's presence to itself. The frame is therefore not an outside contour whose role is to display an inside content: it is a kind of exteriority which permeates the very heart of the story's interiority, an internal cleft separating the story's content from itself, distancing it from its own referential certainty. With respect to the story's content, the frame thus acts both as an inclusion of the exterior and as an exclusion of the interior: it is a perturbation of the outside at the very core of the story's inside, and as such, it is a blurring of the very difference between inside and outside.

No one, then, is left on the "outside" of the story, except the story's inside. Like the circle round the fire, the story's frame thus encloses not only the story's content, but, equally, its readers and its reading. But what if the story's content *were* precisely *its own reading*? What if the *reading* (outside the text) were none other than the story's *content* (inside the text), being also, at the same time, that which compromises that content's inside, preventing it from coinciding with itself, making it ec-centric, exterior to itself? If we stop to consider that this non-presence of the story to itself, this self-exteriority, this ec-centricity and foreignness of the content to itself, can define, as such, precisely, the *unconscious,* we can see that reading, here, might be just the key to an understanding of the essential link between the story and the unconscious. "That is what analytical discourse is all about: reading," says Lacan (*Encore,* p. 29). For has it not become obvious that the chain of narrative voices which transmits *The Turn of the Screw* is also, at the same time, a chain of *readings*? Readings which re-read, and re-write, other readings? In the chain transmission of the story, each narrator, to relay the story, must first be a *receiver* of the story, a *reader* who at once records it and *interprets* it, simultaneously trying to make sense of it and *undergoing* it, as a lived experience, an "impression," a *reading-effect.*

> I asked him if the experience in question had been his own. To this his answer was prompt. "Oh, thank God, no!"
> "And is the record yours? You took the thing down?"
> "Nothing but the impression. I took it here — " he tapped his heart. "I've never lost it" (Prologue, p. 2).

"The safest arena," writes James elsewhere, "for the play of moving accidents and of mighty mutations and of strange encounters, or whatever odd matters, is the field, as I may call it, rather of their second than of their first exhibition":

> By which, to avoid obscurity. I mean nothing more cryptic than I feel myself show them best by showing almost exclusively the way they are felt, by recognising as their *main interest* some *impression strongly made by them* and intensely received. We but too probably break down (...) when we

attempt the prodigy (...) in itself; with its "objective" side too emphasised the report (...) will practically run thin. We want it clear, goodness knows, but we also want it thick, and *we get the thickness in the human consciousness that entertains and records, that amplifies and interprets it.* That indeed, when the question is (...) of the "supernatural", constitutes the only thickness we do get; here *prodigies,* when they come straight, come with an effect imperilled; *they keep all their character,* on the other hand, *by looming through some other history* — the indispensable history of somebody's *normal* relation to something. [23]

The "main interest" of the story is thus the "thickness" it acquires through its own *reading*—through "the human consciousness that entertains and records, that amplifies and interprets it." The very subject-matter of the story of the "supernatural," its narrative condition, is, says James, its way of *"looming through some other history,"* its narration *in the other,* and *out of* the other. And that "other" here is the reader. The reader—i.e., also each one of the narrators: Douglas with respect to the governess's manuscript; "I" with respect to Douglas's account of it. The reader-narrator is here that "other," his personal story is the "other history," and his reading (i.e., his narrative, his telling) is significant to the extent that it *interferes* with the tale it tells. Each one of these superimposed stories, each act of narration and each narrative, is here a *reading of the other;* each reading is a *story in the other,* a story whose signification is interfered with but whose interference is significant, a story whose very meaning *interferes* but whose interference *means.* And this, of course, brings us back to the very question of the unconscious, for what, indeed, is the unconscious if not—in every sense of the word—a *reader*? "In analytical discourse," writes Lacan, "the unconscious subject is presumed to be able to read. And that's what the whole affair of the unconscious amounts to" (*Encore,* p. 38). The story of the unconscious thus resembles James's tale, insofar as they both come to us, constitutively, *through the reader.*

---

[23] Preface to "The Altar of the Dead," in Henry James, *The Art of the Novel, Critical Prefaces,* ed. R. P. Blackmur, New York: Charles Scribner's Sons, 1962, p. 256. Unless otherwise indicated, quotations from James's Prefaces will refer to this collection, hereafter abbreviated *AN.*

Thus it is that the narrator presents us with his own transcription of the manuscript which Douglas, "with *immense effect,* (...) began to *read* to our hushed little circle" (p. 4). Douglas's performance as storyteller, as author-narrator, consists, thereby, of a literal act of *reading.* And if the first-person narrator retransmits the story, communicates to us a reproduction and a reading of that reading, it is doubtless the result of the "immense effect" Douglas's reading produced on him, and which he hopes in turn to produce on us. The very act of telling, of narration, proceeds then from the potentially infinite repercussion of an *effect of reading;* an effect that, once produced, seeks to reproduce itself as an effect yet to be produced—an effect whose *effect* is an effect to produce. Narrative as such turns out to be the trace of the *action* of a reading; it is, in fact, *reading as action.* In Douglas's very first remarks, on the opening page of the prologue, the very *title* of the story is uttered as the mark, or the description, of its own *reading-effect:*

"I quite agree—in regard to Griffin's ghost, or whatever it was—that its appearing first to the little boy, at so tender an age, adds a particular touch. (...) If the child gives the *effect* another *turn of the screw,* what do you say of two children?"

"We say, of course," somebody exclaimed, "that they give two turns! Also that we want to hear about them" (Prologue, p. 1).

It is by virtue of the reading-effect it produces that the text receives its very name, its title. But that title, as a title, is not given to it by the original author of the manuscript: it is added to it "after the fact"—as the alien seal of the reader—by the third narrator, the last reader-receiver in the narrative chain of readings:

The next night, by the corner of the hearth (...) [Douglas] opened the faded red cover of a thin old-fashioad gilt-edged album (...). On the first occasion the same lady put another question. *"What is your title?"*

"I haven't one."

"Oh, *I** have"! *I said.* But Douglas, without heeding me, had begun to *read* with a fine clearness that was like a rendering to the ear of the beauty of his author's hand (Prologue, p. 14; *James's italics; remaining italics mine).

Not only does the title precisely name "the turn of the screw" of its own *effect:* the title is itself the *product* of such an effect, it is itself the *outcome* of a *reading* of the story (and is itself thereby a reading of the story), since the narrative is given its name and title by the reader and not by the author. In this manner the prologue, just as it displaced and dislocated the relationship between the inside and the outside, deconstructs as well the distinction and the opposition between reader and writer. The reader here becomes the author, and the author is in turn a reader. What the narrator perceives in Douglas's reading as "a rendering to the ear of the beauty of his author's hand" is nothing but Douglas's *performance* as a *reader,* which becomes a metaphor of the original author's writing *through* the very act of reading which that writing has inspired and produced as one of its effects. In essence, then, when Douglas answers the question "What is your title?" with "I haven't one," that answer can be understood in two different manners: he has no *name for* his own narrative; or else, he has no *title to* that narrative which is really not his own, he is not *entitled,* therefore, to give it a title, he has no right or authority over it, since he is not its author, since he can only "render the beauty of his author's hand," "represent" the story's author, to the extent that he is the story's reader.

The story, therefore, seems to frame itself into losing not only its origin but also its very title: having lost both its name and the authority of its author, the narrative emerges, out of the turns of its frame, not only authorless and nameless, but also unentitled to its own authority over itself, having no capacity to denominate, no right to *name itself.* Just as the frame's content, the governess's narrative, tells of the *loss of the proprietor* of the *house,* of the "Master" (by virtue of which loss the house becomes precisely *haunted,* haunted by the usurping ghosts of its *subordinates*), so does the framing prologue convey, through the reader's (vocal) rendering of an authorship to which he has no title, the *loss of the proprietor of the narrative.* And this strange condition of the narrative, this strange double insistence, in the frame as in the story, on the absence of the story's master, of the owner of the property, cannot but evoke, once more, the constitutive condition of the unconscious, itself a sort of obscure knowledge which is, precisely, authorless and ownerless, to the extent that it is a knowledge which no consciousness can *master* or *be in possession of,* a knowledge which no conscious subject can attribute to himself, assume as *his own* knowledge. "Any statement of authority," writes Lacan with respect to the discourse of the unconscious, but in terms which can equally describe the very narrative conditions of *The Turn of the Screw*—"Any statement of authority [in this discursive space] has no other guarantee than that of its own utterance." [24]

If the story has thus managed to lose at once its author, its authority, its title, and its origin, *without losing itself*—without being itself suppressed, obliterated or forgotten—, it is because its written record has been repeatedly and carefully *transferred* from hand to hand: bequeathed first by the dying governess to Douglas, and then by the dying Douglas to the narrator. It is thus *death* itself which moves the narrative chain forward, which *inaugurates* the manuscript's *displacements* and the process of the *substitution* of the narrators. By so doing, death paradoxically appears not as an end but rather as a starting point: the starting point of the *transferral* of the story, that is, of its *survival,* of its capacity to go on, to subsist, by means of the repeated *passages* which it effects *from death to life,* and which effect the narrative.

For each of the people who receive and keep the manuscript of the story, that manuscript constitutes, well beyond the death of the addressor—the person who bequeathed it to them—, the survival of the giver's language and the giver's own survival *in* his language: a *return* of the dead *within the text.* And we hardly need recall that it is precisely the return of the dead which provides the central moving force of the narrative being thus transferred: the story of the governess's struggles with the servants' ghosts. While the prologue contains nothing supernatural in itself, it

---

[24] *Ecrits,* Paris: Seuil, 1966, p. 813. Hereafter referred to as *Ecrits.*

Shoshana Felman

curiously foreshadows the question of the return of the dead by making the manuscript itself into a ghost, speaking from beyond several graves.

What, however, is the motivation for the narrative's transmission? For what reason is the manuscript at all transferred? Douglas, quite discreetly, alludes to the reason.

"Then your manuscript—?"
"(...) A woman's. She has been dead these twenty years. She sent me the pages in question before she died." They were all listening now, and of course there was somebody to be arch, or at any rate to draw the inference. But if he put the inference by without a smile it was also without irritation. "She was a most charming person, but she was ten years older than I. She was my sister's governess," he quietly said. "She was the most agreeable woman I've ever known in her position; she would have been worthy of any whatever. It was long ago, and this episode was long before. (...) We had, in her off-hours, some strolls and talks in the garden—talks in which she struck me as awfully clever and nice. Oh yes; don't grin: *I liked her extremely and am glad to this day to think she liked me too. If she hadn't she wouldn't have told me.* She had never told anyone. (Prologue, p. 2).

In an understatement, Douglas lets it be understood that if the manuscript has survived "these twenty years" beyond the death of its author, it is because of the love which had once drawn him to her and which had prompted her in turn to confide to him her ultimate deathbed secret. The cause for the transferral of the manuscript is, therefore, not just death, but love. For Douglas, the manuscript commemorates his encounter with a woman, and with her writing: the story is as such the outcome, the result of love, of death, of writing, of transferring.

If the story's origin is lost, then it is not just because, by virtue of the author's death, it is buried in an unrecoverable, distant past: it is also because that origin cannot be situated as a *fixed point,* but only as a movement, a dynamics: the story's origin is *in transference.* The beginning of the tale, in other words, is not ascribable to any of the narrators, but to the relationship between the narrators. The story's origin is not a *referent,* but the very *act of reference:* the very act—through love and death—of *referring* to *the Other;* the gesture of the transference of a story.

The narrators, in fact, constitute not only a self-relaying *chain* of narrative transmissions, but also a series of pairs or *couples:* the governess and Douglas; Douglas and the first-person narrator. Before the triangular narrative chain comes into being—by means of the repeated and successive transfers of the manuscript due precisely to the disruption of the couples, to the death, each time, of one of the two partners, — the couples, during their lifetime, carry on a relationship which, in both cases, has a discreet erotic connotation but is primarily discursive and linguistic. Such is the relationship between the governess and Douglas:

[and] we had, in her off-hours, some strolls and talks in the garden—talks in which she struck me as awfully clever and nice. Oh yes; don't grin: I liked her extremely and am glad to this day to think she liked me too (Prologue, p. 2).

Later on, it is the same sort of relationship which structures the rapport between Douglas narrating and the first-person narrator listening:

It was *to me in particular* that he appeared to propound this — appeared almost to appeal for aid not to hesitate (. . .). The others resented postponement, but it was just his scruples that *charmed me* (Prologue, p. 2).

In both cases, the couples therefore become couples by virtue of a constitutive situation of dialogue and of *interlocution,* whose discursiveness subtly develops into a discreet game of *seduction.* Indeed, this structuring situation of the couples strikingly calls to mind the psychoanalytical situation *par excellence,* governed as it is by *transference,* in its most strictly analytical sense: it is quite clear that the narrator's fascination with Douglas, as well as Douglas's fascination with the governess, are both transferential fascinations—and so is the governess's fascination with the Master. The tale of transference thus turns out to be the tale of the transference of a tale. This transferential structure will, however, not only motivate, but also modify the narrative, becoming at once its *motive* and its *mask:* putting the narrative in motion as its dynamic, moving force, it will also hide, distort it through the specular mirages of its numerous mirrors of seduction.

The play of seduction is productive of mirages insofar as, inscribed within the very process of narration, it becomes a play of *belief*—belief in the narrator and therefore in the accuracy of his narrative. It is because Douglas is so charmed by the governess, on whom the discursive situation makes him transfer, with whom he becomes narcissistically infatuated, that he *adds faith* to the literality of her narrative and to the authority of her own idealized mirror-image of herself. Vouching for the governess, he grants her story the illusory authority of a delusive *credibility.* Douglas, in other words, endows the governess with a *narrative authority.* Authority as such, so crucial to *The Turn of the Screw,* nonetheless turns out to be itself a fiction, an error in perspective, created by and established through the illusions and delusions of the transferential structure. [25] In the same way, Douglas's account of the governess's story is in turn given authority and credibility by the play of mutual admiration and intuitive understanding between him and his charmed, privileged listener, who will himself become a narrator.

The transferential narrative chain thus consists not only of the echoing effect of voices reproducing other voices, but also of the specular effect of the seductive *play of glances,* of the visual exchange of specular reflections, of the mirror-repetition of a sym-

---

[25] Cf. James's own comments on the "authority" of the governess in the New York Preface: "I recall (...) a reproach made me by a reader capable evidently, for the time, of some attention, but not quite capable of enough, who complained that I hadn't sufficiently 'characterized' my young woman engaged in her labyrinth (...), hadn't in a word invited her to deal with her own mystery as well as with that of Peter Quint (...) I remember well (...) my reply to that criticism. "(...) We have surely as much of her own nature as we can swallow in watching it reflect her anxieties and inductions. It constitutes no little of a character indeed, in such conditions, (...) that she is able to make her particular *credible* statement of such strange matters. She has "authority," which is a good deal to have given her, and I couldn't have arrived at so much had I clumsily tried for more" (*Norton,* pp. 120-121).

metrically—and therefore infinitely—self-reproducing, self-reflecting self-reflections. *The Turn of the Screw,* indeed, in every sense of the word, is a *reflection* of, and on, the act of *seeing.* The story's frame is nothing other than a *frame of mirrors,* in which the narrative is both reflected and deflected through a series of symmetrical, mutual glances of couples looking at themselves looking at themselves.

"... she liked me too. If she hadn't she wouldn't have told me. She had never told anyone. It wasn't simply that she said so, but that I knew she hadn't. I was sure; *I could see.* You'll easily judge why when you hear."
  "Because the thing had been such a scare?"
  He continued to fix me. "You'll easily judge," he repeated; *"you** will."
  I fixed him too. "I see. She was in love."
  He laughed for the first time. "You *are** acute. Yes, she was in love. That is she *had** been. That came out — she couldn't tell her story without its coming out. *I saw it,* and *she saw I saw it;* but neither of us spoke of it (...)" (Prologue, pp. 2-3; *James's italics; remaining italics mine)

What, however, is the nature of the act of "seeing"? This is the crucial question raised by the appearance of the ghosts, not simply because the ghosts only appear when the governess sees them, but also because each of their appearances enacts the same specular confrontation as that between the other couples: the same exchange of symmetrical, dual glances occurs between the governess and the supernatural intruder. In this play of "seeing oneself seen by the other" and of "seeing the other see," through which the prologue, once again, foreshadows the main story, what, then, does "seeing" mean? "I saw it, and she saw I saw it"; "I was sure; I could see"; "He continued to fix me (...) I fixed him too. 'I see. She was in love.'" Clearly, in the play of these Jamesian sentences, "seeing" is *interpreting;* it is *interpreting love;* and it is also interpreting *by means of love.* Thus, in several ways and on several levels, love has here become, in both senses of the word, the *subject* of interpretation. In this double transferential structure, in this double love-relation, between the narrator and Douglas, and between Douglas and the governess, love has become both what is *seen* and what *"can see"*; both what is *read* and what *is reading;* both what is *to be interpreted* in this intense exchange of glances, and what is actively, through that exchange, *doing the interpreting*. Love interprets. And inversely, the interpreter as such, whether or not he knows it, wants it, or intends it, is caught up in a love-relation, in a relationship constitutively transferential.

Transference, says Lacan, is "the acting-out of the reality of the unconscious." [26] On the basis of the literary evidence which we are analyzing, and within the framework of a theory of narrative, we are here prompted to raise the question whether the acting-out of the unconscious is always in effect the acting-out of a *story*, of a narrative; and whether, on the other hand, *all* stories and all narratives imply a transferential structure, that is, a love-relation which both organizes and disguises, deciphers and enciphers them, turning them into their own substitute and their own repetition. *The Turn of the Screw* at any rate would seem to confirm such a hypothesis.

It is therefore no coincidence that the *transferral* of the manuscript should be presided over by a pair of would-be *lovers*, nor that the story should be twice retold (and acted out) for love, precisely, of its previous narrator or teller. Nor is it a coincidence that the transferential couple is here identified with the couple *author-reader*. The love-relation, i.e., the acting out of the unconscious through a relation of performative interpretation, seems to inhere in, and to govern, the relationship between the addressor of the narrative ("author" or narrator) and its addressee (listener-receiver or reader-interpreter).

> I can see Douglas there before the fire (...) looking down at his converser with his hands in his pockets. "Nobody but me, till now, has ever heard. It's quite too horrible." (...) "It's beyond everything. Nothing at all that I know touches it."
>
> "For sheer terror?" I remember asking.
>
> He seemed to say that it wasn't so simple as that; to be really at a loss how to qualify it. *He passed his hand over his eyes*, made a little wincing grimace. "For dreadful — dreadfulness!"
>
> "Oh, how delicious!" cried one of the women.

---

[26] J. Lacan, *Le Séminaire — Livre XI: Les Quatre concepts fondamentaux de la psychanalyse*, Paris: Seuil, 1973, p. 158. This work will henceforth be referred to as *Quatre Concepts*.

He took no notice of her; *he looked at me, but as if, instead of me, he saw what he spoke of.* "For general uncanny ugliness and horror and pain" (Prologue, pp. 1-2).

The play of passionate glances becomes even more complex when the act of looking is revealed to be not so much a passive observation but an active operation of *substitution.* Paradoxically, the intensity of that emotive look directs both the seduction and the story, both the narrative and the emotion toward a rhetorical *place* rather than an individual object: "he looked at me, but *as if, instead of me,* he saw *what he spoke of.*" That sentence has two different implications: 1) "what the narrator *speaks of*" is equivalent to the *place* of the person he addresses, or *speaks to:* if the reader also finds himself in that place (spoken to), then the reader is indeed the *subject* of the story; 2) what Douglas actually "speaks of" is the "general uncanny ugliness and horror and pain" that has to do with *ghosts.* In becoming, by virtue of his *place* ("spoken *to*") the *subject* of the story ("spoken *of*"), the *reader* (as well as the first-person narrator) himself becomes a ghost, occupying the rhetorical *ghostly place,* bound up in the "uncanniness" of the odd relationship between love, death, and substitution.

If, by virtue of the storyteller's transference on the reader, the reader thus becomes the storyteller's *ghost* (the addressee of his unconscious), the reader, in his turn, transfers on the storyteller or the "author," to the extent that he invests the latter with the authority and prestige of the *"subject presumed to know."* "Transference," says Lacan, "is only understandable insofar as its starting point is seen in the subject presumed to know; he is presumed to know what no one can escape: meaning as such." It is, as we have seen, the first-person narrator who, in his role as fascinated reader and admiring interpreter, confers upon Douglas his prestige, upon the narrative its title, and upon the story the authority of the ultimate *knowledge* it is *presumed* to have of its own meaning: " 'The story will tell,' I took upon myself to reply" (p. 10). The "I" of the first-person narrator in his role of reader thus constitutes as the text's *knowledge* what his own reading does *not* know in precisely the same way as a psychoanalytical patient's transferential fantasy attributes to his analyst a knowledge which is really his own story as *unknown*.

In telling at once of transference and through transference, the story acts as a repetitive border-crossing, as a constant shuttle between opposed domains: speech and silence, life and death, inside and outside, consciousness and the unconscious, sleep and wakefulness:

> The case, I may mention, was that of an apparition in just such an old house as had gathered us for the occasion — an appearance, of a dreadful kind, to a little boy *sleeping* in the room with his mother and *waking her up* in the terror of it; *waking her not to dissipate his dread* and soothe him to sleep again, *but to encounter also, herself, (. . .) the same sight* that had shaken him. It was this observation that drew from Douglas — not immediately, but later in the evening — a reply that had the interesting consequence to which I call attention (Prologue, p. 1).

It is noteworthy that, in these opening lines of the prologue, it is a child who is at the origin both of the dream and of the dreamlike tale that follows. But if the child, indeed, *awakens* here his mother, it is only so as to *include her in his dream*, to wake her *into his own sleep*. In straddling, in this manner, the line between waking and sleeping, the child's story thus subverts or at least distorts the possibility of telling the two apart. Like the child, the narrator, too, through the dreamlike narrative which he puts in motion out of his own transferential illusions, can only *wake us* into *his own sleep:* into the transferential dream which becomes our own. What the tale awakens in us is finally nothing other than, precisely, *our own sleep*.

At this juncture, it could be illuminating to recall that the psychoanalytical notion of transference is for the first time brought up by Freud in *The Interpretation of Dreams,* precisely with respect to the question of the *relation between sleeping and waking:* in attempting to explain the interactions and exchanges which occur between sleep and wakefulness, Freud analyzes the role of the "day's residues" and their relation to the "dream wish":

On this view dream might be described as *a substitute for an infantile scene modified by being TRANSFERRED on to a recent experience.* The infantile scene is unable to bring about its own revival and has to be content with returning as a dream. [27]

My supposition is that a conscious wish can only become a dream-instigator if it succeeds in AWAKENING an unconscious wish with the same tenor and in obtaining reinforcement from it (Ibid., p. 591).

It is only possible to do so [to explain the part played by the day's residues] if we bear firmly in mind the part played by the unconscious wish and then seek for information from the psychology of the neuroses. We learn from the latter that an unconscious idea is as such quite incapable of entering the preconscious and that it can only exercise any effect there by establishing a connection with an idea which already belongs to the preconscious, by TRANSFERRING ITS INTENSITY on to it and by getting itself "covered" by it. Here we have the fact of "TRANSFERENCE," which provides an explanation of so many striking phenomena in the mental life of neurotics (*Ibid*, p. 601).

I will be seen, then, that the DAY'S RESIDUES (. . .) not only *borrow* something from the unconscious when they succeed in taking a share in the formation of a dream — namely the instinctual force which is at the disposal of the repressed wish — but that they also *OFFER* THE UNCONSCIOUS something indispensable — namely THE NECESSARY POINT OF ATTACHMENT FOR A TRANSFERENCE (*Ibid.*, p. 603).

Let us summarize what we have learnt so far. (. . .) The unconscious wish links itself up with the day's residues and effects a transference on to them; this may happen either in the course of the day or not until a state of sleep has been established. A wish now arises which has been transferred on to the recent material; or a recent wish, having been suppressed, gains fresh life by being reinforced from the unconscious. This wish seeks to force its way along the normal path taken by thought-processes, through the preconscious (. . .) to consciousness. But it comes up against the censorship. (. . .) At this point it takes on the distortion for which the way has already been paved by the transference of the wish on to the recent material. So far it is on the way to becoming an obsessive idea or a delusion or something of the kind — that is, *a thought* which has been intensified by transference and distorted in its expression by censorship. Its further advance is halted, however, by the sleeping state of the preconscious. (. . .) The dream-process consequently enters on a regressive path, which lies open to it precisely

---

[27] S. Freud, *The Interpretation of Dreams* (trans. James Strachey), New York: Discus/Avon, 1967, p. 585. In this quotation and those that follow from *The Interpretation of Dreams,* the italics are Freud's; the capitalization is mine.

owing to the peculiar nature of the state of sleep, and it is led along that path by the attraction exercised on it by groups of memories; some of these memories themselves exist only in the form of visual cathexes and not as translations into the terminology of the later systems (. . . .) In the course of its regressive path the dream-process acquires the attribute to representability. (. . .) It has now completed the second portion of its zigzag journey (*Ibid.,* pp. 612-613).

Freud's analysis of the movement of psychic energies back and forth between sleep and wakefulness *via* transference seems perfectly tailored to fit precisely the visual dream-like figures of the *ghosts. Seeing* is thus above all *transferring.* And if, as we have "seen" ourselves from the prologue, seeing is always reading, deciphering, *interpreting,* it is because reading is also transferring: just as a dream is a transference of energy between the "day's residue" and the unconscious wish, so does the act of reading invest the conscious, daylight signifiers with an unconscious energy, transfer on recent materials the intensity of an archaic sleep. Seeing, thus, is always in some manner sleeping, that is, looking with the very eyes of the unconscious—through the fabric of a dream, reading not literally but rhetorically.

Both senses of the term "transference" in Freud's text—transference as the mainspring of psychoanalysis, as the repetitive structural principle of the relation between patient and analyst, and transference as the rhetorical function of any signifying material in psychic life, as the movement and the energy of displacement through a chain of signifiers—thus come together in the prologue of *The Turn of the Screw:* it is their very interaction which gives rise to the story and carries out the narrative both as a *couple-relation* and as the displacement—the transferral—of a manuscript. The whole story is thus played out in the differential space between the transference of the narrators and the transference of the narrative, between an enterprise of seduction and of narcissistic capture and the displacement of a signifier, the transferral of a text, the work of an effect of writing:

"Well then," I said, "just sit right down and begin."

He turned round to the fire, gave a kick to a log, watched it an instant. Then as he faced us again: "I can't begin. I shall have to send to town. (...) *The story's written*. It's in a locked drawer — it has not been out for years" (Prologue, p. 2).

V. The Scene of Writing: Purloined Letters

> Sans ce qui fait que le dire, ça vient à s'écrire, il n'y a pas moyen de faire sentir la dimension du savoir inconscient.
>
> (J. Lacan, 1974 Seminar)

> ...l'histoire nous laisse ignorer à peu près tout de l'expéditeur, non moins que du contenu de la lettre (...) nous n'en pouvons retenir qu'une chose, c'est que la Reine ne saurait la porter à la connaissance de son seigneur et maître.
>
> (J. Lacan, *Séminaire sur la lettre volée*)

The fact that "the story's written," underlined by the narrative suspense that that fact creates, has two important implications:

1) The story is a *text* and not just a series of events: it has its own *materiality* and its own *place;* it exists as a material object;

2) As a material object, the manuscript is independent of the narrator, who is, rather, himself dependent on *it:* the narrator is dependent on the place and materiality of the written word.

This double implication will in turn have three immediate consequences:

1) It is *impossible* for the narrator to *begin;* there seems to be a problem inherent in the beginning as such, since it is first *postponed,* and then *replaced* by a "prologue": "I can't begin. I shall have to send to town. (...) The story's written," says Douglas. However, when the manuscript has arrived, Douglas explains the need for "a few words of prologue" (p. 4) which will substitute for the beginning, since "the written statement took up the tale at a point after it had, in a manner, begun" (p. 4).

2) The manuscript's place is a "locked drawer"—a closed, secret place: for the story to be told, the lock has to be forced, the hideout *opened up:* a seal of silence must be broken, and the story's "opening" is thus literally and figuratively an *outbreak:*

"The story (. . .) has not been out for years. I could write to my man and enclose the key; he could send down the packet as he finds it." (. . .) he had *broken* a thickness of ice, the formation of many a winter; had had his reasons for a long silence (Prologue, p. 2).

Mrs. Griffin spoke. (. . .)
    ". . . It's rather nice, his long reticence."
    "Forty years!" Griffin put in.
    "With this *outbreak* at last."
    "The *outbreak,*" I returned, "will make a tremendous occasion of Thursday night" (Prologue, p. 3).

3) In order for there to be a narrative at all, Douglas must have the manuscript *sent* to him through the mail. There is thus an *address* on the text: *the story is a letter.* Indeed, it is triply so: sent first by the governess to Douglas, then by Douglas to himself, then by Douglas to the narrator. As a letter, the narrative entails both a *change of location* and a *change of address.*

In fact, the manuscript-letter is itself a story about letters: the first narrative event of the governess's story is the cryptic letter announcing Miles's dismissal from school; then the governess mentions that she intercepts the children's letters to the Master; then there is the troubling question for the governess of the letter Mrs. Grose wants sent to the Master about the goings-on at Bly, which the governess promises to write herself; and finally, the governess's letter to the Master is intercepted and destroyed by Miles.

What is striking about these letters is that they all bear a curious resemblance to the letter of the manuscript itself. They are addressed and sealed:

. . . my letter, *sealed and directed,* was still in my pocket (ch. 18, p. 65).

To open them requires that a seal be broken, that violence be done; the letters' opening instigates a sort of crisis:

> The postbag, that evening (...) contained a letter for me, which, however, in the hand of my employer, I found to be composed but of a few words enclosing another, addressed to himself, with a *seal still unbroken.* "This, I recognize, is from the head-master, and the head-master's an awful bore. Read him, please; deal with him; but mind you don't report (...)" *I broke the seal with a great effort* — so great a one that I was a long time coming to it; took the unopened missive at last up to my room and only *attacked it* just before going to bed. I had better have let it wait till morning, for it gave me a second sleepless night (ch. 2, p. 10).

In the story as in the prologue, the materiality of writing, as the materiality of the manuscript, seems to create a problem of beginnings. Like Douglas, the governess finds it difficult to begin:

> I went so far, in the evening, as to *make a beginning.* (...) I sat for a long time before a *blank sheet of paper* (...). Finally I went out (ch. 17, p. 62).

We will later learn that this letter from the governess to the Master will never be, in fact, more than just an envelope containing that same blank sheet of paper: the beginning as such is only written as *unwritten,* destined to remain anterior and exterior to what can be learned from a letter:

> "I've just begun a letter to your uncle," I said.
> "Well then, finish it!"
> I waited a minute. "What happened *before?*"
> He gazed up at me again. "*Before* what?"
> "*Before* you came back. And *before* you went away." ... he was silent (ch. 17, pp. 64-65).

Insofar as the narrative itself is an effect of writing and as such is dependent on the letter of its text, its very *telling* involves the non-possession of its beginning. If the story is a letter and if a letter is the materialization of the absence of the beginning of a story, then the very act of telling, of narrating, must begin as the transgressive breaking of a seal—the seal of the silence from which the story springs. The story then is nothing but the circulation of a violated letter which materially travels from place to place through the successive changes of its addressees, and through a series of "address-corrections." While the letter is never really begun, it is nonetheless ceaselessly *forwarded*.

The letters *in* the story, then, strikingly resemble the letter of the manuscript of the story. And although these letters either remain unwritten or are intercepted and destroyed, although their content is either missing or undecipherable, their *function* nonetheless, like that precisely of the manuscript-letter which contains them, is to *constitute a narrative*, to *tell the story* of the goings-on which they partake of, the story which has necessitated their being written.

> "Do you mean you'll write?" Remembering she couldn't, I caught myself up. "How do you communicate?
> "I tell the bailiff. *He* writes."
> "And should you like him to *write our story*?"
> My question had a sarcastic force that I had not fully intended, and it made her (. . .) inconsequently break down (. . .).
> "Ah, Miss, *you write!*" (ch. 16, pp. 61-62).

Clearly, what the letter is about is nothing other than the very story which contains it. What the letters are to tell is the telling of the story: how the narrative, precisely, tells itself *as an effect of writing*. The letters in the story are thus not simply *metonymical* to the manuscript which contains them; they are also *metaphorical* to it: they are the reflection *en abyme* of the narrative itself. To read the story is thus to undertake *a reading of the letters,* to follow the circuitous paths of their changes of address.

The first thing such a "letter-reading" must encounter is the fact that, paradoxically enough, it is not what the letters *say* which gets the story started, but what they *don't say*: the letters are as such *unreadable,* illegible as much for the reader as for the characters in the story, who are *all the more* affected by them for not being able to decipher them. The letters are thus unreadable in precisely the same way the unconscious is unreadable: like the letters, the unconscious also governs an entire (hi)story, determines the course of a whole life and destiny, without ever letting itself be penetrated or understood.

If the letters' very resistance to daylight, to transparency and to meaning, is indicative of their participation in an unconscious economy; if, as signifiers *par excellence* of that unconscious economy, they can only be meaningful *through their own censorship,* signify through their own *blacking-out;* if the very story of the unconscious is a story of the circulation of undecipherable letters, —then the crucial theoretical question for both literature and psychoanalysis, for the reader of textual letters as well as for the interpreter of the text of the unconscious, would be the following one: how can *unreadable* letters be *read,* even as they demand to be *read as unreadable*? This question, which is indeed raised by *The Turn of the Screw* on all levels, is crucial as much for the reader as for the characters of the story, whose fortunes are wholly determined by the mystery that the letters at once point to and withhold.

How can we read the unreadable? This question, however, is far from simple: grounded in contradiction, it in fact subverts its own terms: to actually *read* the unreadable, to impose a *meaning* on it, is precisely *not* to read the unreadable *as unreadable,* but to *reduce* it to the readable, to interpret it as if it were of the same order as the readable. But perhaps the unreadable and the readable *cannot* be located on the same level, perhaps they are *not* of the same order: if they could indeed correspond to the unconscious and to the conscious levels, then their functionings would be radically different, and their modes of being utterly heterogeneous to each other. It is entirely possible that the unreadable as such could by no means, in no way, be made *equivalent* to the readable, through a simple effort at better reading, through a simple *conscious* endeavor. The readable and the unreadable are by no means simply *comparable,* but neither are they simply *opposed,* since above all they are not *symmetrical,* they are *not* mirror-images of each other.

Our task would perhaps then become not so much to read the unreadable *as a variant of the readable,* but, to the very contrary, to *rethink the readable itself,* and hence, to attempt to read it *as a variant of the unreadable.* The paradoxical necessity of "reading the unreadable" could thus be accomplished only through a radical modification of the meaning of "reading" itself. To read on the basis of the unreadable would be, here again, to ask not *what* does the unreadable mean, but *how* does the unreadable mean? Not what is the meaning of the letters, but in what way do the letters *escape* meaning? In what way do the letters *signify via,* precisely, their own *in*-significance?

We have seen how the letters become a crucial dramatic element in the narrative plot precisely because of their unreadability: their function of "giving the alarm" (ch. 21, p. 78), of setting the story in motion and keeping it in suspense through the creation of a situation of tension and of contradiction in which ambiguity reigns, is correlative to the persistent opacity of their informative function and to the repeated failure of their attempts at narration, of their endeavor to tell the story of a beginning, to "write a story" which would itself know its own origin and its own cause. But it is precisely *because* the letters *fail* to narrate, to construct a coherent, transparent story, that there is a story at all: there is a story *because* there is an unreadable, an unconscious. Narrative, paradoxically, becomes possible to the precise extent that a story becomes *impossible*—that a story, precisely, *"won't tell."* Narrative is thus engendered by the displacement of a "won't tell" which, being transmitted through letters, forwards itself as a *writing-effect.*

It is indeed the unreadable which determines, in James's text, the narrative structure of the story. The narrative events themselves arise out of the "alarm" the letters invariably produce. And each of the letters will end up, indeed, giving rise to another letter. There is therefore a *chain* of letters, in much the same way as there is a *chain* of narrative voices, of narrators. The letters, however, relay each other or give rise to each other by means of the very *silences,* of the very *ellipses,* which constitute them: the letters are only linked to each other through the very "holes" in their contents. From the enigmatic letter of the Director of Miles's school, to the unfinished letter of the governess to the Master which Miles intercepts and destroys, the story of *The Turn of the Screw* is structured around a sort of necessity short-circuited by an impossibility, or an impossibility contradicted by a necessity, of *recounting an ellipsis,* of writing, to the Master, a letter about the head-master's letter, and about what was missing, precisely, in the head-master's letter: the reasons for Miles's dismissal from school. The whole story springs from the impossibility, as well as from the necessity, of writing *a letter about what was missing in the initial, original letter.*

Thus it is that the whole course of the story is governed by the hole in a letter. The signifying *chain* of letters, constituted less by what the letters *have* in common than by what they *lack* in common, is thus characterized by three negative features which can be seen as its common attributes: 1) the message or content of the letters is elided or suppressed; 2) in place of the missing message, what is recounted is the story of the material movement and fate of the letters themselves: the letters' circuit, however, becomes, paradoxically enough, a short-circuit of the direct contact between receiver and sender; 3) the addressee, who determines the letters' displacements and circuit, becomes the privileged element in each one of the letters: the *address* is the only thing that is readable, sometimes the only thing even *written.* And, curiously enough, *all* the letters in *The Turn of the Screw*—including the one from the school director, forwarded to the governess—are originally addressed to one and the same person: the Master. What is the structural significance of this convergence of the unreadable upon one crucial address?

The need to write to the Master to inform him of the uncanny happenings for which Bly has become the arena, stems from the fact that the Master is the *lawful proprietor* of Bly: for the governess and for the children as well, the Master embodies at once the supreme instance of Law as such and the supreme figure of

Power. But the Master, before the story's beginning, in its unwritten part for which the prologue accounts, had precisely exerted his power and dictated his law to the governess through the express *prohibition* that any letters be addressed to him.

> "He told her frankly all his difficulty — that for several applicants the *conditions* had been *prohibitive*. (. . .) It sounded strange; and all the more so because of his main condition."
> "Which was —?"
> "That she should never trouble him — but never, never; neither appeal nor complain nor write about anything; only meet all questions herself; receive all moneys from his solicitor, take the whole thing over and let him alone. She promised to do this, and she mentioned to me that when, for a moment, disburdened, delighted, he held her hand, thanking her for the sacrifice, she already felt rewarded."
> "But was that all her reward?" one of the ladies asked.
> "She never saw him again" (Prologue, p. 6).

The paradoxical contract between the governess and the Master is thus from the outset a contract of *disconnection,* of *non-correspondence.* Constitutive of an aporia, of a relation of non-relation, the Master's discourse is very like the condition of the unconscious as such: Law itself is but a form of Censorship. But it is precisely this censoring law and this prohibitive contract which constitute, paradoxically, the story's condition of possibility: the condition of possibility of the story of the impossibility of writing the Master a letter about what was initially missing, *not said,* in yet another letter (equally addressed to, but refused by, the Master). Through the Master's inaugural act of forwarding *unopened* to the governess a letter addressed to him from the Director of Miles's school, mastery determines itself as at once a *refusal of information* and a *desire for ignorance.* Through its repressive function of blocking out, of suppressing, the instance of Law is established as the *bar* which will radically separate signifier from signified ($S/_s$),[28] placing the letters, by the same token, under the odd imperative of the *non-knowledge* of their own content, since, written *for* the Master, the

---

[28] Cf. J. Lacan, "L'Instance de la lettre dans l'inconscient" *(Ecrits)*, esp. pp. 497-498 and 502.

letters are, from the outset, *written for their own Censor*. The situation, however, is even more complex than this, since the governess also, quite clearly, falls in love—right away—with the Master. The Master therefore becomes, at the same time, not only an authority figure as well as an instance of prohibition, but also an object of love, a natural focus of transference. Written not only *for* the very personified image of power, but also *for* their own censorship and their own prohibition, the letters addressed to the Master are in fact, at the same time, *requests for love* and demands for attention. What, then, is the nature of a demand addressed both to the instance of power and to the instance of active non-knowledge? What is the status of *love for the Censor*—of *love for what censures love*? And how can one write *to the Censor*? How can one write *for* the very figure who signifies the suppression of what one has to say to him? These are the crucial questions underlying the text of *The Turn of the Screw*. It is out of this double bind that the story is both recounted and written.

The letters to the Master can convey, indeed, nothing but silence. Their message is not only erased; it consists of its own erasure. This is precisely what Miles discovers when he steals the letter the governess has intended to send to the Master:

"Tell me (. . .) if, yesterday afternoon, from the table in the hall, you took, you know, my letter."

(. . .)

"Yes — I took it."

(. . .)

"What did you take it for?"

"To see what you said about me."

"You opened the letter?"

"I opened it."

(. . .)

"And you found *nothing*!" — I let my elation out.

He gave me the most mournful, thoughtful little headshake. *"Nothing."*

"Nothing, nothing!" I almost shouted in my joy.

"Nothing, nothing," he sadly repeated.

I kissed his forehead; it was drenched. "So what have you done with it?"

"I've burnt it" (Ch. 23-24, pp. 84-86). [29]

It is no coincidence, doubtless, that the letters to the Censor end up being intercepted and materially destroyed. Just as the governess intercepts the children's letters to the Master, Miles intercepts the governess's letter to the Master and ends up throwing it into the *fire*. The reader may recall, however, that the fire, as of the very opening line of the prologue, appeared as the center of the narrative space of desire out of which the story springs: "The story had held us, *round the fire,* sufficiently breathless..." Symbolically narrative frame: in the center of the circle, in the center of the prologue, the same central place, with respect to the circle of readers-listeners, as that of the story's content with respect to the narrative frame: in the center of the circle, in the center of the frame, fire and story's content seemed indeed to act as foci—as *foyers*—upon which the space both of narration and of reading seemed to converge. But through Miles's gesture of throwing the governess's letter into the fire, the *fire inside the story* turns out to be, precisely, *what annihilates the inside of the letter;* what materially destroys the very "nothing" which constitutes its *content.* And since the letters in the story are metaphorical to the manuscript of the story as a whole, i.e., to the narrative itself as an effect of writing, we can see that what the fire indeed consumes,

---

[29] The fact that the letter of *Nothing* can in fact signify a *love letter* is reminiscent of Cordelia's uncanny reply to King Lear: by virtue of his imposing paternal and royal authority, King Lear, although soliciting his daughter's expression of love, can symbolically be seen as its censor. In saying precisely "nothing," Cordelia addresses her father with the only "authentic" love letter:

Lear:	...Now, our joy,
	Although the last, not least, to whose young love
	The vines of France and milk of Burgundy
	Strive to be interested, what can you say to draw
	A third more opulent than your sisters? Speak.
Cordelia:	Nothing, my lord.
Lear:	Nothing!
Cordelia:	Nothing.
Lear:	Nothing will come of nothing. Speak again. (*King Lear,* I, i)

in burning up the content of the letter, is nothing other than the very *content* of the story. If the story here is one of letters, it is because, in every sense of the expression, *letters burn.* As that which burns in the letter and which burns up the letter, the fire is the story's center only insofar as it *eliminates the center:* it is analogous to the story's *content* only insofar as it consumes, incinerates at once the content of the story and the inside of the letter, making both indeed impossible to read, *unreadable,* but unreadable in such a way as to hold all the more "breathless" the readers' circle round it. "We do not see what is burning," says Lacan in another context, referring to another fire which, however, is not without resemblance in its fantastic, funereal presence to the one which, here, is burning up the letter—"we do not see what is burning, for the flame blinds us to the fact that the fire catches (. . .) on the real." [30]

> Tout l'âme résumée
> Quand lente nous l'expirons
> Dans plusieurs ronds de fumée
> Abolis en autres ronds
>
> Atteste quelque cigare
> Brûlant savamment pour peu
> Que la cendre se sépare
> De son clair baiser de feu
>
> Ainsi le chœur des romances
> A la lèvre vole-t-il
> Exclus-en si tu commences
> Le réel parce que vil
>
> Le sens trop précis rature
> Ta vague littérature
>
> (Mallarmé) [31]

[30] *Quatre concepts,* p. 58. It is perhaps not indispensable, but neither would it be here out of place to recall the crucial importance of fire in Henry James's life, and its recurrent role, both real and symbolic, as a *castrating agent*: just as James's father lost a leg in attempting to put a fire out, James himself believed he had injured his back in the course of a fire, as a result of which he was afflicted for the rest of his life with a mysterious, perhaps psychosomatic back ailment. Cf. Dr. Saul Rosen-

Shoshana Felman

VI. The Scene of Reading: The Surrender of the Name

> It was a sense instinctive and unreasoned,
> but I felt from the first that if I was on the
> scent of something ultimate I had better
> waste neither my wonder nor my wisdom. I
> *was* on the scent — that I was sure of; and
> yet even after I was sure I should still have
> been at a loss to put my enigma itself into
> words. I was just conscious, vaguely, of being
> on the track of a law, a law that would fit,
> that would strike me as governing the
> delicate phenomena (...). The obsession pays,
> if one will; but to pay it has to borrow.
>
> (H. James, *The Sacred Fount*)

The Turn of the Screw is thus organized around a double mystery: the mystery of the letters' content and the mystery of the ghosts. Like the letters, the ghosts, too, are essentially figures of *silence:*

It was the *dead silence* of our long gaze at such close quarters that gave the whole *horror*, huge as it was, its only note of the unnatural (ch. 9, p. 41).

On the one hand, then, the ghosts—which are, by definition, "horrors" ("What *is* he? He's a horror" [ch. 5, p. 22]; "For the woman's a horror of horrors" [ch. 7, p. 32])—are as *mute*, that is, as *silent* as the letters. And on the other hand, the letters themselves, through their very silence, point to "horrors":

My fear was of having to deal with the intolerable question of the *grounds of his dismissal from school*, for that was really but the question of the *horrors* gathered behind (ch. 15, p. 57).

zweig, "The Ghost of Henry James: A Study in Thematic Apperception" in *Character and Personality*, Dec. 1943.

[31] The whole soul when slow we breathe it out summed up in several rings of smoke abolished into others, attests to some cigar burning cannily as long as the ash falls away from its clear kiss of fire; just so, the chorus of old romances steals to the lip. Exclude them if you begin the real, because vile. A too precise meaning crosses out your vague literature. (My literal translation).

In the governess's eyes, the word "horror" thus defines both what the ghosts *are* and what the letters *suppress,* leave out. Could it not be said, then, that the ghosts, whatever their horror may consist of, act as a kind of pendant to the missing *content* of the letters? Like that content, the ghosts are themselves erased significations, barred signifieds: just as the letter opened by Miles turned out to contain "nothing," the ghost seen by the governess is like "nobody."

"What is he like?"
"I've been dying to tell you, but he's like nobody" (ch. 5, p. 23).

Nothing, nobody; no-thing, no-body: marked by the very sign of negation and denial, prefixed by a "no" which bars them in the very act of calling them up, the ghosts—like the letters—manifest themselves only to negate themselves, but through this self-negation, carry out their own self-affirmation; their mode of being and of self-manifestation is that of their own contradiction. The double scandal implicated by the double reference to the "horrors," qualifying both what the ghosts reveal and what the letters conceal, could thus spring not from any essential *evil* inherent as such in the letters and the ghosts, but precisely from their structural self-contradictory way of functioning. In the ghosts as well as in the letters, it could be nothing other than this *economy* of contradiction which takes on the power to "horrify," to scandalize and to appall.

If the ghosts, themselves marked with the sign of negation, come to fill in—so to speak—the letters' gaps, or at least to occupy a place homologous to the vacant interior of the letters, could it not be said that the ghosts are in reality nothing other than the letters' *content,* [32] and that the letters' content could thus itself be nothing other than a *ghost-effect*? [33]

---

[32] The signifying chain of letters would then by the same token be a chain of ghosts: the return of the erased letter would have something to do with the return of the dead; writing, in its blots, its omissions, and its changes of address, would reveal the insistence and mark the return of that which was considered dead and buried, but which has nonetheless come back; the story of the unconscious would be that of

Shoshana Felman

The suggestion that the ghosts are in fact contained in the letters, that their manifestations have to do with *writing*, is outlined by a remark of the governess herself, concerning Peter Quint:

So I saw him as I see the letters I form on this page (ch. 3, p. 17).

This remark, which creates a relation between the letters and the ghosts through the intermediary verb "to see," seems to posit an equivalence between two activities, both of which present themselves as a mode of seeing:

$$
\begin{array}{ccc}
& \text{as} & \\
\text{so I saw him} & = & \text{I see the letters} \\
\textit{to see ghosts} & = & \textit{to see letters}
\end{array}
$$

But what is "seeing letters," if not, precisely, *reading?* [34] In observing and in "seeing," as she says, the very letters that she forms "on this page" of the manuscript of her narrative, the governess is indeed *reading* her own story, which she is also writing in the form of a *letter* to be sent to Douglas. Contained within the letter,

---

the return of the repressed through the insistence of the signifier. Cf. *The Turn of the Screw*, ch. 13, pp. 50-51: "The element of the unnamed and untouched became, between us, greater than any other, and (...) so much avoidance couldn't have been made successful without a great deal of tacit arrangement. It was as if, at moments, we were perpetually coming into sight of subjects before which we must stop short, turning suddenly out of alleys that we perceived to be blind, closing with a little bang that made us look at each other — for, like all bangs, it was something louder than we had intended — the doors we had indiscretely opened. All roads lead to Rome, and there were times when it might have struck us that almost every branch of study or subject of conversation skirted forbidden ground. Forbidden ground was the question of the return of the dead in general and of whatever, in especial, might survive, in memory, of the friends little children had lost."

[33] Since the letters, as we saw earlier, are metaphorical to the manuscript as a whole, and since the letters' content thus represents the content of the story, the inside of the "frame" outlined by the prologue, it is not surprising that the ghost first appears to the governess as precisely that which fills in a frame: "The man who looked at me over the battlements was as definite as *a picture in a frame*" (ch. 3, p. 16).

[34] The obverse of this equation, which indeed confirms its validity, is illustrated by Mrs. Grose: on the one hand, she never sees any ghosts, and on the other, she "cannot read," she is illiterate:

$$\text{not to read letters} = \text{not to see ghosts}$$

151

the ghosts are thus determined as both a *writing-* and a *reading-effect*.

The governess is in fact revealed to be an avid reader not only of her own story but also of the novels which fill the library at Bly. Is it not significant, indeed, that the ghosts are consistently associated in the governess's mind with the novels she has read? Quint's first appearance immediately calls up the memory of two such novels: [35] the novels constitute *interpretations* of the ghost. The governess's third encounter with the apparition, on the other hand, occurs just after she has sleepily put aside the book she has been reading: through this metonymical, contiguous connection, the ghost, almost directly, seems to spring out of the pages of the book. It is here no longer fiction which interprets ghostly apparitions, but rather the ghost itself which constitutes a possible interpretation of the novel just read.

I sat reading by a couple of candles (...) I remember that the book I had in my hand was Fielding's *Amelia;* also that I was *wholly awake.* I recall further both a general conviction that it was horribly late and a particular objection to looking at my watch. (...) I recollect (...) that, though I was deeply interested in the author, I found myself, *at the turn of a page* and with his spell all scattered, looking straight up from him and hard at the door of my room. (...)
.. . I went straight along the lobby (...) till I came within sight of the tall window that presided over the great *turn of the staircase* (...). *My candle* (...) *went out* (...). Without it, the next instant, I knew that *there was a figure on the stair.* I speak of sequences, but I require no lapse of seconds to stiffen myself for a third encounter with Quint (ch. 9, pp. 40-41).

To see ghosts, then, is to read letters, and to read letters is to stay up late at night: reading has to do with night as such, just as ghosts have to do with darkness. To read (to see letters, to see

---

[35] "Was there a 'secret' at Bly — a mystery of Udolpho or an insane, an unmentionable relative kept in unsuspected confinement?" (ch. 4, p. 17) The allusions here are to Ann Radcliffe's *Mystery of Udolpho,* which depicts the presence of a ghost in an uncanny, supernatural environment, and to Charlotte Bronte's *Jane Eyre,* which tells of a romance precisely between a governess and her Master, untimely cut off by the revelation of the Master's former marriage to a woman, now mad, who is being sequestered in his house.

Shoshana Felman

ghosts) is thus to *look into the dark,* to see in darkness ("My candle (...) went out. (...) Without it, the next instant, I knew there was a figure on the stair"). In order to look into the dark, to see in darkness (in order to read), should the eyes be opened or should they, on the contrary, be closed? The governess tells us that her eyes were open, that she was "wholly awake." If, however, a suspicion could arise that this was somehow not quite the case, the ghost itself would turn out to be nothing but a *dream induced by letters;* reading itself could then be suspected of being prey to sleep-apparitions, apparitions which would inextricably attend and suffuse the written word as such. [36]

The governess is thus a *reader,* undergoing the effects of letters; of letters which come through the mail or are written to be mailed, as well as those which can be read on the printed pages of a book. The governess's very first question, upon receipt of the letter from the head-master of Miles's school, is indeed the question *par excellence* of the interpreter:

What does it mean? The child's dismissed his school (ch. 2, p. 10).

In her pursuit of *meaning*—the meaning of the ghosts as well as that of the letters—, in her constant efforts at *deciphering* the goings-on at Bly, the governess's whole adventure turns out to be, essentially, a *reading-adventure,* a quest for the definitive, literal or proper meaning of words and of events.

I had restlessly *read into* the facts before us almost all the *meaning* they were to receive from subsequent and more cruel occurrences (ch. 6, pp. 27-28).

I (...) *read into* what our young friend had said to me the *fullness of its meaning* (ch. 15, p. 57).

[36] Cf. indeed the description of the Master: "a figure as had never risen, save in a *dream* or an old *novel*" (prologue, p. 4), and that of the house at Bly: "I had a view of a castle of romance inhabited by a rosy sprite, such a place as would somehow (...) take all colours out of storybooks and fairy-tales. *Wasn't it just a storybook over which I had fallen a-doze and a-dream?* No..." (ch. 1, p. 10)

I *extracted a meaning* from the boy's embarrassed back (ch. 23, p. 82).

I suppose I now *read into* our situation a clearness it couldn't have had at the time (ch. 23, p. 84).

The search for meaning is prompted by a perception of *ambiguities:*—Ambiguities in the letters:

Deep obscurity continued to cover the region of the boy's conduct at school (ch. 4, p. 19).

—Ambiguities in the ghosts:

... I caught at a dozen possibilities (...) that I could see, in there having been in the house (...) a person of whom I was in ignorance. (...) My office seemed to require that there should be no such ignorance and no such person. (...) This visitant (...) seemed to fix me (...) with just the question, just the scrutiny (...) that his own presence provoked (ch. 3, p. 17).

—Ambiguities in the spoken word:
... my impression of her having accidentally said more than she meant (.. .)
   I don't know what there was in this brevity of Mrs. Grose's that struck me as ambiguous. (...) I felt that (...) I had a right to know (ch. 2, pp. 12-13).

Thus, "seeing ghosts" and "seeing letters" both involve the perception of ambiguous and contradictory signifiers, the perception of *double* meanings. The act of reading and interpreting those ambiguities, however, reveals itself paradoxically to be an act of *reducing* and *eliminating* them:

I (...) opened my letter again to repeat it to her. (...) "Is he really bad?"
   The tears were still in her eyes. "Do the gentlemen say so?"
   "They go into no particulars. They simply express their regret that it should be impossible to keep him. *That can have but one meaning* (...): that he's an injury to the others" (ch. 2, p. 11).

There was *but one* sane inference: (...) we had been, collectively, subject to an intrusion (ch. 4, p. 18).

I had an *absolute certainty* that I should see again what I had already seen (ch. 6, p. 26).

I began to take in with *certitude* and yet without direct vision, the presence, a good way off, of a third person. (...) There was *no ambiguity* in anything (ch. 6, p. 29).

"If I had ever doubted, all my doubt would at present have gone. I've been living with the miserable *truth,* and now it has only too much *closed round me...."* (ch. 20, p. 7).

In her endeavor to reduce the contradictory and the ambiguous to "but one meaning," the governess's method of reading her own adventure is thus not substantially different from that of James's readers, the critics of the text:

But what if there is one thing (...) that cannot be read in either of two senses, that can be read *only in one sense?* (A. J. A. Waldock, *Casebook,* p. 172).

The *determining unambiguous passages* from which the critics might work are so plentiful that it seems hardly good critical strategy to use the ambiguous ones as points of departure (Robert Heilman, FR, MLN, p. 436).

In anticipating once again the strategies of its own reading, the text becomes a challenge to the reader, an invitation to a second-degree reading, which would attempt to read the text's own critical reading of its reading: the way in which the text *puts in perspective,* and reflects upon, its own dramatization of the quest for proper meaning, of the determining transition from a perception of the equivocal to the establishment of meaning as univocal, of the very process of truth's closing around the reader:

"If I had ever doubted, all my doubt would at present have gone. (...) Truth (...) has only too much closed round me" (ch. 20, p. 73).

The elimination of uncertainty and doubt, the acquisition of *certainty* and *clearness* about the meaning of what had nonetheless appeared at first to be ambiguous and obscure—the successful culmination, in other words, of the reading process—is time and again formulated in the text as an epistemological assertion, as a cognitive achievement, as a claim to *knowledge:*

"He was looking for little Miles." A portentous clearness now possessed me. *"That's* whom he was looking for."

"But how do you know?"

"I know, I know, I know!" My exaltation grew. "And *you* know, my dear!" (ch. 6, pp. 25-26; James's italics).

The reader's *certainty* is thus correlative to his claim to *know:* knowing, indeed, is first and foremost knowing *meaning.* "I don't *know* what you *mean,* protests Flora (ch. 20, p. 73). "Knowing," however, is acquired by means of "seeing":

Mrs. Grose, of course, could only gape the wider. "Then *how do you know?"*

"I was there — *I saw with my eyes"* (ch. 7, pp. 30-31).

"For the woman's a horror of horrors."

"Tell me *how you know,"* my friend simply repeated.

"Know? By *seeing* her! By the way she looked" (ch. 7, p. 32).

If "to know" is to know *meaning,* "to see" is, on the other hand, to perceive a figure *as a sign:*

There was a figure in the ground, a figure *prowling for a sight* (ch. 10, p. 44).

Seeing, in other words, is of the order of the *signifier* (that which is perceived as a *conveyer* of signification, in the very *process* of signifying), while *knowing,* on the other hand, is of the order of the *signified* (that which *has been meant;* the accomplished meaning which, as such, is mastered, known, possessed). "Knowing," therefore, is to "seeing" as the signified is to the signifier: the signifier is the *seen,* whereas the signified is the *known.* The signifier, by its very nature, is ambiguous and obscure, while the signified is certain, clear, and unequivocal. Ambiguity is thus inherent in the very essence of the act of seeing:

... there are depths, depths! The more I go over it, the more I see in it, and the more I see in it, the more I fear. I don't know what I *don't* see — what I *don't* fear! (ch. 7, p. 31; James's italics).

By the same token, ambiguity is fundamentally excluded from the act and the domain of "knowing":

The way this *knowledge* gathered in me was the strangest thing in the world (...). I began to take in with *certitude* (...) the presence (...) of a third person (ch. 6, p. 29).

The reading strategy employed by the governess entails, thereby, a dynamical relation between *seeing* and *knowing,* a conversion of the act of seeing into the fact of knowing. We will now attempt to analyze more closely, within the very lexical tracks outlined by the vocabulary of the text, the functioning of this conversion and of this strategy, in order to explore the ways in which it governs the narrative diachrony, shaping it indeed into the story of the progress of a reading-process toward its ineluctable end.

Reading, then, begins with an awareness, with a perception of ambiguous signifiers: an enigmatic letter, an unfamiliar and uncanny ghost. The *meaning* they imply is a *knowledge* from which the governess is barred ("He's—God help me if I *know what* he is!"; ch. 5, p. 22). If it is precisely out of *lack of knowledge* that the reading-process springs, the very act of reading implies at the same time the assumption that knowledge *is,* exists, but is *located in the Other:* in order for reading to be possible, there has to be knowledge in the Other (in the text, for instance), and it is that knowledge in the Other, of the Other, which must be *read,* which has to be appropriated, taken from the Other. The governess naturally thus postulates that the signified she is barred from, the sense of what she does not know, exists and is in fact possessed by—or possessing—someone else. Knowledge haunts. The question of meaning as such, which seems indeed to haunt the pages of *The Turn of the Screw,* can thus be formulated as the question: *"What is it that knows?"* "If the unconscious has taught us anything," writes Lacan, "it is first of all this: that somewhere, in the Other, 'it' knows. 'It' knows because 'it' is supposed by those signifiers the subject is constituted by (...). The very status of knowledge implies that some sort of knowledge already exists, in the Other, waiting to be taken, seized." (*Encore,* p. 81, 89.)

Through reading, the governess tries indeed to seize the Other's knowledge, to read in the Other the signified she seeks. First she aims at seizing Mrs. Grose's knowledge:

> Then *seeing* in her face that she already, in this (...) found a touch of picture, I quickly added stroke to stroke (...).
> "You *know* him then?"
> (...)
> "You *do know* him?"
> She faltered but a second. "*Quint! she cried*" (ch. 5, pp. 23-24).

But it is most especially the knowledge of the children which the governess seeks to read:

> "They *know;* it's too monstrous: they know, they know!" (ch. 7, p. 45; James's italics).
> I was ready to *know* the very worst that was to be *known.* What I had then had an ugly *glimpse* of was that my eyes might be sealed just while theirs were most opened. (...)
>   What it was most impossible to get rid of was the cruel idea that whatever I had seen, Miles and Flora saw *more* * — things terrible and unguessable and that sprang from dreadful passages of intercourse in the past (ch. 13, pp. 52-53; * James's italics).

Having been the witnesses or the accomplices of the presumed liaison between the two dead servants, the children, in the governess's eyes, are in possession of a knowledge which is at once *knowledge of meaning* and *knowledge of sex:* "They know—it's too monstrous: they know, they know!" The very predicate of knowledge, while still maintaining here its cognitive sense or value, equally rejoins its Biblical, archaic, sense: "to know," indeed, is both "to possess valuable information," and "to have sexual intercourse with." The presumed knowledge of the Other, which the governess attempts to *read,* has to do, in some odd way, both with cognition and with pleasure, both with sense and with the senses: that which must be read is, uncannily, both an epistemological and a carnal knowledge.

Shoshana Felman

The children become, then, in the governess's eyes, endowed with the prestige of the "subjects presumed to know." The reader will recall, however, that "the subject presumed to know" is what sustains, according to Lacan, precisely the relationship of *transference* in psychoanalytical experience: "I deemed it necessary," says Lacan, "to support the idea of transference, as indistinguishable from love, with the formula of the subject presumed to know (...). The person in whom I presume knowledge to exist, thereby acquires my love" (*Encore,* p. 64). "Transference *is* love (...) I insist: it is love directed toward, addressed to, knowledge." [37] Presuming the child to know, the governess does indeed—unwittingly—fall in love with him, and her love, her fascination, is directed toward his knowledge:

> It was extraordinary how my absolute conviction of his secret precocity (...) made him (...) appear as accessible as an older person—forced me to treat him as an intelligent equal (ch. 17, p. 63).

> ... Miles stood again with his hands in his little pockets (...) We continued silent while the maid was with us — as silent, it whimsically occurred to me, as some young couple who, on their wedding journey, at the inn, feel shy in the presence of the waiter (ch. 22, p. 81).

As was the case in the prologue, we find ourselves again dealing with a relationship of *reading* which as such entails a relationship of *transference:* reading is again revealed to be the repetition of a love story, the story of a love addressed to and directed toward the knowledge of the Other. The governess's reading, her search for a signified located in the knowledge of the Other, thus paradoxically places her in the role not of analyst but of analysand, of *patient* with respect to the children presumed to know, who hence themselves occupy unwittingly the very place, the very structural position, of the *analyst.*

But of course this is not the way the governess herself sees things. In her view, it is the children who are the "patients," whereas she herself is, to the contrary, the therapist:

---

[37] J. Lacan, "Introduction à l'édition allemande des *Ecrits,*" *Scilicet* N° 5 (Paris: Seuil, 1975), p. 16.

His clear, listening face, framed in its smooth whiteness, made him for the minute as appealing as some wistful *patient in a children's hospital;* and I would have given, as the resemblance came to me, all I possessed on earth really to be the nurse or the sister of charity who might have helped to *cure* him (ch. 17, p. 63).

Toward the end of the novel, the governess does indeed come up with what she calls a "remedy" (ch. 21, p. 76) to cure Miles. The remedy she has in mind is a *confession:*

"I'll get it out of him. He'll meet me — he'll confess. If he confesses, he's saved" (ch. 21, pp. 78-79).

It is thus in her capacity as a therapist, as a soul-doctor, that the governess brings about the story's dénouement in the form of a confession intended as a cure. The importance she thereby attributes to the therapeutic value of language and of *speech* as such, to the exorcistic power of Miles's mere *naming* of the evil which possesses him, could be suggestive of a remote resemblance with the therapeutic project of the psychoanalytical "talking cure."

It is, however, not only as a would-be "therapist," but also as a *reader* that the governess desires to bring about Miles's confession: in demanding from the child the *whole truth* about *what he knows,* she seeks, precisely, to appropriate the knowledge that the Other is presumed to have: to force that knowledge to *reveal itself,* to reveal itself, indeed, both as cognition and as pleasure. Miles's expected double confession, the revelation of his misdeeds at school and the avowal of his complicity with the ghosts, would enable the governess to decipher, i.e., to *read,* both the *meaning* of the ghosts and the *content* of the letters. The child's confession would thus constitute the crowning achievement of the governess's enterprise of reading: the definitive *denomination*—by means of language—of both *truth* and *meaning.*

They are in my ears still, his *supreme surrender of the name* and his tribute to my devotion (ch. 24, p. 88).

This victory, this ultimate triumph of reading through the "supreme surrender of the name," remains, however, highly ambiguous and doubly problematic in the text. On the one hand, the very act of naming, which the governess takes to be the decisive *answer* to her questions, is in the child's mouth, in reality, itself a question:

"It's *there* — the coward horror, there for the last time!"

At this (...) he was at me in a white rage, bewildered, glaring vainly over the place and missing wholly, though it now, to my sense, filled the room (...). "It's *he*?"

I was so determined to have all my proof that I flashed into ice to challenge him. "Whom to you mean by 'he'?" — "Peter Quint — you devil!" His face gave again, round the room, its convulsed supplication. "*Where?*" (ch. 23, p. 88; James's italics).

If the act of naming does indeed name the final truth, that truth is given not as an answer to the question about meaning, but as itself a *question* about its *location*. "Where?" asks Miles—and this interrogation is to be his last word, the last word, indeed, of his "confession." The final meaning, therefore, is not an answer, but is itself a question, which also questions its own pursuit. In considering that question as an answer, the governess in effect stifles its nonetheless ongoing questioning power.

On the other hand, the governess's triumph both as a reader and as a therapist, both as an interpreter and as an exorcist, is rendered highly suspicious by the death of what she had set out at once to *understand* and to *cure*. It therefore behooves the reader of *The Turn of the Screw* to discover the meaning of this murderous effect of meaning; to understand how a child can be killed by the very act of understanding.

VII. *A Child is Killed*

> Insupportable est la mort de l'enfant: elle réalise le plus secret et le plus profond de nos vœux (...)
>
> Il est remarquable que, jusqu'à ce jour, on se soit plus volontiers arrêté (...) dans la

> constellation oedipienne, [sur les] fantasmes
> du meurtre du père, de prise ou de mise en
> pièces de la mère, laissant pour compte la
> tentative de meurtre d'Oedipe-enfant dont
> c'est l'échec qui a assuré et déterminé le
> destin tragique du héros.
>
> (Serge Leclaire, *On tue un enfant*)

What, indeed, is the cause of Miles's death? The final paragraph suggests that he is accidentally suffocated by the governess in the strength of her passionate embrace:

> The *grasp* with which I *recovered* him might have been that of catching him in his fall. I *caught* him, yes, I *held* him — it may be imagined with what a passion; but at the end of a minute I began to feel what it truly was that I *held*. We were alone with the quiet day, and his little heart, dispossessed, had stopped (ch. 23, p. 88).

The word "grasp," which commands this *closing* paragraph, thus appears to account for Miles's death. Interestingly enough, this same word "grasp" also commands the *opening* paragraph of the last chapter. It is as though the beginning and end of the last chapter were both placed in the grasp of the word "grasp," as though that word had as its role at once to introduce and to bring to a conclusion the story's final act. Here is then the opening sentence of the last chapter:

> My *grasp* of how he received this suffered for a minute from something that I can only describe as a fierce split of my attention — a stroke that, at first, as I sprang straight up, reduced me to the mere blind movement of *getting hold of him, drawing him close* and, while I just fell for support against the nearest piece of furniture, instinctively keeping him with his back to the window (ch. 24, pp. 84-85).

In spite of the apparent symmetry of its two occurrences, however, the word "grasp" does not have the same meaning in both cases: in the opening sentence ("my *grasp* of how he received this") the word is used in its *abstract* sense of "comprehension," "understanding"; in the closing sentence ("the *grasp* with which I recovered him"), it is used in its *concrete,* physical sense of "clasp," "hold."

Shoshana Felman

In repeating the word "grasp" in its two different senses in these two symmetrical, strategic points of the final chapter, James's text seems to *play* upon the two connotations, to play them off against each other in order to reveal their fundamental interaction and their complicity. The implicit question behind this semantic play which frames the novel's ending thus becomes: what does a "grasp" involve? What is the relation and the interaction between the act of understanding ("my grasp of how he received this") and the act of clasping in one's arms, to the point of suffocating ("the grasp with which I recovered him")? Curiously enough, in a very different context, it is precisely by a similar double image highlighting the interaction between the mental and physical act of grasping that Cicero chooses to reflect upon the very nature of understanding: "Except for the sage," he writes, "no one knows anything, and that fact was demonstrated by Zeno by means of a gesture. He held up his hand, its fingers extended. That's representation, *visum,* he said. Then he curled back his fingers a bit. That's assent, *assensus.* Next, he completely closed his hand and made a fist, and declared that that was comprehension, *comprehensio.* That's why he gave it the name *catalepsis,* [38] which had not been used before him. Finally, he brought his left hand toward his right hand and grasped his fist tightly; that, he said, was science, *scientia,* something none but the sage possess." [39] It is thus the governess's very "science" which seems to kill the child. Just as Cicero illustrates the act of comprehension by the image of a closed fist, James seems to literalize and at the same time ironize the same act by the suffocating gesture of a tightly closed embrace.

Mightn't one, to reach his mind, risk the stretch of a stiff arm across his character? (ch. 22, p. 111).

...the grasp with which I recovered him (...), I caught him, yes, I held him... (ch. 23, p. 88).

[38] Etymologically, "a seizing."
[39] Cicero, quoted by J.-A. Miller, "Théorie de Lalangue (rudiment)," in *Ornicar* N° 1 (Jan. 1975) p. 22.

163

The comprehension ("grasp," "reach his mind") of the meaning the Other is presumed to know, which constitutes the ultimate aim of any act of reading, is thus conceived as a violent gesture of appropriation, a gesture of domination of the Other. Reading, in other words, establishes itself as a relation not only to *knowledge* but equally to *power*; it consists not only of a search for meaning but also of a struggle to control it. Meaning itself thus unavoidably becomes the outcome of an act of violence:

> To do it in *any* * way was an *act of violence,* for what did it consist of but the obtrusion of the idea of grossness and guilt on a small helpless creature who had been for me a revelation of the possibilities of beautiful intercourse? (. . .) I suppose I now *read into our situation a clearness* it couldn't have at the time (ch. 23, p. 84; * James's italics; other italics mine).

But why is violence necessary in order for meaning to appear as "clearness" and as light? What is the obstacle to clearness which the violence of the act of reading must eliminate? What does comprehension ("my grasp of how he received this") suffer from before the physical pressure of its embrace ("the grasp with which I recovered him") insures its triumph? Let us take another look at the opening lines of the last chapter:

> My grasp of how he received this *suffered* for a minute from something that I can describe only as a *fierce split of my attention* — a stroke that at first, as I sprang straight up, reduced me to the mere blind movement of getting hold of him, drawing him close and, while I just fell for support against the nearest piece of furniture, instinctively keeping him with his back to the window (ch. 24, pp. 84-85).

Just before this passage, the governess has asked Miles the decisive question of whether he did steal her letter. But her ability to *grasp* the effect of her own question on Miles suffers, as she herself puts it, from a "fierce *split* of her attention": her attention is *divided* between Miles and the ghost at the window, between a conscious signifier and the unconscious signifier upon which the latter turns, between a conscious perception and its fantasmatic double, its contradictory extension toward the prohibited unconscious desire which

Shoshana Felman

it stirs up. Thus divided, her attention fails to "grasp" the child's reaction. The failure of comprehension therefore springs from the "fierce split"—from the *Spaltung*—of the subject, from the *divided state* in which meaning seems to hold the subject who is seeking it. [40] But it is precisely this division, this castrating "split," which must be reduced or dominated, denied or overcome, by the violence of a suffocating hold.

> . . . something that I can describe only as a fierce split of my attention — a stroke that at first (. . .) reduced me to the mere blind movement of getting hold of him, drawing him close . . .

> . . . yet I believe that no woman so overwhelmed ever in so short a time recovered her command of the *act*. (ch. 24, p. 84-85; James's italics).

James originally wrote "recovered her *grasp* of the act." It is in the revised New York edition that "grasp" is replaced by "command." But what *act* is it of which the governess regains her *understanding* ("grasp"), i.e., her *control* ("command")?

> It came to me in the very horror of the immediate presence that the *act* would be, seeing and facing what I saw and faced, *to keep the boy himself unaware* (ch. 24, p. 85).

It should be remembered that in this final chapter the entire effort of the governess aims at *reading* the knowledge of the child, and thus at naming truth and meaning. But in this passage, paradoxically

---

[40] Like the ghost, Miles's language (which is responsible for his dismissal from school and is thus related to the missing content of the letter) equally *divides* the "attention" of the governess and her "grasping" mind, by manifesting a *contradiction* — a split within language itself — between the statement and the utterance of the child, between the speaker and his speech : " 'What did you do?' 'Well — I said things.' 'But to whom did you say them?' . . .) '[To] those I liked.' Those he liked? I seemed to float not into clearness, but into a darker obscure (. . .) there had come to me out of my very pity the appalling alarm of his being perhaps innocent. (. . .) He turned to me again his little beautiful fevered eyes. 'Yes, it was too bad (. . .). What I suppose I sometimes said. To write home.' "*I can't name*," comments the governess, "the exquisite pathos of the *contradiction* given to *such a speech by such a speaker*" (ch. 24, p. 87). "What the unconscious forces us to examine," writes Lacan, "is the law according to which no utterance can ever be reduced simply to its own statement" (*Ecrits*, p. 892).

enough, the very act of *reading* the child's knowledge turns out to be an act of suppressing, or *repressing,* part of that knowledge: of "keeping the boy himself *unaware.*" As an object of suppression and of repression, the knowledge of the child itself becomes thereby the very emblem of the unconscious; of the unconscious which is always, in a sense, the knowledge of a child about to die and yet immortal, indestructible; the knowledge of a child dead and yet which one has always yet to kill. "The unconscious," says indeed Lacan, "is knowledge; but it is a knowledge one cannot know one knows, a knowledge which cannot tolerate knowing it knows" [41]—a knowledge, in other words, which cannot tolerate, and which escapes, in every sense, conscious *reflection.*

> What was prodigious was that at last, by my success, his sense was sealed and his communication stopped: *he knew that he was in presence, but knew not of what* (...). My eyes went back to the window only to see that the air was clear again (...). There was nothing there. I felt that the cause was mine and that I should surely get *all* * (ch. 24, pp. 85-86; * James's italics; other italics mine).

The act of reading, the attempt to grasp and hold the signified, goes thus hand in hand with the repression or obliteration of a signifier—a repression the purpose of which is to eliminate meaning's *division.* "The act would be, *seeing* and facing what I *saw* and faced, to keep the boy himself unaware (...). My eyes went back to the window only to *see* that the air was clear again. (...) There was nothing there." *To see* (and by the same token, *to read*: "to see letters," "to see ghosts") is therefore paradoxically not only *to perceive,* but also *not to perceive*: to *actively* determine an area as *invisible,* as *excluded* from perception, as external by definition to visibility. To see is to draw a *limit* beyond which vision becomes barred. The rigid *closure* of the violent embrace implied by the act (by the "grasp") of understanding is linked, indeed, to the violence required to impose a *limit,* beyond which one's eyes must *close.* For it is not the closing of one's eyes which determines the invisible

Shoshana Felman

as its empirical result; it is rather the invisible (the repressed) which predetermines the closing of one's eyes. The necessity of shutting one's eyes actively partakes, indeed, of the very act of seeing, knowing, reading:

> ...my equilibrium depended on the success of my rigid will, the will *to shut my eyes as tight as possible* to the truth that what I had to deal with was, revoltingly, against nature. I could only get on at all by taking nature into my confidence and my account (...). No attempt, none the less, could well require more tact than just this attempt to supply, one's self, *all* * the nature. How could I put even a little of that article into a *suppression of reference* to what had occurred? How, on the other hand, could I *make a reference* without a *new plunge into the* hideous *obscure?* (ch. 22, p. 80; * James's italics; other italics mine).

To grasp: to close one's arms, to stifle. To see: to close one's eyes, to suppress a reference, or else to make a reference and by that very act to take "a new plunge into the obscure," that is, into the invisible. Paradoxically enough, however, it is precisely the imposition of a limit beyond which vision is prohibited which dispels the "split of attention" and at the same time the split of meaning, and which hence makes possible the illusion of total *mastery* over meaning as a whole, as an unimpaired *totality*[42]:

> My eyes went back to the window only to see that the air was clear again. (...) There was nothing there. I felt that the cause was mine and that I should surely get *all* (ch. 24, p. 86; James's italics).

> I seemed to myself to have *mastered* it, to *see it all* (ch. 21, p. 78).

The principle of totality being the very principle of a *boundary* and of the repression inherent in it, the text's irony here lies in the

---

[42] Totality as such is both *unique* (since it includes *everything*, nothing is left outside it) and *univocal* (continuous, *coherent*, undivided, homogeneous). Thus it is that the governess can say: "That can have *but one* meaning (...) to put the thing with some *coherence* ..." (ch. 2, p. 11). "The principle of coherence," writes E. D. Hirsch, "is precisely the same as the principle of a boundary. Whatever is continuous with the visible part of an iceberg lies inside its boundaries, and whatever lies within these falls under the criterion of continuity. The two concepts are codefining" (E. D. Hirsch, *Validity in Interpretation*, New Haven: Yale University Press, 1967, p. 54).

suggestion that the illusion of total *mastery,* of "seeing *all,*" is in reality a counterpart to the act of *"shutting one's eyes* as tight as possible to the truth." Now, to *master,* to become a Master, is inevitably in this text also to become *like the Master.* As the reader will recall, the Master is indeed the incarnation of the very principle of *censorship* and of the imposition of a *limit,* as constitutive of authority as such: of the authority of *consciousness* itself as *mastery.* But his is a mastery which exerts its authority not as an imperative to *know,* but as an imperative *not* to know. To "master," therefore, to understand and *"see it all,"* as the governess complacently puts it to herself, is in this text, ironically enough, to occupy the very place of *blindness*: of the blindness to which the Master voluntarily commits himself at the outset of the story, by ordering the suppression of all information, [43] by prohibiting the governess from informing him of anything at all. Through the governess's own action, the quest for mastery will thus repeat itself as a form of blindness:

> . . . a stroke that reduced me to the mere *blind* movement of getting hold of him, drawing him close (. . .) instinctively keeping him with his back to the window.
> (. . .)
> He almost smiled at me in the desolation of his surrender. (. . .) I was *blind* with *victory* (ch. 24, p. 85, 87).

To master, to "see *all,*" is thus not only to be blind with victory, but also, and quite literally, to be triumphant *out of* blindness.

The violence of the blind grip through which the governess seizes Miles recalls the image of the quasi-compulsive clasping of a sinking

---

[43] This suppression of information is also the function of the *Masters* (the head-masters) of Miles's school, since their letter suppresses all mention of the grounds of the child's dismissal: "I turned it over. 'And these things came round — ?' 'To the *masters?* Oh yes!' he answered very simply. 'But I didn't know they'd tell.' 'The *masters?* They didn't — *they've never told.* That's why I ask you.'" (ch. 24, p. 87) The word "Master" thus comes to signify, in James's text, at once the principle of authority and the principle of repression, — the very principle of the *authority to repress:* to repress at once mentally and physically, in a psychoanalytical but equally in a political sense (cf. Miles's dismissal from school and, ultimately, his murder).

boat's helm which the governess evokes so as to metaphorically justify in her own eyes her quest for mastery, her effort to control the situation:

It was in short by just clutching the helm that I avoided total wreck (ch. 22, p. 79).

This metaphor of the boat recurs several times in the text. Marking here the ending of the story, it is also found at the beginning, at the conclusion of the very first chapter:

It was a big, ugly (...) house, (...) in which I had the fancy of our being almost as lost as a handful of passengers in a great drifting ship. Well, I was, strangely, at the helm! (ch. 1, p. 10).

The metaphor of the helm serves to bring out the underlying inter-dependence between meaning and power: to clutch the helm, to steer the ship, is in effect to guide it, to give it a *direction* and a *sense,* to *control* its direction or its sense. Indeed, throughout the story, the governess's very act of reading consists in her *imposing meaning,* in her imposing sense both as a *directive* and as a *direction* upon the others:

This is why I had now given to Mrs. Grose's steps *so marked a direction* — a direction that made her, when she perceived it, oppose a resistence (...).
"You're *going to the water,* Miss? — you think she's *in* *? (ch. 19, p. 68; * James's italics).

I could only get on at all by taking "nature" into my confidence (...), by treating my monstrous ordeal as *a push in a direction unusual* (ch. 22, p. 80).

"Is she *here* *?" Miles panted as he caught with his sealed eyes the *direction* of my words" (ch. 24, p. 88; * James's italics).

In "clutching the helm," in giving direction to the ship she steers, the governess, whose reading alone indeed commands the situation, clutches at power as sense, and at sense as power: she leads us to believe, along with those under her direction, that if her power is as such meaningful, it is because it is meaning itself which is in power; that it is her sense which commands, and that her command indeed *makes sense*: "She has 'authority'," writes James, "which is a good deal to have given her"; "It constitutes no little of a character indeed (...) that she is able to make her particular *credible* statement of such strange matters" (New York Preface, p. 121). Putting into effect the very title of her function, the "governess" does *govern*: she does indeed clutch at the helm of the boat with the same kind of violence and forceful determination with which she ultimately grips the body of little Miles. The textual repetition of the metaphor of the boat thus serves to illustrate, through the singular gesture of grasping the rudder-bar, the very enterprise of reading as a political project of sense-control, the taking over of the very power implied by meaning.

Curiously enough, the image of the boat recurs in yet another strategic, although apparently unrelated context in the story: in the incident beside the lake during which the governess comes upon Flora playing (under the influence, thinks the governess, of Miss Jessel) with two pieces of wood out of which she is trying to construct a toy boat:

> [Flora] had picked up a small flat piece of wood, which happened to have in it a *little hole* that had evidently suggested to her the *idea of sticking in another fragment* that might *figure as a mast* and *make the thing a boat*. This second morsel, as I watched her, she was very markedly and intently attempting to *tighten in its place*.
> (. . .)
> I got hold of Mrs. Grose as soon after this as I could (. . .)
> I still hear myself cry as I fairly threw myself into her arms: "*They know* — it's too monstrous: they know, they know!"
> "And what on earth — ? (. . .)
> "Why, all that *we* * know — and heaven knows what else besides!"
> (ch. 6-7, p. 30; * James's italics; other italics mine).

This incident is crucial, not only because it constitutes for the governess a decisive proof of the children's knowledge, but also because, implicitly but literally, it evokes an image related to the very *title* of the story: in attempting to fit the stick into the hole as a mast for her little boat, Flora "tightens it in its place" with a gesture very like that of *tightening a screw.*

But what precisely does this gesture mean? The screw—or the mast—is evidently, in this incident, at least to the governess's eyes, a phallic symbol, a metaphor connoting sexuality itself. This phallic connotation, the reader will recall, was pointed out and underlined, indeed, by Wilson. Wilson's exegesis, however, viewed the sexual reference as an *answer,* as the literal, proper meaning which it sufficed to *name* in order to understand and "see it all," in order to put an end to all textual questions and ambiguities. As an emblem of the sexual act, Flora's boat was for Wilson a simple indication of the literal object—the real organ—desired by the governess without her being able or willing to admit it. But it is precisely *not* as an unequivocal *answer* that the text here evokes the phallus, but on the contrary rather as a *question,* as a figure—itself ambiguous—produced by the enigma of the *double meaning* of the metaphorical equation: phallus=ship's mast. To say that the mast is in reality a phallus is no more illuminating or unambiguous than to say that the phallus is in reality a mast. The question arises not of what the mast "really is" but of what a phallus—*or* a mast—might be, if they can thus so easily be interchangeable, i.e., signify what they are not. What is the meaning of this movement of *relay* of meaning between the phallus and the mast? And since the mast, which is a figure of the phallus, is also a figure of the *screw,* it seems that the crucial question raised by the text and valorized by its title might be: what is, after all, a *screw* in *The Turn of the Screw?*

Let us take another look at Flora's boat. It is as a phallic symbol that the boat disturbs the governess and convinces her of the perversity of the children: "They know—it's too monstrous: they know, they know!" The screw, or the phallic mast, thus constitutes for the governess a *key to meaning,* a *master-signifier:* the very key to what the Other knows.

In such a context it is no longer possible to be insensitive to the remarkable phonetical resemblance between the word "mast" and the word "master," which it cannot but bring to mind: indeed, if the mast is a kind of "master," i.e., a dominant element determining both the structure and the movement of a boat, the Master is himself a kind of "mast" which at once determines and supports the structure and the movement of the entire story of *The Turn of the Screw*. As one of the principal elements in a ship, the mast is thus not unrelated to the helm which the governess clutches with the same convulsive grasp as that with which she seizes Miles (who is himself a little Master). [44]

Now, to suggest that all these metaphorical elements—*Miles* in the governess's arms, the tightly gripped *helm* in the uncanny drifting ship, the little *mast* in Flora's boat, and the *screw* in *The Turn of the Screw*—refer alternately to the phallus *and* to the Master (as well as to one another), is to set up a *signifying chain* in which the phallus (or the screw, or the mast, or the Master), far from incarnating the unambiguous literal meaning behind things, symbolizes rather the incessant *sliding* of signification, the very principle of movement and displacement which on the contrary *prevents* the chain (or the text) from ever stopping at a final, literal, fixed meaning. The phallus, far from being a real object, is in fact a *signifier*; a signifier which only appears to become a Master—a key to meaning and a key to the knowledge of the Other—by virtue of its incarnating, like the Master, the very function of the semiotic *bar*—the very principle of imposition of a limit, the principle of censorship and of repression which forever *bars* all access to the signified as such. [45]

---

[44] Cf.: "At this, with one of the quick *turns* of simple folk, she suddenly flamed up. '*Master* Miles! — *him** an injury?'" (ch. 2, p. 11).

[45] Cf. J. Lacan, *The Meaning of the Phallus (La Signification du Phallus):* "In Freudian thought, the phallus is not a fantasy, if a fantasy is understood to be an imaginary effect. Nor is it as such an object (partial, internal, good, bad, etc.) if the term is used to designate the reality involved in a relationship. It is still less the organ, penis or clitoris, which it symbolizes. It is not without cause that Freud took his reference from the *simulacrum* it was for the ancients. For the phallus is a signifier (. . .). It can only play its role under a veil, that is, as itself the sign of the latency which strikes the signifiable as soon as it is raised to the function of a signifier (. . .). It then becomes that which (. . .) bars the signified. (*Ecrits,* pp. 690-692).

"The question is," said Alice, "whether you can make words mean so many different things."

"The question is," said Humpty Dumpty, "which is to be master — that's all." [46]

In reaching out both for the master and for the mast, in aspiring to *be,* in fact, herself a master and a mast, in clasping Miles as she would clutch at the ship's helm, the governess becomes, indeed, the *Master* of the ship, the Master of the *meaning* of the story (a master-reader) in two different ways: in clutching the helm, she *directs* the ship and thus apparently determines and controls its sense, its meaning; but at the same time, in the very gesture of directing, steering, she also masters meaning in the sense that she represses and limits it, striking out its other senses; in manipulating the rudder bar, she also, paradoxically, *bars* the signified. While the governess thus believes herself to be in a position of command and mastery, her *grasp* of the ship's helm (or of "the little Master" or of the screw she tightens) is in reality the grasp but of a *fetish,* but of a *simulacrum* of a signified, like the simulacrum of the mast in Flora's toy boat, erected only as a filler, as a stop-gap, designed to fill a hole, to close a gap. The screw, however, by the very gesture of its tightening, while seemingly filling the hole, in reality only makes it deeper.

I was blind with victory, though even then *the effect that was to have brought him so much nearer* was already that of an *added separation* (ch. 24, p. 87).

The grasp with which I recovered him might have been that of catching him in his fall. I caught him, yes, I held him, it may be imagined with what a passion; but at the end of a minute I began to feel *what it truly was that I held.* We were alone with the quiet day, and his little heart, dispossessed, had stopped (ch. 24, p. 88).

Even though, within this ultimate blind grip of comprehension, the "name" has been "surrendered" and meaning at last *grasped,* the governess's very satisfaction at the successful ending of the

[46] Lewis Carroll, *Through the Looking-Glass,* VI.

reading process is compromised by the radical frustration of a tragic loss: the embrace of meaning turns out to be but the embrace of death; the grasp of the signified turns out to be the grasp but of a corpse. The very enterprise of appropriating meaning is thus revealed to be the strict appropriation of precisely *nothing*—nothing alive, at least: "le démontage impie de la fiction et conséquemment du mécanisme littéraire," writes Mallarmé, "pour étaler la piece principale ou rien (...) le conscient manque chez nous de ce qui là-haut éclate." [47]

Literature, suggests thus Mallarmé, like the letters of *The Turn of the Screw*, contains precisely "nothing"; fiction's mainspring is but "nothing," because consciousness in us is lacking, and cannot account for, "that which bursts." But what, precisely, bursts or splits, if not consciousness itself through the very fact that, possessing *nothing* (as it does in the end of *The Turn of the Screw*), it is dispossessed of its own mastery? What is it that bursts and splits if not consciousness itself to the extent that it remains estranged from that which splits, estranged, in other words, from its own split? When Miles dies, what is once again radically and unredeemably *divided*, is at once the unity of meaning and the unity of its possessor: the governess. The attempt to *master* meaning, which ought to lead to its *unification*, to the *elimination* of its contradictions and its "splits," can reach its goal only at the cost, through the infliction of a new wound, of an added split or distance, of an irreversible "separation." The seizure of the signifier creates an unrecoverable *loss*, a fundamental and irreparable *castration:* the tightened screw, the governed helm, bring about "the supreme surrender of the name," *surrender* meaning only by *cleaving* the very *power* of their holder. Meaning's *possession* is itself ironically transformed into the radical *dispossession* of its possessor. At its final, climactic point, the attempt at *grasping* meaning and at *closing*

---

[47] "The impious dismantling of fiction and consequently of the literary mechanism as such in an effort to display the principal part or nothing, (...) the conscious lack(s) within us of what, above, bursts out and splits": Mallarmé, *La Musique et les Lettres,* in *Oeuvres Complètes* (Paris: Pléiade, 1945), p. 647; my translation.

the reading process with a *definitive* interpretation in effect discovers—and comprehends—only death.

The Turn of the Screw could thus be read not only as a remarkable *ghost* story but also as a no less remarkable *detective* story: the story of the discovery of a *corpse* and of a singularly redoubtable crime: *the murder of a child.* As in all detective stories, the crime is not uncovered until the end. But in contrast to the classical mystery novel plot, *this* crime is also not *committed* until the end: paradoxically enough, the process of detection here *precedes* the committing of the crime. As a *reader,* the governess plays the role of the detective: from the outset she tries to *detect,* by means of logical inferences and decisive "proofs," both the *nature of the crime* and the *identity of the criminal.*

I remember (...) my thrill of joy at having brought on a *proof* (ch. 20, p. 71.)

I was so determined to have all my *proof,* that I flashed into ice to challenge him (ch. 24, p. 88).

It didn't last as *suspense* — it was superseded by horrible *proofs* (ch. 6, p. 28).

Ironically enough, however, not knowing what the crime really consists of, the governess-detective finally ends up *committing it herself.* This unexpected and uncanny turn given by James's story to the conventions of the mystery novel is also, as it happens, the constitutive narrative peripeteia of one of the best known detective stories of all time: *Oedipus Rex.* In James's text as well as in Sophocles's, the self-proclaimed detective ends up discovering that he himself is the author of the crime he is investigating: that the crime is his, that he is, himself, the criminal he seeks. "The interest of crime," writes James, in a discussion of modern mystery dramas, "is in the fact that it compromises the criminal's personal safety":

The play is a tragedy, not in virtue of an avenging deity, but in virtue of a preventive system of law; not through the presence of a company of fairies, but through that of an admirable organization of police detectives. Of course, *the nearer the criminal and the detective are brought home to the reader, the more lively his "sensation".* [48]

The Turn of the Screw appears indeed to have carried this ideal of proximity or "nearness" (of the criminal and the detective to the reader) to its ultimate limits, since the criminal himself is here as *close* as possible to the detective, and the detective is only a detective in his (her) function *as a reader.* Incarnated in the governess, the detective and the criminal both are but dramatizations of the *condition of the reader.* Indeed, the governess as at once detective, criminal, and reader is here so intimately "brought home" to the reader that it is henceforth *our own* search for the mysterious "evil" or the hidden meaning of *The Turn of the Screw* which becomes, in effect, itself nothing other than a repetition of the crime. The reader of *The Turn of the Screw* is also the detective of a crime which in reality is his, and which "returns upon himself." For if it is by the very act of forcing her suspect to confess that the governess ends up committing the crime she is investigating, it is nothing other than the very *process of detection* which *constitutes the crime.* The detection process, or reading process, turns out to be, in other words, nothing less than a peculiarly and uncannily effective *murder weapon.* The story of meaning as such (or of consciousness) thus turns out to be the uncanny story of the crime of its own detection.

Just as, in the end, the *detective* is revealed to be the *criminal,* the doctor-therapist, the would-be *analyst,* herself turns out to be but an analysand. *The Turn of the Screw* in fact deconstructs all these traditional oppositions; the exorcist and the possesssed, the doctor and the patient, the sickness and the cure, the symptom and the proposed interpretation of the symptom, become here interchangeable, or at the very least, undecidable. Since the governess's "remedy" is itself a sympton, since the patient's "cure" is in effect his murder, nothing could indeed look more like *madness* than the very self-assurance of the project (of the notion) of *therapy* itself.

[48] From a review of "Aurora Floyd," by M. E. Braddon, in *Norton,* p. 98.

There can be no doubt, indeed, that the ship is really drifting, that the governess is in command but of a "drunken boat." Sailing confidently toward shipwreck, the helm that the governess violently "grasps" and "clutches" is indeed the helm of a phantom ship.

DU FOND DU NAUFRAGE

(...)

LE MAITRE

(...)

jadis il empoignait la barre

(...)

hésite
cadavre par le bras

écarté du secret qu'il détient

(...)

Fiançailles

dont

le voile d'illusion rejailli leur hantise
ainsi que le fantôme d'un geste

chancellera
s'affalera

folie [49]

VIII. Meaning and Madness: the Turn of the Screw

> Les hommes sont si nécessairement fous que
> ce serait être fou par un autre tour de folie
> de n'être pas fou.
>
> (Pascal)

> But this is exactly what we mean by operative
> irony. It implies and projects the possible
> other case.
>
> (H. James, Preface to "The Lesson
> of the Master")

---

[49] FROM THE BOTTOM OF A SHIPWRECK / THE MASTER / formerly he gripped the helm / hesitates / a corpse by the arm / distanced from the secret he holds / Betrothal of which / the spewed forth veil of illusion their obsession / as the ghost of a gesture / will collapse / madness (Mallarmé, *Un Coup de dés,* in *Oeuvres Complètes,* ed. cit., pp. 459-464; translation mine).

The fundamental metaphor of the title—*The Turn of the Screw*— has thus itself been given an unexpected turn of the screw: on the *sexual* level, the seizure of the phallic signifier as a *master*-signifier —as the very fetish of plenitude and potency—amounts to a void, to a castrating *loss* of potency; on the *cognitive* level, the grasp of the signifier as a key to meaning—as the final proof that everything *makes sense*—amounts to a loss of common sense, to the interpreter's loss of his senses, and to the ultimate non-sense of death. By the turn of the screw given to "the turn of the screw," the delusory, self-evident metaphor of control (over the screw) turns out to be an essential metaphor of loss—the loss, precisely, of control over the *mechanical* functioning of a machine. The manipulator of the screw, who believes himself to be in control of its successive turns, in control of an enterprise of fixity and closure, discovers that, in reality, he himself is nothing but a screw, a cog in the wheel of a machine that runs by itself, automatically and repetitively.

> We had, all three, with *repetition,* got into such splendid training that we went, each time, *almost automatically,* to *mark the close* of the incident, *through the very same movements* (ch. 13, p. 53).

The "incident," however, is never "closed," since the movement of the screw constitutes in fact not a circle but a spiral which never closes: as a perfect illustration of the Freudian concept of the repetition compulsion, the spiral consists of a series of repeated circlings in which what turns is indeed bound to *re-turn,* [50] but in which what circularly thus returns only returns so as to *miss* anew its point of departure, to miss the closing point, the completion (or perfection) of the circle. The successive turns and returns of the spiral *never meet,* never touch or cross one another; hence, what

---

[50] Cf. ch. 13, p. 72: "All roads lead to Rome, and there were times when it might have struck us that almost every (...) subject of conversation skirted forbidden ground. Forbidden ground was the question of the *return* of the dead ... Cf. also The New York Preface: "To bring the bad dead back to life for a *second round* of badness is to warrant them as indeed prodigious" (p. 122).

the spiral actually *repeats* is a missed meeting with itself, a *missed encounter with what returns*. The screw, in order to precisely function properly, be operative, can by no means *close* the circle; it can but repeat it; it can but repeat the turn and repeat its own returns, and its own repetition of its turns, "through the very same movements."

No longer a *substantial* metaphor, the figure of a *substance* (which, like the phallic mast on Flora's boat, is designed to fill a hole, to be the central plenitude supporting and securing an enterprise of fixity), the turning screw turns out to be a *functional* metaphor, the figure of a dynamic *functioning:* it is not so much the screw itself that counts, as the very turning *movement* of its twists and whirls, and the very turns it at the same time marks and misses. It is, indeed, quite striking that the ghosts' appearances so very often have to do—in all senses of the word—with *turns:*

... I could take a *turn into the grounds* and enjoy, almost with a sense of property (...), the beauty and dignity of the place. (...) One of the thoughts that (...) used to be with me (...) was that it would be (...) charming (...) suddenly to meet someone. Someone would appear there at the *turn of a path* (...). What arrested me on the spot (...) was the sense that my imagination had, in a flash, *turned real*. He did stand there (...) at the very top of the tower... (ch. 3, pp. 13-16).

I sat reading (...). I found myself, at the *turn of a page* (...) looking (...) hard at the door of my room. (...) I went straight along the lobby (...) till I came within sight of the tall window that presided over the great *turn of a staircase*. (...) I require no lapse of seconds to stiffen myself for a third encounter with Quint (ch. 9, pp. 40-41).

But what, in fact, is the significance of a *turn,* if not that of a *change,* precisely, of *direction,* the modification of an orientation, that is, both a *displacement* and a *choice of sense,* of meaning? And if indeed what is at stake in *The Turn of the Screw* is the question of *sense* in *all* its senses (meaning, sanity, direction), it is not surprising to discover that the text is organized as a veritable *topography of turns*. The screw, however, *turns in place:* the topography of turns and of circular returns is in reality but the tight enclosure of a labyrinth:

It was a *tighter place* still than I had yet *turned round in* (ch. 22, p. 79).

The labyrinth thus annihilates the value, or the meaning, of its turns: while a turn as such indicates *direction, sense,* the topographical economy of a labyrinth on the contrary implies the *loss* of all *sense of direction.* And the loss of the sense of direction is, or can be, indeed fatal: it is just such a state of disorientation which brings about, in fact, the very death of Peter Quint:

Peter Quint was found (...) stone dead on the road from the village: a catastrophe explained (...) by a visible wound to his head; such a wound as might have been produced — and as, on the final evidence, *had* * been — by a *fatal slip,* in the dark and after leaving the public house, on the steepish icy slope, *a wrong path altogether,* at the bottom of which he lay. The icy slope, *the turn mistaken* at night and in liquor, *accounted for much* — practically, *in the end* and after the inquest and boundless chatter, *for everything* (ch. 6, p. 28; * James's italics; other italics mine).

If the "wrong path" or "the turn mistaken" can "account for much," or even, "in the end (...) for everything"—notably for the *accident of death*—, could they not account equally "in the end" for the novel's *end,* for that other *accident* of *the death of little Miles,* doubled as it is by a "second death" of Peter Quint, by the disappearance of the ghost? The parallel, in any case, is striking. The hypothetical, possible *madness* of the governess could then itself be accounted for "in the end" by a "turn mistaken," by a misguided choice of sense or of direction, indeed by nothing other than a fatal, deadly *reading mistake.* The semantic charge of the word "turn" itself in fact connotes the possible resonance of "an attack of madness" (cf. "turns of hysteria"), upon which the text occasionally seems to play. At the crucial moment when the governess is furiously accusing Flora of *seeing* Miss Jessel and of refusing to admit it, Mrs. Grose, who, like the girl, sees nothing, protests against the governess's accusation:

"*What a dreadful turn,* to be sure, Miss! Where on earth do you see anything?" (ch. 20, p. 72).

180

Shoshana Felman

Does the word "turn" here mean "a turning point," "a change of meaning," "a turn of events," or "a turn of hysteria," "an attack of nervousness," "a fit," "a spell"? And if it means a turning point (a change of meaning), does it designate a simple *reorientation* or a radical *disorientation,* i.e., a delirious twist and *deviation?* Or does the "turn" name, precisely, the textual ironic figure of its own rhetorical capacity to *reverse itself,* to turn meaning into madness, to "project the possible other case" or other turn? Whatever the case, the metaphor of the "turn of the screw," in referring to a *turn*—or a twist—of sense, establishes an ironical equivalence between direction and deviation, between a turn of sense and a turn of madness, between the turn of an interpretation and the turning point beyond which interpretation becomes delirious. The governess herself is in fact quite aware of the possibility of madness, of her own madness, as the very risk involved in reading, as the other turn—the other side of the very coin of meaning:

I began to watch them in a stifled suspense, a disguised excitement that might well, had it continued too long, have *turned to* something like *madness.* What saved me, as I now see, was that it *turned to* something else altogether (...) it was superseded by horrible proofs. Proofs, I say, yes — from the moment I really *took hold* (ch. 6, p. 28).

To "take hold"—to seize the screw and tighten it once more so as to gain control of sense, of meaning—is thus conceived as a means of preserving and securing lucidity and sanity, as a gesture of protection against the threat of madness. The question of "taking hold" is often, in effect, associated with the very question of *equilibrium:*

I had felt it again and again — how *my equilibrium depended on the success of my rigid will* (...). I could only get on at all (...) by treating my monstrous ordeal as a push in a direction unusual, of course, and unpleasant, but demanding, after all (...) only *another turn of the screw* of ordinary human virtue (ch. 22, p. 80). [51]

[51] Cf. ch. 24, p. 88: "The grasp with which I recovered him might have been that of *catching him in his fall.* I caught him, yes, *I held him...*" and ch. 24, p. 85: "... the mere blind movement of *getting hold* of him (...) while I just *fell for support* against the nearest piece of furniture..."

The expression "turn of the screw" is, indeed, itself twice used explicity in the text, in two entirely different contexts. The question thus arises whether, within their very differences, these two textual uses of the expression are nonetheless linked to each other in a revealing way. In the context just quoted, we have seen that the "turn of the screw" is directly linked to the question of *equilibrium,* of balance, and therefore also to the question of the loss of balance, of the loss of equilibrium, to the very possibility of *madness;* in the other context—that of the prologue—the expression "turn of the screw" is, on the other hand, used in relation to the question of the reception of the story, of the narrative's impact on its listeners (readers), of the tale's *reading-effect.* From one context to the other, from the story to its "frame," it is once again *reading* and *madness* which interact and confront each other through the differential repetition of the expression "turn of the screw." But their interaction, this time, also implicates *us* as the story's readers, places *us* in the same boat as the governess, since the prologue's use of the expression "turn of the screw" names the "effect" produced precisely on its readers by the very story of *The Turn of the Screw.* Douglas, in this manner, introduces the story he is about to tell:

"I quite agree — in regard to Griffin's ghost (...) — that its appearing first to the little boy, at so tender an age, adds a particular touch. But it's not the first occurrence of its charming kind that I know to have involved a child. If the child *gives the effect another turn of the screw,* what do you say to *two* * children?"

"We say, of course," somebody exclaimed, "that they give *two turns!* [52] Also that we want to hear about them." (Prologue, p. 1; * James's italics; other italics mine.)

[52] If the presence of a child in a ghost story gives a "turn of the screw" to the effect of horror produced upon the reader, the presence of *two* children obviously does not, however, give that effect *"two* turns." The listener's response does not correspond to Douglas's intention in asking the question. The expression "to give a turn of the screw" is a cliché which as such produces meaning only as a reified *unit,* but cannot be divided into its component parts, is not susceptible to modification; it is thus impossible to say "to give two turns of the screw" — or at any rate to say it is to disrupt the cliché's ordinary meaning. As a stereotype signifying "a strengthening (of the effect)," the expression "to give a turn

In what way, however, does the turn of the screw given by the children to the story's reading-effect more specifically refer to the turn of the screw given by the governess to "ordinary human virtue"? Like the story's reader, dramatized in the frame by the listener who replies "two turns!," the governess is herself essentially a *reader,* engaged in an interpretative entreprise. Now, what the governess precisely tells us of the "turn of the screw of ordinary human virtue," is that this turn of the screw is designed to insure her very *equilibrium.* Her equilibrium indeed depends on the strength of her "rigid will," on her capacity to withstand "a push in a direction unusual" by tightening the screw, on her mastery of the screw's direction and of its meaning, on the strength and rigidity of her "hold": "ordinary human virtue," in other words,

of the screw" is not mathematizable: like the act of turning the screw itself, the cliché lends itself not to *addition* but to *repetition;* in order to indicate an *added strengthening,* it is only possible to *repeat* the *same* cliché: not "give *two* turns," but, as the governess and Douglas both put it, "give *another* turn of the screw." The answer to Douglas's question can only *repeat* the terms of its formulation: "two children would indeed give the effect *another* turn of the screw." In this sense, Douglas's question is a *rhetorical* one — an *affirmation* which in truth does not ask nor call for an answer. In addition, if the effect of horror is linked to the presence of a child, the relation of effect to cause (of horror to child) is not *quantitative,* but *qualitative:* what produces the effect is not the *number* of children, but *childhood* as such. The number "two" used by Douglas is not meant as an enumeration, as a *quantitative* measure, but as a superlative, as a *qualitative* measure. Douglas's proposal to outdo the previous narrative constitutes not an *arithmetical* but a *rhetorical* outbidding. Douglas is tantalizing the hushed little circle with a better, more thrilling version of the *same* type of ghost story: the *two* children, in this sense, amount to the *same.*

The listener's interpretation (2 children = 2 turns) is thus a reading-mistake, an error of interpretation. The error lies in taking rhetoric as such (the rhetorical question as well as the rhetorical outbidding) *literally.*

In answering "two turns!," the reader thus produces a difference, or a split, in the text's very relation (or identity) to itself. Curiously enough, however, this *misreading,* this misguided suggestion that the story will have "two turns" — two different senses or directions — rejoins in fact precisely the fundamental *reality* of the text, the very *truth* of its duplicity and of its ambiguity. The text itself could thus say of its reader as the governess says of Miles: "horrible as it was, his lies made up my truth" (ch. 2, p. 84).

In including at its very outset its own misreading, in dramatizing its own rhetoricity as a potentiality for error which, however, effectively deconstructs the decidable polarity between truth and error, the very metaphor of "the turn of the screw," through the turn of the screw given to its meaning by its own enunciation, thus refers at once to a reading-effect and to a reading-mistake.

is nothing other than an enterprise of mastery, a *system of control over meaning*. But in what way does the governess's reading strategy relate to the position of the reader in the story's frame? How is this *hold* on meaning at the very heart of the story linked with the turn of the screw of its reading-effect? Does the turn of the screw of the reading-effect itself involve some kind of a *hold?*

Indeed, while the ending of the story recounts the way in which the governess-reader takes *hold* at once of meaning and of the child ("I caught him, yes, I *held* him"), the beginning of the story, in a strikingly parallel way, introduces in its very first sentence, another type of hold implied by reading: *"The story had held us,* round the fire, sufficiently breathless..." (Prologue, p. 1). With respect to the hold defining the reading-enterprise ("another turn of the screw of ordinary human virtue"), the hold defining the reading-effect is thus reversed: while the governess as a reader strives to *get hold of the story,* the reading-effect is such that it is rather the story itself which *takes hold of its readers.* The reading-enterprise and the reading-effect turn out to be diametrically opposed: to *hold* the signifier (or the story's meaning) is in reality but to *be held* by it. This, then, is the final turn of the screw of the metaphor of the turn of the screw: the reader who tries to take hold of the text can but find himself taken in *by* it. As a performative (and not a cognitive) figure of the ironic textual force of reversal and of chiasmus, of the subversion of the subject by the very irony of language, the "turn of the screw"—or *The Turn of the Screw—acts out,* indeed, the very narrative—or tale—of reading, as precisely *the story of the subversion of the reader.* While the reader thus believes he holds and comprehends the story, it is in effect the story which holds and comprehends the reader. But what, precisely, is the story's hold on us? In what way are we at once held and comprehended by the story?

Shoshana Felman

IX. *The Madness of Interpretation: Literature and Psychoanalysis*

> "Do you know what I think?"
>
> "It's exactly what I'm pressing you to make intelligible."
>
> "Well," said Mrs. Briss, "I think you are crazy."
>
> It naturally struck me. "Crazy?"
>
> "Crazy."
>
> I turned it over. "But do you call that intelligible?"
>
> She did it justice. "No; I don't suppose it *can* be so for you if you *are insane*."
>
> I risked the long laugh which might have seemed that of madness. " 'If I am' is lovely." And whether or not it was the special sound, in my ear, of my hilarity, I remember just wondering if perhaps I mightn't be.
>
> (H. James, *The Sacred Fount*)

The indication that *The Turn of the Screw* is constructed as a *trap* designed to close upon the reader is in fact, as we saw earlier, explicitly stated by James himself:

It is an excursion into chaos while remaining, like Blue-Beard and Cinderella, but an anecdote — though an anecdote amplified and highly emphasized and *returning upon itself;* as, for that matter, Cinderella and Blue-Beard return. I need scarcely add after this that it is a piece of ingenuity pure and simple, of cold artistic calculation, an *amusette* * to *catch those not easily caught* (the "fun" of the *capture* of the merely witless being ever but small), the jaded, the disillusioned, the fastidious. (The New York Preface, p. 120; * James's italics; other italics mine.)

What is interesting about this trap is that, while it points to the possibility of two alternative types of reading, it sets out, in capturing *both* types of readers, to eliminate the very demarcation it proposes. [53] The alternative types of reading which the trap at once

---

[53] These two types of reading thus recall the illusory "two turns" which the mistaken reader in the frame attributes to the screw of the text's effect. (Cf. Prologue, p. 1, and, above, note 52.) But we have seen that the "two turns" in fact amount to the same: based on the symmetry implied by the "*two* children," the apparent *difference* between the "two

elicits and suspends can be described as the *naive* ("the capture of the merely witless") and the *sophisticated* ("to catch those not easily caught... the jaded, the disillusioned, the fastidious"). The trap, however, is specifically laid not for naiveté but for *intelligence* itself. But in what, indeed, does intelligence consist, if not in the determination to *avoid the trap?* "Those not easily caught" are precisely those who are *suspicious,* those who sniff out and detect a trap, those who refuse to be *duped:* "the disillusioned, the jaded, the fastidious." In this sense the "naive reading" would be one which would *lend credence* to the testimony and account of the governess, whereas the "disillusioned" reading would on the contrary be one which would suspect, demystify, "see through" the governess, one which, in fact, would function very much like the reading carried out by Wilson, who in effect opens his discussion by *warning* us precisely against a *trap* set by the text, a "trick of James's":

> A discussion of Henry James's ambiguity may appropriately begin with *The Turn of the Screw.* This story (...) perhaps *conceals another horror behind the ostensible one.* (...) It is a not infrequent *trick of James's* to introduce sinister characters with descriptions that at first sound flattering, so *this need not throw us off.* (*Wilson,* p. 102.)

Since the trap set by James's text is meant precisely for "those not easily caught"—those who, in other words, watch out for, and seek to avoid, all traps,—it can be said that *The Turn of the Screw,* which is designed to snare *all* readers, is a text particularly apt to catch the *psychoanalytic* reader, since the psychoanalytic reader is, *par excellence,* the reader who *would not be caught,* who would not be made a *dupe.* Would it be possible then to maintain that *literature,* in *The Turn of the Screw,* constitutes *a trap for psychoanalytical interpretation?*

turns" is purely *specular*. This is the final irony of the figure of the turn of the screw: while appearing to double and to multiply itself, the turn of the screw only *repeats* itself; while appearing to "turn," to *change* direction, sense, or meaning, the turning sense in fact does not change, since the screw *returns upon itself*. And it is precisely through such a "return upon itself" that the trap set by the text, says James, catches the reader.

186

Let us return, one last time, to Wilson's reading, which will be considered here not as a model "Freudian reading," but as the illustration of a prevalent tendency as well as an inherent temptation of psychoanalytical interpretation as it undertakes to provide an "explanation," or an "explication" of a literary text. In this regard, Wilson's later semi-retraction of his thesis is itself instructive: convinced by his detractors that for James the ghosts were real, that James's *conscious* project or intention was to write a simple ghost story and not a madness story, Wilson does not, however, give up his theory that the ghosts consist of the neurotic hallucinations of the governess, but concedes in a note:

One is led to conclude that, in *The Turn of the Screw,* not merely is the governess self-deceived, but that James is self-deceived about her. (*Wilson,* note added 1948, p. 143.)

This sentence can be seen as the epitome, and as the verbal formulation, of the desire underlying psychoanalytical interpretation: the desire to be *non-dupe,* to interpret, i.e., at once uncover and avoid, the very traps of the unconscious. James's text, however, is made of traps and dupery: in the first place, from an analytical perspective, the governess is *self-deceived;* duping us, she is equally herself a *dupe* of her own unconscious; in the second place, in Wilson's view, James himself is self-deceived: the author also is at once our duper and the dupe of his unconscious; the reader, in the third place, is in turn duped, deceived, by the very rhetoric of the text, by the author's "trick," by the ruse of his narrative technique which consists in presenting "cases of self-deception" "from their own point of view" (*Wilson,* p. 142). Following Wilson's suggestions, there seems to be only one exception to this circle of universal dupery and deception: the so-called Freudian literary critic himself. By avoiding the double trap set at once by the unconscious and by rhetoric, by remaining himself *exterior* to the reading-errors which delude and blind both characters and author, the critic thus becomes the sole agent and the exclusive mouthpiece of the *truth* of literature.

This way of thinking and this state of mind, however, strikingly resemble those of the governess herself, who is equally preoccupied by the desire, above all, not to be made a dupe, by the determination to avoid, detect, demystify, the cleverest of traps set for her credulity. Just as Wilson is distrustful of James's narrative technique, suspecting that its rhetoric involves a "trick," i.e., a strategy, a ruse, a wily game, the governess in turn is suspicious of the children's rhetoric:

"It's a game," I went on, "it's a policy and a fraud" (ch. 12, p. 48).

And just as Wilson, struck by the *ambiguity* of the text, concludes that the governess, in saying *less* than the truth, actually says *more* than she means,— the governess herself, struck by the ambiguity of Mrs. Grose's speech, concludes in a parallel fashion that Mrs. Grose, in saying less than *all*, nonetheless says *more* than she intends to say:

...my impression of her having accidentally said more than she meant...

I don't know what there was in this brevity of Mrs. Grose's that struck me as ambiguous (ch. 2, pp. 12-13).

I was (...) still haunted with the shadow of something she had not told me (ch. 6, p. 27).

Like Wilson, the governess is *suspicious* of the ambiguity of signs and of their rhetorical reversibility; like Wilson, she thus procedes to *read* the world around her, to *interpret* it, not by looking *at* it but by seeing *through* it, by demystifying and *reversing* the values of its outward signs. In each case, then, it is *suspicion* which gives rise as such to *interpretation*.

But isn't James's reader-trap, in fact, a *trap set for suspicion?*

...an *amusette* * to catch those not easily caught (...). Otherwise expressed, the study is of a conceived "tone," the tone of *suspected* and felt *trouble,* of an inordinate and incalculable sore — the tone of tragic, yet of exquisite, mystification. (New York Preface, p. 120; * James's italics; other italics mine.)

The Turn of the Screw thus constitutes a trap for psychoanalytical interpretation to the extent that it constructs a trap, precisely, for suspicion. It has indeed been said of psychoanalysis itself that it is a veritable "school of suspicion." [54] But what, exactly, is suspicion? "Oran," reads the opening line of Camus' *The Plague*, "was a city without suspicion." Brought by "the Plague," suspicion will then signify, in this case, the awakening of consciousness itself through its mêlées with death, with fear, with suffering—the acquisition of a keen awareness of the imminence of a catastrophe of unknown origin, which has to be prevented, fought against, defeated. If it is thus the plague which brings about suspicion, it is well known, indeed, that Freud himself, at the historic moment of his arrival in the United States, said precisely that he had brought with him, ironically enough, "the plague" ... Psychoanalysis, therefore, could very accurately be described as a "school of suspicion," a school which teaches an awareness of the Plague. What, however, is the alternative to suspicion? James's text can perhaps provide an answer. In the New York Preface, to begin with, the alternative to the suspicious reader was incarnated in the so-called "witless" reader ("the 'fun' of the capture of the merely witless being ever but small"); suspicion would thus seem to be equivalent to "wit," to the *intelligence* of the reader. In the text of *The Turn of the Screw* itself, moreover, the alternative to the suspicion of the governess is, symmetrically, the naive *belief* of Mrs. Grose, who unsuspectingly lends credence to whatever the governess may choose to tell her. And, as if the very name of Mrs. Grose were not a sufficient clue to James's view of the attitude of *faith* which he thus opposes to suspicion, the fact that Mrs. Grose *does not know how to read* ("my counselor couldn't read!" ch. 2, p. 10) clearly suggests a parallel with the "witless" reader which the New York Preface in its turn opposes to the suspicious, unbelieving reader, the one who is precisely difficult to catch. Psychoanalysis, therefore, is strictly speaking a "school of suspicion" to the extent that

[54] The formula is Paul Ricoeur's.

it is, in effect, a *school of reading*. Practiced by Wilson as well as by the governess, but quite unknown to Mrs. Grose, "suspicion" is directed, first and foremost, toward the non-transparent, arbitrary nature of the sign: it feeds on the discrepancy and distance which separates the signifier from its signified. While suspicion constitutes, thereby, the very motive of the process of interpretation, the very moving force behind the "wit" of the discriminating reader, we should not forget, however, that the reader is here "caught" or trapped, not *in spite of* but *by virtue of, because of* his intelligence and his sophistication. Suspicion is itself here part of the mystification ("the tone of *suspected* and felt trouble... the tone of tragic, yet of exquisite, *mystification*"): the alert, suspicious, unduped reader is here just as "caught," as mystified, as the naive believer. Like faith (naive or "witless" reading), suspicion (the intelligence of reading) is here a *trap*.

The trap, indeed, resides precisely in the way in which these two opposing types of reading are themselves inscribed and comprehended in the text. The reader of *The Turn of the Screw* can choose either to *believe* the governess, and thus to behave like Mrs. Grose, or *not to believe the governess,* and thus to behave precisely *like the governess*. Since it is the governess who, within the text, plays the role of the suspicious reader, occupies the *place* of the interpreter, to *suspect* that place and that position is, thereby, *to take it*. To demystify the governess is only possible on one condition: the condition of *repeating* the governess's very gesture. The text thus constitutes a reading of its two possible readings, both of which, in the course of that reading, it deconstructs. James's trap is then the simplest and the most sophisticated in the world: the trap is but a text, that is, an invitation to the reader, a simple invitation to undertake its reading. But in the case of *The Turn of the Screw,* the invitation to undertake a reading of the text is perforce an invitation to *repeat* the text, to enter into its labyrinth of mirrors, from which it is henceforth impossible to escape.

It is in just the same manner as the governess that Wilson, in his reading, seeks to avoid above all being duped: to avoid, precisely, being the governess's dupe. Blind to his own resemblance with the governess, he repeats, indeed, one after the other, the procedures and delusions of her reading strategy. "Observe," writes Wilson, "from a Freudian point of view, the significance of the governess's interest in the little girl's pieces of wood" (*Wilson*, p. 104). But to "observe" the *signified* behind the wooden *signifier*, to observe the meaning, or the significance, of the very *interest* shown for that signifier, is precisely what the governess herself does, and invites others to do, when she runs crying to Mrs. Grose, "They know—it's too monstrous: they know, they know!" (ch. 7, p. 30). In just the same manner as the governess, Wilson equally *fetishizes* the phallic simulacrum, delusively raises the mast in Flora's boat to the status of Master-Signifier. Far from following the incessant slippage, the unfixable movement of the signifying chaim from link to link, from signifier to signifier, the critic, like the governess, seeks to *stop* the meaning, to *arrest* signification, by a grasp, precisely, of the Screw (or of the "clue"), by a firm hold on the Master-Signifier:

What if the hidden theme (...) is *simply sex* again? ... the *clue of experience* ... (*Wilson*, p. 115.)

When one has once *got hold* of *the clue to this meaning* of *The Turn of the Screw,* one wonders how one could ever have missed it. (*Wilson*, p. 108.)

Sharing with the governess the illusion of having understood *all*, of having *mastered* meaning by clutching at its clue, at its master-signifier, Wilson could have said, *with* the governess and *like* her, but *against* her:

I seemed to myself to have mastered it, to see it all (ch. 21, p. 78).

In Wilson's case as in the governess's, the move toward mastery, however, is an aggressive move, an "act of violence," which involves a gesture of repression and of *exclusion*. "Our manner of excluding," writes Maurice Blanchot, "is at work precisely at the very moment we are priding ourselves on our gift of universal comprehension." In their attempt to elaborate a speech of mastery, a discourse of *totalitarian* power, what Wilson and the governess both *exclude* is nothing other than the threatening power of rhetoric itself—of sexuality as *division* and as meaning's *flight,* as contradiction and as ambivalence; the very threat, in other words, of the unmastery, of the impotence, and of the unavoidable castration which inhere in *language.* From his very *grasp* of meaning and from the grasp of his interpretation, Wilson thus excludes, *represses,* the very thing which led to his analysis, the very subject of his study: the role of language in the text, "the ambiguity of Henry James":

> Henry James never seems aware of the amount of space he is wasting through the long abstract formulations that do duty for concrete details, the unnecessary circumlocutions and the gratuitous meaningless verbiage — the *as it were's* and *as we may say's* and all the rest — all the words with which he pads out his sentences and which themselves are probably symptomatic of a tendency to stave off his main problems. (*Wilson,* p. 129; author's italics.)

As Jean Starobinski puts it elsewhere, "The psychoanalyst, the expert on the rhetoric of the unconscious, does not himself wish to be a rhetorician. He plays the role that Jean Paulhan assigns to the terrorist as such: he demands that one speak in clear language." [55] In demanding that the text "speak in clear language," Wilson thus reveals the *terroristic status* of his psychoanalytic exegesis. But the governess as well demands "clear language": she terrorizes in effect the child into "surrendering the name," into giving, that is, to the ghost its *proper name.* Wilson's treatment of the text indeed corresponds point for point to the governess's treatment of the child: Wilson, too, forces, as it were, the text to a *confession.* And what, in fact, is the main effort of the analytical interpreter as such, if not, at all events, to extort the *secret* of the text, to compel the language of the text—like that of the child—to confess or to avow: to avow its *meaning* as well as its *pleasure;*

---

[55] Jean Starobinski, *La Relation critique* (Paris: Gallimard, 1970), p. 271; my translation.

to avow its pleasure and its meaning to the precise extent that they are *unavowable*.

It is thus not insignificant for the text's subtle entrapment of its psychoanalytical interpretation that the governess ends up *killing the child*. Neither is it indifferent to the textual scene that the Latin word for child, *infans*, signifies, precisely, "one incapable of speaking." For would it not be possible to maintain that Wilson, in pressing the text to confess, in forcing it to "surrender" its *proper* name, its explicit, literal meaning, himself in fact commits a *murder* (which once more brings up the question of *tact*), by suppressing within language the very silence which supports and underlies it, the silence *out of which* the text precisely speaks?

... a stillness, a pause of all life, that had nothing to do with the more or less noise we at the moment might be engaged in making ... (ch. 13, p. 53).

As the figure of a *knowledge which cannot know itself,* which cannot reflect upon nor name itself, the child in the story incarnates, as we have seen, *unconscious* knowledge. To "grasp" the child, therefore, as both the governess and Wilson do, to press him to the point of suffocating him, of killing or of stifling the silence within him, is to do nothing other than to submit, once more, the silent speech of the unconscious to the very gesture of its *repression*.

Here, then, is the crowning aberration which psychoanalysis sometimes unwittingly commits in its mêlées with literature. In seeking to "explain" and *master* literature, in refusing, that is, to become a *dupe* of literature, in killing within literature that which makes it literature—its reserve of silence, that which, within speech, is incapable of speaking, the literary silence of a discourse *ignorant of what it knows*—the psychoanalytic reading, ironically enough, turns out to be a reading which *represses the unconscious,* which represses, paradoxically, the unconscious which it purports to be "explaining." To *master,* then, (to become the Master) is, here as elsewhere, to *refuse to read* the letters; here as elsewhere, to "see it all" is in effect to "shut one's eyes as tight as possible to the truth"; once more, "to see it all" is in reality to *exclude;* and to exclude, specifically, the unconscious.

Thus repeated on all levels of the literary scene, by the governess as well as by her critics, in the story as well as in its reading, this basic gesture of repression, of exclusion, is often carried out under the auspices of a label which, while naming that which is cast out, excluded, also at the same time sanctions the exclusion. That subtle label is the term "madness" used by the interpreter to mark that which is repressed as indeed *foreclosed,* external to, shut out from, meaning. Wilson thus suggests that the governess is *mad,* i.e., that her point of view *excludes* her, and hence should be excluded, from the "truth" and from the meaning of her story. But the governess herself in her own reading, indeed, refers no less insistently to the question of insanity, of madness. She is preoccupied, as we have seen, by the alternative of madness and of sense as mutually exclusive; she is quite aware, in fact, that the possibility of her own madness is but the converse—the other side, the other turn—of her seizure and *control* of sense, of her "grasp" of and her firm "hold" [56] on meaning, a hold involving the *repression* of otherness as such, an exclusion of the Other. To "grasp," "get hold" of sense will therefore also be to *situate* madness—*outside,* to shut it out, to *locate* it— in the Other: to cast madness as such onto the other insofar as the Other in effect *eludes one's grasp.* The governess indeed maintains that the children are no less than *mad;* [57] when Mrs. Grose urges her to write to the Master about the children's strange behavior, the governess demurs:

---

[56] Cf. ch. 6, p. 28: "... a suspense (...) that might well (...) have *turned* into *something like madness.* (...) It *turned* to *something else altogether* (...) from the moment I really *took hold.*" Cf. also ch. 12, p. 48: "I go on, I know, as if I am *crazy,* and it's a wonder I'm not. What I've seen would have made *you* so; but it only made me more lucid, made me *get hold* of still other things..."

[57] To begin with, she claims they are "possessed," that is, *unseizable,* possessed precisely *by the Other:* "Yes, *mad* as it seems! (...) They haven't been good — they've only been absent. (...) They're simply leading a life of their own. They're not mine — they're not ours. They're his and they're hers!" (ch. 12, pp. 48-49).

Shoshana Felman

"By writing to him that his house is poisoned and his little nephew and niece *mad?*"

"But if they *are*, Miss?"

"And if I am myself, you mean? That's charming news to be sent him by a person (...) whose prime undertaking was to give him no worry" (ch. 12, pp. 49-50).

It is thus *either* the governess *or* the children who are mad: if the children are *not* mad, the governess could well be; if the children *are* mad, then the governess is truly in the right, as well as in her right mind. Hence, to *prove* that the children *are* mad (that they are *possessed* by the Other—by the ghosts) is to prove that the governess is *not* mad: to point to the madness of the other is to deny and to negate the very madness that might be lurking in the self. The Other's madness thus becomes a decisive proof and guarantee of one's own sanity:

Miss Jessel stood before us (...). I remember (...) my thrill of joy at having brought on a *proof*. She was there, and I was justified; *she was there, so I was neither cruel nor mad* (ch. 20, p. 71).

Thus, for the governess to be in *possession* of her *senses*, the *children* must be *possessed* and *mad*. The governess's very *sense*, in other words, is founded on the children's *madness*. Similarly but conversely, the story's very *sense*, as outlined by Wilson, by the *logic* of his reading, is also, paradoxically, *based on madness*—but this time on the madness of the *governess*. Wilson, in other words, treats the governess in exactly the same manner as the governess treats the children. It is the governess's madness, that is, the exclusion of her point of view, which enables Wilson's reading to function as a *whole,* as a system at once *integral* and *coherent* —just as it is the *children's* madness, the exclusion of *their* point of view, which permits the governess's reading, and its functioning as a *totalitarian* system. [58]

[58] Cf.: " 'It's a game,' I went on, — 'it's a policy and a fraud!' (...) 'Yes, *mad* at it seems!' The very act of bringing it out really helped me to trace it — follow it up and *piece it all together*" (ch. 12, pp. 48-49).

"It is not by locking up one's neighbor," as Dostoievsky once said, "that one can convince oneself of one's own soundness of mind." This, however, is what Wilson seems precisely to be doing, insofar as he is duplicating and *repeating* the governess's gesture. This, then, is what psychoanalytical interpretation might be doing, and indeed is doing whenever it gives in to the temptation of *diagnosing* literature, of indicating and of *situating madness* in a literary text. For in shutting madness up in literature, in attempting not just to explain the literary symptom, but to explain away the very symptom of literature itself, psychoanalysis, like the governess, only diagnoses literature so as to *justify itself,* to insure its own *control* of meaning, to deny or to negate the lurking possibility of its own madness, to convince itself of its own incontrovertible soundness of mind.

The paradoxical trap set by *The Turn of the Screw* is therefore such that it is precisely by proclaiming that the governess is mad that Wilson inadvertently *imitates* the very madness he denounces, unwittingly *participates in it.* Whereas the diagnostic gesture aims to situate the madness in the other and to disassociate oneself from it, to exclude the diagnosis from the diagnosed, here, on the contrary, it is the very gesture of exclusion which includes: to exclude the governess—as mad—from the place of meaning and of truth is precisely to repeat her very gesture of exclusion, to *include oneself,* in other words, within her very madness. Unsuspectingly, Wilson himself indeed says as much when he writes of another Jamesian tale:

The book is not merely mystifying, but maddening. (*Wilson,* p. 112.)

Thus it is that *The Turn of the Screw* succeeds in *trapping* the very analytical interpretation it in effect *invites* but whose authority it at the same time *deconstructs.* In inviting, in *seducing* the psychoanalyst, in tempting him into the quicksand of its rhetoric, literature, in truth, only invites him to *subvert himself,* only lures psychoanalysis into its necessary self-subversion.

Shoshana Felman

In the textual mechanism through which the roles of the governess and of the children become reversible, and in the text's tactical action on its reader, through which the roles of the governess and of her critic (her demystifier) become symmetrical and interchangeable, — the textual dynamic, the rhetorical operation at work consists precisely in the *subversion* of the *polarity* or the *alternative* which opposes as such analyst to patient, symptom to interpretation, delirium to its theory, psychoanalysis itself to madness. That psychoanalytical theory itself occupies precisely a symmetrical, and hence a specular, position with respect to the madness it observes and faces, is in fact a fundamental given of psychoanalysis, acknowledged both by Freud and by Lacan. Lacan as well as Freud recognize indeed that the very value—but equally the risk—inherent in psychoanalysis, its insightfulness but equally its blindness, its truth but also its error, reside precisely in this turn of the screw : "The discourse of the hysteric," writes Lacan, "taught [Freud] this other substance which entirely consists in the fact that such a thing as a signifier exists. In taking in the effect of this signifier, within the hysteric's discourse, [Freud] was able to give it that *quarter-turn* which was to turn it into analytical discourse" (*Encore,* p. 41). Freud, in turn, acknowledges a "striking similarity" between his own psychoanalytical theory and the delirious ravings of President Schreber: "It remains for the future to decide," writes Freud, "whether there is more delusion in my theory than I should like to admit, or whether there is more truth in Schreber's delusion than other people are as yet prepared to believe." [59]

It is doubtless no coincidence, therefore, that the myth of Oedipus—the psychoanalytical myth *par excellence*—should happen to recount not only the *drama of the symptom* but equally the very *drama of interpretation*. The tragedy of Oedipus is, after all, the story no less of the analyst than of the analysand: it is specifically, in fact, the story of the deconstruction, of the subversion of

[59] S. Freud, *Three Case Histories* (ed. Philip Rieff), New York: Collier Books, 1963, p. 182.

the polarity itself which distinguishes and which opposes these two functions. The very *murder* that Oedipus commits is indeed constitutive in the story, just as much of the impasse of the interpreter as of the tragedy of the interpreted. For it is the murder which founds the rhetorical movement of substitution as a *blind* movement, leading blindly to the commutation, or to the switch between interpreter and interpreted: it is by murdering that the interpreter takes the place, precisely, of the symptom to be interpreted. Through the blind substitution in which Oedipus unwittingly takes the place of his victim, of the man he killed, he also, as interpreter (as the detective attempting to solve the crime), and equally unwittingly, comes to occupy the place and the position of the very *target* of the blow that he *addresses to the Other*. But Wilson also is precisely doing this, unknowingly assuming the position of the target, when he inadvertently repeats the gesture of the governess at whom he aims his blow, thereby taking her *place* in the textual structure.

It is through *murder* that Oedipus comes to be *master*. It is by *killing literary silence,* by stifling the very silence which inhabits literary language as such, that psychoanalysis *masters* literature, and that Wilson claims to *master* James's text. But Oedipus becomes master only to end up *blinding himself.* To blind oneself: the final gesture of a master, so as to delude himself with the impression that he still is in control, if only of his self-destruction, that he still can master his own blindness (whereas his blind condition in reality preexisted his self-inflicted blindness), that he still can master his own loss of mastery, his own castration (whereas he in reality *undergoes* it, everywhere, from without); to blind oneself, perhaps, then, less so as to punish, to humiliate oneself than so as to persist, precisely, in *not seeing,* so as to deny, once more, the very truth of one's castration, a castration existing outside Oedipus's gesture, by virtue of the fact that his conscious mastery, the mastery supported by his consciousness, finds itself subverted, by virtue of the fact that the person taken in by the trap of his detection is not the Other, but he himself, — by virtue of the fact that he *is* the Other. And isn't this insistence on not seeing, on not knowing, precisely what describes as well the function of the Master in *The Turn of the Screw*? In its efforts to master literature, psychoanalysis—like Oedipus and like the Master —can thus but blind itself: blind itself in order to deny its own castration, in order not to see, and not to read, literature's subversion of the very possibility of psychoanalytical mastery. The irony is that, in the very act of judging literature from the height of its masterly position, psychoanalysis—like Wilson—in effect rejoins within the structure of the text the masterly position, the specific place of the Master of *The Turn of the Screw:* the place, precisely, of the textual *blind spot.*

Now, to occupy a blind spot is not only to be blind, but in particular, to be blind to one's own blindness; it is to be unaware of the fact that one occupies a spot *within* the very blindness one seeks to demystify, that one is *in* the madness, that one is always, necessarily, *in* literature; it is to believe that one is on the *outside,* that one *can* be outside: outside the traps of literature, of the unconscious, or of madness. James's reader-trap thus functions by precisely luring the reader into attempting to avoid the trap, into believing that there *is* an outside to the trap. This belief, of course, is itself one of the trap's most subtle mechanisms: the very act of trying to escape the trap is the proof that one is caught in it. "The unconscious," writes Lacan, "is most effectively misleading when it is caught in the act." [60] This, precisely, is what James suggests in *The Turn of the Screw.* And what James in effect *does* in *The Turn of the Screw,* what he undertakes through the performative action of his text, is precisely to mislead us, and to catch us, by on the contrary inviting us to *catch the unconscious in the act.* In attempting to escape the reading-error constitutive of rhetoric, in attempting to escape the rhetorical error constitutive of literature, in attempting to master literature in order *not to be its dupe,* psychoanalysis, in reality, is *doubly duped:* unaware

[60] *Scilicet* No 1, p. 31 ("La Méprise du sujet supposé savoir").

of its own inescapable participation *in* literature and *in* the errors and the traps of rhetoric, it is blind to the fact that it itself exemplifies no less than the *blind spot* of rhetoricity, the spot where any affirmation of mastery in effect amounts to a self-subversion and to a self-castration. *"Les non-dupes errent"* [non-dupes err], says Lacan. If James's text does not explicitly make such a statement, it enacts it, and acts it out, while also dramatizing at the same time the suggestion that this very sentence—which entraps us in the same way as does the "turn of the screw"—this very statement, which cannot be affirmed without thereby being negated, whose very diction is in fact its own contradiction, constitutes, precisely, the position *par excellence* of *meaning* in the *literary utterance:* a rhetorical position, implying a relation of mutual subversion and of radical, dynamic contradiction between utterance and statement.

The fact that literature has no outside, that there is no safe spot assuredly outside of madness, from which one might demystify and judge it, locate it in the Other without oneself participating in it, was indeed ceaselessly affirmed by Freud in the most revealing moments of his text (and in spite of the constant opposite temptation—the mastery temptation—to which he at other times inevitably succumbed). Speaking of *The Sandman* and of Nathanael's uncanny madness—a madness textually marked, in Hoffmann's rhetoric, by the metaphor of Nathanael's distorted vision, due to the glasses bought from the Sandman (from the optician Coppola) and through which Nathanael at times chooses to behold the world which surrounds him; glasses through which he looks, at any rate, before each of his attacks of madness and of his attempts at murder, — Freud emphasizes the fact that the reader is rhetorically placed *within* that madness, that there is no place from which that madness can be judged *from the outside:*

...We perceive that he [Hoffmann] means to *make us, too, look through the fell Coppola's glasses* (...)

Shoshana Felman

> We know now that we are not supposed to be looking on at the products of a madman's imagination behind which we, with the superiority of rational minds, are able to detect the sober truth... [61]

In a parallel manner, *The Turn of the Screw* imposes the governess's distorted point of view upon us as the rhetorical *condition* of our perception of the story. In James's tale as in Hoffmann's, madness is uncanny, *unheimlich,* to the precise extent that it *cannot be situated,* coinciding, as it does, with the very space of reading. Wilson's error is to try to *situate* madness and thereby situate *himself outside it*—as though it were possible, *in* language, to *separate* oneself from language; as though the reader, looking through the governess's madness and comprehended by it, could situate *himself* within it *or* outside it with respect to it; as though the reader could indeed know *where* he is, what his place is and what his position is with respect to the literary language which itself, as such, does not know what it knows. Thus it is that when, in another of James's novels, *The Sacred Fount,* the label "madness" is ironically applied to the narrator as the last word—the last judgment in the book,

"You *are* crazy, and I bid you good night" [62] —

the narrator, indeed, experiences this last word as the loss of his capacity to situate himself: "Such a last word," he remarks, "(...) put me altogether nowhere." [63]

"It's a game," says the governess of the behavior of the children that in her turn she claims to be "mad",

— "It's a *game,* it's a *policy* and a *fraud*" (ch. 12, p. 48).

— "It's all a mere mistake and a worry and a joke," (ch. 20, p. 72)

[61] S. Freud, "The Uncanny" (trans. Alix Strachey) in *Freud on creativity and the Unconscious,* New York: Harper Torchbooks, 1958, p. 137.
[62] H. James, *The Sacred Fount,* New York: Charles Scribner's Sons, 1901, p. 318.
[63] *Ibid.,* p. 319.

answers, indirectly, Mrs. Grose, when she realizes that it is the governess who is mad, and that the children are but the victims of her delirium. The "mistake," the "worry" and the "joke," in Mrs. Grose's mouth, refer to, and affirm, the non-existence of the ghosts; they thus describe, accuse, excuse, the governess's madness. This ambiguous description of the error at the heart of *The Turn of the Screw* as at once tragic and comic, as both a "worry" and a "joke," is also implicit in James's statement in the New York Preface:

> The study is of a conceived "tone," the tone of suspected and felt trouble, of an inordinate and incalculable sore—*the tone of tragic, yet of exquisite, mystification* (p. 120).

The mystification is indeed exquisitely sophisticated, since it *comprehends* its very *de-mystification*. Since Wilson's gesture repeats the governess's, since the critic here participates in the madness he denounces, the psychoanalytical (or critical) *demystification*, paradoxically enough, ends up reproducing the literary *mystification*. The very thrust of the mystification was, then, to make us believe that there is a radical difference and opposition between the turn of the screw of mystification and the turn of the screw of demystification. But here it is precisely literature's mystification which demystifies and catches the "demystifier," by actively, in turn, *mystifying him*. Thus, paradoxically enough, it is mystification which is here demystifying, while demystification itself turns out to be but mystifying. The demystifier can only err within his own mystification.

"We could very well wonder," writes Lacan of Poe's *Purloined Letter* but in terms applicable equally to *The Turn of the Screw*, "whether it is not precisely the fact that *everyone is fooled* which constitutes here the source of our pleasure." [64] If the literary mystification is, in James's terms, "exquisite," it is indeed because it constitutes a source of pleasure. The mystification is a game, a joke; to play is to be played; to comprehend mystification is to

---

[64] J. Lacan, "Séminaire sur *La Lettre volée*," *Ecrits*, p. 17.

be comprehended *in* it; entering into the game, we ourselves become fair game for the very "joke" of *meaning*. The joke is that, by meaning, everyone is fooled. If the "joke" is nonetheless also a "worry," if, "exquisite" as it may be, mystification is also "tragic," it is because the "error" (the madness of the interpreter) is the error of life itself. "Life is the condition of knowledge," writes Nietzsche; "Error is the condition of life—I mean, ineradicable and fundamental error. The knowledge that one errs does not eliminate the error." [65]

X. *A Ghost of a Master*

> The whole point about the puzzle is its ultimate insolubility. How skillfully he managed it (. . .). The Master indeed.
> (Louis D. Rubin, Jr., *One More Turn of the Screw*)

> Note how masterly the telling is (...) still we must own that something remains unaccounted for.
> (Virginia Woolf, *Henry James's Ghosts*)

> The postbag (...) contained a letter for me, which, however, in the hand of my employer, I found to be composed but of a few words enclosing another, addressed to himself, with a seal still unbroken. "This, I recognize, is from the head-master, and the head-master's an awful bore. Read him, please; deal with him; but mind you, don't report. Not a word. I'm off!"
> (H. James, *The Turn of the Screw*)

Thus it is that within the space of a joke which is also a worry, within the space of a pleasure which is also a horror, Henry James, Master of ceremonies, himself takes pleasure in turning the screw, in tightening the spring of our interest:

[65] F. Nietzsche, *The Will to Power*.

That was my problem, so to speak, and my *gageure* — (...) to work my (...) *particular degree of pressure on the spring of interest*. (Preface to "The Golden Bowl," *AN*, p. 331.)

— "You almost *killed* me,"

protests, in Mozart's opera *Don Giovanni*, the valet of Don Giovanni, Leporello;

— "Go on, — You are mad,
It was only a *joke*,"

replies his Master with a laugh. If the joke in *The Turn of the Screw* is equally a deadly, or a ghostly one, it is because the author —the master-craftsman who masters the "turns" of the game—has chosen indeed to *joke with death* itself. It is in his capacity as master of letters that James turns out to be a master of ghosts. Both ghosts and letters are, however, only "operative terms": the operative terms of the very movement of death within the signifier, of the capacity of *substitution* which founds literature as a paradoxical space of pleasure and of frustration, of disappointment and of elation:

What would the operative terms, in the given case, prove, under criticism, to have been — a series of *waiting satisfactions* or an array of *waiting misfits*? The misfits had but to be positive and concordant, in the special intenser light, to represent together *(as the two sides of a coin show different legends)* just so many *effective felicities* and *substitutes*. (...) Criticism after the fact was to find in them arrests and surprises, emotions alike of disappointment and of elation: all of which means, obviously, that the whole thing was a *living* * affair. (Preface to "The Golden Bowl," *AN*, pp. 341-342; * James's italics; other italics mine.)

If death is but a joke, it is because death is, in a sense, as Georges Bataille has put it, "an imposture." Like the ghosts, death is precisely what cannot die: it is therefore of death, of ghosts, that one can literally say that they are "a *living* affair," an affair of the living, the affair, indeed, of living.

Master of letters and of ghosts alike, James, in contrast to his interpreters, lets himself become as much as possible a *dupe,* precise-

Shoshana Felman

ly, of their literality. It is as the dupe of the very letter of his text
that James remains the Master, that he deflects all our critical as-
saults and baffles all our efforts to master him. He proclaims to
know nothing at all about the content—or the meaning—of his
own letter. Like the letters in the very story of *The Turn of the
Screw,* his own letter, James insists, contains precisely *nothing.* His
text, he claims, can, to the letter, be taken as

a poor pot-boiling *study of nothing* at all, *qui ne tire pas à conséquence.* *
It is but a monument to my fatal technical passion, which prevents my
ever giving up anything I have begun. So that when *something that I have
supposed to be a subject turns out on trial to be none, je m'y acharne
d'autant plus.* * (Letter to Paul Bourget, August 19, 1898; *Norton,* p. 109;
* James's italics; other italics mine.)

As regards a presentation of things so fantastic as in that wanton little
tale, I can only blush to see real substance read into them. (Letter to
Dr. Waldstein, October 21, 1898; *Norton,* p. 110.)

My values are positively all blanks save so far as an excited horror, a
promoted pity, a created expertness (...) proceed to read into them more
or less fantastic figures. (New York Preface, p. 123.)

Master of his own fiction insofar as he, precisely, *is* its dupe, James,
like the Master in *The Turn of the Screw,* doesn't want to *know*
anything about it. In his turn, he refuses to read our letters, send-
ing them back to us unopened:

I'm afraid I don't quite *understand* the principal question you put to me
about "The Turn of the Screw." However, that scantily matters; for in
truth I am afraid (...) that I somehow can't pretend to give any coherent
account of my small inventions "after the fact." (Letter to F. W. Myers,
December 19, 1898, *Norton,* p. 112.)

Thus it is that James's very mastery consists in the denial and
in the deconstruction of his own mastery. Like the Master in his
story with respect to the children and to Bly, James assumes the
role of Master only through the act of claiming, with respect to
his literary "property," the "license," as he puts it, "of discon-
nexion and disavowal" (Preface to "The Golden Bowl," *AN,* p. 348).
Here as elsewhere, "mastery" turns out to be self-dispossession.

Dispossessing himself of his own story, James, more subtly still, at the same time dispossesses his own story of its master. But isn't this precisely what the Master does in *The Turn of the Screw,* when, dispossessing the governess of her Master (himself), he gives her nothing less than "supreme authority"? It is with "supreme authority" indeed that James, in deconstructing his own mastery, vests his reader. But isn't this gift of supreme authority bestowed upon the reader as upon the governess the very thing that will precisely *drive them mad?*

That one should, as an author, *reduce one's reader* (...) *to such a state of hallucination* by the images one has evoked (...) — nothing could better consort than *that* (...) with the desire or the pretention to cast a literary spell. (Preface to "The Golden Bowl," *AN,* p. 332.)

It is because James's mastery consists in knowing that mastery as such is but a *fiction,* that James's law as master, like that of the Master of *The Turn of the Screw,* is a law of flight and of *escape.* [66] It is, however, through his escape, through his *disappearance* from the scene, that the Master in *The Turn of the Screw,* in effect, *becomes a ghost.* And indeed it could be said that James himself becomes a phantom master, a Master-Ghost *par excellence* in terms of his own definition of a ghost:

Very little appears to be [*done*] — *by the persons appearing;* (...) This *negative quantity* is large — (...). Recorded and attested "ghosts" are in other words (...), above all, *as little continuous and conscious and responsive,* as is consistent with their taking the trouble — and an immense trouble they find it, we gather — to appear at all. (The New York Preface, p. 121.)

Now, to state that the Master has become himself a ghost is once again to repeat the very statement of *The Turn of the Screw:* there are *letters* from the moment there is no Master to receive them—or to *read* them: letters exist because a Master ceases to exist. We could indeed advance this statement as a definition of

[66] Cf. "Our noted behaviour at large may show for ragged, because it perpetually *escapes our control;* we have again and again to consent to its appearing in undress — that is, in no state to brook criticism." "It rests altogether with himself [the artist] not to (...) 'give away' his importances." (*AN,* p. 348)

Shoshana Felman

literature iself, a definition implicated and promoted by the practice
of Henry James: literature (the very literality of letters) is nothing
other than the Master's death, the Master's transformation into a
ghost, insofar as that death and that transformation define and
constitute, precisely, *literality* as such; literality as that which is
essentially impermeable to analysis and to interpretation, that which
necessarily remains unaccounted for, that which, with respect to
what interpretation does account for, constitutes no less than *all
the rest:* "All the rest is literature," writes Verlaine. [67] "The rest,"
says the dying artist in James's novel *The Middle Years,* "the rest
is the madness of art": the *rest,* or literality, that which will forever make us *dupe,* insofar as the very knowledge it conveys but
cannot know, the knowledge which *our* knowledge cannot integrate,
dispossesses us both of our mastery and of our Master. "That all
texts see their literality increase," writes Lacan, "in proportion to
what they properly imply of an actual confrontation with truth, is
that for which Freud's discovery demonstrates the structural reason"
(*Écrits,* p. 364). To quote James again:

It's not that the muffled majesty of authorship doesn't here *ostensibly* *
reign; but I catch myself again shaking it off and disavowing the pretence
of it while I get down into the arena and do my best to live and breathe
and rub shoulders and converse with the persons engaged in the struggle
that provides for the others in the circling tiers the entertainment of
the great game. There is no other participant, of course, than each of the
real, the deeply involved and immersed and more or less bleeding
participants. (Preface to "The Golden Bowl," *AN,* p. 328; * James's italics.)

The deeply involved and immersed and more or less bleeding participants are here indeed none other than the members of the "circle
round the fire" which we ourselves have joined. As the fire within
the letter is reflected on our faces, we see the very madness of our
own art staring back at us. In thus mystifying us so as to demystify
our errors and our madness, it is we ourselves that James makes
laugh—and bleed. The joke is indeed on us; the worry, ours.

[67] "Il faut aussi que tu n'ailles point/ Choisir tes mots sans quelque
méprise/ Rien de plus cher que la chanson grise/ Où l'Indécis au Précis se
joint/ (...) Et tout le reste est littérature." (P. Verlaine, *Art Poétique*)

Gayatri Chakravorty Spivak

The Letter as Cutting Edge

If one project of psychoanalytical criticism is to "submit to this test [of the status of speaking] a certain number of the statements of the philosophic tradition," [1] the American common critic might well fix her glance upon Chapters Twelve and Thirteen of Samuel Taylor Coleridge's *Biographia Literaria*. These two chapters are invariably interpreted as an important paradigmatic statement of the union of the subject and object in the act of the mind, of the organic Imagination, and the autonomous self. Over the last fifty years New Criticism—the line of I. A. Richards, William Empson, and then of Brooks, Ransom, Tate, and Wimsatt has "founded [itself] on the implicit assumption that literature is an autonomous activity of the mind." [2] It is not surprising that this School, which has given America the most widely accepted ground rules of literary pedagogy, is also often a running dialogue with the Coleridge who is taken to be the prophet of the sovereign subject. I quote a passage from Richards, as he proposes to discuss Chapters Twelve and Thirteen: "In beginning now to expound Coleridge's theory of the Imagination, I propose to start where he himself in the *Biographia* . . . really started: that is, with a theory of the act of knowledge, or of consciousness, or, as he called it, 'the coincidence or coalescence of an OBJECT with a SUBJECT'." [3]

[1] Jacques Lacan, "A Jakobson," *Le Séminaire de Jacques Lacan,* ed. Jacques-Alain Miller, Livre XX, *Encore* (1972-1973), Paris, 1975, p. 25. All references to Lacan are in my translation.

[2] Paul de Man, "Form and Intent in the American New Criticism," *Blindness and Insight: Essays in the Rhetoric of Contemporary Criticism,* New York, 1971, p. 21.

[3] Ivor Armstrong Richards, *Coleridge on Imagination,* Indiana University Press, Bloomington, 1960, p. 44. On Coleridge's central role in propagating "organistic formalism," the received opinion is nicely stated in the passage below: "This organistic formalism has many antecedents: it started in Germany late in the eighteenth century and came to England

Gayatri Chakravorty Spivak

The testing of these two chapters of the *Biographia* by the American common critic by the rules of new psychoanalysis is therefore not without a certain plausibility, not to say importance. As I describe that testing, I shall imply its ideology—an ideology of "applying" in critical practice a "theory" developed under other auspices, and of discovering an analogy to the task of the literary critic in any interpretative situation inhabiting any "science of man." At the end of this essay, I shall comment on that ideology more explicitly. For reasons that should become clear as the essay progresses, I shall make no attempt to "situate" Coleridge within an intellectual set, nor deal with the rich thematics of his so-called "plagiarisms."

The *Biographia Literaria* is Coleridge's most sustained and most important theoretical work. It is also a declared autobiography. The critic who has attended to the main texts of the new psychoanalysis has learned that any act of language is made up as much by its so-called substance as by the cuts and gaps that substance serves to frame and/or stop up: "We can conceive of the shutting [*fermeture*] of the unconscious by the action of something which plays the role of diaphragm-shutter [*obturateur*]—the object *a,* sucked and breathed in, just where the trap begins." [4] These problematics might play interestingly in a declared autobiography such as Coleridge's. Armed with this insight, the critic discovers, in Coleridge's text, logical and rhetorical slips and dodges, and what looks very much like a narrative *obturateur*. The text is so packed, and so thoroughly commented upon, that here I outline the simplest blueprint of these moments.

The entire *Biographia* inhabits the narrative structure of *pre*monition and *post*ponement (today we might say difference—

with Coleridge. ... Coleridge, Croce, and French symbolism are the immediate antecedents of modern English and American so-called New Criticism." René Wellek, *Concepts of Criticism,* ed. Stephen G. Nichols, Jr., New Haven and London, 1963, p. 354.

[4] Lacan, "Analyse et vérité," *Séminaire,* ed. Miller, Livre XI, *Les quatre concepts fondamentaux de la psychanalyse* (1964), Paris, 1973, p. 132. The discrepancy between the object *a* and the unconscious is contained in Lacan's optic metaphor, which accomodates the idea of the *angle* of incidence.

certainly avoidance *and* longing) that so many Romantic works share. "Intended in the first place as a preface to the *Sibylline Leaves* (a collection of poems), it grew into a literary autobiography, which came to demand a preface. This preface itself outgrew its purposed limits, and was incorporated in the whole work, which was finally issued in two parts—the autobiography (two vols.) and the poems." [5]

The *Biographia Literaria*, then, is not a bona fide book at all, for it was intended only as a preface, pointing to what would come after it. Only because it failed in its self-effacing task did it become a full-fledged book. Even as such it is un-well-made, for, among other reasons, it contains within it its own failed preface. One cannot situate the book in its own place. It looks forward to its promise and backward at its failure and, in a certain way, marks its own absence: autobiography by default, prefaces grown monstrous. And, even beyond this, the work as it stands is often still presented as a preface: "In the third treatise of my Logosophia," never to be written "announced at the end of this volume, I shall give (deo volente) the demonstrations and constructions of the Dynamic Philosophy scientifically arranged" (179-180). "Be assured, however," Coleridge writes to himself, "that I look forward anxiously to your great book on the CONSTRUCTIVE PHILOSOPHY, which you have promised and announced" (200).

The narrative declaration of the status of the *Biographia Literaria* is thus deliberately evasive, the writing reminder of a gap. Within such a framework, the celebrated chapter on Imagination (XIII) declares its own version of absence. Coleridge tells us that the burden of argumentation in that chapter has been supressed at the request of a friend, (who is, as is well-known, "a figment of Coleridge's imagination," another way of saying "Coleridge himself": "Thus far had the work been transcribed for the press, when I received the following letter from a friend, whose practical judg-

[5] "Introduction," Samuel Taylor Coleridge, *Biographia Literaria*, ed. J. Shawcross, London, 1907, Vol. 1 (hereafter cited in the text by page reference alone), p. lv.

ment I have had ample reason to estimate and revere.... In consequence of this very judicious letter, ... I shall content myself for the present with stating the main result of the Chapter, which I have reserved for that future publication, a detailed prospectus of which the reader will find at the close of the second volume [a fruitless promise]" (198, 201-202).

It would perhaps be more precise to say that the chapter declares its own inaccessibility rather than its proper absence. For it is supposed to exist, and Coleridge's friend, its privileged reader, has read it, but, *because the* BIOGRAPHIA *is an autobiography and a preface,* it must be suppressed: "For who, he [your reader] might truly observe," Coleridge's "friend" observes, "could from your title-page, viz. '*My* Literary Life and Opinions,' published too as introductory to a volume of miscellaneous poems, have anticipated, or even conjectured, a long treatise on ideal Realism..." (200-201). We are assured of the chapter's massy presence in the least refutable way; in terms of money and numbers of pages: "I do not hesitate in advising and urging you to withdraw the Chapter from the present work.... This chapter, which cannot, when it is printed, amount to so little as a hundred pages, will of necessity greatly increase the expense of the work" (200). Those paragraphs, beginning "The IMAGINATION then, I consider," that have been quoted so frequently as "Coleridge's theory of the Imagination," are merely "the main result of the Chapter, which I have reserved [held back] for the future publication, a detailed prospectus [which looks forward] of which the reader will find at the close of the second volume" (201-202).

The greatest instrument of narrative refraction in these chapters, the *obturateur,* if you like, is, of course, the letter that stops publication of the original Chapter Thirteen. The gesture is about as far as possible from "the eternal act of creation in the infinite I AM," (202) the most abundantly quoted Coleridgean formula, descriptive of the primary Imagination. It is a written message to oneself represented as being an external interruption. And, the critic cannot forget that it is this that is presented *in the place* of the organic process and growth of the argument leading to the celebrated conclusions about the nature of the sovereign imagination. Why should a *false* disowning (since the letter is by Coleridge after all) of the name of the self as author, a *false* declaration of the power of another, inhabit the place of the greatest celebration of the self? It is a question that her psychoanalytical studies have prepared our critic to ask.

"I see clearly that you have done too much and yet not enough," Coleridge writes to Coleridge. In these chapters, in addition to the general *narrative* motif of declared and stopped-up vacancy, the reader encounters this particular sort of *rhetorical* oscillation between a thing and its opposite, sometimes displacing that opposition (as here, what is too much is presumably what is not enough, the two can never of course be *the same*), which artfully suggests the absence of the thing itself, at the same time, practically speaking and thanks to the conventions of rhetoric, suggesting its presence. The typical hiding-in-disclosure, the signifier creating "the effect of the signified" by rusing anticipation—that psychoanalysis has taught her to recognize. Here are some of these rhetorical gestures.

Consider the title of Chapter Twelve. "Requests"—looking forward to a future result—and "premonitions"—knowing the result beforehand, concerning the "perusal" *or* "omission" of "the chapter that follows." The first two pages are taken up with "understanding a philosopher's ignorance" *or* being "ignorant of his understanding." The connection between this and what follows is not immediately clear in the text. The distinction seems to be invoked simply to reinforce the rhetorical oscillation. We move next to the request that the reader "will either pass over the following chapter altogether, *or* read the whole connectedly" (162). Even if we overlook the fact that Coleridge will set up numerous obstacles to reading these chapters *connectedly,* and that this request is advanced not in its own proper place, but *"in lieu of* the various requests which the anxiety of authorship addresses to the unknown reader," (162) we might quite justifiably ask, "which following chapter?" Chapter

Twelve, the chapter that has just begun and will immediately follow, or Chapter Thirteen, the chapter that comes *after* this one? I am not suggesting, of course, that common-sensically, we cannot make our choice; but that rhetorically, the request seems to blur the possibility of the presence of the matter under discussion.

Upon the rhetoric of oscillation, Coleridge now imposes the rhetoric of condition. He tells us what kind of reader he does *not* want. "If a man receives as fundamental fact, ... the general notions of matter, spirit, soul, body, action, passiveness, time, space, cause and effect, consciousness, perception, memory and habit," et cetera, et cetera, "to such a mind I would as courteously as possible convey the hint, that for him this chapter was not written" (163). After this sentence, with its significant breakdown in parallelism once it gets to "cause and effect," Coleridge plunges into the language of "more and less" where, if we read closely, we will see that the "not more difficult is it to reduce them" and the "still less dare a favorable perusal be anticipated" do not match: "Taking [these terms] therefore in mass, and unexamined, it requires only a decent apprenticeship in logic, to draw forth their contents in all forms and colours, as the professors of legerdemain at our village fairs pull out ribbon after ribbon from their mouths. And not more difficult is it to reduce them back again to their different genera. ... Still less dare a favorable perusal be anticipated from the proselytes of that compendious philosophy..." (163) The rhetoric of "more and less" is there to beguile us. In itself a device to announce the absence of a thing in its proper measure, here deflected and defective, it leads us into further dissimulative plays of presence and absence.

"But," writes Coleridge in the next paragraph, "it is time to tell the truth." A negative truth, presented in halting alternatives: "it is neither possible or necessary for all men, or for many, to be PHILOSOPHERS" (164). After this divisive move, Coleridge leaves the place of spontaneous consciousness vacant of or inaccessible to human knowledge: "we divide all the objects of human knowledge into those on this side, and those on the other side of the spontaneous consciousness" (164).

Coleridge then assumes what is recognizably the language of philosophical exposition. And here the reader repeatedly meets what must be called logical slippages.

In Chapter Twelve, simply breaking ground for the grand demonstration of Chapter Thirteen, Coleridge submits that "there are two cases equally possible. EITHER THE OBJECTIVE IS TAKEN AS THE FIRST, ... OR THE SUBJECTIVE IS TAKEN AS THE FIRST." For "the conception of nature does not apparently involve the co-presence of an intelligence making an ideal duplicate of it, i.e. representing it" (175). So far so good. Yet a few pages later, Coleridge designates the ground of the first alternative as prejudice, and that of the second simply as ground. The reason being one of compulsion; otherwise thought disappears.

THAT THERE EXIST THINGS WITHOUT US ... remains proof against all attempts to remove it by grounds or arguments ... the philosopher therefore *compels himself* to treat this faith as nothing more than a prejudice ... The other position ... is groundless indeed. ... It is groundless; but only because it is itself the ground of all other certainty. Now the apparent contradiction ... the transcendental philosopher *can solve only* by the supposition ... that it is not only coherent but identical ... with our own immediate self-consciousness (178; italics mine).

Upon this fundamental, compulsive, and necessary desire, the philosopher's desire for coherence and the possibility of knowledge—the desire for the One, Coleridge lays the cornerstone of his argument. And then suggests that to demonstrate the identity of the two positions presented in the passage above is "the office and object of philosophy!" (175-178). An office and object, as the reader sees in the next chapter, that can only be performed by deferment and dissimulation.

Indeed, in this section of Chapter Twelve, Coleridge is preparing us systematically for the analysis of Chapter Thirteen, the chapter to come, and giving us the terms for its analysis—a chapter which he warns most of us against reading, and which is not going to be there for any of us to read anyway. And all through Chapter Twelve, Coleridge grapples with the most patent contradiction in his theory:

The possible priority of the object must be rejected out of hand and the identity of the subject and object, although it may be seen as no more than a compulsive project, must be presented as the theorem of philosophy. This "identity" is itself an infinite and primary property of self-*representation* and self-*signification,* both concepts that are constituted by separation from the self. Yet, despite all this, the identity must be seamless. Now this is of course not a contingency peculiar to Coleridge. If confronted at random with "mind is only what it does, and its act is to make itself the object of its own consciousness," who would assign a proper author?

In the passage I cited above Coleridge comes close to suggesting that the driving force of the philosopher's project is desire. Elsewhere Coleridge will not openly declare that the force that would bring the object and the subject, as well as the divided ground of the self, into unity, is also desire, a desire that Lacan will analyze into the desire of the other and the desire to produce the other as well as to appropriate the other, the object, the object-substitute, as well as the image of the subject or subjects—a play of all that masquerades as the "real." Yet Coleridge's desire for unitary coherence seems constantly to be betrayed by a discourse of division. First the division between a principle and its manifestation. "This principle [of identity] manifests itself..." (183). The manifestation of identity is itself given in *two* pieces, not one, connected by an alternative, supported by the possibility of translation, which would contradict its uniqueness, and, given the multiplicity of languages, would make it in principle open-ended. The first piece is the Latin word *sum,* suggesting on the page its English graphic equivalent: "sum." Its translated substitute breaks the unitary sum into two: "I am." "This principle, and so characterized, manifests itself in the SUM or I AM."

Soon Coleridge neatly turns the table. A few pages back, as we have noticed, he was suggesting that the objective and the subjective positions are alternatives, and "to demonstrate their identity is the office and object of... philosophy." Now, with the most sweeping of intermediate steps, and certainly nothing like a demonstration, Coleridge asserts: "It may be described *therefore* as a perpetual Self-duplication of *one and the same power* into object and subject" (183). The following THESIS, punctuated by "therefores" and "it follows"-es, does not in fact depend upon or look forward to proofs presented in the text, and is stated with such uncharged assurance that it has all the force of law:

> for herein consists the essence of a spirit, that it is self-representative. ... It must follow that the spirit in all the objects which it views, views only itself. ... It has been shown, that a spirit is that, which is its own object, yet not originally an object, but an absolute subject for which all, itself included, may become an object. It must therefore be an ACT. ... Again the spirit ... must in some sense dissolve this identity [of subject and object], in order to be conscious of it. ... But this implies an act, and it follows therefore that intelligence or self-consciousness is impossible, except by and in a will. ... Freedom must be assumed as a *ground* of philosophy, and can never be deduced from it (184-185).

In all this barrage of compulsive argumentation, one tends to forget what is written three pages before, where Coleridge describes the strategy of the imagination that might produce such arguments:

> Equally *inconceivable* is a cycle of equal truths without a common and central principle. ... That the absurdity does not so immediately strike us, that it does not seem equally *unimaginable,* is owing to a surreptitious act of the imagination, which, instinctively and without our noticing the same, not only fills up the intervening spaces, and contemplates the *cycle* ... as a continuous *circle* giving to all collectively the unity of their common orbit; but likewise supplies ... the one central power, which renders the movement harmonious and cyclical (181).

Does it help our critic to speculate that the instinctive, surreptitious, and unnoticed imagination, filling up the gaps in the centerless cycle of equal—infinitely substitutable—truths, each signifying the next and vice versa, might follow the graph that Lacan has plotted in "La Subversion du sujet et la dialectique du désir?" Would Coleridge have welcomed Lacan's notion of the *points de capiton*—quilting buttons: "by means of which the signifier stops the otherwise indefinite sliding of signification?" [6]

[6] Lacan, "La Subversion," *Écrits,* Paris, 1966, p. 805.

Gayatri Chakravorty Spivak

The critic cannot know the answer to that question. But she can at least see that for Coleridge, if the controlling imagination or self-consciousness is not taken as performing its task of fixing those conditions of intelligibility, what results is chaos, infinite way-stations of sliding signification. Coleridge, in an older language, calls this fixing or stabilizing the location of ground. "Even when the Objective is assumed as the first, we yet can never pass beyond the principle of self-consciousness. Should we attempt it, we must be driven back from ground to ground, each of which would cease to be a Ground the moment we pressed on it. We must be whirl'd down the gulf of an infinite series." But whereas Lacan or Derrida would see the protective move against such a threat as simply that, and perhaps as a "characteristic" of text or subject, Coleridge speaks of it in the language of necessity and norm:

But this would make our reason baffle the end and purpose of all reason, namely, unity and system. Or we must break off the series arbitrarily, and affirm an absolute something that is in and of itself at once cause and effect..., subject and object, or rather the identity of both. *But as this is inconceivable, except in a self-consciousness, it follows* ... that ... we arrive at ... a self-consciousness in which the principium essendi does not stand to the principium cognoscendi in the relation of cause to effect, but both the one and the other are co-inherent and identical (187).

Here Coleridge glosses over the possibility that if the principle of being (essence, truth) is not the cause of the principle of knowing, the two principles might very well be discontinuous rather than identical, simply on the ground that such a discontinuity would be "inconceivable." But in an argument about knowing and being, inconceivability and unreasonableness are not argument enough. One must allow the aporia to emerge. Especially since, a page earlier, Coleridge had excused himself precisely on the ground of the difference, rather than the identity, between these two principles: "We are not investigating an absolute principium essendi; for then, I admit, many valid objections might be started against our theory; but an absolute principium cognoscendi" (186). The difference—at the sensible frontier of truth and knowledge[7]—that must be covered over by an identity worries Coleridge.

And it is this gap between knowing and being that the episode of the imaginary letter occludes. At the end of Chapter Twelve, Coleridge invokes, in a sentence that seems strangely unrelated to the rest of the page, an overtly theological rather than merely logical authority for thinking unity rather than difference: "I will conclude with the words of Bishop Jeremy Taylor: he to whom all things are one, who draweth all things to one, and seeth all things in one, may enjoy true peace and rest of spirit" (194). But by the end of Thirteen, the imaginary friend, the self's fiction, takes the place of God's instrument, the good Bishop. A fallen discourse of "being as mere existence," the autobiographical anecdote, a letter from the world of others, interrupts the discourse of knowing, and prevents the movement whereby its presentation would (if it could) be identical with its proof, and halts on a promise: a promise to read and to write.

A reader of Lacan can interpret this textual gesture yet another way: the eruption of the Other onto the text of the subject. Read this way, what is otherwise seen as merely an interruption of the development of the *argument* about the imagination may not only be seen as a keeping alive, by unfulfillment, of the desire that moves the argument, but also as the ruse that makes possible the establishment of the *Law* of the imagination. The author's friend, the self split and disguised as the Other, can in this view be called the "Legislator," he who at once dictates the author's course of action and makes it possible for the law to be erected. Seeking to bring his text to the appropriate conclusion—the ex cathedra paragraphs on the Imagination—the subject in this view must ask the Other (no longer the object but what seems another subject) "What is your wish?" (My wish is that you should suppress this chapter.) "By means of which is yet more marked than revealed the true function of the Father which at bottom is to unite (and

[7] *Ibid.*, p. 795.

not to oppose) a desire to the Law." [8] Coleridge's text desires to be logically defective and yet be legislative. The path to such conclusions as "the IMAGINATION, then ..." and so forth, is paved with logical dissimulation. By demanding that the path be effaced, the Lawgiver allows the unacknowledgeable desire to be united with the Law (rather than the argument, which is the text's ostensible desire) of the Imagination. The richness of the text is increased when we realize that the Law in question is not any law, but the Law of the sovereignty of the Self, and that Coleridge's text narrates this legislation in terms of an author who, rusingly, "fathers" the Legislator rather than vice versa, and that that fathering is disavowed. A labyrinth of mirrors here ...

In Coleridge our critic seems confronted with an exemplum. Mingling the theory and the narrative of the subject, Coleridge's text seems to engage most profitably with the work of the new psychoanalysis. The double-edged play of the desire for a unitarian theory and a desire for discontinuity seems accessible to that work.

If our critic does follow the ideology I have predicted for her, she will proceed to search through the basic texts of Lacan for the meaning of her reading, and realize that she has related Coleridge's chapters to the two great psychoanalytic themes: castration and the Imaginary, the second specifically articulated by Lacan.

Although inevitably positioned and characterized by its place in the "symbolic" world of discourse, the subject nonetheless desires to touch the "real" world by constructing object-images or substitutes of that "real" world and of itself. This is the place of the Imaginary, and, according to Lacan, all philosophical texts show us its mark. "In all that is elaborated of being and even of essence, in Aristotle for example, we can see, reading it in terms of the analytic experience, that it is a question of the object *a*." [9] Coleridge, by declaring carefully that he will write on knowing, not being, does not seem to have escaped that mark. For all discourse, including

[8] *Ibid.*, p. 824.
[9] "Le Savoir et la vérité," *Encore,* p. 87.

the authors of discourses, are discourses of being in a certain way, and must therefore harbor the fascinating antagonist of discourse, the production of the Imaginary. Hence Lacan's question: "Is to have the *a*, to be?" [10]

The "friend" who shares in the responsibility of authorship might be a specular (thus objectified) as well as a discursive (thus subjectivized) image of the subject. "The *I* is not a being, it is a presupposition with respect to that which speaks." [11] "That subject which believes it can have access to [or accede to] itself by being designated in a statement [*énoncé*], is nothing other than such an object. Ask the person inflicted with the anguish of the white page, he will tell you who is the turd of his fantasy." [12]

That curious detail in the "friend's" letter that suddenly describes the missing chapter in terms of money and number of pages and reduces the great thought on thought to a massy thing also fits into these thematics. Lacan says again and again that the imaginary is glimpsed only through its moments of contact with the symbolic. That sentence in the letter might indeed be such a moment.

The letter as a whole is the paradigm of the "symbolic," a message conveyed in language—a collection of signifiers, a representative signifier, if such a thing can be said. As we have seen, it halts the fulfillment of the author's apparent desire to present the complete development of his theory of the Imagination, even as it encourages and promises further writing and reading. It is an instrument with a cutting edge.

The critic knows that, in psychoanalytic vocabulary, all images of a cutting that gives access to the Law is a mark of castration. It is the cut in Coleridge's discourse that allows the Law to spring forth full-fledged. The removal of the phallus allows the phallus

---

[10] *Ibid.*, p. 91. My deliberately clumsy translation tries to, but does not quite catch the play in French: both, "Is to have the *a*, being?" and, "Is to have the *a*, to be the *a*?" The (sup)posing of the subject for the subject relates to what is in question in Coleridge's text here.

[11] "Ronds de ficelle," *Ibid.*, p. 109.

[12] "Subversion," *Écrits*, p. 818.

to emerge as the signifier of desire. "Castration means that, in order to attain pleasure on the reversed scale of the Law of desire, [orgasmic] pleasure [*jouissance*] must be refused." [13] As subsequent critical reception of Coleridge has abundantly demonstrated, the letter, by denying the full elaboration of a slippery argument, has successfully articulated the grand conclusion of Chapter Thirteen with what came before. Thus is castration, as a psychoanalytic concept, both a lack and an enabling: "let us say of castration that it is the absent peg which joins the terms in order to construct a series or a set or, on the contrary, it is the hiatus, the cleavage that marks the separation of elements among themselves." [14]

*

As American common critics read more and more of the texts of the new psychoanalysis, and follow the ideology of application-by-analogy, exegeses like this one will proliferate. [15] And so will gestures of contempt and caution against such appropriations by critics closer to the French movement. I propose at this point to make a move toward neutralizing at once the appropriating confidence of the former and the comforting hierarchization of the latter and ask what this sort of use of a psychoanalytic vocabulary in literary criticism might indeed imply.

It is conceivable that a psychoanalytic reading of a literary text is bound to plot the narrative of a psychoanalytic scenario in the production of meaning, using a symbological lexicon and a structural diagram. Literary critics with more than the knowledge of the field allowed our whipping-girl, as well as the great psychoanalysts using literature as example seem to repeat this procedure. As a matter of fact, Freud on *The Sand-Man*, or Lacan on "The Purloined Letter"

---

[13] *Ibid.*, p. 827. I am moved by Derrida's argument, general rather than psychoanalytic, for rewriting the thematics of castration as the thematics of the hymen ("La double séance," *La Dissémination*, Paris, 1972) or of "anthérection" (*Glas*, Paris, 1974). But since this essay is the story of a common critic armed with a specifically psychoanalytic vocabulary, I do not broach that re-inscription here.

[14] Serge Leclaire, *Psychanalyser*, Paris, 1968, pp. 184-185.

[15] For a typical reading that has not been alerted to the importance of letters and cuttings, see Owen Barfield, *What Coleridge Thought*, Middletown, Connecticut, 1971, pp. 26-27.

are more than most aware of this bind. The tropological or narratological crosshatching of a text, given a psychoanalytic description, can be located as stages in the unfolding of the psychoanalytic scenario. There are a few classic scenarios, the most important in one view being the one our critic has located in Coleridge: the access to law through the interdict of the father—the passage into the semiotic triangle of Oedipus: "The stake [setting into play—en jeu] of analysis is nothing else—to recognize what function the subject assumes in the order of symbolic relations which cover the entire field of human relations, and whose initial cell is the Oedipus complex, where the adoption of one's sex is decided." [16]

To plot such a narrative is to uncover the text's intelligibility (even at the extreme of showing how textuality keeps intelligibility forever at bay), with the help of psychoanalytic discourse, at least provisionally to satisfy the critic's desire for mastery through knowledge, even to suggest that the critic as critic has a special, if not privileged, knowledge of the text that the author either cannot have, or merely articulates. The problematics of transference, so important to Freud and Lacan, if rigorously followed through, would dismiss such a project as trivial, however it redefines the question of hermeneutic value. Lacan explains the transference-relationship in terms of the Hegelian master-slave dialectic, where both master and slave are defined and negated by each other. And of the desire of the master—here analyst or critic—Lacan writes: "Thus the desire of the master seems, from the moment it comes into play in history, the most off-the-mark term by its very nature." [17]

What allows the unconscious of patient and analyst to play is not the desire of the master but the production of transference, interpreted by master *and* slave as being intersubjective. Lacan

---

[16] Lacan, "Analyse du discours et analyse du moi," *Séminaire,* ed. Miller, Livre I, *Les Écrits techniques de Freud* (1953-1954), Paris, 1975, p. 80. Again, our critic would probably not enter into the sweeping commentary-critique of the position implied by Lacan's remark launched by Gilles Deleuze and Felix Guattari in *L'Anti-Oedipe: capitalisme et schizophrénie,* Paris, 1972, or by schizo-analysis in general.

[17] "De l'interprétation au transfert," *Quatre concepts,* p. 230.

cautions as much against a misunderstanding of transference as he emphasizes its importance in analysis. It is not a simple displacement or identification that the neutral analyst manipulates with care. He is as much surrendered to the process of transference as the patient. The analyst can neither know nor ignore his own desire within that process: "Transference is not the putting into action that would push us to that alienating identification which all conformization constitutes, even if it were to an ideal model, of which the analyst in any case could not be the support."[18] "As to the handling of transference, my liberty, on the other hand, finds itself alienated by the doubling that my self suffers there, and everyone knows that it is there that the secret of analysis should be looked for."[19]

I do not see how literary criticism can do more than *decide* to deny its desire as master, nor how it can not attend to the conditions of intelligibility of a text. The text of criticism is of course surrendered to the play of intelligibility and unintelligibility, but its decisions can never be more self-subversive than to question the status of intelligibility, or be more or less deliberately playful. Even when it is a question of isolating "something irreducible, *nonsensical,* that functions as the originally repressed signifier," the analyst's function is to give that irreducible signifier a "significant interpretation." "It is not because I have said that the effect of interpretation is to isolate in the subject a heart, a *Kern,* to use Freud's expression, of *non-sense,* that interpretation is itself a nonsense."[20] As Serge Leclaire stresses in *Psychoanalyser,* the psychoanalyst cannot get around the problem of reference. On the other hand, it seems to me important that, in the service of intelligibility, using a text as the narrative of a scenario or even the illustration of a principle, the new psychoanalysis would allow us to doubt the status, precisely, of the intelligence, the meaning of knowledge, the knowledge of meaning. "As it [the Hegelian dialectic] is deduced, it can only be the conjunction of the symbolic with a real from

[18] "Analyse et vérité," *Quatre concepts*, p. 133.
[19] "La direction de la cure," *Écrits*, p. 588.
[20] "De l'interprétation," *Quatre concepts*, p. 226.

which there is nothing more to be expected. ... This eschatological excursion is there only to designate what a yawning chasm separates the two relations, Freudian and Hegelian, of the subject to knowledge." [21]

Like philosophical criticism, psychoanalytical criticism of this sort is in the famous double bind. All precautions taken, literary criticism *must* operate as if the critic is responsible for the interpretation, and, to a lesser extent, as if the writer is responsible for the text. "If then psychoanalysis and philosophy both find themselves today obliged to break with 'sense,' to 'depart' radically from the epistemology of presence and consciousness, they both find themselves equally struggling with the difficulty (impossibility?) of placing their discourse on a level with their discoveries and their programs." [22] What can criticism do?—but *name* frontier concepts (with more or less sophistication) and thus grant itself a little more elbow room to write *intelligibly*: Bloom's Scene of Instruction, de Man's Irony, Kristeva's *chora,* Lacan's *réel.* Or try frontier styles: Lacan's Socratic seminars of the seventies, Derrida's "diphallic" *Glas,* and, alas, the general air of coyness in essays like this one. At least double-bind criticism, here using a psychoanalytic vocabulary, invites us to think—even as we timidly or boisterously question the value of such a specular invitation—that Coleridge was thus double-bound: Imagination his frontier-concept, the self-effacing/affecting literary (auto)biography his frontier style.

There is yet another angle to the appropriation of the idea of transference to the relationship between text and critic: "It is fitting here then, to scrutinize the fact—which is always dodged, and which is the reason rather than the excuse for transference—that nothing can be attained *in absentia, in effigie.* ... Quite on the contrary, the subject, in so far as it is subjected to the desire of the analyst, desires to deceive him through that subjection, by winning his affection, by himself proposing that essential duplicity [*fausseté*] which is love. The effect of transference is this effect of deceit

---

[21] "Subversion," *Écrits,* pp. 798, 802.
[22] Shoshana Felman, "La Méprise et sa chance," *L'Arc* 58 *(Lacan),* p. 46.

in so far as it is repeated at present here and now." [23] Philosophically naive as it may sound, it cannot be ignored that the book cannot think it speaks for itself in the same way as the critic. Now Jacques Derrida has shown carefully that the structure of "live" speech and "dead" writing are inter-substitutable. [24] But that delicate philosophical analysis should not be employed to provide an excuse for the will to power of the literary critic. After all, the general sense in which the text and the person share a common structure would make criticism itself absolutely vulnerable. And also, the meaning of the Derridean move, when written into critical practice, would mean, not equating or making analogical the psychoanalytic and literary-critical situation, or the situation of the book and its reader, but a perpetual deconstruction (reversal and displacement) of the distinction between the two. The philosophical rigor of the Derridean move renders it quite useless as a passport to psychoanalytic literary criticism.

Nor will the difference between text and person be conveniently effaced by refusing to talk about the psyche, by talking about the text as part of a self-propagating mechanism. The disjunctive, discontinuous metaphor of the subject, carrying and being carried by its burden of desire, does systematically misguide and constitute the machine of the text, carrying and being carried by its burden of "figuration." One cannot escape it by dismissing the former as the residue of a productive cut, and valorizing the latter as the only possible concern of a "philosophical" literary criticism. This opposition too, between subject "metaphor" and text "metaphor," needs to be indefinitely deconstructed rather than hierarchized.

And a psychoanalytic procedure, which supplements the category of substitution with the category of desire and vice versa, is a way to perform that deconstruction. The transference situation will never more than lend its aura to the practice of literary criticism. We know well that all critical practice will always be defeated by the

---

[23] "De l'interprétation," *Quatre concepts*, p. 229.
[24] Generally in the first part of *De la grammatologie*, Paris, 1967, and more specifically, apropos of Husserl, in *La Voix et le phénomène*, Paris, 1967, Chapter VII.

possibility that one might not know if knowledge is possible, by its own abyss-structure. But within our little day of frost before evening, a psychoanalytical vocabulary, with its charged metaphors, gives us a little more turning room to play in. If we had followed only the logical or "figurative" (as customarily understood) inconsistencies in Chapters Twelve and Thirteen of the *Biographia Literaria* we might only have seen Coleridge's prevarication. It is the thematics of castration and the Imagination that expose in it the play of the presence and absence, fulfillment and non-fulfillment of the will to Law. The psychoanalytical vocabulary illuminates Coleridge's declaration that the *Biographia* is an autobiography. The supplementation of the category of substitution by the category of desire within psychoanalytic discourse allows us to examine not only Coleridge's declaration but also our own refusal to take it seriously.

In the long run, then, the critic might have to admit that her gratitude to Dr. Lacan would be for so abject a thing as an instrument of intelligibility, a formula that describes the strategy of Coleridge's two chapters: "I ask you to refuse what I offer you because that is not it." [25]

[25] Lacan, "Ronds de ficelle," *Encore,* p. 114. The curious construction leads into the labyrinth by denying the very gift it offers. Need I mention that this formula — taken from one of Lacan's recent seminars — invokes the entire Lacanian thematics of the unconscious producing its own slippage as it positions the subject by the production of the sliding signifier? The *locus classicus* is still the much earlier "L'instance de la lettre dans l'inconscient ou la raison depuis Freud," *Écrits,* pp. 493-528 (translated by Jan Miel as "The Insistence of the Letter in the Unconscious," *Structuralism,* ed. Jacques Ehrmann, New York: Doubleday, 1970, pp. 101-137).

Roger Dragonetti

The Double Play of Arnaut Daniel's *Sestina* and Dante's *Divina Commedia*

S e s t i n a

1 Lo ferm voler q'el cor m'intra
2 no·m pot ies becs escoissendre ni ongla
3 de lausengier, qui pert per mal dir s'arma;
4 e car non l'aus batr'ab ram ni ab verga,
5 sivals a frau, lai on non aurai oncle,
6 iauzirai ioi, en vergier o dinz cambra.

II 7 Qan mi soven de la cambra
8 on a mon dan sai que nuills hom non intra
9 anz me son tuich plus que fraire ni oncle,
10 non ai membre no·m fremisca, neis l'ongla,
11 aissi cum fai l'enfas denant la verga:
12 tal paor ai no·l sia trop de l'arma.

III 13 Del cors li fos, non de l'arma,
14 e cossentis m'a celat dinz sa cambra!
15 Que plus mi nafra·l cor que colps de verga
16 car lo sieus sers lai on ill es non intra;
17 totz temps serai ab lieis cum carns et ongla,
18 e non creirai chastic d'amic ni d'oncle.

IV 19 Anc la seror de mon oncle
20 non amei plus ni tant, per aqest'arma!
21 C'aitant vezis cum es lo detz de l'ongla,
22 s'a liei plagues, volgr'esser de sa cambra;
23 de mi pot far l'amors q'inz el cor m'intra
24 mieills a son vol c'om fortz de frevol verga.

V 25 Pois flori la seca verga
26 ni d'en Adam mogron nebot ni oncle,
27 tant fin' amors cum cella q'el cor m'intra
28 non cuig fos anc en cors, ni eis en arma;
29 on q'ill estei, fors en plaz', o dins cambra,
30 mos cors no·is part de lieis tant cum ten l'ongla.

VI 31   C'aissi s'enpren e s'enongla
    32   mos cors en lei cum l'escorss' en la verga;
    33   q'ill n'es de ioi tors e palaitz e cambra,
    34   e non am tant fraire, paren ni oncle:
    35   q'en paradis n'aura doble ioi m'arma,
    36   si ia nuills hom per ben amar lai intra.

Envoi 37   Arnautz tramet sa chansson d'ongl'e d'oncle,
      38   a grat de lieis que de sa verg'a l'arma,
      39   son Desirat, cui pretz en cambra intra.

Author's Translation of the *Sestina* *

I   The firm desire which enters into my heart,/ no beak can break, nor nail/ of the slanderer-flatterer who through slander loses his soul./ And since I do not dare to beat him with branch or rod,/ at least, by fraud, there where I will have no uncle,/ I will enjoy the joy in a garden or in a chamber.

II   When I remember the chamber/ where, to my disadvantage, I know that no man enters,/ all being more hostile to me than brother and uncle,/ I do not have a limb which does not tremble, even up to the nail,/ like a child who dreads the rod/ I have such fear that my soul does not break.

III   That the body might break rather than the soul/ and that she might receive me secretly into her chamber./ And more than a blow from a rod it breaks my heart/ that her servant never enters there where she is./ I will always be with her as flesh and nail/ and will never listen to the remonstrance of friend or uncle.

IV   Never the sister of my uncle/ did I love as much with that soul./ As near as the finger is to the nail,/ if I pleased her, I would be to her chamber./ Love which enters into my heart can bend me at its will/ more than a strong man a frail rod.

V   Since the dry rod blossomed/ and from Adam descended nephews and uncles/ a love so pure as that which enters my heart,/ I believe, was never in body or in soul;/ wherever she might be,

---

* This English version is a translation of the author's French version of the Provençal original. For other translations or commentaries, see Frederick Goldin, *Lyrics of the Troubadours and Trouveres*, Garden City, N. Y.: Anchor-Doubleday, 1973, pp. 220-223; *Introduction à l'étude de l'ancien provençal*, F. R. Hamlin, P. T. Ricketts, and J. Hathaway, eds., Geneva: Droz, 1967, pp. 198-200; Arnaut Daniel, *Canzoni*, Gianluigi Toja, ed., Florence: Sansoni, 1960, pp. 373-385. (Tr.)

outside in the plaza or inside the chamber,/ my heart does not separate from there the space of a nail.

VI   For thus takes root and grips with the nail/ my heart in her like the bark on the rod/ because she is for me the tower, palace, and chamber of joy/ and I do not love brother or parent or uncle as much:/ in paradise my soul will have a double joy/ if ever someone, through loving well, enters there.

Envoi   Arnaut sends his song of nail and of uncle/ for the pleasure of her who has the soul through her rod,/ his Desired, whose worth enters the chamber.

Arnaut Daniel's fame is due in large part to the setting of the encounter between Dante and the Provençal poet in canto XXVI of *Purgatorio*. It is in this place, near the terrestrial paradise, that the troubadour—by virtue of being an exemplary character—illustrates a dimension of poetic language. Dante fixes, with one decisive stroke, the measure of Arnaut's work through the go-between of the poet Guido Guinizelli, who designates the troubadour as "a better craftsman of the mother tongue" (l. 117). [1]

In this episode, Arnaut expresses and names himself in Provençal: *Ieu sui Arnaut* (l. 142). One must note that by the effect of a homophony the author of the sacred poem brings about a very beautiful marriage of the name of the river of his native city, the Arno, and the name of the troubadour, Arnaut (pronounced Arnô). This osmosis between the two poetic idioms [2] permits Dante to reinforce his tie to the Provençal master. And is it not by way of a suggestion of the flow [*cours*] of water that there reaches us the lament of the troubadour "who, singing, weeps and follows his course (or his discourse)" *?

Ieu sui Arnaut, que plor e vau cantan (l. 142).

----

[1] Except where noted by an asterisk, English translations of passages from the *Divina Commedia* are taken from Charles S. Singleton's translation, *The Divine Comedy*, 3 vols., Princeton, N. J.: Princeton University Press, 1970-1975. — Tr.

[2] Concerning this subject, see our work, *Dante, pèlerin de la Sainte Face* (*Romanica Gandensia*, vol. XI), Ghent: Rijksuniversiteit te Gent, Faculteit der Letteren en Wijsbegeert, 1968, pp. 228-231.

This metaphor of the river, ascribed to the master's rhetoric, is moreover found again, explicitly formulated, in the homage which Dante renders Virgil: "Are you, then, that Virgil, that fount which pours forth so broad a stream of speech?" (*Inf.* I, 79-80).

The *De vulgari eloquentia* furnishes us with other evidence of Dante's admiration for the work of the Provençal master.[3] For Dante, Arnaut Daniel represents an illustrious model not only because the song *L'aur'amara* exemplifies—as a love song—one of the three arguments that one can treat in an illustrious vernacular; and, furthermore, not only because the song *Sols sui* offers the perfect example "of the highest construction"; but above all because, in the bulk of his songs, Arnaut adopts the undivided strophe called *coblas dissolutas* in Old Provençal.[4] Dante cites the song *Si 'm fos Amors de ioi donar tan larga* by way of example of this strophe.[5]

Now Dante pretends to have imitated this undivided strophe, of which Arnaut made great use, in his own sestina, *Al poco giorno e al gran cerchio d'ombra.*[6] Such a claim nevertheless surprises the reader a bit, by reason of the fact that the strophic structure of the song *Al poco giorno* ... does not entirely correspond to the form of the *coblas dissolutas* of the song which Dante pretends to imitate. On the other hand, it depends very precisely (as Marigo has observed) on the *retrogradatio cruciata* present in the only sestina which Arnaut Daniel composed, precisely that one which is the object of our study: *Lo ferm voler q'el cor m'intra.*[7] Indeed, as Marigo again notes, the strophic form used by the Provençal master in

---

[3] See the following passages in Aristides Marigo's edition (Florence: Lemonnier, 1938): II, ii, 1; II, vi, 6; II, xiii, 1-3. For the French translation, see the *Œuvres complètes*, André Pezard, ed., Paris: Gallimard (Bibliothèque de la Pléiade), 1965. (For the English translation, see *A Translation of the Latin Works of Dante Alighieri*, London: The Temple Classics, 1940, pp. 1-115. [Tr.]).

[4] Marigo, p. 264, n. 7.

[5] *Ibid.*, II, xiii, 1-3.

[6] The song *Al poco giorno* . . is part of a group of songs which are called, following Vittorio Imbriani, *Rime petrose*, for the reason that they celebrate a cruel woman assimilated, because of her hardness, to a stone. On this subject, see Gianfranco Contini's edition, in *Letteratura italiana delle origini*, Florence: Sansoni, 1970.

[7] Marigo, pl. 264, n. 7.

Roger Dragonetti

Lo ferm voler... is the only example of the strophe called *retrogradatio cruciata* which we know of in Arnaut Daniel and also in all troubadour lyrics.

Consequently, a question is raised. Why is it that Dante had preferred to connect openly his sestina *Al poco giorno...* to a common form (which he did not follow), while the true model, that is, the ignored sestina *Lo ferm voler...*, was certainly of a nature—given its exceptional character—to stimulate Dante's poetic instinct and his desire to be in his turn unique in the empire of literature?

Be that as it may, what is important here is that Dante not only became the imitator of Arnaut, but also issued a kind of challenge (perhaps not the only one) in composing, in addition to a sestina, a double sestina. [8]

These tokens of admiration are all the more impressive because they come from a poet who raised his own mother tongue to a very high degree of perfection. Thus one must ask oneself the reasons for this admiration. Why did the sestina retain the poet's attention so strongly, in preference to other poetic forms? Why did Dante accord to Arnaut the privilege of placing him at the summit of *Purgatorio* in order to close the series of poets of *la fin'amor*? For what reason, finally, does this encounter in the circle of Purgatory not give rise to any commentary on the part of Dante-persona?

It is understood that we do not in any manner have the pretention of surveying the question of the relations of Dante and Arnaut, [9] at least if "surveying" is taken in another sense than that of "searching." At the very most, it is a matter here of inquiring into one of the aspects of imitation.

We will first present an analysis of Arnaut Daniel's *Sestina,* taking into account certain analogies which it presents with the work of the Florentine poet.

[8] Cf. *Le rime,* CII, Gianfranco Contini, ed., Turin, 1965.
[9] Cf. Arnaut Daniel, *Canzoni,* Gianluigi Toja, ed., Florence: Sansoni, 1960, and especially his chapter, "Dante e Arnaut," pp. 65-99.

Numerous studies (to which we refer the reader) have been devoted to the metrical structure of the sestina, and they have rightly not failed to emphasize the technical virtuousity of the troubadour. [10] Without entering into the complexity of the structure, we can say that the *Sestina* is a poem composed of six strophes comprising six lines apiece, built on six rhyme words which displace themselves from strophe to strophe. As for the *envoi* which closes the poem, it is composed of three lines in which the six rhyme words return in pairs. These rhymes, presented in the first strophe in the order of succession of *intra, ongla, arma, verga, oncle, cambra,* come to undergo a rotational movement thanks to which each of them, beginning with the last, will wind up ending the first line of the successive strophes.

In order to obtain the order of succession from strophe to strophe, it will suffice to join the different rhymes of the strophe at hand according to a spiral movement which begins with the periphery:

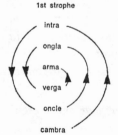

1st strophe

intra
ongla
arma
verga
oncle
cambra

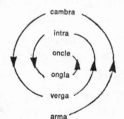

the order of succession of the 2nd strophe

cambra
intra
oncle
ongla
verga
arma

the order of the 3rd strophe (etc.)

arma

cambra

verga

intra

ongla

oncle

[10] *Ibid.,* "Versificazione e tecnica metrica di Arnaud — La sestina," pp. 50 ff.

Roger Dragonetti

In the total economy of the poem, this rhythm ends in the suppression of all hierarchy within the rhymes, and thus in a sort of
equality. In what follows we shall better see how this rhythm which
produces equivalences comes to repeat itself at other levels of reading, although already in the *envoi* the paired state of the rhymes
gives another figure to this parity.

In the meantime, there remains the fact that the rhyme *intra,*
which opens and closes the poem, enjoys a certain privilege with
regard to the others, if only because its status as a verb distinguishes it from the other five, which are all substantives. Moreover,
the verb *intrar,* "to enter," is susceptible of offering multiple possibilities of signification to the poet. Beginning with the common
Latin etymology which gives rise to the two Old Provençal forms,
intrar and *entrar,* as well as to the adverb and preposition *entre,*
one can imagine a play of interferences in their respective significations, that is to say, between the meaning of the verb which stands
for penetration, that of the adverb which expresses the space
between, and that of the preposition indicating distance within
proximity. We shall see the sestina invite us to take account of
these semantic slidings.

In Dante, the corresponding verb *intrare* undergoes a curious
transformation. With the insertion of a vowel, Dante coins a remarkable neologism *intrear* in order to designate the movement of
co-penetration which is unique to the *trinity (Par.* XIII, 57). In the
wake of this thought, the verb *internare* inscribes itself as well, by
which Dante expresses at once the interiorization of the eternal
light *(etterna)* and the *ternary* relation of the divinity:

> Nel suo profondo vidi che s'interna
> Legato con amore in un volume
> Ció che per l'universo si squaderno (*Par.,* XXXIII, 85-87);
>
> (In its depth I saw in-tern/in-trine/in-three itself,
> Bound by love in one volume,
> That which throughout the universe dis-quarto-es/dis-quire-s itself). *

If one takes into account the word *volume* which evokes the image
of rolling up of scrolls and of meaning, we find again in these lines,

in another form, the fundamental model of the rhythm of the un-folding and of the contracting of the six rhymes of the sestina, reduced practically to *three* in the *single* strophe of the *envoi*.

These initial considerations lead us to think that if the terza rima is the metrical form which best corresponds to the sacred poem, founded on the number 3, the sestina ought to be able to justify its form by way of the symbolism of the number six.

One knows the importance which arithmological discourses car-ried during the Middle Ages. Isidore of Seville considered the six to belong among the three perfect numbers (6, 28, 496) less than, respectively, 10, 100, and 1000. For they are in fact the only ones which have the power to reconstitute the original number by way of the sum of their divisors. Thus for the six: $1 + 2 + 3 = 6$.[11] If something analogous to this can be said of the *Sestina,* it could be that its metrical form corresponds to an integral order of the word.

Very curiously, Dante seems to have taken account of the per-fection of the number six in calculating the manifestation of the poetic word and the divine word in the *Divina Commedia.* Let us refer to "the fair school" of the circle of Limbo. Virgil indicates to Dante the four most illustrious poets of antiquity: Homer, Ho-race, Ovid, and Lucan. Greeted by the noble company, Dante de-clares himself to be "sixth amid so much wisdom": *Si ch'io fui sesto fra cotanto senno* (*Inf.* IV, 95).

In this same episode, the name of *altissimo poeta* [great poet] which "a single voice has uttered" goes to Virgil and "to each of these poets":

---

[11] Isidore of Seville, *Etymologiae,* vol. I, W. M. Lindsay, ed., Oxford: Clarendon Press, 1911, III, v, 11: "Perfectus numerus est, qui suis partibus adinpletur, ut senarius: habet enim tres partes, sextam, tertiam et dimidiam: sexta eius unum est, tertia duo, dimidia tres. Haec partes in summam ductae, id est unum et dua et tria simul eundem consummant perfeciuntque senarium. Sunt autem perfecti numeri intra denarium VI, intra centenarium XXVIII, intra millenarium CCCCXCVI." (A perfect number is one which completes itself from its parts, as with six: for it has three parts, a sixth, a third, and a half, its sixth being one, its third two, its half three. Com-puting these parts into a total, that is, summing up one and two and three together, they bring about six. And thus the perfect numbers less than ten, one hundred, and one thousand are 6, 28, and 496.)

Roger Dragonetti

Però che ciascun meco si convene
Nel nome che sonò la voce sola
Fannomi onore [...] (91-93).

Thus, at the heart of the six great men of poetry, an equality is installed in the opening of a single poetic space. This rhythmic movement in which unity unfolds multiplicity is similar to that of the compass which describes the circle. Now, *sesto* in Italian is the homonym of "sixth" and of "sextant." In a language no less indeterminate than that which designates the *altissimo poeta,* Dante uses the word *sesto* in canto XIX of *Paradiso* as a metaphor of creation:

[...] Colui che volse il sesto
à lo stremo del mondo [...] (40, 41);
(He that turned his compass
around the limit of the world).

The indeterminacy which affects the passages just cited, as well as the equivocation of the word *sesto,* [12] provokes [13] a certain sliding in between the image of God-artist and that of the artist-god, or even between the figure of the *auctor* (he who holds power) and that of the *autor* (the poet), as it follows from that distinction established by Dante in a passage from the *Convivio.* [14] Dante derives the word *autor,* in the sense of poet, from the verbal form *avieo* which means "I bind or join." In a breath joining the five vowels *(a-v-i-e-o),* Dante presents himself here again as "the sixth" and

[12] We refer the reader to our work *Dante, pèlerin,* where we constantly pointed out the ambiguity of Dante's poetic language. Yet the ultimate Christian reference of the *Divina Commedia* was not put into question as we will do here. A prolonged critical meditation on medieval texts has caused a new problematic to appear to us which we are tempted to extend to all poetry of that period which is called "religious." In the meantime, this hypothesis being open to confirmation only through systematic analysis of the works, we propose a contribution in this direction in future studies. Concerning the subject of the word *sesto* and of the metaphor of the circle, see *Dante, pèlerin,* pp. 323 ff.

[13] Throughout this translation, the French verb "provoquer" is rendered as "provoke," and not as the alternative "cause," for it is precisely the pro-vocation of language, rather than some mechanistic causality, to which the author is addressing himself in this essay. — Tr.

[14] *Convivio,* Busnelli and Vandelli, eds., Florence, 1954, IV, 3-5.

235

as a "compass" if one takes into account the analogous circle which they describe. [15]

Thus one sees that Dante associates the perfection of the circle and that of the number six with the integrity of a poetic place. At present it is a matter of knowing whether the *Sestina* did not offer to Dante a paradigm of this perfect number dividing and unifying itself by way of a virtual point of intensity figured by the compass. Following the metaphor, the harmonic chamber of the *Sestina* would be equivalent to the space of the total word.

If one now refers to this poem, one will notice that it is the rhyme-word *intra* which assumes the function of primacy in governing all the analogies connected with the power and the impotence of the poetic word. This is why the word *intra* is treated in a positive form when it is a matter of the love which "enters" in the heart of the poet:

> Lo ferm voler q'el cor m'intra (I, 1);
> [...] l'amor q'inz el cor m'intra (IV, 23);
> tant fin'amors cum cella q'el cor m'intra (V, 27);

and in a negative form when to the contrary it concerns the lover desirous of penetrating into the lady's chamber:

> on a mon dan sai que nuills hom non intra (II, 8);
> car la sieus sers lai on ill es non intra (III, 16).

This is as much as saying that penetration is possible only in a dream chamber, a fictive chamber where the poet, in the absence of all power and sheltered from all interdiction including that of "the uncle, will enjoy—but fraudulently—the object of his desire":

> Sivals a frau, lai on non aurai oncle,
> iauzirai ioi, en vergier o dinz cambra (I, 5-6).

One must note that in the *envoi*, the ambivalence of the possessive of attribution which accompanies the *senhal "son" Desirat*

---

[15] Cf. "Le sens du cercle et le poète," in our *Aux frontières du langage poétique* (*Romanica Gandensia*, vol. IX), Ghent, 1961, pp. 79-92.

["his "Desired] inserts itself in an equivocal syntactic structure which allows one to appose the *senhal* to the song as well as to the lady. This leads to two superimposed readings, thanks to which the difference between the dream chamber and that into which the poet does not enter tends to efface itself. Indeed, one can read:

Arnaut sends his song of the nail and of the uncle to please his Desired, (i.e.) that one who posseses the poet's soul and whose worth enters into the chamber;

as well as:

Arnaut sends his song of the nail and of the uncle, (i.e.) the song of his desire, *his Desired,* the worth of which (of the song) alone can enter into the chamber to please that one who possesses the poet's soul.

Consequently, that unique chamber, where the worth which is sung and that of the poet who sings it fuse, becomes the place of accomplishment of that *ben amar* which ought to remove the interdiction, as l. 36 allows one to suppose: *Si ia nuills hom per ben amar lai intra* (VI). Thus, by the play of reflexivity, one arrives at an apparent tautology which is nothing other than the *intra*-penetration of the song in/to itself.

To have this poetic chamber coincide with the other prohibited one; to resolve the oppositions of contraries; to contract the unfolding of the compass or of the *Sestina* into a geometric place where the desire of the subject and the object of desire con-fuse into a single, lone sign, into a single, lone de-signation, namely, *son Desirat*—all this supposes, poetically, the symbolic action of a *verbal* force which, penetrating the words with its own life, abolishes differences of meaning in them just as the giratory movement of the rhymes had suppressed metrical hierarchies. We shall now see the effect on the words which this verbal force exercises.

The attentive reader notices quickly enough that the rotation of the rhymes provokes a semantic circulation such that each rhyme-word winds up becoming the mirroring of all the others. Beginning with the homonym *arma* signifying at once "soul" [*anima, âme*] and "weapon" or "arm" in Old Provençal, the respective meanings of amity and of hostility come to color the other words. That the word *arma* can be discussed in this contrary double meaning appears evident as soon as one discovers that the *lausengier*, the enemy of the poet, can lose both his "soul" and his "arm" (that is, his *ongla;* cf. str. I) in that combat fought with blows of the beak and the claws. It will be noticed that the homonym produced the effect of a synonymity between *arma* and *ongla*. On the other hand, this conflict, in which the nail and the beak are associated within slander (*mal dir*, l. 3) as breaking *(escoissendre),* is opposed to that *ben amar* which, as we have seen, allows a victory of union to be foreseen thanks to the worth of the *chanson d'ongl'e d'oncle.*

Now if one reads through the sestina, one sees that the *verga,* a punitive weapon in the first three strophes, turns toward an image of amity in the other three. A metaphor for the body of the poet (IV), for the Virgin (V), and for the lady (VI), the *verga*—after having assumed negative and positive meanings—joins itself in the double-rhyme of the *envoi* to the homonym *arma,* which itself retains the possibility of a double reading throughout the poem. We shall only explicate lines 12 and 13 in their two meanings, because they raise difficulties for translators, while in all the other verses the word *arma* easily allows for the substitution of the meaning of amity for that of *power*. The two lines in question, which follow one another in the poem,

> Tal paor ai no·l sia trop de l'arma
> Del cors li fos non de l'arma,

we understand as follows: "I am so afraid that she makes me fear that my soul might break/ and I would wish that this fear would be of the body and not of the soul"; as well as: ("Because of the force of the blows) I fear that the arm might break/ and I would wish that the body (of the enemy) would break, and not his arm."

A progressive discharging of hostility in favor of amity may be pointed out as well concerning the subject of the *oncle*. An eminently interdictive power in the first three strophes, first associated with that of the *lausengier* and of the enemy brother, the figure of the uncle joins, in strophe IV, with that of the mother and becomes a reference of filial love: "never have I so loved the sister of my uncle" (lines 19 and 20). In the following strophe the *oncle* inscribes himself in the Adamic lineage, another term of comparison destined to valorize the hyperbolic love of the poet: "Never has the love which I experience been felt by the nephews or the uncles descended from Adam" (lines 26 and 27). One will note that, thus formulated, the difference between the uncle and the nephew shades off, for every man becomes a nephew from the ascending perspective, and an uncle from the inverse perspective of the lineage of Adam. Also, it is through the effect of this reversibility that the enemy uncle can, from the sixth strophe on, be integrated with all love, of which that of the poet for his lady remains the standard: "and I do not love as much brother, parent, or uncle" (l. 34).

These progressive slidings from one rhyme to another, from one meaning to its contrary, have the end-effect of making all the rhyme-words into a metaphor of amorous desire. There is no doubt that the word *ongle* lost all of its aggression in becoming in turn an image of the poet and of the lady. She, who resides in the forbidden chamber, has come to con-fuse herself with her own locale: "For she is the tower of my joy, the palace and the chamber" (l. 33). Whether one envisages this place as an open or closed space, "where she might be outside in the plaza or inside the chamber" (l. 29), the difference from the parallel place of the poet who enjoys himself "in the garden or in the chamber" (l. 6) tends to efface itself, as we have seen, in the *envoi.*

This overview—which ought to permit us to show how, with purely exterior metrical aid, the subtle language weaves itself in with the rhythmic number—does not yet suffice for an understanding of all of the "fraud" which subtends the strategy of writing. One would be mistaken, for example, to believe that the "verbal" action of the word *intra* limits itself to the symbolic function of the compass. The double semantic field of "penetration" and the "space-between," to which we alluded above, enjoys its effects not only in that fusing of amity and enmity (of which the hyperbolic comparison maintains the *décalage* in preventing total superposition), but also in the literal signifier which the *inter*penetration of the words brings to view.

This "fraud" of writing resides, among other places, in the occultation of the vowel *a* in the paronyms *ongl(a)* and *oncle* which serve to designate the "song *d'ongl'e d'oncle.*" The difference between the doublets *d'ongl'e/d'oncle*—to which, by this fact alone, the denomination of the song finds itself reduced—becomes, so to speak, imperceptible to vision and to hearing. And is it not of this minimal distance that the nail becomes the metaphor and the measure in strophe V: "And I will not distance myself from her the space of a nail"?

Ceaselessly camouflaged, the interval between the poet and the lady, between the nephew and the uncle, or between *intrar* and *entre* projects itself onto different planes only to disappear—thanks to another ruse—at the moment when the poet borrows the divine mode of the INcarnation in order to feign the intra-penetration of the irreconcilables of the poem in the mode of fiction and of writing. This displacement of the theological utterance into the element of poetic metaphoricity is the "di-version" or *trope* which provokes the literary *perversio* of the *versus* [verse].

The taking-root of the poetic word in the lady-chamber "like the bark on the branch" (l. 32) follows the mystery of the Word incarnated in the Virgin, evoked by the dry branch which blooms again (l. 25). And so it is the *Verbal* force of the word *intra* which produces the mutation of the substantive *ongla* into the verb *enongla,* mimicking the in-carnation: "For thus my heart takes root in her and grips with its nail like the bark on the branch" (lines 31, 32).

All of this then happens as if the mastery of the pygmalion-poet had animated the inert words in the course of mobilizing them in the round of the rhymes and of their meanings, and at the same time had vivified that refuge-chamber in which the poet—separate and without knowledge of the enemy—had simulated union through this very artifice.

Now this artifice covers up the homonym *intra* as well. The manifest sense of the verb *intrar* signifying penetration toward the interior only served to divert attention from the adverbial and prepositional form *entre*. In sum, it is a matter of masking the form of the *ad-verb* under that of the *verb*, the *ad-verb* which designates proximity but also the insuperable interval, the discontinuity, the irreducible space-between metaphorized by "the space of a nail." And is it not the case that the *senhal*, "his Desired"—where the signatory of the song and the unattainable person to whom it is addressed come to con-fuse—was the privileged sign, capable of assembling in the fictive unity of the ternary *envoi*, the near homonymy of *ongla* and *oncle*, the near synonymity of *verga* and *arma*, and the near identity of the place and its motor manifestation, *cambra intra*?

But what then is this "paradise" which the poet hopes to join (str. IV)? Can we still affirm that it concerns a paradise in the Christian sense of the word? What is that double joy which tends to con-fuse with the *eloquence* of the song of "doubles"?

It is the word itself designating the place of the "double joy" which seems to bring us the answer to these question. For after this vertigo of rhymes, this *paradise* increasingly resembles the place where the tension of words comes to resolve itself, namely, that one himself who, literally, names the *parity* of *eloquence: para-dis*.

If one grants that the poetics of the *Sestina* were able to furnish incentive to Dante's literary thought, one could go further and say that this formal poetics offers one of the most accomplished models of that which is inherent in the essence of medieval courtly poetry. By this we mean to say that Arnaut Daniel's *Sestina* implicitly envelopes a conception of literature, concerning which we propose to offer in this second part of our study several reflections relating to the *Divina Commedia,* it being understood that each point ought to be systematically developed.

241

However slightly the reader might be familiar with the rhetoric of *la fin'Amor* of the troubadours, he will easily recognize the traditional commonplaces of the love song: the lady, the chamber, the *lausengier,* the lover, etc. But perhaps one has not been sufficiently struck by that figure of the uncle which the *Sestina* treats by turns as adversary and as friend of the poet. What function does this familial relation exercise in the song?

First of all, one can find in Claude Lévi-Strauss' *Elementary Structures of Kinship* [16] the important role which the maternal uncle plays for primitive peoples, he being an eminent substitute for paternal authority with regard to the sister and to the nephew. But the privilege accorded to this line of kinship is equally valid for classical antiquity [17] and for medieval civilization. The maternal uncle-nephew relationship abounds in medieval literature [18] and the question is thus to know, in our matter at hand, what such a familial relation signifies when it functions as a textual metaphor.

One must first note that in certain cases the reciprocal tenderness of the maternal uncle and the nephew can cover over an incestuous filiation and a secret antagonism comparable to that which the father-son relationship engenders in its oedipal relations with the mother. But let us guard ourselves against a univocal interpretation, as each triangulation in medieval literature presents a particular textual configuration which demands a specific reading.

One knows, for example, that Charlemagne is the maternal uncle of Roland, but that since the tenth century a legend—that of St. Giles—had it that Roland was the incestuous son of Charlemagne and his sister Gisèle. [19] Gawain, the dear nephew of his uncle

[16] Paris: Presses Universitaires de France, 1941, Ch. XXVI, p. 536. (English translation of rev. ed., Boston: Beacon Press, 1969.) Cf. also *Anthropologie Structurale,* Paris: Plon, 1958, Ch. II, pp. 49-55. (English translation, New York: Basic Books, 1963.)
[17] Cf. Émile Benveniste, "La paternité," in *Vocabulaire des institutions indoeuropéennes,* vol. I, Paris: Éditions de Minuit, 1969, pp. 207 ff.
[18] Cf. Reto Bezzola, in *Mélanges Frappier,* vol. I, pp. 89-111, and W. O. Farnsworth, *Uncle and Nephew in Old French Chansons de geste,* New York: Columbia University Press, 1913.
[19] Cf. R. Lejeune, "Le péché de Charlemagne et la Chanson de Roland," in *Hommage à Damaso Alonso,* vol. II, Madrid, 1961, pp. 339-371.

Roger Dragonetti

Arthur, passes for the incestuous son of the king. [20] The same thing goes for Arthur's other nephew, Mordred, [21] to whom Dante refers at the very bottom of hell, in a context which figures the most extreme narcissism — the reciprocal murder of father and son. [22] If Mordred brings to light the transgression of the incestuous son with regard to the father and the uncle, Tristan, *poet and musician,* belongs to the line of nephews in which the contestation is more latent. [23] From an inverse perspective one could yet cite the relationship of Peleus, uncle of Jason, who drives his nephew to his destruction while hiding his heinous feelings behind the appearance of love. [24]

What relationships do these several examples of familial figures entertain with the text? Surely they are figures of the text itself or, more exactly, the metaphorical projection of interdictive and transgressive forces which govern the narrative field. Whether it concerns the uncle or the father, the law which they represent is defied: by way of the different metaphors which result from the mad effort of the hero (Roland), in open combat (Mordred), and finally in that double language which Tristan addresses to Isolde, knowing that the king hidden in the tree can also find satisfaction in hearing it.

Unjustifiable and beyond the law, the work of literature—at once innocent, guilty, and crafty—for this very reason ceaselessly cloaks itself in an apparent legitimacy by feigning to serve one or another political, religious or pedagogic cause; or, what is more, in adopting the appearance of a fervent imitation of the master, it hides a secret rivalry underneath the seduction.

That which, after the troubadours, the poets of *courtly* poetry designated in the *mother* tongue with the name of "Lady," "sister,"

[20] J. Marx, *La légende arthurienne et le Graal,* Paris: Presses Universitaires de France, 1952, p. 67, n. 2.
[21] Cf. *La Mort le Roi Artu,* Jean Frappier, ed., Paris: Droz, 1964, p. 245, n. 191.
[22] *Inf.* XXXII, 61; see also *Dante, pèlerin,* p. 46, n.
[23] Apropos of this subject, see our study, "Le lai narratif de Marie de France," in *Mélange Gagnebin,* Lausanne: L'Age d'homme, 1973.
[24] Benoit de Saint Maure, *Le Roman de Troie,* Léopold Constans, ed., Paris: Firmin Didot, 1904-1912.

"Queen," "Virgin," is not a feminine persona, still less the imaginary double of a referent, but rather the symbol of the distant essence of Poetry. The quest for that object which is rooted in the desire of writing opens—against the law of textual structure metaphorized by the uncle, the father, the master—the disruptive space of the desiring word, the inter-speech [*entre-dit*] where that which is refused by the uncle (the brother of the sister) is musically granted by the sister in the distance of poetic speech: "All that which the brother refuses me, I hear the sister grant to me."

> Que tot com lo fraire me desditz
> Aug autrejar a la seroz. [25]

This is what Jaufré Rudel wrote at the beginning of the twelfth century, he being the troubadour who, following Guillaume IX, founded the poetic language of the *distant love* [*amour lointain*].

Thus that which, since the troubadours, the poets of the Middle Ages called "sister," "lady," or quite simply *she*, was always—whatever the proper name might be—that *Unknown* which made of literature a work without a graspable object, a chivalry of writing, endlessly rebegun, unfinished, unfinishable—where the thirst for integrity (at once destructive and constitutive of literature), the gratuitousness, the trickery, the lie, and the truth blended their stage effects in the lyric or narrative adventure of *la fin'Amor*.

It is then easy to understand why incest (albeit hidden) appears in literature with such frequency. It is because the poet maintains a relationship of what could be called "consanguinity" with that "feminine possibility" [26] of which he has himself engendered the fiction, and which assumes in the literature the figure of the mother, the sister, the uncle, or the poet.

This allows us to begin to see the whole range which ought to be given to the familial metaphor of the *Sestina,* where the *sivals a*

<hr>

[25] Jaufré Rudel, *Les Chansons,* Alfred Jeanroy, ed., Paris: Honoré Champion (C.F.M.A.), 1974, p. 15.
[26] Mallarmé, "Le Nénuphar blanc," in *Œuvres complètes,* Henri Mondor and G. Jean-Aubry, eds., Paris: Gallimard (Bibliothèque de la Pléiade), 1945, p. 284; cf. also our study in *Yale French Studies, 54, Mallarmé.*

frau marks the character of infraction which obtains in the poetic act, for the poet appears quite like the one who fraudulently transgresses the interdictive law of the uncle, guardian of the forbidden chamber (str. II).

The familial love that the nephew officially brings to his uncle is that which ought to permit him to remain in the proximity of the lady without giving rise to suspicions. In order to conceal his game, the nephew often simulates submission or naïveté, or encloses himself within silence.

To illustrate an aspect of this attitude, one could refer here to Dante's words on the subject of the Franciscans (those naïves of Christianity) who are "following the spouse (here, Christ), so does the bride (Lady Poverty) delight them": "dietro a lo sposo, sì la sposa piace" (*Par.* XI, 84).

The secret aim consists of rejoining the poetic essence of femininity while feigning to be subject to the holder of the law. This is what comes out of a poem of Guinizelli's as well. The poet had taken his lady for an angel, and excuses himself for this before God:

> Tenea d'angel sembianza
> Che credea fosse del tuo regno; [27]
> (She had the appearance of an angel
> So that I thought she was of your realm).

If Dante places the "better craftsman of the mother tongue" at the very top of the steps of Purgatory—that is, Arnaut Daniel who had practiced the poetics of heights so as better to imitate the distance of his narcissistic desire from the diversion of the high lady— it is that Dante recognized in this religion of *la fin'Amor* an art of divine resemblance in which St. Bernard, the Christian mystic, alone could challenge Arnaut at the summit of Paradise. One has perhaps not sufficiently insisted upon the narcissistic coloring which Dante has glittering in the signifier of the prayer which St. Bernard ad-

---

[27] In L. di Benedetto, ed., *Rimatori del dolce stil nuovo*, Turin: Unione typografico-editrico torinese, 1925, p. 61.

dresses to the Virgin, whatever the doctrinal intention of these verses might be:

> Vergine madre, figlia del tuo figlio,
> Umile a alta più che creatura (*Par.* XXXIII, 1, 2);
> (Virgin mother, daughter of thy son,
> humble and *exalted* more than any creature [our italics]).

Now this face of the Virgin—which, as Dante says, is the one "which most resembles Christ" (*Par.* XXXII, 85, 86)—provokes through the specular effects of the signifier a dangerous resemblance between the doctrinal signified of the Christian word and of the Virgin, and the poetic signified of the feminine thought of the poet.

This androgyny of the text·is moreover very close to the hermaphroditism of the poets whom Dante most admired, and of Dante himself, for they fairly acknowledge that their "sin was hermaphrodite" (*Purg.* XXVI, 82). Furthermore, in the same episode of *Purgatorio,* Dante, divided into two in the fantasy of the two sons of Lycurgus, embraces his father Guinizelli as if it were an instance of embrancing a mother:

As in the sorrow of Lycurgus two sons became on beholding their mother again, so I became, but I do not rise to such heights, when I hear name himself the father of me and of others my betters who ever used sweet and gracious rhymes of love (*Purg.* XXVI, 94 ff.).

This encounter of Dante and Guinizelli takes place in the circle of the lustful ones and the sodomites. The scene leads to the understanding that perversion, sodomy and lust have a link with the highest act of literature. Desire of the Other, will not literature always be only a *comedy* in the invisible mirror of the self?

In all its equivocation, this is indeed what characterizes the great song of the poetics of *la fin'Amor.* Dante plays with these spellbinding effects in his meeting with Paolo and Francesca in the circle of the lustful in *Inferno.* At once fascinated and bewildered, Dante denounces the seduction performed by Lancelot's courtly book: "A Gallehaut [= go-between] was the book and he who wrote it" (*Inf.* V, 137).

Roger Dragonetti

This power of the *autor* is often reconciled with, and at once distinguished from, the political (or theological) power of the *auctor*. [28] Doublets of the *autor/auctor* genre figure frequently in the *Divina Commedia* and especially in the dantesque *Para/dis:*

> of caesar or of poet (*Par.* I, 29);
> I was Caesar, and am Justinian (*Par.* VI, 10); [29]
> Through you I was a poet, through you a Christian (*Purg.* XXII, 73);
> I became at once a Christian and Cacciaguida (*Par.* XV, 135).

From this discordant assemblage there arises, we believe, the misapprehension of the other poets of *Purgatorio* concerning the true "dictator," who—exactly as the prophecy of Christ on the part of Pope Adrian allows to be understood—risks letting himself be captured in an image: "I see [...] in his vicar Christ made captive" (*Purg.* XX, 86, 87).

These interferences between poetry, Christianity, and imperialism, which the paternal figure collects, better explain—when conjoined with the hermaphroditism—why in the circle of the lustful in *Purgatorio,* the residence of courtly poetry, there are also the sodomites, whose fault is denounced like that same one which earned Caesar the surname of "queen": "The people who do not come with us offended in that for which Caesar in his triumph once heard 'Queen' cried out against him" (*Purg.* XXVI, 76-78).

The game which consists of substituting simulacra of the father for the authentic, elusive father, and according to which Dante-author projects in turn his doubles under the figures of such masters as Virgil, Brunetto Latini, Guinizelli, Arnaut, Statius, all great representatives of the art of rhetoric, this game conceals, under one form or another, the desire to assign to literature a paternity at once absolute and impossible, a paternity of which the *Seignorie* of the lady is the other face.

---

[28] See above, p. 235.
[29] Concerning this subject, see our study, "Le Style suave dans le Banquet et dans la Divine Comédie," in *Psicoanalisi e strutturalismo di fronte a Dante,* vol. III, Florence: Oslchki, 1972.

Now in *Paradiso* all the masters have disappeared, and it is the *auctoritas* of theology, especially that of St. Thomas and St. Bonaventura, which is going to take over the guard from the rationalist pagan current represented by Virgil and from the courtly mystical current which had led to Arnaut Daniel.

It is also to redress that offence against the father that Dante is begged to intervene in his favor by Guinizelli's penitent soul. Dante is asked to recite a *Pater nostra* when he arrives at the end of his voyage: "Now, if you have such ample privilege that you are permitted to go to the cloister wherein Christ is abbot of the college, say there a paternoster for me" (*Purg.* XXVI, 127-130).

The strange thing is that, having arrived up there, Dante will not recite the *Pater noster,* but rather the *Ave Maria* with St. Bernard. Dante draws out of his own words a theologic-christian scenario in which even the prayer enters into the game of this grand opera.

The lady in whom Dante's desire is rooted is the only pole of attraction in the *Divina Commedia.* The attraction of the *disiato riso* [longed-for smile] and of the courtly book—denounced as fascination in the Francesca episode [30]—persists up to the summit of the dantesque *Para/dis,* exactly there where the perilous resemblance between the poetic word and the language of prayer allows Dante, the courtly lover, to celebrate (under the aspect of the Virgin) the lady of his thoughts in communion with St. Bernard, the mystical lover.

This is to recognize that the paradise of Dante-Orpheus is not that of Christian theology, but that of courtly literature, for which Arnaut Daniel had furnished the prestigious model in his *Sestina.* The proof of this is that scramble of figures provoked by a subtle play of substitutions which recalls, in the mystic rose, [31] the vertigo

[30] Concerning this subject, see our study "L'épisode de Francesca selon la convention courtoise," in *Aux frontières,* pp. 93-116.

[31] *Par.* XXXI, 52-60: "My look had now taken in the general form of Paradise as a whole, and on no part as yet had my sight paused; and I turned with rekindled will to ask my lady about things as to which my mind was in suspense. One thing I purposed, and another answered me:

Roger Dragonetti

of the rotation of rhymes and their meanings in Arnaut's poem: Beatrice, the guide of Dante's gaze and word, has given way to St. Bernard; his charity fuses with that of the *Veronica nostra,* an ambiguous verbalization in which the love of the lover of the Virgin and that of Veronica for Christ tend to con-fuse with the *image* of the divine Word.[32]

If Arnaut's *verbal* dynamics had produced that reversibility in the Adamic line which rendered uncle equal to nephew, those of Dante set up another reversibility within the courtly line of the *gente francesca* (= the French), of which *Francesca da Rimini* and St. *Francis,* the son of *Pietro Bernardone* (as Dante designates him[33]), would be—according to the etymological process of a poetic geneology—the most stunning figures, and Arnaut Daniel and St-Bernard the most sublime.

In the *Divina Commedia* Dante represents the Christian drama of salvation in an image so near its supernatural mystery that one could be tempted to confuse the poetic version of the prayer to the Virgin by the character of St. Bernard with the authentic *Ave Maria.* This proximity of the poetic version of salvation to its supernatural mystery in its radical difference—which as such is destructive of all literature—this formidable nearness Dante accomplishes to the extreme. This is why, through this play of resemblances, Dante at the summit of his *para-dis* surpasses that summit of Purgatory where Arnaut Daniel resides. This is to say that the courtly art of Dante—an art centered on the glorification of the lady, even if it orients itself toward the divine Word—no more escapes than did Arnaut's courtly art from that diversion, the fraud of which the troubadour inscribed in his *Sestina.* And furthermore, the perfection with which the art of the divine *comedy* conceals its own "fraud" makes all the more imperceptible that "space of a nail" which

I thought to see Beatrice, and I saw an elder, clad like the folk in glory." See also *Par.* XXXIII, 115-132.

[32] Concerning St. Bernard, see our commentary in *Dante, pèlerin,* pp. 301 ff.

[33] *Par.* XI, 89. Note that in l. 79 of the same canto, Dante names two other Franciscans: *Bernardo* and *Silvestro.* Concerning *Silvestro* and the relation of his name to Statius, see *Dante, pèlerin,* p. 268.

separates theological language from its metaphorical substitutes. For this new Orpheus substitutes a different grace for the supernatural grace of the Word, one which along the fiction of the Christian in quest of his salvation does not cease, at the same time, to divert the reader from it, in drawing him toward the pleasure of Poetry, even if the place represented is that of the most horrible tortures.

In pushing these reflections still further, one comes to ask whether Dante, the avowed and devoted disciple of Virgil, could not be the inverted image of the poet Statius. The conversion of Statius to Christianity is paradoxical insofar as it is provoked by the fidelity of the disciple to the pagan master.[34] Statius openly acknowledges to Virgil: "Through you I was a poet, through you a Christian" (*Purg.* XXII, 73); and he also does not hide from him that his attraction toward Christianity was motivated by "the *consonance* between the master's word and that of the new preachers":

> e la parola tua sopra toccata
> si consonava a'nuovi predicanti (*Purg.* XXII, 79, 80).

But following Virgil's reproach, who remarks to him that, after his conversion, he had not allowed the language of a believer to show through his work which remained pagan, Statius acknowledges his fear of exposing himself and his decision to remain "a secret Christian": "Ma per paura chiuso cristian fu'mi" (*Purg.* XXII, 90).

According to our hypothesis, Dante—in opposition to the "secret Christian" represented by his enigmatic guide who comes to double in *Purgatorio* for the figure of Virgil—would have substituted his own image of a "secret pagan," that is, that of a new disciple of Virgil constructing a musical architecture which recovers an untamable desire for Poetry from the casing of religious orthodoxy.

From this, *Inferno* and *Paradiso* come to reflect the opposite poles of their discourse in that place of *Purgatorio* which constitutes

---

[34] Concerning Statius, see the chapters, "La Stanza de Stace" and "La Source silencieuse," in *Dante, pèlerin.*

the space-between at the heart of the sacred poem (and with reason), where the courtly poets reside who had promoted the reversible poetry of False Semblance and Beautiful Semblance. Statius and Dante, the two disciples of Virgil, remain faithful to their master, all the while subverting his teaching—each according to his own style of false and beautiful "seeming."

Meanwhile, the relationship between disciple and master (insofar as Statius does not renounce the paganism of his work; insofar as during the whole course which he travels with Virgil, he leaves to his master the initiation of speech, so far as to enclose himself within silence after the master's return to Limbo) evokes by displacement the behavior of Dante in regard to Arnaut Daniel: a parallel silence on the part of the Florentine poet follows the disappearance of the troubadour into the fire which "purifies" [*affine*] him.

Enlarging the discussion a bit, one could see that silence and the celebrating word are the two sides of the same rhetoric of imitation. The courtly lyric often opposes, in the same song, the authentic poet who keeps silent about the love which inspires him, and that other one, called the *lausengier,* who makes flattery his profession.

Here we are touching not only upon the most secret province of courtly poetry, but also upon another aspect of the hermaphroditism of desire. For this continually acknowledged conflict between hollow rhetoric and the unspeakable in the language of love, in which the feminine essence is figured by the lady—in short, the antagonism which divides the *autor* into poet and *lausengier*—doubles itself in another conflict, albeit never manifest as such, which is that of the *auctor.* We mean to say that the word of power, just like the word of love, supposes a *lausengier,* one who will assume the figure of the disciple, faithful and submissive, celebrating in an inveigling rhetoric the no less fascinating rhetoric of the Master. During this second conflict, the silent rival of the *lausengier* remains perpetually withdrawn, so well in fact that his hidden desire of subversion does not allow itself to be revealed except through the grace of certain blank spaces of language.

If one then refers to the model of the "secret Christian" and of the "hidden pagan," as an example of the dissimulation implicit in the double play of writing, one recognizes that the importance which Dante accords to his masters does not allow itself to be measured by the breath of the devoted ceremony with which he surrounds them. For Statius and Arnaut impose themselves on Dante's admiration and imitation more than Virgil or Guinizelli—the former by his art of dissimulation, the latter by that verbal dynamic which allows for the "fraud" inherent in writing. And it is doubtless for this reason that Dante-persona envelopes these two poets in a zone of silence and addresses no eulogy to them within the space of the *Divina Commedia.*

We would be tempted to understand analogously the silence which Dante, in *De vulgari eloquentia,* maintains concerning the poem of *Ferm voler . . .*, which he imitated most faithfully in his own sestina—and which, perhaps, he surpassed most secretly in that *para/dis* where the mother tongue, glorified in its poetic being, mimicks its own redemption in the double writing of *la fin'Amor* while playing with and against theology, with and against the Father, a divine *comedy.*

Translated by Timothy Bahti

Charles Méla

Perceval

> Au Nom du Père etc...
> Ihre Namen machen die Kinder zu "Reve-
> nants." *(Die Traumdeutung)*

Since death had preceded the hand of the master from Champagne, *le Conte du Graal* was left unfinished,[1] although others followed on interminably with continuations of their own.[2] The "matière de Bretagne" took another course and was oriented entirely towards an enigma henceforth shrouded in religious mystery. Now, at the end of the evolution of the Arthurian romance, we find in the Cistercian edition of the *Queste del Saint Graal,* in place of the enchantment of fairy love, another *merveille,* the divine *semblances,* reserved for the chosen ones. The *roman* indeed began when a hero, whose name was lost, unknown or silenced, came into Fairyland; but if he found perfect joy only to live out its misfortune, the path, which would later confront Perceval with the Names of the Father in the desert of Repentance, had been traced out in Chrétien de Troyes' earlier works. The Arthurian legend was then invaded by *senefiance,* and *senefier* was understood to be of the order of what is intimated as well as heralded. It was Robert de Boron who was responsible for this, when soon after in *le roman de l'Estoire dou*

[1] Between 1181 and 1190, ed. Lecoy, CFMA, 2 vol., Paris, 1972-75; trans. L. Foulet, Nizet, Paris, 1970. Cf. J. Frappier, *Chrétien de Troyes,* Hatier, Paris, 1968 and *Chrétien de Troyes et le mythe du Graal,* SEDES, Paris, 1972.

[2] *Les Continuations* (c. 1190-1200), ed. W. Roach, 4 vol., Philadelphia, 1949-71; Robert de Boron, *Le roman de l'Estoire dou Graal* (c. 1200), ed. Nitze, CFMA, Paris, 1927; *le Didot-Perceval* (before 1214), ed. W. Roach, Philadelphia, 1941; *Perlesvaus* (c. 1220-1225?), ed. Nitze, 2 vol., Chicago, 1931; le Lancelot-Graal (c. 1220-1225): *The Vulgate Version of the Arthurian Romances,* ed. Sommer, 7 vol., Washington, 1908-16; *La Queste del Saint-Graal* (c. 1225-1235), ed. Pauphilet, CFMA, Paris, 1949.

Graal, he reinvented the Gospels, supported by the Apocryphia, in order to inscribe the "Greal" within them. The *Saint Vessel,* which caught Christ's blood and *agrée* to sight, carried away with it, in the moment of its eclipse as well as that of its return, the mystery of the tortured and glorious Body. Later on, Galaad, virgin and chaste, was preferred to Perceval, whom Chrétien's story had compromised with Blanchefleur. The ambiguity was, in fact, only displaced: Galaad had as his father the lustful Lancelot, the *fin amant* haloed with shame.

In the same way, Perceval, who just after setting forth from his mother's manor came upon the lily-white fairy, prostrated himself one day at the feet of the hermit, his maternal uncle. In the meanwhile, his course had run aground at the Castle of the Fisher King, as he remained captivated by the sight of the cortege of the Bleeding Lance and the Luminous Grail, under the very eyes of the invalid with the impotent body. Here still remained linked the paths which would later diverge. The shadow of a sexual enigma would not yet yield to the infinite light of religious Mystery, although its persistance is justly measured against a proliferation of meaning, posited in a story set adrift and therefore impossible to conclude unless it be by the division of the celestial *Queste* of the Mystery of the Trinity and the worldly catastrophe of the *Mort Artur.*

In order to revive this very enigma, let us consider Perceval according to Claude Lévi-Strauss (*Anthropologie structurale II,* Plon, 1973, p. 34) as if he were "un Œdipe inversé." In both cases, words are lacking, but instead of a question without its response, the response awaits its question: the sexual relationship is compromised, it is no longer abusive, but lacunary; the seasonal rhythm is broken and either eternal summer decays in its excess, or eternal winter languishes in its sterility. One would have thus an example of the process particular to mythic thought which delimits with negative truths the only possible path of equilibrium, as it calls forth the extreme terms in order to show them to be untenable: it admits neither Oedipus nor Perceval.

But a literary text, regardless of its assumption of reordering its assertion, continually returns to stumble upon an undomptable peculiarity which undoes it entirely. It attempts to claim a sense for what it constructs, one in which to orient and even direct the reader, but it cannot prevent the return of this destructive panic within the text. The matter of the text conjures up, not without good reason, what the pleasure of the text on the other hand invites us to mis-know, since art deludes anguish owing to the meaning its letter chances upon. But the artifice, giving play to the system while at the same time leaving something to be desired, steals the text away from the grasp of meaning which encloses it. Whether it is fable or fantasy, literature incessantly refers to that moment, arbitrary or accidental, which governs the writing process and reproduces within itself, in the course of a destiny's retelling, or in the starry burst of a vision, some obscure disaster thwarting or scattering the novelistic or poetic representation. It is this "lapse" in the narrative or this splitting up of the poem which makes a tale out of what is impossible to tell, or a spell of what is (m)(d)ispelled, but which will be taken into account, if not made into debris, by the interweaving of the story or by the strategies of the mingled letters and sounds of the poem. One is made to wait for something which, although it never comes, indicates that moment in the text where it seems suddenly to be marked by/with absence or even to break open. For *récit* is the anagram of *écrit* just as *image* comes from a practice of *magie*. The worst would be then, out of fear of being made a fool, for one to believe himself capable of deciphering what in the text is shown to bear the mark of the Unconscious, when on the contrary he must learn to count himself among those playing out the game within the text to the end only of finding himself at the mercy of the representations therein exchanged, and being put, once again, in pla(y)(ce) as the subject. [3] If one is thus

---

[3] Exemplaire donc le décompte de J. Lacan lecteur de *Lol V. Stein:* "Ceci légitime que j'introduise ici M. Duras ... dans un troisième ternaire dont l'un des termes est le ravissement de Lol V. Stein pris comme objet dans son nœud même et où me voici le tiers à y mettre un ravissement, dans mon cas décidément subjectif" (in *M. Duras,* éd. Albatros, Paris 1975,

oriented according to the "point of view" of a fictional being and captured in the *donné à voir* on the screen of the poem, he is ultimately nothing more than a gaze appearing in only those places marking his absence—the ellipses of the story or the blanks of the page.

When Freud interprets a work of art, he would sooner, being under its spell, make an entire "novel" of it (cf. GW, VIII, 207).[4] Psychoanalysis re-establishes only what is consonant with the Unconscious of the reader, and the act of putting into words forestalls the refusal to know anything of it precisely in order to leave the question intact. The investigation of *Moses* begins with the crushing, stony immobility where Law triumphs, while in the case of the painting of *Saint Anne,* pervaded by death, Freud is instead concerned with an oneiric fusion with disquieting continuations. *Saint John* and *Bacchus* "do not lower their eyes, but look at us with a mysteriously conquering gaze," when the anonymous author of the *Moses* article would have preferred to "hold fast under the angered and scornful gaze of the hero." As for Moses' finger confining the undulating mass of his beard to no more than the present trace of his past rage, is it not for Freud, contrasted with the representation of the London Cartoon in which the raised finger of Saint Anne separates, as if they were reflections of each other, the child-like heads of Jesus and John?

---

p. 94. Nous lui sommes redevable de la présente méthode, si elle ne défaille pas : à notre seul compte, le pire . . . .

[4] Le "roman psychanalytique" dont Sarah Kofman relève l'expression, nous l'entendrions surtout comme "le roman familial" de celui qui remuait l'Achéron. Aucune avancée ne s'accomplit en tout cas sans que son tremblement ne s'en livrât à la faveur d'une œuvre d'art: le "vautour" maternel de Léonard et le narcissime; l'avertissement du *Moïse* et la fonction symbolique, en attendant *L'Homme Moïse* et le passage de la mère au père comme progrès de la *Geistigkeit.* Mais encore le mot de Heine sur son lit de mort, sobrement, intensément admiré par Freud qui vient de situer le tiers comme "théâtre" du *mot d'esprit* (cf. Gallimard, p. 171); Gradiva, libérant, récidivant l'amour, à l'instar du transfert dans la cure et pourquoi pas Ibsen, occasion d'un "long séjour au monde de la fiction" pour l'énigme de Rebecca? Goethe, encore, à propos de *Poésie et Vérité,* au-delà de l'expérience médiatrice de la mort imaginaire pour "plus de lumière" (cf. J. Lacan, *Le mythe individuel du névrosé*).

Charles Méla

The analytic intervention into the reader's pleasure reopens the gap of desire, inasmuch as the work had been the very stage of its forgetting. If writing is erasing, the reading is seeing nothing, since nothing is put forward but for being masked (cf. *Hamlet, Rosmersholm*). A third moment is required in order to confront this effect of lack precisely where it is written out in full. Moreover, the method invoked in *Moses* demands that one pay attention to these secondary details, to these "minutiae" which for example render a painting authentic, but which remain unnoticed or disdained in the impression of the whole picture. The *rebut* of the observation (Moses' index finger, the Horn of the Tablets) re-presents under the veil of the work, what is only ever inscribed in this mark of loss by means of its absence. Moses, reinvented by Freud breaks only his passion, not the Tablets; for he is there to transmit what comes to him from an Other, even if only by his very failure to do so.

Let us then in the present analysis delineate those shadows obscuring the *Conte du Graal,* and allow ourselves to thus be trapped in a story where the infinite reflections of what can only ever be written as pure loss are mirrored. Is it a metaphor that Perceval will have nothing else to read in Blanchefleur's face? The very style of the work perfectly imitates the adventure, just as the hero's gaze takes in our desire. In fact, the novel invents the hero's *Enfances* in its very inability ever to begin. Nature is reborn in the maternal forest which the Celtic child runs through at will, abandoning himself to the joy of the moment and to the free will of his body: ordinarily, however, an Arthurian novel opens in Arthur's court and is anchored there while he awaits the news from the Otherworld which will carry the narrative far afield. Moreover, the irrupting plenitude with which *Perceval* begins is immediately hollowed out by the abyss of an unfathomable event which happened before the time of the story itself, beyond its scope as well as the understanding of its hero who is called "le fils de la *Veuve* dame de la *Gaste* Forêt solitaire" (vv. 74-75). In this case, however, the *merveille* sits in wait for the wild child in the darkest heart of the forest; but to our surprise, it is a most banal and not at all supernatural matter: armed knights in search of adventure. Yet, what is usual for others slips into the world of fantasy for him who, at his mother's manor, learned nothing of the world of men. He is excited and fascinated by the pure brillance of the coats of mail and the helmets, and by the weapons whose red color is resplendent in the fiery sunlight. "Je vois Dieu" he avows to himself in the presence of the Master Knight; and when the latter denies it, he goes even further: "Vous êtes plus beau que Dieu—Ah! que je voudrais être pareil à vous, brillant et fait comme vous l'êtes!" (vv. 177-79). Without paying attention to the questions put to him, he gives himself over entirely to what he sees, internalizing these ordinary objects named for him for the first time, as he places his hand upon them: "lance," "écu," "haubert." "Etes-vous ainsi né?" (v. 280) he adds, as if these beings who appeared *ex nihilo* were sons of their own arms and as if their bodies existed but for the emblems they bore of their great power. The one who bears the name of "knight," however, sends the *nice,* the "little fool," to King Arthur, who knighted him. That is, he sends him to a prestigious name, one which arranges the entire symbolic system, presides over its rites and orders its meaning. What then were these Breton knights doing as they wandered through a forest, which was not their homeland, if not looking for adventure, that is for an occasion to show valor in ladies' service (vv. 182-83)?

The knights' weapons abruptly disturbed the protected retreat of the Veuve Dame and awakened there an echo of the Father, absent for the "son" whose blood nonetheless carried the traits of his lineage. At first an accomplice of the young hunter's gestures, the forest now echoed the "names" banished until that moment by a mother's efforts. But the intruding signs dazzled his eyes while remaining opaque to his consciousness, since the youth was subjugated by them without understanding anything about them. What then are signs which make no sense, but which invade one's senses, if not pure signifiers whose very unreadability is their *jouissance?* A use of language which was not defective as in this case (vv. 238-39), nor as was lacking later on (v. 3591), would have on the contrary admitted that far from delivering the thing itself, the sign strikes it with an irremediable absence. This would have been to symbolize it. But the hero comes into being in a way which is impious, deviant and, as the rest of the story demonstrates, profoundly culpable.

The weeping mother's mourning is like the funereal reverse side of the *nice*'s initial jubilation. Does she not give him to understand that whoever proposes himself as a master necessarily carries within himself a sense of tragic unhappiness, and that no one who had not previously interiorized mourning would know how to prevail at bearing the lance? But didn't she believe that she had been able to undo destiny? As she stammers the beloved name of *Beau fils* and embraces him vainly, hoping to retain him, he has already set out to the unique rhythm of a line exultant with cruel joy: "Tu as vu, je crois, les anges dont chacun se plaint et qui tuent tout ce qu'ils atteignent?" (vv. 396-98).

> Voir non ai, mere, non ai, non!
> Chevalier dient qu'il ont non.
>
> vv. 399-400

Thus proffered, the name itself—Knight—is deadly, since she collapses immediately before dying, sealing in this way the sin which will later weigh heavily on Perceval's tongue. At least she had attempted to warn him, in an ultimate effort, evoking again, through an enigmatic story, a sparse fragment of a past which is incomprehensible to the young man: the paternal tragedy which took place among the Isles of the Sea and in the remote time of Uter Pandragon, that she would have wished to be a dead letter.

Le Conte du Graal, remains, from one part to the next, haunted by the Father's vacant place. When the vision of the Angel of Fire reveals to the spellbound son the image of the Master Knight who engages him on the path of a deadly rivalry, the mother weeps for her dead ones, and asks him to renounce his pledge, recalling the vanished father, the gentleman maimed between his limbs (vv. 433-35), who did not outlive his oldest son killed in battle and found among the ravens, the orbits of his eyes hollow. But while the buried memory returns in horror and suffering, the Name of the Father is never uttered. Although she teaches that it is by his name that one recognizes the man, his son still remains ignorant of who he is: "beau fils," "beau frère," "beau sire," one slips from one to the other as if nothing can anchor his identity which is subject to the will of his fantasy. Besides, what is it worth, this name — Perceval the Gallois (v. 3561)—about which he will one day have an intuition, just after having discovered, "en un val" (vv. 3026, 3044), the mysterious castle? Is it not in fact the destiny of the Welsh youth in the Waste Forest to *percer* the secret of the *Val* where the Rich Fisher King lives (cf. Wolfram, Book III)? "Perceval l'infortuné," his cousin immediately rectifies, knowing of his failure at the Fisher King's castle. Also, as the name "Perlesvaus" (*Perlesvaus,* 1.460) indicates, he has lost *(perdu)* the *Val* of his obscure origins. But how not to understand in another way the syllable which echoes the *Père* forever lost and whose name re-opens, at the center of the story, a gap which is impossible to close and consequently becomes an unextinguishible source of imaginary errings? Nothing happens henceforth to the hero which does not appear to be an unrecognizable transposition of a lost truth. The Castle of the Fisher King is only the mirror where the diverse reflections of a single event, which it repeats and conceals, are assembled together. Perceval is called upon to come forward as a consciousness in this locus of Knowledge which does not know itself, but if he arrives too early, in order to learn too late, is it not clear that the two will never coincide and that consciousness comes forth only from a deficiency, or rather from the horror of knowing? What then did the hero see, when he remained mute at the Castle of the Enigma? At the very least, his mother, completing finally his religious instruction, limits on the other hand the field into which the irruption of the Knight-God introduced the Welsh youth: to the adoration of the God of Glory is added the story of the anguish and the death of His Son, whose Body was tormented for a long time and is the Holy Relic of which the suffering Church is the locus and the memory. No more than yet another landmark on an errant path which affirms itself as error only inasmuch as it orients itself towards God.

Two episodes follow, both to be united under the heading of one same failing, in its two aspects of *Amors* and *Armes,* the "rape" of the Damsel of the Tent and the murder of the Red Knight amid a fatal burst of redness, bathed in golden light. First to offer itself along the path of this bumpkin torn from his mother, the marvelous tent, where the sleeping maiden lay near the stream in the flowering prairie, indicates that the adventure, finally at hand although upside-down, is, as always in these novels, feminine. The Fairy of the Golden Island in the *Bel Inconnu,* the daughter of the Fairy King in *Sir Launfal,* the Fairy lover of the *Lai de Lanval,* each offers the perfect delights of her lustful bed only to the man who, pledged to combat, has lost her for this very reason. The loves of Morgane the Fay, illicit, incestuous or infamous, were still cursed in order that one might know of just what buried happiness existence is composed. Happily for him, the *nice,* not at all that naïve when he flirted with his mother's chamber-maidens, is under the spell of the sexual interdiction echoed by the maternal discourse: that she forbid him, when he left, the *sorplus* (v. 546) prevents him from going any further at that moment when he would have had his way with the fair lady just as he did with her pâtés. The hand to hand combat, or the theft of the ring wrenched from her finger is only a ridiculous and yet monstrous simulacrum of the sexual act, his behavior being determined by the letter of an instruction to such an extent that its comes to display the contrary. The interdiction maintains a point of suspense here only in order to create the locus wherein the subject will have to recognize his desire as an index. But he may nonetheless miss his chance. The episode is therefore incomplete inasmuch as no battle with the Proud Knight is associated with an unrecognized sexual desire. Further on, the hero will come upon the same characters again as much in order to repair his mistake as to gain a consciousness of the relationship, yet to be established, between *Armes* and *Amors.*

Inversely, when the Red Knight appears at the moment which the logic of the narrative had reserved for the Proud Knight, as if he were his double, love is no longer the key, as it was when Erec challenged Yder or when Yvain challenged the Guardian of the Fountain. As for the Welsh youth, his only care is "les armes," not in the sense of a feat of strength to be accomplished, but literally, as the dazzling armor he dreams to wear. There is no place for a woman in this narcissistic *jouissance* which he takes in his own image. The episode is, in fact, crucial since finally the hero comes to Arthur's court where the novel might find again its predetermined framework: the opening of the *Bel Inconnu,* according to an identical proceeding, re-establishes, moreover, the expected configuration, in this case deliberately compromised, even caricatured. But does it not remain essential that the youth, who has gone off in search of Arthur, not know how to see or recognize him, for he sits among his diminished court, worried, silent and helpless to face the affront inflicted by the Red Knight, waiting for the appearance of the hero destined to restore the Golden Cup to him? Why should the king himself respond to a greeting from one who remains deaf to the reiterated signs of adventure as well as to the calls of pain? That he not be visible to the new arrival has a meaning, for his mourning is not of the visible order but requires the heart's intuition. It was instead the fleeting quality of the Red Arms, carried by an immobile knight, lance in hand, which occupied the front stage to the point of relegating him in this way to the shadow of a secondary place. The Golden Cup illuminates nonetheless the scene, but the youth has eyes only for the redness which is detached from it. Perceval remains on the side of Red and color, not on the side of Gold and light (Arthur, one learns later, had intended the golden arms for him). Doubtless, he is going to kill the Red Knight (but with a javelin, an unworthy arm, and in a bloody parody of battle) in order to substitute himself for him, rather than to submit him to the Round Table. The Red Armor appropriated his entire being instead of the Golden Cup opening up the path of adventure and revealing to him the nature of desire.

Who then is the Red Knight? His arms recall those of Mabonagrain, the Knight of the Enchanted Garden, an inversely symmetrical reflection of Erec and his adventure; and his role recalls that of Méléagant, a knight of too great stature just as the preceding one, the mortal enemy of Lancelot: each is, for the hero, the fatal figure of his double. Moreover is he not just like the Proud Knight, one of those *chevaliers faés,* threatening friends of enchanted maidens in the depths of woods or near streams, whom the Knights of the Round Table, in the course of their wanderings, force into King Arthur's service and into renewing his glory (cf. *l'Élucidation*)? They are the other of the Arthurian world which the latter must constantly vanquish. Finally, according to *Sir Percyvelle of Gales,* he was long ago the murderer of the hero's father; the Proud Knight of the Glade, on the other hand, if one is to believe Gauvain (v. 4073 ff.), was the most prestigious of the knights of the Isles of the Sea, precisely what the *nice's* mother had already said of his father (v. 414 ff.). Now, the conquering youth puts on the red armor and, upon setting out from the court, becomes the Red Knight for the others. In this way he changes identity without however finding his own: he has come to that place never occupied by anyone other than for their own misfortune. Yet he must still be pierced by and assume this misfortune, affirming his being only through the very pain of his existence in order to be truly identified as a knight. For want of this, comes the hilarious scene of divestiture: the youth is unable to remove the dead man's armor, just as he is unable to ungird his sword, for

> Ce dedanz et ce defors/ est trestot un
>
> vv. 1138-39

The armor adheres to the corpse, arms and body being comically one. But he refuses on the other hand to remove his rustic maternal clothing, obstinate in layering the emblems of knighthood upon those signs of savagery: when the *draps* cling in this way to his skin, they form a queer pair with *les armes*. But to have changed them would have been truly to change, as much a death to himself and to his *niceté*. It would have meant distinguishing the inside from the outside, and at the same time symbolizing it as that living thing which is transformed and dies ("la mue psychologique" as J. Frappier would have it), instead of being fixed in the brilliant rigidity of a cadaver. Under his helmet, does the Red Knight in fact have a face?

To the stray laugh of the naïve youth's eyes, however, responded the prophetic laughter of the maiden, just as the idiot's discourse saluted in him the coming of the most accomplished of knights. The hero's destiny is revealed through madness, a destiny he will later recognize in the destruction of his captivated self. The tears of that maiden, abused because of him, call thus for the coming of a man, just as the image of Arthur, which radiated suddenly with all the nobility of a Sarastro, or the symbol of the Sword which, unlike the Lance, is not seen at first, and like the hero will one day be broken, remain in waiting. *Niceté* or the Virgin Sword: such is the still absent mark of lack.

The story is organized now around other representations: the deep, black water, an insuperable barrier; the Castle of the Otherworld (with four towers, deserted or invisible), the seat of the adventure; the Waste Land, whose spell is to be broken. It is during this part that the hero gains in truthfulness without ever achieving anything, whether he assumes consecutively the aspect of knight, lover or chosen one.

After the Knight-God, the Damsel of the Tent and King Arthur, now there are Gornemant, the gentleman, Blanchefleur, the beloved one, and the Rich Fisher King. Is this to say that everything simply begins again? This sequel is inscribed within another framework, for the novel, like the polyphonic song which Chrétien alludes to in *Yvain*, reconciles several voices. Against a background of plains and rivers, stands a towered castle high above a rock, its main part dominating majestically the tumultuous mixing of river and ocean waters. This sovereign quality, imposing to the eyes of the traveler, is perceived at the very instant of its birth (cf. vv. 1322-24). Also, the voice of his blood-line speaks irresistibly within Perceval and the astonished world discovers suddenly about this novice knight the proudest bearing ever encountered. One single demonstration by his new master sufficed for the pupil who owed to his nature the task of equalling the best. The hero was once again captivated by the spectacle of the bearing of arms: each gesture, through a slow motion, fixed itself eternally in his memory and was played out according to a ritual in which knighthood, once again, renewed a pact made at its inception. The hero gave evidence of the same eagerness as on the first day, under the charm of a similar vision of *Armes*. His impatient hands took the Master's weapons, and he now learns from a master how to manage them. The hope of becoming a knight and a Red Knight is completed by the certainty of having been born a knight and of experiencing this. The scene however develops inversely to the first, renewing the rupture which ought to have been other. Before seeing, the youth must speak: Gornemant is not armed until after an exchange of words in which the Welsh youth participated rather than playing a deaf ear. Would he finally leave the imaginary in order to accede to the symbolic? Having arrived as "le valet gallois aux armes de sinople teintes" (v. 1219), he leaves "nouveau chevalier" (v. 1697): the ritual of dubbing presides over this changing of status. The gentleman recognized him to be a fool because of the language he used when greeting him was punctuated with allusions to his mother's advice. The *nice*'s discourse had to be detached from his mother, for one speaks only in the name of the Father. If he must, the hero will henceforth mention only the "vavasseur qui lui chaussa l'éperon." Already, in response to the question of where he came from, he no longer answers from the mother-like forest, but rather from Arthur's court. And if he had taught himself to put on his armor, he now gives in to his master's demands and renounces his mother's coarse garments. Finally, he does not forget to ask the gentleman's name, who, in giving him his sword, confers upon him "l'Ordre de Chevalerie" of which it is a symbol of honor. The old man who plays this role in *Sir Percyvelle* is the hero's *paternal* uncle: Gornemant, doubtless, re-presents the way of the Father, where the word prevails. To identify oneself with a knight implies then that one has renounced *niceté*, and entering into morality, far from rivalry, means counting oneself among the others: one cuts oneself off from oneself. It is only that slight difference between one who wields swords and one who wields (s)words that make a knight. This, moreover, is meaningful only inasmuch as one does not lose sight of what is at stake: Gornemant, the master, is still the host who gives lodging to the hero on the threshold of his adventure, and he is also the uncle of the Lady of the Waste Castle towards which Perceval finally directs his steps. A woman, Blanchefleur, incarnates then the place where truth finds its touchstone. It is remarkable that Perceval is finally troubled about having seen his mother fall, the day he divested himself of his simplemindedness. He is henceforth capable of being moved by the spectacle of mourning and tears, and the thought of the Widowed Lady of the Waste Forest leads him to the adventures, first of the Waste Castle where Blanchefleur grieves, and then of the *Val Perdu* where the invalid king suffers. But, having trained himself with his mother's pillows and boards, he pretended too quickly with Gornemant to know everything about the handling of a sword. And being forbidden by the *vavasseur* to speak too much, conveying the maternal interdiction of the amorous *sorplus,* keeps him from excess only in order to leave solely to his discernment, and at his own expense, the moment of avoiding the too little, sexually and linguistically.

In *Sir Percyvelle,* Lufamour whom the hero is engaged to serve, is the "Queen of Maydenlande." Morgane, first silhouetted behind the Damsel of the Tent, now appears through Blanchefleur. Beaurepaire concentrates all the signs of adventure: the perilous bridge, the empty castle, the maiden in the window, the funereal welcome, the four sergeants with axes, etc. But, as for Gornemant, the repetition counts only at the cost of its difference: here *Amors* and

Charles Méla

Armes enter into an indissoluble relationship and the young knight is elevated to the Arthurian conception of love, as the rused denegation of the damsel attests:

> Ne dites mie
> que je deveigne vostre amie
> *par tel covant* et *par tel loi*
> que vos ailliez morir por moi.

vv. 2111-14

This episode extends over almost one third of the Perceval section, recalling the unique adventure reserved for the heros of preceding novels: the sparrow hawk and "la pucelle au blanc chainse" (Erec) or the Magic Fountain (Yvain). It even condenses the two separate moments belonging to the Breton novel, since Blanchefleur's tears are a call at first for valor, but then become an invitation to renunciation, just as, at Enide's side, Erec abandoned himself to *récréance*. Perceval will thus have learned all at one time that if it has no other end term than the fairy, wandering itself is without end. To remain with Blanchefleur would be to lose himself, but to pursue his wandering would be to lose her. From now on, the hero, dispossessed of his self by the hostess' grace, should no longer remain in one place in order not to belie the experience of desire which he now recognized. At this instant, as if it were a disquieting obligation (cf. v. 2950), the recollection of his mother, which will guide him to the Graal, confronts the *aise* which he would have forever tasted in the perfect forgetting (v. 2911). An entire population, returned from exile, salutes him, Yvain's or Lancelot's equal, as their savior; and the novice knight, instead of killing them and after trying unsatisfactory solutions, sends those he conquered to Arthur's court and restores its meaning. It is the locus of any language in which are gathered the stories of the Otherworld, the Voices of the Fays, or the echoes of glory, but also a place where the hero is always absent, in order to leave there only his renown. When he leaves Beaurepaire which he rendered to life, the Red Knight, the *nice,* took on a man's flesh. A woman's face, as well as the nocturnal whiteness of her body and her mournful tears, had allowed this miracle to take place. Yet, the hero's ecstasy at the sight of Blanchefleur is completely other than his fascination with the Red Armor: seeing is no longer the greed which anticipates possession, but the rapture which opens an insuperable distance within which another dispossesses one of oneself (v. 1824). Just as his body is disquieted, so the hero awakens to desire. The *nice* for whom a bed is prepared, completely ignorant of amorous delights, sinks quickly into sleep, too sure of missing nothing: "de rien n'était-il donc en souci" (v. 1942). Stealing into his bed, the maiden awakens in him all the gentle desire tormenting his heart. But eroticism is pushed back into the fringes of the story, for this sleepless night is inhabited by words and filled with tears of misfortune. An absence to oneself, in the agitation of the senses, disquiets the soul: thus consciousness (moral included) comes upon the marks left by desire. If the knight is resplendent in the brillance of his armor, it is because the night has swallowed up his heart. The Red Armor symbolizes then the desert of any joy, for he who bears it lives henceforth haunted by the misfortune of the Waste Land.

The Damsel's tent reflected the accursed colors of *jouissance* for a mind obsessed by the dream of the Knight-God. Blanchefleur's face displaces the representation, produces, as if it were a recall, the future vision of the cortege at the castle of the Maimed King and prepares for the assumption of misfortune. Red is still the dominate color, but it is no longer the Red of murderous armor and weapons in the golden solar radiance of a summer's day, but that of blood. And it is blood not only flushing a face luminous with whiteness, the blush of a complexion in which life trembles, a promise of the joy of love, but it is also blood flowing from a wound, truth of the suffering enclosed by night or iced by a winter morning. In these reflections of sacrifice, Perceval can now perceive Blanchefleur, whose blood pulses in order that life re-flower where the desert reigned. But the knight who had left the gentleman owing him nothing for his art of wielding a sword, left the Waste Castle a virgin and will remain mute at the castle of the Rich Fisher King.

At the moment of truth, the story folds back upon itself, the vision of the marvelous cortege and the castle of the maternal uncle recalls that of the armed angels in the mother's forest, and the sad words of the maiden faithful to her dead man, those of the Widowed Lady faithful to the memory of the father. But at the same time, the representations which have appeared during the adventure are joined and exchanged, for the mysterious spectacle draws Blanchefleur's face in outline, and through the womanly grieving one can glimpse the murderer's silhouette. Finally, the enigmatic fisherman, and the damsel in the forest, are, on his mother's side, the hero's cousins, as if no echo or appeal whatsoever from his father could ever reach him which did not harken back to the profound distress of a barren maternal land.

As he invokes, during his prayer to see his mother again one day, "le roi de gloire," God, "le sien père" (v. 2975), a deep and rapid water bars his way: he then imagines that his mother awaits him on the opposite bank. But there is neither ford nor bridge, and the castle where there is lodging, which the fisherman points out to him through a breach in the rock, is located on the same bank he is following. If the thought of his mother, the torment of his soul, reopens the right path for him, he is not allowed to return to her; and the Castle of Nowhere, where one expects to hear from him the name which would have broken the spell, is interposed and *forbids him to cross the deep water.* But the tower which comes into view, flanked by its turrets, like Gornemant's donjon, appears nonetheless in the depths of a valley where an instant before nothing had been visible. In order to return the father to his rightful place, he must yet *pierce the invisible,* and Perceval, who is vainly impatient: "Que suis-je venu quérir?" (v. 3034), ignores this. During the welcome which is finally his, one perceives first, as if in superimposition, a reminder of his arrival at Arthur's: the courtliness and the discomfort of the king, the same square hall, the signs of destiny (from the laugh of the damsel to the Sword of the *sore pucelle*), the mysterious equivalence between the Golden Cup and the light of the Grail, which illuminates the Red Knight and the Bleeding Lance. The fate of this world is played out in the other: if the hero does not live as intimately as possible with his fear of the Waste Land, it is the entire world, as symbolized by Arthur's realm, which will become wasted land. But the scene is, moreover, ordered as was the evening during which Blanchefleur was revealed to him: the solitude before being given lodging by a mourning host, the dazzling nocturnal vision, the guest's silence, the preparations for the repast and the care taken at bed-time, the movement from one chamber to another (whether it is a lady's or an old spiritual man's). Truthfully, all that matters here is in the details: from the white hair of the gentleman dressed in black sable and crimson, as the hostess appeared not so long ago between two hoary gentlemen, to the ebony and ivory table, precious materials which served, like the stones and the gold of the grail, to form the hyperbolic portrait of the beloved woman. One discovers in both instances the unrivaled *Merveille* of Redness within Whiteness: the blood, beaded along the white lance. In fact, is not the stroke of genius worthy of immortalizing Chrétien de Troyes, according to his wish, that of having thus rhymed the mysterious cortege with Blanchefleur's face in order that it become its *semblance?*

In the course of the feast, when the Lance arrives, the story is fixed, as the actors themselves, in this immobile flow of blood which defies time and fills up one's gaze. Given over completely to what he sees, Perceval remains speechless and comes back to himself only too late to ask the proper questions. The aggressive youth, who upon seeing the master's arms, demanded the why of everything, is nothing more than a mute knight, strangely passive when the Arm endowed with the power of Redness returns. He dreamed of possessing the weapon of death, and here he is possessed by it. The deadly *merveille* appropriated the woman's colors; the Accursed Lance is the *Semblant* which captivates his sight. But the Grail? This dish upon which the food is presented, followed by the carving platter *(taillor),* appears only in a second moment, distinct from that of the Lance, and at the same time like a profusion, an over-abundance of light, and like a movement, a passing from one place to another. It would be proper to ask why the Lance is bleeding, but, with respect to the Grail, what does one do with it and to whom is it carried? So much light emanates from the Grail only in order that the guest know that he is being watched by the suffering king, anxious to have his question, and that he thus undo his own gaze from the vision of the Lance, break the spell with his word, and learn of the Dolorous Stroke which it dealt. For want of this, Perceval awakens the following morning in an empty castle and cries out to the invisible gate-keeper as he leaves: "Où es-tu quand je ne te vois?" (v. 3404). What exactly should he have seen? His cousin's revelations, immediately afterwards, emphasize the physical anguish of the Fisher King and the sexual nature of his infirmity. But what should he have known? The hermit will later reveal to him the identity of the mysterious person, his mother's brother, to whom one serves the Grail and who is nourished from it, like a pure spirit. One must certainly add under this sacred heading, the gift of the Fabulous Sword made to the hero, brought by his niece, the blond maiden, and presented to him before the arrival of the sacred cortege. The Lance comes then between the Sword, symbol of goodness, and the Grail, revelation of his kinship. To what end then is the Grail King redoubled? For the son of the Widowed Lady, to go beyond the immediate scene (as far as the invisible old man, his uncle) would have led him back to the absent Father in order that his name come back to him, but to see the invalid who was close beside him (the Fisher King, his cousin) would have allowed him to see himself and to enable him to be moved by the spectacle which offered itself to his eyes. As if a mirror image, the *valet* (v. 3179) who holds the Lance firmly recalls the *valet* (v. 3190) subjugated by the prodigy, but what is one to make then of the blood flowing onto the bearer's hand? Instead, the Grail is between the hands of a damsel who partakes of its luminosity: why is she described as was Blanchefleur, "bele et jointe et bien

acesmée" (v. 3211; vv. 1793-94)? Doubtless, the wound of the Fisherman is itself the analogue of the father's, but was he not struck with a javelin, the weapon *par excellence* of the Welsh youth, with which the latter brought down the Red Knight? If he testifies without Perceval's knowledge to what was his murderous rage, he is still the victim of his own silence, telling of his culpability. And, if for his cousin, he is the image of his sin, does he not represent to him his own castration?

Echoing the tardy awakening of the hero, the weeping maiden appears embracing the beheaded knight under the oak: only death resounds here, and malediction. The hero is uneasy now: who killed the knight? As he learns further on, he is dead in his stead, paying for a fault for which only he is responsible (v. 3880). Just as the blood of the Lance rebounded upon him, the recumbant figure confronts him with his own death. For whom does his cousin weep if not for him, "Perceval l'infortuné," in whose eyes the head cut from the knight should be symbolic? The fabulous vision of the cortege, heavy with his silence, relives through the word in the dialogue he engages, while the octosyllabic meter bursts open and breaks into pieces under the harassment of his questions.

It is unusual in Chrétien's work that the story be twice told; the novel of the Grail henceforth progresses only through its own repetition: the episode of the Proud Knight reminds him of his fault, the drops of blood on the snow offer the *semblance* of Blanche-fleur, the Loathly Damsel brings back what was repressed. The story is now only the memory where abounds what had come to pass in order to force Perceval's consciousness. The echo of the cortege comes again in his cousin's words, set within the evocation of the maimed king who receives the name of Fisher King and the revela-tion of Perceval's sin, guilty of his mother's death, which explains his *méchéance* soon after the intuition of his own name. But what of these names which seem to be surnames, "fisherman" and "dis-coverer" (*Perce*val), the ones which always leave gaping the place of the Name of the Father? Rigorously, the episode, which opened with the spectacle of the beheaded knight, closes with an allusion

to the Sword which will be broken and resoldered only at the cost
of great pain. Perceval does not hear: upon hearing the news of
his mother's death, he acted inversely to his cousin, refusing that
his life be preoccupied any more with death:

<blockquote>
Les morz as morz, les vis as vis

v. 3616
</blockquote>

At the very least, through her appeal to avenge the dead man, the
maiden orients him, unaware, towards that Other who was also
once upon a time the victim of the lineage of the Proud Knight
of the Glade.

By means of an effect of *conjointure,* the last three episodes are
bathed in an Arthurian light. Each obeys the same schema: a vision
(misery, grace or horror), a dialogued exchange (challenge, courtliness or shame) and an emotion which upsets the court (regret,
joy or impatience). The Proud Knight and his damsel and the Red
Knight dreaming over the snow offer in diptych a representation
of sexual impossibility, contrasted through hate or *Fine Amour.*
In both instances, there is the solitude of the wood haunted by the
unhappy woman or of the snow-covered prairie where Blanchefleur
relives; the "traces" of tears which have hollowed out a woman's
face or of blood on the snow in the likeness *(semblance)* of the
beloved, and a story of sexual violence, this *mêlée* of man and
woman, or of the flight of the falcon who throws the wild goose,
dazzled by the light, to the ground amid the trampled snow. In
the same way that Erec re-established, according to the model of the
courtly lover and the Arthurian knight, the love of the Fay of
the Garden and the Red Knight (Mabonagrain), under the aegis
of Arthur, Perceval reconciles the Proud Knight and the Damsel of
the Tent. But the jealous man has nonetheless decried the depths
of hate which incite the *mêlée* of the sexes: the man not forgiving
the woman for having made a comic conqueror of him, the woman
not admitting that she owes him anything in this affair; she would
like to have put nothing into it, in order to *be* everything for

herself, he would not have wanted that in escaping from him, she caused him to doubt that he *had* everything (vv. 3845-58). Perceval's ecstasy, finally worthy of Lancelot, reflects on the contrary an experience of absence and a representation of loss. In the eyes of Gauvain henceforth present,

> Li chevaliers d'aucune *perte*
> estoit *pansis* qu'il avoit fete.
>
> vv. 4336-37

Everything begins with a hunting scene just as at the inception of the novel, and not without the falcon, deadly to the wild goose, rekindling the memory of the brute who in the isolated prairie threw the tearful damsel beneath him without however assaulting her. Perceval sets out only to stop abruptly before the traces of battle in the snow: what he sees and what takes him away from himself is an object, itself absent. It is as if his eyes were accustomed to seeing the invisible, for he is dazzled by the one who is there only by means of an immaterial reflection, when the precious drops of blood evaporate in the sun. But this *semblance* of the beloved's face is itself a reflection of a reflection, since the blood mingled with the snow had sprung from a wound recalling the Redness wept by the Lance. The *semblance* of Blanchefleur is the putting into absence of the *Semblant* of the Lance; it is written out in the snow like a metaphor of desire, when the blood shed by a woman prevails over the renounced redness of Arms. For Perceval, would one forget it?, stands erect, immobile, his red stature amid the white prairie: he leans on his *lance* called to the rhyme by the *semblance* of the three drops of blood in order to conceal it from sight (vv. 4177, 4305, 4399). Curiously, although he is observed by all, mention is never made during the entire episode of the red color of his armor; and when Gauvain leads him to Arthur, he has rid him beforehand of this armor in order to clothe him elegantly in courtly garments.

Thus Perceval is susceptible to moral and amorous representations, whether he has finally answered for his actions, or apprehended himself in the other, whether he revealed himself capable of emotion and humor, or poetry and courtliness. Nothing however is accomplished, for if he broaches the truth, he has not put himself into the game nor recognized himself as having fallen short and being accursed. The representation of desire is not yet affirmed in the mark which bruises his flesh and stupefies his spirit. The Grail, too soon forgotten by him recalls itself suddenly to mind in the middle of the Arthurian reunion; but instead of the maiden carrying the Grail, the Loathly Damsel (the same person, according to *Peredur*) now re-presents it: a vision of horror in the place of the *Merveille,* just as Fortune, bald from behind and hairy from in front, depicts it. Against this infernal background is detached the guilty silence of the chosen one under the spell of the Lance. Why was the Lance bleeding? Who was the rich man served by the Grail? How could Perceval not have felt the horror of knowing something, when what fascinated him then now returned to petrify him, uncovering the fear of the Waste Land and the devastation, henceforth promised to the world (daughters without fathers, wives without husbands, a land without a master), harbored by the dazzling *Semblant* of the Lance. Accursed be he, she cried to the banished man,

> Qui voit
> si bel tans que plus ne covaigne
> *si atant tant que plus biaux vaïgne!*

> vv. 4638-4640

It was necessary to detach his gaze from the vision, instead of being suspended to it, in the funereal desire of seeing more of it, when nothing other than the sexual mutilation of the Fisherman concerned him, nor did anything await him beyond the "rich man" but the estranged name of the Father. The ugly messenger has holes in place of her eyes, fixing Perceval with the same hollow orbits as his older brother, who once upon a time wanted, just as he does now, to bear the father's arms.

The *Unheimlichkeit* undoes the fantasy and threatens the representation itself. The story is disseminated in as many *merveilles* which suddenly invade the land of Logres, proliferating there and dispersing Arthur's court: the Proud Castle, the Perilous Mount, the Damsel of Montesclaire. What is one to think of the promise made by Perceval, who alone among the others engaged himself in the henceforth impossible quest for the Grail and the Lance? He, who was forgetful of his mother, then indifferent as to the fate of the Fisherman, as if he were a stranger to the affair, would from now on give his life to this quest, in innumerable adventures (not told) but for another forgetting: having become this time a stranger to himself, he loses the memory of God and of His cross. One last time, the story begins again and, on the path of the lost one, the hermit, his uncle, holds up the Name of God. Everything is turned back and the circle is closed in the inverse direction: Perceval is now the armed knight who goes through the desert, to the surprise of the penitents, ladies with knights among them. Instead of being enraptured by the appearance of the Knight-God, he learns that the true divinity has hidden himself in the body of a man; instead of angels who sow death, one speaks of God dead on the cross Who returns the dead to life (and according to the author's wish, articulated in the prologue, his novel will be a germ of life in fertile lands); instead of the fantasy of being born completely armed, there is the mystery of the Incarnation, God born of a Virgin; instead of untimely questions, he asks the penitents what they asked the hermit. As if awaking from a bad dream, he comes back to the time of men upon learning that it is Holy Friday. Five years of wandering thus opened the same empty parenthesis as the years of infancy in the Waste Forest. At the recollection of his sins, the hero who had never cried for anyone finally receives the gift of tears and cries for himself. Only then does he come into the presence of the hermit, his maternal uncle, a saintly man (un "saint homme") living by divine glory (v. 6095), who exhorts him to humility in front of God and reveals to him the identity of the invisible Grail King, another saintly man nourished only by the host, a brother also of his mother. According to this pious model, the hero worships the almightiness of the true God which he renounced for himself. And in order to imprint his heart with fear, the hermit murmurs in his ear the oration forbidden to the lips of man, "des Noms Nostre Seignor" (v. 6263), while the repenter *reconnut*

> que Deux au vandredi recut
> mort et si fut crocefïez

vv. 6283-85

For lack of the Name of the Father, the Holy Man imposes the Names of God within the maternal orbit; in place of the sexual wound, the Body of Christ as martyr calls for atonement and tears.

The structure of the Perceval section appears thus:

(maternal manor; Waste Forest)	(Castle of the Fisherman King; Lost Vale)	(Hermitage; Desert)
the Knight-God (names of the Arms)	the Lance (Name of the Father?)	the Saintly Man (names of God)
the fantasy of the Red Armor	the invisible host	the Crucifixion
	the Maimed King (castration?) the Grail	

The episode of the hermit comes in the middle of Gauvain's adventures when the story is wandering about and redoubling itself endlessly. Holiness tolls the death knell of the *Féerie,* at the very moment when it overflows like the strange dream of this accursed story, inasmuch as Gauvain is accused of having traitorously killed the father of the King of Escavalon, the youth of ineffable beauty. In Escavalon however, after having chased the white doe and after having encountered the Huntsman King incognito, he learns of love's joy beside the latter's sister who welcomes him as a brother and who would have given herself to him if there had not suddenly appeared an old man of biblical mien who cursed her. According to *Sir Gawain and the Green Knight,* one knows that the hero escapes the beheading promised him in return by the Green Knight, his future host, under the lineaments of the Huntsman, a monstrous figure of the Dreadful Father, only because he resisted the seduction of the unfaithful wife, alias Morgane the Fay. It is true that for having accepted her green silk belt, he will remain marked by a gash on the neck. Is it chance if, like the Proud Knights of *Perceval*, Meliant de Lis and Greoreas, through their amorous excess or their sexual violence, are placed in opposition to the paternal figures of Tiebaut (Bran?) and Arthur? By means of a redoubling analogous to that of the master of the Grail, the Huntsman became the son of the dead king and his beauty reflected to Gauvain his own image, just as his cousin's had recalled to Perceval his own castration. Did not the tournament of Tintagel recall the celebrated beauty of Arthur's nephew? Now, in a second time of his adventures, which redoubles the first, Gauvain, unlike Perceval, crosses the deep water in order to find on the other side a fertile land, abounding in game. There in the Palace of Marvels, from which emerge to the waist, as one would say of the river itself, dazzling damsels, after the trial of the Marvelous Bed (a stream of arrows and lion's claws), the Mothers whom one believed dead await him. The realm of the White-Haired Queen is a fantasized world of death where one would hope to be able to vanish. But after his victory, Gauvain, who like the Fisher King had donned the black sable and the red *sanguine*, must break the spells which are similar to those Perceval provoked by his failure. He owes it to the Scornful Damsel, who incessantly harassed him and made fun of him, that he did not delay in this closed paradise and that he encountered at the Perilous Ford, in the figure of Guiromelant, a being as beautiful as the King of Escavalon, who hated him for a similar reason, but who loved the one Gauvain knew not to be his own sister, at the risk of begging for her love as he did the Damsel of Escavalon. Since he asked the necessary questions, he avoids incest, and in convoking Arthur's court in order to watch his duel with Guiromelant, he breaks the imprisonment of the Enchanted Palace. Did he not with the same stroke exorcise his double?

Charles Méla

If the adventure of Perceval ends in the horror of the Waste Land where his culpability begins, that of Gauvain goes back further to the time of a rivalry struck by Interdiction. This is why the first, through his failure, produced the second as his unfinished dream.

English adaptation by Catherine Lowe (and the author)

Peter Brooks

Freud's Masterplot

> As if they would confine th' Interminable,
> And tie him to his own prescript.

In one of his best essays in "narratology," where he is working toward a greater formalization of principles advanced by Vladimir Propp and Viktor Shklovsky, Tzvetan Todorov elaborates a model of narrative transformation whereby narrative plot *(le récit)* is constituted in the tension of two formal categories, difference and resemblance. [1] Transformation—a change in a predicate term common to beginning and end—represents a synthesis of difference and resemblance; it is, we might say, the same-but-different. Now "the same-but-different" is a common (and if inadequate, not altogether false) definition of metaphor. If Aristotle affirmed that the master of metaphor must have an eye for resemblances, modern treatments of the subject have affirmed equally the importance of difference included within the operation of resemblance, the chief value of the metaphor residing in its "tension." Narrative operates as metaphor in its affirmation of resemblance, in that it brings into relation different actions, combines them through perceived similarities (Todorov's common predicate term), appropriates them to a common plot, which implies the rejection of merely contingent (or unassimilable) incident or action. The plotting of meaning cannot do without metaphor, for meaning in plot is the structure of action

---

[1] Tzvetan Todorov, "Les Transformations narratives," in *Poétique de la prose* (Paris: Seuil, 1971), p. 240. Todorov's terms *récit* and *histoire* correspond to the Russian Formalist distinction between *sjužet* and *fabula*. In English, we might use with the same sense of distinctions: narrative *plot* and *story*.

I wish at the outset of this essay to express my debt to two colleagues whose thinking has helped to clarify my own: Andrea Bertolini and David A. Miller. It is to the latter that I owe the term "the narratable."

Peter Brooks

in closed and legible wholes. Metaphor is in this sense totalizing. Yet it is equally apparent that the key figure of narrative must in some sense be not metaphor but metonymy: the figure of contiguity and combination, the figure of syntagmatic relations. [2] The description of narrative needs metonymy as the figure of movement, of linkage in the signifying chain, of the slippage of the signified under the signifier. That Jacques Lacan has equated metonomy and desire is of the utmost pertinence, since desire must be considered the very motor of narrative, its dynamic principle.

The problem with "the same-but-different" as a definition of narrative would be the implication of simultaneity and stasis in the formulation. The postulation of a static model indeed is the central deficiency of most formalist and structuralist work on narrative, which has sought to make manifest the structures of narrative in spatial and atemporal terms, as versions of Lévi-Strauss' "atemporal matrix structure." [3] Todorov is an exception in that, faithful to Propp, he recognizes the need to consider sequence and succession as well as the paradigmatic matrix. He supplements his definition with the remark: "Rather than a 'coin with two faces,' [transformation] is an operation in two directions: it affirms at once resemblance and difference; it puts time into motion and suspends it, in a single movement; it allows discourse to acquire a meaning without this meaning becoming pure information; in a word, it makes narrative possible and reveals its very definition." [4] The image

[2] See Roman Jakobson, "Two Types of Language and Two Types of Aphasic Disturbances," in Jakobson and Halle, *Fundamentals of Language* (The Hague: Mouton, 1956). Todorov in a later article adds to "transformation" the term "succession," and sees the pair as definitional of narrative. He discusses the possible equation of these terms with Jakobson's "metaphor" and "metonymy," to conclude that "the connection is possible but does not seem necessary." (Todorov, "The Two Principles of Narrative," *Diacritics*, Fall, 1971, p. 42.) But there seem to be good reasons to maintain Jakobson's terms as "master tropes" referring to two aspects of virtually any text.

[3] See Claude Lévi-Strauss, "La Structure et la forme," *Cahiers de l'Institut de science économique appliquée*, 99, série M, no. 7 (1960), p. 29. This term is cited with approval by A. J. Greimas in *Sémantique structurale* (Paris: Larousse, 1966) and Roland Barthes, in "Introduction à l'analyse structurale des récits," *Communications* 8 (1966).

[4] Todorov, "Les Transformations narratives," *Poétique de la prose*, p. 240. Translations from the French, here and elsewhere, are my own.

of a double operation upon time has the value of returning us to the evident but frequently eluded fact that narrative meanings are developed in time, that any narrative partakes more or less of what Proust called "un jeu formidable ... avec le Temps," and that this game of time is not merely in the world of reference (or in the *fabula*) but as well in the narrative, in the *sjužet,* be it only that the meanings developed by narrative *take time:* the time of reading. [5] If at the end of a narrative we can suspend time in a moment where past and present hold together in a metaphor which may be the very recognition which, said Aristotle, every good plot should bring, that moment does not abolish the movement, the slidings, the errors and partial recognitions of the middle. As Roland Barthes points out, in what so far must be counted our most satisfactory dynamic analysis of plot, the proairetic and hermeneutic codes— code of actions, code of enigmas and answers—are irreversible: their interpretation is determined linearly, in sequence, in one direction. [6]

Ultimately—Barthes writes elsewhere—the passion that animates us as readers of narrative is the passion for (of) meaning. [7] Since for Barthes meaning (in the "classical" or "readable" text) resides in full predication, completion of the codes in a "plenitude" of signification, this passion appears to be finally a desire for the end. It is at the end—for Barthes as for Aristotle—that recognition brings its illumination, which then can shed retrospective light. The function of the end, whether considered syntactically (as in Todorov and Barthes) or ethically (as in Aristotle) or as formal or cosmological closure (as in Barbara H. Smith or Frank Kermode) continues to fascin⌐   ⌐and to baffle. One of the strongest statements of its determi⌐   ⌐ᵒn in narrative plots comes in a passage from Sartre'⌐   ⌐ı bears quotation once again. Roquentin is ref⌐   ⌐ning of "adventure" and the difference be-

---

cited by Gerard Genette in "Discours du récit," *Figures III* (Paris: Seuil, 1972), p. 182. Whereas Barthes maintains in "Introduction à l'analyse structurale des récits" that time belongs only to the referent of narrative, Genette gives attention to the time of reading and its necessary linearity. See pp. 77-78.

[6] See Roland Barthes, *S/Z* (Paris: Seuil, 1970), p. 37.

[7] "Introduction à l'analyse structurale des récits," p. 27.

tween living and narrating. When you narrate, you appear to start with a beginning. You say, "It was a fine autumn evening in 1922. I was a notary's clerk in Marommes." But, says Roquentin:

In reality you have started at the end. It was there, invisible and present, it is what gives these few words the pomp and value of a beginning. "I was out walking, I had left the town without realizing it, I was thinking about my money troubles." This sentence, taken simply for what it is, means that the man was absorbed, morose, a hundred miles from an adventure, exactly in a mood to let things happen without noticing them. But the end is there, transforming everything. For us, the man is already the hero of the story. His moroseness, his money troubles are much more precious than ours, they are all gilded by the light of future passions. And the story goes on in the reverse: instants have stopped piling themselves up in a haphazard way one on another, they are caught up by the end of the story which draws them and each one in its turn draws the instant preceding it: "It was night, the street was deserted." The sentence is thrown out negligently, it seems superfluous; but we don't let ourselves be duped, we put it aside: this is a piece of information whose value we will understand later on. And we feel that the hero has lived all the details of this night as annunciations, as promises, or even that he has lived only those that were promises, blind and deaf to all that did not herald adventure. We forget that the future wasn't yet there; the man was walking in a night without premonitions, which offered him in disorderly fashion its monotonous riches, and he did not choose. [8]

The beginning in fact presupposes the end. The very possibility of meaning plotted through time depends on the anticipated structuring force of the ending: the interminable would be the meaningless. We read the incidents of narration as "promises and annunciations" of final coherence: the metaphor reached through the chain of metonymies. As Roquentin further suggests, we read only those incidents and signs which can be construed as promise and annunciation, enchained toward a construction of significance—those signs which, as in the detective story, appear to be *clues* to the underlying intentionality of event.

The sense of beginning, then, is determined by the sense of an ending. And if we inquire further into the nature of the ending, we no doubt find that it eventually has to do with the human end, with

---

[8] Jean-Paul Sartre, *La Nausée* (Paris: Livre de Poche, 1957), pp. 62-63.

death. In *Les Mots,* Sartre pushes further his reflection on ends. He describes how in order to escape contingency and the sense of being unjustified he had to imagine himself as one of the children in *L'Enfance des hommes illustres,* determined, as promise and annunciation, by what he would become for posterity. He began to live his life retrospectively, in terms of the death that alone would confer meaning and necessity on existence. As he succinctly puts it, "I became my own obituary." [9] All narration is obituary in that life acquires definable meaning only at, and through, death. In an independent but convergent argument, Walter Benjamin has claimed that life assumes transmissible form only at the moment of death. For Benjamin, this death is the very "authority" of narrative: we seek in fictions the knowledge of death, which in our own lives is denied to us. Death—which may be figural but in the classic instances of the genre is so often literal—quickens meaning: it is the "flame," says Benjamin, at which we warm our "shivering" lives. [10]

We need to know more about this death-like ending which is nonetheless animating of meaning in relation to initiatory desire, and about how the interrelationship of the two determines, shapes, necessitates the middle—Barthes' "dilatory space" of retard, postponement—and the kinds of vacillation between illumination and blindness that we find there. If the end is recognition which retrospectively illuminates beginning and middle, it is not the exclusive truth of the text, which must include the processes along the way—the processes of "transformation"—in their metonymical complexity. If beginning is desire, and is ultimately desire for the end, between lies a process we feel to be necessary (plots, Aristotle tells us, must be of "a certain length") but whose relation to originating desire and to end remains problematic. It is here that Freud's most ambitious investigation of ends in relation to begin-

---

[9] Sartre, *Les Mots* (Paris: Gallimard, 1968), p. 171.
[10] Walter Benjamin, "The Storyteller," in *Illuminations,* translated by Harry Zohn (New York: Schocken Books, 1969), p. 101.

Peter Brooks

nings may be of help—and may suggest a contribution to a properly dynamic model of plot.

We undertake, then, to read *Beyond the Pleasure Principle* as an essay about the dynamic interrelationship of ends and beginnings, and the kind of processes that constitute the middle. The enterprise may find a general sort of legitimation in the fact that *Beyond the Pleasure Principle* is in some sense Freud's own masterplot, the text in which he most fully lays out a total scheme of how life proceeds from beginning to end, and how each individual life in its own way repeats the masterplot. Of Freud's various intentions in this text, the boldest—and most mysterious—may be to provide a theory of comprehension of the dynamic of the life-span, its necessary duration and its necessary end, hence, implicitly, a theory of the very narratability of life. In his pursuit of his "beyond," Freud is forced to follow the implications of argument—"to throw oneself into a line of thought and follow it wherever it leads," as he says late in the essay—to ends that he had not originally or consciously conceived.[11] *Beyond the Pleasure Principle* shows the very plotting of a masterplot made necessary by the structural demands of Freud's thought, and it is in this sense that we shall attempt to read it as a model for narrative plot.

Narrative always makes the implicit claim to be in a state of repetition, as a going over again of a ground already covered: a *sjužet* repeating the *fabula*, as the detective retraces the tracks of the criminal.[12] This claim to an act of repetition—"I sing," "I tell"—appears to be initiatory of narrative. It is equally initiatory of *Beyond the Pleasure Principle;* it is the first problem and clue that Freud confronts. Evidence of a "beyond" that does not fit neatly into the functioning of the pleasure principle comes first in

[11] Sigmund Freud, "Beyond the Pleasure Principle" (1920), in *The Standard Edition of the Complete Psychological Works of Sigmund Freud,* ed. James Strachey (London: Hogarth Press, 1955), 18, 59. Subsequent page references will be given between parentheses in the text.
[12] J. Hillis Miller, in "Ariadne's Web" (unpublished manuscript), notes that the term *diegesis* suggests that narrative is a retracing of a journey already made. On the detective story, see Tzvetan Todorov, "Typologie du roman policier," *Poétique de la prose,* pp. 58-59.

the dreams of patients suffering from war neuroses, or from the traumatic neuroses of peace: dreams which return to the moment of trauma, to relive its pain in apparent contradiction of the wish-fulfillment theory of dreams. This "dark and dismal" example is superseded by an example from "normal" life, and we have the celebrated moment of child's play: the toy thrown away, the reel on the string thrown out of the crib and pulled back, to the alternate exclamation of *fort* and *da*. When he has established the equivalence between making the toy disappear and the child's mother's disappearance, Freud is faced with a set of possible interpretations. Why does the child repeat an unpleasurable experience? It may be answered that by staging his mother's disappearance and return, the child is compensating for his instinctual renunciation. Yet the child has also staged disappearance alone, without reappearance, as a game. This may make one want to argue that the essential experience involved is the movement from a passive to an active role in regard to his mother's disappearance, claiming mastery in a situation which he has been compelled to submit to.

Repetition as the movement from passivity to mastery reminds us of "The Theme of the Three Caskets," where Freud, considering Bassanio's choice of the lead casket in *The Merchant of Venice* —the correct choice in the suit of Portia—decides that the choice of the right maiden in man's literary play is also the choice of death; by this choice, he asserts an active mastery of what he must in fact endure. "Choice stands in the place of necessity, of destiny. In this way man overcomes death, which he has recognized intellectually." [13] If repetition is mastery, movement from the passive to the active; and if mastery is an assertion of control over what man must in fact submit to—choice, we might say, of an imposed end—we have already a suggestive comment on the grammar of plot, where repetition, taking us back again over the same ground, could have to do with the choice of ends.

[13] Freud, "The Theme of the Three Caskets" (1913), *Standard Edition*, 12, 299.

Peter Brooks

But other possibilities suggest themselves to Freud at this point. The repetition of unpleasant experience—the mother's disappearance—might be explained by the motive of revenge, which would yield its own pleasure. The uncertainty which Freud faces here is whether repetition can be considered a primary event, independent of the pleasure principle, or whether there is always some direct yield of pleasure of another sort involved. The pursuit of this doubt takes Freud into the analytic experience, to his discovery of patients' need to repeat, rather than simply remember, repressed material: the need to reproduce and to "work through" painful material from the past as if it were present. The analyst can detect a "compulsion to repeat," ascribed to the unconscious repressed, particularly discernable in the transference, where it can take "ingenious" forms. The compulsion to repeat gives patients a sense of being fatefully subject to a "perpetual recurrence of the same thing"; it suggests to them pursuit by a daemonic power. We know also, from Freud's essay on "The Uncanny," that this feeling of the daemonic, arising from involuntary repetition, is a particular attribute of the literature of the uncanny. [14]

Thus in analytic work (as also in literary texts) there is slim but real evidence of a compulsion to repeat which can over-ride the pleasure principle, and which seems "more primitive, more elementary, more instinctual than the pleasure principle which it overrides" (23). We might note at this point that the transference itself is a metaphor, a substitutive relationship for the patient's infantile experiences, and thus approximates the status of a text. Now repetition is so basic to our experience of literary texts that one is simultaneously tempted to say all and to say nothing on the subject. To state the matter baldly: rhyme, alliteration, assonance, meter, refrain, all the mnemonic elements of fictions and indeed most of its tropes are in some manner repetitions which take us back in the text, which allow the ear, the eye, the mind to make connections between different textual moments, to see past and

[14] See Freud, "The Uncanny" (Das Unheimliche) (1919), in Standard Edition, 17, 219-52.

present as related and as establishing a future which will be noticeable as some variation in the pattern. Todorov's "same but different" depends on repetition. If we think of the trebling characteristic of the folk tale, and of all formulaic literature, we may consider that the repetition by three constitutes the minimal repetition to the perception of series, which would make it the minimal intentional structure of action, the minimum plot. Narrative must ever present itself as a repetition of events that have already happened, and within this postulate of a generalized repetition it must make use of specific, perceptible repetitions in order to create plot, that is, to show us a significant interconnection of events. Event gains meaning by repeating (with variation) other events. Repetition is a *return* in the text, a doubling back. We cannot say whether this return is a return *to* or a return *of:* for instance, a return to origins or a return of the repressed. Repetition through this ambiguity appears to suspend temporal process, or rather, to subject it to an indeterminate shuttling or oscillation which binds different moments together as a middle which might turn forward or back. This inescapable middle is suggestive of the daemonic. The relation of narrative plot to story may indeed appear to partake of the daemonic, as a kind of tantalizing play with the primitive and the instinctual, the magic and the curse of reproduction or "representation." But in order to know more precisely the operations of repetition, we need to read further in Freud's text.

"What follows is speculation" (24). With this gesture, Freud, in the manner of Rousseau's dismissal of the facts in the *Discourse on the Origins of Inequality*, begins the fourth chapter and his sketch of the economic and energetic model of the mental apparatus: the system Pcpt-Cs and Ucs, the role of the outer layer as shield against excitations, and the definition of trauma as the breaching of the shield, producing a flood of stimuli which knocks the pleasure principle out of operation. Given this situation, the repetition of traumatic experiences in the dreams of neurotics can be seen to have the function of seeking retrospectively to master the flood of stimuli, to perform a mastery or binding of mobile

Peter Brooks

energy through developing the anxiety whose omission was the cause of the traumatic neurosis. Thus the repetition compulsion is carrying out a task that must be accomplished *before* the dominance of the pleasure principle can begin. Repetition is hence a primary event, independent of the pleasure principle and more primitive. Freud now moves into an exploration of the theory of the instincts. [15] The instinctual is the realm of freely mòbile, "unbound" energy: the "primary process," where energy seeks immediate discharge, where no postponement of gratification is tolerated. It appears that it must be "the task of the higher strata of the mental apparatus to bind the instinctual excitation reaching the primary process" before the pleasure principle can assert its dominance over the psychic economy (34-35). We may say that at this point in the essay we have moved from a postulate of repetition as the assertion of mastery (as in the passage from passivity to activity in the child's game) to a conception whereby repetition works as a process of *binding* toward the creation of an energetic constant-state situation which will permit the emergence of mastery, and the possibility of post-ponement.

That Freud at this point evokes once again the daemonic and the uncanny nature of repetition, and refers us not only to children's play but as well to their demand for exact repetition in storytelling, points our way back to literature. Repetition in all its literary manifestations may in fact work as a "binding," a binding of textual energies that allows them to be mastered by putting them into serviceable form within the energetic economy of the narrative. Serviceable form must in this case mean perceptible form: repetition, repeat, recall, symmetry, all these journeys back in the text, returns to and returns of, that allow us to bind one textual moment to another in terms of similarity or substitution rather than mere

[15] I shall use the term "instinct" since it is the translation of *Trieb* given throughout the Standard Edition. But we should realize that "instinct" is inadequate and somewhat misleading, since it loses the sense of "drive" associated with the word *Trieb*. The currently accepted French translation, *pulsion*, is more to our purposes: the model that interests me here might indeed be called "pulsional."

continguity. Textual energy, all that is aroused into expectancy and possibility in a text—the term will need more definition, but corresponds well enough to our experience of reading—can become usable by plot only when it has been bound or formalized. It cannot otherwise be plotted in a course to significant discharge, which is what the pleasure principle is charged with doing. To speak of "binding" in a literary text is thus to speak of any of the formalizations (which, like binding, may be painful, retarding) that force us to recognize sameness within difference, or the very emergence of a *sjužet* from the material of *fabula*.

We need at present to follow Freud into his closer inquiry concerning the relation between the compulsion to repeat and the instinctual. The answer lies in "a universal attribute of instincts and perhaps of organic life in general," that *"an instinct is an urge inherent in organic life to restore an earlier state of things"* (36). Instincts, which we tend to think of as a drive toward change, may rather be an expression of "the conservative nature of living things." The organism has no wish to change; if its conditions remained the same, it would constantly repeat the very same course of life. Modifications are the effect of external stimuli, and these modifications are in turn stored up for further repetition, so that, while the instincts may give the appearance of tending toward change, they "are merely seeking to reach an ancient goal by paths alike old and new" (38). Hence Freud is able to proffer, with a certain bravado, the formulation: *"the aim of all life is death."* We are given an evolutionary image of the organism in which the tension created by external influences has forced living substance to "diverge ever more widely from its original course of life and to make ever more complicated *détours* before reaching its aim of death" (38-49). In this view, the self-preservative instincts function to assure that the organism shall follow its own path to death, to ward off any ways of returning to the inorganic which are not immanent to the organism itself. In other words, "the organism wishes to die only in its own fashion." It must struggle against

Peter Brooks

events (dangers) which would help it to achieve its goal too rapidly
—by a kind of short-circuit.

We are here somewhere near the heart of Freud's masterplot
for organic life, and it generates a certain analytic force in its
superimposition on fictional plots. What operates in the text through
repetition is the death instinct, the drive toward the end. Beyond
and under the domination of the pleasure principle is this baseline
of plot, its basic "pulsation," sensible or audible through the repetitions which take us back in the text. Repetition can take us both
backwards and forwards because these terms have become reversible: the end is a time before the beginning. Between these two
moments of quiescence, plot itself stands as a kind of divergence
or deviance, a postponement in the discharge which leads back to
the inanimate. For plot starts (must give the illusion of starting)
from that moment at which story, or "life," is stimulated from
quiescence into a state of narratability, into a tension, a kind of
irritation, which demands narration. Any reflection on novelistic
beginnings shows the beginning as an awakening, an arousal, the
birth of an appetency, ambition, desire or intention. [16] To say this is
of course to say—perhaps more pertinently—that beginnings are the
arousal of an intention in reading, stimulation into a tension.
(The specifically erotic nature of the tension of writing and its
rehearsal in reading could be demonstrated through a number of
exemplary texts, notably Rousseau's account, in *The Confessions,*
of how his novel *La Nouvelle Héloïse* was born of a masturbatory
reverie and its necessary fictions, or the very similar opening of Jean
Genet's *Notre-Dame des fleurs;* but of course the sublimated forms
of the tension are just as pertinent.) The ensuing narrative—the
Aristotelean "middle"—is maintained in a state of tension, as a
prolonged deviance from the quiescence of the "normal"—which is
to say, the unnarratable—until it reaches the terminal quiescence
of the end. The development of a narrative shows that the tension is

[16] On the beginning as intention, see Edward Said, *Beginnings: Intention
and Method* (New York: Basic Books, 1975). It occurs to me that the
exemplary narrative beginning might be that of Kafka's *Metamorphosis:*
waking up to find oneself transformed into a monstrous vermin.

291

maintained as an ever more complicated postponement or *détour* leading back to the goal of quiescence. As Sartre and Benjamin compellingly argued, the narrative must tend toward its end, seek illumination in its own death. Yet this must be the right death, the correct end. The complication of the *détour* is related to the danger of short-circuit: the danger of reaching the end too quickly, of achieving the im-proper death. The improper end indeed lurks throughout narrative, frequently as the wrong choice: choice of the wrong casket, misapprehension of the magical agent, false erotic object-choice. The development of the subplot in the classical novel usually suggests (as William Empson has intimated) a different solution to the problems worked through by the main plot, and often illustrates the danger of short-circuit. [17] The subplot stands as one means of warding off the danger of short-circuit, assuring that the main plot will continue through to the right end. The desire of the text (the desire of reading) is hence desire for the end, but desire for the end reached only through the at least minimally complicated *détour,* the intentional deviance, in tension, which is the plot of narrative.

Deviance, *détour,* an intention which is irritation: these are characteristics of the narratable, of "life" as it is the material of narrative, of *fabula* become *sjužet.* Plot is a kind of arabesque or squiggle toward the end. It is like Corporal Trim's arabesque with his stick, in *Tristram Shandy,* retraced by Balzac at the start of *La Peau de chagrin* to indicate the arbitrary, transgressive, gratuitous line of narrative, its deviance from the straight line, the shortest distance between beginning and end—which would be the collapse of one into the other, of life into immediate death. Freud's text will in a moment take us closer to understanding of the formal organization of this deviance toward the end. But it also at this point offers further suggestions about the beginning. For when he has identified both the death instincts and the life (sexual) instincts as conservative, tending toward the restoration of an earlier state of things,

---

[17] See William Empson, "Double Plots," in *Some Versions of Pastoral* (New York: New Directions, 1960), pp. 25-84.

Peter Brooks

Freud feels obliged to deconstruct the will to believe in a human drive toward perfection, an impulsion forward and upward: a force which—he here quotes *Faust* as the classic text of man's forward striving—*"ungebändigt immer vorwärts dringt."* The illusion of the striving toward perfection is to be explained by instinctual repression and the persisting tension of the repressed instinct, and the resulting difference between the pleasure of satisfaction *demanded* and that which is *achieved,* a difference which "provides the driving factor which will permit of no halting at any position attained" (36). This process of subtraction reappears in modified form in the work of Lacan, where it is the difference between *need* (the infant's need for the breast) and *demand* (which is always demand for recognition) that gives as its result *desire,* which is precisely the driving power, of plot certainly, since desire for Lacan is a metonymy, the forward movement of the signifying chain. If Roman Jakobson is able, in his celebrated essay, to associate the metonymic pole with prose fiction (particularly the nineteenth-century novel)—as the metaphoric pole is associated with lyric poetry—it would seem to be because the meanings peculiar to narrative inhere (or, as Lacan would say, "insist") in the metonymic chain, in the drive of desire toward meaning in time. [18]

The next-to-last chapter of *Beyond the Pleasure Principle* cannot here be rehearsed in detail. In brief, it leads Freud twice into the findings of biology, first on the track of the origins of death, to find out whether it is a necessary or merely a contingent alternative to interminability, then in pursuit of the origins of sexuality, to see whether it satisfies the description of the instinctual as conservative. Biology can offer no sure answer to either investigation, but it offers at least metaphorical confirmation of the necessary dualism of Freud's thought, and encouragement to reformulate his earlier opposition of ego instincts to sexual instincts as one between life instincts and death instincts, a shift in the grouping of oppositional

---

[18] See Jakobson, "Two Types of Language...". See, in Lacan's work, especially "Le Stade du miroir" and "L'Instance de la lettre dans l'inconscient," in *Écrits* (Paris: Seuil, 1966).

forces which then allows him to reformulate the libidinal instincts themselves as the Eros "of the poets and philosophers" which holds all living things together, and which seeks to combine things in ever greater living wholes. Desire would then seem to be totalizing in intent, a process tending toward combination in new unities: metonymy in the search to become metaphor. But for the symmetry of Freud's opposition to be complete, he needs to be able to ascribe to Eros, as to the death instinct, the characteristic of a need to restore an earlier state of things. Since biology will not answer, Freud, in a remarkable gesture, turns toward myth, to come up with Plato's Androgyne, which precisely ascribes Eros to a search to recover a lost primal unity which was split asunder. Freud's apologetic tone in this last twist to his argument is partly disingenuous, for we detect a contentment to have formulated the forces of the human masterplot as "philosopher and poet." The apology is coupled with a reflection that much of the obscurity of the processes Freud has been considering "is merely due to our being obliged to operate with the scientific terms, that is to say with the figurative language, peculiar to psychology" (60). *Beyond the Pleasure Principle,* we are to understand, is not merely metapsychology, it is also mythopoesis, necessarily resembling "an equation with two unknown quantities" (57), or, we might say, a formal dynamic the terms of which are not substantial but purely relational. We perceive that *Beyond the Pleasure Principle* is itself a plot which has formulated that dynamic necessary to its own *détour.*

The last chapter of Freud's text recapitulates, but not without difference. He returns to the problem of the relationship between the instinctual processes of repetition and the dominance of the pleasure principle. One of the earliest and most important functions of the mental apparatus is to bind the instinctual impulses which impinge upon it, to convert freely mobile energy into a quiescent cathexis. This is a preparatory act on behalf of the pleasure principle, which permits its dominance. Sharpening his distinction between a *function* and a *tendency,* Freud argues that the pleasure principle is a "tendency operating in the service of a function whose

Peter Brooks

business it is to free the mental apparatus entirely from excitation or to keep the amount of excitation in it constant or to keep it as low as possible" (62). This function is concerned "with the most universal endeavour of all living substance—namely to return to the quiescence of the inorganic world." Hence one can consider "binding" to be a preliminary function which prepares the excitation for its final elimination in the pleasure of discharge. In this manner, we could say that the repetition compulsion and the death instinct serve the pleasure principle; in a larger sense, the pleasure principle, keeping watch on the invasion of stimuli from without and especially from within, seeking their discharge, serves the death instinct, making sure that the organism is permitted to return to quiescence. The whole evolution of the mental apparatus appears as a taming of the instincts so that the pleasure principle—itself tamed, displaced —can appear to dominate in the complicated *détour* called life which leads back to death. In fact, Freud seems here at the very end to imply that the two antagonistic instincts serve one another in a dynamic interaction which is a perfect and self-regulatory economy which makes both end and *détour* perfectly necessary and interdependent. The organism must live in order to die in the proper manner, to die the right death. We must have the arabesque of plot in order to reach the end. We must have metonymy in order to reach metaphor.

We emerge from reading *Beyond the Pleasure Principle* with a dynamic model which effectively structures ends (death, quiescence, non-narratability) against beginnings (Eros, stimulation into tension, the desire of narrative) in a manner that necessitates the middle as *détour*, as struggle toward the end under the compulsion of imposed delay, as arabesque in the dilatory space of the text. We detect some illumination of the necessary distance between beginning and end, the drives which connect them but which prevent the one collapsing back into the other: the way in which metonymy and metaphor serve one another, the necessary temporality of the same-but-different which to Todorov constitutes the narrative transformation. The model suggests further that along the way of the path from beginning to end—in the middle—we have repetitions serving to bind the energy of the text in order to make its final discharge more effective. In fictional plots, these bindings are a system of repetitions which are returns to and returns of, confounding the movement forward to the end with a movement back to origins, reversing meaning within forward-moving time, serving to formalize the system of textual energies, offering the possibility (or the illusion) of "meaning" wrested from "life."

As a dynamic-energetic model of narrative plot, then, *Beyond the Pleasure Principle* gives an image of how "life," or the *fabula,* is stimulated into the condition of narrative, becomes *sjužet:* enters into a state of deviance and *détour* (ambition, quest, the pose of a mask) in which it is maintained for a certain time, through an at least minimally complex extravagance, before returning to the quiescence of the non-narratable. The energy generated by deviance, extravagance, excess—an energy which belongs to the textual hero's career and to the readers' expectation, his desire of and for the text—maintains the plot in its movement through the vacillating play of the middle, where repetition as binding works toward the generation of significance, toward recognition and the retrospective illumination which will allow us to grasp the text as total metaphor, but not therefore to discount the metonymies that have led to it. The desire of the text is ultimately the desire for the end, for that recognition which is the moment of the death of the reader in the text. Yet recognition cannot abolish textuality, does not annul the middle which, in its oscillation between blindness and recognition, between origin and endings, is the truth of the narrative text.

It is characteristic of textual energy in narrative that it should always be on the verge of premature discharge, of short-circuit. The reader experiences the fear—and excitation—of the improper end, which is symmetrical to—but far more immediate and present than—the fear of endlessness. The possibility of short-circuit can of course be represented in all manner of threats to the protagonist or to any of the functional logics which demand completion; it

Peter Brooks

most commonly takes the form of temptation to the mistaken erotic object choice, who may be of the "Belle Dame sans merci" variety, or may be the too-perfect and hence annihilatory bride. Throughout the Romantic tradition, it is perhaps most notably the image of incest (of the fraternal-sororal variety) which hovers as the sign of a passion interdicted because its fulfillment would be too perfect, a discharge indistinguishable from death, the very cessation of narrative movement. Narrative is in a state of temptation to over-sameness, and where we have no literal threat of incest (as in Chateaubriand, or Faulkner), lovers choose to turn the beloved into a soul-sister so that possession will be either impossible or mortal: Werther and Lotte, for instance, or, at the inception of the tradition, Rousseau's *La Nouvelle Héloïse,* where Saint-Preux's letter to Julie following their night of love begins: "Mourons, ô ma douce amie." Incest is only the exemplary version of a temptation of short-circuit from which the protagonist and the text must be led away, into *détour,* into the cure which prolongs narrative.

It may finally be in the logic of our argument that repetition speaks in the text of a return which ultimately subverts the very notion of beginning and end, suggesting that the idea of beginning presupposes the end, that the end is a time before the beginning, and hence that the interminable never can be finally bound in a plot. Analysis, Freud would eventually discover, is inherently interminable, since the dynamics of resistance and the transference can always generate new beginnings in relation to any possible end. [19] It is the role of fictional plots to impose an end which yet suggests a return, a new beginning: a rereading. A narrative, that is, wants at its end to refer us back to its middle, to the web of the text: to recapture us in its doomed energies.

One ought at this point to make a new beginning, and to sketch the possible operation of the model in the study of the plot of a fiction. One could, for instance, take Dickens' *Great Expectations.* One would have to show how the energy released in the text by

[19] See Freud, "Analysis Terminable and Interminable" (1937), in *Standard Edition,* 23, 216-53.

its liminary "primal scene"—Pip's terrifying meeting with Magwitch in the graveyard—is subsequently bound in a number of desired but unsatisfactory ways (including Pip's "being bound" as apprentice, the "dream" plot of Satis House, the apparent intent of the "expectations"), and simultaneously in censored but ultimately more satisfying ways (through all the returns of the repressed identification of Pip and his convict). The most salient device of this novel's "middle "is literally the journey back—from London to Pip's home town—a repeated return to apparent origins which is also a return of the repressed, of what Pip calls "that old spell of my childhood." It would be interesting to demonstrate that each of Pip's choices in the novel, while consciously life-furthering, forward oriented, in fact leads back, to the insoluble question of origins, to the palindrome of his name, so that the end of the narrative—its "discharge"— appears as the image of a "life" cured of "plot," as celibate clerk for Clarrikers.

Pip's story, while ostensibly the search for progress, ascension, and metamorphosis, may after all be the narrative of an attempted homecoming: of the effort to reach an assertion of origin through ending, to find the same in the different, the time before in the time after. Most of the great nineteenth-century novels tell this same tale. Georg Lukács has called the novel "the literary form of the transcendent homelessness of the idea," and argued that it is in the discrepancy between idea and the organic that time, the process of duration, becomes constitutive of the novel as of no other genre:

Only in the novel, whose very matter is seeking and failing to find the essence, is time posited together with the form: time is the resistance of the organic — which possesses a mere semblance of life — to the present meaning, the will of life to remain within its own completely enclosed immanence. . . . In the novel, meaning is separated from life, and hence the essential from the temporal; we might almost say that the entire inner action of the novel is nothing but a struggle against the power of time. [20]

[20] Georg Lukács, *The Theory of the Novel*, trans. Anna Bostock (Cambridge, Mass.: MIT Press, 1971), p. 122.

The understanding of time, says Lukács, the transformation of the struggle against time into a process full of interest, is the work of memory—or more precisely, we could say with Freud, of "remembering, repeating, working through." Repetition, remembering, reënactment are the ways in which we replay time, so that it may not be lost. We are thus always trying to work back through time to that transcendent home, knowing of course that we cannot. All we can do is subvert or, perhaps better, pervert time: which is what narrative does. [21]

To forgo any true demonstration on a novel, and to bring a semblance of conclusion, we may return to the assertion, by Barthes and Todorov, that narrative is essentially the articulation of a set of verbs. These verbs are no doubt ultimately all versions of desire. Desire is the wish for the end, for fulfillment, but fulfillment delayed so that we can understand it in relation to origin, and to desire itself. The story of Scheherezade is doubtless the story of stories. This suggests that the tale as read is inhabited by the reader's desire, and that further analysis should be directed to that desire, not (in the manner of Norman Holland) his individual desire and its origins in his own personality, but his transindividual and intertextually determined desire as a reader. Because it concerns ends in relation to beginnings and the forces that animate the middle in between, Freud's model is suggestive of what a reader engages when he responds to plot. It images that engagement as essentially dynamic, an interaction with a system of energy which the reader activates. This in turn suggests why we can read *Beyond the Pleasure Principle* as a text concerning textuality, and conceive that there can be a psychoanalytic criticism of the text itself that does not become—as has usually been the case—a study of the psychogenesis of the text (the author's unconscious), the dynamics of literary response (the reader's unconscious), or the occult motivations of the characters (postulating an "unconscious" for them). It is rather

---

[21] Genette discusses Proust's "perversion" of time in "Discours du récit," p. 182. "Remembering, Repeating, and Working Through" *(Erinnern, Wiederholen und Durcharbeiten)* (1914) is the subject of one of Freud's papers on technique. See *Standard Edition*, 12, 145-56.

the superimposition of the model of the functioning of the mental apparatus on the functioning of the text that offers the possibility of a psychoanalytic criticism. And here the superimposition of Freud's psychic masterplot on the plots of fiction seems a valid and useful maneuver. Plot mediates meanings with the contradictory human world of the eternal and the mortal. Freud's masterplot speaks of the temporality of desire, and speaks to our very desire for fictional plots.

Jean-Michel Rey

Freud's Writing on Writing

What of the continuous work—all the more effective for being lateral and/or implicit—of the various contradictions at work within a theoretical system?

Such a question opens up the possibility of introducing some preliminary remarks concerning the position and function of "literature" in the apparatus of psychoanalysis. For if it is undeniable that "literature" occupies a relatively privileged place in psychoanalytic theory—sometimes even without Freud's knowledge or recognition—it is nonetheless true that, at the same time, literature is submitted to divergent interpretations and thus becomes, in view of the totality of the Freudian corpus, a paradoxical space verging on contradiction itself. A labor of "reading" at the borders of knowledge, at the uttermost boundaries of the symbolic, *would* thus be particularly required by the object designated "literature." Now it seems that such a reading is never explicitly programmed by Freud, even though literature imposes itself periodically with insistence within the totality of the Freudian context. That is to say that it represents a determinant strategic stake which weighs heavily upon the elaboration of psychoanalytic discourse, and which even punctuates the different stages of its constitution. It does so in its status as a limit-object which has nevertheless the essential advantage of being always familiar. In what sense can "literature" participate within the "psychic" economy and thereby perhaps inflect the course of psychoanalytic knowledge? [1] Why is literature the locus of an apparently always possible recognition?

---

[1] The English expressions "knowledge," "field of knowledge," and "science" are used in different instances to render the same French word, "*savoir*"; the reader should realize that the necessity of choosing one reading or another at any one point is not present for the French reader,

That a field of knowledge might be traversed by a network of contradictions or of paradoxes which it is structurally incapable of mastering, or even of perceiving and apprehending consistently at the time of its construction; that this impossibility also constitutes both the effectiveness of such a science—which bears upon the formations of the unconscious—and its most remarkable novelty, without forgetting that it would obviously be impossible for this science to escape involvement with the very things it discovered; [2] that no text called "theoretical" could possibly be homogeneous and linear and, consequently, immediately transparent to its author; that belatedness [*l'après-coup, Nachträglichkeit,* deferred action] is necessarily an integral part of any scriptural practice and that this belatedness continually causes the postponement of the moment of comprehension, of interpretation, indeed the moment of the conclusion itself—Freud was obliged to take into account precisely all these empirical and lateral "discoveries" which marked out the course of his theoretical progress, not without detours to be sure. He was obliged to calculate as exactly as possible their practical import, notably with regard to the mode of exposition *(Darstellung)* of his object. It is as if the very richness of this object, its character at once familiar and strange, near and distant, the singularity of its occurrence and the generality of its functioning—as if all this, little by little, compelled Freud to recognize the existence of a close connection between *Darstellung* and writing.

---

for whom the associations of "knowledge," "science," and "knowing" are all there in each case. Moreover, as a result of the growth of influence in France both of Georges Bataille and of numerous French readers of Freud, the noun *"savoir"* has been devalorized and has acquired connotations that are less immediate for the reader of English but which may be suggested by this text. — Tr.

[2] Freud never ceased to encounter this reverse effectiveness of the unconscious upon the elaboration of his theory, e.g., in the following form: "Every science is based on observations and experiences arrived at through the medium of our psychical apparatus. But since *our* science has as its subject that apparatus itself, the analogy ends here. We make our observations through the medium of the same perceptual apparatus, precisely with the help of the breaks in the sequence of 'psychical' events: we fill in what is omitted by making plausible inferences and translating it into conscious material" (*An Outline of Psycho-Analysis,* G. W., XVII, 81; S. E., XXIII, 159).

However, the economy of psychoanalytic discourse does not permit a direct recognition of such a connection, for here too belatedness is at work. Moreover, within such a context certain elements can impose themselves with a sort of blinding obviousness—Freud says *überdeutlich* in this regard—as though in opposition to the conceptual or "scientific" resources that Freud had at his disposal. Is "literature" dependent upon this *Überdeutlichkeit,* upon this blinding clarity which *throws off* interpretation and as a result of which the notion of "literature" or that of "literary fiction" is never examined in its essence but is understood only in a dogmatic mode?

(A whole study could be undertaken of this: how it happens that from the earliest stages of its constitution psychoanalysis, a new kind of science, is accompanied or reflected by a sort of internal working out of dogma, regarding literature in particular. In this perspective, it would be necessary to undertake a detailed reading of the *Minutes of the Vienna Psychoanalytic Society:* [3] for the first psychoanalysts, literature seems to play a decisive, catalytic role, provoking discussions in which absolutely contradictory points of view confront one another, even though the first principles of psychoanalytic theory are applied quite mechanically. The theoretical stakes in these discussions are considerable.)

Thus one can speak of an *uneven development* of Freudian theory which affects its concepts (since they are taken over from previously constituted fields of knowledge) as well as its modes of discursivity, its borrowings of vocabulary or its metaphors as well as its procedures of description. By what avenues does this uneven development come to affect "external" objects, for example literature, to which this theory is applied or extended? If for Freud the literary object is both over-determined and under-determined, it is necessary to situate the forms of such a contradiction and to analyze its consequences for the totality of the apparatus of psychoanalytic theory, and specifically for the practice of *Deutung.* This is a necessary condition for understanding, for example, the

---

[3] Four volumes have appeared, edited by Herman Nunberg and Ernst Federn, published by International Universities Press, New York.

admission of failure with which the 1928 text "Dostoievsky and Parricide" opens: "Leider muss die Analyse vor dem Problem des Dichters die Waffen strecken" ["Before the problem of the creative artist analysis must, alas, lay down its arms"] (*Gesammelte Werke* [henceforth G. W.], XIV, 399; *Standard Edition* [henceforth S. E.], XXI, 177). To lay down arms and thereby to leave the field free—but for whom?—even though for more than thirty years there were attempts to beleaguer [*investir*] it on all sides, multiplying perspectives and indirections, and indeed ruses, designed to integrate it within the apparatus of psychoanalysis in such a way that literature might appear, within a henceforth familiar space, to be in strict continuity with the dream, the phantasy, and the myth. Does this mean that the *Dichter* presents psychoanalytic interpretation with problems that it cannot resolve, or even perceive, and that Freud had to make numerous theoretical detours, multiple attempts, before he could arrive at this impasse? Or does this mean that literature solicits from science a different approach, a less direct one for example, from which psychoanalysis could not escape undamaged? What could guarantee the integrity and the "autonomy" of Freudian theory? Before coming to such questions, it must be recalled that Freud knew very early that he was a writer, although this occurred in a negative mode.

Freud Writes

In a letter to Fliess on the subject of the *Traumdeutung*, which he was writing at the time, Freud says: "The matter about dreams I believe to be unassailable; what I dislike about it is the style [*der Stil*]. I was quite unable to express myself with noble simplicity, but lapsed into a facetious, circumlocutory straining after the picturesque [*in witzelnde, bildersuchende Umschreibungen*]. I know that, but the part of me that knows it and appraises it is unfortunately not the part that is productive" (11 September 1899).[4]

---

[4] Quotations from Freud's letters to Fliess are taken from Freud, *The Origins of Psycho-Analysis*, tr. Eric Mosbacher and James Strachey (New York: Basic Books, 1954). — Tr.

Jean-Michel Rey

From a quite ordinary stylistic fault—who has ever been able to write without the assistance of periphrasis?—from a displeasure felt in the face of the necessary detours of discursivity, indeed of any form of exposition *(Darstellung)*, from a deep-seated dissatisfaction at having to use *witzelnde* terms and at perceiving the lack of strict and properly defined concepts—from the perception therefore of what determines the momentary texture of his writing, Freud immediately draws a conclusion about the very subject of writing, in a word, its *topography* [*topique*]. [5] In a certain place I am able to recognize the constitutive lacks of my writing, but it is obviously on a different stage that the writing takes place. Where I know, I do not write; where I write, I can know only belatedly [*après-coup*], as if in a different context. What is written can thus have the durable value of a symptom: that which, proceeding from "myself," teaches me where I am (not); as though I could signify to myself, by this detour, the thing that institutes me as a subject: a splitting [*clivage*], and, moreover, one that becomes progressively readable in other configurations of the psyche. Only the future can —perhaps—signify it, and not say it explicitly, inasmuch as belatedness very clearly cannot be calculated. A subject can thus, by and in the "events" of his writing, make his own splittings signify to him, and even submit them to representation without his knowledge. However, it takes time to read such "symptoms": see, for example, what Freud says in the preface to the second edition of the *Traumdeutung* about the "further subjective significance" of the book. (What can an "author" do who rereads himself?)

If this is correct, this fault and this displeasure—which is no small matter—can exist only as the reverse or the other side of an "ideal," the necessary complement, within the psychoanalytic order at least, i.e., within the representation that it proposes of the "apparatus of the mind," of any topography. What I write signifies

[5] From his earliest psychoanalytic writings onward, Freud makes use of a variety of "topographical" models to portray the interworkings of an array of "agencies" *(Instanzen)* in the apparatus of the mind. One such topography includes the unconscious, the preconscious, and the conscious; another, the id, the ego, and the superego.—Tr.

for me also, in other forms, the supplementary image of what I am not, the image of my desire, which is fragmented because it is contradictory. As though the person who writes had also to confront constantly, with the "arms" that writing can furnish him, all the figures of the "super-ego" (paternity, legitimacy, tradition . . .),[6] as though he had to traverse them with full knowledge of the facts, at the risk there too of being constrained to recognize the essential contradiction between his "desire" and his lack of mastery over what he does. Certainly never before Freud had "theoretical" discourse been comprehended to this extent in its value as a symptom, understood as a "representation" in a certain mode of the splittings of the subject. Certainly never had the eccentric position of the subject with regard to the discourse he is supposed to carry on, with regard to the "knowledge" he is supposed to avail himself of, been designated with such force. This immutable Freudian topography imposes itself first, chronologically as well as logically, by means of the figures of writing, of "style," of "form," of "mastery." The "discovery" of the formations of the unconscious is reduplicated in practice by a problematic of writing and, even more, by an unheard-of disjunction of writing and knowledge, related to this theoretical innovation, the split subject. In another letter to Fliess Freud writes something that is just as fundamental: "Somewhere inside me there is a feeling for form [*Formgefühl*], an appreciation of beauty as a kind of perfection [*Art der Vollkommenheit*]; and the tortuous sentences of the dream-book, with its high-flown, indirect phraseology, its squinting at the point, have sorely offended one of my ideals [*Ideal*]. And I do not think I am going far wrong if I interpret this lack of form [*Formmangel*] as a sign of deficient mastery of the material [*ein Zeichen fehlender Stoffbeherrschung*]" (letter of 21 September 1899).

One might say of this contradiction, of which there are many confirmations in Freud's writings, that it signs the discourse of psychoanalysis as though *from within,* affixing a constant signature

---

[6] It would be necessary to show how the texts of modernity (Kafka, Joyce, Artaud, Bataille, etc.) traverse these different "figures."

which establishes at the interior of this discourse a certain continuity and a tacit coherence, indeed which supplies it with a
determinate base: viz., that psychoanalysis is *first of all* what
Freud's phantasies made him write and "represent." This conversion
of phantasy into writing implies that, on the part of its author, the
specific (non-formal) dimension of *"Darstellung"* is taken primarily
into account, insofar as *Darstellung* necessarily interferes (it remains
to be seen in what ways) with the phantasy and/or the desire of
anyone who writes. This is undoubtedly the only instance in the
history of theoretical systems of such an involvement of the subject
and his writing process in an imbrication that is never resolved
once and for all. It is an imbrication whose lateral effects continue
to appear as the "science" of psychoanalysis develops and as, consequently, the object appears in a larger number of figures; or,
even more, as the subject learns—if only in rereading himself—the
nature of writing in this context, and what functions, according to
Freud's remarkable expression, as "linguistic compliance" *(sprach-
liches Entgegenkommen),* [7] which comes to surprise the subject in
his own language—and what is more, to precede him there. And,
following a discursive practice that is very common in Freud, it is
necessary to generalize such a process, i.e., to extricate it from
the "subjective" veinstone in which it is embedded, to understand
it therefore as particularly significant or symptomatic of the economy of the psyche in general. This means that such a process
does not proceed according to a logic of example or illustration,
but that it comes to subvert progressively the traditional relationship of the part to the whole. "There is often something in the
material itself [*im Stoff selbst*] which takes charge of one and diverts
one from one's first intentions. Even such a trivial achievement
[*so unscheinbare Leistung*] as the arrangement of a familiar piece
of material is not entirely subject to an author's own choice [*Will-
kür des Autors*]; it takes what line it likes and all one can do is

---

[7] A term that is essential for understanding the novelty of what psychoanalysis reveals about the functioning of language.

ask oneself after the event [*nachträglich*] why it has happened in this way and no other" (G.W., XI, 393; S.E., XVI, 379).

How can literature find a place in such an apparatus? From what places is a reading of literature possible?

Literaturdeutung

It is well known that the *Traumdeutung* refers on several occasions to Greek tragedy or even to *Hamlet,* for the purpose of comparison, and that on these occasions some general statements about literature are proposed. Without being able to go into detail here (it would be necessary in particular to bring out the decisive role of *"Stoff,"* the semantic material which, prior to any "secondary elaboration," to any screen or veil, constitutes the most general hidden meaning, the equivalent of the very truth of the text), without being able to reconstitute this theoretical texture, this thematic matrix which Freud sets up and which persists to the end, [8] I shall cite only a single, particularly significant statement about *Oedipus Rex.* "The action of the play consists in nothing other than the process of revealing, with cunning delays and ever-mounting excitement [*schrittweise gesteigerte und kunstvoll verzögerte Enthüllung*]—a process that can be likened to the work of a psycho-analysis—that Oedipus himself is the murderer of Laïus, but further that he is the son of the murdered man and of Jocasta" (G.W., II/III, 268; S.E., IV, 261-62). [9] Thus Freud summarizes the plot of the tragedy; thus he *interprets* the effective meaning of the decisive reference text of psychoanalysis. It is a strange movement

---

[8] Thus, as though the elaboration of the science of psychoanalysis did not end up modifying this thematism, or even did not permit one to see its faults.

[9] Let us recall also that much later on Freud compares the rhythm of scientific work to that of a psychoanalysis: "Progress in a scientific work is just as it is in analysis. We bring expectations with us into the work, but they must be forcibly held back. By observation, now at one point and now at another, we come upon something new; but to begin with the pieces do not fit together. We put forward conjectures, we construct hypotheses [*Hilfskonstruktionen*], which we withdraw if they are not confirmed, we need much patience and readiness for any eventuality, we renounce early convictions so as not to be led by them into overlooking unexpected factors ..." (G. W., XV, 188; S. E., XXII, 174).

however, about which Freud remains silent for the most part, without speaking of the excessive simplification that such a schematic account represents, or of the levelling of textual differences or of what takes place in the translation of a Greek text. For, on the one hand, in practice nothing seems to distinguish a brief summary from interpretation as such (Where does interpretation begin? Upon what elements does it bear? What can guarantee a reading of this type? etc.); and, on the other, Freud never examines directly the status of the "comparison" which is at the basis of this major statement. "The process of revealing . . . that can be likened to the work of a psycho-analysis": does this mean that the tragedy *Oedipus Rex* enunciates as many elements—but in other terms, in a fundamentally different context, in another linguistic apparatus, and according to a different "logic"—as psychoanalysis itself and its present "knowledge"? For, as a matter of fact, this knowledge— what will take subsequently the name of the "Oedipus complex"— is derived in large part from the legend of Oedipus and, what is more, if one follows Freud exactly, from that economy of deferral which forms the texture of the tragedy.

This "example" thus provides an opportunity to ask the question (but it is presumably something entirely different that concerns Freud and the "future" of psychoanalytic theory) that Freud is so close to comprehending, yet that seems to be the blind spot in his discovery of the unconscious: of what "displacement" in the symbolic order is interpretation *(Deutung)* apparently the most consistent and the most systematic effect? What precisely does the "work of a psycho-analysis" accomplish if it is *practically forced* to repeat what is *already* formulated elsewhere, under other names or in other words, in a mythic context, or more clearly in "literary" forms or in symbolic figures? Where is the material derived from—material in the sense of *Stoff* just as much as of *"Thema"* or of *"Motiv"* as elements that are inductive of interpretation—the material that constitutes the object peculiar to psychoanalytic deciphering? How then are we to conceive of the advent of psychoanalysis *historically* if in fact it alleges Greek tragedy and mythology as its antecedents, if it writes its genealogy by means of recourse to literature?

For everything proceeds as if factual continuity, in large measure postulated, existed between what Greek tragedy represents and what psychoanalysis "discovers" by other roads, particularly the royal road of the interpretation of dreams. The story of Oedipus would thus be the abridged version, the *ante litteram* formulation of one of the essential mechanisms of the general economy of the psyche; as though it were necessary therefore to presuppose a sort of "atemporality" of desire and of phantasy for which literature would be in short the privileged expression, on condition, to be sure, of conceiving it as a particular illumination, as a determinate perspective regarding a content that is always the same. In this way it is possible to understand Freud's insistence on performing repeatedly a thematic interpretation of literary texts, that is, an approach that brings to the fore a content that corresponds, detail for detail, to that of dreams, of phantasies, of myths. The poet, Freud says in the same passage of the *Traumdeutung,* who brings to light the guilt of Oedipus, makes us look into ourselves and recognize impulses which, although suppressed, are still present (G.W., II/III, 269; S.E., IV, 263). This expressive and semantic conception of literature permits Freud to establish, for example, an almost immediate parallel between *Oedipus Rex* and *Hamlet,* upstream from languages, symbolic systems, modes of representation, prior to every formal or textual effect; it gives primacy to a content the equivalent of which one could find in anybody's phantasies, save for a few subtle differences. That is to say that there is in Freud an astounding failure to recognize the formal work of which literature is capable, the power that a fictional text can deploy for representation, the syntactic and semantic transformations of which fiction is the locus. But that is to recognize *at the same time* that literature constitutes for the psychoanalytic apparatus a constant point of support, a necessary reference, a perpetual solicitation, a space of renewed disquiet. "But just as all neurotic symptoms, and, for that matter, dreams, are capable of being 'over-interpreted'

Jean-Michel Rey

[*Überdeutung*] and indeed need to be, if they are to be fully understood, so all genuinely creative writings [*dichterische Schöpfung*] are the product of more than a single motive [*Motiv*] and more than a single impulse in the poet's mind, and are open to more than a single interpretation [*mehr als eine Deutung*]" (G. W., II/III, 272; S. E., IV, 266).

Thus, at the very moment when he is interpreting a series of "literary" texts dogmatically, i. e., by inferring their meaning from another context (that of the content of dreams and of myths), Freud indicates programmatically the possibility of other interpretations; and this because of what the decipherment of the dream and of the logic of neurosis was able to teach him, that is, principally, the overdetermination of all the events in the economy of the psyche, i.e., "overinterpretation." Is it necessary henceforth to generalize this theoretical element and to affirm as a consequence that when "literature" is involved the status of interpretation is perforce implicated, and in a number of ways?

Who, writing in fiction or in theory, can in practice be the same age as his discoveries?

The Mention of the Phantasy

Let us undertake a sinuous traversal of a text such as "Der Dichter und das Phantasieren" ["Creative Writers and Day-dreaming"] (dated 1908), whose importance, in my opinion, comes from the fact that it brings together "hypotheses" of different provenance, at the very limit of what is compatible—as though it were a question here of the experimental testing of the "overinterpretation" to which "literature" seems to be subjected. But this text represents a rather massive displacement of the perspective put into operation in the *Traumdeutung*, since the question it introduces amounts to wondering "from what sources the creative writer draws his material [*seine Stoffe nimmt*]"—another variant concerning *"Stoff"*—and since the phantasy seems to offer a temporary answer which has the additional advantage of sketching a new problematic. Deliberately leaving aside the totality of the text—and specifically the essential relationship of the phantasy to time, what Freud calls the *"Zeitmarke"* of the phantasy—I content myself with emphasizing several terms of the conclusion.

Freud notes in the first place a certain imbalance with regard to the title. The fact that he has spoken more of the phantasy than of the *"Dichter,"* he says, merely reflects the state of development of psychoanalytic knowledge. Indeed, this is the time when the notion of the phantasy is being profoundly remodeled, and in particular is becoming more specific as to the import of the phantasy, as is seen in the text of the same date entitled "Hysterische Phantasien und ihre Beziehung zur Bisexualität" ["Hysterical Phantasies and Their Relation to Bisexuality"], [10] the last stage before the decisive turning-point of 1915 with the elaboration of the notion of the "primal phantasy" *(Urphantasie).* But such an admission can have another significance: the Freudian approach to literature is partly dependent upon the various developments of psychoanalytic theory, or at least upon a certain number of its concepts and notions. This allows us to explain, in part, the variations in point of view with regard to the literary object; for, for example, the development resulting in the notion of the "primal phantasy" does not in the least affect the conception of literature.

"All I have been able to do is to throw out some encouragements and suggestions which, starting from the study of phantasies, lead on to the problem of the writer's choice of his literary material [*Problem der dichterischen Stoffwahl*]. As for the other problem —by what means the creative writer achieves the emotional effects [*Affektwirkungen*] in us that are aroused by his creations—we have as yet not touched on it at all. But I should like at least to point out to you the path that leads from our discussion of phantasies to the problem of poetic effects [*poetische Effekte*]" (G. W., VII, 222; S. E., IX, 152).

Thus the question becomes a multiple one, touching simultaneously the phantasy, the "choice of material," and the "poetic

[10] Elsewhere I have proposed a reading of this text: see my *Parcours de Freud* (Paris: Galilée, 1974), pp. 15-55.

Jean-Michel Rey

effect." How can a literary text in general—beyond the special case of *Oedipus Rex,* which prefigures [11] an event, in the psyche, of far-reaching consequence—have a real effectiveness, it being understood that such a text implies a phantasmatic dimension? If one approaches this question by way of the "choice of literary material," at least two remarks must be made. First of all, such an expression is not to be taken literally, or else we introduce a very great ambiguity. Is it not instead necessary to see here a transfer from one of the essential motifs of psychoanalysis, the "choice of neurosis"? In which case, the notion of "liberty"—"liberty of the author," and in "Das Unheimliche" ["The Uncanny"] even "liberty of fiction"—becomes invalidated in practice. Secondly, an entirely different dimension is introduced, albeit allusively, by this approach: [12] one that consists in conceiving literature's specific mode of historicity, the transference and displacement of "themes" within a tradition, the symbolic heritage that literature can represent, the modification by fiction of familiar motifs. In other words, how can filiation take effect within the field of "literature" if one postulates literature as inseparable from myths, from legends, hence from a symbolic context within which, according to Freud, it becomes meaningful? Not to forget, as I indicated above, that psychoanalytic theory itself also proceeds, in its own way and according to a discourse that it constitutes and borrows, from this same symbolic context. Beyond literature, it would be necessary to investigate this conspiracy of psychoanalysis with the various artistic practices. For if literature plays a predominant role for psychoanalysis, it is doubtless able to do so for the very reason of its "material": language. With the most rigorous necessity, psychoanalysis encounters, in unforeseeable ways, the dimension of linguistic usage, which Freud indicates by reviving an old term, *"Sprachgebrauch."* [13] Both from this point of view and in attempting to go beyond the Freudian

[11] It is obvious that one can speak of prefiguration only in terms of what psychoanalysis teaches us.

[12] But such a dimension is far from being taken into consideration in the totality of psychoanalytic theory.

[13] A term of the first importance which, although derived from a traditional field, introduces an entirely new dimension into the context of psycho-

impasses, what could a history of literature possibly be? Or, *what is a dictionary?* Although it is likely that the notion of *Sprach-gebrauch* or linguistic usage remains inadequate for interpreting the formal work of literary fiction, it has nevertheless the considerable advantage of forcing what is ordinarily meant by the term "language" to vary almost indefinitely. We know, moreover, that the notion of *Sprachgebrauch* constitutes the necessary starting-point of the trajectory of "Das Unheimliche," insofar as this text grazes the dictionary after having asserted the absence of a "core" of meaning in the word itself which would authorize its use as a concept and, especially, before coming to render explicit the "logic" of this term by recourse to "literary fiction" (the term is Freud's), at least programmatically, viz., the "privileges of fiction" *(die Vorrechte der Fiktion)* (G. W., XII, 266; S. E., XVII, 251) ...as though in response to the "privilege of the writer" *(das Vorrecht des Dichters—*G. W., VII, 38; S. E., IX, 14) spoken of at the beginning of *Delusions and Dreams in Jensen's "Gradiva."* [14]

What of the poetic effectiveness of the literary text, if precisely by this detour Freud rediscovers the dimension of *Darstellung,* but this time accentuated entirely differently? Although we experience no pleasure at the account that the awakened dreamer can give of his phantasies, Freud says, things are quite different in the case of the *"Dichter."* In other words, the *presentation [mise en scène]* that the writer can give of his own phantasies seduces us; it becomes, as though self-evidently, an object of pleasure proceeding doubtless "from a number of sources which mingle" *(aus vielen Quellen zusammenfliessende Lust).* Thus Freud speaks as if fiction succeeded in changing the affective value of phantasies *by working at their very source* [15] (Where is the origin of pleasure? How can

analysis. An entire reading of "Das Unheimliche" would be possible on the basis of this decisive term. What does the traversal of dictionaries represent?

[14] Yet these "privileges" are described by Freud only in a superficial way, notably with terms as lax as "liberty" or "creation."

[15] In a meeting of the Vienna Psychoanalytic Society devoted to Wedekind's play, *Frühlingserwachen,* Freud speaks of "the poetic source" (*"poetische Quelle"*) of the phantasy, without really being able to specify what he means by such an expression (*Minutes of the Vienna Psychoanalytic Society,* I, 114).

what is displeasure for one "system" become pleasure for another? We know how important these questions are in the perspective of topography.)—as though fiction necessarily succeeded in representing phantasies under the sign of pleasure by a sort of constant conversion. This is tantamount to underscoring—which does not mean explaining—the predominant role of *Darstellung* as the locus where the contradictions at play between the different instances are levelled, as the space where the general economy of the psyche becomes readable—but at what price? This constitutes a displacement of what had until then constituted the dominant logic of *Darstellung.*

It is in this way that Freud lays the foundations of a veritable *Ars poetica,* whose technique can take two principal paths.

First: "The writer softens [*mildert*] the egotistical character of the daydream by changes and disguises [*Verhüllungen*]" (G.W., VII, 223; S. E., IX, 153). Now it is by these *metaphorical terms*—metaphors that have at least a long history, that of the metaphysical definition of truth—that Freud always designated the constitutive processes of literature. In fact, three terms constantly recur in this connection within the Freudian text: *Milderung—Verhüllung—Verkleidung.* In other words, literature softens, veils, clothes what it exposes: the themes that it constitutes or borrows elsewhere. Despite appearances, the example of *Oedipus Rex,* which unveils the logic of its own structure, does not contradict this law, to the extent that this unveiling is deferred in the narrative itself, which is moreover reduced, according to Freud, to this operation. Literary fiction thus proceeds by covering up again the very thing that it enunciates, more or less in each case. And it seems that the literary examples analyzed by Freud have this in common, that they produce only a minimal veiling. [16] If this is the case, it must be admitted that

---

[16] This is especially the case, according to Freud, with Jensen's "Gradiva," which through the metaphor of burial, is very close to designating or representing the very process of repression. "In his last simile [*Gleichnis*] ... the author has presented us with the key to the symbolism of which the hero's delusion made use in disguising [*Verkleidung*] his repressed memory. There is, in fact, no better analogy for repression. ... The author was well justified, indeed, in lingering over the valuable

Freud does not really take into account the different degrees of veiling that the literary text is capable of effecting; or rather that he takes this factor into account only to infer from it certain general characteristics of literature (e.g., in "Das Unheimliche" Freud does not notice the central function of the curtain in "The Sandman," nor, moreover, does he consider in this same text the occurrence of the terms *heimlich* and *unheimlich* and the structuring function they are capable of assuming in Hoffmann's story)—generalities of which one finds almost identical formulations here and there.

It is, however, a subtle economy of art in the poet [*feine ökonomische Kunst des Dichters*] that he does not permit his hero [Shakespeare's Richard III] to give open and complete [*restlos*] expression to all his secret motives. By this means he obliges us to supplement [*ergänzen*] them; he engages our intellectual activity, diverts it from critical reflection and keeps us firmly identified with his hero. (G.W., X, 369; S.E., XIV, 315)

It is in fact a case of multiple motivation [*mehrfache Motivierung*], in which a deeper motive comes into view behind the more superficial one. Laws of poetic economy [*Gebote der poetischen Ökonomie*] necessitate this way of presenting [*gestalten*] the situation, for this deeper motive could not be explicitly enunciated. It had to remain concealed, kept from the easy perception of the spectator or the reader ... (G. W., X, 387; S. E., XIV, 329)

Or this, which is presented as a law: "But poetic treatment is impossible without softening and disguise" *(Aber ohne Milderung und Verhüllung ist die poetische Bearbeitung nicht möglich)* (G.W., XIV, 412; S.E., XXI, 188).

---

similarity..." (G. W., VII, 65-66; S. E., IX, 40). And we know how much this "analogy" will dominate the mode of interpretation that Freud proposes, notably the effacement of the fictional dimension. Let us recall, by the way, a remark of Freud's about Schreber, in which one of the essential models of interpretation is indicated: Schreber "himself not infrequently presses the key into our hands, by adding a gloss, a quotation or an example to some delusional proposition in an apparently incidental manner or even by expressly denying some parallel to it that has arisen in his own mind. For when this happens, we have only to follow our usual psycho-analytic technique — to strip his sentence of its negative form [*negative Einkleidung*], to take his example as being the actual thing, or his quotation or gloss as being the original source — and we find ourselves in possession of what we are looking for, namely a translation [*Übersetzung*] of the paranoiac mode of expression into the normal one" (G. W., VIII, 269; S. E., XII, 35).

Jean-Michel Rey

Poetische Bearbeitung, literarische/poetische Produktion, dichterische/poetische Darstellung, poetische Ökonomie/Kombination, ökonomische Kunst: all these notions which always return in connection with "literature" merely ratify the same law which for Freud is at the base of every literary production: *the economy of indirect representation,* indeed, in the extreme case, the economy of dissimulation. The text of fiction comes into being only by representing its themes or operations by successive indirections, by interposing superficial motifs, the better to dissemble the most essential ones. The literary theme never appears as such, offered to the perception of the reader. Now this characteristic is nothing other than the most general mark of the productions of the unconscious. One may then wonder what makes possible the actual differentiation of "literary production" *(literarische Produktion)* from the other formations of the unconscious, save the fact that the writer can perform this operation of *Milderung/Verhüllung/Verkleidung* "consciously" (in part at least). [17] This question is all the more necessary as Freud seems to be content to reinscribe, in this context, the notion of *"Darstellung"* by merely adding an adjective to it *(poetische / dichterische / literarische)* that neither modifies nor affects its meaning in the slightest, because *this adjective remains indeterminate and practically tautological.* For example,

---

[17] Let us recall in this connection a very significant remark from "Das Unheimliche." In this essay, as you know, Freud attempts an interpretation of Hoffmann's "The Sandman" based upon the principle of the symbolic equivalence between fears for one's eyes and the castration complex. After noting some of the secondary themes of the story, Freud writes: "Elements in the story like these, and many others, seem arbitrary and meaningless [*bedeutungslos*] so long as we deny all connection between fears about the eye and castration; but they become intelligible [*sinnreich*] as soon as we replace the Sandman by the dreaded father at whose hands castration is expected." A long note follows, but only the beginning of it concerns me here: "In fact, Hoffmann's imaginative treatment [*Phantasiebearbeitung*] of his material has not made such wild confusion of its elements [*Elemente des Stoffes*] that we cannot reconstruct their original arrangement [*ursprüngliche Anordnung*]" (G. W., XII, 243-44; S. E., XVII, 232). It is thus as though all the work of fiction consisted of nothing more than a more or less marked recasting of the original elements of the theme. The operation of "jumbling" could in that case always be deciphered. One can also get an inkling here of what Freud means by the term "liberties of the writer": the possiblity of encoding a familiar theme.

Freud writes laconically of *Hamlet,* "In the English play the presentation is more indirect..." (*Die Darstellung des englischen Dramas ist indirekter...*) (G.W., XIV, 412; S.E., XXI, 188), as though there might exist elsewhere a direct *"Darstellung."* (Note that this remark exceeds the present framework, that it points to a much larger problem which Freudian theory has never ceased to encounter. In a word, what is involved is the status of the "negative" notions in the psychoanalytic corpus and, first and foremost, the notion of the un-conscious. A simple reference in this connection, to what Freud asserts about the "negative" word *unheimlich:* "The prefix 'un-' ['*un-*'] is the token of repression" [G.W., XII, 259; S.E., XVII, 245].) Everything proceeds as though the principal notions that articulate the science of psychoanalysis *(Phantasie, Ökonomie, Produktion, Bearbeitung,* and especially *Darstellung)* could be reused, without modification or rectification, to circumscribe the field of literature, which would then supposedly become the locus of an extension, or of an application, of categories or notions that are already entirely constituted and that possess a generality sufficient to include a domain like that of literary fiction. Unless what is involved—but it would be necessary to inflect the apparatus of psychoanalytic theory in a completely different way—is the very profound conspiracy that links psychoanalysis, partly without its knowledge, to literary production, in which case (but this proceeds from a different story and implies rather complex operations) it would be necessary, e.g., to understand the notion of *"Darstellung"* on the basis of what literary fiction can reveal about it, insofar as literature historically precedes the "discovery" of psychoanalysis, its appearance on stage, its bursting into the space of the symbolic. This is another way of saying that, by way of the recourse to literature, the science of psychoanalysis is (partially) capable of reconstructing its "own" genealogy, of reconstituting what can appear henceforth as its "prehistory." More than any other science—but it would be necessary from this point of view to investigate Marxism very closely, considering for example Marx's statement that he did not discover class struggle, the pivotal element of his whole system,

Jean-Michel Rey

and moreover his emphasis, which could not possibly be an accident, on how much the object owes to its *Darstellung*—more than any other theory, psychoanalysis is forced to incorporate as much as possible its "historical" precedents (at least, what it is capable of interpreting as such) and is constrained to understand as much as possible the places from which it proceeds and the symbolic stakes that it displaces. For all these elements form, in different ways, an integral part of its "object," although it is never capable of adding them up entirely, nor of calculating in practice their actual import, for it is through them that psychoanalysis is sustained, and it is on the basis of them that it is formulated. Psychoanalysis still has much to teach us concerning the blind spots on the basis of which any theoretical discourse—including psychoanalysis itself—is structured.

A disconcerting theoretical praxis which, in its encounters with existing fields of knowledge (even today), opens up no breach where one might have expected it, but, on the contrary, tends to find its way in by means of familiar, acceptable references: psychoanalysis could never possibly dispose of the question of *Darstellung*, in relation to which it is inscribed like an intaglio, even if it massively displaces the economy of *Darstellung* itself. We know, for example, the enormous difficulties that Freud encountered (especially after the break with Jung) in characterizing the symbolic—notably its perpetual availability [18]—and its relations to language, more precisely to its particularly baffling and unforeseeable "suppleness," "plasticity," and "compliance." At the same time—as Freud was always convinced—to be understood and accepted, psychoanalytic theory must ceaselessly work for recognition by means of familiar, ordinary elements: either by images and metaphors in use in contemporary fields of knowledge, or else, and more broadly, by what literature presents that is most consistent, by what literature possesses that is most adequate to the productions of the unconscious. This is in addition to the fact that in literature we find an articulation

[18] Freud makes a considerable number of brief suggestions on this subject in the *Introductory Lectures on Psycho-Analysis* of 1916-1917.

and stratification of themes at work, themes that resemble to the point of confusion the conscious-unconscious relation such as Freud continually discovers or rediscovers it elsewhere, in the "discourse" of his patients. How then is one to evaluate, to measure, the theoretical yield or profit that literature can provide? Why not speak, as if in response to the *"Lustgewinn"* ["yield of pleasure"] discussed in connection with the *Witz* [joke], of something that could be temporarily called *"Wissensgewinn,"* a "yield of knowledge" for which literary fiction would be the privileged argument? [19] If, as a text cited earlier says, a superficial motive can be a screen concealing a more profound one, we have a right to demand, says Freud, that "the explicit motive shall not be without an internal connection [*innerer Zusammenhang*] with the concealed one, but shall appear as a mitigation of, and a derivation from [*Milderung und Ableitung*], the latter. And if we rely on the fact that the dramatist's [Ibsen's] conscious creative combination [*bewusste poetische Kombination*] arose logically from unconscious premises [*unbewusste Voraussetzungen*]..." (G.W., X, 387; S.E., XIV, 329).

We find here as everywhere the same economy of indirect representation, with a different modulation in each context. By this "indirectness" we mean that without which the theme that is said to be "literary" would be thoroughly unreadable, untenable, indeed strictly impossible—perhaps like the "real" itself, access to which is always in the control of the phantasy. For Freud continually encounters at every level an analogous "logic": either what forms a screen in the "memory" of a subject, or what proceeds from the "detour" by which thought is constituted; or else what can take

---

[19] In the fundamental text of 1911 entitled "Formulations on the Two Principles of Mental Functioning" ("Formulierungen über die zwei Prinzipien des psychischen Geschehens") Freud writes as follows on the subject of the religious doctrine of man's reward in the next life: "Following consistently along these lines, *religions* have been able to effect absolute renunciation of pleasure in this life by means of the promise of compensation in a future existence; but they have not by this means achieved a conquest of the pleasure principle [*Überwindung des Lustprinzips*]. It is *science* which comes nearest to succeeding in that conquest; science too, however, offers intellectual pleasure [*intellektuelle Lust*] during its work and promises practical gain in the end [*endlichen praktischen Gewinn verspricht*]" (G. W., VIII, 236; S. E., XII, 223-24).

Jean-Michel Rey

place only by deferring its arrival and appearing where the subject does not expect it, in an unforeseen form; or else what is derived from a defense which is entirely necessary for the economy of the psyche. *Is it possible that literary fiction has something to do with apotropaic logic?* If literature, according to Freud, can produce a greater number of *unheimlich* effects than can life itself, what in turn might be its effectiveness upon the totality of the psycho-analytic apparatus? How, even beyond what Freud says, can we determine the differential practice that constitutes "literary fiction"? Let us recall that in "Das Unheimliche" Freud goes as far as to say that it is psychoanalysis itself which has become "*unheimlich*" by the very fact of what it *discovers (Aufdeckung),* as though it merely reproduced on a shifted plane what had always been "know-able" but had not been directly asserted. It would thus be necessary to investigate the strange symmetry within the Freudian apparatus between, on the one hand, the literary process as a practice of *Mil-derung / Verhüllung / Verkleidung* and the *thematic density* that actually accompanies it, and, on the other hand, the gesture of inter-pretation as "unveiling," that is to say as *Enthüllung, Entkleidung,* or *Aufdeckung.* This symmetry, which forms one of the most tena-cious theoretical invariants of the Freudian text and which effec-tively commands the conception of *Deutung,* would have to be in-vestigated throughout the rest of Freud's writings. Still, this is the text in which it is gone into most rigorously and in which the complicity it represents can make it possible to read the contra-dictions from which it proceeds. Might the recourse to literary fiction be the most subtle means for shading over these "contradic-tions," i.e., for making them appear elsewhere?

I now come to the second path of the *Ars poetica* set forth at the end of "Der Dichter und das Phantasieren."

Second, then: "The writer ... bribes us by the purely formal—that is, aesthetic—yield of pleasure [*rein formaler, d.h. ästhetischer Lustgewinn*] which he offers us in the presentation of his phan-tasies [*Darstellung seiner Phantasien*]. We give the name of an *in-centive bonus* [*Verlockungsprämie*], or a *fore-pleasure* [*Vorlust*], to

321

a yield of pleasure such as this, which is offered to us so as to make possible the release [*Entbindung*] of still greater pleasure arising from deeper psychical sources. In my opinion, all the aesthetic pleasure which a creative writer affords us has the character of a fore-pleasure of this kind, and our actual enjoyment [*Genuss*] of an imaginative work proceeds from a liberation of tensions in our minds" (G.W., VII, 223; S.E., IX, 153).

Note first of all the implicit reference in this statement to the text entitled *Jokes and Their Relation to the Unconscious* (1905), in which Freud proposes the central notion of the "principle of fore-pleasure" to characterize the fact that a small amount of pleasure—which in practice may be nothing more than a simple *word*—permits the liberation of a considerable quantity of pleasure which would otherwise have remained inaccessible and thereby permits a partial evasion of the process of repression. This amazing bit of arithmetic, arrived at by Freud's classification and analysis of the different figures and techniques of the "*Witz*," leads in practice to the subversion of the traditional logical relation of the part to the whole. We have instead a sort of *occasional logic,* insofar as language—each language—offers its innumerable resources (semantic, syntactic, rhetorical, lexical, etc.) to the subject, permitting him thereby to bring about, within his own symbolic space, tiny significant displacements which are at the same time vectors of pleasure. A mental *event* of far-reaching consequence, the *Witz* reveals at its leisure the relations that every subject can have with his own language, the manner in which he is capable of investing it, what he finds in it capable of temporarily overthrowing the code. If language proves to be compliant, the *Witz* knows how to profit from that compliance up to the limits of nonsense; it is as if the *Witz* disconcerted "memory," thwarting every paradigmatic chain and every convention of significance [*convention signifiante*]. [20]

---

[20] If one carries this suggestion to the extreme, this might mean that everything concerning the *Witz* could serve to determine what is understood today by the term *text.* I shall return to this point elsewhere.

Jean-Michel Rey

Now, rather paradoxically, neither in "Der Dichter und das Phantasieren" nor elsewhere does Freud take up again these elements which touch language so closely. Moreover, whereas he uses the metaphor of the *"Text"* to describe the *Witz*, this metaphor is totally absent when he is dealing with literary fiction. This is a strange silence, one which has as its consequence the practice of plot-summary, as when Freud deals with Jensen's "Gradiva" or Hoffmann's "Sandman"; a summary that follows the articulations of the narrative and elucidates the principal *and* secondary themes with a view to transcribing them in psychoanalytic terms, at the risk of introducing into this framework *reliefs*[21] which may possibly displace the processes and the stakes of interpretation—at the risk, indeed, of twisting, here and there, the principle of the thematic approach. Still, such detours do have their importance—if only to shake up, indirectly, theoretical certitudes, convictions, or beliefs[22]—and they do introduce parentheses, margins, all with a certain suggestive value, into the apparatus of psychoanalytic theory. No discourse can be sustained except by such counterpoints, by remarks that oppose its explicit logic, by disparate details that suspend or defer any immediate perception of its law. And we know how attentive Freud was to this unforeseeable punctuation which marks the development of knowledge, to what extent therefore he is not a Hegelian but a writer, to what extent he was able to recognize chance where it occurred, i.e., able not to be a religious

[21] In a reading of a fragment of "Das Unheimliche," I proposed this term to characterize one of the movements of the text: "La psychanalyse à hauteur de fiction," *Dialectiques* 7.

[22] In a letter to Jung dated 16 April 1909, Freud analyzes a *conviction* that plays a decisive role in his own history. He writes at the end of this analysis: "I incline to explain such obsessions as this with number 61 [the one that Freud has just deciphered] by two factors, first heightened unconsciously motivated attention of the sort that sees Helen in every woman, and second by the undeniable 'compliance of chance' [*Entgegenkommen des Zufalls*], which plays the same part in the formation of the delusions as somatic compliance in that of hysterical symptoms, and linguistic compliance in the generation of puns [*das sprachliche beim Wortwitz*]" (*The Freud/Jung Letters,* ed. William McGuire, tr. Ralph Manheim and R. F. C. Hull [Princeton: Princeton University Press, 1974]). The likening of these three dimensions would merit a detailed demonstration.

man.[23] Still, unlike what is put into operation in the case of the dream or of the *Witz*, or even more broadly in the case of the totality of the psychoanalytic "object," the metaphor of "work" never finds its place in the field of literary fiction. This is another disconcerting omission, one which might lead one to think that literary fiction constitutes a world apart, that it does not proceed, like every form of psychical economy, from a process of work, from an articulation of contradictory instances, from the processes of repression, and thus from a perpetually rich and complex relationship to the logic of the unconscious. But on the basis of this obvious, even blinding, omission, which dominates a traditional conception of literature, one can formulate a further question in the face of the totality of Freud's discoveries: *who can say, perceive, or know himself on a level with what he writes, with what writes him?*

One might suspect that the recourse to the "purely formal yield of pleasure" would permit evasion of, indeed escape from the thematic inflation which seems to be the rule with Freud. But in fact this is not at all the case, and this inflation weighs so heavily that it reappears, most often moreover in a totally explicit way, in the most varied contexts. It is as if—a simple hypothesis which one would have to test both in the case of Freud and in that of literary practice—this inflation corresponded to a diffuse but tenacious ideology that literature itself had contributed historically to constituting and imposing. In any case, a text like "The Moses of Michelangelo" repeats and emphasizes, in connection with artistic practices, the same priority of meaning and content *(Sinn und Inhalt);* not, to be sure, without adding a "subjective" remark concerning the inseparability of "pleasure" and "knowledge"—which abundantly confirms the primacy and the immediacy of the theme of the work of art in general.

[23] "If one considers chance to be unworthy of determining our fate, it is simply a relapse into the pious view of the Universe..." (G.W., VIII, 210; S.E., XI, 137).

Jean-Michel Rey

I have often observed that the subject-matter of works of art has a stronger attraction for me than their formal and technical qualities [*formale und technische Eigenschaften*], though to the artist their value lies first and foremost in these latter. I am unable rightly to appreciate [*das richtige Verständnis fehlt mir*] many of the methods used and the effects obtained in art.... Nevertheless, works of art do exercise a powerful effect upon me.... This has occasioned me, when I have been contemplating such things, to spend a long time before them trying to apprehend them in my own way, i.e. to explain to myself [*mir begreiflich machen*] what their effect is due to. Wherever I cannot do this, as for instance with music, I am almost incapable of obtaining any pleasure [*genussunfähig*]. Some rationalistic, or perhaps analytic turn of mind in me rebels against being moved by a thing without knowing why I am thus affected and what it is that affects me. (G. W., X, 172; S. E., XIII, 211)

And then Freud speaks immediately in the same context of our "state of intellectual bewilderment" ("*Ratlosigkeit unseres begreifenden Verstandes*"). It is all as though artistic pleasure were necessarily accompanied—at least for the "discoverer" of psychoanalytic interpretation—by the mediation of the concept *(begreifen—Begriff)* and by the precise recognition of the specific effectiveness of the work of art, as though emotion could take place only within the space of a field of knowledge already safely mapped out with all the warning lights in place, a science that is already rationalized and all the more capable of rendering intelligible the "intention" of a work because the theme of the work in question is resonant with the subject. To be more specific, a particularly convoluted dialectic is at work, or even *is produced,* between pleasure and the "analytic turn of mind," and this happens for the benefit of interpretation, but not without residue and not without secondary benefits. For example, at the same time as the subject is, or discovers himself to his surprise to be, *implicated* by the "content" of the work of art—and there would be a great deal to say about the relationship of Freud to the figure of Moses—his comprehension can be thrown off the track and thus his enjoyment "almost" done away with, and this process is capable of recurring in different modes. Nevertheless, this "rationalistic turn of mind" and this capacity of interpretation have no choice but to reckon with time, and they must perforce reckon with the contradiction that pleasure opposes to

325

them in practice—aside from the fact, constantly brought out by Freud, that the unconscious is ignorant both of time and of contradiction.

The dream from which psychoanalysis itself proceeds, i.e., the contradictory locus from which it originates and to which it always returns, has certainly in part the omnipotence of "rationalism" as its object: the constant necessity of its passage to its limits, the possibilities that it is incapable of effecting or producing *with a view towards* interpreting what has always been more or less known by other figures, in different modalities, and thus also under other names. A decisive practice which, it seems, only psychoanalysis puts into operation so radically: that of *designation*, of *denomination*. [24] The constant production and introduction of other names border on the most striking gestures of writing and touch on that continual recasting of the symbolic for which literary fiction is the privileged locus of operation. If there is at the very basis of psychoanalysis the wild dream of an omnipotence of interpretation, this dream must of necessity be turned upside down and become its opposite (or be entirely displaced), most often unbeknownst even to whoever thinks he can master it, in accordance with a process to which psychoanalysis ought to have accustomed us. But historically for such a dream to produce an articulated science and to become the motor of a theoretical system, it had to lean, more or less deliberately, on familiar elements, supposedly already known, thereby becoming integrated within a code of sufficient symbolic resonance to open the door to other less familiar "data," which are characterized by an actual strangeness. In more ways than one, literary fiction seems to me to participate in this process of buttressing [*étayage,* anaclisis] from which the apparatus of psychoanalytic theory never ceases to draw support—even beyond what Freud is capable of acknowledging to situate his debt to literature, beyond what he can "know" of it discursively. This is in any case a strange oscillation on Freud's part. Sometimes, indeed, he min-

---

[24] "This piece of insight into psychical dynamics cannot fail to affect terminology and description" (G.W., XIII, 241; S.E., XIX, 15).

Jean-Michel Rey

imizes the import and the effectiveness of literary fiction in order to make of it nothing more than one of the areas to which an established science applies, as if Freud himself as a subject were not implicated in the slightest thereby. Sometimes, *on the contrary,* he places literature on equal footing with psychoanalytic theory, yet without inferring all the possible consequences of this equality. (But what permits the delimitation of the possible terrain that a new theoretical space is capable of surrounding or occupying [*investir, besetzen,* cathectizing], and thus the circumscription of its structural "impossibilities"? This question becomes explicit and primordial with the sudden emergence, under the name we all know, of a theory of the formations of the unconscious. In the face of this, what position can literature occupy if it takes place only by infinitizing itself, if it is produced only by endlessly annulling the subject of writing?)

At the end of a detour in a presentation, Freud writes: "After this long digression into literature [*Dichtung*], let us return to clinical experience—but only to establish in a few words the complete agreement [*die volle Übereinstimmung*] between them" (G.W., X, 389; S.E., XIV, 331).

Must one take Freud literally when, as here for example, he notes this "complete agreement"? Supposing that were necessary— but is not his statement one of merely programmatic value?—one cannot in any case isolate such a proposition from the context of the totality of psychoanalysis, *that is,* from that very thing which permits Freud to formulate any given *remark* concerning the general organization of his discourse, the displacements that it occasions, and indeed the mode of reading that it solicits. "The case histories I write ... read like short stories [*wie Novellen*]" (G.W., I, 227; S.E., II, 160).

If in making these statements [in *Leonardo da Vinci and a Memory of His Childhood*] I have provoked the criticism ... that I have merely written a psycho-analytic novel [*psychoanalytischer Roman*], I shall reply that I am far from over-estimating the certainty of these results. (G. W., VIII, 207; S. E., XI, 134)

It would still be necessary to take into account the remark that opens the text on Jensen's "Gradiva," in the very passage in which Freud understands his "knowledge" as being outflanked by that of fiction, and in which he "learns" that fiction encroaches upon his own discoveries, anticipates them in its own way, thereby twisting the act of interpretation unforeseeably and forcing it to shift to a new location and indeed to find new resources.

> But creative writers are valuable allies and their evidence is to be prized highly, for they are apt to know a whole host of things between heaven and earth of which our philosophy [*Schulweisheit*] has not yet let us dream. In their knowledge of the mind they are far in advance of us everyday people, for they draw upon sources which we have not yet opened up for science. (G. W., VII, 33; S. E., IX, 8)

From such a confrontation Freud hopes for nothing less than an insight into the "nature of poetic production" [*Natur der dichterischen Produktion*].

It would still be necessary to see how Freud manages to adjust to being so outflanked, that is, how he succeeds, *except for some details,* in integrating all this in the perspective of *Deutung,* and to see what the subsequent fortunes of this *Deutung* will be—in the "case" of *das Unheimliche,* for example. But that is another story, or rather the same story read differently on the basis of different references, if it is true that *das Unheimliche*—the word, that is—cannot be translated.

Translated by G.W. Most and James Hulbert

Philippe Sollers

Freud's Hand

I

Why not say that the history of the analytical movement is the history of the crisis of making a community out of it? That's true for Freud; it's true for Lacan. Analysis, in its very foundation, dissolves any possible community, and it could be said that that is in fact what makes it infinite, that it cannot resolve itself to being one, that it *resists*. A resistance to the dissolution of the letter in the unconscious. A resistance to the fact of signature. Wherever there is a regrouping around such a dissolution-in-action of the social bond, there lies the crisis of analysis. At that point, it is not long before its representations begin to circulate on the market.

A community of the signifier can but be imaginary. An equals sign cannot be put between two discursive "reals"—just as there can be no common sexual denominator, no common sexual measure. This means that there are as many sexualities as there are sexed individuals. And consequently, as many discourses, and resistances to discourses, to mark it. Men, women, categories of the homo or the hetero: a whirlwind of counter-cathexes, of counter-invest-ments, designed to try at all costs to preserve the mirage of a universal common measure. We live in a time when this type of *massage* actually appears as such.

He's and she's have only one thing on their minds: measuring the without-measure, obtaining at last the fingerprint of their sex put into words. The unconscious seems to them to be collective *in spite of all*. Whereas it only happens, can only be passed, from *one* to *one*. Nothing proves nor ever will prove that one had anything to do with the other. The time it takes to dream upon this is called an analytical cure.

Look at the patients, the analysands, of a same analyst; or look at the analysts among themselves. What are they thinking about? About the key to the safe that might, all at once, fall to them. That is why it all came to pass around Freud's death, and is once more coming to pass around Lacan's. Until the next one comes along, provided he exists, for after all it's not inconceivable that things always coming in threes might be valid everywhere except in analysis.

If the unconscious lets itself be reached only by one and one alone, that is true for the analysands, for the analysts, and, from that point on, one can ask: what can they be doing together except working things out in such a way as to oversee the impasses of that truth, to bring it about as late as possible, to the fewest "ones" possible?

One, indeed, may pass away, and no one, perhaps, will ever hear of it again.

Lacan sometimes jokes about this situation, saying that the analyst's place is that of a saint. The more saints, the merrier, he says, but of course no one has ever seen saints laughing together, and no saint in fact has ever been able to stand another saint. This is moreover precisely how the Church has functioned: by means of struggles between saints. It follows, then, that you have a dogma to settle the question for the best: the doctrine of the communion of the saints. After all, they had to end up getting together some-where: in heaven. The only hitch is: hell exists, heaven doesn't. The general belief is of course rather the opposite. As for purgatory, its name is: the State. Which explains why it is so hard to get rid of, especially since it easily turns to hell from time to time, just to keep us aware of the problem.

All I wanted to say here is that it is psychoanalysis which has everything to say about the Church, the army, the group, the university, and in general about any institution whatsoever, official or unofficial.

Philippe Sollers

That would not necessarily be the case if analysts were merely people who listen. But they are rather obliged to mouth silently what they hear, and there is where the irreducible difference awaits them.

Someplace, the social bond is loosened: I think that place is also the horizon of literature. Its ground is the Loneman, the Only-One [*l'Un-Seul*]. Coming, that is, from the other side, the dead. (...)

II

(...)

When speaking of castration, one must insist: the *mother's* castration. The reign of the fetish, instituted and consolidated by the belief in the maternal phallus, is threatened by that encounter with the void, and Freud even says: as though the throne and the altar were in danger. All around this question, there is panic. That is why the social bond is absolutely, intrinsically, homosexual in nature. To strengthen the social bond is to build on the sublimation of homosexual drives. This is true of men as well as of women, at this point of repeated immaturation. The formula for the survival of the species is inscribed within that point in the form of permanent misunderstanding, a vanishing point and therefore also a point of return. The species keeps returning upon itself, aiming for that point. "As though the vagina had never been discovered..." Witness Freud, remarking with startling succinctness that Wolf Man "had sided with the intestine and the father, against the vagina and god." A whole history.

The mother's pleasure, the mother's *coming* [*jouissance*], signs, or doesn't sign, the father's, which is much more mysterious, shrouded in the silence of origins. The walls have ears for the woman's coming, but as for the man's, who is to witness it? I am speaking of the man's coming as *avowed* by a woman. Unbearable.

Women these days are making much of Freud's stumblings against the enigma of femininity, of feminine pleasure. Not surprisingly, a lot of men are ready to take up the refrain. But actually all they are doing is broadening and deepening Freud's indirect influence. When Freud affirms that there is only one libido, and that it is masculine, this obviously does not signify for him a valorization of the libido. He does not say that it is "good"; in fact he rather intimates that it can be something of a bother. When he speaks of penis-envy, on the woman's side, he never fails to specify the male counter-term: the feminine position with respect to the father.

The father's pleasure [*jouissance*] is more repressed than the mother's. For the mother *comes* only on the rebound from the fact that the man becomes increasingly what takes the place of god. But what the pleasurable coming of god might be, heaven knows, is impenetrable, utterly unfathomable. What you have instead, as it were, is feminine pleasure as a lure, a mirage, a retro-vibration. Man's route toward god consists in sorting out this concert. But since god does not exist (save for every woman), it can't be said that this is an enviable route. Poor man: that's why he owes it to himself to die.

It will indeed become more and more apparent (this, in my opinion, is the meaning of the current feminine rough-housing) that women, in the final analysis, have rigorously nothing to do with sexuality, that sexuality doesn't interest them, that their problem lies utterly elsewhere. Some people, strangely enough, are stupefied by this. In other words, centuries-old illusions on the subject are starting to crumble. As a result, there isn't much for a man to do besides to advise analysis. For a woman either, of course, but there it's problematic. If they could just rid themselves a bit of their obsession with the male homosexual, that would be almost enough.

Lacan—this much is clear—has succeeded in oedipizing his day. To the point that a book has been produced entitled "anti-oedipus," whose subtitle, readable between the lines, is: pro-lacan. Oedipus was old, not beefy enough for Lacan: that is all being modernized. Why? Because Lacan, not contenting himself with picking up the profound thread of Freud's discovery, has restored to it the specific dimension of utterance as such. Not only in theory: what is touched

Philippe Sollers

upon and tampered with is style. A style makes all the denials of which it is the object in fact work *for* it. And analysis, essentially, only advances, only takes place, through this type of skid. This is a far cry from any thesis, dissertation, or theoretical discussion on Freud: the "Freud-effect" is first and foremost an effect of writing. Again, the question of "literature" is on the horizon.

And here we are once again brought back to the problem of what is at stake in the written work, in the "writ" [*l'écrit*]. That's where it's all happening. Curious, isn't it, that philosophy and psychoanalysis should meet somewhere in that vicinity. To the point that henceforth one might say that *philosophy has become that which speaks of psychoanalysis in the name of literature.* Literature, as for that, says nothing, or almost nothing: it inscribes itself; it writes.

III

(...) The analyst has to deal with discourses which seek, even unwittingly, to interpret themselves. Wherever there is a cry for interpretation, there is, in effect, analysis. Explicit, implicit, avowed or refused. Pretentions to suspend interpretation are 999 times out of 1000 unjustified. And yet, it can happen: once, on rare occasions. Interpretation integrates itself into the written work, and that is when the writ can interpret the interpreter. The analyst, at that point, does not reach the interpretation. The criterion: the writ refuses no interpretation, it doesn't compete with analysis. On the contrary.

Then begins a new, a brand new dialectic between analysis and the written work. A written work can produce analytical effects which remain outside the scope of analysis. But the written work can never be in (the) *place* of analysis. Any writ whatever is interpretable in analytical terms. The point is to begin *with* interpretation.

There is nothing to "save" with respect to analysis. No little metaphysical cranny for madness, for art, for literature. Any writing can fully accept analytical interpretation. I would even say that, from now on, it must. This is why philosophical discourse today is losing ground. Philosophy, in one fell swoop, has two enormous stones to swallow: the Freudian unconscious and this new form of writing (initiated by Mallarmé, Artaud, Joyce). The philosopher chooses to contest the validity of analysis in the name of these experiments in the experience of writing. But for this, he needs the guarantee that the one who transmits the written work will keep his mouth shut about analysis. But what if the written work sides with analytical interpretation? The philosopher feels double-crossed. But at the same time, the analyst is uneasy. Observe this tri-polar mechanism. The analyst must keep his practice distinct from any philosophical recuperation. The philosopher must prevent his discourse from vanishing under analytical interpretation. The subject of the written work does not need to speak *through* philosophy; he, too, has a practice to defend, a rupture. Thus, sometimes you find the analyst and the writing subject siding against philosophical discourse; at other times the analyst and the philosopher side against the writing subject. Then again, sometimes philosophical discourse and the subject of the written work band together against the analyst, whenever the latter (and this is often the case) loses all consciousness of the historical context in which all these operations are taking place.

Analysis, philosophy, the written work: the extremes meet in their absolute separation (analysis and writ). In the middle is the philosopher, seated between two chairs. He envies both places at once. The analyst, for his part, blinds himself in thinking that his place is the place of places. The subject of the writ knows himself (rarely) to be out(side) of place. Whence his relation to the psychotic field, whose impact may perhaps be philosophically narrow (and the philosopher profits from this), but at the same time crucial for the practice of analysis (which sees itself questioned by it).

If an analyst is only as good as his relation to psychosis, his question is the writing which *passes through it*. As for the philosopher, he is there, like habit, to try to fill in the gaps.

I leave aside scientific discourse, about which the analytically engaged writing has no reason to complain (it draws from science as much as it likes). Philosophy, on the other hand, is definitively rattled by it. And analysis has not yet finished exploring its knots.

The writ which passes through the psychotic field may end up simply remaining there. But it sets off, in passing, a mass of neurotic and perverse (phobic, fetishistic, hysterical, obsessional) counter-investments which seal its function as one of *incuration*. The writ must bring investments of writing under cure. The cure always functions somewhere as a demand to be "raised" ["*relevé*," *aufgehoben*] out of the writ. But it is also possible to think that the analyst finds his way back into *his* cure *via* the writ. Which, however, puts him no less in a state of incuration than the analysand who does not recognize himself as such. But here is the main point: the process of putting-on-trial is not the same in each case. The analysand imagines that giving up writing is impossible. The analyst, on the other hand, can consent to do so (uneasily).

The writ "of passage" functions on the basis of the resistances it meets and indeed provokes. Like the cure, but on another level. Analysis and the writ thus act as "controls" for each other. But only the writ can admit it. That's only *logical*.

IV

(...) Imagine, if you will, Freud's hand in the act of writing his five case histories. Hans, the little finger; Schreber, the long one, between the two thieves, fingered by the Index and the ring: Wolf Man, Rat Man. And finally Dora, the thumb, opposable to all the others. Next, imagine that hand in the mirror: you now have the written work of our time. That is, what is real of it *besides*, its weight, its relief, its consequence.

The hysteric touches and thumbs through everything. Phobia whispers secrets to the ear. The two columns of obsessional neurosis hold up the sexo-social edifice. In the middle is the memorable obelisk of unsurpassable paranoia, with which all the other discourses are *woven* if you know how to listen between the threads.

Join the thumb and middle finger: Dora and Schreber form a circle. That's where we have to try to think *in spite of all*.

Analysis, and the writ in the mirror, and vice versa, inevitably lead to the loneman [*l'un-seul*]. On the side of the real which can be grasped as a symptom, this loneman is produced in the form of the one-woman [*l'une-femme*].

The loneman and the one-woman, radically other with respect to each other, are as much outside-of-men as they are outside-of-women. Around these two edges, around these two sides indefinitely pushed apart, is the whirlwind of transference.

The one-woman constitutes a problem not only for the male community, but also, and this will become increasingly apparent, for any eventual community of women as well; the last bastion of the lure of a common measure. This is where all the current blabbering comes from.

Women have no more desire to have anything to do with the one-woman than men with the loneman. One-womans and lonemans don't do anything (in) common: this lONEman/ONE-woman is in fact multiple, precluding any possible unification; for this multiple, there can be no *accounting*.

Observe Schreber in his aborted reach toward the loneman: humbly hoping, perhaps with time, after all those "outlines of femininity" had been completed, to become the absolute and ultimate one-woman, the new, impossible, virgin.

Witness some women in their dizzy messianism actually suspecting that the one-woman, somewhere, is possible. But she is never quite sufficiently themselves. And why not? Because of that loneman who blocks the horizon and who always can rub up against another woman (anxiety). Dora becomes Aimée, but it is still she. Feminine paranoia is the order of the day. Notably, it is there that one must dig if one seeks to learn more about fascist microbiology. Puppet men, women struck with terror, with respect to the virtual one-woman who reaches toward the loneman seen as god who does not exist.

A regressive refuge is in sight: a refuge of a schizophrenic type, with the advantage that it erases sexual division to a maximum degree and perpetuates an air of the sacred. But paranoia, for its part, makes the difference. One can speak in general terms of "the schizoid," but not of "the paranoid" *in general.* Paranoia is always masculine or feminine (or: exclusive).

And here we come back to the writ. It is not surprising that there should have been such confusion over automatic writing, the *tablettes,* the "cut-up," the entrance and exit of mediums. The hysteric would content herself if necessary with just being listened to more and more. *Le* paranoid is totally engaged in the rationalization of the divine writing that racks him. But *la* paranoid does not let herself be fooled. It is the writ which will be charged with all erotomania: the incessant, dictated writ, fabulating, fabricating, or falling apart. [1] FP (feminine paranoia) does not, so to speak, have the possibility of perversion as a limit of balance (there is a play with eviration). What is at stake here, radically, is that all this traces itself *sotto voce,* a wild, borderless inscription.

Is *la* paranoid keeping watch over *all* writing? What about the analyst's, then? Isn't that what gives Lacan's its value: precisely in shaking up that watch? The university takes care of putting it to sleep.

One who writes touches these shadows.

Translated by Barbara Johnson

[1] Freud makes the following suggestion: that writing was invented by women through the weaving and braiding of their pubic hairs. And consequently: there is a maximal cathexis or investment in (the) place of the missing penis, transferred masturbation tracing thought, the "magic" threshold. Man, in turn, would write himself all the more in assuming the "potential" of this lack.

Fredric Jameson

Imaginary and Symbolic in Lacan:

Marxism, Psychoanalytic Criticism, and the Problem of the
Subject

The attempt to coordinate a Marxist and a Freudian criticism confronts—but as it were explicitly, thematically articulated in the form
of a problem—a dilemma that is in reality inherent in all psychoanalytic criticism as such: that of the insertion of the subject, or,
in a different terminology, the difficulty of providing mediations
between social phenomena and what must be called private, rather
than even merely individual, facts. Only what for Marxist criticism
is already overtly social—in such questions as the relationship of
the work to its social or historical context, or the status of its
ideological content—is often merely implicitly so in that more
specialized or conventional psychoanalytic criticism which imagines
that it has no interest in extrinsic or social matters.

In "pure" psychoanalytic criticism, indeed, the social phenomenon with which the private materials of case history, of individual fantasy or childhood experience, must initially be confronted
is simply language itself. Even prior to the establishment of those
official social phenomena which are the literary forms and the
literary institution as such, language—the very medium of univer-
sality and of intersubjectivity—constitutes that primary social
instance into which the pre-verbal, pre-social facts of archaic or
unconscious experience find themselves somehow inserted. [1] Anyone

---

[1] See Hegel, *Phenomenology of Mind*, Chapter I ("Certainty at the
Level of Sense Experience") for the classic description of the way in which
the unique experience of the individual subject (sense-perception, the feeling
of the here-and-now, the consciousness of some incomparable individuality)
turns around into its opposite, into what is most empty and abstract, as it
emerges into the universal medium of language. And see, for a demonstration of the social nature of the object of linguistic study, V. N. Voloshinov,
Marxism and the Philosophy of Language (New York: Seminar Press, 1973).

Fredric Jameson

who has ever tried to recount a dream to someone else is in a position to measure the immense gap, the qualitative incommensurability, between the vivid memory of the dream and the dull, impoverished words which are all we can find to convey it: yet this incommensurability, between the particular and the universal, between the *vécu* and language itself, is one in which we dwell all our lives, and it is from it that all works of literature and culture necessarily emerge.

What is so often problematical about psychoanalytic criticism is therefore not its insistence on the subterranean relationships between the literary text on the one hand and the "obsessive metaphor" or the distant and inaccessible childhood or unconscious fascination on the other: it is rather the absence of any reflection on the transformational process whereby such private materials become public—a transformation which is often, to be sure, so undramatic and inconspicuous as the very act of speech itself. Yet insofar as speech is pre-eminently social, in what follows we will do well to keep Durkheim's stern warning constantly before us as a standard against which to assess the various models psychoanalytic criticism has provided: "Whenever a social phenomenon is directly explained by a psychological phenomenon, we may be sure that the explanation is false." [2]

I

In any case, it was Freud himself who, as so often, first sensed the methodological problems raised by the application of psychoanalytic techniques to those intersubjective objects which are works of art or literature. It has not sufficiently been observed that his major statement in this area, the essay "Creative Writers and Day-Dreaming" (1907), far from using the identification of literary productivity with private fantasy as a pretext for "reducing" the former to the latter, on the contrary very specifically enumerates the

[2] Emile Durkheim, *Les Règles de méthode sociologique* (Paris: Alcan, 1901), p. 128.

theoretical difficulties such an identification must face. His point is that it is by no means so easy as it might seem to reconcile the collective nature of literary reception with that fundamental tenet of psychoanalysis which sees the logic of the wish-fulfillment (or of its more metaphysical contemporary variant, "le désir"), as the organizing principle of all human thought and action. Freud tirelessly stresses the infantile egotism of the unconscious, its *Schadenfreude* and its envious rage at the gratifications of others, to the point where it becomes clear that it is precisely the fantasy or wish-fulfilling component of the literary work which constitutes the most serious barrier to its reception by a public: "You will remember how I have said that the day-dreamer carefully conceals his phantasies from other people because he feels he has reasons for being ashamed of them. I should now add that even if he were to communicate them to us he could give us no pleasure by his disclosures. Such phantasies, when we learn them, repel us or at least leave us cold." [3] Here again the dream provides a useful confirmation, and anyone who has had to listen to the dream narratives of other people can readily weigh that monotony against the inexhaustible fascination of our own dream memories. Thus, in literature, the detectable presence of self-dramatizing, and most often, self-pitying, fantasies is enough to cause a withdrawal from the implied contract of reading. The novels of Baron Corvo may serve as illustrations, or most best-sellers; even in Balzac, a good many thinly disguised wish-fulfillments become the object of what is at best amused complicity on the reader's part, but at the worst outright embarrassment. [4]

[3] Sigmund Freud, *Standard Edition* (London: Hogarth Press, 1959), Vol. IX, p. 152.
[4] It is true that the taboo on biographical criticism ought to make statements of this kind inadmissible; yet, particularly in a period in which literary biography is flourishing as never before, it is perhaps time to have a closer look at the ideological function of that taboo. It should be observed that, where the older biographical criticism understood the author's life as a context, or as a cause, as that which could explain the text, the newer kind understands that "life," or rather its reconstruction, precisely as one further text in its turn, a text on the level with the other literary texts of the writer in question and susceptible of forming a larger corpus of study with them. In any case, we need a semiotic account of the status

Freud does not conclude, but proposes a two-fold hypothesis for exploration as to the nature of the poetic process itself, which he characterizes as "the technique of overcoming the feeling of repulsion in us which is undoubtedly connected with the barriers that rise between each single ego and the others... The writer softens the character of his egoistic day-dreams by altering and disguising it, and he bribes us by the purely formal—that is, aesthetic—yield of pleasure which he offers us in the presentation of his phantasies. We give the name of an *incentive bonus,* or a *fore-pleasure,* to a yield of pleasure such as this, which is offered to us so as to make possible the release of still greater pleasure arising from deeper psychical sources." [5] Repression of the private or individual relevance of the fantasy, or in other words, its universalization, on the one hand; and the substitution of a formal play for the immediate gratification of wish-fulfilling content on the other—these two "methods" as Freud calls them correspond to a dual interpretive system that runs through all of his reading of texts—from those of dreams all the way to literary and cultural objects, but most strikingly, perhaps, in *Jokes and their Relation to the Unconscious:* namely, an account of the wish-fulfillment in terms of its content, in other words, the nature of the wish being fulfilled, and the symbolic ways in which it may be said to reach fulfillment, side by side with an explanation of the "supplement" of a more purely formal pleasure to be derived from the work's organization itself and the psychic economy the latter realizes. It is thus perhaps not too far-fetched to see at work in this two-fold account of the poetic process the subterranean presence of those primordial Freudian powers of Displacement and Condensation; gratification of the wish by its displacement and disguise, and a simultaneous release of psychic energy owing to the formal short-cuts and superpositions

of what are here designated as "autobiographical" passages, and of the specificity of those registers of a text in which authorial wish-fulfillment — in the form of complacency, self-pity and the like — is deliberately foregrounded.

[5] Freud, p. 153. The mechanisms outlined here are much closer to the model of *Jokes and the Unconscious* — its object a message and a communication situation — than to that of *The Interpretation of Dreams.*

of overdetermination. For the moment, however, we must retain, not Freud's solution, but rather his formulation of the problem in terms of a dialectic between individual desire and fantasy and the collective nature of language and reception.

It cannot be said that the literary criticism of orthodox Freudianism—even at its best—has followed the example of Freud himself in these reflections; rather, it has tended to remain locked within the categories of the individual and of individual experience (psychoanalyzing, as Holland puts it, either the character, or the author, or the public), without reaching a point at which those categories themselves become problematical. It is rather in some of the oppositional, or heretical, applications of psychoanalytic method to literature that we will be likely to find suggestive hints towards a further specification of the problem itself.

Thus, for example, Sartre may be said to have pioneered a psychobiographical method which cuts across some of the false problems of an orthodox psychoanalytic and a traditional biographical criticism alike. In both Sartre and Erikson, indeed, the conventional opposition between the private and the public, the unconscious and the conscious, the personal or unknowable and the universal and comprehensible, is displaced and reanchored in a new conception of the historical and psychic situation or context. Now the meaning of Genêt's style or Luther's theological propositions is no longer a matter for intuition, for the instinctive sensibility of analyst or interpreter in search of a hidden meaning within the outer and external one; rather, these cultural manifestations and individual productions come to be grasped as responses to a determinate situation and have the intelligibility of sheer gesture, provided the context is reconstructed with sufficient complexity. From an effort at empathy, therefore, the process of analysis is transformed into one of a hypothetical restoration of the situation itself, whose reconstruction is at one with comprehension *(Verstehen).* [6]
Even the problem of evaluation (the greatness of Luther's political

---

[6] For good and for ill, Sartre's theory of language has much in common with that of Dilthey.

Fredric Jameson

acts, of Genêt's formal innovations) becomes linked to the way in which each articulates the situation and may thus be seen as an exemplary reaction to it: from this point of view the response may be said to structure and virtually to bring to being for the first time an objective situation lived in a confused and less awakened fashion by their contemporaries. The concept of the context or situation here is thus not something extrinsic to the verbal or psychic text, but is generated by the latter at the very moment in which it begins to work on and to alter it. It should be added that in both Sartrean and Eriksonian reconstructions, the family proves to be the central mediatory institution between the psychic drama and that social or political realm (papal authority for Luther, nineteenth century class society for Flaubert), in which the psychic drama is ultimately acted out and "resolved."

At least for Sartre, however, this valorization of the situation goes hand in hand with a radical depersonalization of the subject. Here, despite the Lacanian polemic against the Cartesianism of *Being and Nothingness* and against the alleged ego-psychologizing of the psychobiographies and the evident revisionism of Sartre's early attacks on the Freudian concept of the Unconscious, it must be observed that another Sartre—that of *The Transcendence of the Ego*—was an important predecessor in precisely that struggle against ego psychology in which Lacan and his group have for so long been engaged. In that work, as well as in the chapter on the psyche in *L'Etre et le néant* which prolongs it, the ego in the traditional sense—character, personality, identity, sense of self—is shown to be an object for consciousness, part of the latter's "contents," rather than a constitutive and structuring element of it. A distance thus emerges within the subject between pure consciousness and its ego or psyche which is comparable to that separating the subject (S) and the ego *(a')* in Lacan's L-schema. Sartre's "Cartesianism" is not properly understood unless the attendant stress on the impersonality of consciousness is also grasped, on its utter lack of quality or individuating attributes, its "nature" as a mere speck or point without substance or consistency, in terms of which you, I, Luther,

Genêt, Flaubert, are all radically equivalent and indistinguishable. We are thus entitled to speak of an insertion of the subject here, both in the relationship of the historical figure to his situation and in the project of the psychobiography as a reconstruction of it: the opposition of particular to universal has been transformed into the relationship of an impersonal and rigorously interchangeable consciousness to a unique historical configuration. This said, it must also be noted that the psychobiographical form remains shackled to the categories of individual experience, and is thus unable to reach a level of cultural and social generalization without passing through the individual case history (a survival of the classical existential insistence on the primacy of individual experience which continues to govern both the *Critique de la raison dialectique* and the presentation of nineteenth century objective spirit—there called "objective neurosis"—in volume III of *L'Idiot de la famille*).

In contrast, the synthesis of Marx and Freud projected by the Frankfurt School takes as its province the fate of the subject in general under late capitalism. In retrospect, their Freudo-Marxism has not worn well, often seeming mechanical in those moments in Adorno's literary or musical studies when a Freudian scheme is perfunctorily introduced into a discussion of cultural or formal history. [7] Whenever Adorno or Horkheimer found their historical analyses upon a specific diagnosis, that is, on a local description of a determinate configuration of drive, repressive mechanism, and anxiety, Durkheim's warning about the psychological explanation of social phenomena seems to rematerialize in the middle distance.

---

[7] So for example, in his discussion of the sacrificial dance in Stravinsky's *Sacre du printemps,* Adorno observes: "The pleasure in a condition that is void of subject and harnessed by music is sadomasochistic. If the liquidation of the young girl is not simplistically enjoyed by the individual in the audience, he feels his way into the collective, thinking (as the potential victim of the collective) to participate thereby in collective power in a state of magical regression." (*Philosophy of Modern Music* [New York: Seabury, 1973]. p. 159) I am tempted to add that recourse to the hypothesis of a sadomasochistic or aggressive impulse is always a sign of an unmediated and psychologizing ideology (on the other hand, Adorno's use of the concept of "regression" is generally mediated by the history of form, so that regression to archaic instincts tends to be expressed by or to result in regression to earlier and cruder formal techniques, etc.).

Fredric Jameson

What remains powerful in this part of their work, however, is a more global model of repression which, borrowed from psychoanalysis, provides the underpinnings for their sociological vision of the total system or "verwaltete Welt" (the bureaucratically "administered" world system) of late capitalism. The adaptation of clinical Freudianism proves awkward at best precisely because the fundamental psychoanalytic inspiration of the Frankfurt School derives, not from diagnostic texts, but rather from *Civilization and Its Discontents,* with its eschatological vision of an irreversible link between development (or "Kultur" in the classical German sense of the word as technological and bureaucratic "progress") and ever-increasing instinctual renunciation and misery. Henceforth, for Adorno and Horkheimer, the evocation of renunciation will function less as psychic diagnosis than as cultural criticism; and technical terms like repression come to be used less for their own denotative value than as instruments for constructing, a contrario, a new Utopian vision of "bonheur" and instinctual gratification. Marcuse's work can then be understood as an adaptation of this Utopian vision to the quite different condition of the "société de consommation," with its "repressive desublimation," its commercialized permissiveness, so different from the authoritarian character structures and the rigid instinctual taboos of an older European industrial society.

If the Sartrean approach tended to emphasize the individual case history to the point where the very existence of more collective structures becomes problematical, the Frankfurt School's powerful vision of a liberated collective culture tends to leave little space for the unique histories—both psychic and social—of individual subjects. We must not forget, of course, that it was the Frankfurt School which pioneered the study of family structure as the mediation between society and the individual psyche;[8] yet even here the

[8] See "Authority and the Family", in Max Horkheimer, *Critical Theory* (New York: Seabury, 1972), pp. 47-128; and also Martin Jay, *The Dialectical Imagination* (Boston: Little, Brown, 1973), chapters 3-5. The appeal to the institution of the family as the primary mediation between childhood psychic formation and class realities is also an important feature of Sartre's program

results now seem dated, partly owing to precisely that decay of family structure in modern times which they themselves denounced. Partly, however, this relative obsolescence of their finding is owing to a methodological shift for which they themselves are responsible, namely the change of emphasis—particularly in the American period —from the family as a social institution to more properly psychological concepts like those of the authoritarian personality or the fascist character structure. Today, however, when it is ever clearer just how banal evil really is, and when we have repeatedly been able to observe the reactionary uses of such psychological interpretations of political positions (e.g., the student revolt as an Oedipal manifestation), this will no longer do. Frankfurt School Freudo-Marxism ended up as an analysis of the threats to "democracy" from right-wing extremism which was easily transferred, in the 1960's, to the Left; but the original Freudo-Marxian synthesis—that of Wilhelm Reich in the 1920's—evolved as an urgent response to what we would today call the problems of cultural revolution, and addressed the sense that political revolution cannot be fulfilled until the very character structures inherited from the older, pre-revolutionary society, and reinforced by its instinctual taboos, have been utterly transformed in their turn.

A rather different model of the relationship between individual psychology and social structure from either that of Sartre or of the Frankfurt School may be found in a remarkable and neglected work of Charles Mauron, *Psychocritique du genre comique* [Paris: Corti 1964]. Mauron's work cuts across that static opposition between the individual and the collective whose effects we have observed in the preceding discussion by introducing between them the mediation of a generic structure capable of functioning both on the level of individual gratification and on that of social structuration.

Comedy is in any case a unique and privileged type of cultural and psychic material, as the lasting theoretical suggestiveness of Freud's joke book may testify. Nor is Mauron's Oedipal interpreta-

for a reform of Marxist methodology in *Search for a Method* (New York: Vintage, 1968), pp. 60-65.

tion of classical comedy as the triumph of the young over the old particularly novel for the Anglo-American reader (a similar analysis of comedy is to be found in Northrop Frye's work). Even here, however, the psychoanalytic reading raises the fundamental issue of the status of character as such and of the categories that correspond to it: are the characters of classical comedy—hero-protagonist, love object, split drives or fragments of libidinal energy, the father as super-ego or as Oedipal rival—all structurally homogeneous with each other as in other forms of representation, or is there some more basic structural discontinuity at work here which the theatrical framework serves to mask?

It is precisely such a discontinuity which Mauron sees as constituting the originality of the Aristophanic form, in contrast to the classical theater of Molière or of Roman comedy. He shows that the fundamental Oedipal analysis can be made to apply to Old Comedy only if the framework of representation and the primacy of the category of character be broken: the place of the love object of Oedipal rivalry is then seen to be taken, not by another individual character, as in the heroines of Molière or of Plautus, but rather by the *polis* itself, that is, by an entity that dialectically transcends any individual existence. Aristophanic comedy thus reflects a moment of social and psychic development which precedes the constitution of the family as a homogeneous unit, a moment in which libidinal impulses still valorize the larger collective structures of the city or the tribe as a whole; and Mauron's analysis may be profitably juxtaposed with the results of the investigation by Marie-Cecile and Edmond Ortigues of the functioning of the Oedipus complex in traditional African society: "The question of the Oedipus complex cannot be assimilated to a characterology, or to a genetic psychology, or to a social psychology, or to a psychiatric semiology, but circumscribes the fundamental structures according to which, for society as well as for the individual, the problem of evil and suffering, the dialectic of desire and demand, are articulated... The Oedipus complex cannot be reduced to a description of the child's attitudes towards his or her father and mother...

The father is not only a second mother, a masculine educator; rather, the difference between the father and the mother, insofar as it projects that of man and woman in society as a whole, is part of the logic of a structure which manifests itself at several levels, both sociological and psychological ... The principal distinction [between the manifestation of the Oedipal problem in Senegalese society and that of Europe] lies in the form taken by guilt. Guilt does not appear as such; in other words, as the absence of depression and of any delirium of self-denunciation testifies, it does not appear as a splitting of the ego, but rather under the form of an anxiety at being abandoned by the group, of a loss of object." [9] The source of these modifications is then seen by the Ortigues to be the ancestor cult, into which much of the authority function of the Western father figure is absorbed: "It is the collectivity which [in Senegalese society] takes the death of the father upon itself. From the outset traditional Senegalese society announces that the place of each individual in the community is marked by reference to an ancestor, the father of the lineage ... Society, by presenting the law of the fathers, thus in a sense neutralizes the diachronic series of generations. In effect the death fantasies of the young Oedipal subject are deflected onto his collaterals, his brothers or his contemporaries. Instead of developing vertically or diachronically in a conflict between generations, aggressivity tends to be restricted to a horizontal expression within the limits of a single generation, in the framework of a solidarity and rivalry between collaterals." [10]

The methodological recourse to formally different textual structures, as in Mauron, or sociologically different contexts, as in *Oedipe africain,* thus has the merit of freeing the psychoanalytic model from its dependency on the classical Western family, with its ideology of individualism and its categories of the subject and (in matters of literary representation) of the character. It suggests

---

[9] Marie-Cécile and Edmond Ortigues, *Œdipe africain* (Paris: Plon, 1966), pp. 301-303.
[10] Ortigues, p. 304.

in turn the need for a model which is not locked into the classical opposition between the individual and the collective, but is rather able to think these discontinuities in a radically different way. Such is indeed the promise of Lacan's conception of the three orders (the Imaginary, the Symbolic, and the Real), of which it now remains for us to determine whether the hypothesis of a dialectically distinct status for each of these registers or sectors of experience can be maintained within the unity of a single system.

II

For the difficulties involved in an exposition of the three orders spring at least in part from their inseparability. According to Lacanian epistemology, indeed, acts of consciousness, experiences of the mature subject, necessarily imply a structural coordination between the Imaginary, the Symbolic, and the Real. "The experience of the Real presupposes the simultaneous exercise of two correlative functions, the imaginary function and the symbolic function." [11] If the notion of the Real is the most problematical of the three—since it can never be experienced immediately, but only by way of the mediation of the other two—it is also the easiest to bracket for purposes of this presentation. We will return to the function of this concept—neither an order nor a register, exactly— in our conclusion; suffice it to underscore here the profound heterogeneity of the Real with respect to the other two functions,

[11] Serge Leclaire, "A la recherche des principes d'une psychothérapie des psychoses", La Solution psychiatrique (1958), p. 383. Besides Lacan's early work (in the Ecrits [Paris: Seuil, 1966] and above all the first volume of the Séminaire, Les Ecrits techniques de Freud [Paris: Seuil, 1975], I have found the following works the most useful on the Imaginary/Symbolic distinction: Anika Rifflet-Lemaire, Jacques Lacan (Brussels: Dessart, 1970 — the most complete exposition of Lacan's thought to date); A. G. Wilden, The Language of the Self (Baltimore: Johns Hopkins, 1968 — still the best introduction to Lacan in English); Edmond Ortigues, Le Discours et le symbole (Paris: Aubier, 1962); Louis Althusser, "Freud and Lacan", in Lenin and Philosophy (New York: Monthly Review, 1971); and the above-mentioned article of Leclaire. An English translation of Lacan's "The Mirror phase as Formative of the Function of the I" may be found in New Left Review, #51 (September-October, 1968).

between which we would then expect to discover a similar disproportion.

Yet to speak of the Imaginary independently of the Symbolic is to perpetuate the illusion that we could have a relatively pure experience of either. If, for instance, we overhastily identify the Symbolic with the dimension of language and the function of speech in general, then it becomes obvious that we can hardly convey any experience of the Imaginary without presupposing the former. Meanwhile, insofar as the Imaginary is understood as the place of the insertion of my unique individuality as *Dasein* and as *corps propre,* it will become increasingly difficult to form a notion of the Symbolic Order as some pure syntactic web, which entertains no relationship to individual subjects at all.

In reality, however, the methodological danger is the obverse of this one, namely, the temptation to transform the notion of the two orders or functions into a binary opposition, and to define each relationally in terms of the other—something it is even easier to find oneself doing when one has begun by suspending the Real itself and leaving it out of consideration. We will however come to learn that this process of definition by binary opposition is itself profoundly characteristic of the Imaginary, so that to allow our exposition to be influenced by it is already to slant our presentation in terms of one of its two objects of study.

Fortunately, the genetic preoccupations of psychoanalysis provide a solution to this dilemma: for Freud founded his diagnosis of psychic disorders, not only on the latter's own aetiology, but on a larger view of the process of formation of the psyche itself as a whole, and on a conception of the stages of infantile development. And we shall see shortly that Lacan follows him in this, rewriting the Freudian history of the psyche in a new and unexpected way. But this means that, even if they are inextricable in mature psychic life, we ought to be able to distinguish Imaginary from Symbolic at the moment of emergence of each; in addition, we ought to be able to form a more reliable assessment of the role of each in the economy of the psyche by examining those moments in which their

Fredric Jameson

mature relationship to each other has broken down, moments which present a serious imbalance in favor of one or the other registers. Most frequently, this imbalance would seem to take the form of a degradation of the Symbolic to an Imaginary level: "The problem of the neurotic consists in a loss of the symbolic reference of the signifiers which make up the central points of the structure of his complex. Thus the neurotic may repress the signified of his symptom. This loss of the reference value of the symbol causes it to regress to the level of the imaginary, in the absence of any mediation between self and idea." [12] On the other hand, when it is appreciated to what degree, for Lacan, the apprenticeship of language is an alienation for the psyche, it will become clear that there can also be a hypertrophy of the Symbolic at the Imaginary's expense which is no less pathological; the recent emphasis on the critique of science and of its alienated "sujet supposé savoir" is indeed predicated on this overdevelopment of the Symbolic function: "The symbol is an imaginary figure in which man's truth is alienated. The intellectual elaboration of the symbol cannot disalienate it. Only the analysis of its imaginary elements, taken individually, reveals the meaning and the desire that the subject had hidden within it." [13]

Even before undertaking a genetic exposition of the two registers, however, we must observe that the very terms themselves present a preliminary difficulty which is none other than their respective previous histories: thus Imaginary surely derives from the experience of the image—and of the imago—and we are meant to retain its spatial and visual connotations. Yet as Lacan uses the word, it has a relatively narrow and technical sense, and should not be extended in any immediate way to the traditional conception of the imagination in philosophical aesthetics (nor to the Sartrean doctrine of the "imaginaire," although the latter's material of study is doubtless Imaginary in Lacan's sense of the term).

[12] Rifflet-Lemaire, p. 364.
[13] A. Vergote, quoted in Rifflet-Lemaire, p. 138.

The word Symbolic is even more troublesome, since much of what Lacan will designate as Imaginary is traditionally designated by expressions like symbol and symbolism. We will want to wrench the Lacanian term loose from its rich history as the opposite number to allegory, particularly in Romantic thought; nor can it maintain any of its wider suggestion of the figural as opposed to the literal meaning (symbolism versus discursive thought, Mauss' symbolic exchange as opposed to the market system, etc.). Indeed, we would be tempted to suggest that the Lacanian Symbolic Order be considered as having nothing to do with symbols or with symbolism whatsoever in the conventional sense, were it not for the obvious problem of what then to do with the whole classical Freudian apparatus of dream symbolism proper.

The originality of Lacan's rewriting of Freud may be judged by his radical reorganization of this material which had hitherto —houses, towers, cigars and all—been taken to constitute some storehouse of universal symbols. Most of the latter will now be understood rather as "part-objects" in Melanie Klein's sense of organs and parts of the body which are libidinally valorized; these part-objects then, as we shall see shortly, belong to the realm of the Imaginary rather than to that of the Symbolic. The one exception —the notorious "phallic" symbol dear to vulgar Freudian literary criticism—is the very instrument for the Lacanian reinterpretation of Freud in linguistic terms, for the phallus—not, in contradistinction to the penis, an organ of the body—now comes to be considered neither image nor symbol, but rather a signifier, indeed the fundamental signifier of mature psychic life, and thus one of the basic organizational categories of the Symbolic Order itself. [14]

[14] The fundamental text here is Ernest Jones, "The Theory of Symbolism," in *Papers on Psychoanalysis* (Boston: Beacon Press, 1961); to juxtapose this essay, one of the most painfully orthodox in the Freudian canon, with the Lacanian doctrine of the Signifier which appeals to it for authority, is to have a vivid and paradoxical sense of the meaning of Lacan's "return to the original Freud." This is also the place to observe that the feminist attacks on Lacan, and on the Lacanian doctrine of the Signifier, which seem largely inspired by A. G. Wilden, "The Critique of Phallocentrism" (in *System and Structure* [London: Tavistock, 1972], pp. 278-301), tend to be

Fredric Jameson

In any case, whatever the nature of the Lacanian Symbolic, it is clear that the Imaginary—a kind of pre-verbal register whose logic is essentially visual—precedes it as a stage in the development of the psyche. Its moment of formation—and that existential situation in which its specificity is most strikingly dramatized—has been named the "mirror stage" by Lacan, who thereby designates that moment between six and eighteen months in which the child first demonstrably "recognizes" his or her own image in the mirror, thus tangibly making the connection between inner motricity and the specular movements stirring before him. It is important not to deduce too hastily from this very early experience some ultimate ontological possibility of an ego or an identity in the psychological sense, or even in the sense of some Hegelian self-conscious reflexivity. Whatever else the mirror stage is, indeed, for Lacan it marks a fundamental gap between the subject and its own self or *imago* which can never be bridged: "The important point is that this form [of the subject in the mirror stage] fixed the instance of the ego, well before any social determination, in a line of fiction which is forever irreducible for the individual himself—or rather which will rejoin the subject's evolution in asymptotic fashion only, whatever the favorable outcome of those dialectical syntheses by which as an ego he must resolve his discordance with his own reality." [15] In our present context, we will want to retain the words "dans une ligne de fiction," which underscore the psychic function of narrative and fantasy in the attempts of the subject to reintegrate his or her alienated image.

The mirror stage, which is the precondition for primary narcissism, is also, owing to the equally irreducible gap it opens between the infant and its fellows, the very source of human aggressivity; and indeed, one of the original features of Lacan's early teaching is its insistence on the inextricable association of these two drives. [16]

---

vitiated by their confusion of the penis as an organ of the body with the phallus as a signifier.

[15] "Le stade du miroir," *Ecrits*, p. 94.

[16] Insofar as this insistence becomes the basis for an anthropology or a psychology proper — that is, for a theory of human nature on which a

How could it indeed be otherwise, at a moment when, the child's investment in images of the body having been achieved, there does not yet exist that ego formation which would permit him to distinguish his own form from that of others? The result is a world of bodies and organs which in some fashion lacks a phenomenological center and a privileged point of view: "Throughout this period the emotional reactions and verbal indications of normal transitivism [Charlotte Bühler's term for the indifferentiation of subject and object] will be observed. The child who hits says he has been hit, the child who sees another child fall begins to cry. Similarly, it is by way of an identification with the other that the infant lives the entire spectrum of reactions from ostentation to generosity, whose structural ambiguity his conduct so undisguisedly reveals, slave identified with despot, actor with spectator, victim with seducer." [17] This "structural crossroads" (Lacan) corresponds to that pre-individualistic, pre-mimetic, pre-point-of-view stage in aesthetic organization which is generally designated as "play," [18] whose essence lies in the frequent shifts of the subject from one fixed position to another, in a kind of optional multiplicity of insertions of the subject into a relatively fixed Symbolic Order. In the realm of linguistics and psychopathology, the fundamental document on the effects of "transitivism" remains Freud's "A Child is Being Beaten," which has had considerable emblematic significance for recent theory. [19]

A description of the Imaginary will therefore on the one hand require us to come to terms with a uniquely determinate configuration of space—one not yet organized around the individuation of

political or a social theory may then be built — it is ideological in the strict sense of the term; we are thus entitled to find Lacan's stress on the "pre-political" nature of the phenomenon of aggressivity (see *Le Séminaire*, Livre I, p. 202) somewhat defensive.

[17] "L'Aggressivité en psychanalyse," *Ecrits*, p. 113.

[18] Hans-Georg Gadamer, "Der Begriff des Spiels," in *Wahrheit und Methode* (Tübingen: Mohr, 1965), pp. 97-105.

[19] Freud, *Standard Edition*, Vol. XVII, pp. 179-204; and compare Jean-Louis Baudry's discussion of the 1911 essay, "On the Mechanism of Paranoia," in his "Ecriture, fiction, idéologie" in *Tel Quel: Théorie d'ensemble* (Paris: Seuil, 1968), pp. 145-146.

my own personal body, or differentiated hierarchically according to the perspectives of my own central point of view—yet which nonetheless swarms with bodies and forms intuited in a different way, whose fundamental property is, it would seem, to be visible without their visibility being the result of the act of any particular observer, to be, as it were, already-seen, to carry their specularity upon themselves like a color they wear or the texture of their surface. In this—the indifferentiation of their *esse* from a *percipi* which does not know a *percipiens*—these bodies of the Imaginary exemplify the very logic of mirror images; yet the existence of the normal object world of adult everyday life presupposes this prior, imaginary, experience of space: "It is normally by the possibilities of a game of imaginary transposition that the progressive valorization of objects is achieved, on what is customarily known as the affective level, by a proliferation, a fan-like disposition of all the imagination equations which allow the human being, alone in the animal realm, to have an almost infinite number of objects at his disposition, objects isolated in their form." [20]

The affective valorization of these objects ultimately derives from the primacy of the human *imago* in the mirror stage; and it is clear that the very investment of an object world will depend in one way or another on the possibility of symbolic association or identification of an inanimate thing with the libidinal priority of the human body. Here, then, we come upon what Melanie Klein termed "part-objects"—organs, like the breast, or objects associated with the body, like feces, whose psychic investment is then transferred to a host of other, more indifferent contents of the external world (which are then, as we shall see below, valorized as good or as evil). "A trait common to such objects, Lacan insists, is that they have no specular image, which is to say that they know no alterity. 'They are the very lining, the stuff or imaginary filling of the subject itself, which identifies itself with these objects.'" [21] It is from Mel-

---

[20] *Le Séminaire*, I, p. 98.

[21] Rifflet-Lemaire, op. cit., p. 219; and see for an analysis of schizophrenic language in terms of part-objects, Gilles Deleuze, "Préface," to Louis Wolfson, *Le Schizo et les langues* (Paris: Gallimard, 1970).

anie Klein's pioneering psychoanalysis of children that the basic features of the Lacanian Imaginary are drawn: there is, as we might expect for an experience of spatiality phenomenologically so different from our own, a logic specific to Imaginary space, whose dominant category proves to be the opposition of container and contained, the fundamental relationship of inside to outside, which clearly enough originates in the infant's fantasies about the maternal body as the receptacle of part-objects (confusion between childbirth and evacuation, etc.).[22]

This spatial syntax of the Imaginary order may then be said to be intersected by a different type of axis, whose conjunction completes it as an experience: this is the type of relationship which Lacan designates as aggressivity, and which we have seen to result from that indistinct rivalry between self and other in a period that precedes the very elaboration of a self or the construction of an ego. As with the axis of Imaginary space, we must again try to imagine something deeply sedimented in our own experience, but buried under the adult rationality of everyday life (and under the exercise of the Symbolic): a kind of situational experience of otherness as pure relationship, as struggle, violence, and antagonism, in which the child can occupy either term indifferently, or indeed, as in transitivism, both at one. A remarkable sentence of St. Augustine is inscribed as a motto to the primordiality of this rivalry with the imagoes of other infants: "I have myself seen jealousy in a baby and know what it means. He was not old enough to speak, but, whenever his foster-brother was at the breast, would glare at him pale with envy [et intuebatur pallidus amaro aspectu conlactaneum suum]."[23]

Provided it is understood that this moment is quite distinct from that later intervention of the Other (Lacan's capital A, the

[22] The archetypal realization of these fantasies must surely be Philip Jose Farmer's classic story "Mother" (in *Strange Relations* [London: Panther, 1966]), which has the additional interest of being a historic document of the psychological or vulgar Freudian *Weltanschauung* of the 1950's and in particular of the ideology of "momism" elaborated by writers like Philip Wylie.
[23] St. Augustine, *Confessions*, Book I, part 7, quoted in *Ecrits*, p. 114.

parents) which ratifies the assumption of the subject into the realm of language or the Symbolic Order, it will be appropriate to designate this primordial rivalry of the mirror stage as a relationship of otherness: nowhere better can we observe the violent situational content of those judgements of good and evil which will later on cool off and sediment into the various systems of ethics. Both Nietzsche and Sartre have exhaustively explored the genealogy of ethics as the latter emerges from just such an archaic valorization of space, where what is "good" is what is associated with "my" position, and the "bad" simply characterizes the affairs of my mirror rival. [24] We may further document the archaic or atavistic tendencies of ethical or moralizing thought by observing that it has no place in the Symbolic Order, or in the structure of language itself, whose shifters are positional and structurally incapable of supporting this kind of situational complicity with the subject momentarily occupying them.

The Imaginary may thus be described as a peculiar spatial configuration, whose bodies primarily entertain relationships of inside/outside with one another, which is then traversed and reorganized by that primordial rivalry and transitivistic substitution of imagoes, that indistinction of primary narcissism and aggressivity, from which our later conceptions of good and evil derive. This stage is already an alienation—the subject having been captivated by his or her specular image—but in Hegelian fashion it is the kind of alienation from which a more positive evolution is indistinguishable and without which the latter is inconceivable. The same must be said for the next stage of psychic development, in which the Imaginary itself is assumed into the Symbolic Order by way of its alienation into language itself. The Hegelian model of dialectical history—as Jean Hyppolite's interventions in Lacan's first Seminar make clear —remains the fundamental one here: "This development [of the human anatomy and in particular the cortex] is lived as a temporal

---

[24] See in particular *The Genealogy of Morals* and *Saint Genêt*. Neither fully realizes his intent to transcend the categories of "good and evil": Sartre for reasons more fully developed below, Nietzsche insofar as his philosophy of history aims at reviving the more archaic forms of rivalry rather than dissolving them.

dialectic which decisively projects the formation of the individual as history: the *mirror stage* is a drama whose internal dynamic shifts from insufficiency to anticipation—a drama which, for its subject, caught in the mirage of spatial identification, vehiculates a whole series of fantasies which range from a fragmented image of the body to what we will term an orthopedic form of its unity, and to that ultimate assumption of the armature of an alienating identity, whose rigid structure will mark the subject's entire mental development. Thus the rupture of the circle in which *Innenwelt* and *Umwelt* are united generates that inexhaustible attempt to square it in which we reap the ego." [25]

The approach to the Symbolic is the moment to suggest the originality of Lacan's conception of the function of language in psychoanalysis. For neo-Freudianism, it would seem that the role of language in the analytical situation or the "talking cure" is understood in terms of what we may call an aesthetic of expression and expressiveness: the patient unburdens himself or herself, his "relief" comes from his having verbalized (or even, according to a more recent ideology, from having "communicated"). For Lacan, on the contrary, this later exercise of speech in the analytical situation draws its therapeutic force from being as it were a completion and fulfillment of the first, imperfectly realized, accession to language and to the Symbolic in early childhood.

For the emphasis of Lacan on the linguistic development of the child—an area in which his work necessarily draws much from Piaget—has mistakenly been criticized as a "revision" of Freud in terms of more traditional psychology, a substitution of the psychological data of the mirror stage and of language acquisition for the more properly psychoanalytic phenomena of infantile sexuality and the Oedipus complex. Obviously Lacan's work must be read as presupposing the entire content of classical Freudianism, otherwise it would be simply another philosophy or intellectual system. The linguistic materials are not intended, it seems to me, to be

[25] "Le stade du miroir," *Ecrits,* p. 97.

substituted for the sexual ones; rather we must understand the Lacanian notion of the Symbolic Order as an attempt to create mediations between libidinal analysis and the linguistic categories, to provide, in other words, a transcoding scheme which allows us to speak of both within a common conceptual framework. Thus, the very cornerstone of Freud's conception of the psyche, the Oedipus complex, is transliterated by Lacan into a linguistic phenomenon which he designates as the discovery by the subject of the Name-of-the-Father, and which consists, in other words, in the transformation of an Imaginary relationship to that particular imago which is the physical parent into the new and menacing abstraction of the paternal role as the possessor of the mother and the place of the Law. (Meanwhile, we have already seen above how this conception allows the Ortigues to posit a continuing validity for the Freudian notion of the Oedipus complex in a social and familial situation in which many of the more parochial and purely European features of this relationship no longer obtain.)

The Symbolic Order is thus, as we have already suggested, a further alienation of the subject; and this repeated emphasis further serves to distinguish Lacan's position (what we have called his Hegelianism) from many of the more facile celebrations of the primacy of language by structuralist ideologues. Perhaps the link with Lévi-Strauss' primitivism may be made across Rousseau, for whom the social order in all its repressiveness is intimately linked with the emergence of language itself. In Lacan, however, an analogous sense of the alienating function of language is arrested in Utopian mid-course by the palpable impossibility of returning to an archaic, pre-verbal stage of the psyche itself (although the Deleuze-Guattari celebration of schizophrenia would appear to attempt precisely that). Far more adequately than the schizophrenic or natural man, the tragic symbol of the unavoidable alienation by language would seem to have been provided by Truffault's film, *L'Enfant sauvage*, in which language learning comes before us as a racking torture, a palpably physical kind of suffering upon which the feral child is only imperfectly willing to enter.

The clinical equivalent of this agonizing transition from the Imaginary to the Symbolic is then furnished by an analysis, by Melanie Klein, of an autistic child, which makes it clear that the "cure," the accession of the child to speech and to the Symbolic, is accompanied by an increase, rather than a lessening, of anxiety. This case history (published in 1930 under the title "The Importance of Symbol-Formation in the Development of the Ego") may also serve to correct the imbalance of our own presentation, and of the very notion of a "transition" from Imaginary to Symbolic, by demonstrating that the acquisition of the Symbolic is rather the precondition for a full mastery of the Imaginary as well. In this case, the autistic child is not only unable to speak but unable to play as well—unable, that is, to act out fantasies and to create "symbols," a term which in this context means object substitutes. The few meager objects handled by Dick all represent in a kind of undifferentiated state "the phantasied contents [of the mother's body]. The sadistic phantasies directed against the inside of her body constitute the first and basic relation to the outside world and to reality." [26] Psychic investment in the external world—or in other words, the development of the Imaginary itself—has been arrested at its most rudimentary form, with those little trains that function as representations of Dick and of his father and the dark space or station that represents the mother. The fear of anxiety prevents the child from developing further symbolic substitutes and expanding the narrow limits of his object world.

Melanie Klein's therapy then consists in the introduction into this impoverished realm of the Symbolic Order and of language; and that, as Lacan observes, without any particular subtlety or precautions ("Elle lui fout le symbolisme avec la dernière brutalité, Melanie Klein, au petit Dick! Elle commence tout de suite par lui flanquer les interprétations majeures. Elle le flanque dans une verbalisation brutale du mythe oedipien, presque aussi révoltante pour

---

[26] Melanie Klein, *Contributions to Psychoanalysis 1921-1945* (London: Hogarth Press, 1950), p. 238.

Fredric Jameson

nous que pour n'importe quel lecteur"). [27] Verbalization itself super-poses a Symbolic relationship upon the Imaginary fantasy of the train rolling up to the station: "The station is mummy; Dick is going into mummy." [28]

It is enough: from this point on, miraculously, the child begins to develop relationships to others, jealousies, games, and much richer forms of substitution and of the exercise of language. The Symbolic now releases Imaginary investments of ever new kinds of objects, which had hitherto been blocked, and permits the development of what Melanie Klein in her paper calls "symbol formation." Such symbol or substitute-formation is a fundamental precondition of psychic evolution, since it can alone lead the subject to love objects which are equivalents for the original, now forbidden or taboo, maternal presence: Lacan will then assimilate this process to the operation of the trope of metonymy in the linguistic realm, [29] and the profound effects of this new and complex "rhetorical" mechanism—unavailable in the pre-verbal realm of the Imaginary, where, as we have seen, only the rudimentary oppositions of inside/outside and good/bad are operative—may serve to underscore and to dramatize the extent of the transformation language brings to what without it could not yet have been called desire.

We may now attempt to give a more complete picture of Lacan's conception of language, or at least of those features of articulate speech which are the most essential in the structuration of the psyche and may thus be said to constitute the Symbolic Order. It will be convenient to consider these features in three groups, even though they are obviously all very closely interrelated.

---

[27] *Le Séminaire,* I, p. 81.
[28] Melanie Klein, p. 242.
[29] See "L'Instance de la lettre dans l'inconscient," *Ecrits,* p. 515 (or "The Insistence of the Letter in the Unconscious," *Yale French Studies* [36/37, 1966], p. 133). But see, for a powerful critique of the Lacanian figural mechanism, Tzvetan Todorov, *Théories du symbole* (Paris: Seuil, 1977), ch. 8 esp. pp. 302-305; and for a more general analysis of Lacan's linguistic philosophy, Henri Meschonnic, *Le Signe et le poème* (Paris: Gallimard, 1975), pp. 314-322.

The first of these groups—we have already seen it at work in the Oedipal phenomenon of the Name-of-the-Father—may be generalized as that naming function of language which is not without its profound consequences for the subject himself. For the acquisition of a name results in a thorough-going transformation of the position of the subject in his object world: "That a name, no matter how confused, designates a particular person—this is precisely what the passage to the human state consists in. If we must define that moment in which man [sic] becomes human, we would say that it is at that instant when, as minimally as you like, he enters into a symbolic relationship." [30] It would seem fair to observe that Lacan's attention to the components of language has centered on those kinds of words, primarily names and pronouns, on those slots which, like the shifters generally, anchor a free-floating syntax to a particular subject, those verbal joints, therefore, at which the insertion of the subject into the Symbolic is particularly detectable.

Even here, however, we must distinguish among the various possible effects of these types of words: nouns, in particular the Name-of-the-Father itself, awaken the subject to the sense of a function which is somehow objective and independent of the existence of the biological father. Such names thus provide a liberation from the here-and-now of the Imaginary; for the separation, through language, of the paternal function from the biological father is precisely what permits the child to take the father's place in his turn. The Law, as Lacan calls it, the order of abstraction, is thus also what releases the subject from the constraints of his immediate family situation and from the "bad immediacy" of the pre-Symbolic period.

Pronouns, meanwhile, are the locus for a related, yet distinct, development which is none other than the emergence of the Unconscious itself. Such is indeed for Lacan the significance of the bar which divides signifier from signified in the semiotic fraction: the

---

[30] *Le Séminaire*, I, p. 178.

Fredric Jameson

pronoun, the first person, the signifier, results in a division of the subject or *Spaltung* which drives the "real subject" as it were underground, and leaves a "representative"—the ego—in its place: "The subject is figured in symbolism by a stand-in or substitute [un tenant-lieu], whether we have to do with the personal pronoun 'I', with the name that is given him, or with the denomination 'son of'. This stand-in is of the order of the symbol or the signifier, an order which is only perpetuated laterally, through the relationships entertained by that signifier with other signifiers. The subject mediated by language is irremediably divided because it has been excluded from the symbolic chain [the lateral relations of signifiers among themselves] at the very moment at which it became 'represented' in it." [31] Thus, the discontinuity insisted on by linguists between the *énoncé* and the subject of the enunciation (or, by Humboldt's even broader distinction between language as *ergon* or produced object, and language as *energeia* or force of linguistic production) corresponds to the coming into being of the Unconscious itself, as that reality of the subject which has been alienated and repressed through the very process by which, in receiving a name, it is transformed into a representation of itself.

This production of the Unconscious by way of a primary repression which is none other than the acquisition of language is then reinterpreted in terms of the communicational situation as a whole; and Lacan's redefinition of the signifier, "the signifier is what represents the subject for another signifier," [32] now illuminates what it may be artificial to call a different form of linguistic alienation than either of the above features, but what is certainly a distinct dimension of that alienation, namely, the coming into view of the inescapable mediation of other people, and more particularly of the Other with a capital O or A, or in other words the parents: yet here the Law represented by the parents, and in particular by the father, passes over into the very nature of language itself, which

[31] Rifflet-Lemaire, p. 129.
[32] "Subversion du sujet et dialectique du désir dans l'inconscient freudien," *Ecrits*, p. 819.

the child receives from the outside and which speaks him just as surely as he learns to speak it. At this third moment of the subject's alienation by language we therefore confront a more complex version of that strategy which we have elsewhere described as the fundamental enabling device of structuralism in general, namely, the possibility—provided by the ambiguous nature of language itself—of imperceptibly shifting back and forth between a conception of speech as a linguistic structure, whose components can then be tabulated, and that which, now on the contrary understanding speech in terms of communication, permits a virtual dramatization of the linguistic process (sender/receiver, destinaire/destinateur, etc.). [33] Lacan's "capital A" is the locus of this superposition, constituting at one and the same time the dramatis personae of the Oedipal situation (but most particularly the father or his substitutes) and the very structure of articulate language itself.

So it is that this third aspect of Symbolic alienation, the alienation by the Other, passes over into the more familiar terms of the accounts of the "chaîne du signifiant" given in Lacan's mature doctrine, [34] which, embattled in a struggle against ego psychology, and emerging from a long polemic with the neo-Freudian emphasis on the analysis of resistances and the strengthening of the subject's ego, has found its fundamental principle and organizing theme in "a conception of the function of the signifier able to demonstrate the place at which the subject is subordinated to it to the point of being virtually subverted [suborné]." [35] The result is a determination of the subject by language—not to say a linguistic determinism —which results in a rewriting of the classical Freudian Unconscious

[33] *The Prison-House of Language* (Princeton: Princeton University Press, 1972), p. 205. This is the place to add that, while I would maintain my position on the other thinkers there discussed, I no longer consider the account of Lacan given in that book to be useful or adequate: let the present essay serve as its replacement.

[34] Its fundamental texts are now available in English: "The Function of Language in Psychoanalysis" or so-called "Discours de Rome" (translated in Wilden, *The Language of the Self*); "The Insistence of the Letter" (see note 29 above) and the "Seminar on The Purloined Letter'," in *Yale French Studies*, 48 (1972), pp. 39-72.

[35] "La Direction de la cure et les principes de son pouvoir," *Ecrits*, p. 593.

Fredric Jameson

in terms of language: "the Unconscious," to quote what must be Lacan's best-known sentence, "is the discourse of the Other." [36] For those of us still accustomed to the classical image of the Freudian Unconscious as a seething cauldron of archaic instincts (and inclined, also, to associate language with thinking and consciousness rather than the opposite of those things), the Lacanian redefinition must inevitably scandalize. As far as language is concerned, the references to Hegel have a strategic role to play in confronting this scandal with the philosophically more respectable idea of alienation in general, and alienation to other people in particular (the Master/Slave chapter is of course the basic text here): thus, if we can bring ourselves to think of language itself as an alienating structure, particularly in those features enumerated above, we are halfway towards an appreciation of this concept.

The other half of the way, however, presents the more serious obstacle of our preconceptions, not about language, but rather about the Unconscious itself. To be sure, the relationship between the Unconscious and the instincts will seem less problematical when we recall the enigma posed by Freud's notion of the *Vorstellungsrepräsentanz* (or "ideational representative"), [37] one of those rare moments in which, as with his hypothesis of the death wish, Freud himself seems terminologically and theoretically inarticulate. Yet the function of the concept seems clear: Freud wants to avoid giving the impression that instincts or drives *(Triebe)* are conceivable in a pure state, even for the purposes of building a model of the psyche, and his tautological term is meant to underscore the indissociable link, no matter how far back we go in the history of the psyche, between the instincts to be found there and the fantasies or objects to which they are bound and through which alone they must express themselves. What is this to say but that the instincts, indeed, the libido itself, no matter how energetically boiling, cannot be conceived independently of their representations,

[36] As, e.g., in "Subversion du sujet et dialectique du désir," *Ecrits*, p. 814.

[37] Freud, *Standard Edition*, Vol. XIV, pp. 152-153. This is the term Lacan translates as "le tenant lieu de la représentation."

in short, that, in Lacanian terms, no matter how archaic they may be, the instincts are already of the order of the signifier? So it is that the place A of the Lacanian topology indifferently designates the Other (the parents), language, or the Unconscious, now termed the "treasurehouse of the signifier," or in other words, the lumber-room in which the subject's most ancient fantasies or fragments of fantasy are still stored. Two well-known, if less well understood, graphs illustrate this topology, in dynamic as well as in static forms. The static version is, of course, the so-called L-schema,[38] in which the subject's conscious desire, which he understands as a relation-ship between the desired object (a) and his ego or self *(a')*, is mediated by the more fundamental relationship between the real subject (S) and the capital A of the Other, language or the Un-conscious. In the dynamic version of this topology (the so-called "graphe du désir"),[39] this structure of the subject is as it were put in motion by the movement of desire, considered as a *parole* or act of enunciation: the inexhaustible fascination of this graph comes from the difficulty of thinking its intersections, in which the speech act of the subject, on its way from sender to receiver, is traversed by the retroactive effect of the "chain of the signifier" travelling, *nachträglich,* in the opposite direction, in such a way that the capital A constitutes the source and the fulfillment of both trajectories.

Still, it will be observed that even if language can be invested to this degree with the content of the subject's alienations, it re-mains to square the Lacanian linguistic bias with the predominantly sexual emphasis of psychoanalysis' inaugural period. Even if, in other words, one were willing to grant the phallus provisional status as a signifier, the relationship between language and sexuality remains to be defined, the suspicion lingering that a system which permits you to talk about language instead of sexuality must betray a revisionist, if not a downright idealistic, impulse. The connection

[38] *Ecrits*, p. 53.
[39] *Ecrits*, pp. 805-817; but see also J. B. Pontalis' comptes rendus of the 1957 and 1958 seminars, *Bulletin de psychologie* XI/4-5, p. 293, and XIII/5, pp. 264-265.

Fredric Jameson

is made by way of the distinction between need ("pure" biological phenomenon) and demand (a purely interpersonal one, conceivable only after the emergence of language): sexual desire is then that qualitatively new and more complex realm opened up by the lateness of human maturation in comparison with the other animal species, in which a previously biological instinct must undergo an alienation to a fundamentally communicational or linguistic relationship—that of the demand for recognition by the Other—in order to find satisfaction. Yet this alienation also explains why, for Lacan, sexual desire is structurally incapable of ultimate satisfaction: "plaisir" —as the momentary reduction of a purely physical tension—not being the same as "jouissance," which involves that demand for recognition by the Other which in the very nature of things (in the very nature of language?) can never be fulfilled. This structural distance between the subject and his own desire will then serve as the enabling mechanism for the Lacanian typology of the neuroses and the perversions; and nowhere is Lacan more eloquent than in his defense of the ontological dignity of these primordial malfunctionings of the human psyche: "Hieroglyphics of hysteria, blazons of phobia, labyrinths of the *Zwangsneurose*—charms of impotence, enigmas of inhibition, oracles of anxiety—armorial bearings of character, seals of self-punishment, disguises of perversion—these are the hermetic elements that our exegesis resolves, the equivocations that our invocation dissolves, the artifices that our dialectic absolves, in a deliverance of the imprisoned sense, which moves from the revelation of the palimpsest to the pass-word of the mystery and the pardon of speech." [40]

Meanwhile, this conception of desire as a proto-linguistic demand, and of the Unconscious as a language or "chain of signifiers," then permits something like a rhetorical analysis of psychic processes to come into being. As is well known, not only is desire for Lacan a function of metonymy, the symptom is a product of metaphor, and the entire machinery of the psychic life of the mature subject

[40] Wilden, "The Function of Language in Psychoanalysis," p. 44, translation modified.

—which consists, as we have seen above, in the infinite production of substitutes, or, in other words, in Melanie Klein's "symbol-formation"—may be said to be figural in its very essence, figuration being that property of language which allows the same word to be used in several senses. The correlative of the chain of signifiers is thus the conception of a "glissement du signifié" or slippage of signifieds which allows the psychic signifier to be displaced from one object to another. Here once again, the material of the Imaginary serves as a useful contrast by which to define the Symbolic: for not only does the latter, with its slippage of signifieds, know a structural malfunction in the language of the schizophrenic (whose syntagmatic experience of the signifying chain has broken down, on account of a radical *forclusion* or expulsion of the Other), it may be said to have something like a zero degree in the so-called animal languages which constitute the very prototype of the code proper to the Imaginary, involving no demands on the Other, but simply a fixed one-to-one relationship between signifier and signified, between signal and place, from which the more properly human phenomenon of figuration is absent. [41]

Displacement of the subject and redefinition of the Unconscious as a language, topology and typology of desire and of its avatars —this brief sketch of "Lacanianism" would not be complete without a mention of that third overriding preoccupation of Lacan's life work—the one which it is most tempting and convenient for laymen to overlook, namely, the strategy of the analytic situation itself, and in particular the role to be played in it by the analyst's interventions and the nature of transference. It is clear that in the Lacanian scheme of things, the uniqueness of the analytic situation —its emblematic as well as therapeutic value—derives from the fact that it is the one communicational situation in which the Other is

[41] Wilden, p. 61ff. (or *Ecrits*, p. 297); here and elsewhere, Lacan bases a whole phenomenology of Imaginary space on ethological data. It would be suggestive, but not altogether accurate, to claim that the Imaginary and animal or "natural" languages alike are governed by *analog* rather than *digital* logic. See Thomas A. Sebeok, *Perspectives in Zoosemiotics* (The Hague: Mouton, 1972), esp. pp. 63-83, and also A. G. Wilden "Analog and Digital Communication," in *System and Structure*, pp. 155-190.

Fredric Jameson

addressed without being functionally involved: the analyst's silence thus causes the structural dependency of the subject on the capital A of the Other's language to become visible as it never could in any concrete interpersonal situation. So the subject's gradual experience of his or her own subordination to an alienating signifier is at one with the theorist's denunciation of philosophies of the subject and his Copernican attempt to assign to the subject an ec-centric position with respect to language as a whole.

We may now ask what, apart from the incidental mention of phenomena like that of animal language, above, can be said to be the place of the Imaginary in the later teaching; and we shall later on have occasion to see that its gradual eclipse in Lacan's later work is not foreign to a certain overestimation of the Symbolic which may be said to be properly ideological. For the moment, we may suggest that Imaginary thought patterns persist into mature psychic life in the form of what are generally thought of as ethical judgments—those implicit or explicit valorizations or repudiations in which "good" and "bad" are simply positional descriptions of the geographical relationship of the phenomenon in question to my own Imaginary conception of centrality: it is a comedy we may observe, not only in the world of action, but also in that of thought, where, in that immense proliferation of private languages which characterizes the intellectual life of consumer capitalism, the private religions which emerge around thinkers like the one presently under consideration are matched only by their anathematization by the champions of rival "codes." The Imaginary sources of passions like ethics may always be identified by the operation of the dual in them, and the organization of their themes around binary oppositions; the ideological quality of such thinking must however be accounted for, not so much by the metaphysical nature of its categories of centrality, as Derrida and Lyotard have argued, as rather by its substitution of the categories of individual relationships for those—collective—of history and of historical, transindividual phenomena.

This view of ethics would seem to find confirmation in Lacan's essay, "Kant avec Sade," in which the very prototype of an attempt to construct a rationally coherent (or in other words, Symbolic) system of ethics by the first-named is thoroughly discredited by a structural analogy with the delirious rationality of the second. By attempting to universalize ethics and to establish the criteria for universally binding ethical laws which arè not dependent on the logic of the individual situation, Kant merely succeeds in stripping the subject of his object (a) in an effort to separate pleasurability from the notion of the Good, thereby leaving the subject alone with the Law (A): "Cannot moral law be said to represent desire in that situation in which it is not the subject, but rather the object, which is missing?" [42] Yet this structural result turns out to be homologous with perversion, defined by Lacan as the fascination with the pleasure of the Other at the expense of the subject's own, and illustrated monotonously by the voluminous pages of Sade.

Whatever the philosophical value of this analysis, in the present context it has the merit of allowing us to conceive the possibility of transforming the topological distinction between Imaginary and Symbolic into a genuine methodology. "Kant avec Sade" would seem indeed to be the equivalent in the realm of moral philosophy of those logical paradoxes and mathematical "travaux pratiques" which have so disoriented the readers of Lacan in other areas. Thus, for example, we find a properly psychoanalytic reflection on the timing of the analytical situation unexpectedly punctuated by a me-ditation on a logical puzzle or metalogical paradox (see "Le Temps logique"), whose upshot is to force us to reintroduce the time of the individual subject back into what was supposed to be a universal or impersonal mental operation. Elsewhere the experiment is re-versed, and the laws of probability are invoked to demonstrate the Symbolic regularity (in Freudian terms, the repetitive structure) of what otherwise strikes the subject as sheer individual chance. Lacan has however explained himself about these excursions, designed, he

[42] "Kant avec Sade," *Ecrits,* p. 780.

says, to lead "those who follow us into places where logic itself is staggered by the glaring incommensurability between Imaginary and Symbolic; and this, not out of complacency with the resultant paradoxes, nor with any so-called intellectual crisis, but rather on the contrary to restore its illicit glitter to the structural gap [*béance*] thereby revealed, a gap perpetually instructive for us, and above all to try to forge the method of a kind of calculus able to dislodge its secret by its very inappropriateness." [43]

In the same way, "Kant avec Sade" transforms the very project of a moral philosophy into an insoluble intellectual paradox by rotating it in such a way that the implicit gap in it between subject and law catches the light. It is time to ask whether a similar use of the distinction between Imaginary and Symbolic may not be possible in the realm of aesthetic theory and literary criticism, offering psychoanalytic method a more fruitful vocation than it was able to exercise in the older literary psychoanalyses.

III

We cannot do so, however, before first asking whether, alongside that Freudian criticism, of which everyone—for good or ill—has a fairly vivid idea what it ends up looking like, a properly Lacanian criticism is also conceivable. Yet it is here that the ambiguity of Lacan's relations to his original—is he rewriting him or merely restoring him?—becomes problematical: for at the point of interpretation, either the attempt at a Lacanian reading simply resolves into the classic themes of all psychoanalytic literary criticism since Freud—the Oedipus complex, the double, splitting, the phallus, the lost object, etc.—or else, trying to keep faith with the linguistic inspiration of "L'Instance de la lettre," it exercises the distinction between metaphor and metonymy to the point where the orthodox psychoanalytic preoccupations seem to have been forgotten without a trace. [44] In part, of course, this methodological

---

[43] "Subversion du sujet et dialectique du désir," *Ecrits*, p. 820.
[44] The aesthetic chapters of Guy Rosolato, *Essais sur le symbolique* (Paris: Gallimard, 1969), may serve to document this proposition; they

fluctuation can be accounted for by what we have suggested above, namely, that on the level of interpretive codes Lacan's position is not one of substituting linguistic for classical psychoanalytic concepts, but rather of mediating between them: and this is clearly a matter of some tact which cannot be successfully realized on the occasion of every text.

But there is another, more structural, side to this problem, which raises the question of the syntagmatic organization of the work of art, rather than the issue—a more properly paradigmatic one—of the interpretive schemes into which it is to be "transcoded" or interpreted. Freud's own two greatest narrative readings, that of Jensen's *Gradiva* and that of Hoffmann's *Sandmann,* turn on delusions which either come to appeasement or culminate in the destruction of the subject. They thus recapitulate the trajectory of the cure, or of the illness, or—ultimately, and behind both—of the evolution and maturation of the psyche itself. We have here, therefore, narratives which formally require the final term of a norm (maturity, psychic health, the cure) towards which to steer their itineraries, whether catastrophic or providential; of that ultimate norm itself however, the narrative can have nothing to say, as it is not a realm, but rather only an organizational device or term limit.

also suggest that our frequent discomfort with psychoanalytic criticism may spring just as much from those ahistorical and systematizing categories of an older philosophical aesthetics in which it remains locked, as from its Freudian interpretative scheme itself. It will indeed have become clear that in the perspective of the present essay all of that more conventional Freudian criticism — a criticism which, above and beyond some "vision" of human nature, offers the critic a privileged interpretative code and the ontological security of some ultimate content — must for this very reason be understood as profoundly ideological. What now becomes clearer is that the structural oscillation here referred to in Lacanian conceptuality itself — the strategic alternation between linguistic and "orthodox Freudian" codes — often determines a slippage in the literary or cultural analyses of its practitioners whereby the properly Lacanian tension (or "heterogeneity") tends to relax into more conventional Freudian interpretations: I will argue elsewhere for example that something like this is happening in the best of the recent work of the so-called Tel Quel group after their movement away from historical materialism.

Fredric Jameson

It would not be difficult to imagine a Lacanian criticism—although I do not know that there has been one [45]—in which the transition from the Imaginary to the Symbolic described above played an analogous role in organizing the syntagmatic movement of the narrative from disorder to the term limit of the Symbolic Order itself. The risk of an operation like this lies clearly in the assimilation of what is original in Lacan to the more wide-spread and now conventionalized structuralist paradigm of the passage from nature to culture; and this is surely the moment to ask ourselves whether the Lacanian emphasis on the Law and on the necessity of the castration anxiety in the evolution of the subject— so different in spirit from the instinctual and revolutionary Utopias of Brown's polymorphous perversity, Reich's genital sexuality and Marcuse's maternal super-id—shares the implicit conservatism of the classical structuralist paradigm. Insofar as the Lacanian version generates a rhetoric of its own which celebrates submission to the Law, and indeed, the subordination of the subject to the Symbolic Order, conservative overtones and indeed the possibility of a conservative misappropriation of this clearly anti-Utopian scheme are unavoidable. On the other hand, if we recall that for Lacan "submission to the Law" designates, not repression, but rather something quite different, namely alienation—in the ambiguous sense in which Hegel, as opposed to Marx, conceives of this phenomenon— then the more tragic character of Lacan's thought, and the dialectical possibilities inherent in it, become evident.

Indeed, the one sustained literary exegesis that Lacan has published, the seminar on Poe's "Purloined Letter," [46] suggests that

[45] But see the chapter on Michel Leiris in Jeffrey Mehlman, *A Structural Study of Autobiography* (Ithaca: Cornell University Press, 1974) and my own "Balzac and Lacan: Imaginary and Symbolic in *La Rabouilleuse*, in *Social Science Information*, Vol. XVI, No. 1, 1977, pp. 59-81 (or in my forthcoming book *The Political Unconscious: Studies in the Ideology of Form*); and see also Christian Metz, "The Imaginary Signifier," *Screen*, Summer, 1975, Vol. 16, No. 2, pp. 14-76. With respect to this last, not strictly speaking, an analysis of an individual work, it may be observed that the structural discontinuity, in film, between the visual plenitude of the filmic image and its "diegetic" use in the narrative of a given film makes it a privileged object for the exercise of the Lacanian dual registers.
[46] *Ecrits*, pp. 11-41 (for English translation, see note 34 above).

for Lacan, in contradistinction to Freud himself, the norm *can* be the locus of a properly narrative exploration, albeit one of a uniquely didactic or "illustrative" type. [47] Poe's story is for Lacan the occasion of a magistral demonstration of the way "a formal language determines the subject:" [48] the three distinct positions structurally available in relationship to the Letter itself, or the signifier—that of the king, that of the queen, and that of the Minister—proving, when in the sequel to the narrative, the places change, Dupin taking the place of the Minister, who then moves to that previously held by the queen, to exercise a structurating power over the subjects who momentarily occupy them. So the signifying chain becomes a vicious circle, and the story of the norm itself, of the Symbolic Order, is not that of a "happy end," but rather of a perpetual alienation. Obviously, Lacan's interpretation of the narrative is an allegorical one, in which the signified of the narrative proves to be simply language itself. Once again, the relative richness of the reading derives from the dramatic structure of the communicational process and the multiplicity of different positions available in it; but while more lively on account of the musical chairs being played in it, Lacan's exegesis in this respect rejoins that now conventional structuralist conception of the auto-referentiality of the text which we have shown at work in *Tel Quel* and Derrida, as well as in Todorov's interpretations. [49] Read in this way—but as we will suggest later, it is not the only way one can read Lacan's essay—the "Seminar on 'The Purloined Letter',", by its programmatic demonstration of the primacy of the signifier, furnishes powerful ammunition for what must properly be called, in distinction to its other achievements, the ideology of structuralism (it may rapidly be defined here as that systematic substitution of "referent" for "signified" which allows one to pass logically from the properly

[47] See Jacques Derrida, "The Purveyor of Truth," in *Yale French Studies*, #52 (1975), esp. pp. 45-47. But it might be argued against Derrida that it was Poe himself who first opened up this gap between the abstract concept and its narrative illustration in the lengthy reflections on detection and ratiocination with which the tale is interlarded.
[48] "Présentation de la suite," *Ecrits*, p. 42.
[49] See *The Prison-House of Language*, pp. 182-183, 197-201.

Fredric Jameson

linguistic assertion that the signified is an effect of the organization of signifiers to the quite different conclusion that therefore the "referent"—i.e., history—does not exist). Yet the present context suggests an explanation for this excess charge of ideology, this ideological effect, vehiculated or produced by Lacan's exposé: indeed, its opening page, with its polemic repudiation of those "imaginary incidences [which], far from representing the essence of our experience, reveal only what remains inconsistent in it," [50] makes a diagnosis of an overestimation of the Symbolic at the expense of the Imaginary in its presentation wellnigh inescapable.

We have thus, strengthened by this detour through Lacan's own literary criticism, returned to our hypothesis that whatever else it is, the distinction between the Imaginary and the Symbolic, and the requirement that a given analysis be able to do justice to the qualitative gap between them, may prove to be an invaluable instrument for measuring the range or the limits of a particular way of thinking. If it is always unsatisfying to speculate on what a Lacanian literary criticism ought to be in the future, if it is clear that the "Seminar on 'The Purloined Letter'" cannot possibly constitute a model for such criticism, since on the contrary the literary work is in it a mere pretext for a dazzling illustration of a non-literary thesis, then at least we may be able to use the concept

---

[50] "Seminar on 'The Purloined Letter'," p. 39 (or *Ecrits*, p. 11). Derrida's reading (see note 47 above), which emphasizes the moment of "dissemination" in the Poe story (in particular, the generation of doubles ad infinitum: the narrator as the double of Dupin, Dupin as the double of the Minister, the story itself as the double of the two other Dupin stories, etc.), thus in opposition to the Lacanian seminar foregrounds what we have learned to identify as the Imaginary, rather than the Symbolic, elements of Poe's text. Whatever the merits of the polemic here engaged with Lacan, as far as the tale itself is concerned, there emerges a sense of the tension between these two kinds of elements which suggests that it is not so much Lacan, as rather Poe's text itself that tends towards a suppression of the traces of just this Imaginary "drift" of which Derrida here reminds us; and that it is precisely the "work" of the text itself to transform those Imaginary elements into the closed Symbolic circuit which is Lacan's own object of commentary. This is why it does not seem quite right to conclude, from such a re-emphasis on the Imaginary and "disseminatory," that "the opposition of the imaginary and symbolic, and above all its implicit hierarchy, seem to be of very limited relevance" (Derrida, pp. 108-109). On the contrary, it is precisely from this opposition that the exegetical polemic here launched by Derrida draws its interest.

of the two orders or registers as a means for demonstrating the imbalance of other critical methods, and of suggesting ways in which they may be coordinated, and an eclectic pluralism overcome. So, for instance, it seems abundantly clear that the whole area of image-study and image-hunting must be transformed, when we grasp the image content of a given text, not as so many clues to its ideational content (or "meaning"), but rather as the sedimentation of the imaginary material on which the text must work, and which it must transform. The relationship of the literary text to its image content is thus—in spite of the historic preponderance of the sensory in modern literature since Romanticism—not that of the production of imagery, but rather of its mastery and control in ways which range from outright repression (and the transformation of the sensory image into some more comfortable conceptual symbol) to the more complex modes of assimilation of surrealism and, more recently, of schizophrenic literature.[51] Only by grasping images— and also the surviving fragments of authentic myth and delusion —in this way, as that trace of the Imaginary, of sheer private or physiological experience, which has undergone the sea-change of the Symbolic, can criticism of this kind recover a vital and her- meneutic relationship to the literary text.

Yet image criticism raises a problem which we have postponed until this time, namely, how, as a matter of critical practice now rather than abstract theory, to identify Imaginary materials as such, particularly insofar as the same contents can at different times or in different contexts have been part of an imaginary experience as well as of a symbolic system? Leclaire's useful example of the bronze ashtray[52] enumerates this gradual shifting of registers as the initial perception of the shape and the blackened metal surface of the object, of its density in the hand and its slickness for the eye, then is slowly by means of names ranged in the various sym-

---

[51] Reread from this perspective, Walter Benjamin's seminal essay on *Elective Affinities* ("Goethe's *Wahlverwandtschaften*," in *Schriften*, Vol. I [Frankfurt: Suhrkamp, 1955], pp. 55-140) takes on a suggestively Lacanian ring.

[52] Leclaire, p. 382.

bolic systems in which it seems to find a momentary home, first as a functional object ("ashtray"), then as an antique, further as the specimen of a particular style of rural furnishing, and so forth. This distinction between the experience of immediate sense perception and the various systems of abstraction into which the name of an object allows it to be inserted, has already become familiar to us.

It should, however, be possible to formulate more specific rules for the determination of the respective Imaginary or Symbolic function of a given object, such as the following one: "The same term may be considered imaginary if taken absolutely and symbolic if taken as a differential value correlative of other terms which limit it reciprocally." [53] This excellent formula, which we owe to Edmond Ortigues, should probably not be generalized into the kind of ahistorical system he goes on to offer us, in which the Imaginary becomes the regime of the eye, the Symbolic that of the ear and of language; in which the "material imagination," with its fascination with a single sense plenum, is opposed to all those differential systems which are essentially linguistic and social in character. Such an opposition is unfortunately, as we have come to learn, a properly Imaginary one. Yet the formula usefully insists on the tendency of the Imaginary object to absolutize itself, to exclude relationship and to overshadow the perceptual apparatus in a free-standing and isolated way, in contrast to the ways in which elements of Symbolic systems are always implicitly or explicitly embedded in a complex of binary oppositions and subjected to the whole range of what Greimas calls the "play of semiotic constraints."

The problem with such a definition is that when we reintroduce the subject into such relationships, the proportions change, and what it was useful to designate in terms of the isolation of the single Imaginary object, now becomes a two-term relationship, while the binary systems of the Symbolic must now be understood as introducing a third term into the hitherto duplex logic of the Imag-

[53] Edmond Ortigues, *Le Discours et le symbole,* p. 194.

inary: "This is the sense of J. Lacan's definition of the essence of the Imaginary as a 'dual relationship,' an ambiguous redoubling, a 'mirror' reflection, an immediate relationship between the subject and its other in which each term passes immediately into the other and is lost in a never-ending play of reflections. Imagination and desire are the realities of a finite being which can emerge from the contradiction between self and other only by the genesis of a third term, a mediatory 'concept' which, by determining each term, orders them into reversible and progressive relations which can be developed in language. The whole problem of symbolization lies here, in this passage from a dual opposition to a ternary relation, a passage from desire to the concept." [54] On the other hand, as we have suggested above, to stage the relationship in terms of so radical an opposition is somehow covertly to reintroduce Imaginary thinking itself into a thought which was apparently attempting to overcome it; nor is it really a question of repudiating the Imaginary and substituting the Symbolic for it—as though the one were "bad" and the other "good"—but rather of elaborating a method which can articulate both, while preserving their radical discontinuity with each other.

In this perspective, returning now to our critique of current literary methods, it becomes clear that above and beyond image criticism, it is phenomenology itself which must become the object of critical reconsideration, insofar as its fundamental materials of analysis—the lived experience of time and space, of the elements, of the very texture of subjectivity—are drawn almost exclusively from the Imaginary realm. Phenomenological criticism, whose program was heralded by Husserl's well-known slogan of a "return to things," clearly had a role to play as a kind of therapeutic corrective to overly intellectualized conceptions of the work of art, as

---

[54] *Ibid.*, p. 205. The difference between an Imaginary study of the image and a Symbolic one may be dramatized by juxtaposing properly Imaginary works like Gaston Bachelard's *L'Eau et les rêves* (or its equivalent in the Anglo-American criticism of writers like G. Wilson Knight), with the new iconographic studies of the same image patterns, as in Alistair Fowler, "Emblems of Temperance in *The Faerie Queene,* Book II," *Review of English Studies,* n.s., Vol. II (1960), pp, 143-149.

Fredric Jameson

an attempt to restore the authenticity of lived experience and sensory plenitude to the aesthetic text.

In retrospect, however, the aesthetic developed by the phenomenologists, and in particular by Merleau-Ponty, with its notion of the primacy of perception in the elaboration of the languages of art, would seem to be the very prototype of a theory of the Symbolic conceived almost exclusively from the perspective of the Imaginary. On the other hand, it cannot be said that in its most rigorous form, phenomenological criticism as such has been widely applied in the United States; what has tended to replace it, but sometimes to claim its authority, is the far more obviously ideological interpretation of works in terms of the "self" and its various identity crises. On readings of this kind—which have obviously become the dominant academic interpretive ideology, along with so-called "pluralism"—readings whose interminable oscillation between the subject, the ego, and the other reflects the optical illusions of the Imaginary register itself, the full force of the Lacanian denunciation of ego psychology may be allowed to fall. [55]

We must, however, specify an important variant of this approach which, framed in proto-social terms, has genuinely political consequences. This approach—the reading of cultural phenomena in terms of otherness—derives from the dialectic of the relationship to the Other in Sartre's *Being and Nothingness*, and beyond that, from the Hegelian account of the Master and the Slave in the *Phenomenology*. It is a dialectic which, particularly as developed in *Saint Genêt*, seemed to lay the basis for an aggressive critique of the relations of domination: hence, in particular, its extension by Frantz Fanon to the whole realm of Third World theory and of the psychopathology of the colonized and the colonial other; and something like just such a theory of otherness must surely always be implicit in a politics which for whatever reason substitutes categories

[55] It does not follow that as literary critics and theorists we have any business idly perpetuating the Lacanian polemic in the field of psychoanalytic criticism proper: rigorous work like that of Ernst Kris or Norman Holland deserves to be studied in its own tems and not in those of some (properly Imaginary) feud between rival standard-bearers.

of race for those of class, and the struggle for colonial independence for that of the class struggle proper.

Meanwhile, the work of Michel Foucault testifies to the growing influence of a similar theory of otherness in the analysis of culture and history, where it has taken on the more structural form of a theory of exclusion. So, following Sartre's analysis of criminality in *Saint Genêt*, Foucault showed how a society developing a conception of Reason found it necessary to devise one of insanity and abnormality as well, and to generate marginal realities against which to define itself; and his more recent work on emprisonment and incarceration proper rejoins what has become one of the most significant currents of American political reality since Attica, namely, the movement within the prisons themselves.

On the other hand, it cannot be denied that *"Saint Genêt* is the epic of the 'stade du miroir' " [56]; and political reality, as well as the theoretical framework offered here, suggests that the Lumpen-politics, the politics of marginality or "molecular politics" (Deleuze), of which such theories are the ideology, and which is in some ways the successor to the student movements of the 1960's both here and in France, is essentially an ethical—when not an overtly anarchist—politics dominated by the categories of the Imaginary. Yet, in the long run, as we shall see in our concluding section, an ethical politics is a contradiction in terms, however admirable may be its passions and the quality of its indignation.

Such are, then, some of the forms taken in recent criticism by what we may diagnose as an over-estimation of the Imaginary at the expense of the Symbolic. That it is not simply a question of method or theory but has implications for aesthetic production may be suggested by the example of Brecht, whose conception of an anti-Aristotelian theater, an aesthetic which refuses spectator empathy and "identification" has raised problems that are clarified by our present context: we would suggest, indeed, that the Brechtean

[56] Mehlman, p. 182. Mehlman's critique of the limits of Sartre's Hegelianizing conceptual instruments in *Saint Genêt* (and most notably of the concept of synthesis) might well have been extended to Hegel himself, whose system in this respect constitutes a veritable *Summa* of the Imaginary.

attack on "culinary" theater—as well as the apparent paradoxes to which the ideal of "epic theater" gives rise—can best be understood as an attempt to block Imaginary investment and thereby to dramatize the problematical relationship between the observing subject and the Symbolic Order or history.

As for the complementary extreme, the over-estimation of the Symbolic itself, it is easier to say what this particular "heresy" or "illusion" looks like since the development of semiotics, whose fundamental program may in this respect be described as a veritable mapping of the Symbolic Order. Its blind spots may therefore be expected to be particularly instructive as to the problems of the insertion of the Imaginary into the model of a Symbolic system: I will here only point to one of them, but it is surely the most important one in the context of literary criticism, namely, the problem of the category of the "character" in a structural analysis of narrative. [57]

For, as the ideologies of "identification" and "point of view" make plain, "character" is that point in the narrative text at which the problem of the insertion of the subject into the Symbolic most acutely arises. It can surely not be solved by compromises like those of Propp and Greimas—whatever their undoubted practical value—in which the anthropomorphic remnant of a "subject" of the action persists beneath the guise of the "function" or the *actant*. What is wanted is not only an instrument of analysis which will maintain the incommensurability of the subject with its narrative representations—or in other words between the Imaginary and the Symbolic in general—but also one which will articulate the discontinuities within the subject's various "representatives" themselves, not only those that Benveniste has taught us to observe between the first and second pronouns on the one hand and the third on the other, but also, and above all, that, stressed by Lacan, between the nom-

---

[57] See for example Roland Barthes, "An Introduction to the Structural Analysis of Narrative," *New Literary History,* Vol. VI, No. 2 (Winter, 1975), pp. 256-260; and François Rastier, "Un concept dans le discours des études littéraires," in *Essais de sémiotique discursive* (Paris: Mame, 1973), pp. 185-206.

inative and the accusative forms of the first person itself. To a certain degree, the theoretical problem of the status of the subject in narrative analysis is itself a reflection of the historical attempt of modernistic practice to eliminate the old-fashioned subject from the literary text. My own feeling is that you cannot deny the possibility of an adequate representation of the subject in narrative on the one hand, and then continue the search for a more satisfactory category for such representation on the other: if this is so, then the notion of some relationship—still to be defined—between the subject and this or that individual character or "point of view" should be replaced by the study of those character systems into which the subject is fitfully inserted. [58]

In a more general way, however, this dilemma suggests that the most crucial need of literary theory today is for the development of conceptual instruments capable of doing justice to a post-individualistic experience of the subject in contemporary life itself as well as in the texts. Such a need is underscored by the persistent contemporary rhetoric of a fragmentation of the subject (most notably perhaps, in the *Anti-Oedipe* of Deleuze and Guattari, with their celebration of the schizophrenic as the "true hero of desire"); but it is not satisfied any more adequately by the (still very abstract) Marxist conviction that the theory as well as the experience of the decentering of consciousness must serve "to liquidate the last vestiges of bourgeois individualism itself and to prepare the basis for some new post-individualistic thought mode to come". [59] At the least, however, and whatever their practical value as analytic machinery turns out to be, the Lacanian graphs of a properly structural "subversion of the subject" allow us in retrospect to measure both the anticipatory value, but also the Hegelianizing limits, of such conceptual precursors as the dialectics of *Saint Genêt*

[58] I have tried to explore the possibility of such an approach in two recent essays: "After Armageddon: Character Systems in Philip K. Dick's *Dr. Bloodmoney*," *Science-Fiction Studies*, 5, (March, 1975), pp. 31-42; and "The Ideology of Form: Partial Systems in *La Vieille Fille*," *Sub-stance*, 15 (Winter, 1976), pp. 29-49.

[59] F. Jameson, "On Goffman's *Frame Analysis*", *Theory and Society*, Vol. III, No. 1 (Spring, 1976), pp. 130-131.

Fredric Jameson

and of René Girard's *Deceit, Desire and the Novel,* as well as of Sartre's later concept of "seriality" in the *Critique,* while suggesting future areas for exploration in Bakhtin's pre-structural notion of a properly dialogical speech and the pre-individualistic forms of social experience from which it springs. [60] It is therefore tempting to reverse Lacan's polemics (in the "Seminar on "The Purloined Letter' " and elsewhere) and to suggest that at a time when the primacy of language and the Symbolic Order is widely understood—or at least widely asserted—it is rather in the underestimation of the Imaginary and the problem of the insertion of the subject that the "un-hiddenness of truth" (Heidegger) may now be sought.

IV

For Derrida's accusation is undoubtedly true, and what is at stake, in Lacan as well as in psychoanalysis in general is truth; even worse, a conception of truth peculiarly affiliated to the classical existential one (that of Heidegger as a veiling/unveiling, that of Sartre as a fitful reclamation from *mauvaise foi*). [61] For that very reason, it seems arbitrary to class as logocentric and phonocentric a thought which—insofar as it is structural—proposes a decentering of the subject, and—insofar as it is "existential"—is guided by a concept of truth, not as adequation with reality (as Derrida suggests), but rather as a relationship, at best an asymptotic approach, to the Real.

This is not the place to deal with Lacan's epistemology, but it is certainly the moment to return to this term, the third of the canonical Lacanian triad, of which it must be admitted that it is at the very least astonishing that we have been able to avoid mentioning it for so long. Just as the Symbolic Order (or language itself) restructures the Imaginary by introducing a third term into the hitherto infinite regression of the duality of the latter's mirror

[60] On seriality, see *Marxism and Form* (Princeton: Princeton University Press, 1971), pp. 247-250. The concept of the dialogical is most fully developed in Mikhail Bakhtin, *Problems of Dostoevski's Poetics* (Ann Arbor, Michigan: Ardis, 1973), pp. 150-169.
[61] Derrida, pp. 81-94.

images, so we may hope and expect that the tardy introduction of this new third term of the Real may put an end to the Imaginary opposition into which our previous discussion of Lacan's two orders has risked falling again and again. We must not, however, expect much help from Lacan himself in giving an account of a realm of which he in one place observes that it—"the Real, or what is perceived as such,—is what resists symbolization absolutely" [62] (it would however be useful to have a compilation of all of these lapidary comments on the Real which are to be stumbled on throughout his work).

Nonetheless, it is not terribly difficult to say what is meant by the Real in Lacan. It is simply History itself: and if for psycho-analysis the history in question here is obviously enough the history of the subject, the resonance of the word suggests that a confronta-tion between this particular materialism and the historical material-ism of Marx can no longer be postponed. It is a confrontation whose first example has been set by Lacan himself, with his suggestion that the notion of the Symbolic as he uses it is compatible with Marxism (whose theory of language, as most Marxists would be willing to agree, remains to be worked out). [63] Meanwhile, it is certain that his entire work is permeated by dialectical tendencies, the more Hegelian ones having already been indicated above; and, beyond this that the fascination of that work lies precisely in its ambiguous hesitation between dialectical formulations and those, more static, more properly structural and spatializing, of his various topologies. In Lacan, however, unlike the other varieties of structural mapping, there is always the proximity of the analytic situation to ensure the transformation of such structures back into "moments"

[62] *Le Séminaire*, I, p. 80.
[63] "La Science et la vérité," *Écrits*, p. 876; and see also the remarks on historiography in the "Discours de Rome" (Wilden, pp. 22ff, p. 50, or *Écrits*, pp. 260ff, p. 287). The problem of the function of a genetic or evolu-tionary set of stages within a more genuinely dialectical conception of historical time is common to both psychoanalysis and Marxism. Lacan's insistence on the purely schematic or operational nature of the Freudian stages (oral, anal, genital) may be compared with Etienne Balibar's reflec-tions on the proper uses of the Marxian evolutionary schema (savage, barbarian, civilized) in *Lire le capital*, Vol. II (Paris: Maspero, 1968), pp. 79-226.

of a more process-oriented type. Thus, in that "Seminar on 'The Purloined Letter'" which we have hitherto taken at face value as a "structuralist" manifesto against the optical illusions of the Signified, other passages on the contrary suggest that the circular trajectory of the Signifier may be a little more closely related to the emergence of a dialectical self-consciousness than one might have thought, and project a second, more dialectical reading superimposed upon the structural one already outlined. In particular, the dilemma of Poe's Minister implies that it is in awareness of the Symbolic that liberation from the optical illusions of the Imaginary is to be sought: "For if it is, now as before, a question of protecting the letter from inquisitive eyes, he can do nothing but employ the same technique he himself has already foiled: leave it in the open. And we may properly doubt that he knows what he is thus doing, when we see him immediately captivated by a dual relationship in which we find all the traits of a mimetic or of an animal feigning death, and, trapped in the typically imaginary situation of seeing that he is not seen, misconstrue the real situation in which he is seen not seeing." [64]

Even if the structural self-consciousness diagnostically implied by such a passage is a properly dialectical one, it would not necessarily follow that the dialectic is a Marxist one, even though psychoanalysis is unquestionably a materialism. Meanwhile the experience of a whole series of abortive Freudo-Marxisms, as well as the methodological standard of the type of radical discontinuity proposed by the model outlined in the present essay, both suggest that no good purpose is to be served by attempting too hastily to unite them into some unified anthropology. To say that both psychoanalysis and Marxism are materialisms is simply to assert that each reveals an area in which human consciousness is not "master in its own house": only the areas decentered by each are the quite different ones of sexuality and of the class dynamics of social history. That these areas know local interrelationships—as

---

[64] "Seminar on 'The Purloined Letter'," *Yale French Studies*, p. 61, or *Écrits*, pp. 30-31.

when Reich shows how sexual repression is something like the cement which holds the authority fabric of society together—is undeniable; but none of these instinctual or ideological ion-exchanges, in which a molecular element of one system is temporarily lent to the other for purposes of stabilization, can properly furnish a model of the relationship of sexuality to class consciousness as a whole. Materialistic thinking, however, ought to have had enough practice of heterogeneity and discontinuity to entertain the possibility that human reality is fundamentally alienated in more than one way, and in ways which have little enough to do with each other.

What one can do, however, more modestly but with better hope of success, is to show what these two systems—each one essentially a hermeneutic—have to teach each other in the way of method. Marxism and psychoanalysis indeed present a number of striking analogies of structure with each other, as a checklist of their major themes can testify: the relation of theory and practice; the resistance of false consciousness and the problem as to its opposite (is it truth or knowledge? science or individual certainty?); the role and risks of the concept of a "midwife" of truth, whether analyst or vanguard party; the reappropriation of an alienated history and the function of narrative; the question of desire and value and of the nature of "false desire;" the paradox of the end of the revolutionary process, which, like analysis, must surely be considered "interminable" rather than "terminable;" and so forth. It is therefore not surprising that these two nineteenth century "philosophies" should be the objects, at the present time and in the present intellectual atmosphere, of similar attacks, which focus on their "naive semanticism."

It is at least clear that the nineteenth century is to be blamed for the absence, in both Marxism and psychoanalysis, until very recently, of a concept of language which would permit the proper answer to this objection. Lacan is therefore in this perspective an exemplary figure, provided we understand his life's work, not as the transformation of Freud into linguistics, but as the disengagement of a linguistic theory which was implicit in Freud's practice but for which he did not yet have the appropriate conceptual instruments; and clearly enough, it is Lacan's third term, his addition of the Real to a relatively harmless conceptual opposition between Imaginary and Symbolic, which sticks in the craw and causes all the trouble. For what is scandalous for contemporary philosophy in both of these "materialisms"—to emphasize the fundamental distance between each of these "unities-of-theory-and-practice" and conventional philosophies as such—is the stubborn retention by both of something the sophisticated philosopher was long since supposed to have put between parentheses, namely a conception of the referent. For model-building and language-oriented philosophies, indeed (and in our time they span an immense range of tendencies and styles from Nietzsche to common language philosophy and from pragmatism to existentialism and structuralism)—for an intellectual climate dominated, in other words, by the conviction that the realities which we confront or experience come before us pre-formed and pre-ordered, not so much by the human "mind" (that is the older form of classical idealism), as rather by the various modes in which human language can work—it is clear that there must be something unacceptable about this affirmation of the persistence, behind our representations, of that indestructible nucleus of what Lacan calls the Real, of which we have already said above that it was simply History itself. If we can have an idea of it, it is objected, then it has already become part of our representations; if not, it is just another Kantian *Ding-an-sich,* and we can probably all agree that that particular solution will no longer do. Yet the objection presupposes an epistemology for which knowledge is in one way or another an identity with the thing: it is a presupposition peculiarly without force over the Lacanian conception of the decentered subject, which can know union neither with language nor with the Real, which is structurally at distance from both in its very being. The Lacanian notion of an "asymptotic" approach to the Real, moreover, maps a situation in which the action of this "absent cause" can be understood as a term limit, as that which can be both indistinguishable from the Symbolic (or the Imaginary) and also independent of it.

The other version of this objection—that history is a text, and that in that case, as one text is worth another, it can no longer be appealed to as the "ground" of truth—raises the issue of narrative fundamental both for psychoanalysis and for historical materialism, and requires us to lay at least the groundwork for a materialist philosophy of language. For both psychoanalysis and Marxism depend very fundamentally on history in its other sense, as story and storytelling: if the Marxian narrative of the irreversible dynamism of human society as it develops into capitalism be disallowed, little or nothing remains of Marxism as a system and the meaning of the acts of all those who have associated their praxis with it bleeds away. Meanwhile, it is clear that the analytic situation is nothing if not a systematic reconstruction or rewriting of the subject's past, [65] as indeed the very status of the Freudian corpus as an immense body of narrative analyses testifies. We cannot here fully argue the distinction between this narrative orientation of both Marxism and Freudianism and the non-referential philosophies alluded to above. Suffice it to observe this: that history is not so much a text, as rather a text-to-be-(re-)constructed. Better still, it is an obligation to do so, whose means and techniques are themselves historically irreversible, so that we are not at liberty to construct any historical narrative at all (we are not free, for instance, to return to theodicies or providential narratives, nor even the older nationalistic ones) and the refusal of the Marxist paradigm can generally be demonstrated to be at one with the refusal of historical narration itself, or at least, with its systematic pre-preparation and strategic delimitation.

In terms of language, we must distinguish between our own narrative of history—whether psychoanalytic or political—and the Real itself, which our narratives can only approximate in asymptotic

[65] The reproach that patients in analysis do not so much rediscover as rather "rewrite" their pasts is a familiar one, argued, however, most rigorously by Jürgen Habermas, in *Knowledge and Human Interests* (Boston: Beacon Press, 1971), pp. 246-273.

Fredric Jameson

fashion and which "resists symbolization absolutely." Nor can the historical paradigm furnished us by psychoanalysis or by Marxism— that of the Oedipus complex or of the class struggle—be considered as anything more Real than a master text, an abstract one, hardly even a proto-narrative, in terms of which we construct the text of our own lives with our own concrete praxis. This is the point at which the intervention of Lacan's fundamental distinction between truth and knowledge (or science) must be decisive: the abstract schemata of psychoanalysis or of the Marxian philosophy of history constitute a body of knowledge, indeed, of what many of us would be willing to call scientific knowledge; but they do not embody the "truth" of the subject, nor are the texts in which they are elaborated to be thought of as a "parole pleine." A materialistic philosophy of language reserves a status for scientific language of this kind, which designates the Real without claiming to coincide with it, which offers the very theory of its own incapacity to signify fully as its credentials for transcending both Imaginary and Symbolic alike. "Il y a des formules qu'on n'imagine pas," Lacan observes of Newton's laws: "Au moins pour un temps, elles font assemblée avec le réel." [66]

The chief defect of all hitherto existing materialism is that it has been conceived as a series of propositions about matter—and in particular the relationship of matter to consciousness, which is to say of the natural sciences to the so-called human sciences [67]—rather than as a set of propositions about language. A materialistic philosophy of language is not a semanticism, naive or otherwise, because its fundamental tenet is a rigorous distinction between the signified

[66] Jacques Lacan, "Radiophonie," *Scilicet* 2/3 (1970), p. 75.
[67] See, for the most powerful of recent attempts to re-invent this older kind of materialism, Sebastiano Timpanaro "Considerations on Materialism," *New Left Review*, 85 (May-June, 1974), pp. 3-22. The reckoning on Timpanaro's attempt to replace human history within the "history" of nature comes due, not in his politics, nor even in his epistemology, but rather in his aesthetics, which, proposing that Marxism now "do justice" to the natural elements of the human condition, to death, sickness, old age and the like, turns out to be nothing more than a replay of existentialism. It is a significant paradox that at the other end of the Marxist spectrum — that of the Frankfurt School — an analogous development may be observed in Herbert Marcuse's late aesthetics.

—the realm of semantics proper, of interpretation, of the study of the text's ostensible meaning—and the referent. The study of the referent, however, is the study, not of the meaning of the text, but of the limits of its meanings and of their historical preconditions, and of what is and must remain incommensurable with individual expression. In our present terms, this means that a relationship to objective knowledge (in other words, to what is of such a different order of magnitude and organization from the individual subject that it can never be adequately "represented" within the latter's lived experience save as a term limit) is conceivable only for a thought able to do justice to radical discontinuities, not only between the Lacanian "orders," but within language itself, between its various types of propositions as they entertain wholly different structural relations with the subject.

The Lacanian conception of science as a historically original form of the decentering of the subject [68]—rather than as a place of "truth"—has much that is suggestive for a Marxism still locked in the outmoded antinomy of that opposition between ideology and science whose bewildering changes are rung in the various and contradictory models of that relationship proposed by Althusser at various stages of his work. And in view of the use to which we shall elsewhere see Althusser put the Lacanian notion of the orders, it is all the more surprising that he should not have profited from a scheme in which knowledge and science, the subject and his or her individual truth, the place of the Master, the ec-centric relationship both to the Symbolic and to the Real, are all relationally mapped.

For clearly, in Marxism as well as in psychoanalysis, there is a problem—even a crisis—of the subject: suffice it to evoke on the level of praxis the intolerable alternative between a self-sacrificing and repressing Stalinism and an anarchistic celebration of the subject's immediate here-and-now. In the area of theory, the crisis in the Marxian conception of the subject finds its most dramatic

---

[68] For the most part, these developments on the subject of science have not yet been published; but see *Le Séminaire*, XX: *Encore* (Paris: Seuil, 1975), pp. 20-21.

expression in the contrast between what we may call the German and the French traditions—the Hegelianizing and dialectical current which, emerging from Lukács' *History and Class Consciousness*, found its embodiment in the work of the Frankfurt School, and that structural and science-oriented reading of Marx which, combining the heritage of Saussure with the lessons of Mao Tse-tung's *On Contradiction* (and also with Lacanian psychoanalysis), informs the theoretical practice of Althusser and his group.

The theme of the subject, indeed, clarifies many of the ambiguities of Althusser's positions. His polemic against that particular ideology of the subject called humanism is to be sure a relatively local one, directed not only against currents in the non- and even anti-Communist left in France, but also against some elements of the PCF itself, most notably Garaudy; while his polemic against Hegel is clearly intended to forestall the use of the early, Hegelianizing Marx, the Marx of the theory of alienation, against the later Marx of *Capital*. [69] Neither of these polemics is particularly relevant to the fortunes of Marxism in the Anglo-American world, where Hegel has never been a name to conjure with in the first place, and where the dominant individualism has never flirted very extensively with the rhetoric of humanism. Our present context, however, makes it easier to see the markings of the Imaginary and its distortion in that "idealism" with which Althusser reproaches Hegel, whose conceptual instruments—totality, negativity, alienation, *Aufhebung*, and even "contradiction" when understood in a fundamentally idealist sense—he takes such pains to distinguish from his own discontinuous and structural ones. [70] To rewrite Althusser's critique in these terms is to escape the antithesis between that affirmation of a "materialist kernel" in Hegel to which he rightly objects, and his own blanket repudiation, and to evolve a more productive way of handling the content of "idealistic" philosophies. Some such approach, indeed, seems implicit in Althus-

[69] See Mark Poster, *Existential Marxism in Postwar France* (Princeton: Princeton University Press, 1975), Chapter Two.
[70] As outlined, for instance, in "Sur la dialectique matérialiste," in *Pour Marx* (Paris: Maspéro, 1965), pp. 161-224.

ser's later conception of history as a "process without a subject"[71] (a polemic aimed at the Hegelianism of Lukács, whose characterization of the proletariat as the "subject of history" is here alluded to). Yet it must not be thought that this difference has to do with the content of a Marxian vision of history which both Lukács and Althusser share: rather, it would seem a question for Althusser of rejecting the use of categories of the subject in the discussion of a collective process structurally incommensurable with them, and with individual or existential experience.[72] Indeed, the Althusserian emphasis on science is in this respect such an extreme overreaction as to leave no place for that very rich field of study which emerged from Lukács' tradition and which is customarily designated as the phenomenology of everyday life.

The lasting achievement of the Frankfurt School, meanwhile, lies in precisely in this area, and in particular, in its vivid demonstration of the reification of the subject under late capitalism—a demonstration that ranges from Adorno's diagnoses of the fetishization of aesthetic perception (and of artistic form) all the way to Marcuse's anatomy of the language and thought patterns of *One-Dimensional Man*. What we must now observe is that the demonstration depends for its force on the hypothesis of some previous historical stage in which the subject is still relatively whole and autonomous. Yet the very ideal of psychological autonomy and individualism in the name of which their diagnosis of the atomized subject of late capitalism is made precludes any imaginative appeal back beyond bourgeois civil society to some pre-individualistic and pre-capitalist social form, since the latter would necessarily precede the constitution of the bourgeois subject itself. Inevitably then, the Frankfurt School drew its norm of the autonomous subject from that period in which

---

[71] Louis Althusser, *Réponse à John Lewis* (Paris: Maspero, 1973), pp. 91-98.

[72] But it would be possible to show that Lukács' critique of bourgeois philosophy in *History and Class Consciousness* turns precisely on the distinction between referent and signified outlined above, particularly in the systematic demonstration of the inner structural limits of that philosophy which takes the place of a more conventional denunciation of the latter's "errors" of content.

the bourgeoisie was itself a rising and progressive class, its psychological formation conditioned by the then still vital structure of the nuclear family; and this is the sense in which their thought has with some justification been taxed as a potentially regressive and nostalgic.

Whereas in France—and here the most dramatic illustrations are to be found rather in the *Tel Quel* group than among the Althusserians—the left-wing celebration of the "end of man" (Foucault) has generated a rhetoric in which it is precisely the so-called autonomous subject (in other words, the ego, the illusion of autonomy) which is denounced as an ideological and a bourgeois phenomenon, and the various signs of its decay—what the Frankfurt School took to be symptoms—welcomed as the harbingers of some new post-individualistic state of things. The historical reasons for this theoretical divergence—the Frankfurt School's experience of the quality of consciousness among the subjects of Nazism, the absence from the France of the *société de consommation* of anything like a countercultural "revolution" in daily life on the American type—do not suffice to solve the theoretical problem of the status the subject ought to have for Marxism today.

The solution can only lie, it seems to me, in the renewal of Utopian thinking, of creative speculation as to the place of the subject at the other end of historical time, in a social order which has put behind it class organization, commodity production and the market, alienated labor, and the implacable determinism of an historical logic beyond the control of humanity. Only thus can a third term be imagined beyond either the "autonomous individualism" of the bourgeoisie in its heyday or the schizoid part-objects in which the fetishization of the subject under late capitalism has left its trace; a term in the light of which both of these forms of consciousness can be placed in their proper historical perspective.

To do so, however, would require the elaboration of a properly Marxist "ideology." It should not, indeed, be forgotten that it is precisely to a Lacanian inspiration that we owe the first new and as yet insufficiently developed conception of the nature of ideology since Marx and Nietzsche: I refer to Althusser's seminal definition of ideology as "the 'representation' of the Imaginary relationship of individuals to their Real conditions of existence." [73] Ideology conceived in this sense is therefore the place of the insertion of the subject in those realms or orders—the Symbolic (or in other words the sychronic network of society itself, with its kinship-type system of places and roles), and the Real (or in other words the diachronic evolution of History itself, the realm of time and death) both of which radically transcend individual experience in their very structure. But if this is how ideology is understood, then it is clear that it has a function to play in every conceivable social order, and not merely those of what Marx called "pre-history" or class societies: the ideological representation must rather be seen as that indispensable mapping fantasy or narrative by which the individual subject invents a "lived" relationship with collective systems which otherwise by definition exclude him insofar as he or she is born into a pre-existent social form and its pre-existent language.

The project of a Marxist ideology, alongside a Marxist "science," is therefore not so contradictory as it might seem. This is not the place to inquire why other ideological traditions—that of anarchist revolt, or even that of Christian poverty and charity—should have known a richer development and have exerted a more powerful influence than that properly communal and collective vision which was generated by Marxism at its moments of greatest intensity, as in the greatest, but also the most obscure, moments of labor militancy, in the brief vitality of the soviets, or in the rich collective innovations of the Chinese experience. To such a vision, to the

[73] Louis Althusser, "Ideology and Ideological State Apparatuses," in *Lenin and Philosophy*, p. 162. It is no accident that both the Marxist conception of ideology and the Lacanian notion of the Imaginary draw heavily on the model of optics: compare the Marxian image of the *camera obscura* and the inversion of the image on the retina (*Marxism and Form*, pp. 369-370) and the Lacanian experiment with the vase of flowers ("Remarque sur le rapport de Daniel Lagache," *Écrits*, pp. 672-677, and *Le Séminaire*, I, pp. 91-95, 142-145, and 187).

theoretical elaboration of such an ideology of the collective, it would seem that the Lacanian doctrine of the decentered subject—particularly insofar as that structural "subversion" of the subject aims, not at renunciation or repression, but rather precisely at the realization of desire—offers a model more than merely suggestive.

John Brenkman

The Other and the One: Psychoanalysis, Reading, the *Symposium*

Why sidetrack an inquiry directed at the points of intersection between psychoanalysis and literary theory by making it pass through a reading of Plato's *Symposium?*

The response must come from more than one angle:

—Psychoanalysis, as a theory and practice, grasps in the processes of desire the mechanism that determines the structure of subjectivity. From Freud's discovery that the dream articulates a *Wunsch* and his development of a therapeutic practice that treats the neurotic symptom as the product of unconscious desire to Lacan's general theory of the "subversion of the subject" and the "dialectic of desire," psychoanalysis has forged a discourse on desire. The *Symposium* elaborates the idealist theory of love and desire with such refinement and so thoroughly that it becomes an integral part of idealism's understanding of itself as a philosophical search for the truth and of its practice as an educational process with specific social aims. Forcing an encounter between these two discourses on desire, an encounter already broached in several of Lacan's texts, promises to uncover the antagonism, or the complicity, between psychoanalysis and idealism.

—It is not possible, in my view, to import psychoanalysis directly into the problematics of literary analysis; literary theory itself is today in the midst of a struggle against its own subservience to a philosophical tradition that it has never thoroughly questioned. An indispensable benchmark here, of course, is the deconstruction of metaphysics as practiced by Jacques Derrida. The project of systematically taking apart the conceptual edifice of Western philosophy and the presuppositions on which it is built cannot be ignored by any literary analysis once we recognize that aesthetics and criticism, since Plato and Aristotle, have been accomplices of the "metaphysics of presence." Derrida has radically shifted the terrain of literature's relation to philosophy. On the one hand, deconstruction treats the philosophical discourse as a text, a signifying production to be read with an eye to its metaphoricity, its stratifications, and the economy of its contradictions. And, on the other hand, in marking philosophy's repression of the concepts and effects of writing, Derrida has allowed the violence of literary writing to disturb the serenity and security of philosophical reflection. In "La double séance," for example, a reading of Mallarmé subverts the Platonic conception of speech, mimesis, and truth. The bearing that psychoanalysis may have on reading literary texts cannot be assessed without asking how it inscribes a reading of philosophy within its own theoretical discourse.

—The *Symposium* is itself situated between philosophy and literature. As a philosophical text, it presents the idealist discourse on desire as it emerges and takes shape through a series of speeches that culminates with Socrates' account of love and philosophy. At the same time the *Symposium stages* this philosophical discussion, giving it the form of drama among its participants, including the drama of their desires and jealousies. Moreover, this drama is filtered through the editing and paraphrase of a narrator, Apollodorus, who did not witness it and whose stake in its outcome is determined perhaps as much by his own love for Socrates as by his philosophical interest. Plato, then, does not simply write a philosophical discourse; he writes the fragmented narrative of a drama in which the course of a philosophical reflection is already interwoven with the paths of desire.

The task of unravelling the knot that binds psychoanalysis to the theoretical practice of reading texts, whether "philosophical" or "literary," has become all the more urgent with the publication of Derrida's "Le facteur de la vérité." [1] Derrida not only tries to identify the ways in which Lacanian psychoanalysis is yet controlled

---

[1] *Poétique*, 21 (1975), pp. 96-147. English translation: "The Purveyor of the Truth," *Yale French Studies*, 52 (1975), pp. 31-113.

by the metaphysics of presence but also draws as sharply as possible the divergence between Lacan's theory and several key motifs of grammatology. Louis Althusser, in an essay designed to make some preliminary connections between Marxism and the work of Freud and Lacan, treats Lacan's borrowing from philosophy in an analogous but more apologetic way, seeing them as the sign of the embattled political and institutional context in which Lacan works:

> Hence the contained passion and passionate contention of Lacan's language, unable to live or survive except in a state of alert and accusation: the language of a man of the besieged vanguard, condemned by the crushing strength of the threatened structures and corporations to forestall their blows, or at least to feint a response before they are delivered, thus discouraging the opponents from crushing him beneath their assault. Hence also the often paradoxical resort to the security provided by philosophies completely foreign to his scientific undertaking (Hegel, Heidegger), as so many intimidating witnesses thrown in the face of part of his audience to retain their respect; and as so many witnesses to a possible objectivity, the natural ally of his thought, to reassure or educate the rest. [2]

Neither Derrida nor Althusser entertains, even momentarily, another possibility, namely, that Lacan's grafting of philosophical concepts onto the theoretical discourse of psychoanalysis may operate according to a strategy that is critical and systematic but that remains to be formulated as such. The elision of this alternative does not seem, initially at least, to stem from the ways in which Derrida and Althusser read philosophy. Indeed, we might have expected just the opposite. Derrida's earlier essay on psychoanalysis, "Freud et la scène de l'écriture," [3] demonstrates that Freud's various models of the "psychic apparatus," from the path-cutting neurones of the *Project for a Scientific Psychology* to the mystic writing-pad, undermine metaphysics to the extent that they do not recapitulate its tendency to give a special value to speech in opposition to writing

---

[2] Louis Althusser, "Freud and Lacan," in *Lenin and Philosophy and Other Essays,* trans., Ben Brewster (New York: Monthly Review Press, 1971), p. 203.
[3] *L'écriture et la différence* (Paris: Seuil, 1967), pp. 293-340. English translation: "Freud and the Scene of Writing," *Yale French Studies,* 48 (1972), pp. 73-117.

in determining the relation between consciousness and language: the critical force of Freud's texts is shown to be rigorous and systematic in spite of the fact that Freud does not address the problem of reading philosophy. Althusser, on the other hand, actually provides the terms with which to get hold of the strategy that determines Lacan's use of "philosophies completely foreign to his scientific undertaking." Althusser argues that the materialist reading of philosophy, as when Marx declares that in part of *Capital* he has "coquetted with modes of expression peculiar to Hegel"[4] or when Lenin takes up the last chapter of the *Science of Logic* to describe the materialist dialectic, is in fact a productive *rewriting*.[5] The thesis I will develop is that Lacan's own flirtation with Plato rewrites the *Symposium* from a materialist viewpoint. It will be necessary to examine one moment in Lacan's relation to Hegel as well. Lacan transforms the Hegelian *Aufhebung*, a prefiguration of which we will find at the very core of Socrates' discourse on desire, when he applies it to the dialectic of desire in the unconscious. "Le facteur de la vérité" has made Lacan's use of Hegel crucial to the entire range of problems we are considering. What will be at stake is whether Lacan's interpretation of the castration complex serves to overturn the metaphysics of presence or is totally recuperated by it. Except for the question of castration, the *Symposium* itself touches on virtually every element to be integrated into a theory of desire.

Those elements, however, remain encased within a conceptual framework the bounds of which are set by Plato's metaphysics of presence. As a result, the misrecognition of the processes of desire is organized into a philosophical reflection that progressively takes on the appearance of total rigor.

The philosophical discussion staged and recounted in the *Symposium* arranges itself around a set of oppositions and values which are never open to question. They function as the string of axiomatic

[4] *Capital, Volume One,* trans., Samuel Moore and Edward Aveling (New York: International Publishers, 1967), p. 20.
[5] Cf., Althusser, "Lenin before Hegel," *Lenin and Philosophy,* pp. 107-125.

or self-evident propositions that every participant weaves into his discourse in a particular way. None of the controversies or rebuttals ever touches on this substratum as such. In fact, the various disputes do no more than secure and solidify this underlying scheme of oppositions and values. And, as we will see, Socrates' contribution, from his refutation of Agathon to his account of Diotima's teachings, is the culminating point of the dialogue precisely to the extent that it refines this scheme into a single and unified system.

The conceptual oppositions in the *Symposium* operate according to the mechanism that Derrida has shown supports all philosophical discourse since Plato; namely, the tendency to designate one term in the opposition as privileged or primary and as free from any necessary entanglement with the inferior or secondary term. Let us at first simply enumerate the oppositions to be analyzed. The distinction between earthly love and heavenly love is promoted by the second speaker, Pausanias, and remains in place from then on; this opposition is itself founded on two others that lie at the heart of Platonic idealism: body/soul and matter/idea. In Socrates' speech the maternal is associated with materiality and put in opposition to the paternal, which supercedes the maternal and becomes, in the realm of ideas, the name for spiritual as opposed to biological reproduction. Sexual difference is never interrogated as such by the *Symposium*. The pair man/woman or male/female is not the result of an active process of differentiation but marks the hierarchical relation between two positive identities or essences. The feminine has nothing to do with the highest form of sexual desire—the relation between two men—and is excluded from spiritual love altogether, whether in Pausanias' understanding of heavenly Love as the offspring of "a goddess whose attributes have nothing of the female, but are altogether male" (181 c)[6] or in Socrates' model of spiritual reproduction as the philosopher's education of a beloved youth. The two oppositions that provoke the

---

[6] All citations of the *Symposium* are from Michael Joyce's translation in *Plato: The Collected Dialogues*, ed., Edith Hamilton and Huntington Cairns (Princeton: Princeton University Press, 1963), pp. 527-574.

greatest controversy are those between harmony and discord and completeness and lack; Eryximachus, Aristophanes, and Socrates evolve very different strategies in order to demonstrate how love is associated with harmony or completeness. And, finally, there is the distinction between lover and beloved which, while belonging to this entire series, does not thoroughly conform to the other oppositions; it will, however, be pivotal to Socrates' effort to fuse a theory of desire with the practice of philosophy.

In order to submit these concepts to a deconstructive reading, it will be necessary to grasp how the value scheme controlling each opposition fixes the meaning of the specific concepts in question. The oppositions just listed, as well as those that have been analyzed by Derrida in "La pharmacie du Platon" (speech/writing, life/death, master/servant), are organized in such a way that one term is relegated to a secondary or derivative status; the valued term can then claim to have preceded the other and to survive it. As the soul precedes and survives the body. To deconstruct such a system entails questioning the secondariness of the second term, in the case of the *Symposium,* the body, matter, the maternal, the feminine, discord, lack, and so on. This does not mean, however, that the value scheme is to be simply reversed, since the reversal will transform the terms themselves by displacing their relation to one another. The "soul" can no longer mean what Socrates wants it to mean once its priority in relation to the body has been called into question. And the concept that has been devalued will not be the same when mobilized in the deconstructive discourse as an instrument for criticizing the system to which it belongs. Having been shaken from its place, the concept receives a "double mark" in the sense that it will always be read and written in two ways, from inside the system and from outside it:

This structure of the *double mark* (*pris* [meaning "taken from" and "caught in"] — borrowed and enclosed — in an oppositional pair, a term keeps its old name in order to destroy the opposition to which it no longer fully belongs, to which it will have *never* actually yielded, the history of this opposition being that of an incessant and hierarchizing struggle) works on the entire field in which these texts move about. It is itself also worked on: the rule according to which each concept necessarily receives two similar marks — repetition without identity — the one inside, the other outside the deconstructed system, must give rise to a double reading and a double writing. [7]

Derrida goes on to warn of a danger that is faced by the three fields of inquiry whose interrelation is our concern: the deconstruction of metaphysics, psychoanalysis, and dialectical-historical materialism. Each of these critical projects draws on the disruptive force of a concept that metaphysics has always tried to subordinate or ignore —writing, practice, the unconscious, matter—and each must guard against allowing that concept to slip back into the place that metaphysics reserves for it or to become attached in a new way to the system of metaphysics:

> We will attempt to determine the law that makes it necessary ... to give the name "writing" to what criticizes, deconstructs, strains the traditional and hierarchized opposition of writing to speech, of writing to the (idealist, spiritualist, phonocentric, and most of all logocentric) system of all its opposing concepts; to give the name "work" or "practice" to what disorganizes the philosophical opposition *praxis/theoria* and does not let itself be *raised* by a process of Hegelian negativity; to give the name "unconscious" to what will never have been the symmetrical negative of potential reservoir of "consciousness;" to give the name "matter" to that which falls outside the classical oppositions and, provided that a recent theoretical advance and philosophical deconstruction are taken into account, should no longer have a reassuring form: neither that of a referent (at least if conceived as a real object or cause that is anterior and external to the system of general textuality), nor that of presence in any of its modes (meaning, essence, objective or subjective existence, form, that is, appearance, content, substance, etc., sensible presence or intelligible presence), nor that of a fundamental or totalizing principle nor even of a last instance. [8]

For now let us heed this warning as it is formulated. My commentary on the *Symposium* will begin, therefore, by working through the preliminary stages of the deconstructive reading, marking not only the text's oppositions and values but also the moments when it is caught off-balance. The instability of the *Symposium* does not

---

[7] "Hors livre," in *La Dissémination* (Paris: Seuil, 1972), p. 10.
[8] *Ibid.,* pp. 10-11.

lie primarily in the disagreements among the participants since, as I have already suggested, these disputes are in general designed to protect the system itself. Rather the text's imbalance stems, on the one hand, from the comedy that occasionally erupts in the drama of the *Symposium,* leaving its developing philosophical argument in suspension, and, on the other hand, from the fact that the corresponding superior and inferior terms of the various oppositions are not always commensurate with one another. Two aspects of the text's structure point to this fundamental instability. The *Symposium* is presented by Plato as though at two removes from the actual gathering. The narrative frame has Apollodorus, who was not present at the symposium, recounting, for his friend Glaucon, the account given to him by Aristodemus, who was there but did not participate in the discussion. The symposium occurred several years earlier, and it is not clear how long ago Apollodorus heard about it. When the narrator, whose own "reliability" is somewhat questionable since he himself is now enamoured with Socrates, gets down to the actual discussion he prefaces his account with a disclaimer: "but before I go on I must make it quite clear that Aristodemus did not pretend to reproduce the various speeches verbatim, any more than I could repeat them word for word as I had them from him" (178 a). Secondly, the drama staged by the *Symposium* undergoes a reversal whose effects on the philosophical discussion are never calculated, by the narrator or by any of the participants. Just as Socrates finishes his speech and is about to entertain an objection from Aristophanes, Alcibiades arrives drunk and pronounces a humorous eulogy of Socrates. His description of Socrates, as lover and as teacher, subverts Socrates' own account of the relation between love and philosophy. While the narrative seems to treat Alcibiades' disruption as no more than a playful, less than meaningful supplement to the seriousness of the philosophical debate, there is a detail that invites us to make the calculations that the text itself shuns. Alcibiades, as he begins, promises Socrates that he is "simply going to tell the truth": "If I say a word that is not the solemn truth I want you to stop me right away and tell me I'm a liar" (214 e). Socrates remains silent throughout. It will be necessary to read the effects of this silence as well as to look behind the artifice by which the narrative, in presenting its own incompleteness as the result of extraneous events, mere chance, lets Socrates' discourse on desire appear triumphant.

Pausanias introduces the distinction between earthly love and heavenly love to correct Phaedrus' eulogizing of love in general as "the ancient source of all our highest good" (178 c): "I am afraid, my dear Phaedrus, that our arrangement won't work very well if it means that we are simply to pronounce a eulogy of Love. It would be all very well if there were only one kind of Love, but unfortunately this is not the case, and we should therefore have begun by stipulating which kind in particular was to receive our homage" (180 c). Like Phaedrus, Pausanias bolsters his argument with a reference to myth, giving the appearance of natural fact to the philosophical opposition that will remain secure throughout the *Symposium* now that it has been put on the right track:

> Now you will all agree, gentlemen, that without Love there could be no such goddess as Aphrodite. If, then, there were only one goddess of that name, we might suppose that there was only one kind of Love, but since in fact there are two such goddesses there must also be two kinds of Love. No one, I think, will deny that there are two goddesses of that name — one, the elder, sprung from no mother's womb but from the heavens themselves, we call the Uranian, the heavenly Aphrodite, while the younger, daughter of Zeus and Dione, we call Pandemus, the earthly Aphrodite. It follows, then, that Love should be known as earthly or as heavenly according to the goddess in whose company his work is done. (180 d, e)

Besides having a kinship with the fundamental Platonic division of body and soul or matter and spirit, Pausanias' distinction is linked with the underlying problem of relating love to the good. While Phaedrus claimed that love is the "source of all our highest good," Pausanias argues that love, in itself, is neither good nor bad: "Now it might be said of any action that the action itself, as such, is neither good nor bad. ... If it is done rightly and finely, the action will be good; if it is done basely, bad. And this holds for loving, for Love is not of himself either admirable or noble, but only when

John Brenkman

he moves us to love nobly" (180 e - 181 a). The opposition good/bad is then fitted to a grid formed by a series of oppositions lined up behind the pair heavenly love/earthly love: the permanent/the transitory, the one/the many, and, as we will see, male/female:

We agreed that love itself, as such, was neither good nor bad, but only in so far as it led to good or bad behavior. It is base to indulge a vicious lover viciously, but noble to gratify a virtuous lover virtuously. Now the vicious lover is the follower of the earthly Love who desires the body rather than the soul; his heart is set on what is mutable and therefore must be inconstant. And as soon as the body he loves begins to pass the first flower of beauty, he "spreads his wings and flies away," giving the lie to all his pretty speeches and dishonoring his vows, whereas the lover who is touched by moral beauties is constant all his life, for he has become one with what will never fade. (183 d, e)

The next speaker, the physician Eryximachus, reaffirms but adjusts the argument set forth by Pausanias. What we find here is an example of the controversies that crop up in the various speeches. The disagreements never bear on the oppositional scheme itself or its values, which remain intact and increasingly secure; they simply involve the best way to associate the privileged terms of the various oppositions with one another—heavenly love, the good, the eternal, the one, the male, etc. Thus Eryximachus, on the one hand, argues that physical as well as spiritual relations can partake of the good, which he defines as healthy moderation, temperance, and balance. Eros as restraint: "the power of Love in its entirety is various and mighty, nay, all-embracing, but the mightiest power of all is wielded by that Love whose just and temperate consummation, whether in heaven or on earth, tends toward the good" (188 d). On the other hand, Eryximachus retains Pausanias' distinction, as well as its mythology, and continues placing a higher value on spiritual love because its inherently temperate nature helps to control the excesses that are encouraged by physical love:

we are justified in yielding to the desires of the temperate — and of the intemperate in so far as such compliance will tend to sober them, and to this Love, gentlemen, we must hold fast, for he is the fair and heavenly one, born of Urania, the Muse of heaven. But as for that other, the earthly

Love, he is sprung from Polyhymnia, the Muse of many songs, and whatever we have to do with him we must be very careful not to add the evils of excess to the enjoyment of the pleasures he affords ... (187 d, e)

The *Symposium*, then, has already made two affirmations—that love takes two distinct forms, the physical and the spiritual, and that spiritual love is more essentially associated with the good. These affirmations amount to a presentation of the self-evident; they affirm by precluding doubt. One question, however, is still left open. Does the superiority of the spiritual separate it from the physical altogether, or does it give spiritual love the power to subjugate physical love to its own aims?

Pausanias is also the first speaker to employ the opposition male/ female. This opposition does not refer to the purely biological difference between the sexes, though based upon it, nor does it address the questions that psychoanalysis will put under the rubric of sexual difference. Pausanias means to designate two positive essences. They stand in hierarchical relation to one another and are attached to the controlling distinction between heavenly and earthly love:

the earthly Aphrodite's Love is a very earthly Love indeed, and does his work entirely at random. It is he that governs the passions of the vulgar. For, first, they are as much attracted by women as by boys; next, whoever they may love, their desires are of the body rather than the soul; and, finally, they make a point of courting the shallowest people they can find, looking forward to the mere act of fruition and careless whether it be a worthy or unworthy consummation. And hence they take their pleasures where they find them, good and bad alike. For this is the Love of the younger Aphrodite, whose nature partakes of both male and female.

But the heavenly Love springs from a goddess whose attributes have nothing of the female, but are altogether male, and who is also the elder of the two, and innocent of any lewdness. And so those who are inspired by this other Love turn rather to the male, preferring the more vigorous and intellectual bent. One can always tell — even among the lovers of boys — the man who is wholly governed by this older Love, for no boy can please him until he has shown the first signs of dawning intelligence, signs which generally appear with the first growth of beard. (181 b, c, d)

In order to attribute masculinity or femininity to love, Pausanias implicitly divides love into the impulse proper and its object and draws yet another distinction, this time between lover and beloved. Earthly love is said to be a mixture of the male and the female because while the lover is male the object of his desire may be a woman. Pausanias grants the capacity to desire only to men; the beloved may be a boy, a man, or a woman, but the lover is always male. There is no room in this scheme for a purely feminine desire —the earthly Aphrodite's "nature partakes of both male and female," and the heavenly Aphrodite's attributes are "altogether male" —since it does not acknowledge that women desire. Heavenly love is purely masculine because both the lover and the beloved are male. Once again all these discriminations rest on the opposition between the body and the soul. Love for a woman can be no more than a bodily desire, whereas only love for a man can be a pure desire of the soul. Note, however, that the two sides of this pairing—body-feminine/soul-masculine—are not strictly parallel. There is something awry in Pausanias' elaborate system of oppositions in that a degraded love for a male would be partly "feminine" because directed toward the beloved's body. Pausanias himself is sensitive to this difficulty, but he does not recognize it as a problem in the logic of his argument. Instead he sees a social and ethical danger to be solved institutionally; the epitome of this danger is love for a boy, boyhood representing an as yet unaccomplished masculinity: "But I cannot help thinking, gentlemen, that there should be a law to forbid the loving of mere boys, a law to prevent so much time and trouble being wasted on an unknown quantity—for what else, after all, is the future of any boy, and who knows whether he will follow the path of virtue or of vice, in body and in soul?" (181 e). Pausanias' speech continues into a digression on the need for laws in Athens to control the practices of those who love mere boys.

When Aristophanes' turn comes he counters the way in which Pausanias has explained the masculine and feminine traits of love. His comic myth of the origin of love proposes that there were once three sexes, the masculine, the feminine, and the hermaphrodite:

First of all I must explain the real nature of man, and the change which it has undergone — for in the beginning we were nothing like what we are now. For one thing, the race was divided into three; that is to say, besides the two sexes, male and female, which we have at present, there was a third which partook of the nature of both, and for which we still have a name, though the creature itself is forgotten. For though "hermaphrodite" is only used nowadays as a term of contempt, there really was a man-woman in those days, a being which was half male and half female.

And secondly, gentlemen, each of these beings was globular in shape, with rounded back and sides, four arms and four legs, and two faces, both the same, on a cylindrical neck, and one head, with one face one side and one the other, and four ears, and two lots of privates, and all the other parts to match. (189 d - 190 a)

Threatened by a possible onslaught, Zeus had them all cut in two "just as you or I might chop up sorb apples for pickling, or slice an egg with a hair" (190 d). For mankind, which descended from these spherical creatures, love is the longing to restore this lost wholeness or oneness, "to re-integrate our former nature, to make two into one, and to bridge the gulf between one human being and another" (191 d). This desire affects both sexes. Aristophanes, unlike Pausanias, is willing to conceive of women as loving:

But if we cling to [Love] in friendship and reconciliation, we shall be among the happy few to whom it is given in these latter days to meet their other halves. Now, I don't want any coarse remarks from Eryximachus. I don't mean Pausanias and Agathon, though for all I know they may be among the lucky ones, and both be sections of the male. But what I am trying to say is this — that the happiness of the whole human race, women no less than men, is to be found in the consummation of our love, and in the healing of our dissevered nature by finding each his proper mate. (193 b, c)

However, Aristophanes does reinstate the value scheme that privileges masculinity and the love between men, on the grounds that the masculine nature is of the highest value to society:

The man who is a slice of the hermaphrodite sex, as it was called, will naturally be attracted by women — the adulterer, for instance — and women who run after men are of similar descent — as, for instance, the unfaithful wife. But the woman who is a slice of the original female is attracted by women rather than by men — in fact she is a Lesbian — while men who are slices of the male are followers of the male, and show their masculinity throughout their boyhood by the way they make friends with men, and the delight they take in lying beside them and being taken in their arms. And these are the most hopeful of the nation's youth, for theirs is the most virile constitution. (191 d - 192 a)

The variations that distinguish the speeches of Aristophanes and Pausanias and the male/female opposition they share pose two questions that must eventually be addressed. The first can be formulated in terms that are thoroughly intrinsic to the concerns and premises of the debate. Aristophanes, in identifying masculine, feminine, and hermaphrodite forms of love, leaves unanswered a question that haunts Pausanias' discourse. How is the debate to make a more systematic connection between three oppositions that are explicitly tacitly accepted by every participant: male/female, soul/body, lover/beloved? The question will remain in suspension until Socrates speaks.

The second problem is apparently extrinsic in that the *Symposium* passes over it in silence. The value given to the male over the female, man over woman, and male homosexuality over heterosexuality or feminine homosexuality obviously registers a purely historical situation—the subordination of women in Greek society. It would be a mistake, however, to claim that the hierarchical opposition male/female is a purely contingent element of the *Symposium*'s discussion. Such a position would ignore that this opposition is solidary with all the others and cannot, therefore, be bracketted as "historical" while the others are accorded the special status of being "philosophical." It is precisely this distinction between the historical and the philosophical, the extrinsic and the intrinsic, that must be questioned—in the name of the "philosophical" rigor of our commentary. We will come back to this problem.

Aristophanes' fable revolves around the attempt to establish desire's relation to some state of wholeness or completeness. This motif first appears with Eryximachus. Using as a model the practice of medicine, whose function is "to reconcile the jarring elements of the body, and force them, as it were, to fall in love with one another" (186 d), the physician argues that love provides physical and spiritual harmony and governs life with temperance and order. Every aspect of human life, and even the life of plants and animals, is under the harmonizing influence of heavenly Love as it seeks to overcome the disruptive effects of earthly Love, "sprung from Polyhymnia, the Muse of many songs." Harmony reconciles by balancing extremes, while discord represents their destructive conflict. However, Eryximachus encounters considerable difficulty in setting up this opposition between harmony and conflict. He refers, almost in passing, to a passage from Heraclitus, hoping to clarify its enigma. Instead, he finds himself faced with the alternative of declaring that the statement is utter nonsense, since in it the concepts of harmony and discord do not guard their integrity as clearly separated opposites, or else of claiming that it is self-evident that the passage must mean something other than what it says. Eryximachus' wavering is indicative of the uneasiness that strikes the logic of identity, with its denial that A can be both A and not-A, when confronted with an affirmation of contradiction. Eryximachus is left trying to silence Heraclitus:

> And so, gentlemen, I maintain that medicine is under the sole direction of the god of love, as are also the gymnastic and the agronomic arts. And it must be obvious to the most casual observer that the same holds good of music — which is, perhaps, what Heraclitus meant us to understand by that rather cryptic pronouncement, "The one in conflict with itself is held together, like the harmony of the bow and the lyre." Or course it is absurd to speak of harmony as being in conflict, or as arising out of elements that are still conflicting, but perhaps he meant that the art of music was to create harmony by resolving the discord between the treble and the bass. There can be no harmony of treble and bass while they are still in conflict, for harmony is concord, and concord is a kind of sympathy, and sympathy between things which are in conflicts is impossible so long as the conflict lasts. (186 e - 187 b)

The text, as though compelled to point to the scar that is left behind when Platonic idealism tries to seal off the effects of pre-Socratic thought, lets Eryximachus' notion of harmony, so crucial to the dialogue's developing theory of desire, be mocked once more by making it the object of Aristophanes' humor. Aristophanes was to speak before Eryximachus but had an uncontrollable fit of hiccups for which the physician prescribed a sequence of treatments: holding the breath, gargling water, "or if it's particularly stubborn

John Brenkman

you'll have to get something you can tickle your nostrils with, and sneeze, and by the time you've done that three or four times you will find that it will stop, however bad it is" (185 e). When Eryximachus has finished, the following exchange takes place between the two of them:

It is for you, Aristophanes, to make good my deficiencies, that is unless you're thinking of some other kind of eulogy. But in any case, let us hear what you have to say — now you've recovered from your hiccups.

To which ... Aristophanes replied, Yes, I'm better now, thank you, but not before I had recourse to sneezing — which made me wonder, Eryximachus, how your orderly principle of the body could have called for such an appalling union of noise and irritation; yet there's no denying that the hiccups stopped immediately when I sneezed.

Now, Aristophanes, take care, retorted Eryximachus, and don't try to raise a laugh before you've started. You'll only have yourself to thank if I'm waiting to pounce on your silly jokes, instead of giving your speech a proper hearing.

Aristophanes laughed. You're quite right, Eryximachus, he said. I take it all back. (188 e - 189 b)

Aristophanes himself, of course, associates love with wholeness. But his point of departure is just the reverse of Eryximachus', for he sees love not as harmony but as the effect of a primordial sense of loss and separation. Through the recourse to the myth that humans descend from spherical beings who were cut in half, Aristophanes can propose that the goal of desire is wholeness or oneness since that was the original condition whose loss gave rise to desire. However, no matter how much Aristophanes exalts love he cannot, given the myth itself, claim that this oneness is ever achieved. Every love relation is but a substitute for the original condition, an approximation rather than a recovery of lost wholeness. This is clear when Aristophanes ponders what would happen if two lovers were actually given the chance to be welded together:

The fact is that both their souls are longing for a something else: a something to which they can neither of them put a name, and which they can only give an inkling of in cryptic sayings and prophetic riddles.

Now, supposing Hephaestus were to come and stand over them with his tool bag as they lay there side by side, and suppose he were to ask, Tell me, my dear creatures, what do you really want with one another?

And suppose they didn't know what to say, and he went on, how would you like to be rolled into one, so that you could always be together, day and night, and never be parted again? . . .

We may be sure, gentlemen, that no lover on earth would dream of refusing such an offer, for not one of them could imagine a happier fate. Indeed, they would be convinced that this was just what they had been waiting for — to be merged, that is, into an utter oneness with the beloved. (192 c, d, e)

This myth is utterly unacceptable to Socrates. He dismisses it as he recounts the discourse in which Diotima taught him about love, "the one thing in the world I understand" (177 d): "I know it has been suggested, she continued, that lovers are people who are looking for their other halves, but as I see it, Socrates, Love never longs for either the half or the whole of anything except the good" (205 d, e). On one level Socrates is simply restoring the notion, already affirmed in earlier speech but obscured by Aristophanes, that love serves the good. More importantly, he is laying the foundation for an argument that will give love an attainable goal as opposed to Aristophanes' myth which can do no more than imagine a lost fullness that love vainly tries to recover. Socrates does not, on the other hand, claim that love *is* the good or the beautiful or the harmonious. To the contrary, like Aristophanes, he defines love as a lack. What follows is an exchange between Agathon and Socrates which, the latter tells us, virtually duplicates his first conversation with Diotima:

Well, then, continued Socrates, desiring to secure something to oneself forever may be described as loving something which is not yet to hand.

Certainly.

And therefore, whoever feels a want is wanting something which is not yet to hand, and the object of his love and his desire is whatever he hasn't got — that is to say, whatever he is lacking in.

Absolutely.

And now, said Socrates, are we agreed upon the following conclusions? One, that Love is always the love of something, and two, that that something is what he lacks.

Agreed, said Agathon. (200 d, e)

John Brenkman

Desire is a lack—a failure-to-be or failure-to-have—that somehow propels the lover toward the good. This journey passes through several stages, and eventually we will have to consider its trajectory; its destination is a vision of the beautiful in its purest form as Idea. When the lover reaches this vision he partakes of the One, which is spiritual rather than material, eternal rather than mortal, permanent rather than transitory, whole rather than fragmentary:

> Nor will his vision of the beautiful take the form of a face, or of hands, or of anything that is flesh. It will be neither words, nor knowledge, nor a something that exists in something else, such as a living creature, or the earth, or the heavens, or anything that is — but subsisting of itself and by itself in an eternal oneness while every lovely thing partakes of it in such sort that, however much the parts may wax and wane, it will be neither more nor less, but still the same inviolable whole. (211 a, b)

Socrates' conception of love differs from those proposed by Phaedrus and Pausanias in that it does not claim that love brings man immediately into contact with the good. Moreover, it finds a third way to dispose of the problem that Eryximachus and Aristophanes have taken up. Eryximachus proposed that love is harmonious, while Aristophanes defined it as the yearning after a wholeness that man primordially lost. Socrates employs the oppositions harmony/discord and completeness/lack, both of which are associated with that between the one and the many, but he does so by defining desire as the lack that pushes the lover toward the vision of the beautiful, which "is in perfect harmony," in its completeness and wholeness. Desire's goal is to abolish itself. In this way the Socratic conception of love forges the concatenation of the axiomatic oppositions and values that organize the other discourses and provides for their synthesis into a coherent system.

Socrates does leave aside one question. And it is a question that may be asked in two radically different ways. Posed from within the philosophical framework that governs the *Symposium*'s discussions, the question bears on the *source* or *origin* of the lack inherent in desire. Asked in this way it must be answered either with a myth, as Aristophanes does, or else with an appeal to yet another opposition that is supposedly axiomatic: the opposition between the human and the divine, in which case we are asked to conceive of the human as a derivation or deviation from the divine which it then seeks to (re)appropriate. This second alternative, which merely retraces the circuit of axioms and values it is intended to explain, is the one that Socrates implicitly chooses even though he does not here evoke the concept of recollection on which this explanation hinges in other texts by Plato. The other way of posing the question is to be found in psychoanalytic theory, whether that of Freud or Lacan, and addresses itself to the biological and social conditions in which the human child's earliest relations to others are formed. In the context determined by these relations and conditions, what is the process that institutes desire as a primordial lack?

For Socrates this question would undoubtedly be improper, even inconceivable, since it eschews any reference to the divine and does not found itself on the separation of body and soul. My intention is not, however, merely to juxtapose two conflicting theories of desire, the Platonic and the psychoanalytic. From the outset the psychoanalytic theory of desire has shaped itself as a critical reversal of the idealist theory. Thus, as Derrida has reminded us, Freud has to wrench the term "the unconscious" from the metaphysical opposition in which it is no more than "the symmetrical negative and potential reservoir of 'consciousness'" in order to give a name to the process or mechanism that is irreducible to "consciousness" and conditions its very possibility. So also we find Lacan taking over the concepts of loss and lack but without attaching them to some original or final fullness or completeness. The other side of this dialectic makes it possible to take Plato's text and, as Lacan has said in a similar context, "read it from the analytic experience." Such a reading, I will argue, amounts to a productive rewriting of the philosophical text from a materialist viewpoint; it lets Freud's discovery of the unconscious disrupt the metaphysical discourse on desire. And, since the idealist discourse is built around a misrecognition of the processes of desire, psychoanalytic theory will achieve a fully critical and dialectical relation to idealism if it can contribute to the analysis of that misrecognition, its formation and structure. Lacan's commentary on the *Symposium* operates according to a system, but it has not been presented systematically; the psychoanalytic reading-rewriting of the *Symposium* has to be constructed, starting from the more or less fragmentary references to it in *Écrits,* the published seminars, and other essays. At times Lacan very directly rewrites Plato, as when he counters Aristophanes's myth by producing a *canular* of his own that is designed to outdo its classical model. More often Lacan initiates a rewriting in the sense of writing what remains unreadable to the *Symposium* itself, that is, what is readable only in the gaps and against the grain of the text's organization. Given the complex form of the dialectic that joins and severs the *Symposium* and the psychoanalytic theory of desire, it will not be a detour to begin with the way Freud and Lacan broach their description of the processes that institute desire.

In the *Interpretation of Dreams,* Freud discovered that the dream articulates a wish or desire that is itself comprised of the articulated connections between "memory traces." Lacan has shown that these unconscious memory traces constitute a network of signifiers in the sense that each element of the unconscious, like the phoneme in language, relates to the others through contiguity (metonymy) and substitution (metaphor), that is, through what Freud called displacement and condensation. Freud's first systematic attempt to depict the process by which these memory traces are inscribed in the unconscious led him to present a model of "the primitive psychical apparatus" in Chapter VII of the *Interpretation of Dreams,* and this was followed, in the second of the *Three Essays on the Theory of Sexuality,* by a more complete set of formulations based on the theory of infantile sexuality. These models envisioned the memory trace as the unconscious recording or inscription of the perception that accompanied an "experience of satisfaction," the prototype for this experience being the gratification provided by the mother's breast. Desire, then, is defined as the seeking after a repetition of that satisfaction by bringing an object into contact with the body in the same way. In the dream, according to this model, the flow of psychical energy toward real objects is reversed and moves backward across the memory traces themselves, repeating the "experience of satisfaction" by hallucinating the original memory trace or some other trace that is associatively connected with it.

Lacan recasts this theoretical problem—particularly in "La direction de la cure" and "La signification du phallus"—by arguing that the child's earliest relation to others generates a dialectical interplay between need, the request for love, and desire. [9] At birth, the infant is not only unable to care for itself but also does not have a command of the language with which it could engage in a communicative exchange with those who care for it. It depends upon a social organization in which it does not yet fully participate. While forced to request that his needs be satisfied, the child does not have at his disposal the collection of signifiers or the rules for their combination that are necessary to form a message capable of communicating the *specific* need (like hunger) that agitates him. The language belongs to the social group and not to him, or, as Lacan puts it, "the storehouse of the signifier" is in the possession of the Other. At first, then, the request that the child proffers, gesturally and vocally, can be no more than a *general* appeal for the mother's presence. The conflict between the specificity of the need and the generality of the request inhabits the first moment of Lacan's dialectic: "the request cancels *(aufhebt)* the particularity of everything that can be granted in response to it by transmuting that response into a proof of love." [10] The mother's response (feeding serving again as the prototype) contains the contradictions that will define sexual life. Her responsive gesture, which already mixes caring for the child's need with showing her love, at the same time crushes his request—silences him and so deprives him of his only means of

---

[9] Cf., Jacques Lacan, *Écrits* (Paris: Seuil, 1966), esp., pp. 620-642 and 690-695.
[10] "La signification du phallus," *Écrits*, p. 691.

John Brenkman

establishing a signifying relation with her—and produces a desire (the oral drive) that exceeds simple biological need.

Freud's own efforts to pinpoint the relation between need and desire revolved around two important but imprecise formulae: (1) that an erotic drive is "at first" attached to a need, as the oral drive is attached to the need for nourishment, and "later" becomes separate from it, as in thumbsucking; and (2) that "The sexual aim of the infantile instinct consists in obtaining satisfaction by means of an appropriate stimulation of the erotogenic zone which has been selected in one way or another. This satisfaction must have previously been experienced in order to have left behind a need for its repetition" [11]—satisfaction itself being experienced only after the fact, since it is the effect of a diminution of excitation. If desire is the seeking after the repetition of a "previously" experienced satisfaction, what could be the "first" experience of satisfaction, and how does desire emerge as different from need?

The Lacanian dialectic of desire addresses these questions by introducing the notion of the lost object. The maternal response to the request for love brings an object (the breast) into contact with a localized zone of the body (the mouth). This object provides an "experience of satisfaction" by stimulating this zone until its excitation passes a certain threshold and subsides; it is the diminution, the return to zero, that is felt as pleasure. "This strikes us as somewhat strange," Freud wrote, "only because, in order to remove one stimulus, it is necessary to adduce another one at the same spot." [12] The unconscious memory trace, or signifier in Lacan's terminology, is inscribed only with the loss of the real object, its disappearance coinciding with the diminution of excitation. The object that causes desire is, therefore, primordially lost, and the signifier, connected in this way to the body, marks its disappearance. Desire arises from this pure loss and is what traverses the gap or space that separates the metonymically linked signifiers in the unconscious. Desire is

[11] *Three Essays on the Theory of Sexuality*, Standard Edition, VII, p. 184.
[12] *Ibid.*, p. 185.

separated from need in this process because of the dissonance between the request and the maternal response to it. Rather than merely answering the *generalized* request for love, the mother's response satisfies the need by provoking and reducing the excitation of a *particular* zone of the body. The particularity that the request abolished "reappears on the other side *(au-delà)* of the request, but conserving the structure that the unconditioned aim of the request for love harbors."[13] The desire that the lost object causes through this dialectic is at once unconditioned in that virtually any object will suffice and conditioned in that the object must gratify a particular zone; moreover, desire is an absolute condition in that, unlike a need, it can never be satisfied:

For the unconditioned aim of the request, desire substitutes the "absolute" condition: this condition sets apart what in the proof of love is refractory to the satisfaction of a need. It is in this way that desire is neither the appetite for satisfaction nor the request for love but rather the difference resulting from the subtraction of the first from the second, the very phenomenon of their splitting *(Spaltung).*[14]

The (unconscious) subject is thus, on the one hand, the effect of speech, that is, of the combinative interplay of the unconscious signifiers whose inscription results from the dialectic that transpires between the body and others. And, on the other hand, the subject depends upon the signifier, which comes to him from the Other, so that he must seek for it in the locus of the Other even though, as an *infans,* he cannot as yet integrate it into his own signifying activity, the request.

It is in order to connect the lost object, or a-object, to the Freudian notion of the libido that Lacan introduces his parody of Aristophanes' myth. It is designed not only to outdo and criticize Aristophanes' story but also to move away from the metaphors in which Freud couched his description of the libido by suggesting that the libido is not so much a field of forces as an organ:

[13] Lacan, "La signification du phallus," p. 691.
[14] *Ibid.*

418

Let me announce straightaway what the point of this elucidation will be by telling you that the libido is not something receding and flowing: it does not break apart or accumulate, like some magnetism; in the centers of localization that the subject offers to it, the libido is to be conceived as an organ, in both senses of the term, organ-part of the body and organ-instrument. [15]

From the other direction, the critique of Aristophanes bears on the notion of the complement, the missing half, which for him defines the source and goal of human love:

Aristophanes' myth gives us, in a moving and deceiving way, the image of the pursuit of the complement, by stating that it is the other, his sexual half, that the living being seeks in love. For this mythic representation of love's mystery, analytic experience substitutes the subject's search not for the sexual complement but for the part of himself that is forever lost because of the very fact that he is but a sexual living being and no longer immortal. [16]

What the living being loses in having to pass through sexual reproduction is the libido insofar as it is

the pure instinct of life — of immortal life, irrepressible life, life without need of any organ, simplified and indestructible life. This is precisely what is subtracted from the living being when it is submitted to the cycle of sexual reproduction. All the forms of the a-object that could be enumerated are the representatives or equivalents of this ... Indeed the breast ... represents that part of himself that the individual loses at birth and that can serve to symbolize the most profound lost object. [17]

To provide an image for this, Lacan picks up on Aristophanes' comparison of primordial man with an egg cut in two with a hair, but he considers two other forms of the egg—the intra-uterine life of the foetus and ... the omelette:

To trespass on the territory of the *Symposium's* Aristophanes, let us recall his primitive two-backed creature, the two halves of which are joined as tightly as those of a Magdeburg sphere; these halves, later separated by

[15] Lacan, *Le Séminaire, Livre XI: Les quatre concepts fondamentaux de la psychanalyse* (Paris: Seuil, 1973), p. 171.
[16] *Ibid.*, p. 187.
[17] *Ibid.*, p. 180.

a surgical intervention on the part of a jealous Zeus, represent what we have become in love, beings longing for an undiscoverable complement.

In considering this sphericity of primordial Man as well as his division, it is the egg that is evoked. . . .

Let us consider this egg in the viviparous womb where it has no need of a shell, and let us recall that each time the membranes are broken it is a part of the egg that is wounded, since the membranes of the fertilized eggs are offspring just as much as the living being that is born with their perforation. Consequently, with the cutting of the cord, what the new-born loses is not, as analysts think, its mother but rather its anatomical complement. What midwives call the *délivre* (after-birth).

Breaking the egg makes Man *(l'Homme)*, but also *l'Hommelette.*

Let us imagine it, a large crêpe moving about like the amoeba, ultra-flat for passing under doors, omniscient in being led by the pure life instinct, immortal in being scissiparous. Here is something you would not like to feel creeping over your face, silently while you are asleep, in order to seal it up. [18]

The pure life instinct, then, is something that is separated from the living being because the latter, in owing its existence to sexual reproduction, is not immortal. The sexual being loses its share in life in order to live. And the libido, instead of being irrepressible life, now becomes an organ attaching itself to the "points of focalization" that the body offers. The instrument (organ) of the libido—*l'homme-lette* or, as Lacan also calls it, to give it a "more decent name," the lamella—finds its function in relation to a part (organ) of the body, the erotogenic zones but also the a-objects themselves, the breast and excrement, for example, which are precisely parts of the body related to the oral and anal zones of erotogeneity. The breast becomes a figure for this pure loss that goes with living simply because in the infant's extra-uterine existence the separation from the breast is the first experience that recapitulates the loss of a part of itself that occurs at birth: "if we recall the parasitic relation to the mother's body that the mammalian organization imposes on its young, from the embryo to the newborn, we will see that the breast is the same kind of organ, to be conceived as the ectopy of one individual on another, as the placenta is in the first

[18] "Position de l'inconscient," *Écrits,* p. 845.

420

John Brenkman

period of growth for a certain type of organism." [19] Lacan criticizes the tendency on the part of Melanie Klein to suggest that the significance of the breast comes from the fact that the infant fantasizes its detachment from the mother's body; what is crucial, to the contrary, is the separation of the breast from the infant, which occurs intermittently with each feeding and permanently with weaning.

Lacan continues to modify the Kleinian terminology in order to establish the relation of the libido to the erotogenic zones and their objects, rejecting the notion of the "partial object" and speaking instead of the partial drive and the a-object. The erotic drives are "partial" in the sense that they function independently of one another and cannot, taken separately or together, represent the reproductive aim of sexuality. The structure of the partial drives (orality, anality, etc.) is a circuit going from the erotogenic zone to the a-object and back to the erotogenic zone, the excitation of which is diminished when the external object stimulates it. This circuit contains all three moments that Freud somewhat misleadingly separates into active, passive, and reflexive impulses. "The lamella has a border [or, rim: *bord*]; it comes to insert itself on the erotogenic zones, that is, on one of the body's orifices.... The erotogenic zones are tied to the unconscious since it is on them that the presence of the living being is fastened to the unconscious. We have discovered that it is precisely the organ of the libido, the lamella, that ties the oral or anal drive to the unconscious." [20] As we have seen, this interaction between the a-objects and the body also gives rise to the signifier. The human subject is an effect of the signifier coming from the Other, that is, from the social group and more specifically from the mother as its representative, the signifier being inscribed in the unconscious as the object-cause of desire is lost. The subject's relation to the signifier introduces a lack in the structure of subjectivity which can now be related to the lack installed by birth itself:

[19] *Ibid.*, p. 848.
[20] *Le Séminaire, Livre XI*, pp. 181-182.

Two lacks overlap here. The one follows from the central insufficiency around which turns the dialectic of the subject's accession to his own being in his relation to the Other — from the fact that the subject depends upon the signifier and that the signifier is at first in the field of the Other. This lack comes to take up again the other, the anterior, real lack, which is to be situated in the advent of the living being itself, in sexual reproduction. The real lack is what the living being loses of his share in life by being reproduced through the paths of sexuality. This lack is real because it relates to something real, which is that the living person, in being a subject in sex, has fallen under the influence of individual death. [21]

The overlapping of these two lacks comprises the dialectical connection between the biological conditions of human life and the social processes that produce the human subject as such. Moreover, the submission of the pure life instinct *(Instinkt, instinct)* to the function of the signifier makes it necessary to propose, as Freud tried to do, a theoretical formulation that links the erotic drive *(Trieb, pulsion)* to the death drive:

If the subject is what I teach you, namely, the subject determined by language and speech, this means that the subject, *in initio,* begins in the locus of the Other inasmuch as the first signifier appears there.

Now, what is a signifier? I have been drilling it into you long enough not to have to articulate it anew here; a signifier is what represents a subject, for what? — not for another subject but for another signifier. To illustrate this axiom, suppose that you discover in the desert a stone covered with hieroglyphs. You do not doubt for an instant that there had been a subject before who wrote them. But to believe that each signifier is addressed to you would be an error — the proof of this being that you do not understand a thing about them. To the contrary, you define them as signifiers because you are sure that each of those signifiers relates to each of the others. This is what is at issue in the subject's relation to the field of the Other.

The subject is born as the signifier arises in the field of the Other. But, for that very reason, the subject — who previously was nothing, except a subject to come — is fixed in the signifier.

The relation to the Other is exactly that which, for us, brings to light what the lamella represents — not the sexual polarity, the relation of the masculine to the feminine, but the relation of the living subject to what he loses in having to pass through the sexual cycle for his own reproduction.

---

[21] *Ibid.,* p. 186.

John Brenkman

> In this way I explain the essential affinity of every drive with the zone of death and bring together the two aspects of the drive — which at once manifests sexuality in the unconscious and represents, in its essence, death. [22]

Lacan's analysis of the libido, the partial drive, the a-object, and the erotogenic zone, including his mythical illustration, breaks out of the confines imposed by the conceptual scheme that regulates the *Symposium,* Aristophanes' myth as well as the other speeches. To begin with, the theory of the lost object establishes the genesis of desire—the question that Socrates does not pose—without having recourse to any original wholeness or unity, as does Aristophanes. The object-cause of desire is lost from the beginning, since the "experience of satisfaction" it affords coincides with its disappearance, its removal from the erotogenic zone. Secondly, the psychoanalytic theory of the signifier overturns the Platonic distinction, so crucial to this dialogue, between the body and soul, matter and spirit. The Lacanian subject is not a soul or spirit; it is a process or function that is instituted by the dialectic to which the biological life of man is submitted when connected to the action of the signifier, which is itself at the heart of the most elementary social practices. The birth of the subject—or, better, the production of the structure and processes of subjectivity—depends upon the signifier that arises out of the interaction between the erotogenic body (its zones) and matter (the a-objects). The subject, then, is the effect of a signifying process that is at once material and social. The psychoanalytic concept of the partial drive wrenches another metaphysical distinction that will play a role in the *Symposium:* life/death. Lacan argues, much as Freud did, that the very fact that a living being is submitted to sexual reproduction separates it from life in any pure form. Death inhabits life, and their conjunction defines the structure of the partial drive. Indeed, Lacan refuses to distinguish, even hypothetically, the erotic and the death drive: "the partial drive is fundamentally a death drive and in itself represents death's share in the life of the sexual being." [23]

[22] *Ibid.,* pp. 180-181.
[23] *Ibid.,* p. 187.

The meshing of the relation to death and the relation to re-production also informs the symbolic organization of culture, kin-ship relations, lineage, paternity, and so on. And again it is a ques-tion of the workings of the signifier:

> There is, of course, no need for a signifier to be a father, any more than to be dead, but without the signifier no one would know anything about either of these states of being....
>
> How in fact could Freud not recognize [the affinity of the two signifying relations we have just evoked] when his reflection led him to join the appearance of the signifier of the Father, as author of the Law, to the death, indeed the murder, of the Father, — thus showing that if this murder is the key moment of the debt whereby the subject is tied, in life, to the Law, then the symbolic Father inasmuch as he signifies this Law is indeed the dead Father. [24]

The point here is that the subject, as he situates himself within the kinship structures that organize human reproduction, comes to re-cognize that the death of the father is already implied in the suc-cession of generations. To become a father is to fall under the mark of death. From this perspective it is possible to analyze an important aspect of Socrates' discourse on love as a narrative that breaks the two sides of the dialectic joining death and reproduction into separate moments in a temporal sequence. After Diotima and Socrates had agreed on the precise relation of love to the good: "In short, that Love longs for the good to be his own forever" (206 a), she went on to explain that loving necessarily involves procreation:

> Well, I'll tell you, then, she said. To love is to bring forth upon the beautiful, in body and in soul.
>
> I'm afraid that's too deep, I said, for my poor wits to fathom.
>
> I'll try to speak more plainly, then. We are all of us prolific, Socrates, in body and in soul, and when we reach a certain age our nature urges us to procreation. Nor can we be quickened by ugliness, but only by the beautiful. Conception, we know, takes place when man and woman come together, but there's divinity in human propagation, an immortal something in the midst of man's mortality which is incompatible with any kind of

[24] Lacan, "D'une question préliminaire à tout traitement possible de la psychose," *Écrits*, p. 556.

discord. And ugliness is at odds with the divine while beauty is in perfect harmony.... So you see, Socrates, that Love is not exactly a longing for the beautiful, as you suggested.

Well, what is it, then?

A longing not for the beautiful itself, but for the conception and generation that the beautiful effects.

Yes. No doubt you're right.

Of course I'm right, she said. And why all this longing for propagation? Because this is the one deathless and eternal element in our mortality. And since we have agreed that the lover longs for the good to be his own forever, it follows that we are bound to long for immortality as well as for the good — which is to say that Love is a longing for immortality. (206 b - 207 a)

Socrates here renews the opposition between the beautiful and the ugly but avoids claiming either that love is the beautiful (as Agathon does) or that the beautiful is the object of love. Rather the beauty of the beloved, whether a woman or a young man, is the occasion for love. The actual motive of love is procreation. Socrates is the first speaker to incorporate the reproductive function into the theory of love. Only Aristophanes has mentioned it, but in a way that grants no necessary connection between love and reproduction. Thus, for example, he says of those lovers who descend from the purely male that "they have no natural inclination to marry and beget children. Indeed, they only do so in deference to the usage of society" (192 a, b). The form that Socrates' argument takes permits him to recognize that desire is founded on a lack but at the same time to reaffirm the already established opposition between the temporal and the eternal. Love, even the relatively devalued love for a woman, is situated on the path between the temporal and the eternal; since its real aim is immortality, love, through procreancy, puts the human in touch with the divine and the eternal. Socrates can secure this reconciliation of the notion of lack with the metaphysical oppositions underlying the entire dialogue only by producing a kind of narrative, a fictive temporality. Whereas the relation to death and the relation to reproduction are actually enfolded in a single moment, Diotima separates them and distributes them along a narrative line. The recognition of death comes first, and the idea of becoming a father comes afterward as a means of surpassing that recognition. In other words, the relation to reproduction follows upon and triumphs over the relation to death.

This severing of the link between sexuality and death becomes all the more decisive when Diotima proceeds to distinguish procreancy of the soul from procreancy of the body. The lover now seeks immortality not by producing mortal offspring, children, but by creating an immortal offspring, "the things of the spirit":

And I ask you, who would not prefer such fatherhood to merely human propagation, if he stopped to think of Homer, and Hesiod, and all the greatest of our poets? Who would not envy them their immortal progeny, their claim upon the admiration of posterity. (209 c, d)

Spiritual fatherhood entails not only a change in the nature of the offspring, wisdom instead of children, but also in the nature of the beloved, who is no longer a woman but a young man to be educated by the philosopher-lover. The beloved, however, is not strictly parallel to the woman in sexual reproduction in that he is not designated as the "mother" of the wisdom and discourse that his education produces. The philosopher-lover himself takes on the attributes of maternity as well as paternity; while "his first ambition is to be begetting" and to "go about in search of the loveliness—and never the ugliness—on which he may beget" (209 b), he is thereby "delivered of the burden he has labored under all these years" (209 c). In the shift from bodily to spiritual procreation, the role of the body is not excluded altogether or from the start. This is clear in Diotima's description of the first step in the philosopher-lover's journey toward vision: "First of all ..., he will fall in love with the beauty of one individual body, so that his passion may give life to noble discourse" (210 a). What the shift from the material to the spiritual has excluded is not the body but the *maternal* body. The feminine body has been replaced by the masculine body of the beloved, and, as part of the same process, maternity has been absorbed into the spiritual paternity of the philosopher-lover. Socrates' discourse in this way succeeds in uniting the hierarchical relations masculine/feminine, spirit/matter, soul/body into a coherent system of interlocking oppositions.

The lover/beloved distinction operates throughout the *Symposium*, but without any real consistency, until Socrates makes it the very cornerstone of both the theory of love and the practice of philosophy. In the model of love as philosophical education, lover and beloved are absolutely distinct. Their separation in turn maintains the separation of soul and body insofar as it is only the beloved's body that plays a role in the process. And even that role is superceded as the lover mounts "the heavenly ladder, stepping from rung to rung — that is, from one to two, and from two to every lovely body, from bodily beauty to the beauty of institutions, from institutions to learning, and from learning in general to the special lore that pertains to nothing but the beautiful itself—until at last he comes to know what beauty is" (211 c).

The *Symposium* does not just set forth the distinction between lover and beloved, it dramatizes in the encounter between Socrates and Agathon, his beloved. Agathon speaks just before Socrates, and his eulogy has stirred all of those present with its eloquence. Socrates then leads Agathon through the series of questions cited earlier and forces him to admit that love is the lack not the possession of the good, the true, the beautiful. At the end of this exchange, the beloved is left in the position of disavowing his entire speech:

To which Agathon could only reply, I begin to be afraid, my dear Socrates, that I didn't know what I was talking about.

Never mind, said Socrates, it was a lovely speech, but there's just one more point. I suppose you hold that the good is also beautiful.

I do.

Then, if Love is lacking in what is beautiful, and if the good and the beautiful are the same, he must also be lacking in what is good.

Just as you say, Socrates, he replied. I'm afraid you're quite unanswerable.

No, no, dear Agathon. It's the truth you find unanswerable, not Socrates. (201 c)

Socrates' soothing comment, "Never mind, it was a lovely speech," is more than a coy mixture of flattery and criticism. It pinpoints the relation that Agathon is supposed to have to him. The beloved's "lovely speech" is precisely like the bodily beauty that attracts Socrates to him. Rhetorical eloquence, his suspicion of which Socrates voices elsewhere as well, is like a body without a soul in that it has no inherent relation to the truth. Just as Agathon finishes his eulogy Socrates feigns amazement at "the sheer beauty of his diction" (198 b). Then he lowers the boom, explaining how he must have misunderstood the entire purpose of a eulogy on love:

I imagined in my innocence that one began by stating the facts about the manner in hand, and then proceeded to pick out the most attractive points and display them to the best advantage. And I flattered myself that my speech would be a great success, because I knew the facts. But the truth, it seems, is the last thing the successful eulogist cares about; on the contrary, what he does is simply to run through all the attributes of power and virtue, however irrelevant they may be, and the whole thing may be a pack of lies, for all it seems to matter. (198 d. e)

Truth is to eloquence as the soul to the body. We should remember that from the outset Socrates has said that "love is the one thing in the world I understand." Socrates' beloved, with his physical beauty and "the sheer beauty of his diction," is precisely in need of a lover whose interest is in spiritual things, wisdom and truth, and who can therefore educate him. The empty eloquence of the beloved awaits the lover's truth, which will fill it; the beautiful body awaits its introduction to wisdom. Socrates, just as he is about to begin his own discourse, which will present the truth about love, has prepared his beloved to be a proper pupil. Through the response to Agathon's speech and the questioning of his arguments, Socrates fixes himself and Agathon in their proper positions in a relation that is as hierarchical as it is philosophical: lover/beloved, mind/body, wisdom/ignorance, truth/rhetoric.

A knowledge of love turns out, of course, to be a knowledge of the path of philosophy itself. Socrates has positioned himself as the subject who's supposed to know; this position is necessary to both his roles, that of philosopher and that of lover. When Alcibiades arrives at the banquet, drunk und uninvited, he launches into a eulogy of Socrates himself, his practice as a philosopher and as a lover. The interpretation of this speech is crucial to a critical reading of the *Symposium,* especially one which, like our own, is designed to reconcile the practice of the deconstructive reading with that of the materialist rewriting. Alcibiades drives a wedge into the finely organized system of Socrates' theory of love, but the precise effects of the violence of his intrusion are left unarticulated by the text. It is as though the *Symposium,* like Socrates himself, stands by in silence even though provoked by Alcibiades to strike back: "if I say a word that is not the solemn truth I want you to stop me right away and tell me I'm a liar" (214 e).

To begin with, Alcibiades pins down the structure of reversals that defines Socrates' "little game of irony" (216 e). He claims that the initial pose Socrates strikes has two aspects each of which is calculated to deceive those around him:

Take my word for it, there's not one of you that really knows him. But now I've started, I'll show him up. Notice, for instance, how Socrates is attracted by good-looking people, and how he hangs around them, positively gaping with admiration. Then again, he loves to appear utterly uninformed and ignorant — isn't that like the Silenus? (216 c, d)

The Silenus is the rough-looking box to which Alcibiades has compared Socrates because, despite its exterior, it contains a treasure of "little figures of the gods." Now, the pose of fascination with beauty and the appearance of ignorance quickly turn, Alcibiades claims, into their opposites once the beloved has come under Socrates' influence. He goes on to recount how Socrates responded to his own futile attempts to make the master acknowledge his youthful beauty:

He heard me out, and then said with that ironical simplicity of his, My dear Alcibiades, I've no doubt there's a lot in what you say, if you're right in thinking that I have some kind of power that would make a better man of you, because in that case you must find me so extraordinarily beautiful that your own attractions must be quite eclipsed. And if you're trying to barter your own beauty for the beauty you have found in me, you're driving a very hard bargain, let me tell you. You're trying to exchange the semblance of beauty for the thing itself. (218 d. e)

Ignorance and lack of beauty suddenly shift from the lover to the beloved, and the lover now presents himself as beautiful as well as knowing. This is what we have just seen Socrates do to Agathon; the strategem began in the same way, for when Socrates takes his place next to Agathon at the beginning of the banquet he poses as the ignorant man hoping to gain wisdom from his beautiful companion. With no little irony he laments that wisdom cannot be transferred from Agathon to himself:

> My dear Agathon, Socrates replied as he took his seat beside him, I only wish that wisdom were the kind of thing one could share by sitting next to someone — if it flowed, for instance, from the one that was full to the one that was empty, like the water in two cups finding its level through a piece of worsted. If that were how it worked, I'm sure I'd congratulate myself on sitting next to you, for you'd soon have me brimming over with the most exquisite kind of wisdom. (175 d, e)

By the time Socrates is ready to speak, his manipulation of the ironic reversal has made Agathon admit total ignorance and await the truth that Socrates has promised him. Only when lover and beloved are properly positioned is it possible for wisdom to flow into the empty and outwardly beautiful form that the youth offers to the philosopher. The implication of all that Alcibiades says, when applied to the account of the evening, is that Socratic irony and the dialectic it produces are a mode of seduction.

The fixed relation between lover and beloved is, I have argued, the cornerstone of Socrates' theory of love. Alcibiades disorients this relation by suggesting that the two positions are reversible in yet another way. Lacan has identified this aspect of Alcibiades' speech, and we will try to calculate its effect on the questions we are discussing. "In his quest," writes Lacan, "Alcibiades lets the cat out of the bag concerning love's deception and its baseness—to love is to want to be loved—, to which he was ready to consent." [25] In-

[25] "Du 'Trieb' de Freud," *Écrits*, p. 853.

deed, the whole thrust of Alcibiades' eulogy is to show that Socrates, as a lover, does not admire the beloved so much as seek his admiration. There are two moments where Alcibiades notes this reversibility of lover and beloved. First he indicates how Socrates' lack of interest in him forced him to act like the lover instead of the beloved: "Well, I realized there was nothing to be gained in that direction, so I decided to make a frontal attack. I asked him to dinner, just as if I were the lover trying to seduce his beloved, instead of the other way round" (217 c). And, conversely, Socrates, in rebuffing his youthful admirers, whose admiration his irony has adduced, acts like the beloved: "I'm not the only one either; there's Charmides, and Euthydemus, and ever so many more. He's made fools of them all, just as if he were the beloved, not the lover" (222 b). The seductive force of Socratic irony is that it presents Socrates as the one who has beauty as well as the one who has wisdom; that is, it makes him the object of others' desire. Alcibiades affirms that he and all the others at the banquet have been "bitten in the heart, or the mind, or whatever you like to call it, by Socrates' philosophy, which clings like an adder to any young and gifted mind it can get hold of, and does exactly what it likes with it" (218 a).

The reciprocality of love, "to love is to want to be loved," defines for Lacan the essentially narcissistic character of love; the lover's ideal image of himself is enhanced and secured insofar as he is loved by the one who prompts his own desire. What, for Socrates, is this ideal image? Precisely that of the master who has access to the truth. That is, the subject who's supposed to know. For Socrates, to be loved, which he deceptively calls having a beloved, is to be granted the status of the one who moves in the element of the soul—truth, wisdom, the eternal, the divine. His *practice* as a philosopher depends upon it. This practice takes the form of education, the process of introducing the beloved into a discourse, fathered by the master, that will eventually lead him to be a philosopher too. It is in this sense then that Socrates wants to present himself as a model with which the beloved can identify. And, to complete the opposition that operates here, the beloved is a kind of servant, reduced at the extreme in Socrates' description to the body that attracts the philosopher-lover and so launches the latter's journey toward the vision that will transcend the material world altogether.

To this point, I have tried to reconcile the critical force of the deconstructive reading with the initial results produced by considering psychoanalysis as a materialist rewriting of the idealist discourse on love. The critical force of deconstruction assuredly lies in its power to disorient and dismantle the philosophical text by tracing the entire series of concepts that owe their existence to a system of presuppositions and values that the text avoids questioning. These presuppositions and values, which are presented by the philosophical text as virtually self-evident, do not, however, arise spontaneously. Even a *pre*supposition already reflects and responds to a particular formation.

Jean-Joseph Goux, in an important work entitled *Économie et Symbolique*, has broached the question of the relation between the metaphysics of presence and the social formations with which it coincides in the West. What follows concerns the relation of Platonic philosophy to the organization of the first form of Western class society:

> Whereas money, as we know since Marx, is objectively only the completed *reflection*, attached to a special commodity, of the relation of all the other commodities, the ideological perception tied to the *fetishism of money* inverts the meaning of this reflection. It makes commodities a simple reflection of the money-form.... In a general manner, the relation between the Platonic Forms (model, ideal standard) and the sensible world is a philosophical corollary, at once faithful and displaced, of the relation, as perceived by the dominant ideology, between the fetishized general equivalents and the relative forms.... The fetishism of the general equivalent not only has, for its effect and cause, the effacement of the genesis of its institution, but it also leads to a decisive reversal between matter and reflection which is at the foundation of idealism. This reversal is the effect of a class perspective: Plato perceives the relations between the universal equivalent and the relative form *from* the universal equivalent, that is, from the perspective of the class holding economic and political power.... For the laboring class, which produces commodities, the relations between general equivalent and

relative form are, to the contrary, perceived from that relative form; money, or the idea, is but the reflection of material reality. [26]

If Socrates' discourse corresponds to the structure of the earliest form of Western class society, the problem that compels our attention has to do with the process by which he assumes that discourse. Our analysis of the *Symposium* thus far would permit an initial formulation: Socrates is secure in his position as a philosophical subject so long as it sustains his ideal image. Such a formulation follows the lead established by Althusser's "Ideology and Ideological State Apparatuses," which connects the subject's imaginary identification with an image (the self) to his ideologically distorted relation to social reality:

> all ideology represents in its necessarily imaginary distortion not the existing relations of production ..., but above all the (imaginary) relationship of individuals to the relations of production and the relations that derive from them. What is represented in ideology is therefore not the system of real relations which govern the existence of individuals, but the imaginary relation of those individuals to the real relations in which they live. [27]

Our reading also makes clear, however, two other points the neglect of which would severely limit the import of this basic formulation: (1) that Socrates arrives at this position only by passing through the paths of desire, and (2) that he can hold firm in this position only if another, the beloved, affirms that he is there. Socrates himself denies both of these necessities at the very moment they make themselves felt. His ironic pose of disinterest in the beloved not only devalues the beloved's beauty but also presents Socrates as the master of his own desire; indeed, his desire lies hidden behind the image of the master just as, in his philosophical argument, the function of the a-object as cause of desire is hidden behind the image of ultimate harmony and oneness. Secondly, Socrates denies the necessity of being loved by the other at the very moment he fixes

---

[26] Jean-Joseph Goux, "Économie monétaire et philosophie idéaliste," in *Économie et symbolique* (Paris: Seuil, 1973), pp. 181-182.

[27] *Lenin and Philosophy*, pp. 164-165.

the relation in which, as lover, he wants to be loved: "It's the truth you find unanswerable, not Socrates." As a philosopher, Socrates must search elsewhere for the *philosophical* support of his position as a subject who pronounces a philosophical discourse. To delineate the function of this "elsewhere," we will have to consider another aspect of the metaphysics of presence and determine the role that psychoanalysis may have in its overthrow.

The scope of Derrida's critique makes it possible to define the conceptual system that has dominated Western philosophy in terms of three interdependent components: the presupposition of presence, the logic of identity by means of which the philosophical discourse seeks to eliminate or resolve all contradiction, and the reference to a transcendental subject as the guarantee of truth, metaphysics having given different names to this subject—the One, God, Spirit, the transcendental ego. For Plato, as for Descartes and Hegel in different ways, this transcendental subjectivity at first has an identity distinct from that of the philosopher. The philosopher's discourse does not, by itself, make the truth its own from the beginning. Truth lies elsewhere, already in the possession of some transcendental Other. The existence of this Other guarantees the truth of the philosophical discourse, and the Other's own self-identity, or presence, guarantees the philosopher's eventual identity with it. This promised unity of the philosophical subject with the transcendental Other would abolish otherness altogether. Let us cite once again Diotima's image of this absorption of the subject in the Other:

> Nor will his vision of the beautiful take the form of a face, or of hands, or of anything that is of the flesh. It will be neither words nor knowledge, nor a something that exists in something else, such as a living creature, or the earth, or the heavens, or anything that is — but subsisting of itself and by itself in an eternal oneness, while every lovely thing that partakes of it in such sort that, however much the parts may wax and wane, it will be neither more nor less, but still the same inviolable whole (211 a, b).

The divine oneness serves to define the endeavor of philosophy itself and orients it toward an escape from the effects of materiality, the body, difference, language, and contradiction, all of which can be superseded because they are no more than divisions and derivatives of the One.

Derrida alludes to this function of the transcendental Other whenever he points up the profound complicity that joins Western philosophy to theology, the obligatory reference that metaphysics makes, whether explicitly or tacitly, to the existence of God. This question, however, usually remains subordinate, perhaps because Derrida's most systematic interrogation of the transcendental subject is directed against Husserlian phenomenology, where the Other produced by the Cartesian cogito is itself denied and the philosophical subject, from the first moment of his reflection, stands in the position of the transcendental ego. In *La voix et le phénomène* the emphasis falls, therefore, on the presupposition of presence and the logic of identity. The strategy behind this procedure is to challenge Husserlian phenomenology on the terrain of its own most basic principles. It is a subversion rather than a frontal attack. Husserl defines, with unprecedented rigor, the conditions under which the transcendental ego can be maintained; it must produce a discourse that entertains no presuppositions and remains free from all contradiction. Derrida shows that the founding moment of pure phenomenology contains a presupposition and so is in contradiction with itself. In the *Cartesian Meditations,* for example, Husserl's very definition of the apodictic evidence that is to guide the presuppositionless philosophy rests on a presupposition, the presupposition of *presence.* As the temporal condition of consciousnes:

> [In transcendental self-experience] the ego is accessible to himself originaliter. But at any particular time this experience offers only a core that is experienced "with strict adequacy," namely the ego's living present (which the grammatical sense of the sentence *ego cogito,* expresses). [28]

And as the immediate presence of what transcendental consciousness intuits:

---

[28] Edmund Husserl, *Cartesian Meditations: An Introduction to Phenomenoloy,* trans., Dorion Cairns (The Hague: Martinus Nijhoff, 1960), pp. 22-23.

We remain aloof from all that [the failings of Descartes], if we remain true to the radicalness of our meditative self-examination and therefore to the principle of pure "intuition" or evidence — that is to say, if we accept nothing here but what we find actually given (and, at first, quite immediately) in the field of the *ego cogito,* which has been opened up to us by epoché, and if accordingly we assert nothing we ourselves do not "see." [29]

La voix et le phénomène shows that this contradiction between the founding principle of pure phenomenology and its inaugural moment inhabits its entire conceptual system. It is as though Husserl's texts are traversed by a crack, or fault, produced by the stress of their own effort to sustain logical rigor and yet not violate the presupposition of presence. A gap thereby opens between what is supposed to be the pure content of transcendental consciousness and the structure and effects of the discourse it ostensibly pronounces—a breach, that is, between the signified (as phenomenology wants to conceive it) and the signifier. The transcendental ego falls apart in turn, since its very possibility is defined as the position of conscious mastery over the discourse. It becomes, then, not the locus of truth, the pure consciousness of what is apodictically present before it in the living present, but a hypothesis or fiction. The transcendental ego is a product of the text and not, as Husserl wants to show, a consciousness that oversees the meaning of a discourse that it pronounces simply in order to put into language a content already fully realized. This second determination of the relation between consciousness and the text is the one that Husserl sets out not only to formulate but also to enact. It is what he wanted to write. What Derrida reads is a text whose internal divisions destroy the position of the transcendental ego.

It is, then, the philosophical subject's own entanglement with the process of writing that poses the greatest threat to the metaphysics of presence. The Husserlian conception of the relation that consciousness has to meaning and to language serves to block the recognition that the philosophical discourse is irreducibly a text;

[29] *Ibid.,* p. 24.

it views language as no more than the contingent form (signifier) through which the content (transcendental signified) of consciousness is communicated, communication itself being an option not a necessity for the philosophical ego. Like Plato and the whole philosophico-theological tradition, Husserl places writing in opposition to the voice or speech as its mere derivative, an inessential repetition of the spoken word. Writing is the signifier of a signifier and so at an unbridgeable distance from the transcendental signified or concept. "Writing" can then be given a double mark as the work of deconstruction takes it up, breaking the hierarchical system that reduces it to a secondary status and so releasing its force as a concept that affirms the primacy of the signifier over the signified, of textuality over consciousness.

Now, Lacan's point of departure is different than that of Derrida but it no less effectively demolishes the Husserlian conception of speech and the subject's relation to the signifier. Lacan turns to the concept of the Other in order to account for three interrelated scenes of communication in which the subject is determined by the signifier: normative linguistic exchange, the dream, and the infant's relation to the mother.

The ordinary spoken discourse exchanged by two subjects has as its ideal norm what Chomsky calls the "immediately comprehensible utterance" or "well-formed sentence." This norm implies that the speaking subject oversees the meaning of his own utterance and understands it at the very moment he proffers it. Husserl turns this hypothetical norm into the model of the subject's relation to discourse, arguing that speech is nothing more than the act of making available to others a meaning that is already constituted in the self, silently and without any necessary recourse to language. This reduction of language stems from the view that speech is simply the dual relation between self and other and that meaning is grasped in consciousness independent of the signifiers that are its vehicle. The signifier is at the subject's disposal but in no way determines subjectivity. Even the linguistic "science" of Saussure falls prey to this metaphysical trap, as Derrida has demonstrated, when it upholds the so-called unity of the sign, the unbreakable link between signified and signifier. [30] To combat this error, Lacan puts a great deal of weight on another aspect of the linguistic theory of Saussure, Hjemlslev, and Jakobson, namely, the discovery that the constituent element of language is the phoneme (or "figura" or "bundle of differences"). The phoneme is a signifier without a signified, the signified being but the effect of the combination and interaction of signifiers.

If the linguistic system, at bottom, is not a collection of signs (signifier/signified) but a collection of signifiers, our description of verbal communication changes drastically. While the participants are positioned in a dual relation in the sense that each is alternately the sender or receiver of the message, they both have recourse to another place or locus from which they draw the signifiers of their utterances and to which they refer to comprehend one another's statements. [31] The most basic linguistic exchange, then, involves more than the dual relation of two subjects, since the very act of speaking or listening puts them in relation to a third. This third, however, is not another subject; it is not a subjective *position* comparable to those occupied by sender and receiver but is rather the *place (lieu)* where the collection of signifiers is already constituted prior to any subject's entry into the speech act. Lacan calls this third, this other scene that makes the scene of communication possible, the Other, designating with the capital "O" a radical degree of otherness that is anterior to any speech relation between the subject and another.

Lacan's frequent use of the phrase "the other scene" does more than allude to Freud's passing remark that the unconscious might

[30] Cf., Derrida, *De la grammatologie* (Paris: Minuit, 1967), pp. 46-50.

[31] For example, in explaining his "graph of desire" in "Subversion du sujet et dialectique du désir dans l'inconscient freudien," Lacan writes: "I will save you some steps by giving you right off the function of the two cross-over points. The one, marked A, is the locus of the treasure of the signifier, which does not mean the code, for it is not that the univocal correspondance of the sign to something is preserved in this locus, but rather that the signifier is constituted by a synchronic and countable collection in which no signifier is sustained except by the principle of its opposition to each of the others." *Écrits*, p. 806.

be called "ein anderer Schauplatz." It gives this formula the scope of a rigorous theoretical concept that links the subject's relation to language with the effects of the unconscious. As we have already seen, the *Interpretation of Dreams* established that the dream articulates a wish or desire and that the unconscious is a network of signifying elements that refer to other signifying elements. As a result, psychoanalytic interpretation does not seek to restore a hidden center of meaning or some original signified but rather reconstitutes the process of the dream's production. The subject through whom this discourse is produced and whose desire it articulates at first *receives* his own message. And, insofar as the dream has undergone distortion, it articulates a desire that the subject does not recognize or assume as his own. This primacy of the signifier over the subject leads Lacan to call the dream and, by extension, the unconscious, "the discourse of the Other." The dream, because the subject experiences in it the effects of discourse long before he learns the language spoken by those around him, permits us to grasp the subject's relation to the signifier in a far more radical way than does any model derived from normative verbal communication. In the dream the subject, far from seeming to oversee the meaning of his own utterance, confronts his message as coming from the Other. The pure subject of the unconscious, the subject who desires, is thus the effect of the discourse of the Other. In this way, basic categories of linguistic theory can be brought into touch with Freud's discovery of the unconscious and kept from being appropriated by any philosophical position which, like Husserl's, gives primacy and autonomy to the relation between consciousness and the transcendental signified: "What is omitted in the banal formulae of modern information theory is that one cannot even speak of a code unless it is already the code of the Other; now, the message is another matter, since it is from the message that the subject is constituted, from which it follows that the subject receives from the Other the very message he sends." [32]

[32] *Ibid.*, p. 807.

We have already seen how the primordial relation of the subject to the signifier emerges from the processes that govern the infant's relation to others—the dialectic of need, the request for love, and desire. This dialectic institutes a fundamental split in the subject's relation to the signifier. The request represents the subject's elementary attempt to construct a message, but in answering this request the mother crushes it, obliterating the subject's effort to enter into a speech relation with her. The sleep of the satiated infant is a condition in which, having faded from his position as a subject who signifies, he dreams and so confronts his own desire as a message coming from the Other. There is, then, an incommensurability between the signifying process that constitutes the subject as a desiring subject and the activity by which he may become a signifying subject. And since the first of these relations of the subject to the signifier is primary—the subject being unable at first to integrate the unconscious signifier of desire into the request—we might formulate this split in the language of Derrida's deconstruction of metaphysics and say that the subject is written before he speaks.

The primacy that psychoanalytic theory accords to the signifier, in the genesis of desire and in the constitution of the subject out of his relation to the Other, also serves to establish the primacy of the material and the social. On the one hand, because the signifying flux that comprises the unconscious is inseparable from the erotogenic zones of the body: "the place of the Other may not be grasped except in the body." [33] And, on the other hand, because the production of desire results from the interaction of the subject's body with the material objects brought to it and taken from it through the socially organized practices of those who care for the child.

Inasmuch as the mother plays a primary role in this process Lacan says that she is "the first real representative of the Other." His analysis of the castration complex develops in terms of the child's relation to the mother and the dialectic of need, the request, and desire. The genitals emerge as a foremost zone of sexual excitation and masturbatory enjoyment at a time when the child is trying

[33] "La logique du fantasme," (pamphlet, n. d.).

to decipher the cultural and social order in which it lives—the significance of kinship relations, sexual reproduction, the difference of the sexes, the contradictions affecting forbidden and permitted desires, and so on. Because the erect penis is the visible evidence, on the body, of desire, the phallus becomes the signifying mark of desire. Moreover, the alternative of the presence/absence of the penis functions as a differential mark that distinguishes the sexes, and this organ gives the child an initial insight into the nature of copulation and generation. However, what gives the phallus its privileged role in the psychic economy is that all aspects of desire are manifested in it. In the dialectic of desire as we have described it thus far, an unconscious signifier is inscribed on one side as the real object giving rise to it is lost on the other. The phallus is *at once* the signifying mark of desire and the symbol for object loss, since it derives its signifying function from the very possibility of its disappearance or absence: "It can only play its role veiled, that is, as itself the sign of the hiddenness with which anything signifiable is struck as soon as it it raised *(aufgehoben)* to the function of a signifier. The phallus is the signifier of this *Aufhebung* itself, which it inaugurates (initiates) by its disappearance." [34] Secondly, the interdiction against masturbation removes the real organ as a source of autoerotic enjoyment: "the interdiction against autoerotism, bearing on a particular organ, which for that very reason acquires the value of an ultimate (or first) symbol of lack *(manque),* has the impact of pivotal experience." [35] The other key moment in the dialectic of desire is the "fading of the subject" which accompanies the first "experiences of satisfaction" in the form of falling asleep and which Freud more generally identified in his definition of pleasure as the effect of the discharge of psychical energy. Because the detumescence of the penis inevitably coincides with genital gratification, the phallus serves as a figure for this fading, the already ambivalent meaning of which (satisfaction/crushing of the request)

[34] La signification du phallus," p. 692.
[35] "Pour une logique du fantasme," *Scilicet,* 2/3 (1970), p. 259. It should be noted that this extremely important essay is the product of an anonymous transcription of parts of Lacan's fourteenth seminar.

is now inserted into the castration complex to the degree that the alternation between erection and detumescence reiterates the alternative of the presence/absence of the penis. [36]

As we have seen, the subject's primordial relation to the Other makes it impossible for him to fully integrate the signifier of his desire into the request for love and so forces him to seek that signifier in the Other. The relation to the mother undergoes a profound change when the phallus emerges as the privileged signifier of desire. The maternal body becomes the actual terrain of the castration complex, the place where the subject searches for the phallus. The incest prohibition plays its role here as well. The child has already experienced its effects to the extent that it regulates the satisfactions that the parents provide and withhold. What the incest taboo forbids is that the mother-child relation be a self-enclosed circuit of desire. The subject, therefore, must make two discoveries: not only that the mother does not *have* the signifier of his desire, but also that he cannot *be* the signifier of her desire. In other words, he must face the impossibility of fully merging desire and the request for love; his attempt to integrate the signifier of desire (the phallus) into his request for the mother's love would require that her love make him the signifier of her own desire. That is, the subject desires the desire of the Other:

The request for love can only suffer from a desire whose signifier is alien to it. If the mother's desire *is* the phallus, the child wants to be the phallus in order to satisfy that desire. In this way the division inherent in desire already makes itself felt in being experienced in the desire of the Other; this division already stands in the way of the subject's being satisfied with presenting to the Other what he may actually *have* which corresponds to this phallus, since what he has counts for no more than what he does not have as far as his request for love is concerned, which would have him be the phallus.

Clinical practice shows us that this ordeal with the desire of the Other is decisive not insofar as the subject learns from it whether or not he has a real phallus but insofar as he learns that the mother does not. [37]

[36] Cf., Guy Rosolato, "La différence des sexes," in *Essais sur le symbolique* (Paris: Gallimard, 1969), p. 16.
[37] "La signification du phallus," p. 692.

John Brenkman

The castration complex, then, hinges on the recognition that the phallic signifier is missing from the material discourse that defines the subject's relation to the Other; its lack is to be discovered in the maternal body to the extent that the mother initially represents the Other.

The Other that philosophical discourse installs is intended to stand above the effects of the signifier. It transcends the philosopher's discourse, which it supposedly precedes and reabsorbs; moreover, it is beyond the touch of the material signifier that is inscribed in the social and unconscious networks that produce the human subject and make possible his entry into discourse as a subject who signifies. If the philosopher is to write or pronounce the metaphysical discourse he must deny the discourse that produces him. That is, he must guard against recognizing the material discourse of the Other in order to put in place the transcendental Other whose existence would guarantee the truth of his own discourse. The antagonism that separates the psychoanalytic conception of the Other from the philosophical is more than that between two contending perspectives. If that were the case psychoanalysis would be no more than the materialist reversal of the idealism that dominates Western philosophy. The psychoanalytic theory of the subject's relation to the Other can also act as a dialectical account of the very process that brings about the philosophical conception of the Other. By means of what operation is philosophy able to refuse to recognize the Other as the social and unconscious processes of matter and so let it appear as a transcendental subject in possession of the truth? Lacan's response: by removing the signifying mark from the Other, an erasure that works "in a manner analogous" to the denial that the mother is castrated: "Philosophy..., once it has marked itself in writing, consists in simultaneously striking any mark from the Other, thereby presenting it as unaffected by the mark." [38]

I want now to argue that the relation indicated by Lacan is more than an analogy. The metaphysical discourse forms itself around the

[38] "Pour une logique du fantasme," pp. 238-239.

refusal to recognize the materiality of discourse and the primacy of the signifier. The philosophical subject could not assume his proper place within this discourse unless the structure of subjectivity already contained, as a possibility, a position that allows the subject to deny that the Other from which he draws his relation to the signifier "is itself already divided by the signifying *Spaltung*."[39] The unconscious denial that the maternal body is inscribed with the mark of castration is, therefore, the precondition, at the level of the subject, for the philosophical exclusion or suppression of the maternal, the body, and the signifying mark.

This relation between the denial of castration and philosophical discourse acquires a specifically social dimension when viewed from the standpoint of the subject's history. It allows us to glimpse how an unconscious formation can, with the help of the educational process that intervenes during latency, be fitted to the exigencies of an existing social and ideological order. The denial that the mother is castrated is an always virtual moment in the structure of the subject's earliest relation to the Other—that is, in the structure of the unconscious—which can then serve to insert the subject within the general ideological discourse of a particular class society and sustain him there as a subject who (re)produces a discourse that legitimates the existing social hierarchy, its relations of production and modes of domination. When this subject is a philosopher his mission is precisely to secure the illusion that this ideological discourse has a privileged connection with truth.

The problem we have just broached has occupied the Marxist theory of ideology from Engels' "Ludwig Feuerbach and the End of Classical German Philosophy" to Althusser's "Ideology and Ideological State Apparatuses." As Goux has shown, there exists a complicity between the philosophical system of Platonic idealism and the social formations of class society. The former "reflects" the latter and gives it legitimacy. The notion of "reflection," however, maps out the problem rather than the solution in that it indicates

---

[39] "La signification du phallus," p. 693.

John Brenkman

the relation between the socio-economic base and the superstructure but does not yet fully account for the process by which they are tied to one another. Jean-Louis Houdebine, writing on Lenin, has pinpointed the problem that our commentary on Lacan must approach:

> In a general manner, one can say that the discovery of a "reflection," at whatever level this operation is performed, always points out that an articulated link exists between at least two systems of relations; the notion of *reflection* functions then as an index (signal) of this articulated link. But when it comes to thinking this articulation as such, that is, of passing from the stage of merely indicating it to the stage where this articulation will be effectively *known* ..., in particular the dialectical mode of the transformations from one system of relations to the other and the logic proper to each of these systems — then only the concept of *process* proves to be genuinely operative, that is, capable of producing the knowledge of such a link. [40]

The very recognition that the superstructure is composed of "systems of relations" remained clouded and imprecise until linguistics and semiology emerged as analytical instruments applicable to ideological and cultural formations. Lévi-Strauss' studies of mythic thought and symbolic exchange in primitive societies, Barthes' analysis of the cultural products and practices of consumer society as a specific mode of semiological connotation, and Derrida's deconstructive reading of philosophy, which treats "concepts" not as instances of consciousness grasping truth or reality but as elements within a textual process—all of these researches have made it possible to consider "ideology" as discourse or semiological operation or text. Lévi-Straus explicitly defines the task of structural anthropology as a contribution to historical materialism:

> Without questioning the undoubted primacy of infrastructures, I believe that there is always a mediator between *praxis* and practices, namely the conceptual scheme by the operation of which matter and form, neither with any independent existence, are realized as structures, that is as entities which are both empirical and intelligible. It is to this theory of super-

[40] Jean-Louis Houdebine, "Sur une lecture de Lénine," in *Théorie d'ensemble*, ed., *Tel Quel* (Paris: Seuil, 1968), pp. 294-295.

structures, scarcely touched on by Marx, that I hope to make a contribution. . . .

All I claim to have shown so far is, therefore, that the dialectic of the superstructure, like that of language, consists in setting up *constitutive units* (which, for this purpose, have to be defined unequivocally, that is by contrasting them in pairs) so as to be able by means of them to elaborate a system which plays the part of synthesizing operator between ideas and facts, thereby turning the latter into signs. [41]

The problem posed by Houdebine bears, then, on the process that links an ideological discourse to the social relations of economic production and exchange. That the analysis of this process must come to terms with the question of the subject is already apparent in Engels' work on ideology. For example, at a point where he is establishing the relation of the state (superstructure) to civil society (infrastructure) he draws on the model of the material forces that determine a subject's action: "As all the driving forces of the actions of any individual person must pass through his brain, and transform themselves into motives of his will in order to set him into action, so also the needs of civil society—no matter which class happens to be the ruling one—must pass through the will of the state in order to secure general validity in the forms of laws." [42] The difficulty of specifying the process by which material forces come to be reflected in consciousness haunts the entire fourth section of "Ludwig Feuerbach and the End of Classical German Philosophy." The question must find a more rigorous form as soon as we recognize that these "reflections" in "consciousness" are so many semiological or textual operations into which a subject enters, as sender or receiver, in such a way as to allow an existing set of relations of production and exchange to be reproduced through him. Restated, the question becomes: By means of what process does matter become meaning?

[41] Claude Lévi-Strauss, *The Savage Mind* (Chicago: University of Chicago Press, 1966), pp. 130-131.

[42] Frederick Engels, *Ludwig Feuerbach and the End of Classical German Philosophy,* in Marx and Engels, *Selected Works* (New York: International Publishers, 1968), p. 626.

John Brenkman

With its materialist theory of the signifier and the subject, psychoanalysis has precisely discovered that, at the base, the unconscious is that through which matter passes in order to become the signifying network that engenders the subject and founds his relation to discourse in general. It is here, then, that we may locate a point of intersection between psychoanalysis and dialectical-historical materialism. The kind of investigation called for would have as its task to determine the specific modes of interaction between the unconscious discourse that engenders the subject and the various discourses in which a particular society's ideological formations reside. [43]

The example at hand may seem limiting in that it connects a particular moment in the subject's relation to the Other, the denial that the mother is castrated, with the most refined of ideological practices, the philosophical text. By the same token, however, the very fact that philosophy stands at such a distance from the socio-

---

[43] The most important work in this direction has undoubtedly been that of Julia Kristeva. See in particular *La révolution du langage poétique* (Paris: Seuil, 1974); "Le sujet en procès," *Tel Quel* 52 (1972), pp. 12-30 and *Tel Quel* 53 (1973), pp. 17-38; "Matière, sens, dialectique," *Tel Quel* 44 (1971), pp. 17-34. I have not taken up an explicit commentary here on Althusser's discussion of ideology and the subject because it would require a careful and critical examination of his concept of the subject. In spite of the allusions to Lacan, Althusser does not really make use of the Lacanian theory of the subject. Failing to take into account Lacan's concept of the division or splitting of the subject, Althusser reduces the "subject" to the Freudian ego as reformulated in Lacan's theory of the mirror stage, that is, to a system of misrecognitions and imaginary identifications. He then makes a complete separation between the "subject" (imaginary identifications) and the "concrete individual." A critical study of this misguided importation of Lacanian psychoanalysis into a supposedly Marxist theory of ideology would, I think, eventually touch on other central formulations in Althusser, especially the elision of the subject from the processes of history and from scientific discourse. My own purpose in this study is to shift the discussion of ideology and the subject away from a narrow consideration of the subject's imaginary identifications, beginning instead with the more fundamental psychoanalytic problematic, namely, the subject's relation to the signifier and to the Other. It is worth noting that earlier, purely structuralist analyses of ideological formations have been led to introduce the question of the subject, particularly at those points where it becomes necessary to interrogate the *effectiveness* of the ideological discourse. Thus, for example, Lévi-Strauss, "The Effectiveness of Symbols," in *Structural Anthropology,* trans. Claire Jacobson and Brooke Grundfest Schoepf (Garden City, N. Y.: Anchor, 1967), pp. 181-201, and Roland Barthes, *Mythologies,* trans. Annette Lavers (New York: Hill and Wang, 1972), pp. 124-125.

economic base would actually define the general import of outlining in terms of Plato's text the interrelation of society, ideology, and the unconscious. That a critical reading of Plato is still relevant to the ideological struggle is itself a sign of what Marxism has called the relative autonomy of the superstructure, especially religion and philosophy, and its tendency to develop unevenly in relation to the infrastructure. This too deserves restatement. It seems to me that Derrida's work furnishes the possibility of a more rigorous model. If Western philosophy since Plato constitutes the era or epoch of the metaphysics of presence, that era, with its own more or less coherent system, coincides, at the superstructural level, with the era of Western class societies. It is against the background of this extensive span of our social and cultural history that the more highly differentiated analyses demanded by Marxism would have to be organized.

Throughout Lacan's analysis of philosophical writing and the operations it performs with respect to the Other, he has in mind Descartes since the certitude that the Cartesian *cogito* promises the philosophical subject ultimately depends upon the existence of God. [44] I want to bring the question back to Plato in order to collate the reading of the *Symposium* that Lacan has initiated with the problematics that concern "Pour une logique du fantasme." More-over, the Platonic text, which itself makes the theory of desire go hand in hand with the foundations of the metaphysics of presence, includes two moments that serve as evidence for the actual connection between the unconscious denial that the mother is castrated and the philosophical presentation of the Other as unmarked and as a "subject who's supposed to know."

As we have seen, Socrates gives meaning to the enterprise of philosophy by pointing to an eternal oneness in which the philosopher may participate. Socrates secures the primacy of the spiritual One, and with it the suppression of materiality, difference, and language, not simply by denying the maternal as such but by assimilating it to the paternal. He removes maternity from the

[44] Cf., *Le Séminaire, Livre XI*, pp. 204-205.

effects of materiality and the signifying mark. Diotima's discourse turns on this elevation of the maternal. At the very moment that she seems innocently enough to draw on the metaphorical resonances of biological reproduction in order to designate the production and reproduction of knowledge, she in fact makes maternity slide from the material realm to the spiritual realm:

Well then, she went on, those whose procreancy is of the body turn to woman as the object of their love, and raise a family, in the blessed hope that by doing so they will keep their memory green, "through time and eternity." But those whose procreancy is of the spirit rather than of the flesh — and they are not unknown, Socrates — *conceive and bear* the things of the spirit. And what are they? you ask. Wisdom and all her sister virtues (208 e - 209 a).

Having given himself to the pursuit of wisdom, the philosopher-lover sets about to reproduce that wisdom through his relation with another—the beloved: "And if any man is so closely allied with the divine as to be teeming with these virtues even in his youth, and if, when he comes to manhood, his first ambition is to be begetting, he too, you may be sure, will go about in search of the loveliness—and never the ugliness—on which he may beget" (209 b). In this act of spiritual procreation, that is, education as the reproduction of wisdom and virtue, the philosophical subject is at once mother and father. Maternity has become absorbed within paternity:

And, as I believe, by constant association with so much beauty, and by thinking of his friend when he is present and when he is away, he will be delivered of the burden he has labored under all these years. And what is more, he and his friend will help each other rear the issue of their friendship — and so the bond between them will be more binding, and their communion even more complete, than that which comes of bringing children up, because they have created something lovelier and less mortal than human seed.

And I ask you, who would not prefer such fatherhood to merely human propagation...? (209 c).

There is a kind of Platonic *Aufhebung* at work here. When the philosophical subject enters the realm of spiritual reproduction, taking as his beloved not a woman but a youth to be educated, the maternal is cancelled and transcended by the paternal and yet conserved within it.

The phallocentrism of the Socratic theory of desire stems from the operation of this *Aufhebung*. Not because the *Aufhebung* draws attention to the phallus but, on the contrary, because it acts to avoid any reference to the phallic function—that is, to the crucial moment in the castration complex where the subject is faced with recognizing and/or denying that the mother is castrated. Since the phallus acquires its function as a signifier only by disappearing, the very elision of any reference to it recapitulates, at the level of the philosophical discourse, the denial of castration at the level of the unconscious discourse. It is for this reason, we might conjecture, that Lacan has seen in the castration complex the crucial point of divergence between Freud and Plato: "Castration is the altogether new motive force that Freud has introduced into desire, giving to the lack in desire the meaning that remains enigmatic in the dialectic of Socartes, although conserved in the account of the Symposium." [45] Even though Socrates defines desire as a lack, as the failure-to-have or the failure-to-be: "And therefore, whoever feels a want is wanting something which is not yet to hand, and the object of his love is whatever he isn't, or whatever he hasn't got" (200 e); he must present this lack as a lack to be filled and so abolished. In the scheme of Platonic idealism, love is merely the path along which the philosopher presses his way toward the vision of fullness, and the journey itself gets under way with the *Aufhebung* of the maternal.

In the formations of the unconscious the phallocentric moment lies in the subject's identification with the phallus as signifier of the Other's desire, an identification that protects him from recognizing that the mother is castrated—that is, that she does not have and he cannot be the signifier of her desire:

The entire problem of the perversions consists in conceiving how the child, in his relation to the mother, a relation constituted in analysis not

[45] "Du 'Trieb' de Freud," p. 853.

by his vital dependence but by his dependence on her love, that is, the desire of her desire, identifies with the imaginary object of this desire inasmuch as the mother herself symbolizes it in the phallus.

The phallocentrism produced by this dialectic is what we want to retain for now. It is, of course, wholly conditioned by the intrusion of the signifier into the psyche of man.[46]

The discourse on desire moves toward phallocentrism not in promoting the phallus to a central role in the theory of desire but in suppressing it. The force of this apparent paradox helps to explain the disarray that has inflicted discussions of the castration complex, from the controversies within the psychoanalytic movement in Freud's time up to the polemics of those who are now trying to gauge the importance of Lacan's interpretation of Freud. It is not surprising that the key element of a theory that shattered the idealist conception of subjectivity should have been attacked as soon as it emerged and remain embattled today. Nor will it be surprising, given the dominance that idealism and the metaphysics of presence in general have exercised throughout the history of Western culture, if the forms of resistance of which it is capable not only define the strategies of its allies but also infiltrate the discourses of its most radical opponents.

Psychoanalysis sets itself apart from Platonic idealism by discovering that the phallus is the signifier of the lack inherent in desire, whether as the failure to have the phallus—in the form of a threat for the little boy, nostalgia for the little girl—or as the failure to be the phallus in the relation of both sexes to the mother. While Socrates introduces the notion of lack, he also, as we have seen, rejects Aristophanes' myth. Aristophanes' speech touches on two aspects of desire that Socrates/ Diotima must keep out of their discourse. It approaches, in however mythifying a way, the question of sexual difference, and secondly it suggests that love is a perpetual seeking after a substitute for something irretrievably lost. The second of these implications in Aristophanes' speech is unacceptable to Socrates on two levels. First, as Diotima's argument suggests,

---

[46] "D'une question préliminaire . . . ," pp. 554-555.

the concept of substitution has no place in a theory of desire that looks forward to complete fulfillment, the ultimate appropriation of the good. Secondly, if we follow Lacan's argument that Aristophanes' story amounts to a philosophico-mythical misinterpretation of the structure of primordial loss and interminable substitution, then we can say that Socrates must refuse to connect the lack inherent in desire with the primordial loss of the object. With this refusal Socrates effectively precludes any reference to the phallus, since the phallic signifier marks just this connection between desire as lack and the primordial object loss that is the cause of desire.

This does not mean that the phallus plays no role in the *Symposium*. It is true that Socrates' discourse forms itself around the suppression of the phallic signifier and that the organization of Plato's text seems to give precedence to this discourse; nevertheless, Socratic speech is not the only voice engendered by Platonic writing. Alcibiades' intrusion not only interrupts Socrates' seduction of Agathon but at the same time disrupts his philosophical speaking as such. This disruption can be read in two ways, with restraint or without restraint. The restrained reading, encouraged by the narrative's organization, would relegate Alcibiades' discourse to a secondary status within a well known set of oppositions: his remarks can easily be viewed as anecdotal rather than philosophical, comic rather than serious, drunken rather than sober, bodily rather than spiritual. The narrative structure of the *Symposium,* its presentation as a second-hand account, further underscores this devaluation of Alcibiades' discourse by helping to explain away the failure of Socrates' speech to maintain its central and triumphant position in the dialogue. Alcibiades, according to this reading, provides a mere side-show on the margins of philosophy. His role is part of the *Symposium*'s entertainment but not its meaning. The unrestrained reading is suggested by Lacan and allows us to calculate the actual damage done to Socratic philosophy by Alcibiades. For Lacan, Alcibiades reintroduces the effects of the phallus into a discourse which, as I have tried to show, denies the phallus in order to secure its philosophical coherence. Let us reset the stage for this reading of Alcibiades' side-show. In "La signification du phallus," Lacan writes, without reference to Plato, that sexual relations

revolve around a being and a having which, in being related to a signifier, the phallus, have the contrary effects of giving reality to the subject in this signifier and making unreal the relations to be signified.

This through the intervention of an appearing that is substituted for having — to protect it from one side, mask the lack of it on the other side — and which has for its effect the projection of the ideal or typical manifestation of each sex's behavior ... entirely into the realm of comedy. [47]

Alcibiades draws out this comedy in the *Symposium,* the humor that disorients Socratic irony. In triggering this interplay of having, being, and appearing, he brings back on stage all that Socrates has tried to sweep away: the lack inherent in desire, the material cause of desire, the phallic signifier. Lacan, just as in general he rewrites the idealist discourse on love, retells the story of Alcibiades' eulogy of Socrates, discerning in it the return of what the Socratic dialogue represses, the a-object, and what it denies, the phallus:

The fantasy, in its structure as I define it, contains the $(-\varphi)$, the imaginary function of castration, in a hidden form that is reversible from one of its terms to the other [i.e., either the barred subject or the object in the formula of the fantasy: $\$ \diamond a$, where the diamond is read as "desire of" from either direction]. Like a complex number, the $(-\varphi)$ alternately imaginarizes (if I be permitted this term) one of those terms in relation to the other.

Included in the object a is the *agalma,* the invaluable treasure that Alcibiades proclaims is enclosed in the rough-looking box that for him forms the figure of Socrates. But let us observe that this is affected by the minus-sign. It is because he has never seen Socrates' cock — I am permitted to say so following Plato who does not spare us the details — that Alcibiades the seducer exalts in him the *agalma,* the marvel that he had wanted Socrates to yield to him by acknowledging his desire: the division of the subject that he carries in himself being acknowledged with bombast on this occasion.

Such is the woman behind her veil: the absence of the penis is what makes her the phallus, the object of desire. . . .

In pointing to his object as castrated, Alcibiades parades as desiring — this does not escape Socrates — for another of the assistants who is present, Agathon, whom Socrates, precursor of analysis and utterly con-

[47] "La signification du phallus," p. 694.

fident of himself in this fine company, does not hesitate to name as the object of the transference. [48]

This interpretation, in spite of its resemblance to psychoanalytic allegoresis, articulates what can be enacted in the *Symposium*'s drama but remains philosophically unspeakable.

While Lacan credits Socrates with identifying the transference at work in Alcibiades' performance, he does not therefore attribute any neurotic mechanism to the latter's behavior. To the contrary, "Alcibiades is by no means a neurotic. It is even because he is the desirer *par excellence* and the man who goes as far as possible in enjoyment that he can in this way ... produce, in contrast to everyone else, the central articulation of the transference, the presentation of the adorned object of his reflections." [49] There is yet another tack to be taken here. Socrates' own discourse, the dialogue that for him structures both philosophy and love, makes use of the transference. Through his dialogue Socrates attempts to induce a transference in his interlocutor. He wants to be the object of a transference love, that is, to be posed by another as the subject who's supposed to know:

The transference is unthinkable unless one grasps its starting-point in the subject who's supposed to know. . . .
What happens? What happens is what we call in its most common form the *transference effect*. This effect is love. It is clear that, like all love, it is to be located within the field of narcissism. To love is to want to be loved.
What emerges in the transference effect is opposed to the process of revealing. Love intervenes in its function, here shown to be essential, in its function of deception. Love is undoubtedly a transference effect, but it is its aspect of resistance. We are bound to await this transference effect in order to be able to interpret, and yet at the same time we know that it closes the subject off from the effect of our interpretation. [50]

As we have seen, the positioning of the philosopher-lover as the subject who is supposed to know, the ideal master, serves to block

[48] "Subversion du sujet . . . ," p. 825.
[49] *Ibid.*, pp. 825-826.
[50] *Le Séminaire, Livre XI*, pp. 228-229.

John Brenkman

any reference to the a-object, the material cause of desire. The Socratic dialectic is mobilized by the transference but in turn freezes it in the first moment of its unfolding; Socrates must sustain in the other the idealizing identification that shuts off any recognition of the a-object and with it the discourse of the unconscious if he is to organize a properly philosophical discourse. The analyst, on the other hand, must work through the dialectic of the transference in a way that opens up interpretation, that is, the laying bare of the unconscious discourse, the network of signifiers caused by the a-object. To do so, the psychoanalytic dialogue must keep separate what the Socratic dialogue would fuse and obscure: "The mainspring of the analytic operation is the preservation of the distance between the *I* [i.e., the identification centered on the ideal signifier] and the *a* [i.e., the a-object]." [51] Hiding the a-object behind the Ego Ideal, the Socratic dialogue constitutes the transferential discourse in its idealist form. The psychoanalytic dialogue, propelling itself toward the dissolution of the transference love and toward the interpretation of the unconscious, is, then, the materialist form of the transferential discourse, the practice that criticizes and overturns idealism itself.

What Alcibiades breaks up is this idealist form of the transferential discourse, itself indistinguishable from Socrates' philosophical method. The mixture of philosophy and literature long recognized as a characteristic of Plato's texts, especially the *Symposium,* here amounts to the conflict between two incommensurable discourses: the one culminating in Socrates' discussion of love, the other bursting forth with Alcibiades' arrival. The organization of the dialogue into an orderly succession of philosophical arguments, even the strategic distractions of a second-hand narration, cannot finally deflect the comic drama of desire through which Alcibiades releases the movement of the lack inherent in desire. Hence Socrates' silence when faced with Alcibiades' monologue. It is this inability of the *Symposium* to protect its idealist discourse on love from the effects of desire that makes possible the materialist read-

[51] *Ibid.,* p. 245.

ing-rewriting that we call psychoanalytic theory. In this sense, it is the force of literary writing in the *Symposium* that clears the path for psychoanalysis.

At the outset, I hesitated to formulate any kind of psychoanalytic approach to literature because this would entail the double danger of reducing the specificity of literature and short-circuiting literary theory's own struggle with philosophy. Our reading of the *Symposium* now makes it possible to argue that the psychoanalytic theory of desire emerges from the subversion that literary writing performs on the discourse of philosophy. It would undoubtedly be prudent to restrict this conclusion to the relation between Lacan and Plato. But, on the other hand, is it not possible to suggest that this kind of interaction between three modalities of writing —philosophy, literature, psychoanalytic theory—is always at work in the texts of Freud and Lacan inasmuch as their writing necessarily occurs within the intertextual network that comprises Western culture?

Barbara Johnson

The Frame of Reference: Poe, Lacan, Derrida

1. *The Purloined Preface*

A literary text which *both* analyzes itself *and* shows that it actually has neither a self nor any neutral metalanguage with which to do the analyzing, calls out irresistibly for analysis. And when that call is answered by two eminent French thinkers whose readings emit an equally paradoxical call-to-analysis of their own, the resulting triptych, in the context of the question of the act-of-reading (-literature), places *its* would-be reader in a vertiginously insecure position.

The three texts in question are Edgar A. Poe's short story *The Purloined Letter*, [1] Jacques Lacan's *Seminar on The Purloined Letter*, [2] and Jacques Derrida's reading of Lacan's reading of Poe, *The Purveyor of Truth* [*Le Facteur de la Vérité*]. [3] In all three texts, it is the *act of analysis* which seems to occupy the center of the discursive stage, and the *act of analysis of the act of analysis* which in some way disrupts that centrality. In the resulting asymmetrical, abyssal structure, no analysis—including this one—can intervene without transforming *and* repeating other elements in the sequence, which is thus not a *stable* sequence, but which nevertheless produces certain regular effects. It is the functioning of this regularity, and the structure of these effects, which will provide the basis for the present study.

---

[1] In *Great Tales and Poems of Edgar Allan Poe*, The Pocket Library, New York, 1951, hereafter designated as "Poe."

[2] In *Écrits* (Paris: Seuil, 1966). Quotations in English are taken, unless otherwise indicated, from the partial translation in *Yale French Studies* 48, *French Freud*, 1973, hereafter designated as "SPL."

[3] This article was published in French in *Poétique* 21 (1975) and, somewhat reduced, in *Yale French Studies* 52, *Graphesis*, 1975. Unless otherwise indicated, references are to the English version, hereafter designated as "PT."

The subversion of any possibility of a position of analytical mastery occurs in many ways. Here, the very fact that we are dealing with *three* texts is in no way certain. Poe's story not only fits into a triptych of its own, but is riddled with a constant, peculiar kind of intertextuality (the epigraph from Seneca which is not from Seneca, the lines from Crébillon's *Atrée* which serve as Dupin's signature, etc.). Lacan's text not only presents itself backwards (its introduction *following* its conclusion), but it never finishes presenting itself (*"Ouverture de ce recueil," "Présentation de la suite," "Présentation"* to the *Points* edition). And Derrida's text is not only preceded by several years of annunciatory marginalia and footnotes, but it is itself structured precisely by its own deferment, its *différance* (cf. the repetition of such expressions as *"Mais nous n'en sommes pas encore là,"* "But we are getting ahead of ourselves," etc.). In addition, all of these texts are characterized by an unusually high degree of apparent digressiveness, to the point of making the reader wonder whether there is really any true subject matter there at all. It is as though any attempt to follow the path of the purloined letter is automatically purloined from itself. Which is, as we shall see, just what the letter has always already been saying.

Any attempt to do "justice" to three such complex texts is obviously out of the question. But it is precisely the *nature* of such "justice" that *is* the question in each of these readings of the act of analysis. The fact that the debate proliferates around a *crime* story—a robbery and its undoing—can hardly be an accident. Somewhere in each of these texts, the economy of justice cannot be avoided. For in spite of the absence of mastery, there is no lack of *effects of power*.

As the reader goes on with this series of prefatory remarks, he may begin to see how contagious the deferment of the subject of the purloined letter can be. But the problem of how to *present* these three texts is all the more redoubtable since each of them both presents itself and the others, and clearly shows the fallacies inherent in any type of "presentation" of a text. The fact that such fallacies are not only inevitable but also *constitutive* of any act of reading—also demonstrated by each of the texts—is small comfort, since the resulting injustices, however unavoidable in general, always appear corrigible in detail. Which is why the sequence continues.

The question of how to present to the reader a text too extensive to quote in its entirety has in fact long been one of the underlying problems of literary criticism. Since a shorter version of the text must somehow be produced, two solutions constantly recur: paraphrase and quotation. Although these tactics are seldom if ever used in isolation, the specific configuration of their combinations and permutations determines to a large extent the "plot" of the critical narrative to which they give rise. The first act of our own narrative, then, will consist of an analysis of the strategic effects of the use of paraphrase vs. quotation in each of the three texts in question.

2. *Round Robbin'*

> *Round robin:* 1) A tournament in which each contestant is matched against every other contestant. 2) A petition or protest on which the signatures are arranged in the form of a circle in order to conceal the order of signing. 3) A letter sent among members of a group, often with comments added by each person in turn. 4) An extended sequence.
>
> —The American Heritage Dictionary

In 1845, Edgar A. Poe published the third of his three detective stories, "The Purloined Letter," in a collective volume entitled— ironically enough, considering all the robberies in the story—*The Gift: A Christmas, New Year, and Birthday Present.* "The Purloined Letter" is a first-person narration of two scenes in which dialogues occur among the narrator, his friend C. Auguste Dupin, and, initially, the Prefect of the Parisian police. The two scenes are separated by an indication of the passage of a month's time. In each of the two dialogues, reported to us verbatim by the narrator, one of the other two characters tells the story of a robbery:

in the first scene, it is the Prefect of Police who repeats the Queen's eyewitness account of the Minister's theft of a letter addressed to her; in the second scene, it is Dupin who narrates his *own* theft of the same letter from the Minister, who had meanwhile read-dressed it to himself. In a paragraph placed *between* these two "crime" stories, the narrator himself narrates a wordless scene in which the letter changes hands again before *his* eyes, passing from Dupin—not without the latter's having addressed not the letter but a *check* to himself—to the Prefect (who will pocket the remainder of the reward) and thence, presumably, back to the Queen.

By thus appearing to repeat to us faithfully every word in both dialogues, the narrator would seem to have resorted *exclusively* to direct quotation in presenting his story. Even when paraphrase could have been expected—in the description of the exact procedures employed by the police in searching unsuccessfully for the letter, for example,—we are spared none of the details. Thus it is all the more surprising to find that there *is* one little point at which direct quotation of the Prefect's words gives way to paraphrase. This point, however brief, is of no small importance, as we shall see. It occurs in the concluding paragraph of the first scene:

> "I have no better advice to give you," said Dupin. "You have, of course, an accurate description of the letter?"
> "Oh, yes!" — And here the Prefect, producing a memorandum-book, proceeded to read aloud a minute account of the internal, and especially of the external, appearance of the missing document. Soon after finishing the perusal of this description, he took his departure, more entirely depressed in spirits than I had ever known the good gentleman before. (Poe, pp. 206-207.)

What is paraphrased is thus the description of the letter the story is about. And, whereas it is generally supposed that the function of paraphrase is to strip off the *form* of a speech in order to give us only its *contents,* here the use of paraphrase does the very opposite: it *withholds* the contents of the Prefect's remarks, giving us *only* their form. And what is swallowed up in this ellipsis is nothing less than the contents of the letter itself. The *fact* that the letter's message is never revealed, which will serve as the basis for Lacan's reading of the story, is thus negatively made explicit by the functioning of Poe's *text* itself, through what Derrida might have called a repression of the written word (a suppression of what is written in the memorandum-book—and in the letter). And the question of the strategic use of paraphrase versus quotation begins to invade not only the critical narrative, but the literary text as well.

Lacan's presentation of Poe's text involves the paraphrase, or plot summary, of the two thefts as they are told to the narrator by the Prefect and by Dupin. Since Derrida, in his critique of Lacan, chooses to *quote* Lacan's paraphrase, we can combine all the tactics involved by, in our turn, *quoting* Derrida's quotation of Lacan's paraphrase of Poe's quoted narrations. [4]

There are two scenes, the first of which we shall straightway designate the primal scene, and by no means inadvertently, since the second may be considered its repetition in the very sense we are considering today.

The primal scene is thus performed, we are told [by neither Poe, nor the scriptor, nor the narrator, but by G, the Prefect of Police who is *mis en scène* by all those involved in the dialogues — J. D. [5]] in the royal *boudoir*, so that we suspect that the person of the highest rank, called the "exalted personage," who is alone there when she receives a letter, is the Queen. This feeling is confirmed by the embarrassment into which she is plunged by the entry of the other exalted personage, of whom we have already been told [again by G — J. D.] prior to this account that the knowledge he might have of the letter in question would jeopardize for the lady nothing less than her honor and safety. Any doubt that he is in fact the King is promptly dissipated in the course of the scene which begins with the entry of the Minister D.... At that moment, in fact, the Queen can do no better than to play on the King's inattentiveness by leaving the letter on the table "face down, address uppermost." It does not, however, escape the Minister's lynx eye, nor does he fail to notice the Queen's distress and thus to fathom her secret. From then on everything transpires like clockwork. After dealing in his customary manner with the business of the day, the Minister draws from his pocket a letter similar in appearance to the one in his view, and, having pretended

---

[4] Such a concatenation could jokingly be called, after the nursery rhyme, "This is the text that Jacques built." But in fact, it is precisely this kind of sequence or chain that is in question here.

[5] We will speak about this bracketed signature later; for the time being it stands as a sign that Derrida's signature has indeed been added to our round robin.

to read it, places it next to the other. A bit more conversation to amuse the royal company, whereupon, without flinching once, he seizes the embarrasing letter, making off with it, as the Queen, on whom none of his maneuver has been lost, remains unable to intervene for fear of attracting the attention of her royal spouse, close at her side at that very moment.

Everything might then have transpired unseen by a hypothetical spectator of an operation in which nobody falters, and whose *quotient* is that the Minister has filched from the Queen her letter and that — an even more important result than the first — the Queen knows that he now has it, and by no means innocently.

A *remainder* that no analyst will neglect, trained as he is to retain whatever is significant, without always knowing what to do with it: the letter, abandoned by the Minister, and which the Queen's hand is now free to roll into a ball.

Second scene: in the Minister's office. It is in his hotel, and we know — from the account the Prefect of Police has given Dupin, whose specific genius for solving enigmas Poe introduces here for the second time — that the police, returning there as soon as the Minister's habitual, nightly absences allow them to, have searched the hotel and its surroundings from top to bottom for the last eighteen months. In vain, — although everyone can deduce from the situation that the Minister keeps the letter within reach.

Dupin calls on the Minister. The latter receives him with studied nonchalance, affecting in his conversation romantic *ennui*. Meanwhile Dupin, whom this pretence does not deceive, his eyes protected by green glasses, proceeds to inspect the premises. When his glance catches a rather crumbled piece of paper — apparently thrust carelessly in a division of an ugly pasteboard card-rack, hanging gaudily from the middle of the mantelpiece — he already knows that he's found what he's looking for. His conviction is reinforced by the very details which seem to contradict the description he has of the stolen letter, with the exception of the format, which remains the same.

Whereupon he has but to withdraw, after "forgetting" his snuff-box on the table, in order to return the following day to reclaim it — armed with a facsimile of the letter in its present state. As an incident in the street, prepared for the proper moment, draws the Minister to the window, Dupin in turn seizes the opportunity to seize the letter while substituting the imitation, and has only to maintain the appearances of a normal exit.

Here as well all has transpired, if not without noise, at least without all commotion. The quotient of the operation is that the Minister no longer has the letter, but, far from suspecting that Dupin is the culprit who has ravished it from him, knows nothing of it. Moreover, what he is left with is far from insignificant for what follows. We shall return to what brought Dupin to inscribe a message on his counterfeit letter. Whatever the case, the Minister, when he tries to make use of it, will be able to read these words, written so that he may recognize Dupin's hand: "...Un dessein si funeste/ S'il n'est digne d'Atrée est digne de Thyeste," [6] whose source, Dupin tells us, is Crébillon's *Atrée*.

Need we emphasize the similarity of these two sequences? Yes, for the resemblance we have in mind is not a simple collection of traits chosen only in order to delete their difference. And it would not be enough to retain those common traits at the expense of the others for the slightest truth to result. It is rather the intersubjectivity in which the two actions are motivated that we wish to bring into relief, as well as the three terms through which it structures them.

The special status of these terms results from their corresponding simultaneously to the three logical moments through which the decision is precipitated and the three places it assigns to the subjects among whom it constitutes a choice.

That decision is reached in a glance's time. For the maneuvers which follow, however stealthily they prolong it, add nothing to that glance, nor does the deferring of the deed in the second scene break the unity of that moment.

This glance presupposes two others, which it embraces in its vision of the breach left in their fallacious complementarity, anticipating in it the occasion for larceny afforded by that exposure. Thus three moments, structuring three glances, borne by three subjects, incarnated each time by different characters.

The first is a glance that sees nothing: the King and the police.

The second, a glance which sees that the first sees nothing and deludes itself as to the secrecy of what it hides: the Queen, then the Minister.

The third sees that the first two glances leave what should be hidden exposed to whomever would seize it: the Minister and finally Dupin.

In order to grasp in its unity the intersubjective complex thus described, we would willingly seek a model in the technique legendarily attributed to the ostrich attempting to shield itself from danger; for that technique might ultimately be qualified as political, divided as it here is among three partners: the second believing itself invisible because the first has its head stuck in the ground, and all the while letting the third calmly pluck its rear; we need only enrich its proverbial denomination by a letter, producing *la politique de l'autruiche*, [7] for the ostrich itself to take on forever a new meaning.

Given the intersubjective modulus of the repetitive action, it remains to recognize in it a *repetition automatism* in the sense that interests us in Freud's text. (SPL, pp. 41-44.)

---

[6] "So infamous a scheme/ If not worthy of Atreus, is worthy of Thyestes."

[7] *La politique de l'autruiche* combines the policy of the ostrich *(autruche)*, others *(autrui)* and Austria *(Autriche)*.

Thus, it is neither the character of the individual subjects, nor the contents of the letter, but the *position* of the letter within the group, which decides what each person will do next. It is the fact that the letter does *not* function as a unit of meaning (a *signified*) but as that which produces certain *effects* (a *signifier*), which leads Lacan to read the story as an illustration of "the truth which may be drawn from that moment in Freud's thought under study—namely, that it is the symbolic order which is constitutive for the subject —by demonstrating (...) the decisive orientation which the subject receives from the itinerary of a signifier" (SPL, p. 40). The letter acts like a signifier precisely to the extent that its *function* in the story does not require that its meaning be revealed: "the letter was able to produce its effects *within* the story: on the actors in the tale, including the narrator, as well as *outside* the story: on us, the readers, and also on its author, without anyone's ever bothering to worry about what it *meant*" (not translated in SPL; *Écrits*, p. 57, translation and emphasis mine). "The Purloined Letter" thus becomes for Lacan a kind of *allegory of the signifier*.

Derrida's critique of Lacan's reading does not dispute the validity of the allegorical interpretation on its own terms, but questions rather its implicit presuppositions and its modus operandi. Derrida aims his objections at two kinds of targets: 1) what Lacan *puts into* the *letter* and 2) what Lacan *leaves out of* the *text*.

1) *What Lacan puts into the letter.* While asserting that the letter's meaning is lacking, Lacan, according to Derrida, makes this lack into *the* meaning of the letter. But Derrida does not stop there: he goes on to assert that what Lacan means by that lack is the truth of lack-as-castration-as-truth: "The truth of the purloined letter is the truth itself (...) What is veiled/unveiled in this case is a hole, a non-being [*non-étant*]; the truth of being [*l'être*], as non-being. Truth is 'woman' as veiled/unveiled castration" (PT, pp. 60-61). Lacan himself, however, never uses the word "castration" in the text of the original Seminar. That it is *suggested* is indisputable, but Derrida, by filling in what *Lacan* left blank, is repeating precisely the gesture of blank-filling for which he is criticizing Lacan.

2) *What Lacan leaves out of the text.* This objection is itself double: on the one hand, Derrida criticizes Lacan for neglecting to consider "The Purloined Letter" in connection with the other two stories in what Derrida calls Poe's "Dupin Trilogy." And on the other hand, according to Derrida, at the very moment Lacan is reading the story as an allegory of the signifier, he is being blind to the disseminating power of the signifier in the *text* of the allegory, in what Derrida calls the "scene of writing." To cut out part of a text's frame of reference as though it did not exist, and to reduce a complex textual functioning to a single meaning, are serious blots indeed in the annals of literary criticism. Therefore it is all the more noticeable that Derrida's own reading of Lacan's text repeats precisely the crimes of which he accuses it: on the one hand, Derrida makes no mention of Lacan's long development on the relation between symbolic determination and random series. And on the other hand, Derrida dismisses Lacan's "style" as a mere ornament, veiling, for a time, an unequivocal message: "Lacan's 'style', moreover, was such that for a long time it would hinder and delay all access to a *unique* content or a single unequivocal meaning determinable beyond the writing itself" (PT, p. 40). The fact that Derrida repeats the very gestures he is criticizing does not in itself invalidate his criticism of their *effects,* but it does problematize his statement condemning their *existence.*

What kind of logic is it that thus seems to turn one-upmanship into inevitable one-downmanship?

It is precisely the logic of the purloined letter.

3. *Odd Couples*

> Je tiens la reine!
> O sûr châtiment...
> —Mallarmé, "L'après-midi d'un faune"

> L'ascendant que le ministre tire de la situation ne tient donc pas à la lettre, mais, qu'il le sache ou non, au personnage qu'elle lui constitue.
> —Lacan, "Séminaire sur 'la Lettre volée' "

We have just seen how Derrida, in his effort to right (write) Lacan's wrongs, can, on a certain level, only repeat them. And how the rectification of a previous injustice somehow irresistibly dictates the *filling in of a blank,* which then becomes the new injustice. In fact, the act of clinching one's triumph by filling in a blank is already prescribed in all its details within Poe's story, in Dupin's unwillingness to "leave the interior blank" (Poe, p. 219) in the facsimile he has left for the Minister, in place of the purloined letter he, Dupin, has just repossessed by means of a *precise* repetition of the act of robbery he is undoing. What is written in the blank is a quotation-as-signature, which curiously resembles Derrida's initialed interventions in the passages he quotes from Lacan, a resemblance on which Derrida is undoubtedly playing. And the *text* of the quotation transcribed by Dupin *says* precisely the structure of rectification-as-repetition-of-the-crime which has led to its being transcribed in the first place:

> —Un dessein si funeste,
> S'il n'est digne d'Atrée, est digne de Thyeste.

Atreus, whose wife was long ago seduced by Thyestes, is about to make Thyestes eat (literally) the fruit of that illicit union, his son Plisthenes. The avenger's plot may not be worthy of *him,* says Atreus, but his brother Thyestes deserves it. What the addressee of the violence is going to get is simply his own message backwards. It is this vengeful anger which, as both Lacan and Derrida show, places Dupin as one of the "ostriches" in the "triad." Not content simply to return the letter to its "rightful" destination, Dupin jumps into the fray as the wronged victim *himself,* by recalling an "evil turn" the Minister once did him in Vienna, and for which he is now, personally, taking his revenge.

Correction must thus posit a previous pretextual, pre-textual crime which will justify its excesses. Any degree of violence is permissible in the act of *getting even* ("To be *even* with him," says Dupin, "I complained of my weak eyes..." [Poe, p. 216]). And Dupin's backwards revision of the story repeats itself in his readers as well. The existence of the same kind of prior aggression on Lacan's part is posited by Derrida in a long footnote in his book *Positions,* in which he outlines what will later develop into *Le Facteur de la Vérité:* "In the texts I have published up to now, the absence of reference to Lacan is indeed almost total. That is *justified* not only by the *acts of aggression* in the form of, or with the intention of, reappropriation which, ever since *De la grammatologie* appeared in *Critique* (1965) (and even earlier, I am told) Lacan has multiplied...." [8] The priority of aggression is doubled by the aggressiveness of priority: "At the time of my first publications, Lacan's *Écrits* had not yet been collected and published..." [9] And Lacan, in turn, mentions in his *Presentation* to the *Points* edition of his *Écrits:* "what I properly call the instance of the letter *before any grammatology.*" [10] The rivalry over something neither man will credit the other with possessing, the retrospective revision of the origins of both their resemblances and their differences, thus spirals backward and forward in an indeterminable pattern of cancellation and duplication. If it thus becomes impossible to determine "who started it" (or even whether "it" was started by either one of them), it is also impossible to know who is ahead, or even whose "turn" it is. This is what makes the business of "getting even" so *odd.*

---

[8] J. Derrida, *Positions,* Minuit, 1972, pp. 112-113 (translation and emphasis mine).

[9] *Ibid.,* p. 113.

[10] J. Lacan, *Écrits,* Seuil ("Points"), 1966, pp. 11 (translation and emphasis mine).

This type of oscillation between two terms, considered as totalities in a binary opposition, is studied by Lacan in connection with Poe's story of the eight-year-old prodigy who succeeded in winning, far beyond his due, at the game of—even and odd. The game consists of guessing whether the number of marbles an opponent is holding is even or odd. The schoolboy explains his success by his *identification* with the physical characteristics of his opponent, from which he deduces the opponent's degree of intelligence and its corresponding line of reasoning. What Lacan shows, in the part of his seminar which Derrida neglects, is that the *mere* identification with the opponent as an *image of totality* is not sufficient to insure success—and in no way explains Dupin's actual strategy— since, from the moment the opponent becomes aware of it, he can then *play* on his own appearance, and dissociate it from the reasoning that is presumed to go with it. (This is, indeed, what occurs in the encounter between Dupin and the Minister: the Minister's *feigned* nonchalance is a true vigilance but a blinded vision, whereas Dupin's *feigned* blindness ("weak eyes") is a vigilant act of lucidity, later to succumb to its own form of blindness.) From then on, says Lacan, the reasoning "can only repeat itself in an indefinite oscillation" (*Écrits,* p. 58: translation mine). And Lacan reports that, in his own classroom tests of the schoolboy's technique, it was almost inevitable that *each* player begin to feel he was losing his marbles ... [11]

But if the complexities of these texts could be reduced to a mere combat between ostriches, a mere game of heads and tails played out in order to determine a "winner," they would have very little theoretical interest. It is, on the contrary, the way in which each mastermind avoids *simply* becoming the butt of his own joke that displaces the opposition in unpredictable ways, and transforms the textual encounter into a source of insight. For if the very possibility of *meeting* the opponent on a common ground, without which no *contact* is possible, implies a certain symmetry,

---

[11] Cf. Lacan's description of the "effect of disorientation, or even of great anxiety," provoked by these exercises (*Écrits,* p. 60).

a sameness, a repetition of the error which the encounter is designed to correct, any true avoidance of that error entails a non-meeting or incompatibility between the two forces. If to hit the target is in a way to become the target, then to miss the target is perhaps to hit it elsewhere. It is not the way in which Lacan and Derrida *meet* each other, but rather the way in which they *miss* each other, which opens up a space for interpretation.

Clearly, what is at stake here has something to do with the status of the number 2. If the face-off between two opponents or polar opposites always simultaneously backfires *and* misfires, it can only be because 2 is an extremely odd number. On the one hand, as a specular illusion of symmetry or metaphor, it can either be narcissistically reassuring (the image of the other as a reinforcement of my identity) or absolutely devastating (the other whose existence can totally cancel me out). This is what Lacan calls the *imaginary* duality. It is characterized by its absoluteness, its independence from any accident or contingency which might subvert the unity of the terms in question, whether in their opposition or in their fusion. To this, Lacan opposes the *symbolic*, which is the entrance of difference or otherness or temporality into the idea of identity—it is not something which *befalls* the imaginary duality, but something which has always already inhabited it, something which subverts not the symmetry of the imaginary couple, but the possibility of the independent unity of any one term whatsoever. It is the impossibility not of the number 2 but of the number 1. Which, paradoxically enough, turns out to lead to the number 3.

If 3 is what makes 2 into the impossibility of 1, is there any inherent increase in lucidity in passing from a couple to a triangle? Is a triangle in any way more "true" than a couple?

It is Derrida's contention that, for psychoanalysis, the answer to that question is "yes." The triangle becomes the magical, Oedipal figure that explains the functioning of human desire. The child's original imaginary dual unity with the mother is subverted by the law of the father as that which prohibits incest under threat of castration, and the child has "simply" to "assume castration" as the necessity of substitution in the object of his desire (the object of desire becoming the locus of substitution and the focus of repetition), after which the child's desire becomes "normalized." Derrida's criticism of the "triangles" or "triads" in Lacan's reading of Poe is based on the assumption that Lacan's use of triangularity stems from this psychoanalytical myth.

Derrida's criticism takes two routes, both of them numerical:

1) The structure of "The Purloined Letter" cannot be reduced to a triangle unless the narrator is eliminated. The elimination of the narrator is a blatant and highly revealing result of the way "psychoanalysis" does violence to literature in order to find its own schemes. What psychoanalysis sees as a triangle is therefore really a quadrangle, and that fourth side is the point from which literature problematizes the very possibility of a triangle. Therefore: $3 = 4$.

2) Duality as such cannot be dismissed or simply absorbed into a triangular structure. "The Purloined Letter" is traversed by an uncanny capacity for doubling and subdividing. The narrator and Dupin are doubles of each other, and Dupin himself is first introduced as a "Bi-Part Soul" (Poe, p. 107), a sort of Dupin Duplex, "the creative and the resolvent." The Minister, D——, has a brother for whom it is possible to mistake him, and from whom he is to be distinguished because of *his* doubleness (poet *and* mathematician). Thus the Minister and Dupin become doubles of each other through the fact of their both being already double, in addition to their other points of resemblance, including their names. "The Seminar," writes Derrida, "mercilessly forecloses this problematic of the double and of *Unheimlichkeit*—no doubt considering that it is confined to the imaginary, to the dual relationship which must be kept rigorously separate from the symbolic and the triangular. (...) All the 'uncanny' relations of duplicity, limitlessly deployed in a dual structure, find themselves omitted or marginalized [in the Seminar]. (...) What is thus kept under surveillance and control is the Uncanny itself, and the frantic anxiety which can be provoked, with no hope of reappropriation, enclosure, or truth, by the infinite play from

simulacrum to simulacrum, from double to double" (omitted in PT; FV, p. 124, translation mine).

Thus the triangle's angles are always already bisected, and 3 = (a factor of) 2.

In the game of odd versus even, then, it would seem that Derrida is playing evens (4 or 2) against Lacan's odds (3). But somehow the numbers 2 and 4 have become uncannily odd, while the number 3 has been evened off into a reassuring symmetry. How did this happen, and what are the consequences for an interpretation of "The Purloined Letter"?

Before any answer to this question can be envisaged, several remarks should be made here to problematize the terms of Derrida's critique:

1) If the narrator and Dupin are a strictly dual pair whose relationship is in no way mediated by a third term in any Oedipal sense, how is one to explain the fact that their original meeting was brought about by their potential rivalry over the same object: "the accident of our both being in search of the *same* very rare and very remarkable volume." Whether or not they ever found it, or can share it, is this not a triangular relationship?

2) Although Lacan's reading of "The Purloined Letter" divides the story into triadic structures, his model for (inter-)subjectivity, the so-called "schema L," which is developed in that part of the Seminar's introduction which Derrida glosses over, is indisputably quadrangular. In order to read Lacan's repeating triads as a triangular, Oedipal model of the subject instead of as a mere structure of repetition, Derrida must therefore lop off one corner of the "schema L" in the same way as he accuses Lacan of lopping off a corner of Poe's text—and Derrida does this precisely by lopping off that corner of Lacan's text in which the quadrangular "schema L" is developed.

But can what is at stake here really be reduced to a mere numbers game?

Let us approach the problem from another angle, by asking two more questions:

1) What is the relation between a divided unity and a duality? Are the two *two*'s synonymous? Is a "Bi-Part Soul," for example, actually composed of two wholes? Or is it possible to conceive of a division which would not lead to two separable parts, but only to a problematization of the idea of unity? This would class what Derrida calls "duality" not in Lacan's "imaginary," but in Lacan's "symbolic."

2) If the doubles are forever redividing or multiplying, does the number "2" really apply? If $1 = 2$, how can $2 = 1 + 1$? If what is uncanny about the doubles is that they never stop doubling up, would the number 2 still be uncanny if it *did* stop at a truly dual symmetry? Isn't it the very limitlessness of the process of the dissemination of unity, rather than the existence of any one duality, which Derrida is talking about here?

Clearly, in these questions, it is the very notion of a number which becomes problematic, and the argument on the basis of numbers can no longer be read literally. If Derrida opposes doubled quadrangles to Lacan's triangles, it is not because he wants to turn Oedipus into an octopus.

To what, then, does the critique of triangularity apply?

The problem with psychoanalytical triangularity, in Derrida's eyes, is not that it contains the wrong number of terms, but that it presupposes the possibility of a successful dialectical mediation and harmonious normalization or *Aufhebung* of desire. The three terms in the Oedipal triad enter into an opposition whose resolution resembles the synthetic moment of a Hegelian dialectic. The process centers on the phallus as the locus of the question of sexual difference: it is when the observation of the mother's lack of a penis is joined with the father's threat of castration as the punishment for incest that the child passes from the *alternative* (thesis vs. antithesis; presence vs. absence of penis) to the *synthesis* (the phallus as a sign of the fact that the child can only enter into the circuit of desire by assuming castration as the phallus' *simultaneous* presence and absence; that is, by assuming the fact that both the subject and the object of desire will always be *substitutes* for something that was never really present). In Lacan's article on "La signification du phallus," which Derrida quotes, this process is evoked in precisely Hegelian terms:

> All these remarks still do nothing but veil the fact that it [the phallus] cannot play its role except veiled, that is to say as itself sign of the latency with which anything signifiable is stricken as soon as it is raised *(aufgehoben)* to the function of signifier.
> The phallus is the signifier of this *Aufhebung* itself which it inaugurates (initiates) by its disappearance. (*Écrits*, p. 692; PT, p. 98.)

"It would appear," comments Derrida, "that the Hegelian movement of *Aufhebung* is here reversed since the latter sublates [*relève*] the sensory signifier in the ideal signified" (PT, p. 98). But then, according to Derrida, Lacan's privileging of the spoken over the written word annulls this reversal, reappropriates all possibility of uncontainable otherness, and brings the whole thing back within the bounds of the type of "logocentrism" which has been the focus of Derrida's entire deconstructive enterprise over the past ten years.

The question of whether or not Lacan's "privileging" of the voice is strictly logocentric in Derrida's sense is an extremely complex one with which we cannot hope to deal adequately here. [12] But what does all this have to do with "The Purloined Letter"?

In an attempt to answer this question, let us examine the way in which Derrida deduces from Lacan's text the fact that, for Lacan, the "letter" is a symbol of the (mother's) phallus. Since Lacan never uses the word "phallus" in the Seminar, this is already an *inter-*

---

[12] Some idea of the possibilities for misunderstanding inherent in this question can be gathered from the following: In order to show that psychoanalysis *represses* "writing" in a logocentric way, Derrida quotes Lacan's statement against tape recorders: "But precisely because it comes to him through an alienated form, even a retransmission of his own recorded discourse, be it from the mouth of his own doctor, cannot have the same effects as psychoanalytical interlocution." This Derrida regards as a *condemnation* of the "simulacrum," a "disqualification of recording or of repetition in the name of the living and present word." But what does Lacan actually *say*? Simply that a tape recording *does not have the same effects* as psychoanalytical interlocution. Does the fact that psychoanalysis is a technique based on verbal interlocution automatically reduce it to a logocentric error? Is it not equally possible to regard what Lacan calls "full speech" as being *full* of precisely what Derrida calls *writing*?

pretation on Derrida's part, and quite an astute one at that, with which Lacan, as a later reader of his own Seminar, implicitly agrees by placing the word "castrated"—which had not been used in the original text—in his "Points" *Presentation.* The disagreement between Derrida and Lacan thus arises not over the *validity* of the equation "letter = phallus," but over its *meaning.*

How, then, does Derrida derive this equation from Lacan's text? The deduction follows four basic lines of reasoning, all of which will be dealt with in greater detail later in the present essay:

1) The letter "belongs" to the Queen as a substitute for the phallus she does not have. It feminizes (castrates) each of its successive holders and is eventually returned to her as its rightful owner.

2) Poe's description of the position of the letter in the Minister's apartment, expanded upon by the figurative dimensions of Lacan's text, suggests an analogy between the shape of the fireplace from the center of whose mantelpiece the letter is found hanging, and that point on a woman's anatomy from which the phallus is missing.

3) The letter, says Lacan, cannot be divided: "But if it is first of all on the materiality of the signifier that we have insisted, that materiality is *odd* [singulière] in many ways, the first of which is not to admit partition" (SPL, p. 53). This indivisibility, says Derrida, is odd indeed, but becomes comprehensible if it is seen as an *idealization* of the phallus, whose integrity is necessary for the edification of the entire psychoanalytical system. With the phallus safely idealized and located in the voice, the so-called "signifier" acquires the "unique, living, non-mutilable integrity" of the self-present spoken word, unequivocally pinned down to and by the *signified.* "Had the phallus been per(mal)chance divisible or reduced to the status of a partial object, the whole edification would have crumbled down, and this is what has to be avoided at all cost" (PT, pp. 96-97).

4) And finally, if Poe's story "illustrates" the "truth," the last words of the Seminar proper seem to reaffirm that truth in no

uncertain terms: "Thus it is that what the 'purloined letter', nay, the 'letter in sufferance' means is that *a letter always arrives at its destination*" (SPL, p. 72, emphasis mine). Now, since it is unlikely that Lacan is talking about the efficiency of the postal service, he must, according to Derrida, be affirming the possibility of unequivocal meaning, the eventual reappropriation of the message, its total equivalence with itself. And since the "truth" Poe's story illustrates is, in Derrida's eyes, the truth of veiled/unveiled castration and of the transcendental identity of the phallus as the lack that makes the system work, this final sentence in Lacan's Seminar seems to affirm both the absolute truth of psychoanalytical theories and the absolute decipherability of the literary text. Poe's message will have been totally, unequivocally understood and explained by the psychoanalytical myth. "The hermeneutic discovery of meaning (truth), the deciphering (that of Dupin and that of the Seminar), arrives itself at its destination" (PT, p. 66).

Thus, the law of the phallus seems to imply a reappropriating return to the place of true ownership, an indivisible identity functioning beyond the possibility of disintegration or unrecoverable loss, and a totally self-present, unequivocal meaning or truth.

The problem with this type of system, counters Derrida, is that it cannot account for the possibility of sheer accident, irreversible loss, unreappropriable residues, and infinite divisibility, which are in fact necessary and inevitable in the system's very elaboration. In order for the circuit of the letter to end up confirming the law of the phallus, it must begin by transgressing it: the letter is a sign of high treason. Phallogocentrism mercilessly represses the uncontrollable multiplicity of ambiguities, the disseminating play of *writing,* which irreducibly transgresses any unequivocal meaning. "Not that the letter never arrives at its destination, but part of its structure is that it is always capable of not arriving there. (. . .) Here dissemination threatens the law of the signifier and of castration as a contract of truth. Dissemination mutilates the unity of the signifier, that is, of the phallus" (PT, p. 66).

In contrast to Lacan's *Seminar,* then, Derrida's text would seem to be setting itself up as a *Disseminar.*

From the foregoing remarks, it can easily be seen that the disseminal criticism of Lacan's apparent reduction of the literary text to an unequivocal message depends for its force upon the presupposition of unambiguousness in *Lacan's* text. And indeed, the statement that a letter always reaches its destination seems straightforward enough. But when that statement is reinserted into its context, things become palpably less certain:

> Is that all, and shall we believe we have deciphered Dupin's real strategy above and beyond the imaginary tricks with which he was obliged to deceive us? No doubt, yes, for if "any point requiring reflection," as Dupin states at the start, is "examined to best purpose in the dark," we may now easily read its solution in broad daylight. It was already implicit and easy to derive from the title of our tale, according to the very formula we have long submitted to your discretion: in which the sender, we tell you, receives from the receiver his own message in reverse form. Thus it is that what the "purloined letter," nay, the "letter in sufferance" means is that a letter always arrives at its destination. (SPL, p. 72.)

The meaning of this last sentence is problematized not so much by its own ambiguity as by a series of reversals in the preceding sentences. If the *best* examination takes place in darkness, what does "reading in broad daylight" imply? Could it not be taken as an affirmation not of actual lucidity but of *delusions* of lucidity? Could it not then move the "yes, no doubt" as an answer not to the question "have we deciphered?" but to the question "shall we *believe* we have deciphered?" And if this is possible, does it not empty the final affirmation of all unequivocality, leaving it to stand with the force of an assertion, without any definite content? And if the sender receives from the receiver his own message backwards, who is the sender here, who the receiver, and what is the message? It is in fact not even clear what the expression "the purloined letter" refers to: Poe's text? the letter it talks about? or simply the *expression* "the purloined letter"?

We will take another look at this passage later, but for the moment its ambiguities seem sufficient to problematize, if not

subvert, the presupposition of univocality which is the very foundation on which Derrida has edified *his* interpretation.

But surely such an oversimplification on Derrida's part does not
result from mere blindness, oversight, or error. As P. de Man says
of Derrida's similar treatment of Rousseau, "the pattern is too
interesting not to be deliberate." [13] Being the sharp-eyed reader that
he is, Derrida's consistent forcing of Lacan's statements into systems
and patterns from which they are actually trying to escape must
correspond to some strategic necessity different from the attentiveness to the letter of the text which characterizes Derrida's way
of reading Poe. And in fact, the more one works with Derrida's
analysis, the more convinced one becomes that although the critique
of what Derrida *calls* psychoanalysis is entirely justified, it does not
quite apply to what Lacan's text is actually saying. What Derrida
is in fact arguing against is therefore not Lacan's *text* but Lacan's
power—or rather, "Lacan" as the apparent cause of certain *effects
of power* in French discourse today. Whatever Lacan's text may *say,*
it *functions,* according to Derrida, as if it said what *he* says it says.
The statement that a letter always reaches its destination may be
totally undecipherable, but its assertive force is taken all the more
seriously as a sign that Lacan himself has everything all figured out.
Such an assertion, in fact, gives him an appearance of mastery like
that of the Minister in the eyes of the letterless Queen. "The ascen-
dancy which the Minister derives from the situation," explains
Lacan, "is attached not to the letter but to the character it makes
him into."

Thus Derrida's seemingly "blind" reading, whose vagaries we
shall be following here, is not a mistake, but the positioning of
what can be called the "average reading" of Lacan's text, which is
the true object of Derrida's deconstruction. Since Lacan's text is
read as if it said what Derrida says it says, its actual textual functioning is irrelevant to the agonistic arena in which Derrida's anal-

[13] Paul de Man, *Blindness and Insight,* Oxford University Press, 1971,
p. 140.

ysis takes place, and which is, in fact, suggested by the very first word of the epigraph: *ils,* "they":

> They thank him for the grand truths he has just proclaimed, — for they have discovered (o verifier of what cannot be verified!) that everything he said was absolutely true; even though, at first, these honest souls admit, they might have suspected that it could have been a simple fiction . . . (PT, p. 31; translation mine.)

The fact that this quotation from Baudelaire refers to Poe and not Lacan does not completely erase the impression that the unidentified "him" in its first sentence is the "Purveyor of Truth" of the title. The evils of Lacan's analysis of Poe are thus located less in the letter of the text than in the gullible readers, the *"braves gens"* who are taken in by it. Lacan's ills are really *ils.*

If Derrida's reading of Lacan's reading of Poe is thus actually the deconstruction of a reading whose status is difficult to determine, does this mean that Lacan's text is completely innocent of the misdemeanors of which it is accused? If Lacan can be shown to be opposed to the same kind of logocentric error that Derrida is opposed to, does that mean that they are both really saying the same thing? These are questions which must be left, at least for the moment, hanging.

But the structure of Derrida's *transference of guilt* from a certain *reading* of Lacan onto Lacan's *text* is not indifferent in itself, in the context of what, after all, started out as a relatively simple crime story. For what it amounts to is nothing less than . . . a *frame.*

4. *The Frame of Reference*

> Elle, défunte *nue* en le miroir, encor
> Que, *dans l'oubli fermé par le cadre,* se fixe
> De scintillations sitôt le septuor.
>
> —Mallarmé, "Sonnet en X"

If Derrida is thus framing Lacan for an interpretative malpractice of which he himself is, at least in part, the author, what can this

Barbara Johnson

frame teach us about the nature of the act of reading, in the context of the question of literature and psychoanalysis?

Interestingly enough, one of the major crimes for which Lacan is being framed by Derrida is precisely the psychoanalytical reading's elimination of the literary text's *frame*. That frame here consists not only of the two stories which precede "The Purloined Letter," but of the stratum of narration through which the stories are told, and, "beyond" it, of the text's entire functioning as *écriture:*

> Without breathing a word about it, Lacan excludes the textual fiction within which he isolates the so-called "general narration." Such an operation is facilitated, too obviously facilitated, by the fact that the narration covers the entire surface of the fiction entitled "The Purloined Letter." But *that* is the fiction. There is an invisible but structurally irreducible frame around the narration. Where does it begin? With the first letter of the title? With the epigraph from Seneca? With the words, "At Paris, just after dark . . ."? It is more complicated than that and will require reconsideration. Such complication suffices to point out everything that is misunderstood about the structure of the text once the frame is ignored. Within this invisible or neutralized frame, Lacan takes the borderless narration and makes another subdivision, once again leaving aside the frame. He cuts out two dialogues from within the frame of the narration itself, which form the narrated history, i.e. the content of a representation, the internal meaning of a story, the all-enframed which demands our complete attention, mobilizes all the psychoanalytical schemes — Oedipal, as it happens — and draws all the effort of decipherment towards its center. What is missing here is an elaboration of the problem of the frame, the signature and the *parergon.* This lack allows us to reconstruct the scene of the signifier as a signified (an ever inevitable process in the logic of the sign), writing as the written, the text as discourse or more precisely as an "intersubjective" dialogue (there is nothing fortuitous in the fact that the Seminar discusses only the two *dialogues* in "The Purloined Letter"). (PT, pp. 52-53, translation modified.)

It is well known that "The Purloined Letter" belongs to what Baudelaire called a "kind of trilogy," along with "The Murders in the Rue Morgue" and "The Mystery of Marie Rogêt." About this Dupin trilogy, the Seminar does not breathe a word; not only does Lacan lift out the narrated triangles (the "real drama") in order to center the narration around them and make them carry the weight of the interpretation (the letter's destination), but he also lifts one third of the Dupin cycle out of an ensemble discarded as if it were a natural, invisible frame. (Not translated in PT; FV p. 123; translation mine.)

In framing with such violence, in cutting a fourth side out of the narrated figure itself in order to see only triangles, a certain complication, perhaps a complication of the Oedipal structure, is eluded, a complication which makes itself felt in the scene of writing. (PT, p. 54; translation entirely modified.)

It would seem, then, that Lacan is here guilty of several sins of omission: the omission of the narrator, of the non-dialogue parts of the story, of the other stories in the trilogy. But does this criticism amount to a mere plea for the inclusion of what has been excluded? No: the problem is not simply quantitative. What has been excluded is not homogeneous to what has been included. Lacan, says Derrida, misses the specifically literary dimension of Poe's text by treating it as a "real drama," a story like the stories a psychoanalyst hears every day from his patients. What has been left out is precisely *literature* itself.

Does this mean that the "frame" is what makes a text literary? Interestingly enough, in a recent issue of *New Literary History* devoted to the question "What is Literature?" and totally unrelated to the debate concerning the purloined letter, this is precisely the conclusion to which one of the contributors comes: "Literature is language (...), but it is language around which we have drawn a *frame*, a frame that indicates a decision to regard with a particular self-consciousness the resources language has always possessed." [14]

Such a view of literature, however, implies that a text is literary because it remains inside certain definite borders: it is a many-facetted object, perhaps, but still, it is an object. That this is not quite what Derrida has in mind becomes clear from the following remarks:

By overlooking the narrator's position, the narrator's involvement in the content of what he seems to be recounting, one omits from the scene of writing anything going beyond the two triangular scenes.

And first of all one omits that what is in question — with no possible access route or border — is a scene of writing whose boundaries crumble off into an abyss. From the simulacrum of an overture, of a "first word," the

[14] Stanley E. Fish, "How Ordinary is Ordinary Language?," *New Literary History,* Vol. V, No. 1, p. 52 (emphasis mine).

narrator, in narrating himself, advances a few propositions which carry the unity of the "tale" into an endless drifting-off course: a textual drifting not at all taken into account in the Seminar. (PT, pp. 100-101; translation modified.)

These reminders, of which countless other examples could be given, alert us to the effects of the frame, and of the paradoxes in the parergonal logic. Our purpose is not to prove that "The Purloined Letter" functions within a frame (omitted by the Seminar, which can thus be assured of its triangular interior by an active, surreptitious limitation starting from a metalinguistic overview), but to prove that the structure of the framing effects is such that no totalization of the border is even possible. Frames are always framed: thus, by part of their content. Pieces without a whole, "divisions" without a totality — this is what thwarts the dream of a letter without division, allergic to division. (PT, p. 99; translation slightly modified.)

Here the argument seems to reverse the previous objection: Lacan has eliminated not the frame but the unframability of the literary text. But what Derrida calls "parergonal logic" is paradoxical precisely because *both* of these incompatible (but not totally contradictory) arguments are equally valid. The total inclusion of the "frame" is both mandatory and impossible. The "frame" thus becomes not the borderline between the inside and the outside, but precisely what subverts the applicability of the inside/outside polarity to the act of interpretation.

The "frame" is, in fact, one of a series of paradoxical "borderline cases"—along with the tympanum and the hymen—through which Derrida has recently been studying the limits of spatial logic as it relates to intelligibility. Lacan, too, has been seeking to displace the Euclidean model of understanding (*comprehension,* for example, means *spatial inclusion*) by inventing a "new geometry" by means of the logic of knots. The relation between these two attempts to break out of spatial logic has yet to be articulated, but some measure of the difficulties involved may be derived from the fact that "to break out of" is still a spatial metaphor. The urgency of these undertakings cannot, however, be overestimated, since the logic of metaphysics, of politics, of belief, and of knowledge itself is based on the imposition of definable objective frontiers and outlines whose possibility and/or justifiability are precisely what is here being put in question. If "comprehension" is the framing of something whose limits are undeterminable, how can we know *what* we are comprehending? The play on the spatial and the criminal senses of the word "frame" with which we began this section may thus not be as gratuitous as it seemed. And indeed, the question of the fallacies inherent in a Euclidean model of intelligibility, far from being a tangential theoretical consideration here, is in fact central to the very plot of "The Purloined Letter" itself. For it is precisely the notion of space as finite and homogeneous which underlies the Prefect's method of investigation: "I presume you know," he explains, "that, to a properly trained police-agent, such a thing as a 'secret' drawer is impossible. Any man is a dolt who permits a 'secret' drawer to escape him in a search of this kind. The thing is *so* plain. There is a certain amount of bulk—of space—to be accounted for in every cabinet. Then we have accurate rules. The fiftieth part of a line could not escape us" (Poe, p. 204). The assumption that what is not seen must be hidden—an assumption Lacan calls the "realist's imbecillity"—is based on a falsely objective notion of the act of *seeing*. The polarity "hidden/exposed" cannot alone account for the fact that the police did *not* find the letter —which was entirely exposed, inside out—let alone the fact that Dupin *did*. A "subjective" element must be added, which subverts the geometrical model of understanding through the *interference* of the polarity "blindness/sight" with the polarity "hidden/exposed." The same problematic is raised by the story of "The Emperor's New Clothes," which Derrida cites as an example of psychoanalysis' *failure* to go beyond the polarity "hidden/exposed" (in Freud's account). We will return to the letter's "place" later on in this essay, but it is already clear that the "range" of any investigation is located not in geometrical space, but in its implicit notion of what "seeing" is.

What enables Derrida to problematize the literary text's frame is, as we have seen, what he calls "the scene of writing." By this he means two things:

1) The textual signifier's resistance to being totally transformed into a signified. In spite of Lacan's attentiveness to the path of the letter in Poe's story as an illustration of the functioning of a signifier, says Derrida, the psychoanalytical reading is still blind to the functioning of the signifier *in the narration itself.* In reading "The Purloined Letter" as an *allegory* of the signifier, Lacan, according to Derrida, has made the "signifier" into the story's truth: "The displacement of the signifier is analyzed as a signified, as the re-counted object in a short story" (PT, p. 48). Whereas, counters Derrida, it is precisely the *textual* signifier which resists being thus totalized into meaning, leaving an irreducible residue: "The rest, the remnant, would be 'The Purloined Letter', the text that bears this title, and whose place, like the once more invisible large letters on the map, is not where one was expecting to find it, in the enclosed content of the 'real drama' or in the hidden and sealed interior of Poe's story, but in and as the open letter, the very open letter which fiction is" (PT, p. 64).

2) The actual writings—the books, libraries, quotations, and previous tales which surround "The Purloined Letter" with a *frame* of (literary) *references.* The story begins in "a little back library, or book-closet" (Poe, p. 199) where the narrator is mulling over a previous conversation on the subject of the two previous instances of Dupin's detective work as told in Poe's two previous tales, the first of which recounted the original meeting between Dupin and the narrator—in a *library,* of course, where both were in search of the same rare *book.* The story's *beginning* is thus an infinitely regressing *reference* to previous writings. And therefore, says Derrida, "nothing begins. Simply a drifting or a disorientation from which one never moves away" (PT, p. 101). Dupin himself is in fact a walking library: books are his "sole luxuries," and the narrator is "astonished" at "the vast extent of his reading" (Poe, p. 106). Even Dupin's last, most seemingly personal words—the venomous lines he leaves in his substitute letter to the Minister—are a *quotation.* A quotation whose transcription and proper authorship are the last things the story tells us. "But," concludes Derrida, "beyond the

quotation marks that surround the entire story, Dupin is obliged to quote this last word in quotation marks, to recount his signature: that is what I wrote to him and how I signed it. What is a signature within quotation marks? Then, within these quotation marks, the seal itself is a quotation within quotation marks. This remnant is still literature" (PT, pp. 112-113).

It is by means of these two extra dimensions that Derrida intends to show the crumbling, abyssal, non-totalizable edges of the story's frame. Both of these objections, however, are in themselves more problematic and double-edged than they appear. Let us begin with the second. "Literature," in Derrida's demonstration, is indeed clearly the beginning, middle, and end—and even the interior—of the purloined letter. But how was this conclusion reached? To a large extent, by listing the books, libraries, and other writings *recounted* in the story. That is, by following the *theme*—and not the functioning—of "writing" within "the content of a representation." But if the fact that Dupin signs with a quotation, for example, is for Derrida a sign that "this remnant is still literature," does this not indicate that "literature" has become not the signifier but the *signified* in the story? If the play of the signifier is really to be followed, doesn't it play beyond the range of the *seme* "writing"? And if Derrida criticizes Lacan for making the "signifier" into the story's *signified,* is Derrida not here transforming "writing" into "the written" in much the same way? What Derrida calls "the reconstruction of the scene of the signifier as a signified" seems indeed to be "an inevitable process" in the logic of reading the purloined letter.

Derrida, of course, implicitly counters this objection by protesting—twice—that the textual drifting for which Lacan does not account should not be considered "the *real subject* of the tale," but rather the "remarkable ellipsis" of any subject. But the question of the seemingly inevitable slipping from the signifier to the signified still remains. And it remains not as an *objection* to the logic of the frame, but as its fundamental *question.* For if the "paradoxes of parergonal logic" are such that the frame is always being framed by part of its contents, it is precisely this slippage between signifier and signified—which is *acted out* by both Derrida and Lacan against their intentions—which best illustrates those paradoxes. Derrida's justification of his framing of the "Lacan" he is reading as neither being limited to the "Seminar" nor as including Lacan's later work, itself obeys the contradictory logic of the frame: on the one hand, Derrida will study that part of Lacan's work which seems to embody a *system* of truth even though other writings might put that system in question, and on the other hand this same part of Lacan's work, says Derrida, will probably some day be called the work of the "young Lacan" by "university types eager to divide up *what cannot be divided*." Whatever Derrida actually thinks he is doing here, his contradictory way of explaining it obeys the paradoxes of parergonal logic so perfectly that this self-subversion may have even been deliberate.

If the question of the frame thus problematizes the object of any interpretation by setting it at an angle or fold [*pli*] with itself, then Derrida's analysis errs not in opposing this paradoxical functioning to Lacan's allegorical reading, but in not following the consequences of its own insight far enough. If the frame is that which makes it impossible for us to know where to begin and when to stop, for example, why does Derrida stop within the limits of the Dupin trilogy? And if the purpose of studying "writing" is to sow an uncanny uncertainty about our position in the abyss, isn't the disseminal library Derrida describes still in a way just a bit too comfortable?

"The Purloined Letter," says Derrida, is signed "literature." What does this mean, if not that the letter's *contents*—the only ones we are allowed to see—are in *another* text? That the locus of the letter's meaning is not *in* the letter, but somewhere else? That the *context* of that meaning is precisely the *way* in which its context is lacking, both through the explicit designation of a proper origin (Crébillon's *Atrée*) *outside* the text and through a substitutive structure from letter to letter, from text to text, and from brother to brother, *within* the text, such that the expressions "outside" and "within" have ceased to be clearly definable? But until we have actually opened that other text, we cannot know the modality of the *precise* otherness of the abyss *to itself*, the way in which the story's edges do not *simply* crumble away.

In order to escape the reduction of the "library" to its thematic presence as a *sign* of writing, let us therefore pull some of the books off the shelves and see what they contain. This is a track neither Lacan nor Derrida has taken, but we will soon see how it in some way enfolds them both.

First of all, the name "Dupin" itself, according to Poe scholars, comes out of *Poe*'s interior library: from the pages of a volume called *Sketches of Conspicuous Living Characters of France* (Philadelphia: Lea & Blanchard, 1841), which Poe reviewed for *Graham's Magazine* during the same month his first Dupin story appeared. André-Marie-Jean-Jacques Dupin, a minor French statesman, is there described as precisely himself a walking library: "To judge from his writings, Dupin must be a perfect living encyclopedia. From Homer to Rousseau, from the Bible to the civil code, from the laws of the twelve tables to the Koran, he has read every thing, retained every thing..." (p. 224). Detective Dupin's "origin" is thus multiply bookish: he is a reader whose writer read his name in a book describing a writer as a reader—a reader whose nature can only be described in writing, in fact, as irreducibly double: "He is the personage for whom the painters of political portraits, make the most enormous consumption of antithesis. In the same picture, he will be drawn as both great and little, courageous and timid, trivial and dignified, disinterested and mercenary, restive and pliable, obstinate and fickle, white and black; there is no understanding it" (p. 210). And the writing which serves as the vehicle of this description of written descriptions of double Dupin, is *itself* double: a translation, by a Mr. Walsh, of a series of articles by a Frenchman whose name is not even known to the translator, but who is said to

Barbara Johnson

call himself "an *homme de rien*, a nobody" (p. 2). "Nobody" thus becomes the proper name of the original author in the series. [15]

But the author of the last word in "The Purloined Letter" is clearly *not* nobody. It is not even Poe; it is Crébillon. What is remarkable about Crébillon's *Atrée*, when read as the context from which Dupin's letter to the Minister has been purloined, is not simply that it tells the story of revenge as a symmetrical repetition of the original crime, but that it does so precisely by means of... a purloined letter. It is a *letter* which informs King Atreus of the extent of his betrayal, and serves as an instrument of his revenge; it is the King himself who has purloined the letter—written by the Queen to her lover Thyestes just before her death. The letter reveals that Plisthenes, whom everyone believes to be Atreus' son, is really the son of his brother Thyestes. Having kept the letter and its message secret for twenty years, Atreus plans to force Plisthenes, unaware of his true parentage, to commit patricide. Thwarted in this plan by Plisthenes' refusal to kill the father of his beloved, Theodamia, who is, unknown to him, his sister, Atreus is forced to produce the letter, reunite the illicit family, and transfer his revenge from Plisthenes' patricide to Thyestes' infantophagy. A Queen betraying a King, a letter representing that betrayal being purloined for purposes of power, an eventual return of that letter to its addressee, accompanied by an act of revenge which duplicates the original crime—"The Purloined Letter" as a story of repetition is *itself* a repetition of the story from which it purloins its last words. The Freudian "truth" of the repetition compulsion is not simply illustrated *in* the story; it is illustrated *by* the story. The story obeys the very law it conveys; it is framed by its own content. And thus "The Purloined Letter" no longer simply repeats its own "primal scene": what it repeats is nothing less than a previous story of repetition. The "last word" names the place where the non-firstness of the "first word" repeats itself.

[15] In a final twist to this *mise en abyme* of writing, the words "by L. L. de Loménie" have been penciled into the Yale library's copy of this book under the title in a meticulous nineteenth-century hand, as the book's "*supplément d'origine*" ...

487

This is not the only instance of the folding-in of the frame of references upon the purloined letter's interior. Another allusion, somewhat more hidden, is contained in the description of the Minister as someone "who dares all things, those unbecoming as well as those becoming a man" (Poe, p. 201). These words echo Macbeth's protestation to his ambitious wife: "I dare do all that may become a man./ Who dares do more is none" (I, vii). The reference to *Macbeth* substantiates Lacan's reading of the description of the Minister as pointing toward femininity: it is indeed Lady Macbeth who dares to do what is unbecoming a man. And what is Lady Macbeth doing when we first catch sight of her? She is reading a letter. Not a *purloined* letter, perhaps, but one which contains the ambiguous letter of destiny, committing Macbeth to the murder of the King, whose place Macbeth will take, and whose fate he will inevitably share. The King seems to be precisely that which cannot remain intact in the face of a letter: Atreus betrayed by his wife's letter to his brother; Duncan betrayed by Macbeth's letter to Lady Macbeth; Macbeth himself betrayed by his own confidence in his ability to read the letter of his Fate. And of course, the King in the "Purloined Letter," whose power is betrayed precisely by his not even knowing about the existence of the letter that betrays him.

The questions raised by all these texts together are legion. What is a man? Who is the child's father? What is the relation between incest, murder, and the death of a child? What is a king? How can we read the letter of our Destiny? What is seeing? ... The cross-roads where these stories come together seems to point to the story of what occurred at another crossroads: the tragedy of *Oedipus Rex*. We seem to have returned to our starting point, then, except for one thing: it is no longer "The Purloined Letter" which repeats the story of Oedipus, but the story of Oedipus which repeats all the letters purloined from "The Purloined Letter" 's abyssal interior.

But that is not where the letter stops. For the very Oedipal reading which Derrida attributes to Lacan is *itself,* according to Derrida, a purloined letter—purloined by Lacan from Marie Bona-

Barbara Johnson

parte's psychobiographical study of the life and works of Edgar Allan Poe: "At the moment when the Seminar, like Dupin, finds the letter where it is to be found, between the legs of the woman, the deciphering of the enigma is anchored in truth (...) Why then does it find, at the same time that it finds truth, the same meaning and the same topos as Bonaparte when, leaping over the text, she proposes a psycho-biographical analysis of 'The Purloined Letter'?" (PT, p. 66). In that analysis, Bonaparte sees Dupin's restitution of the letter to the Queen as the return of the missing maternal penis to the mother. The letter's hiding place in the Minister's apartment, moreover, is "almost an anatomical chart" of the female body—which leads Bonaparte to note that Baudelaire's translation of "hung from a little brass knob just beneath the middle of the mantelpiece" as "suspendu à un petit bouton de cuivre au dessus du manteau de la cheminée" ["*above* the mantelpiece"] is "completely wrong" (quoted in PT, p. 68). Bonaparte's frame of reference—the female body—cannot tolerate this error of translation.

It is by means of a note which Lacan drops on the subject of the letter's position that Derrida is here able to frame Lacan for neglecting to mention his references: "The question of deciding," says Lacan, "whether he [Dupin] seizes it [the letter] above the mantelpiece as Baudelaire translates, or beneath it, as in the original text, may be abandoned without harm to the inferences of those whose profession is grilling [*aux inférences de la cuisine*]." * *Lacan's note: "And even to the cook herself" (SPL, pp. 66-67). In this cavalier treatment of Bonaparte as the "cook," Lacan thus "makes clear" to Derrida "that Lacan had read Bonaparte, although the Seminar never alludes to her. As an author so careful about debts and priorities, he could have acknowledged an irruption that orients his entire interpretation, namely the process of rephallization as the proper course of the letter, the 'return of the letter' restored to its 'destination' after having been found between the legs of the mantelpiece" (PT, p. 68). The *interpretation* of the letter (as the phallus which must be returned to the mother) must *itself* be returned to the "mother" from whom it has been purloined—Marie Bonaparte. Derrida himself thus follows precisely the logic he objects to in Lacan, the logic of rectification and correction: "to return the letter to its proper course, supposing that its trajectory is a line, is to correct a deviation, to rectify a divergence, to recall a direction, an authentic line" (PT, p. 65). But the mere fact that Derrida's critique repeats the same logic he denounces is in itself less interesting than the fact that *this* rectification itself presupposes another, which puts its very foundations in question. For when Lacan says that the question of the exact position of the letter "may be abandoned without harm" to the grillers, Derrida protests, "Without harm? On the contrary, the harm would be decisive, within the Seminar itself: *on* the mantelpiece, the letter could not have been 'between the cheeks of the fireplace', 'between the legs of the fireplace'" (PT, p. 69). Derrida must thus *correct* Lacan's text, *eliminate* its apparent contradiction, in order to return the letter of the interpretation to its rightful owner. And all this in order to criticize Lacan's enterprise as one of rectification and circular return. If "rectification" as such is to be criticized, it is thus difficult to determine where it begins and where it ends. In *rectifying* Lacan's text in order to make it fit into the logic of rectification, Derrida thus problematizes the very status of the object of his criticism.

But if the correction of Lacan's text is thus itself a mutilation which requires correction, how *are* we to interpret the contradiction between Lacan's description of the Minister's apartment as "an immense female body" (SPL, p. 66) and his statement that the letter's exact location does not matter? This, it seems to me, is the crux of the divergence between Derrida's and Lacan's interpretation of what the equation "letter = phallus" *means*.

For Bonaparte, it was precisely the *analogy* between the fireplace and the female body which led to the letter's phallic function. The phallus was considered as a real, anatomical *referent* serving as the model for a figurative representation. Bonaparte's frame of reference was thus *reference* itself.

For Derrida, on the other hand, the phallus' frame of reference is precisely "psychoanalytical theory" 's way of preserving the phallus' referential status *in the act of negating it.* In commenting on Lacan's discussion of "The Meaning of the Phallus," Derrida writes:

> Phallogocentrism is one thing. And what is called man and what is called woman might be subject to it. The more so, we are reminded, since the phallus is neither a phantasy ("imaginary effect") nor an object ("partial, internal, good, bad"), even less the organ, penis or clitoris, which it symbolizes [*Écrits,* p. 690]. Androcentrism ought therefore to be something else.
> Yet what is going on? The entire phallogocentrism is articulated from the starting-point of a determinate *situation* (let us give this word its full impact) in which the phallus *is* the mother's desire inasmuch as she does not have it. An (individual, perceptual, local, cultural, historical, etc.) situation on the basis of which is developed something called a "sexual theory": in it the phallus is not the organ, penis or clitoris, which it symbolizes; but it does to a larger extent and in the first place symbolize the penis. (...) This consequence had to be traced in order to recognize the meaning [the direction, *sens*] of the purloined letter in the "course *which is proper to it.*" (PT, pp. 98-99.)

Thus, says Derrida, it is the very non-referentiality of the phallus which, in the final analysis, insures that the penis is its referent.

Before trying to determine the applicability of this summary to Lacan's actual statements in "The Meaning of the Phallus"—not to mention in the "Seminar"—let us follow its consequences further in Derrida's critique. From the very first words of "The Purveyor of Truth," psychoanalysis is implicitly being criticized for being capable of finding only *itself* wherever it looks: "Psychoanalysis, supposing, finds itself" (PT, p. 31, translation mine). In whatever it turns its attention to, psychoanalysis seems to recognize nothing but its own (Oedipal) schemes. Dupin finds the letter because "he knows that the letter finally *finds itself* where it must *be found* in order to return circularly and adequately to its proper place. This proper place, known to Dupin and to the psychoanalyst who intermittently takes his place, is the place of castration" (PT, p. 60; translation modified). The psychoanalyst's act, then, is one of mere *recognition* of the expected, a- recognition which Derrida finds explicitly stated as such by Lacan in the underlined words he quotes from the Seminar: "Just so does the purloined letter, like an immense female body, stretch out across the Minister's office when Dupin enters. But just so does he already *expect to find it* [emphasis mine—J. D.] and has only, with his eyes veiled by green lenses, to undress that huge body" (PT, pp. 61-62; emphasis and brackets restored).

But if recognition is a form of blindness, a form of violence to the otherness of the object, it would seem that, by eliminating Lacan's suggestion of a possible complication of the phallic scheme, and by lying in wait between the brackets of the fireplace to catch the psychoanalyst at his own game, Derrida, too, is "recognizing" rather than reading. And what *he* recognizes is, as he himself states it, a certain classical conception of psychoanalysis: "From the beginning," writes Derrida early in his study, "*we recognize* the classical landscape of applied psychoanalysis" (PT, p. 45; emphasis mine). It would seem that the theoretical frame of reference which governs recognition is a constitutive element in the blindness of any interpretative insight. And it is precisely that frame of reference which allows the analyst to *frame* the author of the text he is reading for practices whose locus is simultaneously *beyond* the letter of the text and *behind* the vision of its reader. The reader is framed by his own frame, but he is not even in possession of his own guilt, since it is that which prevents his vision from coinciding with *itself*. Just as the author of a criminal frame transfers guilt from himself to another by leaving *signs* which he hopes will be read as insufficiently erased *traces* or *referents* left by the other, the author of any critique is himself framed by his own frame of the other, no matter how guilty or innocent the other may be.

What is at stake here is thus the question of the relation between referentiality and interpretation. And here we find an interesting twist: while criticizing Lacan's notion of the phallus as being too referential, Derrida goes on to *use* referential logic against it. This comes up in connection with the letter's famous "materiality" which Derrida finds so odd. "It would be hard to exaggerate here the scope of this proposition on the indivisibility of the letter, or rather on its identity to itself inaccessible to dismemberment (...), as well as on the so-called materiality of the signifier (the letter) intolerant to partition. But where does this idea come from? A torn-up letter may be purely and simply destroyed, it happens..." (PT, pp. 86-87; translation modified). The so-called materiality of the signifier, says Derrida, is nothing but an *idealization.*

But what if the signifier were precisely what puts the polarity "materiality/ideality" in question? Has it not become obvious that neither Lacan's description ("Tear a letter into little pieces, it remains the letter that it is") nor Derrida's description ("A torn-up letter may be purely and simply destroyed, it happens...") can be read *literally?* Somehow, a rhetorical fold [*pli*] in the text is there to trip us up whichever way we turn. Especially since the expression "it happens" [*ça arrive*] uses the very word on which the controversy over the letter's *arrival* at its destination turns.

Our study of the readings of "The Purloined Letter" has thus brought us to the point where the *word* "letter" no longer has any literality.

But what is a letter which has no literality?

5. A "Pli" for Understanding

> I pull in resolution, and begin
> To doubt the equivocation of the fiend
> That lies like truth.
>
> —Macbeth

> "Why do you lie to me saying you're going to Cracow so I should believe you're going to Lemberg, when in reality you *are* going to Cracow?"
>
> —Joke quoted by Lacan after Freud

The letter, then, is that which poses the question of its own rhetorical status. It moves *rhetorically* through the two long, minute studies in which it is presumed to be the literal object of analysis, *without* having any literality. Instead of simply being explained *by* those analyses, the rhetoric of the letter problematizes the very rhetorical mode of analytical discourse itself. And if "literal" *means "to the letter,"* the literal becomes the most problematically figurative mode of all.

As the locus of rhetorical displacement, in fact, the letter made its very entrance into Poe's story by "traumatizing" the Prefect's discourse about it. After a series of paradoxes and pleas for absolute secrecy, the Prefect describes the problem created by the letter with a proliferation of *periphrases* which the narrator dubs "the cant of diplomacy":

> "Well, then; I have received personal information, from a very high quarter, that a certain document of the last importance has been purloined from the royal apartments. The individual who purloined it is known; this beyond a doubt; he was seen to take it. It is known, also, that it still remains in his possession."
>
> "How is this known?" asked Dupin.
>
> "It is clearly inferred," replied the Prefect, "from the nature of the document, and from the non-appearance of certain results which would at once arise from its passing *out* of the robber's possession — that is to say, from his employing it as he must design in the end to employ it."
>
> "Be a little more explicit," I said.
>
> "Well, I may venture so far as to say that the paper gives its holder a certain power in a certain quarter where such power is immensely valuable." The Prefect was fond of the cant of diplomacy. (Poe, p. 200.)

The letter thus enters the discourse of Poe's story as a rhetorical fold which actually hides nothing, since, although *we* never find out what was written in the letter, it is presumable that the Queen, the Minister, Dupin, the Prefect—who all held the letter in their hands— and even the narrator, who heard what the Prefect read from his memorandum-book, *did.* The way in which the letter dictates a series of *circumlocutions,* then, resembles the way in which the *path* of the letter dictates the characters' *circumvolutions*—not that the letter's contents *must* remain hidden, but that the *question* of whether or not they are revealed is immaterial to the displacement the letter governs. The character and actions of each of the letter's holders are determined by the rhetorical spot it puts them in *whether or not* that spot can be read by the subjects it displaces.

The letter, then, acts as a signifier *not* because its contents are lacking, but because its function is not dependent on the knowledge *or* nonknowledge of those contents. What Lacan means by saying that the letter cannot be divided is thus not that the phallus must remain intact, but that the phallus, the letter, and the signifier *are not substances.* The letter cannot be divided because it only functions *as* a division. It is not something with "an *identity* to itself inaccessible to dismemberment" as Derrida interprets it; it is a *difference.* It is known only in its efects. The signifier is an articulation in a chain, not an identifiable unit. It cannot be known in itself because it is capable of "sustaining itself *only* in a displacement" (SPL, p. 59; emphasis mine). It´ is localized, but only as the non-generalizable locus of a differential relationship. Derrida, in fact, *enacts* this law of the signifier in the very act of opposing it:

> Perhaps only one letter need be changed, maybe even less than a letter in the expression: "missing from its place" [*manque à sa place*]. Perhaps we need only introduce a written "a", i.e. without accent, in order to bring out that if the lack *has* its place [*le manque a sa place*] in this atomistic topology of the signifier, that is, if it occupies therein a specific place of definite contours, the order would remain undisturbed. (PT, p. 45.)

While thus criticizing the *hypostasis* of a lack—the letter as the *substance* of an absence—(which is not what Lacan is saying), Derrida is *illustrating* what Lacan *is* saying about *both* the materiality *and* the localizability of the signifier *as the mark of difference* by operating *on* the letter as a material locus of differentiation: by removing the little signifier " ´," an accent mark which has *no* meaning in itself. [16]

The question of the nature of the "lack," however, brings us back to the complexities of the meaning and place of the "phallus." For while it is quite easy to show the *signifier* as a "difference" rather than a "lack," the question becomes much more tricky in relation to the phallus. There would seem to be no ambiguity in

[16] It is perhaps not by chance that the question here arises of whether or not to put the accent on the letter "a." The letter "a" is perhaps the purloined letter *par excellence* in the writings of all three authors: Lacan's "objet *a*," Derida's "différance," and Edgar Poe's middle initial, A, taken from his foster father, John Allan.

Lacan's statement that "Clinical observation shows us that this test through the desire of the Other is not decisive insofar as the subject thereby learns whether or not he himself has a real phallus, but insofar as he learns *that the mother doesn't*" (*Écrits*, p. 693; translation and emphasis mine). The theory seems to imply that at some point in human sexuality, a referential moment is unbypassable: the *observation* that the mother does not have a penis is *necessary*. And therefore it would seem that the "lack" *is* localizable as the substance of an absence or a hole. To borrow a joke from Geoffrey Hartman's discussion of certain solutionless detective stories, if the purloined letter *is* the mother's phallus, "instead of a whodunit we get a whodonut, a story with a hole in it." [17]

But even on this referential level, is the object of observation really a lack? Is it not rather not an observation at all but already an *interpretation*—an interpretation ("castration") *not* of a lack but precisely of a *difference*? If what is observed is irreducibly anatomical, what is anatomy here but the irreducibility of *difference*? Even on the most elementary level, the phallus is a sign of sexuality *as* difference, and not as the presence or absence of this or that organ.

But Lacan defines the phallus in a much more complicated way than this. For if the woman is defined as "giving in a love-relation that which she does not have," the *definition* of what the woman does not have is not limited to the penis. At another point in the discussion, Lacan refers to "the gift of what one does not have" as "love" (*Écrits*, p. 691). Is "love" here a mere *synonym* of the phallus? Perhaps. But only if we modify the definition of the phallus. "Love" is, in Lacan's terminology, what is in question in the "request for love" [*demande d'amour*], which is "unconditional," the "demand for a presence or an absence" (*Écrits*, p. 691). This *demande* is not only a reference to "what the Other doesn't have," however. It is also language. And language is what alienates human desire such that "it is from the place of the Other that the subject's message is

[17] Geoffrey Hartman, "Literature High and Low: the Case of the Mystery Story," in *The Fate of Reading*, University of Chicago Press, 1975, p. 206.

emitted" (*Écrits*, p. 690). The "demand" is thus a request for the unconditional presence or absence not of an organ but of the Other in answer to the question asked by the subject from the place of the Other. But this *demande* is not yet the definition of "desire." Desire is what is left of the *demande* when all possible satisfaction of "real" needs has been subtracted from it. "Desire is neither the appetite for satisfaction, nor the demand for love, but the difference which results from the subtraction of the first from the second, the very phenomenon of their split [*Spaltung*]" (*Écrits*, p. 691). And if the phallus as a signifier, according to Lacan, "gives the *ratio* of desire," the *definition* of the phallus can no longer bear a *simple* relation either to the body or to language, because it *is* that which prevents *both* the body *and* language from being simple: "The phallus is the privileged signifier of that mark where logos is joined together with the advent of desire" (*Écrits*, p. 692; all translations in this paragraph mine).

The important word in this definition is "joined." For if language (alienation of needs through the place of the Other) and desire (the *remainder* which is left from the subtraction of the satisfaction of real needs from absolute demand) are neither totally separable from each other nor related in the same way to their own division, the phallus is the signifier of the articulation between two very problematic chains. But what is a signifier in this context? "A signifier," says Lacan, "is what represents a subject for another signifier." A signifier *represents*, then, and what it represents is a subject. But it only does so *for* another signifier. What does the expression "for another signifier" mean, if not that the distinction between subject and signifier posed in the first part of the definition is being subverted in the second? "Subject" and "signifier" are co-implicated in a definition which is unable either to separate them totally or to fuse them completely. There are *three* positions in the definition, *two* of which are occupied by the same word, but that word is differentiated from *itself* in the course of the definition—because it begins to take the place of the *other* word. The signifier *for which* the other signifier represents a subject thus acts like a subject because it is the place where the representation is "understood." The signifier, then, situates the place of something like a reader. And the reader becomes the place where representation *would be* understood if there were any such thing as a place beyond representation; the place where representation is *inscribed* as an infinite chain of substitutions whether or not there is any place from which it can be understood.

The letter as a signifier is thus not a thing or the absence of a thing, nor a word or the absence of a word, nor an organ or the absence of an organ, but a *knot* in a structure where words, things and organs can neither be definably separated nor compatibly combined. This is why the exact representational position of the letter in the Minister's apartment both matters and does not matter. It matters to the extent that sexual anatomical difference creates an irreducible dissymmetry to be accounted for in every human subject. But it does *not* matter to the extent that the letter is not hidden *in* geometrical space, where the police are looking for it, or in anatomical space, where a literal understanding of psychoanalysis might look for it. It is located "in" a *symbolic* structure, a structure which can *only* be perceived in its effects, and whose effects are perceived as repetition. Dupin *finds* the letter "in" the symbolic order *not* because he knows where to look, but because he knows *what to repeat*. Dupin's "analysis" is the *repetition* of the scene which led to the necessity of analysis. It is not an interpretation or an insight, but an act. An act of *untying* the knot in the structure by means of the repetition of the act of tying it. The word "analyze," in fact, etymologically *means* "untie," a meaning on which Poe plays in his prefatory remarks on the nature of analysis as "that moral activity which disentangles" (Poe, p. 102). The analyst does not intervene by giving meaning, but by effecting a *dénouement*.

But if the act of (psycho)analysis has no identity *apart from* its status as a repetition of the structure it seeks to analyze (to untie), then Derrida's remarks *against* psychoanalysis as being always already *mise en abyme* in the text it studies and as being only capable

Barbara Johnson

of finding *itself,* are not *objections* to psychoanalysis but in fact a profound insight into its very essence. Psychoanalysis is in fact *itself* the primal scene it is seeking: it is the *first* occurrence of what has been repeating itself in the patient without ever having occurred. Psychoanalysis is not itself the *interpretation* of repetition; it is the repetition of a *trauma of interpretation*—called "castration" or "parental coitus" or "the Oedipus complex" or even "sexuality" —the traumatic deferred interpretation not *of* an event, but *as* an event which never took place as such. The "primal scene" is not a scene but an *interpretative infelicity* whose result was to situate the interpreter in an intolerable position. And psychoanalysis is the reconstruction of that interpretative infelicity not as *its* interpretation, but as its first and last *act.* Psychoanalysis has content only insofar as it repeats the dis-content of what never took place.

But, as Dupin reminds us, "there is such a thing as being too profound. Truth is not always in a well. In fact, as regards the more important knowledge, I do believe that she is invariably superficial" (Poe, p. 119). Have we not here been looking *beyond* Lacan's signifier instead of *at* it? When Lacan insists on the "materiality of the signifier" which does not "admit partition," what is *his* way of explaining it? Simply that the *word* "letter" is never used with a partitive article: you can have "some mail" but not "some letter":

> Language delivers its judgment to whomever knows how to hear it: through the usage of the article as partitive particle. It is there that the spirit — if spirit be living meaning — appears, no less oddly, as more available for quantification than the letter. To begin with meaning itself, which bears our saying: a speech rich with meaning ["plein *de* signification"], just as we recognize a measure of intention ["*de* l'intention"] in an act, or deplore that there is no more love ["plus *d'amour*"]; or store up hatred ["*de la* haine"] and expend devotion ["*du* dévouement"], and so much infatuation ["tant *d'*infatuation"] is easily reconciled to the fact that there will always be ass ["*de la* cuisse"] for sale and brawling ["*du* rififi"] among men.
>
> But as for the letter — be it taken as typographical character, epistle, or what makes a man of letters — we will say that what is said is to be understood *to the letter* [*à la lettre*], that *a letter* [*une lettre*] awaits you

at the post office, or even that you are acquainted with *letters* [*que vous avez des lettres*] — never that there is *letter* [*de la lettre*] anywhere, whatever the context, even to designate overdue mail. (SPL, pp. 53-54.)

If this passage is particularly resistant to translation, that in itself is a result of the fact that its message is in the "superficial" play of the signifier. Like the large letters on the map which are so obvious as to be invisible, Lacan's textual signifier has gone unnoticed in the search for the *signified,* "signifier."

But the question of translation in connection with a message which is so obvious that it goes unseen is not an accident here. For in his discussion of Dupin's statement that " 'analysis' conveys 'algebra' about as much as, in Latin, *'ambitus'* implies 'ambition', *'religio'*, religion, or *'homines honesti'* a set of *'honorable* men' " (Poe, p. 212), Lacan asks:

Might not this parade of erudition be destined to reveal to us the key words of our drama? [18] Is not the magician repeating his trick before our eyes, without deceiving us this time about divulging his secret, but pressing his wager to the point of really explaining it to us without us seeing a thing. *That* would be the summit of the illusionist's art: through one of his fictive creations to *truly delude us.* (SPL, pp. 50-51.)

But the trick does not end there. For has Lacan himself not slipped into the paragraph on the quantification of the letter a parade of "key words" for *his* reading of the situation? "Full of meaning," "intention," "hatred," "love," "infatuation," "devotion," "ass for sale," and "brawling among men"—all of these words occur as the possible *signifieds* of "The Purloined Letter" in the Seminar. But if the key words of a reading of the story thus occur only in the mode of a *play of the signifier,* the *difference* between "signifier" and "signified" in Lacan's text, as well as in Poe's, has been effec-

---

[18] *Ambitus* means "detour"; *religio,* "sacred bond"; *homines honesti,* "decent men." Lacan expands upon these words as the "key words" of the story by saying: "All of this (. . .) does not imply that because the letter's secrecy is indefensible, the betrayal of that secret would in any sense be honorable. The *honesti homines,* decent people, will not get off so easily. There is more than one *religio,* and it is not slated for tomorrow that sacred ties shall cease to rend us in two. As for *ambitus:* a detour, we see, is not always inspired by ambition" (SPL, p. 58).

tively subverted. What the reader finally reads when he deciphers the signifying surface of the map of his misreading is: "You have been fooled." And it is precisely in this discussion of "being fooled" that Lacan, far from excluding the narrator, situates him in the dynamic functioning of the text, as a reader *en abyme* duped by Dupin's trick explanations of his technique, a reader who, however, unconscious of the nonsequiturs he is repeating, is so much in awe of his subject that his admiration blinds *us* to the tricky functioning of what he so faithfully transmits.

To be fooled by a text implies that the text is not constative but *performative,* and that the reader is in fact one of its effects. The text's "truth" is what puts the status of the reader in question, what performs *him* as its "address." Thus "truth" is *not* what the fiction *reveals* as a nudity hidden behind a veil. When Derrida calls Lacan's statement that "truth inhabits fiction" an *unequivocal* expression or revelation of the truth of truth (PT, p. 46), he is simply not seeing the performative perversity of the rest of the sentence in which that "statement" occurs: "It is up to the reader to give the letter (...) what he will find as its last word: its destination. That is, Poe's message deciphered and coming back from him, the reader, from the fact that, in reading it, he is able to say of himself that he is not more feigned than truth when it inhabits fiction" (*Écrits,* p. 10; translation mine). The play between truth and fiction, reader and text, message and feint, has become impossible to unravel into an "unequivocal" meaning.

We have thus come back to the question of the letter's *destination* and of the meaning of the enigmatic "last words" of Lacan's Seminar. "The sender," writes Lacan, "receives from the receiver his own message in reverse form. Thus it is that what the 'purloined letter', nay, the 'letter in sufferance' means is that a letter always arrives at its destination" (SPL, p. 72). What the reversibility of the direction of the letter's movement between sender and receiver has now come to stand for is precisely the fact, underlined by Derrida as if it were an *objection* to Lacan, that *there is no position from which the letter's message can be read as an object:* "no neutralization is possible, no general point of view" (PT, p. 106). This is also precisely the "discovery" of psychoanalysis—that the analyst is *involved* (through transference) in the very "object" of his analysis.

Everyone who has held the letter—or even beheld it—including the narrator, has ended up having the letter addressed to *him* as its destination. The reader is comprehended by the letter: there is no *place* from which he can stand back and observe *it*. Not that the letter's meaning is subjective rather than objective, but that the letter is precisely that which subverts the polarity subjective/objective, that which makes subjectivity into something whose position in a structure is situated by the passage through it of an object. The letter's destination is thus *wherever it is read:* the place it assigns to its reader as his own partiality. Its destination is not a place, decided *a priori* by the sender, because the receiver *is* the sender, and the receiver is whoever receives the letter, including nobody. When Derrida says that a letter *can* miss its destination and be disseminated, he reads "destination" as a place which pre-exists the letter's movement. But if, as Lacan shows, the letter's destination is not its literal addressee, nor even whoever possesses it, but whoever is possessed *by* it, then the very *disagreement* over the meaning of "reaching the destination" is an *illustration* of the non-objective nature of that "destination." The very rhetoric of Derrida's differentiation of his own point of view from Lacan's *enacts* that law:

> Thanks to castration, the phallus always stays in its place in the transcendental topology we spoke of earlier. It is indivisible and indestructible there, like the letter which takes its place. And that is why the *interested* presupposition, never proved, of the letter's materiality as indivisibility was indispensable to this restricted economy, this circulation of propriety.
>
> The difference I am *interested* in here is that, a formula to be read however one wishes, the lack has no place of its own in dissemination. (PT, p. 63; translation modified, emphasis mine.)

The play of *interest* in this expression of difference is too interesting not to be deliberate. The opposition between the "phallus" and "dissemination" is not between two theoretical objects but between two interested positions. And if sender and receiver are merely the two poles of a reversible message, then Lacan's very *substitution* of "destin" for "dessein" in the Crebillon quotation —a misquotation which Derrida finds revealing enough to end his analysis upon—*is* in fact the quotation's message. The sender ("dessein") and the receiver ("destin") of the violence which passes between Atreus and Thyestes are *equally* subject to the violence the letter *is*.

The reflexivity between receiver and sender is, however, not an expression of symmetry in itself, but only an evocation of the interdependence of the two terms, of the *question* of symmetry as a *problem* in the transferential structure of all reading. As soon as accident or exteriority or time or repetition enters into that reflexivity—that is to say, *from the beginning*—, Otherness itself becomes in a way the letter's sender. The message I am reading may be either my own (narcissistic) message backwards or the way in which that message is always already traversed by its own otherness to itself or by the narcissistic message of the other. In any case the letter is in a way the materialization of my death. And once these various possibilities are granted, none of them can function in isolation. The question of the letter's origin and destination can no longer be asked as such. And whether this is because it involves 2, 3 or 4 terms must remain undecidable.

The *sentence* "a letter always arrives at its destination" can thus either be simply pleonastic or variously paradoxical: it can mean "the only message I can read is the one I send," "wherever the letter is, is its destination," "when a letter is read, it reads the reader," "the repressed always returns," "I exist only as a reader of the other," "the letter has no destination," and "we all die." It is not any one of these readings, but all of them and others in their very incompatibility, which *repeat* the letter in its way of reading the act of reading. Far from giving us the Seminar's final truth, these last words *enact* the impossibility of any ultimate analytical metalanguage.

If it at first seemed possible to say that Derrida was opposing the unsystematizable to the systematized, "chance" to psychoanalytical "determinism," or the "undecidable" to the "destination," the positions of these oppositions seem now to be reversed: Lacan's apparently unequivocal ending says only its own dissemination, while "dissemination" has erected itself into a kind of "last word." But these oppositions are themselves misreadings of the dynamic functioning of what is at stake here. For if the letter is precisely that which dictates the rhetorical indetermination of any theoretical discourse about it, then the oscillation between unequivocal statements of undecidability and ambiguous assertions of decidability is precisely one of the letter's inevitable effects. Thus it is, for example, that the "indestructibility of desire," which could be considered a psychoanalytical belief in the return of the *same,* turns out to name repetition as the repetition not of sameness but of *otherness,* which results in the *dissemination* of the subject. And "symbolic determination" is not *opposed* to "chance": it is precisely what emerges as the *syntax* of chance. [19] But "chance," out of which what repeats springs, cannot in any way be "known," since "knowing" is precisely one of its *effects.* We can therefore never be *sure* whether or not "chance itself" exists at all. "Undecidability" can no more be used as a last word than "destination." "*Car,*" said Mallarmé, "*il y a et il n'y a pas de hasard.*" The "undeterminable" is not *opposed* to the determinable; "dissemination" is not *opposed* to repetition. If we could be sure of the difference between the determinable and the undeterminable, the undeterminable would be comprehended within the determinable. What is undecidable is precisely whether a thing is decidable or not.

[19] This is what the mathematical model in the Seminar's "Introduction" clearly shows: beginning with a totally arbitrary binary series, a syntax of regularity emerges from the simple application of a law of combination to the series. When it is objected that that syntax *is not,* unless the subject *remembers* the series, Lacan responds, "That is just what is in question here: it is less out of anything real (. . .), than precisely out of *what never was,* that what repeats itself springs" (*Écrits,* p. 43; translation mine). Memory could thus be considered not as a *condition* of repetition, but as one of its syntactic effects. What we call a random series is, in fact, already an *interpretation,* not a given: it is not a materialization of chance itself, but only of something which obeys our conception of the laws of probability.

504

Barbara Johnson

As a final fold in the letter's performance of its reader, it should perhaps be noted that, in this discussion of the letter as what prevents me from knowing whether Lacan and Derrida are really saying the same thing or only enacting their own differences from themselves, my own theoretical "frame of reference" is precisely, to a very large extent, the writings of Lacan and Derrida. The frame is thus framed again by part of its content; the sender again receives his own message backwards from the receiver. And the true otherness of the purloined letter of literature has perhaps still in no way been accounted for.

JOHN BRENKMAN teaches comparative literature at the University of Wisconsin at Madison. He is co-editor of the journal *Social Text.* His book *Culture and Domination* is forthcoming from Cornell University Press.

PETER BROOKS, author of *The Novel of Worldliness* (Princeton University Press, 1969) and *The Melodramatic Imagination* (Yale University Press, 1976), is Chester D. Tripp Professor of French and Comparative Literature at Yale. He is currently working on a study of narrative plots.

ROGER DRAGONETTI is professor of French at the University of Geneva. His books include *Frontières du langage poétique* ("Romanica Gandensia," 1961), *Dante pélerin de la sainte face* ("Romanica Gandensia," 1968) and *La Vie de la lettre au Moyen Age (le Conte du Graal)* (Seuil, 1980).

SHOSHANA FELMAN is professor of French at Yale University. Her writings include *La "Folie" dans l'oeuvre romanesque de Stendhal* (Corti, 1971), *La Folie et la chose littéraire* (Seuil, 1978), *Le Scandale du corps parlant: Don Juan avec Austin, ou la Séduction en deux langues* (Seuil, 1980), the latter two forthcoming in English from Cornell University Press *(Writing and Madness: Literature/ Philosophy/Psychoanalysis* and *The Literary Speech Act: Don Juan with Austin, or Seduction in Two Languages).* She is currently completing a book on Lacanian psychoanalysis.

FREDRIC JAMESON, professor of French at Yale and co-editor of the journal *Social Text,* is the author of *Marxism and Form* (Princeton University Press, 1971), *The Prison-House of Language* (Princeton University Press, 1972), *Fables of Agression: Wyndham Lewis, the*

Modernist as a Fascist (University of California Press, 1979) and *The Political Unconscious: Narrative as a Socially Symbolic Act* (Cornell University Press, 1981).

BARBARA JOHNSON is associate professor of French and comparative literature at Yale. She is the author of *Défigurations du langage poétique* (Flammarion, 1979), and *The Critical Difference: Essays in the Contemporary Rhetoric of Reading* (Johns Hopkins University Press, 1980), as well as the translator (with a critical introduction) of Jacques Derrida's *Dissemination* (University of Chicago Press, 1981), and the special editor of the forthcoming issue of *Yale French Studies: The Pedagogical Imperative: Teaching as a Literary Genre* (Yale University Press, Spring 1982).

JACQUES LACAN (1901–1981), in his lifetime the incontestable leader of French psychoanalysis, is probably the most influential and controversial psychoanalyst since Freud. A brilliant and provocatively inspiring creative thinker, he was famous not just for his best-selling (although highly sophisticated and stylistically demanding) writings but also for the overcrowded bi-monthly seminar he regularly gave for thirty years, which was freely but devotedly attended by psychoanalysts and by the foremost French philosophers, scholars, writers, and artists, as well as by hundreds of students from all disciplines. His books include the *Ecrits* (Seuil, 1966), the series of his seminars (*Le Seminaire de Jacques Lacan:* edited—out of recordings—by J.-A. Miller), and his medical thesis, *De la Psychose paranoïaque dans les rapports avec le personnalité* (Seuil, 1975). The English translation of Lacan's major work, *Ecrits: A Selection* (trans. A. Sheridan) has been published simultaneously by Tavistock and Norton, 1977; also in English, Lacan's Seminar XI: *The Four Fundamental Concepts of Psycho-Analysis* (Hogarth and I.P.A., 1977). Lacan's study of *Hamlet*—as yet unpublished in French— was generously given by Lacan for the present collection.

CHARLES MÉLA, a medievalist at the University of Paris–Sorbonne, has written on various medieval literary works and is the author of

Blanche Fleur et le Saint-Homme ou la Semblance des reliques: Etude comparée de littérature médiévale (Seuil, 1979).

JEAN-MICHEL REY teaches psychoanalytic theory at the University of Paris–Vincennes. He is the author of *L'Enjeu des signes: Lecture de Nietzsche* (Seuil, 1981), *Parcours de Freud* (Galilée, 1974), and another study of Freud entitled *Des Mots à l'oeuvre* (Aubier Montaigne, 1979).

DANIEL SIBONY, formerly a mathematician and currently a well-known French psychoanalyst, is the editor of the psychoanalytical review *Analytiques* and the author of *Le Nom et le corps* (Seuil, 1974), *La Haine du désir* (Christian Bourgois, 1978), and *L'Autre incastrable* (Seuil, 1978).

PHILIPPE SOLLERS, founder and director of the review *Tel Quel,* is one of the best-known contemporary French writers; his novels include *Drame* (Seuil, 1965), *Nombres* (Seuil, 1968), *Lois* (Seuil, 1972), *H* (Seuil, 1973), and *Paradis* (Seuil, 1981). He has also published works of criticism, among which are *Logiques* (Seuil, 1968), *Sur le matérialisme* (Seuil, 1974), and *Vision à New York* (Christian Bourgois, 1981).

GAYATRI CHAKRAVORTY SPIVAK is professor of comparative literature at the University of Texas at Austin. Her books are *Myself Must I Remake: The Life and Poetry of W. B. Yeats* (Thomas Y. Crowell, 1974) and a translation—with a critical introduction—of Jacques Derrida's *Of Grammatology* (Johns Hopkins University Press, 1976). She is presently writing a book on deconstruction, feminism, and Marxism.